WESTERN CIVILIZATION

IDEAS, POLITICS, AND SOCIETY VOLUME I

SPECIAL EIGHTH EDITION WITH HISTORY OF CHINA

MARVIN PERRY
BARUCH COLLEGE
CITY UNIVERSITY OF NEW YORK

MYRNA CHASE
BARUCH COLLEGE
CITY UNIVERSITY OF NEW YORK

JAMES R. JACOB
JOHN JAY COLLEGE OF
CRIMINAL JUSTICE
CITY UNIVERSITY OF NEW YORK

MARGARET C. JACOB
UNIVERSITY OF CALIFORNIA,
LOS ANGELES

THEODORE H. VON LAUE
LATE OF CLARK UNIVERSITY

GEORGE W. BOCK
EDITORIAL ASSOCIATE

WITH

CHINA

A CULTURAL, SOCIAL, AND POLITICAL HISTORY

PATRICIA BUCKLEY EBREY
UNIVERSITY OF WASHINGTON, SEATTLE

HOUGHTON MIFFLIN COMPANY
BOSTON NEW YORK

WESTERN CIVILIZATION: IDEAS, POLITICS, AND SOCIETY, VOLUME 1 TO 1780, EIGHTH EDITION
by Marvin Perry, Myrna Chase, James R. Jacob, Margaret C. Jacob and Theodore H. Von Laue

Publisher: Charles Hartford
Senior Sponsoring Editor: Nancy Blaine
Senior Development Editor: Jeff Greene
Senior Project Editor: Jane Lee
Editorial Assistant: Kristen Truncellito
Senior Art and Design Coordinator: Jill Haber
Senior Photo Editor: Jennifer Meyer Dare
Composition Buyer: Chuck Dutton
Senior Manufacturing Buyer: Renee Ostrowski
Senior Marketing Manager: Sandra McGuire
Market Specialist: Molly Parke

Text Credits

Page 13: From James B. Pritchard, ed., *The Ancient Near East*. Copyright ©1974 by Princeton University Press. Reprinted by permission of Princeton University Press.
Pages 16, 19: From Adolf Ehrman, ed., *The Ancient Egyptians*, pp. 94, 97, 99, and 76-78. Copyright © 1966. Used by permission of the publishers, Methuen & Co.
Page 18: From John A. Wilson, *The Culture of Ancient Egypt*, 1951, p. 227. Reprinted by permission of the publisher, The University of Chicago Press.
Page 38: From *The TANAKH: The New JPS Translations According to the Traditional Hebrew Text*. Copyright © 1985 by the Jewish Publication Society. Used by permission.
Page 52: From *The Iliad* by Homer, translated by E. V. Rieu, pp. 23, 405. Copyright © 1950. Reproduced by permission of Penguin Books Ltd.
Pages 53, 55: From H. D. F. Kitto, *The Greeks*, pp. 174-175. Copyright © 1957. Reproduced by permission of Penguin Books Ltd.
Page 87: From *Oxford Book of Greek Verse in Translation*, by T. F. Higham and C. M. Bowra (eds.), 1930, p. 211. By permission of Oxford University Press.
Page 88: Reprinted with permission of Pocket Books, an imprint of Simon & Schuster Adult Publishing Group, from Sophocles' *Oedipus the King*, Bernard M. W. Knox, Translator. Copyright © 1959, and renewed © 1987, by Bernard M. W. Knox.
Page 90: From Aeschylus, *The Persians*, translated by Anthony J. Podlecki. Copyright © 1991, published by Bristal Classical Press (Duckworth). Used by permission of the author.
Pages 91-92: From *The Medea*, translated by Rex Warner in *Euripides, Vol.* 3 of Richard Lattimore, *The Complete Greek Tragedies*, p. 96, 101. Copyright © 1959 by The Bodley Head.
Page 128: From Catullus, quoted in E. A. Havelock, *The Lyric Genius of Catullus*, p. 63. Copyright © 1929. Reprinted with permission of Christine M. Havelock.
Page 149: Aeneid of Virgil: A Verse Translation (Paper) by Virgil. Copyright © 1981 by Allen Mandelbaum. Reproduced with permission of Allen Mandelbaum in the format textbook via Copyright Clearance Center.
Page 264: From Helen Waddell, *Medieval Latin Lyrics. Permission to reprint the excerpt from Helen Waddell's translation "Let's away with study..." given by Mary Martin.*
Page 264: From David C. Riede and J. Wayne Baker, *The Western Intellectual Tradition*, Vol. 1, 1980. Reprinted with permission of the author.
Page 265: From Anthony Bonner, ed., *Songs of the Troubadours*, pp. 42-43. Copyright © 1972. Reprinted with permission of the author.
Pages 306-307: From "Hamlet, Prince of Denmark" in *The Complete Plays and Poems of William Shakespeare*, edited by William Allan Neilson and Charles Jarvis Hill, 1942, Houghton Mifflin Company. Reprinted with permission.

CHINA, A CULTURAL, SOCIAL, AND POLITICAL HISTORY
by Patricia Buckley Ebrey

Publisher: Charles Hartford
Senior Sponsoring Editor: Nancy Blaine
Senior Development Editor: Julie Swasey
Senior Project Editor: Jane Lee
Editorial Assistant: Kristen Truncellito
Senior Art and Design Coordinator: Jill Haber
Senior Photo Editor: Jennifer Meyer Dare
Composition Buyer/Manufacturing Coordinator: Chuck Dutton
Senior Marketing Manager: Sandra McGuire
Market Specialist: Molly Parke

Custom Publishing Editor: Todd Corbin
Custom Publishing Production Manager: Christina Battista
Project Coordinator: Jennifer Feltri

Cover Designer: Brian Moore
Cover Image: PhotoDisc

This book contains select works from existing Houghton Mifflin Company resources and was produced by Houghton Mifflin Custom Publishing for collegiate use. As such, those adopting and/or contributing to this work are responsible for editorial content, accuracy, continuity and completeness.

Printed in the United States of America.

ISBN-13: 978-0-618-81297-4
ISBN-10: 0-618-81297-0
N-06804

1 2 3 4 5 6 7 8 9 – CCI – 08 07 06

Houghton Mifflin
Custom Publishing

222 Berkeley Street • Boston, MA 02116

Address all correspondence and order information to the above address.

Brief Contents

Contents

Contents for: CHINA
A Cultural, Social, and Political History

Maps

Chronologies

Preface

Western civilization is a grand but tragic drama. The West has forged the instruments of reason that make possible a rational comprehension of physical nature and human culture, conceived the idea of political liberty, and recognized the intrinsic worth of the individual. But the modern West, though it has unraveled nature's mysteries, has been less successful at finding rational solutions to social ills and conflicts between nations. Science, the great achievement of the Western intellect, while improving conditions of life, has also produced weapons of mass destruction. Though the West has pioneered in the protection of human rights, it has also produced totalitarian regimes that have trampled on individual freedom and human dignity. And although the West has demonstrated a commitment to human equality, it has also practiced brutal racism.

Despite the value that westerners have given to reason and freedom, they have shown a frightening capacity for irrational behavior and a fascination for violence and irrational ideologies, and they have willingly sacrificed liberty for security or national grandeur. The world wars and totalitarian movements of the twentieth century have demonstrated that Western civilization, despite its extraordinary achievements, is fragile and perishable.

Western Civilization: Ideas, Politics, and Society examines the Western tradition—those unique patterns of thought and systems of values that constitute the Western heritage. While focusing on key ideas and broad themes, the text also provides a balanced treatment of economic, political, and social history for students in Western civilization courses.

The text is written with the conviction that history is not a meaningless tale. Without a knowledge of history, men and women cannot fully know themselves, for all human beings have been shaped by institutions and values inherited from the past. Without an awareness of the historical evolution of reason and freedom, the dominant ideals of Western civilization, commitment to these ideals will diminish. Without knowledge of history, the West cannot fully comprehend or adequately cope with the problems that burden its civilization and the world.

In attempting to make sense out of the past, the authors have been careful to avoid superficial generalizations that oversimplify historical events and arrange history into too neat a structure. They strive to interpret and to synthesize in order to provide students with a frame of reference with which to comprehend the principal events and eras in Western history.

Changes in the Eighth Edition

For the eighth edition every chapter has been reworked to some extent. The hundreds of carefully selected modifications and additions significantly enhance the text. Some changes deepen the book's conceptual character, while others provide useful and illustrative historical details. The concluding essays in many chapters have been enlarged and improved. We have been particularly careful to strengthen chapters dealing with intellectual history, the text's distinguishing feature. Each chapter continues to contain a profile of a significant historical figure. Among the new personalities featured are Epicetus, Joan of Arc, Leni Riefenstahl, and Pope John Paul II. Following the suggestions of instructors who have been using the text through many editions, we have dispensed with the review questions at the end of each chapter. Instead, we have inserted several focus questions at the beginning of each chapter that serve to guide students' reading of the chapter. And to help students understand the new terms they will encounter, we have added a glossary.

Specific changes in Chapter 1, "The Ancient Near East," include an expanded treatment of Egyptian religion; as in previous editions, we made a deliberate effort to improve the final section, "The Religious Orientation of the Near East." In Chapter 2, "The Hebrews," we now discuss the scholarly debate initiated by biblical minimalists and have deepened the treatment of the prophets. Added to Chapter 3, "The Greek City-State," is a deeper analysis of the strengths and weaknesses of Athenian democracy. We added material on early Greek philosophy, the Sophists, Socrates, the Greek dramatists, and Thucydides in Chapter 4, "Greek Thought." Here too we have improved the final section, "The Greek Achievement." In Chapter 5, "The Hellenistic Age," more attention has been given to Hellenistic philosophy. Material has been added to the sections on the consequences of expansion and culture in Chapter 6, "The Roman Republic." In Chapter 7, "The Roman Empire," we have expanded the discussions of Neo-Platonism, the reigns of Diocletian and Constantine, the significance of the battle of Adrianople, and the final section, "The Roman Legacy." Changes in Chapter 8, "Early Christianity," include broader treatments of Paul and the appeal of Christianity in the Mediterranean world. The final section, "Christianity and Classical Humanism," has been significantly improved.

An expanded discussion of Muslim religion and culture is the most noteworthy addition to Chapter 9, "The Heirs of Rome." The treatment of medieval commerce and town life has been expanded in Chapter 10, "The High Middle Ages." Also significantly broadened is the treatment of medieval Christian perceptions of the Jew. In Chapter 11, "The Flowering of Medieval Culture," we have added some material on the poetry of university students. Chapter 12, "The Late Middle Ages," contains more material on the adversities of the fourteenth century, but most significant is the enrichment of the final section, "The Middle Ages and the Modern World."

The section on Renaissance art in Chapter 13, "The Renaissance," has been deleted since that topic is covered in the art essays and a new profile of Leonardo da Vinci has been added. The profile of Sir Isaac Newton in Chapter 17 is also new.

In Chapter 19, "The French Revolution," we have expanded the treatment of the relationship of the Enlightenment to the French Revolution and the Terror in the Vendée and enriched the final section, "The Meaning of the French Revolution." Also enriched is the final section, "The Legend and the Achievement," in Chapter 20, "Napoleon." In Chapter 22, "Thought and Culture in the Early Nineteenth Century," we have revised the chapter introduction and the sections on "Romanticism," "Conservatism," and "Liberalism."

In Chapter 24, "Thought and Culture in the Mid-Nineteenth Century," more attention has been given to "Darwinism" and "Religion in a Secular Age." The section on anti-Semitism has been expanded in Chapter 25, "The Surge of Nationalism." In Chapter 28, "Modern Consciousness," we continue to sharpen the treatment of major themes and thinkers. Here too we have enriched the final section, "The Enlightenment Tradition in Disarray."

The most significant changes in Chapter 29, "World War I," are a deeper treatment of the nature of combat and some additions to the final section, "The War and European Consciousness." In Chapter 30, "An Era of Totalitarianism," we have revised the analyses of Stalin's dictatorship, the rise of Hitler, and the Nazi regime. The treatment of the war, including the Holocaust, has been expanded in Chapter 32, "World War II." And, consistent with other chapters, we have improved the last section, "The Legacy of World War II."

In Chapter 34, "The Troubled Present," Russia under President Putin has been revised and updated. A new section, "The European Union," includes the expansion of the EU, a discussion of Euroskepticism among Europeans, and the defeat of the EU constitution. Treatment of the major European countries has been updated. The section dealing with international terrorism by radical Islamic jihadists has been expanded, and considerable space is given to the war in Iraq, including the role of Islamic jihadists in the insurgency.

Distinctive Features

The text contains several pedagogical features, including two new ones mentioned above: focus questions and a glossary. Chapter outlines and introductions provide comprehensive overviews of key themes and give a sense of direction and coherence to the flow of history. Many chapters contain concluding essays that treat the larger meaning of the material. Facts have been carefully selected to illustrate key relationships and concepts and to avoid overwhelming students with unrelated and disconnected data. Appropriate quotations, many not commonly found in texts, have been integrated into the discussion. Each chapter contains notes and an annotated bibliography. And new to this edition, each chapter also begins with focus questions to aid students' reading of the chapter. There is also a comprehensive glossary to help students with unfamiliar terms.

Western Civilization: Ideas, Politics, and Society is available in both one-and two-volume editions, and in a third edition, *From the 1400s*. *From the 1400s* (twenty-two chapters) has been prepared for those instructors whose courses begin with the Renaissance or the Reformation.

Volume 1 of the two-volume edition treats the period from the first civilizations in the Near East through the Age of Enlightenment in the eighteenth century (eighteen chapters). Volume 2 covers the period from the growth of national states in the seventeenth century to the contemporary age (nineteen chapters). Because some instructors start the second half of their course with the period prior to the French Revolution, Volume 2 incorporates the last three chapters of Volume 1: "The Rise of Sovereignty," "The Scientific Revolution," and "The Age of Enlightenment." Volume 2 also contains a comprehensive introduction that surveys the ancient world, the Middle Ages, and the opening centuries of the modern era; the introduction is designed particularly for students who did not take the first half of the course. *From the 1400s* also contains an introduction that covers the ancient world and the Middle Ages.

Ancillaries

We are pleased to introduce an expanded ancillary package that will help students in learning and instructors in teaching:

Online Study Center student website

Online Study Center

Online Teaching Center instructor website
HM ClassPrep with HM Testing (powered by Diploma)
Online Instructor's Resource Manual
Computerized Test Items
PowerPoint maps and images
PowerPoint questions for personal response systems
Blackboard® and WebCT® course cartridges
Eduspace® for World History (powered by Blackboard®)
Map transparencies

The *Online Study Center* is a new companion website for students that features a wide array of resources to help students master the subject matter. The website, prepared by Gregory S. Brown of the University of Nevada, Las Vegas is divided into three major sections: "Prepare for Class" includes material such as learning objectives, chapter outlines, and pre-class quizzes for a student to consult before going to class; "Improve Your Grade" includes self-testing material like interactive flashcards, chronological ordering exercises, web activities, and interactive map and primary source exercises; and "ACE the Test" features our successful ACE brand of practice tests. Students can also find additional text resources such as an online glossary and material on how to study more effectively in the "General Resources" section. For the eighth edition, we have added icons to the text that direct students to relevant exercises and self-testing material located on the *Online Study Center*. Access the *Online Study Center* for this text by visiting college.hmco.com/pic/perrywc8e.

The *Online Teaching Center* is a new companion website for instructors. It features all of the material on the student site plus additional password-protected resources for teaching the course such as an electronic version of the *Instructor's Resource Manual* and *PowerPoint* slides. Access the *Online Teaching Center* for this text by visiting college.hmco.com/pic/perrywc8e.

HM ClassPrep with HM Testing, the latest comprehensive instructor's resource in computerized testing, includes electronic versions of the *Instructor's Resource Manual* and *Test Items*, the *HM Testing* test generation tool, and *PowerPoint* maps and images and questions for use with personal response systems. *HM Testing* (powered by *Diploma*) offers instructors a flexible and powerful tool for test generation and test management. Now supported by the Brownstone Research Group's market-leading *Diploma*™ software, this new version of *HM Testing* significantly improves on functionality and ease of use by offering all the tools needed to create, deliver, and customize multiple types of tests. *Diploma*™ is currently in use at thousands of college and university campuses throughout the United States and Canada.

The *Instructor's Resource Manual,* prepared by John Reisbord, and *Test Items*, prepared by Joseph Y. Appiah of J. Sergeant Reynolds Community College, are both available in electronic format on *HM ClassPrep*™. The *Instructor's Resource Manual* contains advice on teaching the Western civilization course, instructional objectives, chapter outlines, lecture suggestions, paper and class activity topics, primary source and map activities, and suggestions for cooperative learning. The *Test Items* offer multiple-choice, short answer, and essay questions as well as unit, midterm, and final examination questions.

We are pleased to offer a collection of *PowerPoint* maps and images for use in classroom presentations. This collection includes all of the photos and maps in the text, as well as numerous other images from European history. PowerPoint questions and answers for use with personal response system software are also offered to adopters free of charge.

New to this edition, graded homework questions have been developed to work with the *Blackboard®* and *WebCT®* course management systems, as well as with *Eduspace® for Western Civilization*: Houghton Mifflin's Online Learning Tool (Powered by Blackboard®). *Eduspace® for Western Civilization* is a web-based online learning environment that provides instructors with a gradebook and communication capabilities, such as synchronous and asynchronous chats and announcement postings. By pairing these widely recognized course management tools with quality, text-specific and course-wide content, *Eduspace® for Western Civilization* makes it easy for instructors to create all or part of a course online. Developed to meet the unique needs of history curricula, *Eduspace® for Western Civilization* offers access to assignable resources such as over 650 gradable homework exercises, writing assignments, discussion questions for online discussion boards, and tests, which all come ready-to-use. Instructors can choose to use the content as is, modify it, or even add their own. Finally, a set of full-color map transparencies of all the maps in the text is available on adoption.

The text represents the efforts of several authors. Marvin Perry, general editor of the project, wrote Chapters 1–12, 19–20, 22–25, 28–32, the Epilogue, and the section on the American Revolution in Chapter 18. James R. Jacob is the author of Chapters 13 and 15. Margaret C. Jacob wrote Chapters 14 and 16–18. Myrna Chase is the author of Chapters 21, 26–27, and contributed to the section on reform in Britain in Chapter 23. Theodore H. Von Laue wrote much of Chapters 33 and 34 and contributed the sections on tsarist Russia to Chapter 26, and on Communist Russia to Chapter 30. Since his death, Marvin Perry and Angela Von Laue have revised these chapters. Over the years, Marvin Perry and George Bock have edited the manuscript for continuity and clarity.

Acknowledgments

The authors would like to thank the following instructors for their critical reading of sections of the manuscript: Joseph Appiah, J. Sargeant Reynolds Community College; Gregory S. Brown, University of Nevada, Las Vegas; Frank Buscher, Christian Brothers University; Chiarella Esposito, University of Mississippi; L. Edward Hicks, Faulkner University; Donald M. McKale, Clemson University; and Barbara Hensley Shepard, Longwood University. Several of their suggestions were incorporated into the final version.

We are also grateful to the staff of Houghton Mifflin Company who lent their considerable talents to the project. In particular we would like to thank Jeff Greene, senior development editor, for his conscientiousness and concern; Jane Lee, project editor, for her careful attention to detail; Jay Boggis, whose copyediting skills are reflected in the manuscript; and Linda Sykes, for supervising the choice of pictures in the text. This edition rests substantially on the editorial talents of Freda Alexander, who worked closely with us on earlier editions of the text. Both Jean Woy, senior consulting editor, who has been affiliated with the text since the first edition and Nancy Blaine, senior sponsoring editor, continue to recognize and support what we are trying to do—and for this we remain grateful. The death of my long time colleague and friend, Theodore Von Laue, deeply saddens me. Although his special talents are missed, his wife Angela Von Laue has added her literary and research skills to the project. I would like to express my personal gratitude to her and to my good friend George Bock, whose creative insights in previous editions continue to contribute to the text's distinguishing character—a concern for crucial concepts and essential relationships. Our often heated, but always fruitful discussions demonstrate to me the intrinsic value of the Socratic dialogue. And, as always, I am grateful to my wife, Phyllis Perry, for her encouragement and computer expertise, which have saved me much time and frustration.

M. P.

Geography of Europe

The map on the following pages shows the continent of Europe and the countries around the Mediterranean Sea, together with the physical features of the land such as major rivers and other bodies of water, mountains and changes of elevation, and the names of countries and their capitals. A knowledge of the geography of this area will help give a sense of the relationship between geography and history, of how the characteristics of the terrain and the availability of rivers and other bodies of water affected the movement of people and the relationship between people and environment throughout history.

Europe is the smallest continent in the world with the exception of Australia. The other continents are Africa, Asia, North America, South America, and Antarctica. The continent of Europe, which can be viewed as the western extension of the Asian landmass, is distinctive in its configuration. Peninsulas make up a significant portion of the continent's land area. This feature gives Europe an unusually long coastline, equal in distance to one and a half times around the equator (37,877 miles). Europe's western boundary is the Atlantic Ocean, while the Ural Mountains, Ural River, and Caspian Sea—in Russia and Kazakhstan—form its eastern boundary. Europe extends southward to the Caucasus Mountains, the Black Sea, and the Mediterranean Sea. The continent extends to the Arctic Ocean in the north. Off the mainland but considered by geographers to be part of Europe are thousands of islands, most notably the British Isles to the northwest.

North Americans are often surprised to discover the small size of the European continent. The geographic area of France, for example, is less than that of Texas; England is similar in size to Alabama. The distance from London to Paris is about the same as from New York to Boston; the distance from Berlin to Moscow is comparable to that of Chicago to Denver. And the entire continent of Europe is about the size of Canada.

Major Peninsulas and Islands There are five major European peninsulas: the Iberian (Portugal and Spain); the Apennine (Italy); the Balkan (Albania, Bulgaria, Greece, and parts of the former Yugoslavian republics and Turkey); the Scandinavian (Norway and Sweden); and Jutland (Denmark). Ireland and the United Kingdom of England, Wales, and Scotland make up the British Isles. Major islands of the Mediterranean Sea include the Balearic Islands, Corsica, Sardinia, Sicily, Crete, and Cyprus.

Seas, Lakes, and Rivers Europe's irregular coastline encloses large areas of the surrounding waters into bays, gulfs, and seas. In the Mediterranean Sea are located, from west to east, the Tyrrhenian Sea (between Italy and Sicily, and Sardinia and Corsica), the Adriatic Sea (between Italy and the former Yugoslavian republics), the Ionian Sea (between Italy and Greece), and the Aegean Sea (between Greece and Turkey).

The Baltic Sea, in the north, is bordered by Finland, Estonia, Latvia, Lithuania, Poland, Germany, and Sweden, and connected by narrow channels to the North Sea, which lies between Great Britain and the countries of the northwestern mainland. The English Channel separates England and France, and the Bay of Biscay borders the west coast of France and the north coast of Spain. The Black Sea, on the southern border of Russia and the Ukraine, is connected by water passages to the Aegean Sea. The Caspian Sea, which lies partly in Russia and Kazakhstan, and

Elevation
Meters
Feet
4,000
13,120
2,000
6,560
500
1,640
200
656
Sea level
Sea level
Below sea level
Below sea level
National capital
Other city
NORWAY
Oslo
SWEDEN
Stockho
SCOTLAND
North Sea
Balti Sea
NORTHERN IRELAND
UNITED KINGDOM
IRELAND
Dublin
DENMARK
Copenhagen
ENGLAND
WALES
NETHERLANDS
Amsterdam
Thames
London
Elbe
Berlin
ATLANTIC OCEAN
English Channel
Brussels
BELGIUM
GERMANY
POLA
Vistula
Seine
LUXEMBOURG
Luxembourg
Paris
Prague
CZECHOSLOVAKIA
Loire
Rhine
Bay of Biscay
FRANCE
Bern
Vienna
SWITZERLAND
AUSTRIA
Bud
HUNG
ALPS
SLOVENIA
Ljubljana
Zagreb
CROATIA
Rhône
Po
PYRENEES
Ebro
APENNINES
Adriatic Sea
Belgrad
BOSNIA AND HERZEGOVINA
Sarajevo
PORTUGAL
Lisbon
SPAIN
Madrid
Corsica
Tiber
Rome
(YUG
MONTENEGRO
Titograd
ITALY
ALBA
Balearic Is.
Sardinia
Tyrrhenian Sea
GIBRALTAR (Gt. Br.)
Ionian Sea
Algiers
Rabat
Sicily
Tunis
MOROCCO
MALTA
TUNISIA
Tripoli
ALGERIA
LIBYA
0 100 200 300 400 500 Km.
0 100 200 300 400 500 Mi.

LAND
St. Petersburg
Tallinn
ESTONIA
Nizhniy Novgorod
Volga
URAL MTS.
Riga
LATVIA
Moscow
RUSSIA
Vilnius
Minsk
BYELARUS
Ural
KAZAKHSTAN
Kiev
Kharkov
UKRAINE
Dnieper
MOLDOVA
Kishinev
MTS.
ROMANIA
Caspian
Sea
CAUCASUS MTS.
Bucharest
Danube
Black Sea
GEORGIA
Tbilisi
Baku
AZERBAIJAN
ARMENIA
Yerevan
BULGARIA
Sofia
AZERBAIJAN
Ankara
TURKEY
IRAN
Aegean
Sea
Athens
Euphrates
Tigris
SYRIA
Baghdad
IRAQ
CYPRUS
LEBANON
Beirut
Damascus
Crete
Sea
KUWAIT
Kuwait
Jerusalem
Amman
ISRAEL
JORDAN
Cairo
EGYPT
Nile
SAUDI ARABIA

partly in Asia, is the world's largest saltwater lake and is the lowest point in Europe at 92 feet below sea level.

Europe's many rivers have served as transportation routes for thousands of years. Several of the major rivers, including the longest, flow across the Russian plain. The Volga, Europe's longest river (2,194 miles), rises west of Moscow and empties into the Caspian Sea. It is also linked by canals and other river systems to the Arctic Ocean and the Baltic Sea. The Dnieper flows south through the agricultural heartland of the Ukraine into the Black Sea.

Europe's second longest river, the Danube (1,777 miles), is the principal waterway in the southeastern part of the continent. It originates in Germany and flows through Austria, Slovakia, Hungary, the former Yugoslavian republics, Bulgaria, and Romania into the Black Sea. The Rhine winds northward from the Alps through western Germany and the Netherlands into the North Sea, which is also the destination of the Elbe River in eastern Germany. In France, the Rhône flows south into the Mediterranean, and the Seine and Loire flow west to the English Channel and the Bay of Biscay. Other important waterways are the Po in northern Italy, the Vistula in Poland, and the Thames in England.

The proximity of most areas of the European landmass to the coastline or to major river systems is important to understanding the historical development of European civilization. Trading routes and major cities developed along these waterways, and rivers have served as natural boundaries.

LAND REGIONS Europe, despite its small size, presents a wide range of landforms, from rugged mountains to sweeping plains. These landforms can be separated into four major regions: the Northwest Mountains, the Great European Plain, the Central Uplands, and the Alpine Mountain System. The mountains of the Northwest Region cover most of the region, running through northwestern France, Ireland, northern Great Britain, Norway, Sweden, northern Finland, and the northwest corner of Russia.

The Great European Plain covers almost all of the European part of the former Soviet Union, extending from the Arctic Ocean to the Caucasus Mountains. This belt stretches westward across Poland, Germany, Belgium, the western portion of France, and southeastern England.

The Central Uplands is a belt of high plateaus, hills, and low mountains. It reaches from the central plateau of Portugal, across Spain, the central highlands of France, to the hills and mountains of southern Germany, the Czech Republic, and Slovakia.

The Alpine Mountain System is made up of several mountain chains. Included in this system are the Pyrenees between Spain and France, the Alps in southeastern France, northern Italy, Switzerland, and western Austria, and the Apennine range in Italy. Also included are the mountain ranges of the Balkan Peninsula, the Carpathian Mountains in Slovakia and Romania, and the Caucasus Mountains between the Black and Caspian Seas. These mountain ranges have been formidable barriers and boundaries throughout history, affecting the movement of people and the relationship of people to each other and to the land.

When studying the map of Europe, it is important to notice the proximity of western areas of Asia, especially those at the eastern end of the Mediterranean Sea, to areas of North Africa. The cultures of these areas have not only interacted with those of Europe but have also played a significant role in shaping the history of Western civilization.

Western Civilization

Ideas, Politics & Society

Eighth Edition

Part One

The Ancient World: Foundation of the West

to A.D. 500

3000 B.C.

2000 B.C.

1000 B.C.

500 B.C.

100 B.C.

A.D. 200

Politics and Society	Thought and Culture
Rise of civilization in Sumer (c. 3200) Union of Upper and Lower Egypt (c. 2900) Rise of Minoan civilization (c. 2600)	Cuneiform writing in Sumer; hieroglyphics in Egypt
Rise of Mycenaean civilization (c. 2000) Hammurabi of Babylon builds an empire (1792–1750)	*Epic of Gilgamesh* (c. 1900) Code of Hammurabi (c. 1790) Amenhotep IV and a movement toward monotheism in Egypt (c. 1369–1353) Moses and the Exodus (1200s)
The creation of a unified Hebrew monarchy under David (1000–961) Dark Age in Greece (c. 1100–800) Hellenic Age (c. 800–323) Fall of Assyrian empire (612) Persian conquest of Near East (550–525) Formation of Roman Republic (509)	Homer's *Iliad* and *Odyssey* (700s) Age of classical prophecy: flowering of Hebrew ethical thought (750–430)
Persian Wars (499–479) Peloponnesian War (431–404) Conquest of Greek city-states by Philip of Macedon (338) Conquests of Alexander the Great (336–323) Hellenistic Age (323–30) Roman conquest of Carthage and Hellenistic kingdoms (264–146)	Law of the Twelve Tables (c. 450) Rise of Greek philosophy: Ionians, Pythagoreans, Parmenides (500s and 400s) Greek dramatists: Aeschylus, Sophocles, Euripides, Aristophanes (400s) Greek philosophers: Socrates, Plato, Aristotle (400s and 300s) Hellenistic philosophies: Epicureanism, Stoicism, Skepticism, Cynicism
Political violence and civil wars in Rome (88–31) Assassination of Julius Caesar (44) Octavian takes the title Augustus and becomes first Roman emperor (27) Greco-Roman Age (30 B.C.–c. A.D. 500) Pax Romana—the height of Roman Empire (27 B.C.–A.D. 180)	Roman philosophers during the Republic: Lucretius, Cicero (1st cent. B.C.) Rise and spread of Christianity: Jesus (d. A.D. 29); Paul's missionary activity (c. 34–64) Gospel According to Mark (c. 66–70) Roman historians, poets, and philosophers during the Pax Romana: Livy, Tacitus, Virgil, Horace, Ovid, Juvenal, Seneca, Marcus Aurelius
Military anarchy in Rome (235–285) Goths defeat Romans at Adrianople (378) End of Roman Empire in the West (476)	Church fathers: Jerome, Ambrose, Augustine (300s and 400s)

Chapter 1

The Ancient Near East: The First Civilizations

Built as royal tombs, the pyramids at Giza are among the wonders of the ancient world. (Robert Frerck/Woodfin Camp.)

- **Prehistory**
- **The Rise to Civilization**
- **Mesopotamian Civilization**
- **Egyptian Civilization**
- **Empire Builders**
- **The Religious Orientation of the Near East**

Focus Questions

1. What is meant by the term *civilization?* Under what conditions did it emerge?
2. What did Mesopotamian and Egyptian civilizations have in common? How did they differ?
3. In what ways did mythopoeic thought characterize Near Eastern civilization? How does this type of thinking differ from that of science?
4. What elements of Near Eastern civilization were passed on to Western civilization?

Online Study Center

This icon will direct you to interactive map and primary source activities on the website http://college.hmco.com/pic/perrywc8e.

Civilization was not inevitable; it was an act of human creativity. The first civilizations emerged about five thousand years ago, in the Near Eastern river valleys of Sumer and Egypt. Before that time stretched the vast ages of prehistory, when our ancestors did not dwell in cities and knew nothing of writing; some 99 percent of human history took place before the creation of civilization. Today, when human beings have the capacity to destroy civilization, we might reflect on humanity's long and painful climb to a civilized state.

PREHISTORY

The period called the **Paleolithic Age,** or Old Stone Age, began with the earliest primitive toolmaking human beings who inhabited East Africa nearly three million years ago. It ended ten thousand years ago in parts of the Near East when people discovered how to farm. Our Paleolithic ancestors lived as hunters (no doubt also as scavengers) and food gatherers. Because they had not learned how to farm, they did not establish permanent villages. When their food supplies ran short, they abandoned their caves or tentlike structures of branches and searched for new dwelling places.

Human social development was shaped by this three-million-year experience of hunting and food gathering. For survival, groups of families formed bands consisting of around thirty people; members learned how to plan, organize, cooperate, trust, and share. The men hunted for meat, and the women cared for the young, tended the fires, and gathered fruits, nuts, berries, and grain. Hunters assisted each other in tracking and killing game, finding cooperative efforts more successful than individual forays. By sharing their kill and bringing some back to their camp for the rest of the group, they reinforced the social bond. So, too, did women who gathered food for the group. Bands that did not cooperate in the hunt, in food gathering, or in food distribution were unlikely to survive.

Although human progress was very slow during the long centuries of the Paleolithic Age, advances occurred that influenced the future

Chronology 1.1 ❖ The Near East

3200 B.C.*	Rise of civilization in Sumer
2900	Union of Upper and Lower Egypt
2686–2181	Old Kingdom: essential forms of Egyptian civilization take shape
2180	Downfall of Akkadian empire
1792–1750	Hammurabi of Babylon brings Akkad and Sumer under his control and fashions a code of laws
1570	Egyptians drive out Hyksos and embark on empire building
1369–1353	Reign of Amenhotep IV: a movement toward monotheism
1200	Fall of Hittite empire
612	Fall of Assyrian empire
604–562	Reign of Nebuchadnezzar: height of Chaldean empire
550–525 B.C.	Persian conquests form a world empire

*Most dates are approximations

enormously. Paleolithic people developed spoken language and shaped bone, wood, and stone tools that corresponded to ideas in their minds. They preserved their creations and taught other people how to use them. Succeeding generations improved on what they had learned from their ancestors. With these simple but useful tools, Paleolithic human beings dug up roots; peeled the bark off trees; trapped, killed, and skinned animals; made clothing; and fashioned fishnets. They also discovered how to control fire, which allowed them to cook their meat and provided warmth and protection against predators—lions and leopards, for example—that feared fire. From evidence discovered in caves, it is certain that Paleolithic people had domesticated fire about 500,000 years ago. Some evidence points to fire use as far back as 1.5 million years.

Like toolmaking and the control of fire, language was a great human achievement. Language enabled individuals to acquire and share with one another knowledge, experiences, and feelings. Thus, language was the decisive factor in the development of culture and its transmission from one generation to the next. Language helped parents teach their children rules of conduct and religious beliefs, as well as how to make tools and light fires.

Most likely, our Paleolithic ancestors developed mythic-religious ideas to explain the mysteries of nature, birth, sickness, and death. They felt that living powers operated within and beyond the world that they experienced, and they sought to establish friendly relations with these powers. To primitive peoples, the elements—sun, rain, wind, thunder, and lightning—were alive. The natural elements were spirits; they could feel and act with a purpose. To appease these forces of nature, hunters and gatherers made offerings to them. Gradually, there emerged shamans, medicine men, and witch doctors, who, through rituals, trances, and chants, seemed able to communicate with these spirits. Paleolithic people also began the practice of burying their dead, sometimes with offerings, which suggests belief in life after death. Corpses were sometimes dusted with red ocher, which represented blood, a source of life. Another belief is revealed in the many small statues of women, made between forty thousand and twenty-five thousand years ago, that have been found by archaeologists in Europe and Asia. Fashioned from ivory, wood, and clay and often marked by huge breasts and distended stomachs, these fertility figurines represent a mother goddess who gave life, food, and protection.

Between thirty thousand and twelve thousand years ago, Paleolithic people sought out the dark and silent interior of caves, which they probably viewed as sanctuaries, and, with only torches for light, they painted remarkably skillful and perceptive pictures of animals on the cave walls. Even prior to civilization, human beings demonstrated artistic talent, an esthetic sense. When these prehistoric artists drew an animal with a spear in its side, they probably believed that this act would make them successful in hunting; when they drew a herd of animals, they probably hoped that this would cause game to be plentiful. This belief that something done to an image of an animal or a person will produce the same effect on the being itself is called *sympathetic magic*. Hunting societies that endured into the modern world still engaged in rituals designed to protect the hunter and to ensure a kill.

Our knowledge of prehistoric art is being expanded by the discovery in December 1994 of a cave in southern France containing more than two hundred paintings made about thirty thousand years ago. Although not yet completely explored, several factors make this discovery so promising: the number of paintings is considerably greater than that found in the famous caves of Lascaux, also in southern France, and Altamira, Spain; included are images of animals—panthers and owls—not found in other caves; and the site seems to have been undisturbed for thousands of years.

Some ten thousand years ago, the New Stone Age, or **Neolithic Age,** began in the Near East. During the Neolithic Age, human beings discovered farming, domesticated animals, established villages, polished stone tools, made pottery, and wove cloth. So important were these achievements that they are referred to as the Neolithic Revolution.

Agriculture—the deliberate planting and cultivation of crops—first developed in the hilly regions of the Near East, where rainfall was plentiful and wheat and barley grew abundantly in the wild. People there also began to domesticate the sheep and wild goats that roamed the hills. In other parts of the world, farming and the domestication of animals developed independently.

Agriculture and the domestication of animals revolutionized life. Whereas Paleolithic hunters and food gatherers had been forced to use whatever nature made available to them, Neolithic farmers altered their environment to satisfy human needs. Instead of spending their time searching for grains, roots, and berries, women and children grew crops near their homes; instead of tracking animals over great distances, men could slaughter domesticated goats or sheep nearby. (Later, horses, camels, and donkeys were tamed, providing people with a means of transportation.) Since farmers had to live near their fields and could store food for the future, farming led to the rise of permanent settlements. Villages containing as many as two hundred or three hundred people had occasionally emerged in late Paleolithic times, before the discovery of agriculture. Hunter-gatherers built such villages in areas that had an abundant, stable food supply—near a river or lake well stocked with fish, or in a valley with plenty of wild wheat and barley and herds of gazelles or goats. The development of farming greatly speeded the shift to villages. It is likely that trade also impelled people to gather in village communities. Herdsmen, hunters, and food gatherers living in regions rich in salt (needed for preserving food), volcanic glass (used for mirrors, blades, and spearheads), or hematite (an iron ore that was a source of red coloring for pottery) formed trading settlements, which exchanged raw materials for food.

Villages changed the patterns of life. A food surplus freed some people to devote part of their time to sharpening their skills as basket weavers or toolmakers. The demand for raw materials and the creations of skilled artisans fostered trade, sometimes across long distances, and the formation of trading settlements. An awareness of private property emerged. Hunters had accumulated few possessions, since belongings presented a burden in moving from place to place. Villagers, however, acquired property and were determined to protect it from one another and from outsiders—nomadic herdsmen who might raid the village. Hunting bands were egalitarian; generally, no one member had more possessions or more power than another. In farming villages, a ruling elite emerged that possessed wealth and wielded power.

No doubt farming also affected our emotional development. Human beings who had evolved as hunters and foragers, enjoying considerable leisure, personal freedom, independence, and equality, were now forced to adjust to a different tempo of life—unending toil, stifling routine, and the need to obey the commands of the elites. Scholars ponder the psychological dimensions of this shift from the hunter's way of life to sedentary farming.

In recent years, archaeologists have uncovered several Neolithic villages, the oldest of which was established before 8000 B.C. Among the most famous of these sites are Çatal Hüyük in Anatolia (Turkey), Jericho in Palestine, and Jarmö in eastern Iraq. Scholars disagree on whether these communities were just highly developed villages or the first cities. The traditional view is that cities arose about 3000 B.C. in Sumer, the home of the earliest civilization. Some scholars argue that five thousand years before the Sumerian cities Jericho's two thousand inhabitants had created urban life by engaging in trade and embarking on public works. Jericho's walls were six feet six inches thick at the base and in some places twenty feet high. Their construction required cooperation and a division of labor beyond the capacity of an agricultural village. Similar communities, or "primitive cities," spread throughout much of the Near East in late prehistoric times.

Neolithic people made great strides in technology. By shaping and baking clay, they made pottery containers for cooking and for storing food and water. The invention of the potter's wheel enabled them to form bowls and plates more quickly and precisely. Stone tools were sharpened by grinding them on rock. The discoveries of the wheel and the sail improved transportation and promoted trade, and the development of the plow and the ox yoke made tilling the soil easier for farmers.

The Neolithic period also marks the beginning of the use of metals. First used was copper, which was easily fashioned into tools and weapons. Copper implements lasted longer than those made of stone and flint, and they could be recast and reshaped if broken. In time, artisans discovered how to make bronze by combining copper and tin in the proper ratio. Bronze was harder than copper, which made a sharper cutting edge possible.

During the Neolithic Age, the food supply became more reliable, village life expanded, and the population increased. Families that acquired wealth gained a higher social status and became village leaders. Religion grew more formal and structured; nature spirits evolved into deities, each with specific powers over nature or human life. Altars were erected in their honor, and ceremonies were conducted by priests, whose power and wealth increased as people gave offerings to the gods. Neolithic society was growing more organized and complex; it was on the threshold of civilization.

The Rise to Civilization

What we call **civilization** arose some five thousand years ago in the Near East (in Mesopotamia and Egypt) and then later in the Far East (in India and China). The first civilizations began in cities, which were larger, more populated, and more complex in their political, economic, and social structure than Neolithic villages. Because the cities depended on the inhabitants of adjacent villages for their food, farming techniques must have been developed sufficiently to produce food surpluses. Increased production provided food for urban inhabitants, who engaged in nonagricultural occupations; they became merchants, craftsmen, bureaucrats, and priests.

The invention of writing enabled the first civilizations to preserve, organize, and expand knowledge and to pass it on to future generations; it also allowed government officials and priests to conduct their affairs more efficiently. Moreover, civilized societies possessed organized governments, which issued laws and defined the boundary lines of their states. On a scale much larger than Neolithic communities, the inhabitants erected buildings and monuments, engaged in trade and manufacturing, and used specialized labor for different projects. Religious life grew more organized and complex, and a powerful and wealthy priesthood emerged. These developments—cities, specialization of labor, writing, organized government, monumental architecture, and a complex religious structure—differentiate the first civilizations from prehistoric cultures.

Religion was the central force in these primary civilizations. It provided satisfying explanations for the workings of nature, helped ease the fear of death, and justified traditional rules of morality. Law was considered sacred, a commandment of the gods. Religion united people in the common enterprises needed for survival—for example, the construction and maintenance of irrigation works and the storage of food. Religion also promoted creativity in art, literature, and science. In addition, the power of rulers, regarded as gods or their agents, derived from religion.

The emergence of civilization was a great creative act and not merely the inevitable development of agricultural societies. Many communities had learned how to farm, but only a handful made the leap into civilization. How was it possible for Sumerians and Egyptians, the creators of the earliest civilizations, to make that breakthrough? This question has intrigued and baffled historians, and no single explanation is entirely convincing. Most scholars stress the relationship between civilizations and river valleys. Rivers deposited fertile silt on adjoining fields, provided water for crops, and served as avenues for trade. But environmental factors alone do not adequately explain the emergence of civilization. What cannot be omitted is the human contribution: capacity for thought and cooperative activity.

Both the Tigris and Euphrates Rivers in Mesopotamia and the Nile River in Egypt deposited fertile soil when they overflowed their banks. But before these rivers could be of any value in producing crops, swamps around them had to be drained, jungles had to be cleared, and dikes, reservoirs, and canals had to be built. To construct and maintain irrigation works required the cooperation of large numbers of people, a necessary condition for civilization. As anthropologist Robert J. Braidwood says,

> *Whole villages or groups of people had to turn out to fix dikes or dig ditches. The dikes had to be repaired and the ditches carefully cleared of silt each year, or they would become useless. There also had to be hard and fast rules. The person who lived nearest the ditch or the reservoir must not be allowed to take all the water and leave none for his neighbors. It was not only a business of learning to control the rivers and making their waters do the farmer's work. It also meant controlling men. . . . This learning to work together for the common good was probably the real germ of the Egyptian and the Mesopotamian civilizations.*[1*]

In the process of constructing and maintaining irrigation networks, people learned to formulate and obey rules and developed administrative, engineering, and mathematical skills. The need to keep records stimulated the invention of writing. These creative responses to the challenges posed by nature spurred the early inhabitants of Sumer and Egypt to make the breakthrough to civilization, thereby altering the course of human destiny. By the time the Hebrews and the Greeks, the spiritual ancestors of Western civilization, appeared on the stage of history, civilizations had been in existence for some two thousand years.

Civilization also had its dark side. Epidemic disease thrived in urban centers, where people lived close together in unsanitary conditions, drinking contaminated water and surrounded by rotting garbage. Slavery was an essential and accepted feature of early civilizations. The authority wielded by rulers and their officials and the habits of discipline acquired by the community's members made possible the construction of irrigation works, but they were also harnessed for destructive conflicts between states. Such warfare, which involved managing large numbers of combatants, was far more lethal than the sporadic and generally disorganized acts of violence that occurred in Neolithic times. A hostile and aggressive attitude toward members of alien groups has plagued human beings since the rise of civilization. And warfare fascinated the people who created the first civilizations: scribes recounted battle after battle, warrior-kings boasted of their military conquests, and military heroes were held in the highest esteem. Cultural historian Lewis Mumford observes:

> *War was not a mere residue of more common primitive forms of aggression. . . . In all its typical aspects, its discipline, its drill, its handling of large masses of men as units, in its destructive assaults en masse, in its heroic sacrifices, its final destructions, exterminations, seizures, enslavements, war was rather the special invention of civilization: its ultimate drama.*[2]

*Numbered source notes appear at the end of each chapter along with suggested readings.

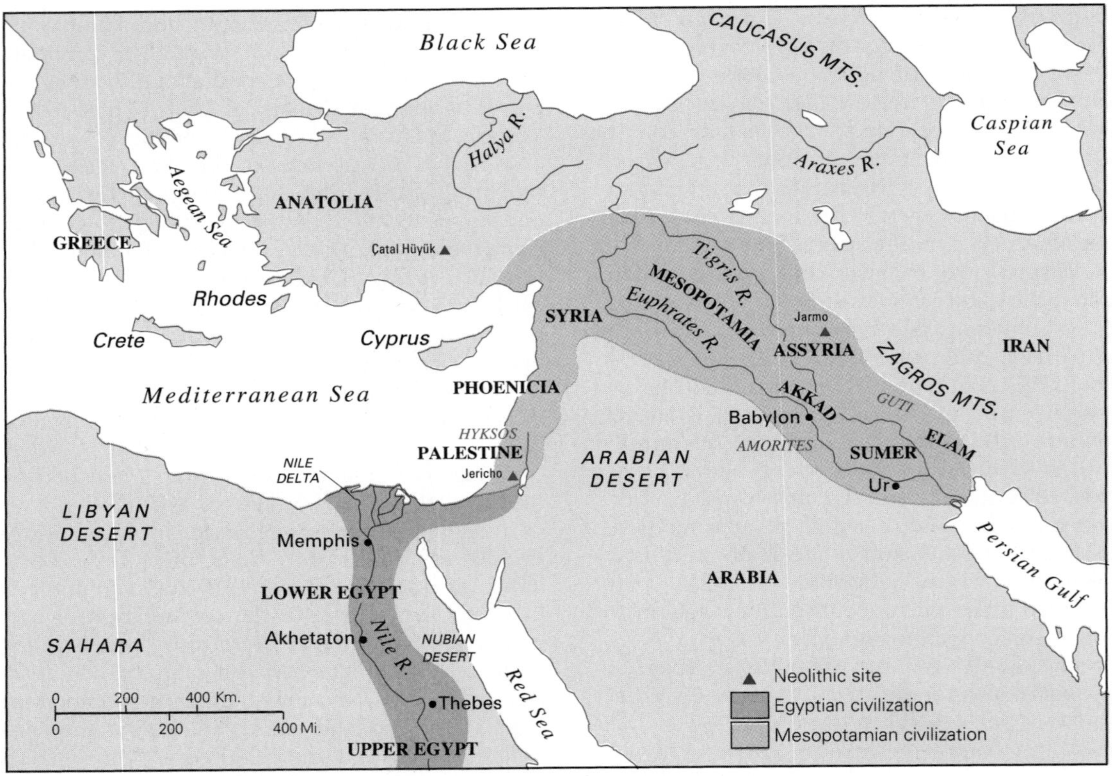

Map 1.1 MESOPOTAMIAN AND EGYPTIAN CIVILIZATIONS The first civilizations emerged in river valleys: Mesopotamia in the valleys of the Tigris and Euphrates Rivers, Egypt in the Nile valley.

MESOPOTAMIAN CIVILIZATION

Mesopotamia is the Greek word for "land between the rivers." It was here, in the valleys of the Tigris and Euphrates Rivers, that the first civilization began. The first to develop an urban civilization in Mesopotamia (modern-day Iraq) were the Sumerians, who colonized the marshlands of the lower Euphrates, which, together with the Tigris, flows into the Persian Gulf. The Sumerians' origin is obscure, although scholars speculate that they migrated from the East, perhaps northern India. They spoke a language unrelated to the tongues of their Semitic neighbors, who had migrated from Arabia into Mesopotamia and adjacent regions.

Through constant toil and imagination, the Sumerians transformed the swamps into fields of barley and groves of date palms. Around 3000 B.C., their hut settlements gradually evolved into twelve independent city-states, each consisting of a city and its surrounding countryside. Among the impressive achievements of the Sumerians were a system of symbol writing (*cuneiform*), in which pictograms and signs for numbers were engraved with a reed stylus on clay tablets to represent ideas; elaborate brick houses, palaces, and temples; bronze tools and weapons; irrigation works; trade with other peoples; an early form of money; religious and political institutions; schools; religious and secular literature; varied art forms; codes of law; medicinal drugs; and a lunar calendar.

Although they spoke a common language and shared the same customs and gods, the Sumerian city-states engaged in frequent warfare with each other, principally over boundaries and water rights (canals built upriver reduced the water available to the cities downriver). Weakened by warfare, the Sumerians lay open to foreign domination.

The history of Mesopotamia is marked by a succession of conquests. To the north of Sumer was a Semitic city called Akkad. About 2350 B.C., the people of Akkad, led by Sargon the Great, the warrior-king, conquered the Sumerian cities. Sargon built the world's first empire, which extended from the Persian Gulf to the Mediterranean Sea. Establishing a pattern that future despotic rulers would emulate, Sargon stationed garrisons in conquered lands and appointed governors and officials to administer the territories, as well as additional bureaucrats to register and parcel out the precious metals, horses, grain, and other commodities exacted from conquered peoples. He also retained a large standing army to quell revolts and to launch new imperialist ventures. The Akkadians adopted Sumerian cultural forms, including cuneiform, and spread them beyond the boundaries of Mesopotamia with their conquests. Mesopotamian religion became a blend of Sumerian and Akkadian elements.

In succeeding centuries, the Sumerian cities were incorporated into various kingdoms and empires. The Sumerian language, replaced by a Semitic tongue, became an obscure language known only to priests, and the Sumerians gradually disappeared as a distinct people. But their cultural achievements endured. Akkadians, Babylonians, Elamites, and others adopted Sumerian religious, legal, literary, and art forms. The Sumerian legacy served as the basis for a Mesopotamian civilization that maintained a distinct style for three thousand years.

WOODEN SOUNDBOX OF A SUMERIAN HARP, UR, C. 2600 B.C. The top panel features a heroic figure embracing two man-faced bulls made from shells inlaid in bitumen. Beneath are three panels with various animals carrying food or drink and musical instruments. The theme may depict a fable of some festive celebration or a ritual myth. (*University Museum, University of Pennsylvania, Negative #S8–22097.*)

Online Study Center **Improve Your Grade**
Interactive Map: Ancient Mesopotamia through the Persian Empire

Religion: The Basis of Mesopotamian Civilization

Religion lay at the center of Mesopotamian life. Every human activity—political, military, social, legal, literary, artistic—was generally subordinated to an overriding religious purpose. Religion was the Mesopotamians' frame of reference for understanding nature, society, and themselves; it dominated and inspired all other cultural expressions and human activities. Wars between cities, for instance, were interpreted as conflicts between the gods of those cities, and victory ultimately depended on divine favor, not on human effort. **Myths**—narratives about the activities of the gods—explained the origins of the human species. According to the earliest Sumerian myths, the first human beings issued forth from the earth like plant life, or were shaped from clay by divine craftsmen and granted a heart by the goddess Nammu, or were formed from the blood of two gods sacrificed for that purpose.

The Mesopotamians believed that people were given life so that they could execute on earth the will of the gods in heaven. No important decisions were made by kings or priests without first consulting the gods. To discover the wishes of the gods, priests sacrificed animals and then examined their livers; or the priests might find their answers in the stars or in dreams.

The cities of Mesopotamia were sacred communities dedicated to serving divine masters, and people hoped that appeasing the gods would bring security and prosperity to their cities. The Sumerians erected ziggurats—huge multilevel mounds—on which temples were built. The ziggurat in Ur measured 205 feet by 140 feet at the base and was about 70 feet high; staircases connected its levels and led to the top platform, on which stood a majestic temple.

The ziggurat was surrounded by low walls enclosing offices and houses for the priests and shops where potters, weavers, carpenters, and tanners performed their crafts. The temple was the religious and economic heart of the city. A particular city belonged to a god, who was the real owner of the land and the real ruler of the city; often a vast complex of temples was built for the god and the god's family. In the temple, the god was offered shelter, food, clothing, and the homage of dutiful servants. Temple priests collected rents, operated businesses, and received contributions for festivals. Most inhabitants of the city worked for the temple priests as tenant farmers, agricultural laborers, or servants. Anxious to curry favor with the gods and goddesses who watched over the fields, peasants surrendered part of their crops to the temple. Priests coordinated the city's economic activity, supervising the distribution of land, overseeing the irrigation works, and storing food for emergencies. Temple scribes kept records of expenditures and receipts. By serving as stewards of the city's deities and managing their earthly estates, the priests sustained civilized life.

The gods and goddesses, invisible to human eyes but omnipresent, controlled the entire universe and everything in it. The moon, the sun, and the storm, the city, the irrigation works, and the fields—each was directed by a god. Mesopotamians saw gods and demons everywhere in nature. There was a god in the fire and another in the river; evil demons stirred up sandstorms, caused disease, and endangered women in childbirth. To shield themselves from hostile forces, Mesopotamians wore charms and begged their gods for help. Each Mesopotamian offered prayers and sacrifices to a personal god or goddess, who provided protection against evil spirits.

Mesopotamians believed that they were manipulated by divine beings. When misfortune befell them, people attributed it to the gods. Even success was not due to their own efforts but to the intervention of a god who had taken a special interest in them. Compared with the gods, an individual was an insignificant and lowly creature.

Uncertainty and danger filled life in Mesopotamia. Sometimes, the unpredictable waters of the rivers broke through the dikes, flooding fields, ruining crops, and damaging cities. At other times, an insufficient overflow deprived the land of water, causing crops to fail. Great windstorms left the countryside covered with a layer of sand, and heavy thunderstorms turned fields into a sea of mud that made travel impossible. Unlike Egypt, which was protected by vast deserts, Mesopotamia had no natural barriers to invasion. Feeling themselves surrounded by unfathomable and often hostile forces, Mesopotamians lived in an atmosphere of anxiety, which permeated their civilization.

Contributing to this sense of insecurity was the belief that the gods had little love for humanity. They had created a "savage, 'man' shall be his name . . . [who] shall be charged with the service of the gods that they might be at ease."[3] Toward humans the gods behaved capriciously, maliciously, and vindictively, and it was difficult to please them.

What do the gods demand of me? Is it ever possible to please them? To these questions Mesopotamians had no reassuring answers, for the gods' behavior was a mystery to mere human beings:

> *What is good for oneself may be offense to*
> *one's god,*
> *What in one's own heart seems despicable*
> *may be proper to one's god.*
> *Who can know the will of the gods in heaven?*
> *Who can understand the plans of the*
> *underworld gods?*
> *Where have humans learned the way of a god?*
> *He who was alive yesterday is dead today.*[4]

A Mesopotamian man or woman hoped to experience the good life by being obedient to his or her older brother, father, foreman, priest, and king and to a personal deity, who could influence the decisions of the other gods. The rewards for obedience were long life, health, and worldly success. But the feeling persisted that happiness was either transitory or beyond reach—a pessimism that abounded in Mesopotamian literature.

A mood of uncertainty and anxiety, an awareness of the cosmos as unfathomable and mysterious, a feeling of dread about the fragility of human existence and the impermanence of human achievement—these attitudes are as old as the first civilization. The *Epic of Gilgamesh*, the finest work of Mesopotamian literature, masterfully depicts this mood of pessimism and despair. The epic deals with a profound theme: the human protest against death. The death of his close friend causes Gilgamesh to face the reality of his own death. "Despair is in my heart. What my brother is now that shall I be when I am dead. . . . I am afraid of death."[5] Gilgamesh yearns for eternal life, but he

King Gudea. Inscriptions written in cuneiform recorded the construction of temples and irrigation works in the Sumerian city-state of Lagash during the reign of King Gudea around 2150 B.C. The inscription on Gudea's image describes a temple dedicated to the goddess Geshtin-anna. (*Louvre © R.M.N.*)

learns that when the gods created human beings, they allotted to them only death. "Where is the man who can clamber to heaven? Only the gods live forever . . . but as for us men, our days are numbered, our occupations are a breath of wind."[6]

And in contrast to the Egyptians, the Mesopotamians had little to look forward to after death. They believed that they would either be confined to a dreary underworld whose rulers would inflict pain on them or be transformed into spirits, flying about and tormenting the living.

Government, Law, and Economy

Kingship, bestowed on a man by the gods, was the central institution in Mesopotamian society. Unlike Egyptian pharaohs, Mesopotamian kings saw themselves not as gods but rather as great men selected by the gods to represent them on earth. Gods governed through the kings, who reported to the gods about conditions in their land (which was the gods' property) and petitioned the gods for advice.

The king administered the laws, which came from the gods. Like everyone else in the land, the king had to obey divine laws. These laws provided Mesopotamians with a measure of security. The principal collection of laws in ancient Mesopotamia was the famous code of Hammurabi (c. 1792–c. 1750), the Babylonian ruler. Unearthed by French archaeologists in 1901–1902, the code has provided invaluable insights into Mesopotamian society. The laws were inscribed on a stone slab (stele), near the top of which Hammurabi was depicted, standing reverently before the throne of Shamash, the sun-god and patron of justice. In typical Mesopotamian fashion, Hammurabi claimed that his code rested on the authority of the gods; to violate it was to contravene the divine order.

The code reveals social status and mores in that area and time. Men were the heads of the family, although efforts were made to protect women and children from mistreatment and poverty. Thus, if a man divorced his wife because she did not bear him a son, he had to provide her with money. Punishments were generally severe—"an eye for an eye and a tooth for a tooth." The code prescribed death for housebreaking, kidnapping, aiding the escape of slaves, receiving stolen goods, and bearing false witness; however, it allowed consideration of extenuating circumstances. Being forgiven by the wronged party could also mitigate the penalty. For example, a wife who committed adultery could be spared execution if pardoned by her husband. Class distinctions were expressed in the code. Penalties varied with the status of both the wrongdoer and the victim. For instance, a person received a harsher punishment for harming a noble than for harming a commoner. Government officials engaging in extortion or bribery were punished severely. The code's many provisions relating to business transactions show the importance of trade to Mesopotamian life.

The economy of Mesopotamian cities depended heavily on foreign and domestic trade. Whereas trade in Egypt was conducted by the state bureaucracy, in Mesopotamia there was greater opportunity for private enterprise. Besides merchants, temple priests engaged in trade because they possessed surplus produce collected as rents from farmers using temple land. Early in Mesopotamian history, merchants were subservient to the king and the temple priests. Over the centuries, however, merchants began to behave as professionals—not just as agents of the palace or temple, but as private entrepreneurs.

Because of trade's importance to the life of the city, governments instituted regulations to prevent fraud. Business transactions had to be recorded in writing, and severe punishments were imposed for dishonesty. A system of weights and measures facilitated trade, and efforts were made to prevent excessive interest rates for loans.

Mesopotamians imported resources not found at home—stone, silver, and timber. In exchange, they exported textiles, fine handicrafts, and (less often because of difficulty in transporting them by donkey) agricultural products. They also imported copper from the Persian Gulf, precious metals from Afghanistan, ivory from Africa and the west coast of India, and cedar and cypress woods, oils, and essences from the Mediterranean coastal areas. Enterprising businessmen set up trading outposts in distant lands, making the Mesopotamians pioneers in international trade.

Writing, Mathematics, Astronomy, and Medicine

The Sumerians established schools, which trained the sons of the upper class in the art of cuneiform writing. Hundreds of tablets on which Sumerian students practiced their lessons have been discovered, testifying to the years of disciplined and demanding work required to master the scribal art. Virtually all scribes were men, but female scribes are at times mentioned in Mesopotamian writings. Noble women in particular were literate.

To assist their pupils, teachers prepared textbooks of word lists and mathematical problems with solutions. In translating Sumerian words into the Akkadian language, they compiled what was probably the world's first dictionary. Students who completed the course of study successfully were employed as archivists, secretaries, or accountants by the temple, the palace, the law courts, or merchants. The Sumerian system of cuneiform writing spread to other parts of the Near East.

The Mesopotamians made some impressive advances in mathematics. They devised multiplication and division tables, including even cubes and cube roots. They determined the area of right-angle triangles and rectangles, divided a circle into 360 degrees, and had some understanding of the principles that centuries later would be developed into the Pythagorean theorem and quadratic equations. But the Babylonians, who made the chief contribution in mathematics, barely advanced to the level of theorizing; they did not formulate general principles or furnish proofs for their mathematical operations.

By carefully observing and accurately recording the positions of planets and constellations of stars, Babylonian sky watchers took the first steps in developing the science of astronomy, and they devised a calendar based on the cycles of the moon. As in mathematics, however, they did not form theories to coordinate and illuminate their data. Believing that the position of the stars and planets revealed the will of the gods, astronomers did not examine the heavens to find what we call cause and effect connections between the phenomena. Rather, they sought to discover what the gods wanted. With this knowledge, people could organize their political, social, and moral lives in accordance with divine commands and escape the terrible consequences that they believed resulted from ignoring the gods' wishes. Thus, despite its impressive achievements, Babylonian astronomy remained essentially a mythical interpretation of the universe.

As was consistent with their religious worldview, the Mesopotamians believed that disease was caused by gods or demons. To cure a patient, priest-physicians resorted to magic; through prayers and sacrifices, they attempted to appease the gods and eject the demons from the sick body. Nevertheless, in identifying illnesses and prescribing appropriate remedies, Mesopotamians demonstrated some accurate knowledge of medicine and pharmacology.

Egyptian Civilization

During the early period of Mesopotamian civilization, the people of another river valley, to the west, put themselves on the path toward civilization. The Egyptians developed their civilization in the fertile valley of the Nile. For good reason, the Greek historian Herodotus called Egypt "the gift of the Nile," for without this mighty river, which flows more than four thousand miles from central Africa northward to the Mediterranean, virtually all Egypt would be a desert. When the Nile overflowed its banks, as it did reliably and predictably, the floodwaters deposited a layer of fertile black earth, which, when cultivated, provided abundant food to support Egyptian civilization. The Egyptians learned how to control the river—a feat that required cooperative effort and ingenuity, as well as engineering and administrative skills.

Online Study Center

Improve Your Grade
Primary Source: The Hymn to the Nile

Nature favored Egypt in a number of ways. Besides water, fish and fowl, and fertile land, the Nile also provided an excellent transportation link between Upper (southern) and Lower (northern) Egypt. Natural barriers—mountains, deserts, cataracts (rapids) in the Nile, and the Mediterranean—protected Egypt from attack, allowing the inhabitants to enjoy long periods of peace and prosperity. Gold, copper, and stone abounded, along with other natural resources. In addition, the climate of Egypt is dry and salutary. To the Egyptians, nature seemed changeless and beneficent. Hence, unlike Mesopotamians, Egyptians derived a sense of security from their environment.

From the Old Kingdom to the Middle Kingdom

About 2900 B.C., a ruler of Upper Egypt, known as Narmer, or Menes, conquered the Nile Delta and Lower Egypt. By 2686 B.C., centralized rule had been firmly established, and great pyramids, which were tombs for the pharaohs, were being constructed. The pyramids required rigorous central planning to coordinate the tens of thousands of laborers drafted to build these immense monuments. During this Pyramid Age, or Old Kingdom (2686–2181 B.C.), the essential forms of Egyptian civilization crystallized.

The Egyptians believed the pharaoh to be both a man and a god, the earthly embodiment of the deity Horus; he was an absolute ruler of the land and held his court at the city of Memphis. The Egyptians regarded the pharaoh as a benevolent protector who controlled the floodwaters of the Nile, kept the irrigation works in order, maintained justice in the land, and expressed the will of heaven. They expected that when the pharaoh died and joined his fellow gods, he would still help his living subjects.

In time, the nobles who served as district governors gained in status and wealth and gradually came to undermine the divine king's authority. The nobles' growing power and the enormous expenditure of Egypt's human and material resources on building pyramids led to the decline of the Old Kingdom. From 2181 to 2040 B.C.—a time called the First Intermediate Period—rival families competed for the throne, thus destroying the unity of the kingdom. The civil wars and the collapse of central authority required to maintain the irrigation system cast a pall over the land, as illustrated in this ancient Egyptian poem:

> *The wrongdoer is everywhere. . . .*
> *Plunderers are everywhere. . . .*
> *Nile is in flood, yet none plougheth*
> *for him. . . .*
> *Laughter hath perished and is no longer*
> *made.*
> *It is grief that walketh through the land, mingled with lamentations. . . .*
> *The storehouse is bare.*[7]

During what is called the Middle Kingdom (2040–1786 B.C.), strong kings reasserted pharaonic rule and reunited the state. The restoration of political stability reinvigorated cultural life and revived economic activity. Pharaohs extended Egyptian control south over the land of Nubia, which became a principal source of gold. A profitable trade was carried on with Palestine, Syria, and Crete.

About 1800 B.C., central authority again weakened. In the era known as the Second Intermediate Period (1786–1570 B.C.), the nobles regained some of their power, the Nubians broke away from Egyptian control, and the Hyksos (a mixture of Semites and Indo-Europeans) invaded Egypt. For centuries, desert and sea had effectively guarded Egypt from foreign invasion, but the Hyksos invaders, using horse and chariot and body armor, ended Egyptian complacency. The Hyksos succeeded in dominating Egypt for about a hundred years. Resentful of foreign rule, the Egyptians became more militant and aggressive; they learned to use the Hyksos' weapons and drove out the invaders in 1570 B.C. The period of empire building known as the New Kingdom (1570–1085 B.C.) then began.

The basic features of Egyptian civilization had been forged during the Old and Middle Kingdoms. The Egyptians looked to the past, believing that the ways of their ancestors were best. For almost three thousand years, Egyptian civilization sought to retain a harmony with the order of nature instituted at creation. Believing that the universe was changeless, the Egyptians did not value change or development—what we call progress—

but venerated the institutions, traditions, and authority that embodied permanence.

Religion: The Basis of Egyptian Civilization

Religion was omnipresent in Egyptian life and accounted for the outstanding achievements of Egyptian civilization. Religious beliefs were the basis of Egyptian art, medicine, astronomy, literature, and government. The great pyramids, which took decades to finish and required the labor of thousands of people, were tombs for the pharaohs, man-gods. Magical utterances pervaded medical practices, for disease was attributed to the gods. Astronomy evolved to determine the correct time to perform religious rites and sacrifices. The earliest examples of literature dealt wholly with religious themes. The pharaoh was a sacrosanct monarch who served as an intermediary between the gods and human beings. Justice was conceived in religious terms, something bestowed by a creator-god. Egyptians appealed to the gods to grant victory in war, provide a bountiful harvest, and protect them from illness and misfortune. The Egyptians developed an ethical code, which they believed the gods had approved. In a number of treatises compiled by high officials, now called *Books of Instruction*, Egyptians were urged to tell the truth and to treat others fairly. In one *Book of Instruction* prepared at the end of the second millennium, the author, in a high ethical tone, enjoined Egyptians to express compassion for the poor, widows, and the handicapped.

Egyptian **polytheism** took many forms, including the worship of animals, for the Egyptians believed that gods manifested themselves in animal shapes. Certain gods were conceived by the Egyptians as taking various forms. Thoth, for example, was represented as the moon, a baboon, an ibis, and an ibis-headed man. The god Amon was depicted both in human form and as a ram. To the Egyptians, these different representations were not contradictory, for they did not seek logical consistency in religion. The Egyptians also believed great powers in nature—sky, sun, earth, the Nile—to be gods or the abodes of gods. Thus, the universe was alive with divinities—there were about two thousand gods in the Egyptian pantheon—and human lives were tied to the movements of the sun and the moon and to the rhythm of the seasons. In the heavens the Egyptians found answers to the great problems of human existence.

A crucial feature of Egyptian religion was the afterlife. Through pyramid-tombs, mummification to preserve the dead, and funerary art, the Egyptians showed their yearning for eternity and their desire to overcome death. Mortuary priests recited incantations to ensure the preservation of the dead body and the continuity of existence. Inscribed on the pyramids' interior walls were "pyramid texts," written in *hieroglyphics*—a form of picture writing in which figures, such as crocodiles, sails, eyes, and so forth, represented words or sounds that would be combined to form words. The texts contained fragments from myths, historical annals, and magical lore and provided spells to assist the king in ascending to heaven.

At first, the Egyptians believed that only the pharaoh and the royal family were immortal. In time, the nobility and then the commoners claimed that they, too, could share in the blessings of the "other world." Prayers hitherto reserved for the pharaoh were, for a fee, recited by priests at the burial of commoners. Egyptians believed that their deceased relatives would intercede with the gods in their behalf. They wrote letters to these spirits, petitioning them for help for such problems as infertility, inheritance of property, and family quarrels. Widows and widowers placed letters in the tomb of a deceased spouse in which they expressed their grief, often with great tenderness. To the Egyptians, the other world contained the same pleasures as those enjoyed on earth—friends, servants, fishing, hunting, paddling a canoe, picnicking with family members, entertainment by musicians and dancers, and good food. However, because earthly existence was not fundamentally unhappy, Egyptians did not yearn for death. Unlike early Christians, they did not reject this world or willingly endure martyrdom in order to enter a higher and better world. The following song, inscribed in a pharaoh's tomb, reveals the Egyptians' relish for life.

> *Enjoy yourself while you live,*
> *put on fine linen*
> *anoint yourself with wonderful ointments,*
> *multiply all your fine possessions on earth,*
> *follow your heart's command on earth*
> *be joyful and make merry.*[8]

Divine Kingship

"What is the king of Upper and Lower Egypt? He is a god by whose dealings one lives, the father and mother of men, alone by himself, without an equal."[9] Divine kingship was the basic institution of Egyptian civilization. Perhaps the requirements of the Egyptian environment helped forge the idea of the pharaoh as a living god because a ruler with supernatural authority, and held in favor by the gods, could hold together the large kingdom and draft the mass labor required to maintain the irrigation system. Numerous priests and a standing army enhanced the pharaoh's authority.

Through the pharaoh, the gods made known their wishes for the Egyptian people. As kingship was a divine, not a manmade, institution, it was expected to last for eternity. The Egyptians rejoiced in the rule of an all-powerful, all-knowing **god-king**, who controlled the Nile, bringing fertility to the land, and could intercede in their behalf with the other deities. And after death, when the pharaoh joined the other gods in the otherworld, he would still assist his subjects. To the Egyptians, the pharaoh was "the herdsman of everyone without evil in his heart."[10] They believed that divine kingship, which was instituted by a creator god, was the only acceptable political arrangement, that it was in harmony with the order of the universe, and that it brought stability and authority to the nation.

Pharaoh Mycerinus and His Queen, c. 2525 b.c. Swelling chests and hips idealize the royal couple's humanity, but the cubic feeling of the sculpture and rigid confidence of the pose proclaim their unquestioned divinity. (*Harvard MFA Expedition. Courtesy Museum of Fine Arts, Boston.*)

The power of the pharaoh extended to all sectors of society. Peasants were drafted to serve in labor corps as miners or construction workers. Foreign trade was a state monopoly. The pharaoh authorized commercial ventures—caravan expeditions south to Nubia for ivory, gold, and ebony and sailing expeditions east to Lebanon for timber. Profits from foreign trade enriched the royal treasury. Although private ownership of land was recognized in practice, in theory all land belonged to the pharaoh. As the supreme overlord, the pharaoh oversaw an army of government officials, who collected taxes, managed construction projects, checked the irrigation works, surveyed the land, kept records, and supervised government warehouses, where grain was stored as insurance against a bad harvest. All Egyptians were subservient to the pharaoh, and there was no conception of political liberty.

Egyptian rulers, like their Mesopotamian counterparts, believed that they had an obligation to render justice. Injustice was seen as an offense against the gods. Most pharaohs took their responsibilities seriously and tried to govern as benevolent protectors of the people.

> *Be not evil, it is good to be kindly. . . . Do right so long as thou abidest on the earth. Calm the weeper, oppress no widow, expel no man from the possessions of his father. . . . Take heed lest thou punish wrongfully. . . . Slay not a man whose good qualities thou knowest. . . . Exalt not the son of one of high degree more than him that is of lowly birth, but take to thyself a man because of his actions.*[11]

Egyptians derived a sense of security from the concept of divine kingship. It meant that earthly government and society were in harmony with the cosmos, a divine order that provided justice and security. The Egyptians believed that the institution of kingship dated from the creation of the universe, that as part of the rhythm of the universe kingship was necessary and beneficial to human beings.

The pharaoh was seen as ruling in accordance with Ma'at, which means justice, law, right, and truth. To oppose the pharaoh was to violate the universal and divinely ordained order of Ma'at and to bring disorder to society. Because the Egyptians regarded Ma'at, which was established with the creation of the universe, as the right order of nature, they believed that its preservation must be the object of human activity—the guiding norm of the state and the standard by which individuals conducted their lives. Those who did Ma'at and spoke Ma'at would be justly rewarded. Could anything be more reassuring than this belief that divine truth was represented in the person of the pharaoh, who guaranteed and defended the sacred order of the universe?

Science and Mathematics

Like the Mesopotamians, the Egyptians made practical advances in mathematics and science. They demonstrated superb engineering skills in building pyramids. For example, the pyramid of Khufu, still the largest stone building ever constructed, contains 2.3 million stone blocks, each averaging 2.5 tons. They fashioned an effective system of mathematics, including geometry for measurements, that enabled them to solve relatively simple problems.

Controlling the floodwaters of the Nile required careful planning. Therefore, it was vital to know when the Nile would begin to overflow. Noting that the Nile flooded after the star Sirius appeared in the sky, the Egyptians developed a calendar by which they could predict the time of the flood. Eventually, they fashioned a calendar of twelve months, each having thirty days. To complete the solar year, they added a separate period of five days after the last month. The Egyptian calendar based on the sun was more accurate than the Babylonian lunar calendar.

In the area of medicine, Egyptian doctors were more capable than their Mesopotamian counterparts. They were able to identify illnesses; they recognized that uncleanliness encouraged contagion; they had some knowledge of anatomy and performed operations—circumcision and perhaps the draining of abscessed teeth. Although the progress of medicine was handicapped by the belief that supernatural forces caused illnesses, there is evidence that some Egyptian doctors examined the body in a scientific way. In a scroll, the Edwin Smith Surgical Papyrus (named after the nineteenth-century American Egyptologist who acquired it), the writer omitted all references to divine intervention in his advice for treating wounds and fractures. He described fractures in a matter-of-fact way and recommended healing them with splints and casts. In another papyrus document (papyrus is writing material made from the stalks of the papyrus plant), the writer identified the various snakes, analyzed the effects of their bites, and listed treatments, including the use of specific drugs—and he did so with only minimum references to magical incantations.

The New Kingdom and the Decline of Egyptian Civilization

The New Kingdom began in 1570 B.C. with the war of liberation against the Hyksos. This war gave rise to an intense militancy, which found

Profile

Hatchepsut

Hatchepsut, daughter of Thutmose I (1493–1482 B.C.), was an exceptional figure in Egyptian history—a female pharaoh. As the wife of her half brother, Thutmose II, she did not produce a male heir. When Thutmose II died after a three-year reign, his infant son by a secondary wife inherited the throne. But because of his tender years, Hatchepsut served as regent. By the seventh year of the regency, Hatchepsut had assumed the royal title of king of Egypt. Although females were not officially barred from becoming pharaohs, it was an unchallenged tradition that this revered position was reserved for men. To legitimize her rule, Hatchepsut had a sequence of pictures carved on the porch of her mortuary temple that told the story of her divine birth. She was conceived when the god Amon-Re, disguised as Thutmose I, visited her mother's boudoir. Amon indicated that he intended to father a female, who one

Erich Lessing/Rijksmuseum van Oudheden, Egyptian Collection/Art Resource, NY.

expression in empire building. Aggressive pharaohs conquered territory that extended as far east as the Euphrates River. From its subject states, Egypt acquired tribute and slaves. Conquests led to the expansion of the bureaucracy, the creation of a professional army to protect the new territorial acquisitions, and the increased power of priests, whose temples, which grew larger and more lavish, shared in the spoils. Foreign slaves acquired from imperial conquests provided much of the labor for the construction of new shrines and temples. The formation of the empire ended Egyptian isolation and accelerated commercial and cultural intercourse with other peoples. During this period, Egyptian art, for example, showed the influence of foreign forms.

A growing cosmopolitanism was paralleled by a movement toward **monotheism** during the reign of Pharaoh Amenhotep IV (c. 1369–1353 B.C.). Amenhotep sought to replace traditional polytheism with the worship of Aton, a single god of all people, a supreme force in nature represented as the sun disk. Amenhotep took the name Akhenaton ("Servant of Aton") and moved the capital from Thebes to a newly constructed holy city called Akhetaten ("Horizon of Aton," which is near modern Tell el-Amarna). The city had palaces, administrative centers, and a temple complex honoring Aton. Akhenaton and his wife, Nefertiti, who played a prominent role in his court, dedicated themselves to Aton—the creator of the world, the maintainer of life, and the god of love, justice, and peace. Akhenaton (or Ikhnaton) also ordered his officials to remove the names and images of other gods from temples and monuments. With awe, Akhenaton celebrated Aton's power and magnificence:

day would rule Egypt. "Come to me in peace, daughter of my loins, . . . thou art the king who takes possession of the diadem [crown] on the Throne of Horus of the Living, eternally."*

Hatchepsut came to be depicted with male attire and a male body. Apparently, by casting off her female appearance, she aimed to be seen as a king, the equal of all other pharaohs, and not as a queen, who was not regarded as divine. Hatchepsut, says Egyptologist Joyce Tyldesley, "needed to make a sharp and immediately obvious distinction between her former position as queen regent and her new role as pharaoh. The change of dress was a clear sign of her altered state."†

During her twenty-year reign, from about 1479 to 1458, Hatchepsut promoted extensive building projects, including her royal tomb, and trading expeditions, particularly to the land of Punt, in modern-day Somaliland. From Punt the Egyptians obtained myrrh and frankincense, precious resins used for making incense that was burned in temple rituals and perfumes and for the mummification of bodies. It was an arduous journey to Punt; the return of the expeditions with these treasures must have greatly increased the prestige of the female pharaoh.

After Hatchepsut's death, her monuments were mutilated and her name and image deleted in a deliberate attempt to obliterate her memory. The campaign was probably initiated by Thutmose III, but his motivation is not clear. Was he demonstrating hatred for his stepmother, who had relegated him to a subordinate role for so many years? Did he try to erase the memory of Hatchepsut in order to prevent the succession in the future of still another female pharaoh in the belief that such a situation was a grave violation of tradition and Ma'at?

---

*Quoted in Joyce Tyldesley, *Hatchepsut: The Female Pharaoh* (New York: Penguin Books, 1998), p. 105.
†Ibid., p. 133.

> *How manifold are thy works!*
> *They are hidden from man's sight.*
> *O sole god, like whom there is no other.*
> *Thou hast made the earth according to thy*
> *desire.*[12]

Akhenaton's "monotheism" had little impact on the masses of Egyptians, who remained devoted to their traditional gods and ancient beliefs, and was resisted by priests, who resented his changes. The new religion could not survive the death of its founder. Akhenaton's successor, Tutankhamen (1352–1344 B.C.), abandoned the capital at Amarna and returned to Thebes. Tutankhamen was succeeded by an elderly relative, who reigned briefly. In 1340, Horemheb (1340–1315 B.C.), an army commander, seized power and had the monuments to Aton destroyed, along with records and inscriptions bearing Akhenaton's name. And the great visionary was vilified as "The Blasphemer."

Historians are not certain why Akhenaton made such a radical break with tradition by propagating the worship of a single god. Was he trying to strike at the priests, whose wealth and prestige had increased considerably with Egypt's conquests? Did the break stem essentially from the vision of a great prophet? But the most significant historical questions concerning Akhenaton are these: First, was Akhenaton's religion genuine monotheism, which pushed religious thought in a new direction? And second, if this was the case, did it influence Moses, who led the Israelites out of Egypt about a century later?

These two questions have aroused controversy among historians. The principal limitation on the monotheistic character of Atonism is that there were really two gods in Akhenaton's religion—

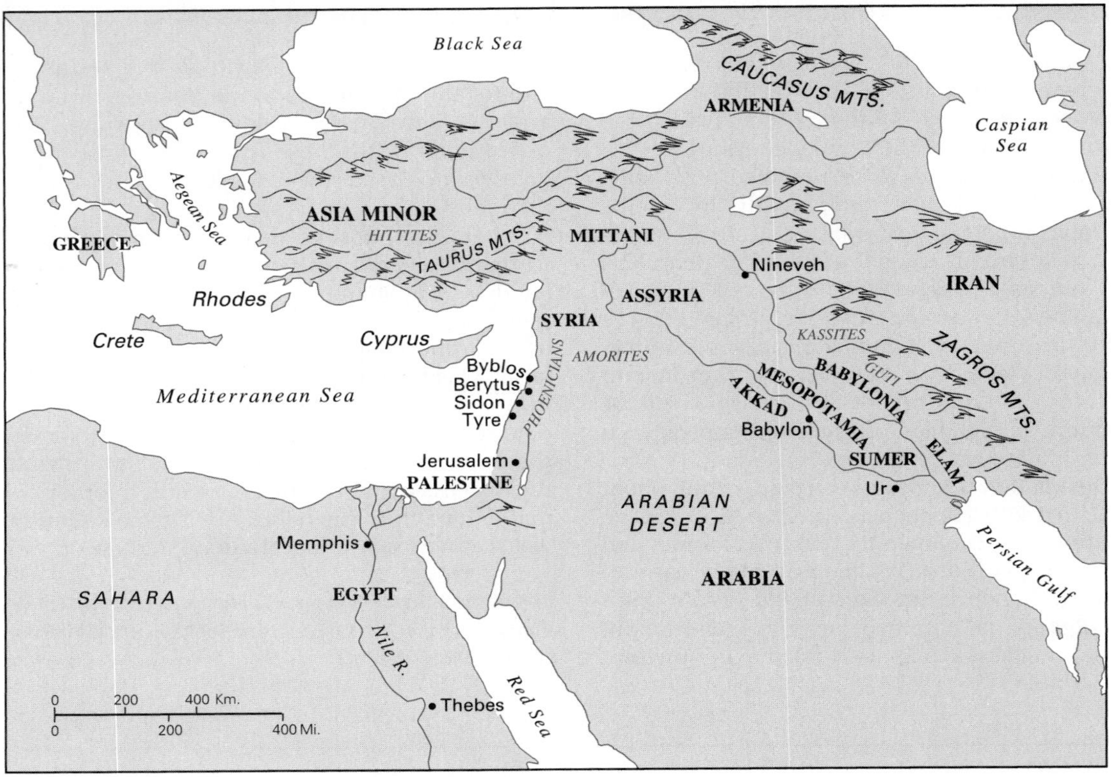

MAP 1.2 **KINGDOMS AND PEOPLES OF THE ANCIENT WORLD** In addition to the Sumerians and Egyptians, founders of the first civilizations, other peoples contributed to the development of civilization in the Near East. The Hebrews conceived the idea of the one God, the Phoenicians invented the alphabet, and the Hittites developed a substantial iron industry.

Aton and the pharaoh himself, who was still worshiped as a deity. Egyptologist John A. Wilson sheds light on this notion. Because Egyptians could not break with the central idea of their civilization, divine kingship, "one could say that it was the closest approach to monotheism possible within the thought of the day. That would still fall short of making it a belief in and worship of only one god."[13] Regarding the relationship of Atonism to a later Hebrew monotheism, Wilson says, "The mechanism of transmission from the faith of Akhenaton to the monotheism of Moses is not apparent."[14] Moreover, the Hebrews never identified God with the sun or any other object in nature.

Late in the thirteenth century B.C., Libyans, probably seeking to settle in the more fertile land of Egypt, attacked from the west, and the Peoples of the Sea, as unsettled raiders from the Aegean Sea area and Asia Minor were called, launched a series of strikes at Egypt. A weakened Egypt abandoned its empire. In the succeeding centuries, Egypt came under the rule of Libyans, Nubians, Assyrians, Persians, and finally Greeks, to whom Egypt lost its independence in the fourth century B.C. Egyptian civilization had flourished for nearly two thousand years before it experienced an almost one-thousand-year descent into stagnation, decline, and collapse. During its long history, the Egyptians tried to preserve its ancient forms, revealed to them by their ancestors and representing for all time those unchanging values that they believed to be the way of happiness.

Empire Builders

The rise of an Egyptian empire during the New Kingdom was part of a wider development in Near Eastern history after 1500 B.C.—the emergence of international empires. Empire building led to the intermingling of peoples and cultural traditions and to the extension of civilization well beyond the river valleys.

One reason for the growth of empires was the migration of peoples known as Indo-Europeans. Originally from a wide area ranging from southeastern Europe to the region beyond the Caspian Sea, Indo-Europeans embarked, around 2000 B.C., on a series of migrations, which eventually brought them into Italy, Greece, Asia Minor, Mesopotamia, Persia, and India. From a core Indo-European tongue emerged the Greek, Latin, Germanic, Slavic, Persian, and Sanskrit languages.

Hittites

Several peoples established strong states in the Near East around 1500 B.C.—the Hurrians in northern Mesopotamia, the Kassites in southern Mesopotamia, and, most importantly, the Hittites in Asia Minor.

Penetrating Asia Minor, Indo-Europeans coalesced with native Hattic-speaking peoples to create the Hittite empire (1450–1200 B.C.). The Hittites ruled Asia Minor and northern Syria, raided Babylon, and challenged Egypt for control of Syria and Palestine.

The Hittites wanted to control the trade routes that ran along the Euphrates River into Syria. In the 1300s, the Hittite empire reached its peak and included much of Asia Minor and northern Syria. The Hittites succeeded because of their well-trained army. Mass attacks by light, horse-drawn chariots demolished enemy lines, while foot soldiers made effective use of the battle-ax and a short curved sword.

The Hittites borrowed several features of Mesopotamian civilization, including cuneiform, legal principles, and literary and art forms. Hittite religion blended the beliefs and practices of Indo-Europeans, native inhabitants of Asia Minor, and Mesopotamians. The Hittites were probably the first people to develop a substantial iron industry. Initially, they apparently used iron just for ceremonial and ritual objects and not for tools and weapons. However, because iron ore was more readily available than copper or tin (needed for bronze), after 1200 B.C. iron weapons and tools spread throughout the Near East, although bronze implements were still used. Around 1200 B.C., the Hittite empire fell, most likely to Indo-European invaders from the north.

Small Nations

During the twelfth century B.C., a temporary lull in empire building permitted a number of small nations in Syria and Palestine to assert their sovereignty. Three of these peoples—the Phoenicians, the Aramaeans, and the Hebrews*—were originally Semitic desert nomads. The Phoenicians were descendants of the Canaanites, a Semitic people who had settled Palestine about 3000 B.C. The Canaanites who had migrated northwest into what is now Lebanon were called Phoenicians.

Settling in the coastal Mediterranean cities of Tyre, Byblos, Berytus (Beirut), and Sidon, the Phoenicians were naturally drawn to the sea. These daring explorers established towns along the coast of North Africa, on the islands of the western Mediterranean, and in Spain, and they became the greatest sea traders of the ancient world. Phoenician merchants exported lumber, glass, copper and bronze utensils, and the purple dye produced from the murex, a mollusk that was plentiful in the coastal waters. The Phoenicians (or their Canaanite forebears) devised the first alphabet—a monumental contribution to writing. Since all words could be represented by combinations of letters, it saved memorizing thousands of diagrams and aided the Phoenicians in transmitting the civilizations of the Near East to the western Mediterranean. Adapted by the Greeks, who added

*The Hebrews are discussed in Chapter 2.

vowels, the phonetic alphabet became a crucial component of European languages.

The Aramaeans, who settled in Syria, Palestine, and northern Mesopotamia, performed a role similar to that of the Phoenicians. As great caravan traders, they carried both goods and cultural patterns to various parts of the Near East. The Hebrews and the Persians, for example, acquired the Phoenician alphabet from the Aramaeans.

Assyria

In the ninth century B.C., empire building resumed with the Assyrians, a Semitic people from the region around the upper Tigris River. The Assyrians carefully planned their military campaigns and excelled in siege weapons—battering rams built on massive wheeled frames—which pulverized city walls that had hitherto resisted attackers. Their soldiers wore armor and wielded iron swords, and charging chariots terrorized the foe's infantry, which generally consisted of farmer-soldiers armed with little more than bows and arrows.

Although they had made forays of expansion in 1200 and 1100 B.C., the Assyrians began their march to "world" empire three centuries later. In the eighth and seventh centuries, the Assyrians became a ruthless fighting machine that stormed through Babylonia, Syria, Palestine, and Egypt. Assyrian kings believed that their gods commanded them to conquer and assisted them in their campaigns. At its height, the Assyrian empire extended from the Iranian plateau in the east to the Egyptian city of Thebes.

How did the Assyrians administer such a vast empire? An Assyrian king, who was the representative and high priest of the god Ashur, governed absolutely. Nobles appointed by the king kept order in the provinces and collected tribute, which they probably used for building palaces, temples, and canals. The Assyrians improved roads, established messenger services, and engaged in large-scale irrigation projects to facilitate effective administration of their conquered lands and promote prosperity. To keep their subjects obedient, the Assyrians resorted to terror and to deportation of troublesome subjects from their home territories. (It is also likely that masses of people were moved around for economic reasons—to replenish a diminishing labor supply.) Assyrian kings boasted of their ruthlessness toward rebellious subjects:

> *13,000 of their warriors I cut down with the sword. Their blood like the water of a stream I caused to run through the squares of their city. The corpses of their soldiers I piled in heaps. . . . [The Babylonian king's] royal bed, his royal couch, the treasure of his palaces, his property, his gods and everything from his palace without number, I carried away. His captive warriors were given to the soldiers of my land like grasshoppers. The city I destroyed, I devastated, I burned with fire.*[15]

Despite an almost all-consuming concern for war, the Assyrians maintained and spread the culture of the past. They copied and edited the literary works of Babylonia, adopted the old Sumerian gods, and used Mesopotamian art forms. The Assyrian king Ashurbanipal (669–626 B.C.) maintained a great library, which contained thousands of clay tablets.

"The king knows that all lands hate us," wrote an official to King Esarhaddon (680–669 B.C.).[16] After a period of wars and revolts weakened Assyria, a coalition of Medes, or Indo-Europeans from Iran, and the Semitic Chaldeans, or Neo-Babylonians, sacked the Assyrian capital of Nineveh in 612 B.C. The conquerors looted and destroyed the city, and the surviving Assyrians fled. Assyrian power was broken.

The Neo-Babylonian Empire

The destruction of the Assyrian empire made possible the rise of a Chaldean empire, which included Babylonia, Assyria, Syria, and Palestine. Under Nebuchadnezzar, who ruled from 604 to 562 B.C., the Chaldean, or Neo-Babylonian, empire reached its height. A talented general and statesman, and a brilliant administrator, Nebuchadnezzar had Babylon rebuilt. The new Babylon that arose on the shore of the Euphrates had magnificent procession-ways that led to palaces and temples. On his palace grounds, Nebuchadnezzar created the famous Hanging Gardens for his Median wife, according to legend. The 350-

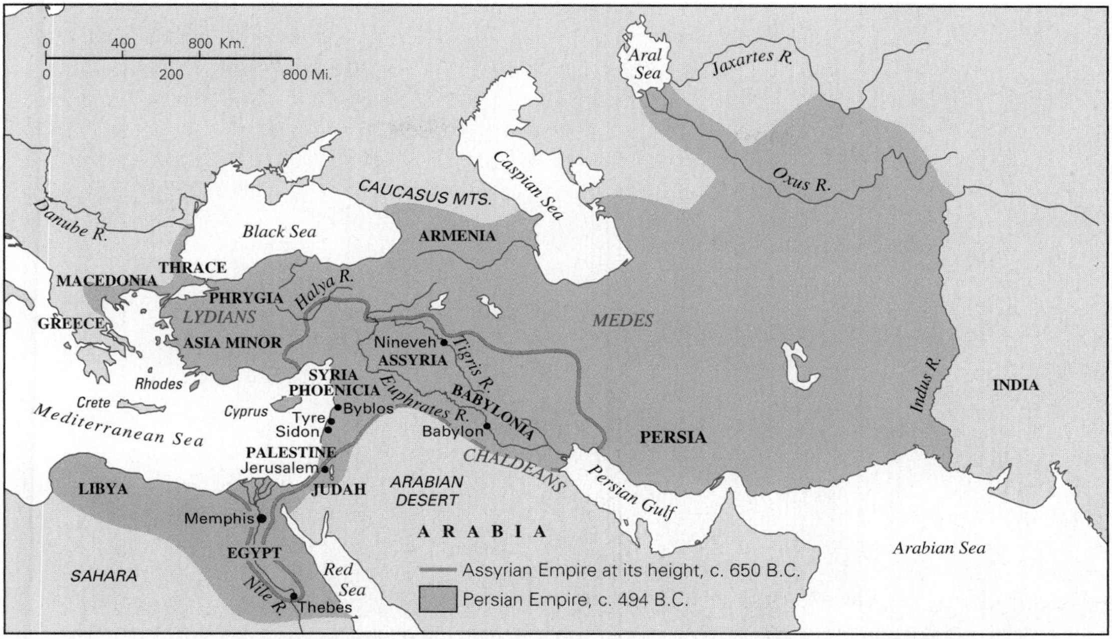

Map 1.3 **The Assyrian and Persian Empires** In the last part of the sixth century B.C., the Persians established the greatest empire of the ancient Near East, conquering all the lands between the Nile in Egypt and the Indus River in India.

foot building was a series of vaulted terraces and was surrounded by a moat of flowing water. Trees, shrubs, and flowers decorated each terrace. In the interior, vaulted halls were stocked with vessels, fabrics, ornaments, and wines gathered from different regions of the empire. Here guests reclined on divans and were attended by slaves.

Persia: Unifier of the Near East

After Nebuchadnezzar's death, the Chaldean empire was torn by civil war and threatened by a new power—the Persians, an Indo-European people who had settled in southern Iran. Under Cyrus the Great and his son and successor, Cambyses, the Persians conquered all lands between the Nile in Egypt and the Indus River in India. This conquest took twenty-five years, from 550 to 525 B.C. The Near Eastern conception of absolute monarchy justified by religion reached its culminating expression in the person of the Persian king, who, with divine approval, ruled a vast empire, "the four quarters of the earth." Persian kings developed an effective system of administration—based in part on an Assyrian model—which gave stability and a degree of unity to their extensive territories. In so doing, they performed a creative act of statesmanship. The Persian empire was divided into twenty provinces (satrapies), each administered by a governor (satrap) responsible to the emperor. To guard against subversion, the king employed special agents—"the eyes and ears of the emperor"—who supervised the activities of the governors. Persian kings allowed the provincials a large measure of self-rule. They also respected local traditions, particularly in matters of religion, as long as subjects paid their taxes, served in the royal army, and refrained from rebellion; and

PERSEPOLIS, IRAN, C. 500 B.C. The Persian ruler Darius (522–486 B.C.) constructed a thirty-acre earthen terrace almost fifty feet above the plain and built there a complex of palaces, reception halls, a treasury, and barracks for his royal guards. Persepolis became the ceremonial center of the vast Persian empire until it was destroyed by Alexander the Great's soldiers. (*Photo Researchers © George Holton.*)

they deliberately tried to win the goodwill of priests in conquered lands.

The empire was bound together by a uniform language, Aramaic (the language of the Aramaeans of Syria), used by government officials and merchants. Aramaic was written in letters based on the Phoenician alphabet. By making Aramaic a universal language, the Persians facilitated written and oral communication within the empire. The empire was further unified by an elaborate network of roads, an efficient postal system, a common system of weights and measures, and an empirewide coinage, based on an invention of the Lydians from western Asia Minor.

Besides providing impressive political and administrative unity and promoting international trade, the Persians fused and perpetuated the various cultural traditions of the Near East. Persian palaces, for example, boasted the terraces of

Babylon, the colonnades of Egypt, the winged bulls that decorated Assyrian palace gates, and the craftsmanship of Median goldsmiths.

The political and cultural universalism of the Persian empire had its counterpart in the emergence of a higher religion, Zoroastrianism. Named for its founder, the Persian prophet Zarathustra (Zoroaster in Greek), who probably lived in the sixth century B.C. (some scholars place him much earlier), this religion taught belief in Ahura Mazda—the Wise Lord—god of light, of justice, wisdom, goodness, and immortality. But, in addition to the Wise Lord, there also existed Ahriman, the spirit of darkness, who was evil and destructive. Ahriman was in conflict with Ahura Mazda. People were free to choose whom they would follow. By choosing Ahura Mazda, they chose good over evil. To serve Ahura Mazda, one had to speak the truth and be good to others; the reward for such behavior was life eternal in paradise, the realm of light and goodness. Followers of the evil spirit could be cast into a realm of darkness and torment. In contrast to the traditional religions of the Near East, Zoroastrianism rejected magic, polytheism, and blood sacrifices and instead stressed ethics.

Persia unified the nations of the Near East into a world-state, headed by a divinely appointed king, and synthesized the region's cultural traditions. Soon it would confront the city-states of Greece, whose political system and cultural orientation differed from that of the Near East.

The Religious Orientation of the Near East

Religion dominated, suffused, and inspired all features of Near Eastern society—law, kingship, art, and science. In the first civilizations, the deepest thoughts of human beings were expressed in the form of religious myths. They were the source of the vitality and creativity of Mesopotamian and Egyptian civilizations. Near Eastern art derived from religion, and science was permeated with it; literature and history dealt with the ways of the gods; and priest-kings or god-kings, their power sanctioned by divine forces, furnished the necessary authority to organize large numbers of people in cooperative ventures. Religion also encouraged and justified wars—including enslavements and massacres—which were seen as conflicts between the gods. Religious beliefs and values served as a powerful social force uniting people into a cohesive community.

A Mythmaking World-View

A religious or **mythopoeic** (mythmaking) **view** of the world gives Near Eastern civilization its distinctive form and allows us to see it as an organic whole. Mesopotamians and Egyptians inherited from their prehistoric ancestors a great variety of communally produced imagery, rituals, and tales accounting for the origin of the world and human life. Giving free play to their imagination, they altered the old myths and elaborated new ones to resolve questions that today we try to answer with science. Mythmaking was humanity's first way of thinking; it was the earliest attempt to explain the beginnings of the universe and human history, to make nature's mysteries and life's uncertainties comprehensible. Appealing primarily to the imagination and emotions, rather than to reason, mythical thinking, as expressed in language, art, poetry, and social organization, has been a fundamental formative element of human culture.

Originating in sacred rites, ritual dances, feasts, and ceremonies, myths narrated the deeds of gods, who, in some remote past, had brought forth the world and human beings. Holding that human destiny was determined by the gods, Near Eastern people interpreted their experiences through myths. Myths also enabled Mesopotamians and Egyptians to make sense out of nature, to explain the world of phenomena. Through myths, the Near Eastern mind sought to give coherence to the universe, to make it intelligible. These myths gave Near Eastern peoples a framework with which to pattern their experiences into a meaningful order, justify their rules of conduct, and try to overcome the uncertainty of existence.

The civilizations of the ancient Near East were based on a way of thinking fundamentally different from the modern scientific outlook. The difference between scientific and mythical thinking is profound. The scientific mind views physical nature as an *it*—inanimate, impersonal, and governed by universal law. The mythmaking mind of the Near East saw every object in nature as a *thou*—personified, alive, with an individual will. It saw gods or demons manipulating things. The world was enchanted, imbued with mysterious spirits. The sun and stars, the rivers and mountains, the wind and lightning were either gods or the dwelling places of gods. Live agents were the forces behind natural events. An Egyptian or a Mesopotamian experienced natural phenomena—a falling rock, a thunderclap, a rampaging river—as life facing life. If a river flooded the region, destroying crops, it was because it wanted to; the river or the gods desired to punish the people.

> *In other words, the ancients told myths instead of presenting an analysis or conclusions. We would explain, for instance, that certain atmospheric changes broke a drought and brought about rain. The Babylonians observed the same facts but experienced them as the intervention of the gigantic bird Imdugud which came to their rescue. It covered the sky with the black storm clouds of its wings and devoured the Bull of Heaven, whose hot breath had scorched the crops.*[17]

The Egyptians believed that Nut, the sky goddess, gave birth to the sun, a deity who sailed west across the celestial sea before descending into his mother's womb to be reborn again in the morning. For the Egyptians, the rising and setting of the sun were not natural occurrences—a celestial body obeying an impersonal law—but a religious drama.

The scientific mind holds that natural objects obey universal rules; hence, the location of planets, the speed of objects, and the onset of a hurricane can be predicted. The mythmaking mind of the ancient Near East was not troubled by contradictions. It did not seek logical consistency and had no awareness of repetitive laws inherent in nature. Rather, it attributed all occurrences to the actions of gods, whose behavior was often erratic and unpredictable. Shamans employed magic to protect people from evil supernatural forces that surrounded them. The scientific mind appeals to reason—it analyzes nature logically and systematically and searches for general principles that govern phenomena. The mythmaking mind appeals to the imagination and feelings and proclaims a truth that is emotionally satisfying, not one that has been arrived at through intellectual analysis and synthesis. Mythical explanations of nature and human experience enrich perception and feeling. Thus, they made life seem less overwhelming and death less frightening.

Of course, Near Eastern people did engage in rational forms of thought and behavior. They certainly employed reason in building irrigation works, preparing a calendar, and performing mathematical operations. Moreover, in their daily life, men and women were often driven by purely pragmatic concerns. Fields had to be planted, goods sold, and household chores attended to. In dealing with these concerns, people did what had to be done in commonsense ways. They planned and prepared, they weighed actions as either beneficial or harmful and behaved accordingly. However, because rational or logical thought remained subordinate to a mythic-religious orientation, they did not arrive at a *consistently* and *self-consciously* rational method of inquiring into physical nature and human culture.

Thus, Near Eastern civilization reached the first level in the development of science—observing nature, recording data, and improving technology in mining, metallurgy, and architecture. But it did not advance to the level of self-conscious philosophical and scientific thought—that is, logically deduced abstractions, hypotheses, and generalizations. Mesopotamians and Egyptians did not fashion a body of philosophical and scientific ideas that were logically structured, discussed, and debated. They had no awareness of general laws that govern particular events. These later developments were the achievement of Greek philosophy. It gave a "rational interpretation to natural occurrences which had previously been explained by ancient mythologies. . . . With the study of nature set free from the control of mythological fancy, the way was opened for the development of science as an intellectual system."[18]

Near Eastern Achievements

Sumerians and Egyptians demonstrated enormous creativity and intelligence. They built irrigation works and cities, organized governments, charted the course of heavenly bodies, performed mathematical operations, constructed large-scale monuments, engaged in international trade, established bureaucracies and schools, and considerably advanced the level of technology. Without the Sumerian invention of writing—one of the great creative acts in history—what we mean by *civilization* could not have emerged.

Many elements of ancient Near Eastern civilization were passed on to the West. The wheeled vehicle, the plow, and the phonetic alphabet—all important to the development of civilization—derive from the Near East. In the realm of medicine, the Egyptians knew the value of certain drugs, such as castor oil; they also knew how to use splints and bandages. The innovative divisions that gave 360 degrees to a circle and 60 minutes to an hour originated in Mesopotamia. Egyptian geometry and Babylonian astronomy were utilized by the Greeks and became a part of Western knowledge. The belief that a king's power came from a heavenly source, a key idea in Western political thought, also derived from the Near East. In Christian art, too, one finds connections to the Mesopotamian art forms—for example, the Assyrians depicted winged angel-like beings.

Both the Hebrews and the Greeks borrowed Mesopotamian literary themes. For example, some biblical stories—the Flood, the quarrel between Cain and Abel, and the Tower of Babel—stem from Mesopotamian antecedents. A similar link exists between the Greek and the earlier Mesopotamian mythologies.

Thus, many achievements of the Egyptians and the Mesopotamians were inherited and assimilated by both the Greeks and the Hebrews, the principal founders of Western civilization. Even more important for an understanding of the essential meaning of Western civilization are the ways in which Greeks and Hebrews rejected or transformed elements of the older Near Eastern traditions to create new points of departure for the human mind.

❖ ❖ ❖

Online Study Center **ACE the Test**

Notes

1. Robert J. Braidwood, *Prehistoric Man* (Glenview, Ill.: Scott, Foresman, 1967), p. 141.
2. Lewis Mumford, *Transformation of Man* (New York: Harper Torchbooks, 1972), pp. 46–47.
3. Excerpted in James B. Pritchard, ed., *Ancient Near Eastern Texts Relating to the Old Testament,* 3rd ed., with supplement (Princeton, N.J.: Princeton University Press, 1969), p. 67.
4. Excerpted in James B. Pritchard, ed., *The Ancient Near East: A New Anthology of Texts and Pictures* (Princeton, N.J.: Princeton University Press, 1975), p. 154.
5. *The Epic of Gilgamesh*, with an introduction by N. K. Sandars (Baltimore: Penguin Books, 1960), p. 94.
6. Ibid., pp. 69, 104.
7. Excerpted in Adolf Ehrman, ed., *The Ancient Egyptians* (New York: Harper Torchbooks, 1966), pp. 94, 97, 99.
8. Quoted in Eugen Strouhal, *Life of the Ancient Egyptians* (Norman: University of Oklahoma Press, 1992), p. 41.
9. Quoted in Frankfort, *Ancient Egyptian Religion* (New York: Harper Torchbooks, 1961), p. 43.
10. Quoted in John A. Wilson, "Egypt," in Henri Frankfort et al., *Before Philosophy* (Baltimore: Penguin Books, 1949), p. 88.
11. Excerpted in Erhman, *The Ancient Egyptians*, pp. 76–78.

12. Quoted in John A. Wilson, *The Culture of Ancient Egypt* (Chicago: University of Chicago Press, Phoenix Books, 1951), p. 227.
13. Ibid., p. 225.
14. Ibid., p. 226.
15. Quoted in Joan Oates, *Babylon* (London: Thames & Hudson, 1979), pp. 110–111.
16. Quoted in Georges Roux, *Ancient Iraq* (Harmondsworth, England: Penguin Books, 1966), p. 278.
17. Frankfort et al., *Before Philosophy*, p. 15.
18. S. Sambursky, *The Physical World of the Greeks* (New York: Collier Books, 1962), pp. 18–19.

Suggested Reading

David, Rosalie A., *The Ancient Egyptians* (1982). Focuses on religious beliefs and practices.

Moscati, Sabatino, *The Face of the Ancient Orient* (1962). An illuminating survey of the various peoples of the ancient Near East.

Oates, Joan, *Babylon* (1979). A survey of the history of Babylon from its origin to Hellenistic times; includes a discussion of the legacy of Babylon.

Saggs, H. W. F., *Civilization Before Greece and Rome* (1989). Focuses on culture and society.

Snell, Daniel C., *Life in the Ancient Near East* (1997). An excellent synthesis.

Stiebing, William H., Jr., *Ancient Near Eastern History and Culture* (2003). A sound general introduction for students.

Strouhal, Eugen, *Life of the Ancient Egyptians* (1992). Daily life of Egyptians; lavishly illustrated.

von Soden, Wolfram, *The Ancient Orient* (1994). A thematic treatment of ancient Mesopotamian civilization.

Chapter 2

The Hebrews: A New View of God and the Individual

A sculptured relief from the triumphal Arch of Titus showing Jewish captives bearing the menorah and vessels from the holy temple burned by the Romans at the end of the Jewish revolt, first century A.D. (Alinari/Art Resource, NY.)

- Outline of Hebrew History
- God: One, Sovereign, Transcendent, Good
- The Individual and Moral Autonomy
- The Covenant and the Law
- The Hebrew Idea of History
- The Prophets
- The Legacy of the Ancient Jews

Focus Questions

1. In what ways did the Hebrew view of God mark a revolutionary break with Near Eastern thought?
2. How did Hebrew religious thought promote the ideas of moral autonomy?
3. What were the unique achievements of the Hebrew prophets?
4. Why are the Hebrews regarded as a principal source of the Western tradition?

Online Study Center

This icon will direct you to interactive map and primary source activities on the website http://college.hmco.com/pic/perrywc8e.

Ancient Mesopotamia and Egypt, the birthplace of the first civilizations, are not the spiritual ancestors of the West. For the origins of the Western tradition, we must turn to the Hebrews and the Greeks. Both Greeks and Hebrews, of course, absorbed elements of the civilizations of Mesopotamia and Egypt, but even more significant is how they transformed this inheritance and shaped world-views that differed markedly from the outlooks of these first civilizations. As Egyptologist John A. Wilson writes,

> *The Children of Israel built a nation and a religion on the rejection of things Egyptian. Not only did they see God as one, but they ascribed to him consistency of concern for man and consistency of justice to man. . . . Like the Greeks, the Hebrews took forms from their great neighbors; like the Greeks, they used those forms for very different purposes.*[1]

In this chapter, we examine one source of the Western tradition, the Hebrews, whose conception of God broke with the outlook of the Near East and whose ethical teachings helped fashion the Western idea of the dignity of the individual.

Outline of Hebrew History*

The Hebrews originated in Mesopotamia and migrated to Canaan, a portion of which was later called Palestine. The Hebrew patriarchs—Abraham, Isaac, and Jacob, so prominently depicted in the Old Testament—were chieftains of seminomadic clans that roamed Palestine and occasionally journeyed to Mesopotamia and Egypt. The early Hebrews absorbed some features of Mesopotamian civilization. For example, there are parallels between biblical law and the Mesopotamian legal tradition. Several

*Since there is a paucity of references to the early Hebrews in nonbiblical sources, scholars have to rely almost entirely on the Hebrew Bible for reconstructing much of the history of the ancient Israelites. The divergence of scholarly opinion regarding the Bible's accuracy and reliability creates additional uncertainty for the historian.

Chronology 2.1 ❖ The Hebrews

1250 B.C.*	Hebrew Exodus from Egypt
1024–1000	Reign of Saul, Israel's first king
1000–961	Creation of a united monarchy under David
961–922	Reign of Solomon: construction of the first temple
750–430	Age of classical prophecy
722	Kingdom of Israel falls to Assyrians
586	Kingdom of Judah falls to Chaldeans; the temple is destroyed
586–539	Babylonian exile
538	Cyrus of Persia allows exiles to return to Judah
515 B.C.	Second temple is dedicated

*Most dates are approximations

biblical stories, including the Garden of Eden and the Flood, derive from Mesopotamian sources.

Some Hebrews journeyed from Canaan to Egypt to be herdsmen and farmers, but they eventually became forced laborers for the Egyptians. Fearful of remaining permanent slaves of the pharaoh, the Hebrews yearned for an opportunity to escape. In the early thirteenth century B.C., an extraordinary leader rose among them, called Moses, who came to his people as a messenger of God. Leading the Hebrews in their Exodus from Egypt,* Moses transformed them during their wanderings in the wilderness of Sinai into a nation, welded together and uplifted by a belief in Yahweh, the one God.

The Israelite Kingdom

The wandering Hebrews returned to Canaan to rejoin other Hebrew tribes that had not migrated to Egypt. The colonization of Canaan, a gradual process, took many generations. In Canaan, the Israelites did not form a state with a central government but were loosely organized into a tribal confederation bound by a commitment to Yahweh. When enemies threatened, the elders of each of the twelve tribes would decide whether to engage in joint action. During emergencies, judges, who were leaders distinguished by their courage and empowered by "the spirit of Yahweh," rallied the clans against the common enemy. The tribal confederation lasted for about two hundred years, until a threat by the Philistines in the late eleventh century B.C. led the Israelites to draw closer together under a king.

Originally from the islands of the Aegean Sea and the coast of Asia Minor, the Philistines (from whom the name *Palestine* derives) had invaded Canaan in the early part of the twelfth century B.C. From the coastal regions, they expanded into the interior, extending their dominion over much of the Israelite territory. During this time of crisis, the twelve tribes united under the leadership of Saul, a charismatic hero, whom they acclaimed as their first king. Under Saul's successor, David, a gifted warrior and a poet, the Hebrews (or Israelites) broke the back of Philistine power and subdued neighboring peoples.

The creation of an Israelite kingdom under David and his son Solomon in the tenth century B.C. was made possible by the declining power of other states in the Near East—Babylonia, Assyria, the Hittite kingdom, and Egypt. Solomon's kingdom engaged in active trade with neighbor-

*Arguing that there is no extrabiblical evidence for the Exodus or even for the presence of Jews in Egypt, some scholars known as biblical minimalists dismiss the Exodus as fiction. Other scholars reject this position, holding that there is evidence of Asiatic slaves toiling in Egypt, some of whom might have been Hebrews. Moreover, assert these scholars, the ancient Hebrews would not have concocted and faithfully preserved such an inglorious history of enslavement unless the biblical account contained a historical core along with the legend and folklore.

WALL PAINTING FROM THE SYNAGOGUE OF DURA-EUROPOS, ROMAN SYRIA, EARLY THIRD CENTURY A.D. Although a strict prohibition of the use of images inhibited representational art among the Hebrews, in Hellenistic times scenes from Hebrew history appeared on the walls and floors of Jewish synagogues. Here the prophet Samuel is depicted anointing David as King of Israel. (*Art Resource, NY.*)

ing states, particularly Tyre (located along the Phoenician coast). Solomon's merchant fleet, built and sailed by Phoenicians, traded with southerly lands bordering the Red Sea. Another sign of economic progress was extensive construction, especially in Jerusalem, the Hebrew spiritual center, where Solomon erected a royal palace and beside it a magnificent temple honoring God.

New cities were built, and Jerusalem grew larger. The use of the iron-tipped plow improved agricultural productivity, which, in turn, contributed to a significant population increase. Under Solomon, Israel also experienced a cultural flowering: some magnificent sections of the Old Testament took form, and music flourished.

Old tribal patterns weakened as urban life expanded and some people gained wealth. Tribal society had been distinguished by a large measure of economic equality, but disparity grew between the rich and the poor, between those who considered themselves aristocrats and the common people.

Under Solomon, ancient Israel was at the height of its power and prosperity.* However, opposition to Solomon's tax policies and his favored

*A minority of scholars reject the Bible's picture of a golden age, holding that both David and Solomon were little more than tribal chieftains.

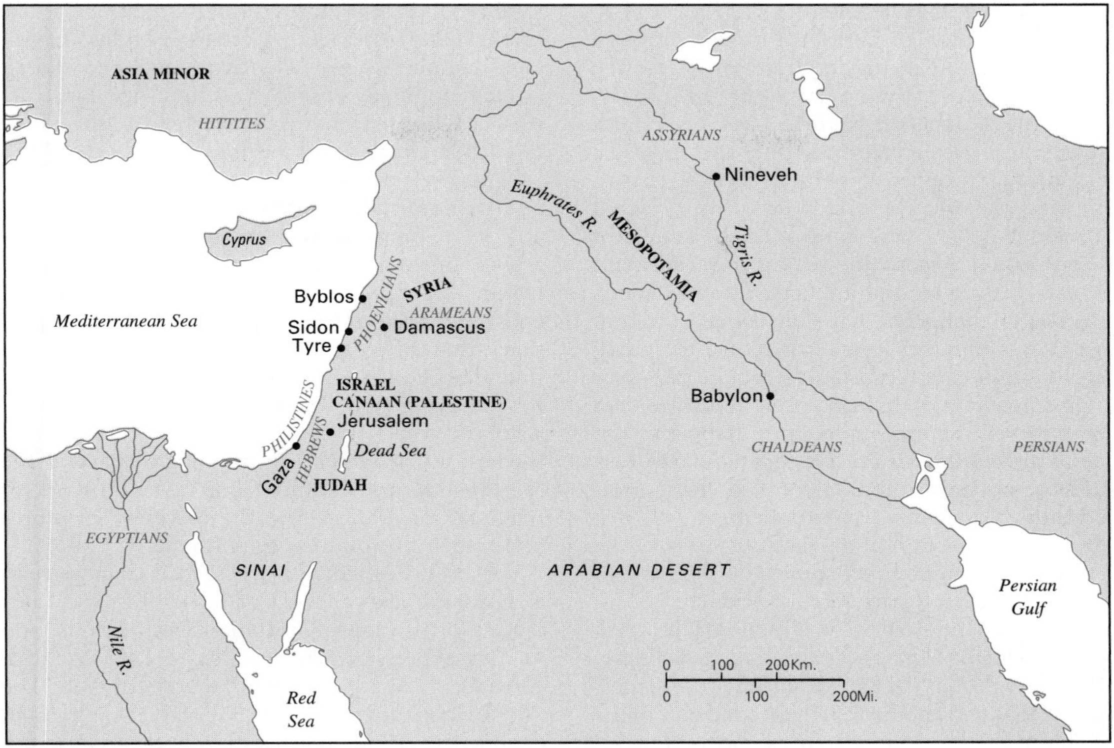

Map 2.1 Hebrews and Other Peoples of the Ancient Middle East
Despite conquest and exile, the Hebrews survived as a people, retained their faith, and remained devoted to their homeland, which, they believed, God had given them.

treatment of the region of Judah in the south led to the division of the kingdom after his death in 922 B.C. The tribes loyal to Solomon's son belonged to the kingdom of Judah, whereas the other tribes organized the northern kingdom of Israel. Both second-rate powers, neither Judah nor Israel could hold on to earlier conquests.

Conquest, Captivity, and Restoration

In 722 B.C., Israel fell to the Assyrians, who deported many Hebrews to other parts of the Assyrian empire. These transported Hebrews—the so-called ten lost tribes—merged with neighboring peoples and lost their identity as the people of God. By 586 B.C., the Chaldeans had conquered Judah, destroyed Solomon's temple, devastated the land, and deported several thousand Hebrews to Babylon. The prophets Isaiah, Ezekiel, and Jeremiah declared that the destruction of Judah was a punishment that the Hebrews had brought on themselves by violating God's laws. This time was the darkest moment in the history of the Hebrews. Their state was gone, neighboring peoples had overrun their land, and their holy temple was in ruins. Thousands had died in battle, had been executed, or had fled to Egypt and other lands, and thousands more were in exile in Babylon. This exile is known as the Babylonian Captivity.

Still, in what is a marvel of history, the Hebrews survived as a people. Although many of the exiles in Babylon assimilated Babylonian ways, some remained faithful to their God Yahweh and the Law of Moses and longed to return to their homeland. Priests struggled to understand the misfortunes that had befallen their people and to prevent the erosion of faith in a foreign environment. They codified ancient traditions, records, and practices, particularly laws, in the process creating the Torah (see below). Thus, their faith enabled them to endure conquest and exile. In Babylon, the prophet known as Second Isaiah comforted the uprooted Hebrews. He declared that soon Yahweh, who controlled the course of history, would restore the erring but repentant Hebrews to their land in a second Exodus. When the Persians conquered Babylon, King Cyrus, in 538 B.C., permitted the exiles to return to Judah, now a Persian province, and to rebuild the temple. The majority of Judeans preferred to remain in prosperous and cosmopolitan Babylon. But some of them did return to Judah, and in 515 B.C., the Hebrews, now commonly called Jews, dedicated the second temple at Jerusalem.

During the first half of the fifth century B.C., the restored Jewish community seemed on the verge of disintegration. Exploitation of the poor created internal tensions; intermarriage with non-Jews grew more frequent; and there was spiritual backsliding, including neglect of the Sabbath. Under the leadership of Nehemiah and Ezra in the second half of the fifth century B.C., administrative reforms were introduced and spiritual life was invigorated. Once again, the Jews had overcome threats to their communal existence.

Online Study Center **Improve Your Grade**
Interactive Map: The Assyrian and Persian Empires

The Hebrew Scriptures

In the following centuries, the Jews would lose their independence to Rome and become a dispersed people. But they never relinquished their commitment to God and his Law as recorded in the Hebrew Scriptures (Old Testament). Called *Tanak* by Jews, the Old Testament consists of thirty-nine books* by several authors who lived in different centuries. Jews call the first five books of the Old Testament—Genesis, Exodus, Leviticus, Numbers, and Deuteronomy—the Torah (which originally meant "teaching" or "instruction"). Often, the Torah is referred to as the Pentateuch, a Greek word meaning "five books."

The Hebrew Scriptures represent Jewish oral and written tradition dating from about 1250 to 150 B.C. Compiled by religious devotees, not research historians, they understandably contain factual errors, imprecisions, discrepancies, legends, and folklore. However, there are also passages that offer reliable history, and historians find the Old Testament an indispensable source for studying the ancient Near East. Literary scholars study it for its poetry, legends, and themes, all of which are an integral part of the Western literary tradition. But it is as a work of religious inspiration that the Hebrew Scriptures attain their profoundest importance.

The Old Testament is the record of more than a thousand years of ancient Jewish history. Containing Jewish laws, wisdom, hopes, legends, and literary expressions, it describes an ancient people's efforts to comprehend the ways of God. The Old Testament emphasizes and values the human experience; its heroes are not demigods but human beings. It depicts human strength as well as weakness. Some passages exhibit cruelty and unseemly revenge against the enemies of Israel, while others express the highest ethical values. As set forth in the Hebrew Scriptures, the Hebrew idea of God and his relationship to human beings is one of the foundations of the Western tradition.

*In ancient times, the number of books was usually given as twenty-four. Certain books are now divided into two parts, and the twelve works by the minor prophets are now counted as individual books.

God: One, Sovereign, Transcendent, Good

The Hebrew view of God evolved through the history and experiences of the Hebrew people. In the days of the patriarchs, before the sojourn in Egypt, the Hebrews most likely were not monotheists. They probably devoted themselves to the god of their particular clan and expressed no hatred for the idolatrous beliefs of neighboring peoples. The chief of each clan established a special attachment to the god of his fathers, hop-

A Dead Sea Scroll, Judea, second century B.C. God's law, as recorded in the Holy Scriptures, still remains a unifying force among Jews. Many ancient Hebrew scrolls were found in caves near the west bank of the Dead Sea beginning in the late 1940s. The scroll depicted here contains the earliest existing copy of a complete Hebrew text of the book of the prophet Isaiah. It barely differs from more modern manuscripts. (© *John Trevor, 1970, Ancient Biblical Manuscript Center, Claremont, CA.*)

ing that the deity would protect and assist the clan. Quite likely, the patriarchs' religion contained spiritual elements that later would aid in the transition to monotheism. But this probability cannot be documented with certainty, for much of patriarchal religion still remains a mystery.

Some historians say that Moses' religion was not pure monotheism because it did not rule out the existence of other gods. According to this view, not until the prophets, centuries later, did the Hebrews explicitly deny that other gods existed and proclaim that Yahweh stood alone. Other scholars believe that Moses proclaimed a monotheistic idea, that this idea became the central force in the life of the Hebrews at the time of the Exodus from Egypt, and that it continues to be central today. John Bright, an American biblical scholar, suggests a judicious balance. The religion of Moses "did not deny the existence of other gods," says Bright, but it "effectively denied them status as *gods*."[2] The Hebrews could serve only Yahweh and "accorded all power and authority to Him." Consequently, Israel was

> *forbidden to approach [other deities] as gods. . . . The gods were thus rendered irrelevant, driven from the field. . . . To Israel only the one God was God. . . . The other gods,*

> *allowed neither part in creation, nor function in the cosmos, nor power over events . . . were robbed of all that made them gods and rendered non-entities, in short, were "undeified." Though the full implications of monotheism were centuries in being drawn, in the functional sense Israel believed in but one God from the beginning.*[3]

The Hebrew view of the one God marked a profound break with Near Eastern religious thought. The gods of other Near Eastern peoples were not truly free; their power was not without limits. Unlike Yahweh, Near Eastern gods were not eternal but were born or created; they issued from some prior realm. They were also subject to biological conditions, requiring food, drink, sleep, and sexual gratification. Sometimes they became ill or grew old or died. When they behaved wickedly, they had to answer to fate, which demanded punishment as retribution; even the gods were subject to fate's power.

The Hebrews regarded God as *fully sovereign.* He ruled all and was subject to nothing. Yahweh's existence and power did not derive from a preexisting realm, as was the case with the gods of other peoples. The Hebrews believed that no realm of being preceded God in time or surpassed him in power. They saw God as eternal and omnipotent, the source of all in the universe, and having a supreme will. He created and governed the natural world and shaped the moral laws that govern human beings. He was not subservient to fate but determined what happened.

Whereas Near Eastern divinities dwelt within nature, the Hebrew God was *transcendent,* above nature and not a part of it. Yahweh was not identified with any natural force and did not dwell in a particular place in heaven or on earth. Since God was the creator and ruler of nature, there was no place for a sun-god, a moon-god, a god in the river, or a demon in the storm. Nature was God's creation but was not itself divine. Therefore, when the Hebrews confronted natural phenomena, they experienced God's magnificent handiwork, not objects with wills of their own. All natural phenomena—rivers, mountains, storms, stars—were divested of any supernatural quality. The stars and planets were creations of Yahweh, not divinities or the abodes of divinities. The Hebrews neither regarded them with awe nor worshiped them. This removal of the gods from nature is a necessary prerequisite for scientific thought.

The Hebrews demythicized nature, but concerned as they were with religion and morality, they did not create theoretical science. As testimony to God's greatness, nature inspired people to sing the praises of the Lord; it invoked worship of God, not scientific curiosity. When Hebrews gazed at the heavens, they did not seek to discover mathematical relationships but admired God's handiwork. The Hebrews did not view nature as a system governed by natural law. Rather, they saw the rising sun, spring rain, summer heat, and winter cold as God intervening in an orderly manner in his creation. The Hebrews, unlike the Greeks, were not philosophers. They were concerned with God's will, not with the human intellect; with the feelings of the heart, not the power of the mind; with righteous behavior, not abstract thought. Human wickedness stemmed not from ignorance but from disobedience and stubbornness.

Unlike the Greeks, the Hebrews did not speculate about the origins of all things and the operations of nature; they knew that God had created everything. For the Hebrews, God's existence was based on religious conviction, not on rational inquiry; on revelation, not reason. It was the Greeks, not the Hebrews, who originated systematic rational thought. But Christianity, born of Judaism, retained the Hebrew view of a transcendent God and the orderliness of his creation—concepts that could accommodate Greek science.

The Hebrews also did not speculate about God's nature. They knew only that he was *good* and that he made ethical demands on his people. Unlike Near Eastern gods, Yahweh was not driven by lust or motivated by evil but was "merciful and gracious, long-suffering, and abundant in goodness and truth . . . forgiving iniquity and transgression and sin" (Psalm 145:8).[4]* In contrast to pagan gods, who were indifferent to human beings, Yahweh was attentive to human needs.

*The Bible passages in this chapter are quoted from *The Holy Scriptures* (published by The Jewish Publication Society of America).

By asserting that God was *one, sovereign, transcendent,* and *good,* the Hebrews effected a religious revolution that separated them entirely from the world-view held by the other peoples of the ancient Near East.

The Individual and Moral Autonomy

This new conception of God made possible a new awareness of the individual, who was seen as the culmination and centerpiece of God's creation. Created in the image of God, the human being is unique, qualitatively different from the rest of animate nature. Only the human being has the power of volition, the power to make choices. The Hebrews believed that God, who possessed total freedom himself, had bestowed on his people moral freedom—the capacity to choose between good and evil. Thus, in confronting God, the Hebrews developed an awareness of *self,* or *I*; the individual became conscious of his or her own person, moral autonomy, and personal worth.

Fundamental to Hebrew belief was the insistence that God did not create people to be his slaves. The Hebrews regarded God with awe and humility, with respect and fear, but they did not believe that God wanted people to grovel before him; rather, he wanted them to fulfill their moral potential by freely choosing to follow or not to follow God's Law. Thus, in creating men and women in his own image, God made them autonomous and sovereign. In God's plan for the universe, human beings were the highest creation, subordinate only to God. Of all his creations, only they had been given the freedom to choose between righteousness and wickedness, between "life and good, and death and evil" (Deuteronomy 30:15). But having the power to choose freely, men and women must bear the responsibility for their choice.

God demanded that the Hebrews have no other gods and that they make no images "nor any manner of likeness, of any thing that is in heaven above, or that is in the earth beneath, . . . thou shalt not bow down unto them nor serve them" (Exodus 20:4–5). Breaking in a revolutionary way with their pagan surroundings, the Hebrews held that the one true God, both omnipotent and invisible, could not be represented in statues or other human creations. The Hebrews believed that the worship of **idols** deprived people of their freedom and dignity; people cannot be fully human if they surrender themselves to a lifeless idol. Hence, the Hebrews had to destroy images and all other forms of idolatry. A crucial element of Near Eastern religion was the use of images—art forms that depicted divinities—but the Hebrews believed that God, the Supreme Being, could not be represented by pictures or sculpture fashioned by human hands. The Hebrews rejected entirely the belief that an image possessed divine powers that could be manipulated for human advantage. Ethical considerations, not myth or magic, were central to Hebrew religious life.

By making God the center of life, Hebrews could become free moral agents; no person, no human institution, no human tradition could claim their souls. Because God alone was the supreme value in the universe, only he was worthy of worship. Thus, to give *ultimate* loyalty to a king or to a general violated God's stern warning against the worship of false gods. The first concern of the Hebrews was supposed to be righteousness, not power, fame, or riches, which were only idols and would impoverish a person spiritually and morally.

There was, however, a condition to freedom. For the Hebrews, people were not free to create their own moral precepts or their own standards of right and wrong. Freedom meant voluntary obedience to commands that originated with God. Evil and suffering were not caused by blind fate, malevolent demons, or arbitrary gods; they resulted from people's disregard of God's commandments. The dilemma is that in possessing freedom of choice, human beings are also free to disobey God, to commit a sin, which leads to suffering and death. Thus, in the Genesis story, Adam and Eve were punished for disobeying God.

For the Hebrews, to know God was not to comprehend him intellectually, define him, or prove his existence; to know God was to be righteous and loving, merciful and just. When men and women loved God, the Hebrews believed, they were uplifted and improved. Gradually, they learned to overcome the worst elements of human nature and to treat other people with respect and compassion. The Jews came to interpret the belief that man was created in God's image to mean that each human being has a divine spark in him or her, giving every person a unique dignity, which cannot be taken away.

By devotion to God, the Hebrews asserted the dignity and autonomy of human beings. Thus, the Hebrews conceived the idea of moral freedom, that each individual is responsible for his or her own actions. These concepts of human dignity and moral autonomy, which Christianity inherited, are at the core of the Western tradition.

JUDAEA CAPTA S(ENATUS) C(ONSULTO). With a commander's baton in hand and his foot upon a helmet, a victorious centurion proclaims Rome's victory over Judea, personified weeping at the foot of the palm tree. The destruction of the city of Jerusalem under Titus was complete, but the ethics of Old Testament writing would become part of the foundation of Western European culture. (*American Numismatic Society.*)

THE COVENANT AND THE LAW

Central to Hebrew religious thought and decisive in Hebrew history was the covenant, God's special agreement with the Hebrew people:

> *And Moses went up unto God, and the Lord called unto him out of the mountain saying: "Thus shalt thou say to the house of Jacob and tell the children of Israel: Ye have seen what I did unto the Egyptians, and how I bore you on eagles' wings, and brought you unto Myself. Now therefore, if ye will hearken unto My voice indeed, and keep My covenant, then ye shall be Mine own treasure from all peoples; for all the earth is Mine; and ye shall be unto Me a kingdom of priests and a holy nation."* (Exodus 19:3–6)

By this act, the Israelites as a nation accepted God's lordship.

The Hebrews came to see themselves as a unique nation, as a "chosen people," for God had given them a special honor, a profound opportunity, and (as they could never forget) an awesome responsibility. The Hebrews did not claim that God had selected them because they were better than other peoples or because they had done anything special to deserve God's election. They believed that God, in a remarkable manner, had rescued them from bondage in Egypt and had selected them to receive the Law so that their nation would set an example of righteous behavior—"a light to the nations," said the prophet Isaiah—and ultimately lead other peoples to acknowledge God and his greatness.

This responsibility to be the moral teachers of humanity weighed heavily on the Hebrews. They believed that God had revealed his Law—including the moral code known as the Ten Commandments—to the Hebrew people as a whole, and obedience to the Law became the overriding obligation of each Hebrew. Violating the Law meant breaking the sacred covenant—an act that could lead to national disaster. As the Law originated with the one God, the necessary prerequisite for understanding and obeying it was surrendering belief in other gods forever, since they were barriers to comprehending and carrying out God's universal Law.

Justice was the central theme of Old Testament ethics. The Israelites, liberated from slavery by a righteous and compassionate God, had a moral responsibility to overcome injustice, to care for the poor, the weak, and the oppressed. Ethical concerns resulted in decrees dealing with economic, social, and political relationships—decrees that were designed to give practical expression to God's universal norms of morality. Because the covenant was made with the entire Hebrew nation, society as a whole had a religious obligation to root out evil and make justice prevail. Duty to God demanded also a duty toward one's neighbor: "Thou shalt surely open thy hand unto thy poor and needy brother, in thy land" (Deuteronomy 15:11). Thus, there were laws to protect the poor, widows, orphans, resident aliens, hired laborers, and slaves. For example, in contrast to ancient Near Eastern law, which regarded slaves as property, biblical legislation emphasized the slave's humanity, although it acknowledged the slave's status as chattel. It called for the punishment of masters who used excessive force against slaves, and it required masters to allow slaves to participate in religious observances and to rest on the Sabbath.

Israelite law incorporated many elements from Near Eastern legal codes and oral traditions. But by making people more important than property, by expressing mercy toward the oppressed, and by rejecting the idea that law should treat the poor and the rich differently, Israelite law demonstrated a greater ethical awareness and a more humane spirit than other legal codes of the Near East:

> *And a stranger shalt thou not wrong, neither shalt thou oppress him; for ye were strangers in the land of Egypt. Ye shall not afflict any widow or fatherless child. (Exodus 22:20–21)*
>
> *If thy brother, a Hebrew man, or a Hebrew woman, be sold unto thee, he shall serve thee six years; and in the seventh year thou shalt let him go free from thee. And when thou lettest him go free from thee, thou shalt not let him go empty; thou shalt furnish him liberally. . . . (Deuteronomy 15:12–14)*
>
> *Thou shalt not curse the deaf, nor put a stumbling-block before the blind, but thou shalt fear thy God: I am the Lord. . . . thou shalt love thy neighbor as thyself. (Leviticus 19:14,18)*

Hebrew law regulated all aspects of daily life, including family relationships. The father had supreme authority in the family, and this authority extended to his married sons and their wives if they remained in his household. Although polygamy was permitted, monogamy was the general rule; adultery was punishable by death.

As in other Near Eastern societies, the Jews placed women in a subordinate position. The husband was considered his wife's master, and she often addressed him as a servant or subject would speak to a superior. A husband could divorce his wife, but she could not divorce him. Only when there was no male heir could a wife inherit property from her husband or a daughter inherit from her father. Women were not regarded as competent witnesses in court and played a lesser role than men in organized worship.

On the other hand, the Jews also showed respect for women. Wise women and prophetesses like Judith and Deborah were respected by the community and were consulted by its leaders. Prophets compared God's love for the Hebrews with a husband's love for his wife. The Book of Proverbs describes a woman of valor:

> *Strength and dignity are her clothing;*
> *And she laugheth at the time to come.*
>
> *She openeth her mouth with wisdom;*
> *And the law of kindness is on her tongue.*
> *She looketh well to the ways of her household,*
> *And eateth not the bread of idleness.*
> *Her children rise up and call her blessed;*
> *Her husband also, and he praiseth her. . . .*
> *(Proverbs 31:25–28)*

Jewish law regarded women as persons, not as property. Even female captives taken in war were not to be abused or humiliated. The law required a husband to respect and support his wife and never to strike her. One of the Ten Commandments called for honoring both father and mother.

The Hebrew Idea of History

Their idea of God made the Hebrews aware of the crucial importance of historical time. Holidays commemorating such specific historical events as the Exodus from Egypt, the receiving of the Ten Commandments on Mount Sinai, and the destruction of Solomon's temple kept the past alive and vital. Egyptians and Mesopotamians did not have a similar awareness of the uniqueness of a given event: to them, today's incident merely reproduced events experienced by their ancestors. To the Jews, the Exodus and the covenant at Mount Sinai were singular, nonrepetitive occurrences, decisive in shaping their national history. This historical uniqueness and importance of events derived from the idea of a universal God profoundly involved in human affairs—a God who cares, teaches, and punishes.

The Jews valued the future as well as the past. Regarding human history as a process leading to a goal, they envisioned a great day when God would establish on earth a glorious age of peace, prosperity, happiness, and human brotherhood. This utopian notion has become deeply embedded in Western thought.

The Hebrews saw history as the work of God; it was a divine drama filled with sacred meaning and moral significance. Historical events revealed the clash of human will with God's commands. Through history's specific events, God's presence was disclosed and his purpose made known. When the Hebrews suffered conquest and exile, they interpreted these events as divine retribution for violating the covenant and the Law, sinful acts that brought down the wrath of God upon them. For the Hebrews, history also revealed God's compassion and concern. Thus, the Lord liberated Moses and the Israelites at the Red Sea and appointed prophets to plead for the poor and the oppressed. The ancient Hebrews, says historian Millar Burrows, were convinced that history was "the work of a personal divine will, contending with the foolish, stubborn wills of men, promising and warning, judging and punishing and destroying, yet sifting, saving, and abundantly blessing those found amenable to discipline and instruction."[5] Because historical events revealed God's attitude toward human beings, these events possessed spiritual meaning and were worth recording, evaluating, and remembering.

Wall Painting from the Synagogue in Dura-Europos, Roman Syria, early third century a.d. This painting shows a Hebrew prophet reading from an open scroll. (*Yale University Art Gallery, Dura-Europos Collection.*)

The Prophets

Jewish history was marked by the emergence of spiritually inspired individuals called prophets, who felt compelled to act as God's messengers. The prophets believed that God had commanded them to speak and had legitimated their words. The prophets cared nothing for money or possessions, feared no one, and preached without invitation. Often emerging in times of social distress and moral confusion, the prophets pleaded for a return to the covenant and the Law. Speaking in God's name, they exhorted the entire nation to make God's religious-moral commands central to its existence. Believing that they had been dispatched by God to rescue the disobedient Hebrews from their headlong rush to destruction, the prophets reminded their brethren that because of their moral deterioration, God, who rules history, would inflict swift and terrible punishment on them. Among the prophets were Amos, a shepherd from Judea in the south; his younger contemporary, Hosea, from Israel in the north; Isaiah of Jerusalem; and Jeremiah, who witnessed the siege of Jerusalem by the Chaldeans in the early sixth century B.C.

Online Study Center

Improve Your Grade
Primary Source: The First Book of Isaiah: Prophesy

The prophets saw national misfortune as an opportunity for repentance and reform. It is God's wish, they said, to forgive human sins and to renew his relationship with a contrite Israel. They were remarkably courageous people who did not quake before the powerful. In the late eighth century B.C., an angry Isaiah warned:

> *The Lord will enter into judgment*
> *With the elders of His people, and the princes thereof.*
> *"It is ye that have eaten up the vineyard;*
> *The spoil of the poor is in your houses;*
> *What mean ye that ye crush my people,*
> *And grind the face of the poor?"*
> *(Isaiah 3:14–15)*

Social Justice

The flowering of the prophetic movement—the age of classical, or literary, prophecy—began in the eighth century B.C. In attacking oppression, cruelty, greed, and exploitation, the classical prophets added a new dimension to Israel's religious development. These prophets were responding to problems emanating from Israel's changed social structure. The general lack of class distinctions characterizing a tribal society had been altered by the rise of Hebrew kings, the expansion of commerce, and the growth of cities. By the eighth century, there was a significant disparity between the wealthy and the poor. Small farmers in debt to moneylenders faced the loss of their land or even bondage; the poor and their families were often dispossessed and enslaved by the greedy wealthy. To the prophets, these social evils were religious sins that would bring ruin to Israel. Amos, a mid-eighth-century prophet, felt a tremendous compulsion to speak out against these injustices. In the name of God, he denounced the pomp of the heartless rich and the hypocrisy of pious Jews who worshiped God in the prescribed manner but neglected their social obligations to their neighbor, and he demanded justice. For Amos, there was no separation between religion and social conduct:

> *I hate, I despise your feasts,*
> *And I will take no delight in your solemn assemblies.*
> *Yea, though ye offer me burnt-offerings and your meal-offerings,*
> *I will not accept them;*
> *Neither will I regard the peace offerings of your fat beasts.*
> *Take thou away from Me the noise of thy songs;*
> *And let Me not hear the melody of the psalteries.*
> *But let justice well up as waters,*
> *And righteousness as a mighty stream.*
> *(Amos 5:21–24)*

God is compassionate, insisted the prophets. He cares for all, especially the poor, the unfortunate, the suffering, and the defenseless. Justice is God's principal concern and his supreme commandment. God's injunctions, declared Isaiah, were to

> *Seek justice, relieve the oppressed,*
> *Judge the fatherless, plead for the widow.*
> *(Isaiah 1:17)*

Prophets stressed the direct spiritual-ethical encounter between the individual and God. Their concern was the inner person rather than the outer forms of religious activity. Holding that the essence of the covenant was universal righteousness, the prophets criticized priests whose commitment to rites and rituals was not supported by a deeper spiritual insight or matched by a zeal for morality in daily life. To

Profile

Jeremiah

In 597 B.C., the Babylonians, under King Nebuchadnezzar, captured Jerusalem, looted the temple, removed many leading citizens to Babylon, and placed Zedekiah on the throne of David as a puppet ruler. In 589 B.C., Zedekiah, ignoring the warnings of the prophet Jeremiah (born c. 645 B.C.), rebelled against Babylonian rule.

Jeremiah began prophesying when still in his teens, exhorting the Hebrews to avoid the evils of idol worship and mistreatment of their fellows. If the people did not change their ways, he warned, a "foe from the north"—clearly, he meant the Babylonians—would devastate the land and even destroy the temple. After the Babylonian conquest, Jeremiah warned Zedekiah to accept Babylonian dominion. Nebuchadnezzar, he said, was fulfilling

By permission of the Warden and Fellows, New College, Oxford.

the prophets, an ethical sin was far worse than a ritual omission. Above all, said the prophets, God demands righteousness, living justly before God. To live unjustly, to mistreat one's neighbors, to act without compassion—these actions violated God's Law and endangered the entire social order.

The prophets thus helped shape a social conscience that has become part of the Western tradition. This revolutionary social doctrine states that everyone has a God-given right to social justice and fair treatment; that each person has a religious obligation to denounce evil and oppose mistreatment of others; and that the community has a moral responsibility to assist the unfortunate. The prophets held out the hope that life on earth could be improved, that poverty and injustice need not be accepted as part of an unalterable natural order, and that the individual was capable of elevating himself or herself morally and could respect the dignity of others.

Universalism

Two tendencies were present in Hebrew thought: **parochialism** and universalism. Parochial-mindedness stressed the special nature, destiny, and needs of the chosen people—a nation set apart from others—for from among all the nations, God had chosen to give it his Law, the Torah. This narrow, tribal outlook was offset by **universalism,** a concern for all humanity, which found expression in the prophets who envisioned the unity of all people under God. Those prophets told of a great "day" when God, for whom all people were equally precious, would establish everlasting justice and peace among all nations:

> *In that day shall there be a highway out of Egypt to Assyria, and the Assyrian shall come into Egypt, and the Egyptian into Assyria; and the Egyptians shall worship with the Assyrians. In that day shall Israel be the third with Egypt and with Assyria. . . . for that*

God's purpose. God imposed the Babylonian yoke on Judah to provide the people with an opportunity for true contrition and spiritual renewal. To oppose Babylon was to contravene God's plan and bring down his wrath on Judah. Jeremiah told King Zedekiah: "Why should you and your people die by the sword, by famine, and by pestilence, as the Lord has spoken concerning any nation that will not serve the king of Babylon?" (27:12).

Jeremiah's political advice angered royal officials and popular prophets, who urged a war of liberation. When Zedekiah rebelled, Nebuchadnezzar responded with force. The enemies of Jeremiah demanded his execution as a traitor, and he was left to die in a deep cistern. However, Zedekiah allowed the prophet to be rescued but placed him under court arrest. Shortly afterward, the Babylonians poured through Jerusalem's breached walls; they burned the city, destroyed the temple, slaughtered nobles, and forcibly removed many people to Babylon. King Zedekiah met a dreadful end. After being forced to watch the execution of his sons, he was blinded and taken in chains to Babylon.

Nebuchadnezzar ordered Jeremiah's release from prison. Remaining in Jerusalem, the prophet sent out a message of hope to the survivors. God had punished you, he told them, because "your guilt is great, because your sins are so numerous" (30:15). But God, who loved the people of Israel "with an everlasting love" (31:3) and also recognized his abiding commitment to them, will one day "restore the fortunes of my people" (30:3). The exiles will be returned, Jerusalem rebuilt, and the temple restored, he prophesied.

> *the Lord of hosts hath blessed him saying: "Blessed be Egypt My people and Assyria the work of My hands, and Israel Mine inheritance." (Isaiah 19:23–24)*

Israel was charged with a sacred mission: to lead in the struggle against idolatry and to set an example of righteous behavior for all humanity.

The prophets were not pacifists, particularly if a war was being waged against the enemies of Yahweh. But some prophets denounced war as obscene and looked forward to its elimination. In a world where virtually everyone glorified the warrior, the prophets of universalism envisioned the day when peace would reign over the earth, when nations

> *. . . shall beat their swords into plowshares,*
> *And their spears into pruning-hooks;*
> *Nation shall not lift up sword against nation,*
> *Neither shall they learn war any more.*
> *(Isaiah 2:4)*

These prophets maintained that when people glorify force, they dehumanize their opponents, brutalize themselves, and dishonor God. When violence rules, there can be no love of God and no regard for the individual.

Individualism

The prophets' universalism was accompanied by an equally profound awareness of the individual and his or her worth to God. Before Moses and the later prophets, virtually all religious tradition had been produced communally and anonymously. The prophets, however, spoke as fearless individuals who, by affixing their signatures to their thoughts, fully bore the responsibility of their religious inspiration and conviction.

The notion of **individualism** is particularly evident in the prophecies of Jeremiah, who in the early sixth century B.C. predicted doom for Judah because of its collective sins in violating God's covenant. In envisioning the day when "everyone shall die for his own iniquity," Jeremiah explicitly emphasized individual responsibility. At that time, God would make a new covenant with the Jews to replace the covenant they had broken. This new covenant would not be written on stone as the Mosaic covenant had been. Rather, it would be a covenant between God and each individual: "I will put My law in their inward parts, and in their heart will I write it" (Jeremiah 31:30–34).

The prophets' emphasis on the individual's responsibility for his or her own actions is a key component of Western thought. In coming to regard God's Law as a *command to conscience, an appeal to the inner person,* the prophets heightened the awareness of the human personality. They indicated that the individual could not know God by merely following edicts and by performing rituals; the individual must experience God. Precisely this *I-Thou* relationship could make the individual fully conscious of self and could deepen and enrich his or her personality. During the Exodus, the Hebrews were a tribal people who obeyed the Law largely out of awe and group compulsion. By the prophets' time, the Jews appeared to be autonomous individuals who heeded the Law because of a deliberate, conscious inner commitment.

The ideals proclaimed by the prophets helped sustain the Jews throughout their long and often painful historical odyssey, and they remain a vital force for Jews today. Incorporated into the teachings of Jesus, these ideals, as part of Christianity, are embedded in the Western tradition.

The Legacy of the Ancient Jews

For the Jews, monotheism had initiated a process of self-discovery and self-realization unmatched by other peoples of the Near East. The great value that westerners give to the individual derives in part from the ancient Hebrews, who held that man and woman were created in God's image and possessed free will and a conscience answerable to God.

Throughout the centuries the Jewish Bible, with its view of God, human nature, divine punishment, and social justice, has played a pivotal and profound role in Jewish life. Moreover, its significance has transcended the Jewish experience; it is also a cornerstone of Western civilization.

Christianity, the essential religion of Western civilization, emerged from ancient Judaism, and the links between the two, including monotheism, moral autonomy, prophetic values, and the Hebrew Scriptures as the Word of God, are numerous and strong. The historical Jesus cannot be understood without examining his Jewish background, and his followers appealed to the Hebrew Scriptures in order to demonstrate the validity of their beliefs. For these reasons, we talk of a Judeo-Christian tradition as an essential component of Western civilization.

The Hebrew vision of a future **messianic age,** a golden age of peace and social justice, is at the root of the Western idea of progress—that people can build a more just society, that there is reason to be hopeful about the future. This way of perceiving the world has greatly influenced modern reform movements.

In seeking to comprehend their relationship to God, the writers of the Hebrew Scriptures produced a treasury of themes, stories, and models of literary style and craftsmanship that have been a source of inspiration for Western religious thinkers, novelists, poets, and artists to the present day. Historians and archaeologists find the Hebrew Scriptures a valuable resource in their efforts to reconstruct ancient Near Eastern history.

❖ ❖ ❖

Online Study Center **ACE the Test**

Notes

1. John A. Wilson, "Egypt—the Kingdom of the 'Two Lands,'" in *At the Dawn of Civilization,* ed. E. A. Speiser (New Brunswick, N.J.: Rutgers University Press, 1964), pp. 267–268. Vol. 1 in *The World History of the Jewish People.*
2. John Bright, *A History of Israel* (Philadelphia: Westminster Press, 1972), p. 154.
3. Ibid.
4. From *The Holy Scriptures* (Philadelphia: The Jewish Publication Society of America, 1917). The scriptural quotations are used in this chapter with the permission of The Jewish Publication Society of America.
5. Millar Burrows, "Ancient Israel," in *The Idea of History in the Ancient Near East,* ed. Robert C. Denton (New Haven, Conn.: Yale University Press, 1955), p. 128.

Suggested Reading

Anderson, Bernhard, *Understanding the Old Testament,* 2nd ed. (1966). An excellent survey of the Old Testament in its historical setting.

Armstrong, Karen, *A History of God* (1994). Changing views of God from the ancient Hebrews until today.

Boadt, Lawrence, *Reading the Old Testament* (1984). A study of ancient Israel's religious experience by a sympathetic Catholic scholar.

Bright, John, *A History of Israel* (1972). A thoughtful, clearly written survey; one of the best of its kind.

Grant, Michael, *The History of Ancient Israel* (1984). A lucid account.

Heschel, Abraham, *The Prophets,* 2 vols. (1962). A penetrating analysis of the nature of prophetic inspiration.

Metzger, Bruce M., and Michael D. Coogan, eds., *The Oxford Companion to the Bible* (1993). A valuable reference work.

Shanks, Hershel, ed., *Ancient Israel* (1999). The revised and expanded edition contains authoritative essays on various phases of the history of ancient Israel. Highly recommended.

Chapter 3

The Greek City-State: Democratic Politics

The Acropolis of Athens. (Robert Harding Picture Library.)

- Early Aegean Civilizations
- The Rise of Hellenic Civilization
- Evolution of the City-State
- Athenian Greatness
- The Decline of the City-States
- The Dilemma of Greek Politics

Focus Questions

1. What were the basic features and limitations of Greek democracy?
2. How did the Greek city-state differ from Near Eastern political arrangements?
3. How did Greek political life demonstrate both the best and the worst features of freedom as well as both the capabilities and limitations of reason?
4. Why is the Greek political experience crucial to the shaping of the Western tradition?

Online Study Center

This icon will direct you to interactive map and primary source activities on the website http://college.hmco.com/pic/perrywc8e.

The Hebrew conception of ethical monotheism, with its stress on human dignity, is one principal source of the Western tradition. The second major source is ancient Greece. Both Hebrews and Greeks absorbed the achievements of Near Eastern civilizations, but they also developed their own distinctive viewpoints and styles of thought, which set them apart from the Mesopotamians and Egyptians. The great achievements of the Hebrews lay in the sphere of religious-ethical thought; those of the Greeks lay in the development of rational thought. As Greek society evolved, says British historian James Shiel, there

> *was a growing reliance on independent reason, a devotion to logical precision, progressing from myth to logos [reason]. Rationalism permeated the whole social and cultural development. . . . Architecture . . . developed from primitive cultic considerations to sophisticated mathematical norms; sculpture escaped from temple image to a new love of naturalism and proportion; political life proceeded from tyranny to rational experiments in democracy. From practical rules of thumb, geometry moved forward in the direction of the impressive Euclidian synthesis. So too philosophy made its way from "sayings of the wise" to the Aristotelian logic, and made men rely on their own observation and reflection in facing the unexplained vastness of the cosmos.*[1]

The Greeks conceived of nature as following general rules, not acting according to the whims of gods or demons. They saw human beings as having a capacity for rational thought, a need for freedom, and a worth as individuals. Although the Greeks never dispensed with the gods, they increasingly stressed the importance of human reason and human decisions. They came to assert that reason is the avenue to knowledge and that people—not the gods—are responsible for their own behavior. In this shift of attention from the gods to human beings, the Greeks broke with the mythmaking orientation of the Near East and created the rational outlook that is a distinctive feature of Western civilization.

Chronology 3.1 ❖ The Greek City-State

1700–1450 B.C.*	Height of Minoan civilization
1400–1230	Height of Mycenaean civilization
1100–800	Dark Age
c. 700	Homer
750–550	Age of Colonization
621	Draco's code of law
594	Solon is elected chief executive
546–527	Under Pisistratus, tyranny replaces oligarchy
507	Cleisthenes broadens democratic institutions
499	Ionians revolt against Persian rule
490	Athenians defeat Persians at battle of Marathon
480	Xerxes of Persia invades Greece; Greek naval victory at Salamis
479	Spartans defeat Persians at Plataea, ending Persian Wars
478–477	Formation of Delian League
431	Start of Peloponnesian War
429	Death of Pericles
413	Athenian defeat at Syracuse
404	Athens surrenders to Sparta, ending Peloponnesian War
399	Execution of Socrates
387	Plato founds a school, the Academy
359	Philip II becomes king of Macedonia
338	Battle of Chaeronea: Greek city-states fall under the dominion of Macedonia
335 B.C.	Aristotle founds a school, the Lyceum

*Some dates are approximations

Online Study Center **Improve Your Grade**
Interactive Map: Ancient Greece from the Aegean through Classical Period

Early Aegean Civilizations

Until the latter part of the nineteenth century, historians placed the beginning of Greek, or Hellenic, history in the eighth century B.C. Now it is known that two related civilizations preceded Hellenic Greece: the Minoan and the Mycenaean. Although the ancient Greek poet Homer had spoken of an earlier Greek civilization in his works, historians believed that Homer's epics dealt with myths and legends, not with a historical past. In 1871, however, a successful German businessman, Heinrich Schliemann, began a search for earliest Greece. Having been enthralled by Homer's epics as a youth, Schliemann was convinced that they referred to an actual civilization.

In excavating several sites mentioned by Homer, Schliemann discovered tombs, pottery, ornaments, and the remains of palaces of what hitherto had been a lost Greek civilization. The ancient civilization was named after Mycenae, the most important city of the time. Mycenaean civilization pervaded the Greek mainland and the islands of the Aegean Sea for much of the second millennium B.C.

In 1900, Arthur Evans, a British archaeologist, made an equally extraordinary discovery. Excavating on the island of Crete, southeast of the Greek mainland, he unearthed a civilization even older than that of the Mycenaean Greeks. The Cretans, or Minoans, were not Greeks and did not speak a Greek language, but their influence on mainland Greece was considerable and enduring. Minoan civilization lasted about 1,350 years (2600 B.C. to 1250 B.C.) and reached its height during the period from 1700 to 1450 B.C.

The centers of Minoan civilization were magnificent palace complexes, whose construction was evidence of the wealth and power of Minoan kings. That the architects of these palaces and the artists who decorated the walls were sensitive to beauty is shown in the ruins uncovered at various Cretan sites. The palaces housed royal families, priests, and government officials and contained workshops that produced decorated silver vessels, daggers, and pottery for local use and for export. Numerous Cretan artifacts have been found in Egypt, Syria, Asia Minor, and Greece, attesting to a substantial export trade.

Judging by the archaeological evidence, the Minoans seemed peaceful. Minoan art did not generally depict military scenes, and Minoan palaces, unlike the Mycenaean ones, had no defensive walls or fortifications. Thus, the Minoans were vulnerable to the warlike Mycenaean Greeks, who invaded and conquered Knossos. The Minoans never recovered from this blow, and within two centuries Minoan civilization faded away.

Who were these Mycenaeans? Around 2000 B.C., Greek-speaking tribes moved southward into the Greek peninsula, where, together with the pre-Greek population, they fashioned the Mycenaean civilization. In the Peloponnesus, the Mycenaeans built palaces that were based in part on Cretan models. In these palaces, Mycenaean kings conducted affairs of state, and priests and priestesses performed religious ceremonies; potters, smiths, tailors, and chariot builders practiced their crafts in the numerous workshops, much like their Minoan counterparts. Mycenaean arts and crafts owed a considerable debt to Crete. A script that permitted record keeping probably also came from Crete. The Mycenaeans were traders, too, exchanging goods with the peoples of Egypt, Phoenicia, Sicily, southern Italy, Macedonia, and the western coast of Asia Minor.

At the apex of Mycenaean society was the king, who headed the armed forces, controlled production and trade, and was the highest judicial authority. Assisting the king were aristocrats, who were officers in the army and held key positions in the administration. The priestesses and priests were also in the upper echelons of the society; they supervised sanctuaries and other properties of the gods. Farmers, stockbreeders, and craftsmen constituted the bulk of the free population. At the bottom of the social pyramid were the slaves—mostly foreign prisoners of war.

Mycenaean civilization, which consisted of several small states, each with its own ruling dynasty, reached its height in the period from 1400 to 1230 B.C. Following that, constant warfare between the Mycenaean kingdoms (and perhaps foreign invasions) led to destruction of the palaces and the abrupt disintegration of the Mycenaean civilization about 1100 B.C. But to the later Greek civilization the Mycenaeans left a legacy of religious forms, pottery making, metallurgy, agriculture, language, a warrior culture and code of honor immortalized in the Homeric epics, and myths and legends, which offered themes for Greek drama.

The Rise of Hellenic Civilization

From 1100 to 800 B.C., the Greek world passed through the Dark Age, an era of transition between a dead Mycenaean civilization and a still unborn Hellenic civilization. The Dark Age saw the migration of Greek tribes from the barren mountainous regions of Greece to more fertile plains, and from the mainland to Aegean islands and the coast of Asia Minor. One group of invaders, the Dorians, penetrated the Peloponnesian peninsula in the south and later founded Sparta. Another group, the Ionians, settled in Attica, where Athens is located, and later crossed to Asia Minor. During this period, the Greeks experienced insecurity, warfare, poverty, and isolation. The bureaucratic system of Mycenaean government had disappeared, extensive trade had ceased, the art of writing had been forgotten, the palace workshops no longer existed, and art had reverted to primitive forms.

After 800 B.C., however, town life revived. Writing again became part of the Greek culture, this time with the more efficient Phoenician script. (Other borrowings from the Near East included artistic imagery and motifs, religious practices, craft skills, and mythological tales that were adapted and transformed by Greek writers.) The population increased dramatically, there was a spectacular rise in the use of metals, and overseas trade expanded. Gradually, Greek cities founded settlements on the islands of the Aegean, along the coast of Asia Minor and the Black Sea, and to the west in Sicily and southern Italy. These colonies, established to relieve overpopulation and land hunger, were independent, self-governing city-states, not possessions of the homeland city-states, although close ties were maintained between the two. During the two hundred years of colonization (750–550 B.C.), trade and industry expanded, the pace of urbanization quickened, and a new class emerged: the merchants, whose wealth derived from goods and money rather than from land. In time, this middle class would challenge the landholding aristocracy.

Homer, Shaper of the Greek Spirit

The poet Homer lived during the eighth century B.C., just after the Dark Age. His great narrative epics, the *Iliad* and the *Odyssey*,* helped shape the Greek spirit and Greek religion. Homer was the earliest molder of the Greek outlook and character. For centuries, Greek youngsters grew up reciting the Homeric epics and admiring the Homeric heroes, who strove for honor and faced suffering and death with courage. Greek thinkers quoted Homer to illustrate moral truths.

In contrast to earlier works of mythology, Homer dealt not just with a hero's actions but also with what the hero thought and felt about his behavior. Homer was a poetic genius who could reveal a human being's deepest thoughts, feelings, and conflicts in a few brilliant lines. His characters, complex in their motives and expressing powerful human emotions—wrath, vengeance, guilt, remorse, compassion, and love—would intrigue and inspire Western writers down to the present.

The *Iliad* deals, in poetic form, with a small segment of the tenth and last year of the Trojan War, which had taken place centuries before Homer's time, during the Mycenaean period. At the very beginning, Homer states his theme:

> *The Wrath of Achilles is my theme, that fatal wrath which, in fulfillment of the will of Zeus, brought the Achaeans [Greeks] so much suffering and sent the gallant souls of many noblemen to Hades, leaving their bodies as carrion for the dogs and passing birds. Let us begin, goddess of song, with the angry parting that took place between Agamemnon King of Men and the great Achilles Son of Peleus.*[2]

The story goes on to reveal the cause and tragic consequences of this wrath. In depriving "the swift and excellent" Achilles of his rightful war-prize (the captive young woman Briseis), King Agamemnon has insulted Achilles' honor and has violated the solemn rule that warrior heroes treat each other with respect. His pride wounded, Achilles refuses to rejoin Agamemnon in battle against Troy and plans to affirm his honor by demonstrating that the Achaeans need his valor and military prowess. Not until many brave men have been slain, including his dearest friend Patroclus, does Achilles set aside his quarrel with Agamemnon and enter the battle.

Homer employs a *particular* event, the quarrel between an arrogant Agamemnon and a revenge-

*Although scholars agree that Homer composed the *Iliad*, some of them hold that the *Odyssey* was probably the work of an unknown poet who lived sometime after Homer; some say that Homer composed both epics in their earliest forms and that others altered them.

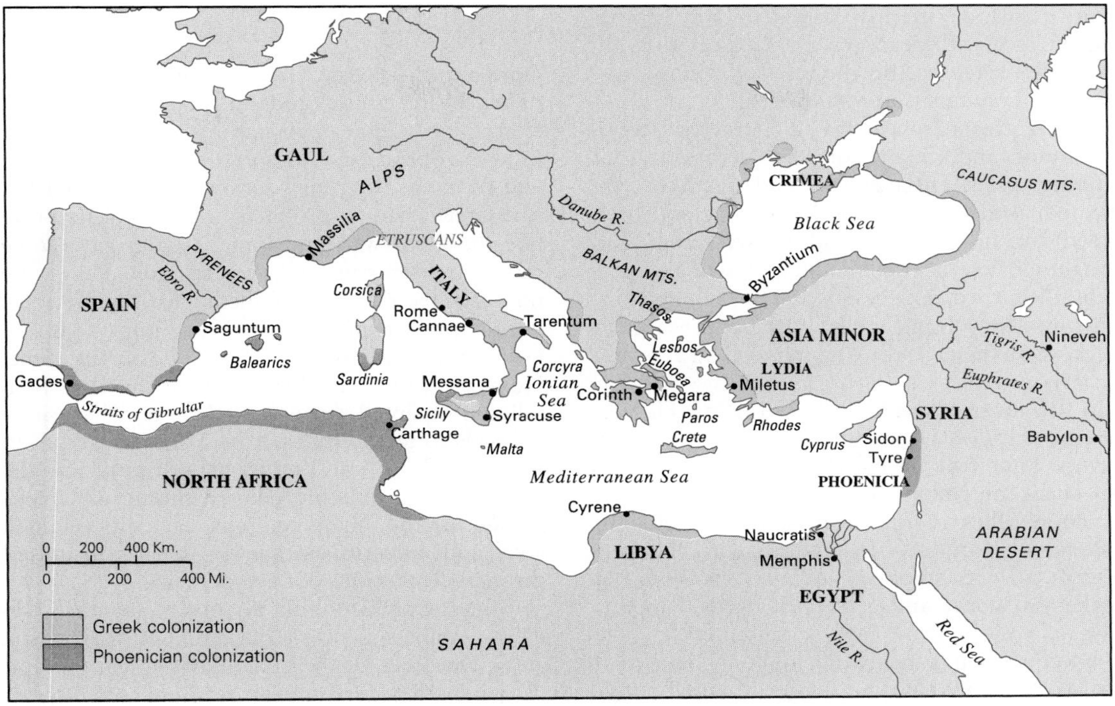

Map 3.1 **Greek Colonization of the Mediterranean Basin** From 750 to 550 B.C., the Greeks colonized the islands of the Aegean, the coasts of Asia Minor and the Black Sea, and, to the west, Sicily and southern Italy.

ful Achilles, to demonstrate a *universal* principle: that "wicked arrogance" and "ruinous wrath" will cause much suffering and death. Homer grasps that there is an internal logic to existence. For Homer, says British classicist H. D. F. Kitto, "actions must have their consequences; ill-judged actions must have uncomfortable results."[3] People, and even the gods, operate within a certain unalterable framework; their deeds are subject to the demands of fate, or necessity. With a poet's intuition, Homer sensed what would become a fundamental attitude of the Greek mind: there is a universal order to things. Later Greeks would formulate Homer's poetic insight in philosophical terms.

Although human life is governed by laws of necessity, the Homeric warrior expresses a passionate desire to assert himself, to demonstrate his worth, to gain the glory that poets would immortalize in their songs—that is, to achieve *areté*, excellence. In the *Iliad*, Hector, prince of Troy, does battle with Achilles, even though defeat and death seem certain. He fights not because he is a fool rushing madly into a fray nor because he relishes combat, but because he is a prince bound by a code of honor and conscious of his reputation and of his responsibility to his fellow Trojans. In the code of the warrior-aristocrats, cowardice brought unbearable shame, and honor meant more than life itself. When Hector knows that he is going to be slain by Achilles, he expresses this overriding concern with heroism and glory: "So now I meet my doom. Let me at least sell my life dearly and have a not inglorious end, after some feat of arms that shall come to the ears of generations still unborn."[4]

Heroism, the pursuit of glory, and war's exhilaration are central to the *Iliad*, but Homer is also sensitive to the suffering caused by war. Battlefields littered with dead and maimed warriors fill soldiers with tears. And the grief of widows, orphans, and parents is unremitting.

Homer grasped war's tragic character: it confers honor and dignity on the victorious, but suffering, grief, enslavement, and death on the defeated. And one day, the hero, who had been lauded for his courage and prowess and had brought glory to his family and city, will also perish by the sword. This is his destiny. Homer's insights into life's tragic nature instructed the great Greek dramatists (see Chapter 4) and future Western writers.

In the warrior-aristocrat world of Homer, **areté** or *excellence* was principally interpreted as bravery and skill in battle. Homer's portrayal also bears the embryo of a larger conception of human excellence, one that combines thought with action. A man of true worth, says the wise Phoenix to the stubborn Achilles, is both "a speaker of words and a doer of deeds." In this passage, we find the earliest statement of the Greek educational ideal: the molding of a man who, says classicist Werner Jaeger, "united nobility of action with nobility of mind," who realized "the whole of human potentialities."[5] Thus, in Homer we find the beginnings of Greek humanism—a concern with man and with his achievements.

To Mesopotamian and Egyptian minds, the gods were primarily responsible for the good or evil that befell human beings. In Homer's work, the gods are still very much involved in human affairs, but Homer also makes the individual a decisive actor in the drama of life. Human actions and human personality are very important. Homer's men demonstrate a considerable independence of will. Human beings pay respect to the gods but do not live in perpetual fear of them; they choose their own way, at times even defying the gods. As British classicist C. M. Bowra notes, "the human actors . . . pursue their own aims and deal their own blows; the gods may help or obstruct them, but success or failure remains their own. The gods have the last word, but in the interval men do their utmost and win glory for it."[6] Homer's view of the eternal order of the world and his conception of the individual striving for excellence form the foundations of the Greek outlook.

Greek Religion

During the Dark Age, Greek religion was a mixture of beliefs and cults of gods and goddesses inherited from the Mycenaean past and from an even older Indo-European past imported from Asia Minor and from the early civilizations of the Near East. The Greeks had no prophets or works of scripture like the Hebrews, but Homer's epics gave some clarity and structure to Greek religion. They were not intended to have any theological significance, but their treatment of the gods had important religious implications for the Greeks. In time, Homer's epics formed the basis of the Olympian religion accepted throughout Greece. The principal gods were said to reside on Mount Olympus in northern Greece, and on its highest peak was the palace of Zeus, the chief deity. Although all Greeks recognized the Olympian gods, each city retained local gods and rituals that had been transmitted through generations by folk memory.

Many Greeks found an outlet for their religious feelings in the sacred ceremonies of mystic cults. Devotees of the cult of Dionysus, the god of wine and agricultural fertility, engaged in ecstatic dances and frenzied prayers for abundant harvests. Participants in the Eleusinian cult felt purified and reborn through their rituals and believed in a happy life after death. The Orphic cult, which was popular in the sixth century B.C., taught the unimportance of earthly life and the need to prepare for life after the grave. The Orphics believed that the soul, which once had enjoyed a happy existence in another world, was imprisoned in the body for an unknown fault, and that if the individual controlled his or her bodily desires, the soul would be liberated after death.

In the early stages of Greek history, most people sought to live in accordance with the wishes of the gods. Through prayer, offerings, and ritual purification, they tried to appease the gods and consulted oracles to divine the future. Although religion pervaded daily life, the Greeks had no official body of priests who ruled religious matters and could intervene in politics. Instead, religious ceremonies were conducted by citizens chosen to serve as priests. Nor was there an official creed with established doctrines. Religion was more social than spiritual; that is, it was more a way of expressing attachment to the community than finding inner peace through personal communion with a higher reality. In time, traditional religion would be challenged and undermined by a growing secular and rational spirit.

Evolution of the City-State

The Break with Theocratic Politics

From 750 B.C. to the death of Alexander the Great in 323 B.C., Greek society consisted of independent city-states. The city-state based on tribal allegiances was generally the first political association during the early stages of civilization. Moreover, Greece's many mountains, bays, and islands—natural barriers to political unity—favored this type of political arrangement.

The scale of the city-state, or *polis*, was small; most city-states had fewer than 5,000 male citizens. Athens, which was a large city-state, had some 35,000 to 40,000 adult male citizens; the rest of its population of 350,000 consisted of women, children, resident aliens, and slaves, none of whom could participate in lawmaking. The citizens of the polis, many of whom were related by blood, knew each other well, and together they engaged in athletic contests and religious rituals. The polis gave individuals a sense of belonging, for its citizens were intimately involved in the political and cultural life of the community.

In the fifth century B.C., at its maturity, the Greeks viewed their polis as the only avenue to the good life—"the only framework within which man could realize his spiritual, moral, and intellectual capacities," in the words of Kitto.[7] The mature polis was a self-governing community that expressed the will of free citizens, not the desires of gods, hereditary kings, or priests. In the **theocracies** of the Near East, religion dominated political activity, and to abide by the mandates of the gods was the ruler's first responsibility. The Greek polis also had begun as a religious institution, in which the citizens sought to maintain an alliance with their deities. But gradually the citizens de-emphasized the gods' role in political life and based government not on the magic powers of divine rulers, but on human intelligence as expressed through the community. Seers, purported to have supernatural skills, might offer advice but could not override the rulings of the Assembly. The great innovation introduced by the Greeks into politics and social theory, says classicist Mason Hammond, was "the view that law did not emanate from gods, or divine rulers, but from the human community."[8] The evolution of the Greek polis from a tribal-religious institution to a secular-rational institution was only a part of the general transition of the Greek mind from myth to reason.

The emergence of rational attitudes did not, of course, spell the end of religion, particularly for the peasants, who remained devoted to their ancient cults, gods, and shrines. Greek commanders and statesmen, at times, were not beyond consulting omens and oracles before making decisions, and considerable public revenue went to the construction of temples and the observance of religious festivals. The Greeks were careful to show respect for the gods, for many believed that these deities could aid or harm a city. Paying homage to the god of the city remained a required act of patriotism, to which Greeks unfailingly adhered.

Thus, the religious-mythical tradition never died in Greece but existed side by side with a growing **rationalism.** As Greek rationalism gained influence, traditional religious beliefs and restrictions either were made to comply more with the demands of reason or grew weaker through neglect and disuse. When Athenian **democracy** reached its height in the middle of the fifth century B.C., religion was no longer the dominant factor in politics. For many Athenians, religion had become largely ceremonial, a way of expressing loyalty to the city. They had come to rely on human reason, not divine guidance, in their political and intellectual life.

Greek political life was marred by violent party conflicts, demagoguery, intercity warfare, and the exploitation of weak states by stronger ones. Nevertheless, the Greek political achievement was extraordinary. What made Greek political life different from that of earlier Near Eastern civilizations, as well as gave it enduring significance, was the Greeks' gradual realization that community problems are caused by human beings and require human solutions. Thus, the Greeks came to understand law as an achievement of the rational mind rather than as an edict imposed by the gods; law was valued because it expressed the will and needs of the community, not out of fear of the divine. The Greeks also valued free **citizenship.** An absolute king, a tyrant who ruled arbitrarily and by decree and who was above the law, was abhorrent.

The ideals of political freedom are best exemplified by Athens. Before turning to Athens, however, let us examine another Greek city, which followed a different political course.

Sparta: A Garrison State

Situated on the Peloponnesian peninsula, farther inland than most Greek cities, Sparta had been settled by Dorian Greeks. The Greek city-states dealt with overpopulation and the need for new agricultural land by founding colonies. Sparta, however, established only one colony, Tarentum, in southern Italy. Sparta's chief means of expansion was to conquer, in the eighth century B.C., its neighbors on the Peloponnesian peninsula, including Messenia. Instead of selling the Messenians abroad, the traditional Greek way of treating a defeated foe, the Spartans kept them as state serfs, or *helots*. Helots were owned by the state rather than by individual Spartans. Enraged by their enforced servitude, the Messenians, also a Greek people, desperately tried to regain their freedom. After a bloody struggle, the Spartans suppressed the uprising, but the fear of a helot revolt became indelibly stamped on Spartan consciousness.

To maintain their dominion over the Messenians, who outnumbered them ten to one, the Spartans—with extraordinary single-mindedness, discipline, and loyalty—transformed their own society into an armed camp. Agricultural labor was performed by helots; trade and crafts were left to the *perioikoi*, conquered Greeks who were free but were not citizens and had no political rights. The Spartans learned only one craft, soldiering, and were inculcated with only one conception of excellence: fighting bravely for their city.

The Spartans were trained in the arts of war and indoctrinated to serve the state. Military training for Spartan boys began at age seven; they exercised, drilled, competed, and endured physical hardships. Other Greeks admired the Spartans for their courage, obedience to law, and achievement in molding themselves according to an ideal. Spartan soldiers were better trained and disciplined and were more physically fit than other Greeks. But the Spartans were also criticized for having a limited conception of areté.

Before Sparta converted itself into a military state, its cultural development had paralleled that of the other Greek cities. By isolating itself economically and culturally from the rest of Greece, however, Sparta became a closed provincial town and did not share in the cultural enlightenment that pervaded the Greek world. A culturally retarded Sparta paid a heavy price for military strength.

By 500 B.C., Sparta had emerged as the leader of the Peloponnesian League, an alliance of southern Greek city-states whose land forces were superior to those of any other combination of Greek cities. Sparta, though, was concerned with protecting its position, not with expansion. Cautious by temperament and always fearful of a helot uprising, Spartans viewed the Peloponnesian League as an instrument for defense rather than aggression.

Athens: The Rise of Democracy

The contrast between the city-states of Athens and Sparta is striking. Whereas Sparta was a land power and exclusively agricultural, Athens, located on the peninsula of Attica near the coast, possessed a great navy and was the commercial leader among the Greeks. Reluctant to send soldiers far from home, where they were needed to control the helots, Sparta's leaders pursued an isolationist foreign policy. The daring and ambitious Athenians, on the other hand, endeavored to extend their hegemony over other Greek cities. Finally, Athenians and Spartans differed in their concept of freedom. To the Spartans, freedom meant preserving the independence of their fatherland; this overriding consideration demanded order, discipline, and regimentation. The Athenians also wanted to protect their city from enemies, but, unlike the Spartans, they valued

SPARTAN WOMAN STATUETTE. Spartan women were expected to marry before the age of twenty and to have children. Moreover, it was assumed that while the men and boys underwent military training, the women would keep the household in order. (*National Archaeological Museum, Athens/Archaeological Receipts Fund.*)

political freedom and sought the full development and enrichment of the human personality. Thus, while authoritarian Sparta became culturally sterile, Athens, with its relatively free and open society, emerged as the cultural leader of Hellenic civilization.

Greek city-states generally moved through four stages: rule by a king (monarchy), rule by landowning aristocrats (oligarchy), rule by one man who seized power (tyranny), and rule by the people (democracy). During the first stage, monarchy, the king, who derived his power from the gods, commanded the army and judged civil cases.

Oligarchy, the second stage, was instituted in Athens during the eighth century B.C. when aristocrats (*aristocracy* is a Greek word meaning "rule of the best") usurped power from hereditary kings. In the next century, aristocratic regimes experienced a social crisis. There was tension between the landholding nobles, who dominated the government, and the newly rich and ambitious merchants, who wanted a share in governing Athens. Furthermore, peasants who borrowed from the aristocracy, pledging their lands as security, lost their property and even became enslaved for nonpayment of their debts. Merchants and peasants also protested that the law, which was based on oral tradition and administered exclusively by aristocrats, was unjust. The embittered and restless middle and lower classes were granted one concession. In 621 B.C., the aristocrats appointed Draco to draw up a code of law. Although Draco's code let the poor know what the law was and reduced the possibilities of aristocratic judges behaving arbitrarily, penalties were extremely severe (hence the word *draconian*), and the code provided no relief for the peasants' economic woes. As the poor began to organize and press for the cancellation of their debts and the redistribution of land, Athens was moving toward civil war.

Solon, the Reformer In 594 B.C., Solon (c. 640–559 B.C.), a traveler and poet with a reputation for wisdom, was elected chief executive. He maintained that the wealthy landowners, through their greed, had disrupted community life and brought Athens to the brink of civil war. Solon initiated a rational approach to the problems of society by de-emphasizing the gods' role in human affairs and attributing the city's ills to the specific behavior of individuals; he sought practical remedies for these ills; and he held that written law should be in harmony with **Diké**, the principle of justice that underlies the human community. At the same time, he wanted to instill in Athenians of all classes a sense of working for the common good of the city.

Solon aimed at restoring a sick Athenian society to health by restraining the nobles and improving the lot of the poor. To achieve this goal, he canceled debts, freed Athenians enslaved for debt, and brought back to Athens those who had been sold abroad; however, he refused to confiscate and redistribute the nobles' land as the

DETAIL OF GREEK KYLIX (CUP) C. 490–480 B.C. The frenzied dancing of the Bacchantes, worshippers of the god Dionysius, is depicted by the vase painter Macron. Maenads (mad-ones) dressed in fawn skins and carrying the *thrysos*, a wand made of vine leaves, leap and carouse in ecstatic orgies with satyrs in worship of the god of wine and sexual liberation. (*The Metropolitan Museum of Art, Rogers Fund, 1906 [06.115.2.].*)

extremists demanded. He permitted all classes of free men, even the poorest, to sit in the Assembly, which elected magistrates and accepted or rejected legislation proposed by a new Council of Four Hundred. He also opened the highest offices in the state to wealthy commoners, who had previously been excluded from these positions because they lacked noble birth. Thus, Solon undermined the traditional rights of the hereditary aristocracy and initiated the transformation of Athens from an aristocratic oligarchy into a democracy.

Solon also instituted ingenious economic reforms. Recognizing that the poor soil of Attica was not conducive to growing grain, he urged the cultivation of grapes for wine and the growing of olives, whose oil could be exported. To encourage industrial expansion, he ordered that all fathers teach their sons a trade and granted citizenship to foreign craftsmen who were willing to migrate to Athens. These measures and the fine quality of the native reddish-brown clay allowed Athens to become the leading producer and exporter of pottery. Solon's economic policies transformed Athens into a great commercial center. However, Solon's reforms did not eliminate factional disputes among the aristocratic clans or relieve much of the discontent of the poor.

Pisistratus, the Tyrant In 546 B.C., Pisistratus (c. 605–527 B.C.), an aristocrat, took advantage of the general instability to become a one-man ruler, driving into exile those who had opposed him. Tyranny thus replaced oligarchy. Tyranny occurred frequently in the Greek city-states. Almost always aristocrats themselves, tyrants generally posed as champions of the poor in their struggle against the aristocracy. Pisistratus sought popular support by having conduits constructed to increase the Athenian water supply; like tyrants in other city-states, he gave to peasants land confiscated from exiled aristocrats and granted state loans to small farmers.

Pisistratus' great achievement was the promotion of cultural life. He initiated grand architectural projects, encouraged sculptors and painters, arranged for public recitals of the Homeric epics, and founded festivals, which included dramatic performances. In all these ways, he made culture, formerly the province of the aristocracy, available to commoners. Pisistratus thus launched a policy that eventually led Athens to emerge as the cultural capital of the Greeks.

Cleisthenes, the Democrat Shortly after Pisistratus' death, a faction headed by Cleisthenes, an aristocrat sympathetic to democracy, assumed leadership. By an ingenious method of redistricting the city, Cleisthenes ended the aristocratic clans' traditional jockeying for the chief state positions, which had caused much divisiveness and bitterness in Athens. Cleisthenes replaced this practice, rooted in tradition and authority, with a new system, rationally planned to ensure that historic allegiance to tribe or clan would be superseded by loyalty to the city as a whole.

Cleisthenes hoped to make democracy the permanent form of government for Athens. To safeguard the city against tyranny, he utilized (or perhaps introduced) the practice of **ostracism.** Once a year, Athenians were given the opportunity to inscribe on a fragment of pottery (*ostracon*) the name of anyone who, they felt, endangered the state. An individual against whom six thousand votes were cast was ostracized, that is, forced to leave Athens for ten years.

Cleisthenes firmly secured democratic government in Athens. The Assembly, which Solon had opened to all male citizens, was in the process of becoming the supreme authority in the state. But the period of Athenian greatness lay in the future; the Athenians first had to fight a war of survival against the Persian Empire.

Athenian Greatness

The Persian Wars

In 499 B.C., the Ionian Greeks of Asia Minor rebelled against their Persian overlord. Sympathetic to the Ionian cause, Athens sent twenty ships to aid the revolt, an act that the Greek historian Herodotus said "was the beginning of trouble not only for Greece, but for the rest of the world as well." Bent on revenge, Darius I, king of Persia, sent a small detachment to Attica. In 490 B.C., on the plains of Marathon, the citizen army of Athens defeated the Persians—for the Athenians, one of the finest moments in their history. Ten years later, Xerxes, Darius' son, organized a huge invasion force—some 250,000 men and more than 500 ships—with the aim of reducing Greece to a Persian province. Setting aside their separatist instincts, many of the city-states united to defend their independence and their liberty. Herodotus viewed the conflict as an ideological clash between Greek freedom and oriental despotism.

The Persians crossed the waters of the Hellespont (Dardanelles) and made their way into northern Greece. Herodotus describes their encounter at the mountain pass of Thermopylae with three hundred Spartans, who were true to their training and ideal of areté and "resisted to the last with their swords if they had them, and if not, with their hands and teeth, until the Persians, coming on from the front over the ruins of the wall and closing in from behind, finally overwhelmed them."[9] Northern Greece fell to the Persians, who continued south, burning a deserted Athens.

When it appeared that the Greeks' spirit had been broken, the Athenian statesman and general Themistocles (c. 527–460 B.C.), demonstrating in military affairs the same rationality that Cleisthenes had shown in political life, lured the Persian fleet into the narrows of the Bay of Salamis. Unable to deploy its more numerous ships in this cramped space, the Persian armada was destroyed by Greek ships sailed by crews who understood what was at stake. In 479 B.C., a year after the Athenian naval victory at Salamis, the Spartans defeated the Persians in the land battle of Plataea. The inventive intelligence with which the Greeks planned their military operations and a fierce desire to preserve their freedom—which, the war made them realize, was their distinguishing attribute—enabled them to defeat the greatest military power the Mediterranean world had yet seen.

The Persian Wars were decisive in the history of the West. Had the Greeks been defeated, it is very likely that their cultural and political vitality would have been aborted. The confidence and pride that came with its astonishing victory, however, propelled Athens into a golden age, which became marred by the Athenian urge for dominance in Greece.

The Persian Wars ushered in an era of Athenian imperialism, which had drastic consequences for the future. Immediately after the wars, more than 150 city-states organized a confederation, the Delian League (named after its treasury on the island of Delos), to protect themselves against a renewed confrontation with Persia. Because of its wealth, its powerful fleet, and the restless energy of its citizens, Athens assumed leadership of the Delian League. Largely thanks to the Athenian fleet, the league was able to drive both pirates and Persians from the Aegean Sea.

Although it had been conceived as a voluntary association of independent Greek states seeking protection against Persia, the league gradually came under the domination of Athens. Athenians also manipulated the league for their own economic advantage, seeing no conflict between imperialism and democracy. They believed that their freedom and prosperity required subduing, exploiting, and enslaving others, and they adhered to the principle that strong states had a natural right to dominate weaker ones. They relished the empire that gave them wealth, power, and glory. Moreover, the Athenians claimed that the other city-states benefited from Athenian hegemony. Athens forbade member states to withdraw, crushed revolts, and stationed garrisons on the territory of confederate states. It used both tribute from members and the league's treasury to finance public works in Athens.

Although member states did receive protection, were not overtaxed, and enjoyed increased trade, they resented Athenian domination. As the Persian threat subsided, hatred for Athenian imperialism grew. In converting the Delian League into an instrument of Athenian imperialism, Athens may have lost an opportunity to perform a great creative act—forming a broad voluntary confederation that might have forestalled the intercity warfare that gravely weakened Hellenic civilization.

The Mature Athenian Democracy

Athenian imperialism was one consequence of the Persian Wars; another was the flowering of Athenian democracy and culture. The Athenian state was a direct democracy, in which the citizens themselves, not elected representatives, made the laws. In the Assembly, which was open to all adult male citizens and which met some forty times a year, Athenians debated and voted on key issues of state; they declared war, signed treaties, and spent public funds. By the middle of the fifth century B.C., the will of the people, as expressed by a majority vote in the Assembly, was supreme. Rejecting the arbitrary rule of tyrants and domination by a small circle of nobles, the Athenians conceived the idea of **isonomy**—equality of political rights for citizens of the polis, that is, the right to vote, to speak before and submit motions to the Assembly, to hold the highest public positions, and to receive equal treatment before the law.

The Council of Five Hundred (which had been established by Cleisthenes to replace Solon's Council of Four Hundred) managed the ports, military installations, and other state properties and prepared the agenda for the Assembly. Because its members were chosen annually by lot and could not serve more than twice in a lifetime, the Council could never supersede the Assembly. Chosen at random, its membership could not become a cabal of the most powerful and ambitious citizens. Some 350 magistrates, also chosen by lot, performed administrative tasks: collecting fines, policing the city, repairing streets, inspecting markets, and so forth. Because of the special competence that their posts required, the ten generals who led the army were not chosen by lot but were elected by the Assembly.

The introduction of pay for government officials marked a great democratic advance. It meant

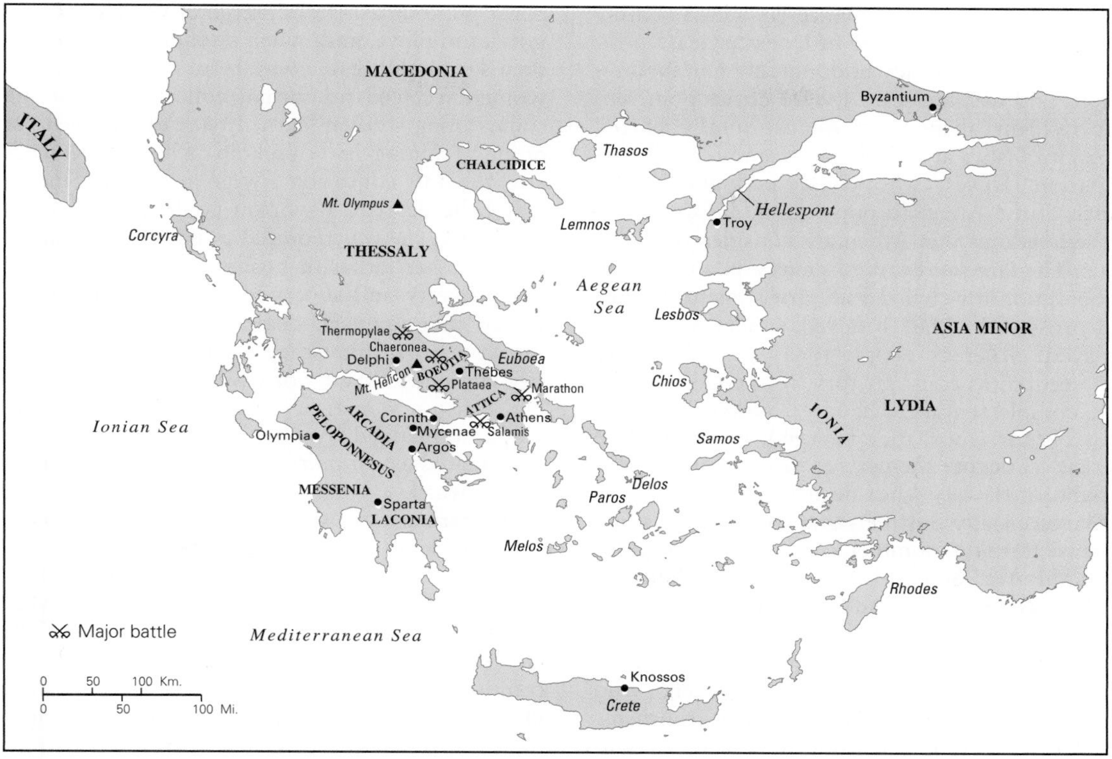

Map 3.2 **The Aegean Basin** This map shows major battle sites. Note also the Hellespont, where Xerxes' forces crossed into Greece, and Ionia, the coast of Asia Minor, where Greek philosophy was born.

that an average person could afford to leave his job for a year in order to serve on the Council of Five Hundred, on a commission overseeing the administration of the city, or in the law courts.

Athens has been aptly described as a government of amateurs. There were no professional civil servants, no professional soldiers and sailors, no state judges—all legal cases were decided by juries chosen by lot—and no elected lawmakers. The duties of government were performed by ordinary citizens. Such a system rested on the assumption that the average citizen was capable of participating intelligently in the affairs of state and that he would, in a spirit of civic patriotism, carry out his responsibilities to his city. In fifth-century Athens, excellence was equated with good citizenship—a concern for the good of the community that outweighed personal aspirations. Indeed, to a surprisingly large number of Athenians, politics was an overriding concern, and they devoted considerable time and thought to civic affairs. Those who allowed private matters to take precedence over the needs of the community were denounced as useless people living purposeless lives.

Although Athens was a democracy in form, in practice aristocrats continued to dominate political life for most of the fifth century. Generals came from noble houses as did the leading voices in the Assembly. This situation was not surprising, for aristocrats took for granted a responsibility to exercise leadership and acquired the education, particularly in public speaking and debate, needed to perform this role. The economic expansion after the Persian Wars produced a wealthy class of tradesmen, who eventually challenged aristocratic dominance in the Assembly during the last third of the fifth century B.C.

Athenian democracy undoubtedly had its limitations and weaknesses. Modern critics point out that resident aliens were almost totally barred from citizenship and therefore from political participation. Slaves, who constituted about one-fourth of the Athenian population, enjoyed none of the freedoms that Athenians considered so precious. The Greeks regarded slavery as a necessary precondition for civilized life; for some to be free and prosperous, they believed, others had to be enslaved. Whereas people today regard slavery and freedom as contradictory, to the Greeks they were complementary. The large number of slaves available for labor, they believed, permitted free citizens to devote themselves to civic affairs and to fight for the city when needed.

Slaves usually did the same work as Athenian citizens: farming, commerce, manufacturing, domestic chores. Some slaves—the three hundred Scythian archers who made up the police force and those sufficiently educated to serve the state as clerks—enjoyed a privileged position. However, slaves, including preadolescent children, who toiled in the mines suffered a grim fate. In Athens, some slaves were Greeks, but most were foreigners. Slaves were generally prisoners of war and captives of pirates. Sometimes they were foreign children sold by their parents or abandoned infants left to die, a not uncommon practice in ancient Greece and Rome. A person finding the infant might eventually sell the child into slavery.

Athenian women were another group denied legal or political rights. Most Greeks, no doubt, agreed with Aristotle, who said: "[T]he male is by nature superior, and the female inferior; and . . . the one rules and the other is ruled."[10] A girl usually was married at fourteen, to a man twice her age, and the marriage was arranged by a male relative. The wedding day might be the first time that the young bride saw her future husband. Although either spouse could obtain a divorce, the children remained with the father after the marriage was dissolved. Wives did not dine with their husbands and spent much of their time in the women's quarters.

Athenian women were barred from holding public office and generally could not appear in court without a male representative. They could not act in plays, and, when attending the theater, they sat in the rear, away from the men. Greek women received no formal education, although some young women learned to read and write at home. Training in household skills was considered the only education a woman needed. Since it was believed that a woman could not act independently, she was required to have a guardian—normally her father or husband—who controlled her property and supervised her behavior. Convinced that financial dealings were too difficult for women and that they needed to be protected from strangers, men, not women, did the marketing. When a woman left the house, she was usually accompanied by a male. The Athenian wife was treated as a minor; in effect, she was her husband's ward.

Modern critics also point out the failure of Hellenic Greeks to arrive at a conception of what seventeenth- and eighteenth-century liberal thinkers were to call natural or inalienable rights and what are now generally known as human rights. The Greeks limited rights to members of a particular community; they had no awareness of the modern idea that all individuals possess as a birthright basic rights that government must respect.

Ancient critics, too, attacked Athenian democracy. Having no confidence in the ability of the common people to govern, these aristocratic critics equated democracy with mob rule. In a democracy, they said, the envious, volatile, and incompetent poor tyrannize the rich; make unwise, impetuous decisions; and are easily manipulated by clever demagogues. A political system that gives power to people of limited merit is destined to fail. The Assembly did at times make rash and foolish decisions and was swayed by the oratory of demagogues. For the most part, however, as British historian A. H. M. Jones concludes,

> *the Assembly seems to have kept its head, and very rarely to have broken its rules of procedure. . . . Moreover, the people demanded high standards of its advisors. . . . It was informed advice, and not mere eloquence, that the people expected from rising politicians, and they saw to it that they got it.*[11]

ATTIC BLACK-FIGURE HYDRIA, C. 510 B.C. This hydria, or water jug, shows women drawing water from a fountainhouse. Trips to the fountainhouse provided one of the few opportunities for women to socialize outside the home. (*William Francis Warden Fund. Courtesy Museum of Fine Arts, Boston.*)

That the Athenians found democracy an indispensable form of government is proved by the paucity of revolts. In the almost two hundred years after Cleisthenes, there were only two attempts to undo the democracy, both made under the stress of the Peloponnesian War and both short-lived.

The flaws in Athenian democracy should not cause us to undervalue its extraordinary achievement. The idea that the state represented a community of free, self-governing citizens remains a crucial principle of Western civilization. Athenian democracy embodied the principle of the legal state—a government based not on force but on laws debated, devised, altered, and obeyed by free citizens.

This idea of the legal state could have arisen only in a society that was aware of and respected the rational mind. In the same way that the Greeks demythicized nature, they also removed myth from the sphere of politics. Holding that government was something that people create to satisfy human needs, the Athenians regarded their leaders neither as gods nor as priests but as men who had demonstrated a capacity for statesmanship. Athens was unique, writes Italian historian Mario Attilio Levi, for Athenians "had the audacity to maintain that human reason is itself the source of legitimacy and therefore of the right to govern and command, in a world in which the only recognized source of legitimacy was the gods."[12]

Both democratic politics and systematic political thought originated in Greece. There people first asked questions about the nature and purpose of the state, rationally analyzed political institutions, speculated about human nature and justice, and discussed the merits of various forms of government. It is to Greece that we ultimately trace the idea of democracy and all that accompanies it: citizenship, constitutions, equality before the law, government by law, reasoned debate, respect for the individual, and confidence in human intelligence.

But there is a fundamental difference between the Greek concept of liberty and our own. We are concerned with protecting the individual from the state, which we often see as a threat to personal freedom and a hindrance to the pursuit of our personal lives. Identifying the good of the individual with the good of the community, the Greeks were not concerned with erecting safeguards against the state; they did not view the state as an alien force, to be feared or to be protected against. Rather, they saw it as a moral association, a second family, which taught proper conduct and enabled them to fulfill their human potential. Given this orientation, they were not much interested in human rights.

Pericles: Symbol of Athenian Democracy

Pericles (c. 495–429 B.C.), a gifted statesman, orator, and military commander, was the central figure in Athenian life during the middle of the fifth century B.C. So impressive was his leadership that this period is called the Age of Pericles. During these years, Athenians achieved greatness in politics, drama, sculpture, architecture, and thought.

In the opening stage of the monumental clash with Sparta, the Peloponnesian War (431–404 B.C.), Pericles delivered an oration in honor of the Athenian war casualties. The oration, as reconstructed by Thucydides, the great Athenian historian of the fifth century B.C., contains a glowing description of the Athenian democratic ideal, which encompassed both civic and personal freedom:

> *We are called a democracy, for the administration is in the hands of the many and not of the few. But while the law secures equal justice to all alike in their private disputes, the claim of excellence is also recognized; and when a citizen is in any way distinguished, he is [selected for] public service . . . as the reward of merit. Neither is poverty a bar, but a man may benefit his country whatever may be the obscurity of his condition. . . . There is no exclusiveness in our public life, and in our private intercourse we are not suspicious of one another, nor angry with our neighbor if he does what he likes; we do not put on sour looks at him which though harmless are unpleasant. . . . a spirit of reverence pervades our public acts; we are prevented from doing wrong by respect for authority and for the laws. . . .*[13]

Throughout the speech, Pericles contrasted the narrow Spartan concept of excellence with the Athenians' humanistic ideal of the full development of the human personality. Unlike Sparta, Athens valued both political freedom and cultural creativity; indeed, as Pericles recognized, freedom released an enormous amount of creative energy, making possible Athens' extraordinary cultural accomplishments. "Our love of what is beautiful does not lead to extravagance, our love of the things of the mind does not make us soft," continued Pericles in praise of Athenian society.[14]

Online Study Center

Improve Your Grade
Primary Source: The Funeral Oration of Pericles (Thucydides)

The Decline of the City-States

Although the Greeks shared a common language and culture, they remained divided politically. A determination to preserve city-state sovereignty prevented them from forming a larger political grouping, which might have contained the intercity warfare that ultimately cost the city-state its vitality and independence. But the creation of a Pan-Hellenic union would have required a radical transformation of the Greek character, which for hundreds of years had regarded the city-state as the only suitable political system.

The Peloponnesian War

Athenian control of the Delian League engendered fear in the Spartans and their allies in the Peloponnesian League. Sparta and the Peloponnesian states decided on war because they felt that a dynamic and imperialistic Athens threatened their independence. At stake for Athens was hegemony over the Delian League, which gave Athens political power and contributed to its economic prosperity. Neither Athens nor Sparta anticipated the catastrophic consequences that the war would have for Greek civilization.

The war began in 431 B.C. and ended in 404 B.C., with a temporary and uneasy interlude of peace from 421 to 414 B.C. Possessing superior land forces, the Peloponnesian League invaded Attica and set fire to the countryside. In 430 B.C., a plague, probably coming from Ethiopia by way of Egypt, ravaged Athens, killing about one-third of the population, including its leader, Pericles (in 429 B.C.). Because of Athenian sea power and

Grecian Warriors. The Greek warriors in this vase painting have weapons and armor very much like that used by the Greeks in the Persian Wars. (*Vatican Collection/Scala/Art Resource, NY.*)

Spartan inability to inflict a crushing defeat on Athenian ground troops, the first stage of the war ended in stalemate. In 421 B.C., the war-weary combatants concluded a peace treaty.

What led to the resumption of the war and the eventual defeat of Athens was the Athenian expedition against Sicily and its largest city, Syracuse. Athenians were intoxicated by an imperialist urge to extend the empire in the west and by prospects of riches. Swayed by speeches that stirred the emotions, the Athenian populace, believing disaster to be impossible and forsaking caution and reason, approved the Sicilian venture. In the words of Thucydides,

> *There was a passion for the enterprise which affected everyone alike. . . . The result of this excessive enthusiasm of the majority was that the few who actually were opposed to the expedition were afraid of being thought unpatriotic if they voted against it, and therefore kept quiet.*[15]

Launched with extravagant expectations, the Sicilian expedition ended in dismal failure. Athens and its allies lost fifty thousand men and two hundred ships in the venture; the expedition also cost Athens all hope of victory in the struggle with Sparta. Fearful that victory in Sicily would increase Athenian manpower and wealth, Sparta in 414 B.C. had again taken up the sword. Strengthened by financial support from Persia and by the defection of some Athenian allies, Sparta moved to end the war. Finally, with its navy decimated and its food supply dwindling, besieged Athens surrendered. in 404 B.C. Sparta dissolved the Delian League, left Athens with only a handful of ships, and forced the city to pull down its long walls—ramparts designed to protect it against siege weapons. But the Spartans refused to massacre Athenian men and enslave the women and children, as some allies had urged.

The Peloponnesian War shattered the spiritual foundations of Hellenic society. During the course of the long war, men became brutalized, selfish individualism triumphed over civic duty, moderation gave way to extremism, and politics degenerated into civil war.

The deterioration of Greek political life was exemplified by conflicts between oligarchs and democrats. Oligarchs, generally from the wealthier segments of Greek society, wanted to concentrate power in their own hands by depriving the lower classes of political rights. Democrats, generally from the poorer segment of society, sought to preserve the political rights of adult male citizens. Strife between oligarchs and democrats was quite common in the Greek city-states even before the Peloponnesian War. Both sides sought to dominate the Assembly and to manipulate the courts; both resorted to bribery and at times even assassinated opponents. During the Peloponnesian War, these party conflicts erupted into civil war in many cities, including Athens. The moral basis of Hellenic society was wrecked. In the words of Thucydides,

> *Love of power, operating through greed and through personal ambition, was the cause of all these evils. To this must be added the violent fanaticism which came into play once the struggle had broken out. Leaders of parties in professing to serve the public interest . . . were seeking to win the prizes for themselves. In their struggle for ascendancy nothing was barred; terrible indeed were the actions to which they committed themselves, and in taking revenge they went further still. Here they were deterred neither by the claims of justice nor by the interests of the state. . . . Thus neither side had any use for conscientious motives; more interest was shown in those who could produce attractive arguments to justify some disgraceful action. As for the citizens who held moderate views, they were destroyed by both the extreme parties. . . . As the result of these revolutions, there was a general deterioration of character throughout the Greek World.*[16]

Athens shared the political problems of the Greek world during the war. Pericles had provided Athenians with effective leadership in the three decades prior to the war; when the Assembly seemed to support unwise policies, he had won it over with sound arguments. After his death in 429 B.C., the quality of leadership deteriorated. Succeeding statesmen were motivated more by personal ambition than by civic devotion; rather than soberly examine issues, they supported policies that would gain them popularity. Without Pericles' wise statesmanship, the Assembly at times acted rashly, as it did in the case of the Sicilian expedition.

Taking advantage of the decline in morale after the failure of this expedition, oligarchs gained control of Athens in 411 B.C.; a body of citizens, known as the Four Hundred, wielded power. Seeking to deprive the lower classes of political influence, the Four Hundred restricted citizenship to four thousand men. But the crews of Athenian ships, loyal to democracy, challenged the authority of the Four Hundred, who were forced to flee.

After the defeat of Athens in 404 B.C., oligarchs again gained control, this time with the support of Sparta. A ruling council of thirty men, the so-called Thirty Tyrants, held power. Led by Critias, an extreme antidemocrat, the Thirty trampled on Athenian rights, confiscating property and condemning many people to death. In the winter of 404–403 B.C., returned exiles led an uprising against the Thirty, who were unseated.

The Fourth Century

The Peloponnesian War was the great crisis of Hellenic history. The city-states never recovered from their self-inflicted spiritual wounds. The civic loyalty and confidence that had marked the fifth century B.C. waned, and the fourth century was dominated by a new mentality, which the leaders of the Age of Pericles would have abhorred. A concern for private affairs superseded devotion to the general good of the polis. Increasingly, professionals, rather than ordinary citizens, administered the tasks of government, and mercenaries began to replace citizen soldiers.

The political history of the fourth century can be summed up briefly. Athens, the only state that might have united the Greek world, had lost its chance. A culturally sterile, provincial-minded, and heavy-handed Spartan government lacked the talent to govern the Greeks. In many cities, Sparta replaced democratic governments with pro-Spartan oligarchies under the supervision of a Spartan governor. But Spartan hegemony was short-lived; before long, the Greek city-states had thrown off the Spartan yoke. The quarrelsome city-states formed new systems of alliances and persisted in their ruinous conflicts. Some Greek thinkers, recognizing the futility of constant war, argued that peace should be the goal of Greek politics. But their efforts were in vain.

In addition to wars between city-states, fourth-century Greece experienced a new outbreak of civil wars between rich and poor. Athens largely escaped these ruinous conflicts, but they engulfed many other cities. With good reason, Greek thinkers regarded social discord as the greatest of evils.

While the Greek cities battered one another in fratricidal warfare, a new power was rising in the north—Macedonia. To the Greeks, the Macedonians, a wild mountain people who spoke a Greek dialect and had acquired a sprinkling of Hellenic culture, differed little from other non-Greeks, whom they called barbarians. In 359 B.C., at the age of twenty-three, Philip II (382–336 B.C.) ascended the Macedonian throne. Having spent three years as a hostage in Thebes, Philip had learned the latest military tactics and had witnessed firsthand the weaknesses of the warring Greek states. He converted Macedonia into a first-rate military power and began a drive to become master of the Greeks.

Patient, deceitful, clever, and unscrupulous, Philip gradually extended his power over the Greek city-states. The Greeks did not correctly assess Philip's strength and were slow to organize a coalition against Macedonia, despite the efforts of Demosthenes (c. 384–322 B.C.), the Athenian orator and patriot, who urged the Greeks to unite against this threat to their freedom. In 338 B.C., at Chaeronea, Philip's forces inflicted a decisive defeat on the Greeks, and all of Greece was his. The city-states still existed, but they had lost their independence. The world of the small, independent, self-sufficient polis was drawing to a close, and Greek civilization was taking a different shape.

The Dilemma of Greek Politics

Philip's conquest of the city-states points to fundamental weaknesses of Greek politics. Despite the internal crisis and persistent warfare, the Greeks were unable to fashion any other political framework than the polis. The city-state was fast becoming an anachronism, but the Greeks were unable to see that, in a world moving toward larger states and empires, the small city-state could not compete. An unallied city-state, with its small citizen army, could not withstand the powerful military machine that Philip had created. A challenge confronted the city-states: the need to shape some form of political union, a Pan-Hellenic federation, that would end the suicidal internecine warfare, promote economic well-being, and protect the Greek world from hostile states. Because they could not respond creatively to this challenge, the city-states ultimately lost their independence to foreign conquerors.

The waning of civic responsibility among the citizens was another reason for the decline of the city-states. The vitality of the city-state depended on the willingness of its citizens to put aside private concerns for the good of the community. However, although Athens had recovered commercially from the Peloponnesian War, its citizens had suffered a permanent change in character; the abiding devotion to the polis, which had distinguished the Age of Pericles, greatly diminished during the fourth century. The factional strife, the degeneration of politics into personal ambition, the demagoguery, and the fanaticism that Thucydides had described persisted into the fourth century and were aggravated by the economic discontent of the poor. The Periclean ideal of citizenship dissipated as Athenians neglected the community to concentrate on private affairs or sought to derive personal profit from public office. The decline in civic responsibility could be seen in the hiring of mercenaries to replace citizen soldiers and in the indifference and hesitancy with which Athenians confronted Philip. The Greeks did not respond to the Macedonian threat as they had earlier rallied to fight off the Persian menace because the quality of citizenship had deteriorated.

Greek political life demonstrated the best and worst features of freedom. On the one hand, as Pericles boasted, freedom encouraged active citizenship, reasoned debate, and government by law. On the other, as Thucydides lamented, freedom could degenerate into factionalism, demagoguery, unbridled self-interest, and civil war. Because monarchy deprives people of freedom and self-rule, the Greeks regarded monarchy as a form of government appropriate for uncivilized barbarians. But their political experience showed that free men in a democracy are susceptible to demagogues, will base political decisions on keyed-up emotions rather than on cool reasoning, and are capable of behaving brutally toward political opponents. Moreover, Greek democracy, which valued freedom, was unable to overcome a weakness that has afflicted despotic monarchies: an incautious attitude toward power that cause the state to overreach itself. Such an attitude

Profile

Demosthenes

Art Resource, NY.

Debates in the Assembly stimulated the development of oratory as an art form in Athens and other city-states. Demosthenes (384–322 B.C.), the greatest of the Greek orators, earned his reputation through disciplined effort, for he was not a naturally gifted speaker. When he first addressed the Assembly, wrote Plutarch, the second-century A.D. biographer, he was "derided for his strange and uncouth style, which was cumbered with long sentences and tortured with formal arguments to a most harsh and disagreeable excess. Besides, he had, it seems, a weakness in his voice, a perplexed and indistinct utterance and a shortness of breath, which by breaking and disjointing his sentences, much obscured the sense and meaning of what he spoke."* But the very determined Demosthenes practiced constantly until he perfected his enunciation and delivery.

Demosthenes' fame rests mainly on his Philippics—speeches delivered over a ten-year period warning Greeks of the threat posed by Philip of Macedon. He urged the city-states of Greece to unite against the common enemy and

demonstrated a self-destructive **hubris,** excessive pride or arrogance, that Greek moralists warned against. This is how Thucydides interpreted Athens' disastrous Sicilian expedition during the Peloponnesian War. Driven by a mad passion to possess what was beyond their reach, the Athenians brought ruin to their city.

The Athenians, who saw no conflict between imperialism and democracy, considered it natural for stronger states to dominate weaker ones, an attitude that helped to precipitate the destructive Peloponnesian War. A particularly egregious example of this outlook occurred during that war when Athenians decided to invade the island of Melos despite the assurances of the Melians that they represented no threat to Athens. As reported by Thucydides, the Athenian envoys told the Melians that "the strong do what they have the power to do, and the weak accept what they have to accept."[17] When the Melians resisted, the Athenians slaughtered the men, enslaved the women and children, and colonized the territory.

Greek politics also revealed both the capabilities and the limitations of reason. Originally, the polis was conceived as a divine institution in which the citizen had a religious obligation to obey the law. As the rational and secular outlook became more pervasive, the gods lost their authority. When people no longer regarded law as an expression of sacred traditions ordained by the

lamented the deterioration of the Greek character since the heroic struggle against Persia.

> *And we, the Greek community . . . instead of sending embassies to one another about [the danger] and expressing indignation, are in such a miserable state, so intrenched in separate towns, that to this day we can attempt nothing that interest or necessity requires; we cannot combine, or form any association for succour and alliance; we look unconcernedly on the man's growing power, . . . not caring or striving for the salvation of Greece.*†

A passionate patriot, Demosthenes warned his fellow citizens that Philip, an autocratic king, wanted to conquer Athens and put an end to Athenian democracy.

> *there is nothing which [Philip] strives and plots against so much as our constitution, nothing in the world he is so anxious about, as its destruction. . . . first then you must assume that he is an irreconcilable enemy of our constitution and democracy; secondly, you must be convinced that all his operations and contrivances are designed for the injury of our state.*‡

Demosthenes negotiated an alliance between Thebes and Athens, but the two were defeated by Philip at Chaeronea in 338 B.C. Demosthenes, who witnessed the battle, delivered a funeral oration for the Greek dead, but the speech is lost. After the death of Alexander the Great in 323 B.C., Demosthenes helped to organize Greek resistance to Macedonian rule. The Greeks were defeated the following year, and Antipater, the Macedonian governor of Greece, ordered the execution of Demosthenes and other orators who had urged war. The aging orator and passionate patriot took poison.

Demosthenes' speeches served as a model for subsequent orators, including Cicero, Rome's greatest orator. In modern times, patriots and lovers of freedom have evoked Demosthenes' devotion to his city and its free institutions.

---

*Plutarch, *The Lives of Noble Grecians and Romans,* trans. John Dryden, rev. A. H. Clough (New York: Modern Library, n.d.), p. 1025.

†*Demosthenes' Orations,* intro. by John Warrington (London: Dent, Everyman's Library, 1954), Third Philippic, pp. 195–196.

‡Ibid., Fourth Philippic, p. 209.

gods but saw it as a merely human contrivance, respect for the law diminished, weakening the foundations of the society. The results were party conflicts, politicians who scrambled for personal power, and moral uncertainty. Recognizing the danger, conservatives insisted that law must again be conceived as issuing from the gods and the city must again treat its ancient traditions with reverence. Although the Greeks originated the lofty ideal that human beings could regulate their political life according to reason, their history, marred by intercity warfare and internal violence, demonstrates the extreme difficulties involved in creating and maintaining a rational society.

❖ ❖ ❖

Online Study Center **ACE the Test**

Notes

1. James Shiel, ed., *Greek Thought and the Rise of Christianity* (New York: Barnes & Noble, 1968), pp. 5–6.
2. Homer, *The Iliad*, trans. E. V. Rieu (Baltimore: Penguin Books, 1950), p. 23.
3. H. D. F. Kitto, *The Greeks* (Baltimore: Penguin Books, 1957), p. 60.
4. Homer, *The Iliad,* p. 405.
5. Werner Jaeger, *Paideia: The Ideals of Greek Culture,* trans. Gilbert Highet (New York: Oxford University Press, 1945), 1:8.
6. C. M. Bowra, *Homer* (London: Gerald Duckworth, 1972), p. 72.
7. Kitto, *The Greeks*, p. 78.
8. Mason Hammond, *The City in the Ancient World* (Cambridge, Mass.: Harvard University Press, 1972), p. 189.
9. Herodotus, *The Histories*, trans. Aubrey de Sélincourt (Baltimore: Penguin Books, 1954), p. 493.
10. Aristotle, *Politics*, in *Basic Works of Aristotle*, ed. Richard McKeon (New York: Random House, 1941), p. 1132.
11. A. H. M. Jones, *Athenian Democracy* (Oxford: Basil Blackwell, 1969), pp. 132–133.
12. Mario Attilio Levi, *Political Power in the Ancient World* (New York: Mentor Books, 1968), pp. 122–123.
13. Thucydides, *The Peloponnesian War*, trans. B. Jowett (Oxford: Clarendon Press, 1881), bk. 11, chap. 37.
14. Thucydides, *History of the Peloponnesian War*, trans. Rex Warner (Baltimore: Penguin Books, 1954), p. 118.
15. Ibid., p. 382.
16. Ibid., p. 210.
17. Ibid., p. 360.

Suggested Reading

Frost, Frank J., *Greek Society* (1987). Social and economic life in ancient Greece.

Hooper, Finley, *Greek Realities* (1978). A literate and sensitive presentation of Greek society and culture.

Kitto, H. D. F., *The Greeks* (1957). A stimulating survey of Greek life and thought.

Meier, Christian, *Athens: A Portrait of the City in Its Golden Age* (1999). Rich in details and interpretation.

———, *The Greek Discovery of Politics* (1990). Answers the question: How was it that Greek civilization, unlike all others preceding it, gave birth to democracies?

Stockton, David, *The Classical Athenian Democracy* (1990). The evolution and nature of Greek democracy.

Chapter 4

Greek Thought: From Myth to Reason

Theater at Epidaurus, Greece, c. 350 B.C. (Hirmer Fotoarchiv, München.)

- **Philosophy**
- **Art**
- **Poetry and Drama**
- **History**
- **The Greek Achievement: Reason, Freedom, Humanism**

Focus Questions

1. How did the Pre-Socratic thinkers make the transition from myth to reason?
2. How did the Sophists and Socrates advance the tradition of reason and humanism?
3. Why is Plato's *Republic* considered a milestone in the emergence of political thought?
4. What do Plato and Aristotle have in common? How do they differ?
5. How did Greek drama, art, and historiography contribute to the tradition of reason and humanism?

Online Study Center

This icon will direct you to interactive map and primary source activities on the website http://college.hmco.com/pic/perrywc8e.

The Greeks broke with the mythopoeic outlook of the Near East and conceived a new way of viewing nature and human society, which is the basis of the Western scientific and philosophical tradition. After an initial period of mythical thinking, by the fifth century B.C., the Greek mind had gradually applied reason to the physical world and to all human activities. This emphasis on reason marks a turning point for human civilization.

The development of rational thought in Greece was a process, a trend, not a finished achievement. The process began when some thinkers rejected mythical explanations for natural phenomena. The nonphilosophical majority never entirely eliminated the language, attitudes, and beliefs of myth from their lives and thought. For them the world remained controlled by divine forces, which were appeased through cultic practices. Even in the mature **philosophy** of Plato and Aristotle, mythical modes of thought persisted. What is of immense historical importance, however, is not the degree to which the Greeks successfully integrated the norm of reason, but the fact that they originated this norm, defined it, and consciously applied it to their intellectual and social life.

Philosophy

The first theoretical philosophers in human history emerged in the sixth century B.C., in the Greek cities of Ionia in Asia Minor. Curious about the essential composition of nature and dissatisfied with earlier creation legends, the Ionians sought physical, rather than mythic-religious, explanations for natural occurrences. In the process, they arrived at a new concept of nature and a new method of inquiry. They maintained that nature was not manipulated by arbitrary and willful gods, nor was it governed by blind chance. The Ionians said that there is an intelligible pattern to nature; that nature contains a hidden structure—principles of order or general laws—that governs phenomena; and that these fundamental rules were ascertainable by the human mind. They implied that the origin, composition, and structure of the world can be investigated rationally and systematically. Thus, in seeking to account for rainbows, earthquakes, and eclipses, the Ionians posited entirely naturalistic explanations that relied on observation, had an awareness of cause and effect, and excluded the gods. This new outlook marks the beginning of scientific thought.

What conditions enabled the Greeks to make this breakthrough? Perhaps their familiarity with Near Eastern achievements in mathematics and science stimulated their ideas. But this influence should not be exaggerated, says Greek scholar John N. Theodorakopoulos, for Egyptians and Mesopotamians "had only mythological systems of belief and a knowledge of practical matters. They did not possess those pure and crystal-clear products of the intellect which we call science and philosophy. Nor did they have any terminology to describe them."[1] Rooted in mythological thinking, the ancient Near East experienced no eruption of theorizing about nature in pristine philosophical and scientific terms as Greece did beginning in the sixth century B.C. Perhaps the poets' conception of human behavior as subject to universal destiny was extended into the philosophers' belief that nature was governed by law. Perhaps the breakthrough was fostered by the Greeks' freedom from a priesthood and rigid religious doctrines that limit thought. Or perhaps Greek speculative thought was an offspring of the city, because if law governed human affairs, providing balance and order, should not the universe also be regulated by principles of order?

Online Study Center **Improve Your Grade**
Interactive Map: Ancient Greece from the Aegean through Classical Period

The Cosmologists: A Rational Inquiry into Nature

The first Ionian philosophers are called cosmologists because they sought to discover the underlying principles of the universe: how nature came to be the way it was. They held that some single, eternal, and imperishable substance, which underwent various modifications, gave rise to all phenomena in nature.

Ionian philosophy began with Thales (c. 624–548 B.C.) of Miletus, a city in Ionia. He was a contemporary of Solon of Athens and concerned himself with understanding the order of nature. Thales said that water was the basic element, the underlying substratum of nature, and that through some natural process—similar to the formation of ice or steam—water gave rise to everything else in the world.

Thales revolutionized thought because he omitted the gods from his account of the origins of nature and searched for a natural explanation of how all things came to be. He broke with the commonly held belief that earthquakes were caused by Poseidon, god of the sea, and offered instead a naturalistic explanation for these disturbances: that the earth floated on water and when the water experienced turbulent waves the earth was rocked by earthquakes. Thales was the first person to predict an eclipse of the sun. To do this, he had to dismiss traditional mythical explanations and to grasp a crucial scientific principle—that heavenly objects move in regular patterns, which can be known.

Anaximander (c. 611–547 B.C.), another sixth-century Ionian, rejected Thales' theory that water was the original substance. He rejected any specific substance and suggested that an indefinite, undifferentiated substance, which he called the Boundless, was the source of all things. He believed that from this primary mass, which contained the powers of heat and cold, there gradually emerged a nucleus, the seed of the world. According to Anaximander, the cold and wet condensed to form the earth and its cloud cover, while the hot and dry formed the rings of fire that we see as the moon, the sun, and the stars. The heat from the fire in the sky dried the earth and shrank the seas. From the warm slime on earth arose life, and from the first sea creatures there evolved land animals, including human beings. Anaximander's account of the origins of the universe and nature understandably contained fantastic elements. Nevertheless, by offering a natural explanation for the origin of nature and life and by holding that nature was lawful, it surpassed the creation myths.

Like his fellow Ionians, Anaximenes, who died around 525 B.C., made the transition from myth to reason. He also maintained that a primary substance, air, underlay reality and accounted for nature's orderliness. Air that was rarefied became fire, whereas wind and clouds were formed from condensed air. If the process of condensation continued, it produced water, earth, and eventually stones. Anaximenes also rejected the old belief that a rainbow was the goddess Iris; instead, he saw it as the consequence of the sun's rays falling on dense air.

The Ionians have been called "matter philosophers" because they held that everything issued from a particular material substance. Other sixth-century B.C. thinkers tried a different approach. Pythagoras (c. 580–507 B.C.) and his followers, who lived in the Greek cities in southern Italy, did not find the nature of things in a particular substance but in mathematical relationships. The Pythagoreans discovered that the intervals in the musical scale can be expressed mathematically. Extending this principle of structure and proportion found in sound to the universe at large, they concluded that the cosmos also contained an inherent mathematical order and harmony. Thus, the Pythagoreans shifted the emphasis from matter to form, from the world of sense perception to the logic of mathematics. The Pythagoreans were also religious mystics who believed in the immortality and transmigration of souls. Consequently, they refused to eat animal flesh, fearing that it contained former human souls.

Parmenides (c. 515–450 B.C.), a native of the Greek city of Elea in southern Italy, argued that the fundamental view of the Ionians that the universe underwent change and development over time was utterly mistaken. In developing his position, Parmenides applied to philosophical argument the **logic** used by the Pythagoreans for mathematical thinking. In putting forth the proposition that an argument must be consistent and contain no contradictions, Parmenides became the founder of formal **logic.**

Despite appearances, asserted Parmenides, reality—the cosmos and all that is within it—is one, eternal, and unchanging. It is made known not through the senses, which are misleading, but through the mind; not through experience, but through reason. Truth could be reached through abstract thought alone. Parmenides' concept of an unchanging reality apprehended by thought alone influenced Plato and is the foundation of **metaphysics**—the branch of philosophy that attempts to define ultimate reality, or Being.

Parmenides' thought also had religious implications. Although he did not refer to True Being as God, he did ascribe to it the attributes of oneness, transcendence, permanence, and perfection. Such a description of Being abounds with religious meaning. Particularly as developed by Plato, the quest for Being would greatly influence religious thought, including Christian theology, in the ancient world.

Democritus (c. 460–370 B.C.), from the Greek mainland, renewed the Ionians' concern with the world of matter and reaffirmed their confidence in knowledge derived from sense perception—and the senses indicated that change did occur in nature, in contrast to Parmenides' view. But Democritus also retained Parmenides' reverence for reason. His model of the universe consisted of two fundamental realities: empty space and an infinite number of atoms. Eternal, indivisible, and imperceptible, these atoms moved in the void. All things consisted of atoms, and combinations of atoms accounted for all change in nature. In a world of colliding atoms, everything behaved according to mechanical principles. (Of course, Democritus' atomic theory did not derive from any empirical evidence of atoms but was purely speculative.)

Concepts essential to scientific thought thus emerged in embryonic form with Greek philosophers: natural explanations for physical occurrences (Ionians), the mathematical order of nature (Pythagoras), logical proof (Parmenides), and the mechanical structure of the universe (Democritus). By giving to nature a rational, rather than a mythical, foundation and by holding that theories should be grounded in evidence and that one should be able to defend them logically, the early Greek philosophers pushed thought in a new direction. This new approach allowed a critical analysis of theories, whereas myths, accepted unconditionally on faith and authority, did not promote discussion and questioning. Greek thinkers established the crucial principle that a proposition is not considered true unless it can be supported by logic or empirical evidence. For the most part, the early Greek philosophers rejected the old mythical explanations of nature. Nevertheless, when they proclaimed the unity and orderliness of nature and asserted that an ultimate reality underlies the finite world, they were also expressing ideas integral to religious thought.

VASE PAINTING, 520–510 B.C. In this scene painted by the potter Sosias, Achilles is binding up the wounds of his dear friend Patroclus. The artist's careful attention to detail, both physical and psychological, is seen in Patroclus' turned head and open mouth and his propping of the wounded arm. (*Antikenmuseum der Staatlichen Museen/Preussischer Kulturbesitz, Berlin.*)

These early philosophers made possible theoretical thinking and the systematization of knowledge—as distinct from the mere observation and collection of data. The systematization of knowledge extended into several areas. Greek mathematicians, for example, organized the Egyptians' practical experience with land measurements into the logical and coherent science of geometry, in which each statement followed logically from given assumptions. They established mathematics as a body of theoretical knowledge, an ordered system based on fundamental premises and necessary connections, and they developed logical procedures for arriving at mathematical proofs. Both Babylonians and Egyptians had performed fairly complex mathematical operations, but unlike the Greeks, they made no attempt to prove underlying mathematical principles—to demonstrate that certain conclusions must flow from certain hypotheses. In another area, Babylonian priests observed the heavens for religious reasons, believing that the stars revealed the wishes of the gods. The Greeks used the data collected by the Babylonians, but not for a religious purpose; rather, they sought to discover the geometrical laws that govern the motions of heavenly bodies.

A parallel development occurred in medicine. No Near Eastern medical text explicitly attacked magical beliefs and practices. In contrast, Greek doctors, because of the philosophers' work, were able to distinguish between magic and medicine. The school of the Greek physician Hippocrates (c. 460–c. 377 B.C.), located on the island of Cos, off the Asia Minor coast, was influenced by the thought of the early Greek cosmologists. Hippocratic physicians recorded in detail their observations of ill patients, classified symptoms, and predicted the future course of the disease. They also denounced supernatural and magical explanations and cures. The following tract from the school of Hippocrates on epilepsy, which was considered a sacred disease, illustrates the development of a scientific approach to medicine:

> *I am about to discuss the disease called "sacred." It is not, in my opinion, any more divine or sacred than any other disease, but has a natural cause, and its supposed divine origin is due to men's inexperience, and to their wonder at its peculiar character. Now . . . men continue to believe in its divine origin because they are at a loss to understand it. . . . My own view is that those who first attributed a sacred character to this malady were like the magicians, purifiers, charlatans, and quacks of our own day; men who claim great piety and superior knowledge. Being at a loss, and having no treatment which would help, they concealed and sheltered themselves behind superstition, and called this illness sacred, in order that their utter ignorance might not be manifest.*[2]

The Sophists: A Rational Investigation of Human Society

In their effort to understand the external world, the cosmologists had created the tools of reason. These early Greek thinkers were developing a new and profound awareness of the mind's capacity for theoretical thinking. And equally important, they were establishing the mind's autonomy—its ability to inquire into any subject, relying solely on its own power to think. Greek thinkers then turned away from the world of nature and attempted a rational investigation of people and society, dismissing efforts to explain the social world through inherited beliefs about the gods. The Sophists exemplifed this shift in focus. They were professional teachers who wandered from city to city teaching rhetoric, grammar, poetry, gymnastics, mathematics, and music. The Sophists insisted that it was futile to speculate about the first principles of the universe, for such knowledge was beyond the grasp of the human mind. Instead, they urged that individuals improve themselves and their cities by applying reason to the tasks of citizenship and statesmanship. The Western humanist tradition owes much to the Sophists who examined, at times with great insight, political and ethical concerns, cultivated the minds of their students, and invented formal secular education.

The Sophists answered a practical need in Athens, which had been transformed into a wealthy and dynamic imperial state after the Persian Wars. Because the Sophists claimed that they could teach *political* areté—the skill to formulate the right laws and policies for cities and the art of eloquence and persuasion needed for success in public life—they were sought as tutors by politically ambitious young men, especially in Athens.

Traditionally, the Greeks had drawn a sharp distinction between Greeks, the bearers of an enlightened civilization, and uncivilized and immoderate non-Greeks, whom they called barbarians, and held that some people were slaves by nature. The dramatist Euripides expressed these sentiments: "It is natural for Hellenes to rule barbarians and not . . . for barbarians to rule Hellenes. They are a slave race, Hellenes are free."[3] Some Sophists in the fourth century B.C. arrived at a broader conception of humanity. They asserted that slavery was based on force or chance, that people were not slaves or masters by nature, and indeed that all people, Greek and non-Greek, were fundamentally alike.

The Sophists were philosophical relativists—that is, they held that no truth is universally valid. Protagoras, a fifth-century Sophist, said that "man is the measure of all things." By this he meant that good and evil, truth and falsehood, are matters of community and individual judgment; there are no universal standards that fit all people at all times. Human laws and ethical beliefs have evolved according to a particular community's needs; they are simply human contrivances and conventions, not objective truths or standards written into nature.

In applying reason critically to human affairs, the Sophists attacked the traditional religious and moral values of Athenian society. Some Sophists taught that speculation about the divine was useless. Others went further, asserting that religion was just a human invention to ensure obedience to traditions and laws. Thus, the Sophist Critias (c. 480–403 B.C.) argued that to deter people from committing "open crimes of violence, . . . a wise and clever man invented fear (of the gods) for mortals, that there might be some means of frightening the wicked, even if they do anything or say or think it in secret. Hence he introduced the Divine (religion), saying that there is a God flourishing with immortal life, . . . who will hear everything said among mortals, and will be able to see all that is done."[4]

The Sophists also applied reason to law, with the same effect: the undermining of traditional authority. The laws of a given city, they asserted, did not derive from the gods; nor were they based on any objective, universal, and timeless standards of justice and good, for such standards did not exist. Each community determined for itself what was good or bad, just or unjust. Beginning with this premise, some Sophists simply urged that laws be changed to meet new circumstances. Some radical Sophists argued that law was merely something made by the most powerful citizens for their own benefit. (Or they said that law was a clever invention of the weak in order to check the strong, who benefited from natural advantages.) This view had dangerous implications: first, law did not need to be obeyed since it rested on no higher principle than might; and second, the strong should do what they have the power to do, and the weak must accept what they cannot resist. Both interpretations were disruptive of community life, for they stressed the selfish interests of the individual over the general welfare of the city.

Some Sophists combined this assault on law with an attack on the ancient Athenian idea of **sophrosyne**—moderation and self-discipline—

because it denied human instincts. Instead of moderation, they urged that individuals should maximize pleasure and trample underfoot the traditions that restricted them from fully expressing their desires. As these radical Sophists saw it, the concept of sophrosyne was invented by the weak to enslave nobler natures.

In subjecting traditions to the critique of reason, the radical Sophists triggered an intellectual and spiritual crisis. Their doctrines encouraged loss of respect for authority, disobedience to law, neglect of civic duty, and selfish individualism. These attitudes became widespread during and after the Peloponnesian War, dangerously weakening community bonds.

Socrates: The Rational Individual

In attempting to comprehend nature, the cosmologists had discovered theoretical reason. The Sophists then applied theoretical reason to society. In the process, they created a profound problem for Athens and other city-states: the need to restore the authority of law and a respect for moral values. Conservatives argued that the only way to do so was by renewing allegiance to the sacred traditions that the Sophists had undermined.

Socrates, one of the most extraordinary figures in the history of Western civilization, took a different position. Born in Athens, probably in 469 B.C., about ten years after the Persian Wars, he was executed in 399 B.C., five years after the end of the Peloponnesian War. His life spanned the glory years of Greece, when Athenian culture and democracy were at their height, as well as the tragic years of the lengthy and shattering war with Sparta.

Both the Sophists and Socrates continued the tradition of reason initiated by the cosmologists, but unlike the cosmologists, both felt that knowledge of the individual and society was more important than knowledge of nature. For both, the old mythological traditions, which had served as a foundation for religion and morality, were no longer valid. Socrates and the Sophists endeavored to improve the individual and thought that this could be accomplished through education. Despite these similarities, Socrates' teaching marks a profound break with the Sophist movement.

Socrates attacked the Sophists' **relativism,** holding that people should regulate their behavior in accordance with universal values. As he saw it, the Sophists taught skills but had no insights into questions that really mattered: What is the purpose of life? What are the values by which man should live? How does man perfect his character? Here the Sophists failed, said Socrates; they taught the ambitious to succeed in politics, but persuasive oratory and clever reasoning do not instruct a man in the art of living. He felt that the Sophists had attacked the old system of beliefs but had not provided the individual with a satisfactory replacement.

Socrates' central concern was the perfection of individual human character, the achievement of moral excellence. Moral values, for Socrates, did not derive either from a transcendent God, as they did for the Hebrews, or from an inherited mythic-religious tradition. They were attained when the individual regulated his life according to objective standards arrived at through rational reflection: that is, when reason became the formative, guiding, and ruling agency of the soul. For Socrates, true education meant the shaping of character according to values discovered through the active use of reason.

Socrates wanted to subject all human beliefs and behavior to the scrutiny of reason and in this way remove ethics from the realm of authority, tradition, dogma, superstition, and myth. He believed that reason was the only proper guide to the most crucial problem of human existence: the question of good and evil. Socrates taught that rational inquiry—a questioning mind—was a priceless tool, allowing one to test opinions, weigh the merit of ideas, and alter beliefs on the basis of knowledge. To Socrates, when people engaged in critical self-examination and strove tirelessly to perfect their nature, they liberated themselves from prevailing opinions and conventions and based their conduct on convictions that they could rationally defend. Socrates believed that people with questioning minds could not be swayed by sophistic eloquence nor delude themselves into thinking that they knew something when they really did not.

Socrates' fundamental premise was that wrong thinking resulted in wrongdoing and, conversely, that knowledge of what is right gave one the

THE PARTHENON, ATHENS, 447–432 B.C. A masterpiece of the Doric style, the great temple dedicated to Athena Parthenos (the Maiden), the patron goddess of the city, was constructed through the efforts of Pericles. Its cult statue and the sculptural reliefs under its roofline were designed by the outstanding sculptor of the age, Phidias. In post-Hellenistic times, it served as a Christian church and then as a mosque, until it was destroyed in 1687. Between 1801 and 1812, the marble reliefs were removed by the Englishman Lord Elgin and now reside in the British Museum, in London. (*Hirmer Fotoarchiv, München.*)

strength of will to do what is right. Critics, including religious thinkers, have castigated this assumption as naive, arguing that Socrates credited others with his own extraordinary inner strength and underestimated the immense power of instinct and passions, which drive people, even those who know better, to do what is wrong.

Dialectics. In urging Athenians to think rationally about the problems of human existence, Socrates offered no systematic ethical theory, no list of ethical precepts. What he did supply was a method of inquiry called **dialectics,** or logical discussion. As Socrates used it, a dialectical exchange between individuals (or with oneself), a

Portrait Statuette of Socrates, 200 B.C. Socrates wanted to apply reason to accepted beliefs. In this way human beings could confront the most crucial questions of human existence, particularly that of good and evil.
(*British Museum, London/HIP/Art Resource, NY.*)

dialogue, was the essential source of knowledge. It forced people out of their apathy and smugness and made them aware of their ignorance. It compelled them to examine their thoughts critically, confront illogical, inconsistent, dogmatic, and imprecise assertions, and express their ideas in clearly defined terms.

Dialectics affirmed that the acquisition of knowledge was a creative act. The human mind could not be coerced into knowing; it was not a passive vessel into which a teacher poured knowledge. The dialogue compelled the individual to play an active role in acquiring ideas and values by which to live. In a dialogue, individuals became thinking participants in a quest for knowledge. Through relentless cross-examination, Socrates induced his partner in discourse to explain and justify his opinions rationally, for only thus did knowledge become a part of one's being.

Dialogue implied that reason was meant to be used in relations between human beings and that they could learn from each other, help each other, teach each other, and improve each other. It implied further that the human mind could and should make rational choices. To deal rationally with oneself and with others is the distinctive mark of being human. Through the dialectical method, people could make ethical choices, impose rules on themselves, and give form to their existence.

For Socrates, the highest form of excellence was taking control of one's life and shaping it according to ethical values reached through reflection. The good life, the moral life, is attained by the exercise of reason and by the development of intelligence—this precept is the essence of Socratic teaching. Socrates made the individual the center of the universe, reason central to the individual, and moral worth the central aim of human life. In Socrates, Greek **humanism** found its highest expression.

Condemned to Death. Socrates devoted much of his life to what he believed was his mission: pricking the conscience of complacent Athenians and persuading them to think critically about how they lived their lives. "No greater good can happen to a man than to discuss human excellence every day,"[5] he said. Always self-controlled and never raising his voice in anger, Socrates engaged any willing Athenian in conversation about his values. Unlike the Sophists, who were paid professional teachers, Socrates never accepted a fee for his instruction. Through probing questions, he tried to stir people out of their complacency and make them realize how directionless and purposeless their lives were.

For many years, Socrates challenged Athenians without suffering harm, for Athens was generally distinguished by its freedom of speech and thought. In the uncertain times during and immediately after the Peloponnesian War, however, Socrates made enemies. Several of the young men close to him were antidemocrats still mistrusted by some as a threat to the recently restored democracy. When Socrates was seventy, he was accused of corrupting the youth of the city and of not believing in the city's gods but in other, new divinities. Underlying these accusations was the fear that Socrates was a troublemaker, a subversive, a Sophist who threatened the state by subjecting its ancient and sacred values to the critique of thought.

Socrates denied the charges and conducted himself with great dignity at his trial, refusing to grovel and beg forgiveness. Instead, he defined his creed:

> *If you think that a man of any worth at all ought to . . . think of anything but whether he is acting justly or unjustly, and as a good or a bad man would act, you are mistaken. . . . If you were therefore to say to me, "Socrates, . . . We will let you go, but on the condition that you give up this investigation of yours, and philosophy. If you are found following these pursuits again you shall die." I say, if you offered to let me go on these terms, I should reply: . . . As long as I have breath and strength I will not give up philosophy and exhorting you and declaring the truth to every one of you whom I meet, saying, as I am accustomed, "My good friend, you are a citizen of Athens . . . are you not ashamed of caring so much for making of money and for fame and prestige, when you neither think nor care about wisdom and truth and the improvement of your soul?"*[6]

Convicted by an Athenian court, Socrates was ordered to drink poison. Had he attempted to appease the jurors, he probably would have been given a light punishment, but he would not disobey the commands of his conscience and alter his principles even under threat of death. Socrates' friends wanted to arrange his escape from prison, but he refused, for this would mean violating the city's laws—an act he considered unconscionable.

Socrates did not write down his philosophy and beliefs. We are able to construct a coherent account of his life and ideals largely through the works of his most important disciple, Plato.

Plato: The Rational Society

Plato (c. 429–347 B.C.) used his master's teachings to create a comprehensive system of philosophy, which embraced both the world of nature and the social world. But Plato had a more ambitious goal than Socrates' moral reformation of the individual. He tried to arrange political life according to rational rules and held that Socrates' quest for personal morality could not succeed unless the community was also transformed on the basis of reason. Many of the problems discussed by Western philosophers for the past two millennia were raised by Plato. We focus on two of his principal concerns, the theory of Ideas and the theory of the just state.

Theory of Ideas. Socrates had taught that universal standards of right and justice exist and are arrived at through thought. Building on the insights of his teacher Socrates and of Parmenides, who said that reality is known only through the mind, Plato postulated the existence of a higher world of reality, independent of the world of things that we experience every day. This higher reality, he said, is the realm of Ideas, or Forms—unchanging, eternal, absolute, and universal standards of beauty, goodness, justice, and truth. To live in accordance with these standards constitutes the good life; to know these Forms is to grasp ultimate truth.

Truth resides in this world of Forms and not in the world made known through the senses. For example, a person can never draw a perfect square, but the properties of a perfect square exist in the world of Forms. Also, a sculptor observes many bodies, and they all possess some flaw; in his mind's eye, he tries to penetrate the world of Ideas and to reproduce with art a perfect body. Again, the ordinary person only forms an opinion of what beauty is from observing beautiful things; the philosopher, aspiring to true knowledge, goes beyond what he sees and tries to grasp with his mind the Idea of beauty. Similarly, the ordinary individual has only a superficial understanding of justice or goodness; a true conception of justice or goodness is available only to the philosopher, whose mind can leap from worldly particulars to an ideal world beyond space and time.

Plato saw the world of phenomena as unstable, transitory, and imperfect, whereas his transcendent realm of Ideas was eternal and universally valid. For him, true wisdom was to be obtained through knowledge of the Ideas, not the imperfect reflections of the Ideas perceived with the senses.

A champion of reason, Plato aspired to study human life and arrange it according to universally valid standards. In contrast to Sophist relativism, he maintained that objective and eternal standards do exist. Although Plato advocated the life of reason and wanted to organize society according to rational rules, his writing also reveals a religious-mystical side. At times, Plato seems like a mystic seeking to escape from this world into a higher reality, a realm that is without earth's evil and injustice.

Because Platonism is a two-world philosophy, which believes in a higher world as the source of values and in the soul's immortality, it has had an important effect on religious thought. Christian (as well as Jewish and Muslim) thinkers could harmonize Plato's stress on a higher nonmaterial reality and an immortal soul with their faith. In subsequent chapters, we examine the influence of Platonic otherworldliness on later philosopher-mystics and Christian thinkers.

The Just State. In adapting the rational legacy of Greek philosophy to politics, Plato constructed a comprehensive political theory. What the Greeks had achieved in practice—the movement away from mythic and theocratic politics—Plato accomplished on the level of thought: the fashioning of a rational model of the state.

Like Socrates, Plato attempted to resolve the problem caused by the radical Sophists: the undermining of traditional values. Socrates tried to dispel this spiritual crisis through a moral transformation of the individual, whereas Plato wanted the entire community to conform to rational principles. Plato said that if human beings are to live an ethical life, they must do so as citizens of a just and rational state. In an unjust state, people cannot achieve Socratic wisdom, for their souls will mirror the state's wickedness.

Plato had experienced the ruinous Peloponnesian War and the accompanying political turmoil. He saw Athens undergo one political crisis after another; most shocking of all, he had witnessed Socrates' trial and execution. Disillusioned by the corruption of Athenian morality and politics, Plato refused to participate in political life. He came to believe that under the Athenian constitution neither the morality of the individual Athenian nor the good of the state could be enhanced, and that Athens required moral and political reform founded on Socrates' philosophy. Like Socrates, and in contrast to the Sophists' relativism, Plato sought permanent truth and moral certainty.

In his great dialogue *The Republic,* Plato devised an ideal state based on standards that would rescue his native Athens from the evils that had befallen it. *The Republic* attempted to analyze society rationally and to reshape the state so that individuals could fulfill the best within themselves and attain the Socratic goal of moral excellence. For Plato, the just state could not be founded on tradition (for inherited attitudes did not derive from rational standards) or on the doctrine of might being right (a principle taught by radical Sophists and practiced by Athenian statesmen). A just state, for Plato, conformed to universally valid principles and aimed at the moral improvement of its citizens, not at increasing its power and material possessions. Such a state required leaders distinguished by their wisdom and virtue, rather than by sophistic cleverness and eloquence.

Fundamental to Plato's political theory as formulated in *The Republic* was his criticism of Athenian democracy. An aristocrat by birth and temperament, Plato believed that it was foolish to expect the common man to think intelligently about foreign policy, economics, or other vital matters of state. Yet the common man was permitted to speak in the Assembly, to vote, and to be selected, by lot, for executive office. A second weakness of democracy was that leaders were chosen and followed for nonessential reasons, such as persuasive speech, good looks, wealth, and family background.

A third danger of democracy was that it could degenerate into anarchy, said Plato. Intoxicated by liberty, the citizens of a democracy could lose all sense of balance, self-discipline, and respect for law:

> *The citizens become so sensitive that they resent the slightest application of control as intolerable tyranny, and in their resolve to have no master they end up by disregarding even the law, written or unwritten.*[7]

As liberty leads to license, Plato continued, the democratic society will deteriorate morally.

> *The parent falls into the habit of behaving like the child, and the child like the parent: the father is afraid of his sons, and they show no fear or respect for their parents, in order to assert their freedom. . . . To descend to smaller matters, the schoolmaster timidly flatters his pupils, and the pupils make light of their masters. . . . Generally speaking, the young . . . argue with . . . [their elders] and will not do as they are told; while the old, anxious not to be thought disagreeable tyrants, imitate the young and condescend to enter into their jokes and amusements.*[8]

As the democratic city falls into disorder, a fourth weakness of democracy will become evident. A demagogue—often a wealthy, handsome, war hero of noble birth with an ability to stir the multitude with words—will be able to gain power by promising to plunder the rich to benefit the poor. Increasingly the tyrant throws off all constraints and uses his authority to satisfy his desire for power and possessions. To retain his hold over the state, the tyrant

> *begins by stirring up one war after another, in order that the people may feel their need of a leader, and also be so impoverished by taxation that they will be forced to think of nothing but winning their daily bread, instead of plotting against him.*[9]

Because of these inherent weaknesses of democracy, Plato insisted that Athens could not be saved by more doses of liberty. He believed that Athens would be governed properly only when the wisest people, the philosophers, attained power:

> *Unless either philosophers become kings in their countries or those who are now called kings and rulers come to be sufficiently inspired with a genuine desire for wisdom; unless, that is to say, political power and philosophy meet together . . . there can be no rest from troubles . . . for states, nor yet, as I believe, for all mankind.*[10]

Plato rejected the fundamental principle of Athenian democracy: that the average person is capable of participating sensibly in public affairs. People would not entrust the care of a sick person to just anyone, said Plato, nor would they allow a novice to guide a ship during a storm. Yet in a democracy, amateurs were permitted to run the government and to supervise the education of the young. No wonder Athenian society was disintegrating. Plato felt that these duties should be performed only by the best people in the city, philosophers, who would approach human problems with reason and wisdom derived from knowledge of the world of unchanging and perfect Ideas. Only these possessors of truth would be competent to rule, said Plato. Whereas Socrates believed that all people could base their actions on reason and acquire virtue, Plato maintained that only a few were capable of philosophical wisdom and that these few were the state's natural rulers.

The organization of the state, as formulated in *The Republic,* corresponded to Plato's conception of the individual soul, of human nature. Plato held that the soul had three major capacities: reason (the pursuit of knowledge), spiritedness (self-assertion, courage, ambition), and desire (the "savage many-headed monster" that relishes food, sex, and possessions). In the well-governed soul, spiritedness and desire are guided by reason and knowledge—standards derived from the world of Ideas.

Plato divided people into three groups: those who demonstrated philosophical ability should be rulers; those whose natural bent revealed exceptional courage should be soldiers; and those driven by desire, the great masses, should be producers (tradespeople, artisans, or farmers). In what was a radical departure from the general attitudes of the times, Plato held that men and women should receive the same education and have equal access to all occupations and public positions, including philosopher-ruler.

Plato felt that the entire community must recognize the primacy of the intellect and sought to create a harmonious state in which each individual performed what he or she was best qualified to do and preferred to do. This would be a just state, said Plato, for it would recognize human inequalities and diversities and make the best possible use of them for the entire community. Clearly, this conception of justice was Plato's response to the radical Sophists, who taught that justice consisted of the right of the strong to rule in their own interest or that justice was doing whatever one desired.

In *The Republic*, philosophers were selected by a rigorous system of education open to all children. Those not demonstrating sufficient intelligence or strength of character were to be weeded out to become workers or warriors, depending on their natural aptitudes. After many years of education and practical military and administrative experience, the philosophers were to be entrusted with political power. If they had been properly educated, the philosopher-rulers would not seek personal wealth or personal power; they would be concerned with pursuing justice and serving the community. To prevent the philosopher-rulers from pursuing their own interests rather than the good of the community, they would not be permitted to own property or to have families. Since the children they sired would come from a community of wives, no one would know which child was his.

The philosophers were to be absolute rulers. Although the people would lose their right to participate in political decisions, they would gain a well-governed state, whose leaders, distinguished by their wisdom, integrity, and sense of responsibility, would seek only the common good. Only thus could the individual and the community achieve well-being.

Plato repudiated the fundamental principles of a free community: the right to participate in government, equality before the law, and checks on leaders' power. Even freedom of thought was denied the great mass of people in Plato's state. Philosopher-rulers would search for truth, but the people were to be told clever stories—"noble lies," Plato called them—to keep them obedient. However, the philosopher-rulers, said Plato, would not be seekers of power or wealth. It would not be in their character as wise and virtuous people, the best products of polis education, to behave like ruthless tyrants.

The purpose of *The Republic* was to warn Athenians that without respect for law, wise leadership, and proper education for the young, their city would continue to degenerate. Plato wanted to rescue the city-state from disintegration by recreating the community spirit that had vitalized the polis—and he wanted to recreate it not on the basis of mere tradition but on a higher level, with philosophical knowledge. The social and political institutions of Athens, Plato thought, must be reshaped according to permanent and unalterable ideals of truth and justice, and this could be done only when power and wisdom were joined. He aimed to fashion a just individual and a just state by creating conditions that permitted reason to prevail over the appetites, self-interest, and class and party loyalties.

Online Study Center

Improve Your Grade
Primary Source: Plato on the Equality of Women in His Republic

Aristotle: A Synthesis of Greek Thought

Aristotle (384–322 B.C.) stands at the apex of Greek thought because he achieved a creative synthesis of the knowledge and theories of earlier thinkers. Aristotle studied at Plato's Academy for twenty years. Later, he became tutor to young Alexander the Great, the son of Philip of Macedon. Returning to Athens after Alexander had inherited his father's throne, Aristotle founded a school, the Lyceum.

The range of Aristotle's interests and intellect is extraordinary. He was the leading expert of his time in every field of knowledge, with the possible exception of mathematics. Even a partial listing of his works shows the universal character of his mind and his all-consuming passion to understand the worlds of nature and of humankind: *Logic, Physics, On the Heavens, On the Soul, On the Parts of Animals, Metaphysics, Nicomachean Ethics, Politics, Rhetoric,* and *Poetics.*

Aristotle undertook the monumental task of organizing and systematizing the thought of the Pre-Socratics, Socrates, and Plato. He shared with the natural philosophers a desire to understand the physical universe; he shared with Socrates and Plato the conviction that reason was a person's highest faculty and that the polis was the primary formative institution of Greek life. Out of the myriad of Aristotle's achievements, we discuss only three: his critique of Plato's theory of Ideas, his ethical thought, and his political thought.

Critique of Plato's Theory of Ideas. Like Democritus before him, Aristotle renewed confidence in **sense perception,** for which Plato had little respect; he wanted to swing the pendulum back from Plato's higher world to the material world. Possessing a scientist's curiosity to understand the facts of nature, Aristotle appreciated the world of phenomena, of concrete things. He respected knowledge obtained through the senses, as the following selection from his observations of a hen's embryo shows:

> *With the common hen after three days and three nights there is the first indication of the embryo. . . . Meanwhile the yolk comes into being . . . and, the heart appears, like a speck of blood, in the white of the egg. This point beats and moves as though endowed with life.*[11]

Aristotle retained Plato's stress on universal principles, but he wanted these principles to derive from human experience with the material world. To the practical and empirically minded Aristotle, the Platonic notion of an independent and separate world of Forms beyond space and time seemed contrary to common sense. To comprehend reality, said Aristotle, one should not escape into another world. For him, Plato's two-world philosophy suffered from too much mystery, mysticism, and poetic fancy; moreover, Plato undervalued the world of facts and objects revealed through sight, hearing, and touch, a world that was important to Aristotle. Like Plato, Aristotle desired to comprehend the essence of things and held that understanding universal principles is the ultimate aim of knowledge. But unlike Plato, he did not turn away from the world of things to obtain such knowledge.

For Aristotle, the Forms were not located in a higher world outside and beyond phenomena but existed in things themselves. He said that through human experience with such things as men, horses, and white objects, the essence of man, horse, and whiteness can be discovered through reason; the Form of Man, the Form of Horse, and the Form of Whiteness can be determined. These universals, which apply to all men, all horses, and all white things, were for both Aristotle and Plato the true objects of knowledge. For Plato, these Forms existed independently of particular objects; the Forms for men or horses or whiteness or triangles or temples existed, whether or not representations of these Ideas in the form of material objects were made known to the senses. For Aristotle, however, universal Ideas could not be determined without examination of particular things. Whereas Plato's use of reason tended to stress otherworldliness, Aristotle tried to bring philosophy back to earth.

By holding that certainty in knowledge comes from reason alone and not from the senses, Plato was predisposed toward mathematics and metaphysics—pure thought, which transcends the world of change and material objects. By stressing the importance of knowledge acquired through the rational examination of sense experience, Aristotle favored the development of empirical sciences—physics, biology, zoology, botany, and other disciplines based on the observation and investigation of nature and the recording of data. Aristotle maintained that theory must not conflict with facts and must make them more intelligible, and that it was the task of science to arrange facts into a system of knowledge.

Ethical Thought. Like Socrates and Plato, Aristotle believed that a knowledge of **ethics** was possible and that it must be based on reason, for this is what distinguishes human beings from other forms of life. For him, ethical thought derived from a realistic appraisal of human nature and a commonsense attitude toward life. In *Nicomachean Ethics,* he offered this appraisal, as well as a practical guide to proper conduct. The good life, for Aristotle, was the examined life; it meant making intelligent decisions when confronted with specific problems. Individuals could achieve happiness when they exercised the distinctively human trait of reasoning, when they applied their knowledge relevantly to life, and when their behavior was governed by intelligence and not by whim, tradition, or authority.

Aristotle recognized that people are not entirely rational, that the human personality reveals a passionate element, which can never be eradicated or ignored. Aristotle held that surrendering completely to desire meant descending to the level of beasts, but that denying the passions and living as an ascetic was a foolish and unreasonable rejection of human nature. He maintained that by proper training people could learn to regulate their desires. They could achieve moral well-being, or virtue, when they avoided extremes of behavior and rationally chose the way of moderation, which he defined as the mean between two extremes. For example, in one extreme, some people "become angry at the wrong things, more than is right, and longer, and cannot be appeased until they inflict vengeance or punishment." In the other extreme, foolish and slavish people endure every insult without defending themselves. Between these extremes is "the man who is angry at the right thing and with the right people, and, further as he ought, when he ought, and as long as he ought. . . . [T]he good-tempered man tends to be unperturbed and not to be led by passion."[12] "Nothing in excess" is the key to Aristotle's ethics.

Aristotle believed that the contemplative life of the philosopher would yield perfect happiness. The pursuit of philosophical wisdom and beauty, he stated, offered "pleasures marvelous for their purity and their enduringness."[13] But Aristotle did not demand more from an individual than human nature would allow. He did not set impossible standards for behavior, recognizing that all persons cannot pursue the life of contemplation, for some lack sufficient leisure or intelligence. However, by applying reason to human affairs, all individuals could experience a good life.

Political Thought. Aristotle's *Politics* complements his *Ethics*. To live the good life, he said, a person must do so as a member of a political community. Only the polis would provide people with an opportunity to lead a rational and moral existence, that is, to fulfill their human potential. With this assertion, Aristotle demonstrated a typically Greek attitude. At the very moment when his pupil Alexander the Great was constructing a world-state that unified Greece and Persia, Aristotle defended the traditional system of independent city-states. Indeed, his *Politics* summed up the polis-centered orientation of Hellenic civilization.

Also in typically Greek fashion, Aristotle did not want women to participate in the political life of the city. Unlike Plato, who, in *The Republic* gave women an equal opportunity with men to become philosopher-rulers, Aristotle, in his *Politics,* put women in an inferior category and maintained that the free male should rule over women. Though Aristotle taught that all human beings share in a rational soul, he felt that women, along with children and slaves, shared in it to a lesser degree:

> *[A]lthough the parts of the soul are present in all of them, they are present in different degrees. For the slave has no deliberative faculty at all; the woman has, but it is without authority, and the child has, but it is immature. . . . Clearly, then, moral virtue belongs to all of them; but the temperance of a man and of a woman, or the courage and justice of a man and of a woman, are not, as Socrates maintained, the same; the courage of a man is shown in commanding, of a woman in obeying. . . . All classes must be deemed to have their special attributes, as the poet says of women, "Silence is a woman's glory," but this is not equally the glory of man.*[14]

Like Plato, Aristotle presumed that political life could be rationally understood and intelligently directed. In *Politics,* as in *Ethics,* he adopted a commonsense, practical attitude. He did not aim at utopia but wanted to find the most effective form of government for most men in normal circumstances. Exemplifying the polis outlook, Aristotle held that enhancing the good of the community is nobler and more virtuous than doing good for oneself, however worthy the act.

Aristotle emphasized the importance of the rule of law. He placed his trust in law rather than in individuals, for they are subject to passions. Aristotle recognized that at times laws should be altered, but he recommended great caution; otherwise, people would lose respect for law and legal procedure:

> *For the law has no power to command obedience except that of habit, which can only be given by time, so that a readiness to change from old to new laws enfeebles the power of the law.*[15]

Tyranny and revolution, Aristotle said, can threaten the rule of law and the well-being of the citizen. To prevent revolution, the state must maintain

> *the spirit of obedience to law, more especially in small matters; for transgression creeps in unperceived and at last ruins the state. [This cannot be done] unless the young are trained by habit and education in the spirit of the constitution. [To live as one pleases] is contradictory to the true interests of the state. . . .*
>
> *Men should not think it slavery to live according to the rule of the constitution, for it is their salvation.*[16]

Aristotle held "that the best political community is formed by citizens of the middle class [those with a moderate amount of property], and that those states are likely to be well-administered in which the middle class is large and stronger if possible than the other classes [the wealthy and the poor]." Both the rich, who excel in "beauty, strength, birth, [and] wealth," and the poor, who are "very weak or very much disgraced [find it] difficult to follow rational principle. Of these two the one sort grow into violence and great criminals, the other into rogues and petty rascals." The rich are unwilling "to submit to authority . . . for when they are boys, by reason of the luxury in which they are brought up, they never learn even at school, the habit of obedience." Consequently, the wealthy "can only rule despotically." On the other hand, the poor "are too degraded to command and must be ruled like slaves."[17] Middle-class citizens are less afflicted by envy than the poor and are more likely than the rich to view their fellow citizens as equals.

Art

The classical age of Greek art spans the years from the end of the Persian Wars (479 B.C.) to the death of Alexander the Great (323 B.C.). During this period, standards were established that would dominate Western art until the emergence of modern art in the late nineteenth century.

Greek art coincided with Greek achievement in all other areas. Like Greek philosophy and politics, it too applied reason to human experience and made the transition from a mythopoeic-religious world-view to a world perceived as orderly and rational. It gradually transformed the supernatural religious themes with which it was at first preoccupied into secular human themes. Classical art was representational—that is, it strove to imitate reality, to represent the objective world realistically, as it appeared to the human eye.

Artists carefully observed nature and human beings and sought to achieve an exact knowledge of human anatomy; they tried to portray accurately the body at rest and in motion. They knew when muscles should be taut or relaxed, one hip lower than the other, the torso and neck slightly twisted—in other words, they succeeded in transforming marble or bronze into a human likeness that seemed alive. Yet although it was realistic and naturalistic, Greek art was also idealistic, aspiring to a finer, more perfect representation of what was seen, depicting the essence and form of a thing more truly than it actually appeared. Thus, a Greek statue resembled no specific individual but revealed a flawless human form, without wrinkles, warts, scars, or other imperfections.

In achieving an accurate representation of objects and in holding that there were rules of beauty that the mind could discover, the Greek artist employed an approach consistent with the new scientific outlook. The Greek temple, for example, is an organized unity obeying nature's laws of equilibrium and harmony; classical sculpture captures the basic laws that govern life in motion. Such art, based on reason, which draws the mind's attention to the clear outlines of the outer world, also draws attention to the mind itself, making human beings the center of an intelligible world and the masters of their own persons.

Greek artists, just like Greek philosophers, proclaimed the importance and creative capacity of the individual. They exemplified the humanist spirit that characterized all aspects of Greek culture. Classical art placed people in their natural environment, made the human form the focal point of attention, and exalted the nobility, dignity, self-assurance, and beauty of the human being.

Poetry and Drama

Through their awareness of human personality, poets and dramatists, like philosophers and artists, gave expression to the rise of the individual. One of the earliest and best of the Greek poets was Sappho, a woman who lived around 600 B.C. on the island of Lesbos. Sappho established a school to teach music and singing to well-to-do girls and to prepare them for marriage. With great tenderness, Sappho wrote poems of friendship and love: "Some say the fairest thing on earth is a troop of horsemen, others a band of foot-soldiers, others a squadron of ships. But I say the fairest thing is the beloved."[18] And of her daughter Cleïs, she wrote:

> *I have a child; so fair*
> *As golden flowers is she,*
> *My Cleïs, all my care.*
> *I'd not give her away*
> *For Lydia's* wide sway*
> *Nor lands men long to see.*[19]

Sappho's love poetry, addressed also to women, indicates that she was bisexual. This form of sexual behavior was tolerated in ancient Greece, says classicist Lyn Hatherly Wilson, "because it was not procreative, because it did not alter a woman's virginal status, or affect her entry into marriage and male/female relations, except in ways that were considered positive."[20] Sappho was the most prominent female poet in the ancient world. She was depicted on coins and in art, and Plato praised the beauty of her lyric poetry. Sometimes, however, she was treated in an uncomplimentary way by comic playwrights who thought it inappropriate for a woman to write poetry. Her influence endured for centuries: the Roman poets Catullus, Horace, and Ovid alluded to her.

Pindar (c. 518–438 B.C.) was another Greek lyric poet. In his poem of praise for a victorious athlete, Pindar expressed the aristocratic view of excellence. Although life is essentially tragic—triumphs are short-lived, misfortunes are many, and ultimately death overtakes all—man must still demonstrate his worth by striving for excellence:

> *He who wins of a sudden, some noble prize*
> *In the rich years of youth*
> *Is raised high with hope; his manhood takes*
> *wings;*
> *He has in his heart what is better than wealth*
> *But brief is the season of man's delight.*
> *Soon it falls to the ground;*
> *Some dire decision uproots it.*
> *—Thing of a day! such is man: a shadow in a*
> *dream.*
> *Yet when god-given splendour visits him*
> *A bright radiance plays over him, and how*
> *sweet is life!*[21]

The high point of Greek poetry is drama, an art form that originated in Greece. The Greek dramatist portrayed the sufferings, weaknesses, and triumphs of individuals. Just as a Greek sculptor shaped a clear visual image of the human form, so also a Greek dramatist brought the inner life of human beings, their fears and hopes, into sharp focus and tried to find the deeper meaning of human experience. Thus, both art and drama evidenced the growing self-awareness of the individual.

Drama originated in the religious festivals honoring Dionysus, the god of wine and agricultural fertility. A profound innovation in these sacred performances, which included choral songs and dances, occurred in the last part of the sixth century B.C. when Thespis, the first actor known to history, stepped out of the chorus and engaged it in dialogue. By separating himself from the choral group, Thespis demonstrated a new awareness of the individual.

With only one actor and a chorus, however, the possibilities for dramatic action and human conflicts were limited. Then Aeschylus introduced a second actor in his dramas, and Sophocles a third. Dialogue between individuals thus became possible. The Greek actors wore masks, and by changing them, each actor could play several roles in the same performance. This flexibility allowed the dramatists to depict the clash and interplay of human wills and passions on a greater scale. By the middle of the fifth century B.C., tragedies were performed regularly as civic festivals. The audience sat on wooden bleachers in an open-air, hillside theater (*theatron*). The acoustics of these stone theaters was so superb that a clear voice projected from the front could be heard, without amplification, in the last row. In the staging of these tragedies, the all-male chorus generally danced and sang in a circular area called the *orchestra* ("dancing place"), which encircled an altar. Their costumes con-

*Ancient country in Asia Minor.

Profile

Hesiod

The poet Hesiod (c. 700 B.C.) lived on a farm in Boetia, in central Greece, and wrote two major poems. *Theogony* deals with the formation of the universe, and *Works and Days* depicts the life of peasants.

Theogony is replete with mythical imagery, but for several reasons scholars regard it as a precursor of Greek philosophy. First, in explaining the origins of the world through the genealogy of the gods, Hesiod produced an ordered and structured mythology that can be interpreted as nascent rational speculation. Second, the gift of law bestowed by Zeus on humanity can be viewed as an early expression of natural law—the recognition of both a physical and a moral order inherent in the universe. Crucial for philosophic thought, the concept of natural law that Hesiod expressed in mythical-religious terms was explicitly formulated in the rational categories of philosophy by Greek thinkers after Hesiod.

Whereas Homer's epics concentrate on heroes striving to win honor as defined by a chivalric aristocratic ideal, Hesiod's later poem, *Works and Days,* describes the daily ordeal of common folk struggling to feed their families. A man of the soil, Hesiod maintains that honest labor promotes the good life.

Although he was generally pessimistic, Hesiod believed that human beings could improve their lot if they embraced justice, which "is proved the best thing they have." An awareness of justice is what distinguishes human beings from other creatures:

You, Perses, should store away in your mind
all that I tell you,
and listen to justice, and put away
all notions of violence.
Here is the law, as Zeus established it
for human beings;
as for fish, and wild animals, and the flying
birds,
they feed on each other, since there is no idea
of justice among them;

sisted of goat skins (only later did the costumes become elaborate), larger-than-life masks, and elevated shoes.

Because of the grandeur of the dramatists' themes, the eminence of their heroes, and the loftiness of their language, Greek spectators felt intensely involved in the lives portrayed. What they were witnessing in a **tragedy** went beyond anything in their ordinary lives, and they experienced the full range of human emotions.

A development parallel to Socratic dialectics—dialogue between thinking individuals—occurred in Greek drama. Through the technique of dialogue, early dramatists first pitted human beings against the gods and destiny. Later, by placing characters in conflict with each other, dramatists arrived at the idea of individuals as active subjects responsible for their behavior and decisions, which were based on their own feelings and thoughts. Greek tragedy evolved as a continuous striving toward humanization and individualization.

Like the natural philosophers, Greek dramatists saw an inner logic in the universe and called it Fate or Destiny. When people were stubborn, narrow-minded, arrogant, or immoderate, they were punished. The order in the universe required it, said Sophocles:

The man who goes his way
Overbearing in the word and deed,
Who fears no justice,
Honors no temples of the gods—
May an evil destiny seize him.
And punish his ill-starred pride.[22]

In being free to make decisions, the dramatist says, individuals have the potential for greatness, but in choosing wrongly, unintelligently, they bring disaster on themselves and others. Also like

Art Resource, NY.

but to men he gave justice, and she in the end is
proved the best thing
they have. If a man sees what is right and
is willing to argue it,
*Zeus of the wide brows grants him prosperity.**

Human beings are faced with the choice between *Diké* (straight judgment and justice), which safeguards society, and *Hubris* (excessive pride), which destroys it. Honoring justice is what distinguishes a civilized society from a state of savagery.

Throughout *Theogony* and *Works and Days,* Hesiod used the language and imagery of myth to express curiosity about the genesis of the universe, concern for justice, and awareness of a universal moral order. In succeeding centuries, Greek thinkers would discuss these issues using the language and categories of philosophy.

*Hesiod, *Works and Days,* in *Hesiod,* trans. Richard Lattimore (Ann Arbor: University of Michigan Press, 1973), p. 51.

philosophy, Greek tragedy entailed rational reflection. Tragic heroes were not passive victims of fate. They were thinking human beings who felt a need to comprehend their position, explain the reasons for their actions, and analyze their feelings.

The essence of Greek tragedy lies in the tragic hero's struggle against cosmic forces and insurmountable obstacles, which eventually crush him. But what impressed the Greek spectators (and impresses today's readers and viewers of Greek drama) was not the vulnerability or weaknesses of human beings, but their courage and determination in the face of these forces.

Aeschylus

Aeschylus (525–456 B.C.), an Athenian nobleman, had fought in the battle of Marathon. He wrote more than eighty plays, of which only seven survive. They have common themes. As an Athenian patriot, Aeschylus urged adherence to traditional religious beliefs and moral values. Like Solon, the statesman, he believed that the world was governed by divine justice, which could not be violated with impunity; when individuals evinced *hubris* (overweening pride or arrogance), which led them to overstep the bounds of moderation, and to set themselves above the gods, they must be punished. Another principal theme was that through suffering came knowledge: the terrible consequences of sins against the divine order should remind all to think and act with moderation and caution.

Aeschylus' play *The Persians* dealt with an actual event, the defeat of Xerxes, the Persian emperor, by the Greeks. Xerxes' intemperate ambition to become master of Asia and Greece conflicted with the divine order of the universe. For this hubris, Xerxes must pay:

FLOOR MOSAIC DEPICTING DIONYSUS, THE PATRON GOD OF THE THEATER. The panther's snarl, claws, and craning neck convey a fierceness that vividly contrasts with Dionysus' serene manner. (*Archeological Receipts Fund, Athens.*)

A single stroke has brought about the ruin of great
Prosperity, the flower of Persia fallen and gone.[23]

The suffering of Xerxes should make people aware of what they can and cannot do:

And heaps of corpses even in generations hence
Will signify in silence to the eyes of men
That mortal man should not think more than mortal thoughts.
For hubris blossomed forth and grew a crop of ruin,
And from it gathered in a harvest full of tears.

In face of this, when Xerxes, who lacks good sense, returns
Counsel him with reasoning and good advice,
To cease from wounding God with overboastful rashness.[24]

Whereas Aeschylean drama dealt principally with the cosmic theme of the individual in conflict with the moral universe, later dramatists, while continuing to use patterns fashioned by Aeschylus, gave greater attention to the psychology of the individual.

Sophocles

Another outstanding Athenian dramatist was Sophocles (c. 496–406 B.C.). His greatness as a playwright lay in both the excellence of his dramatic technique and the skill with which he portrayed character. The people that he created possessed violent passions and tender emotions; they were noble in their nature, though their actions showed human frailty. Sophocles consciously formulated a standard of human excellence: individuals should shape their character in the way a sculptor shapes a form, according to laws of proportion. Sophocles felt that when these principles of harmony were violated by immoderate behavior, a person's character would be thrown off balance and misfortune would strike. The physical world and human activities obey laws, said Sophocles, and human beings cannot violate these laws with impunity.

Whereas Aeschylus concentrated on religious matters and Euripides (see below) dealt with social issues, Sophocles wrote about the perennial problem of well-intentioned human beings struggling valiantly, but unwisely and vainly, against the tide of fate. His characters, bent on some action fraught with danger, resist all appeals to caution and inescapably meet with disaster.

In *Oedipus Rex,* first performed about 429 B.C., Sophocles probes deeply into the human psyche. Oedipus is warned not to pursue the mystery of his birth but insists on searching for the truth about himself: "Nothing will move me. I will find the whole truth." (He had unsuspectingly killed his father and married his mother.*) For this determination, born more of innocence than arrogance, he will suffer. Events do not turn out, as Oedipus discovers, the way a person thinks and desires that they should; the individual is impotent before a relentless fate, which governs human existence. It seems beyond imagining that Oedipus, whom all envied for his intelligence, courage, and good works, would suffer such dreadful misfortune.

But tragedy also gives Oedipus the strength to assert his moral independence. Although struck down by fate, Oedipus remains an impressive figure. The tragedy's catharsis (the purging of the audience's emotions through a work of art) comes from Oedipus' choice of his own punishment, self-inflicted blindness. Oedipus demonstrates that he still possesses the distinctly human qualities of choosing and acting, that he still remains a free man responsible for his actions. Despite his misery, Oedipus is able to confront a brutal fate with courage and to demonstrate nobility of character.

In *Antigone,* Sophocles raised a question that is timeless: Should individual conscience, which is prompted by a higher law, prevail over the laws of the state when the two are in conflict?

Euripides

The rationalist spirit of Greek philosophy permeated the tragedies of Euripides (c. 485–406 B.C.). Like the Sophists, Euripides subjected the problems of human life to critical analysis and challenged human conventions. It was this critical spirit that prompted the traditionalist Aristophanes (see below) to attack Euripides for introducing the art of reasoning into tragedy. The role of the gods, women's conflicts, the horrors of war, the power of passion, and the prevalence of human suffering and weakness were carefully scrutinized in Euripides' plays. Euripides blends a poet's insight with a psychologist's probing to reveal the tangled world of human passions and souls in torment. Thus, in *Medea,* he presents the deepest feelings of a Greek woman:

> *It was everything to me to think well of one*
> *man,*
> *And he, my own husband, has turned out*
> *wholly vile.*
> *Of all things which are living and can form a*
> *judgement*
> *We women are the most unfortunate crea-*
> *tures.*
> *Firstly, with an excess of wealth it is required*

*Sigmund Freud's interpretation of the Oedipus story has had a profound impact on psychoanalytic theory: "[Oedipus'] destiny moves us only because it might have been ours. . . . It is the fate of all of us, perhaps, to direct our first sexual impulse towards our mother and our first hatred and . . . murderous wish against our father. Our dreams convince us that this is so" (*The Interpretation of Dreams*).

For us to buy a husband and take for our bodies
A master; for not to take one is even worse.
And now the question is serious whether we take
A good or bad one; for there is no easy escape
For a woman, nor can she say no to her marriage.
She arrives among new modes of behaviour and manners,
And needs prophetic power, unless she has learnt at home,
How best to manage him who shares the bed with her.
And if we work out all this well and carefully,
And the husband lives with us and lightly bears his yoke,
Then life is enviable. If not, I'd rather die.
A man, when he's tired of the company in his home,
Goes out of the house and puts an end to his boredom
And turns to a friend or companion of his own age.
But we are forced to keep our eyes on one alone.
What they say of us is that we have a peaceful time
Living at home, while they do the fighting in war.
How wrong they are! I would very much rather stand
Three times in the front of battle than bear one child.[25]

Euripides recognized the power of irrational, demonic forces that seethe within people—what he called "the bloody Fury raised by fiends of Hell."[26] A scorned Medea, seeking revenge against her husband by murdering their children, says:

I know indeed what evil I intend to do,
But stronger than all my afterthoughts is my fury,
Fury that brings upon mortals the greatest evils.[27]

In his plays, Euripides showed that the great tragedy of human existence is that reason can offer only feeble resistance against these compelling, relentless, and consuming passions. The forces that destroy erupt from the volcanic nature of human beings.

A second distinctive feature of Euripidean tragedy is its humanitarianism. No other Greek thinker expressed such concern for a fellow human being, such compassion for human suffering. In *The Trojan Women,* Euripides depicted war as agony and not glory, and the warrior as brutish and not noble. He described the torments of women, for whom war meant the loss of homes, husbands, children, and freedom. In 416 B.C., Athens massacred the men of the small island of Melos, sold its women and children into slavery, and sacked the city. *The Trojan Women,* performed a year later, warned Athenians:

How are ye blind,
Ye treaders down of cities, ye that cast
Temples to desolation, and lay waste
Tombs, the untrodden sanctuaries where lie
The ancient dead; yourselves so soon to die![28]

By exposing war as barbaric, Euripides was expressing his hostility to the Athenian leaders who persisted in continuing the disastrous Peloponnesian War.

Aristophanes

Aristophanes (c. 448–c. 380 B.C.) was the greatest of the Greek comic playwrights. He lampooned Athenian statesmen and intellectuals, censured government policies, and protested against the decay of traditional Athenian values. Behind Aristophanes' sharp wit lay a deadly seriousness, for there was much in Athens during the Peloponnesian War that angered him. As an aristocrat, he was repelled by Cleon, the common tanner who succeeded Pericles. As an admirer of the ancient values of honor, duty, and moderation, he was infuriated by corruption, which he attributed to the Sophists. As a man of common sense, he recognized that the Peloponnesian War must end. In the process of serving as a social critic, Aristophanes wrote some of the most hilarious lines in world literature.

In *Lysistrata,* an antiwar comedy, the women of Greece agree to abstain from having sexual relations with their husbands to compel the men to make peace. Lysistrata reveals the plan:

> *For if we women will but sit at home,*
> *Powdered and trimmed, clad in our daintiest lawn,**
> *Employing all our charms, and all our arts*
> *To win men's love, and when we've won it, then*
> *Repel them firmly, till they end the war,*
> *We'll soon get Peace again, be sure of that.*[29]

After the plan has been implemented, many women, now sexually frustrated, seek to desert the temple where they have gathered. But the men also suffer:

> *Oh me! these pangs and paroxysms of love,*
> *Riving my heart, keen as a torturer's wheel!*[30]

Through these unorthodox methods, the women achieve their goal, peace. Performed during the darkest days of the war, this play reminded its audiences to concentrate their efforts in the real world on securing peace.

In *The Clouds,* Aristophanes ridiculed the Sophist method of education both for turning the youth away from their parents' values and for engaging the youth in useless, hair-splitting logic. To Aristophanes, the worst of the Sophists was Socrates, who is depicted in *The Clouds* as a fuzzy-minded thinker with both feet planted firmly in the clouds. Socrates is made to look ridiculous, a man who walks on air, contemplates the sun, and teaches such absurd things as "Heaven is one vast fire extinguisher" or "How many feet of its own a flea could jump." The Sophists in the play teach only how "to succeed just enough for my need and to slip through the clutches of the law." A student of these Sophists becomes "a concocter of lies . . . a supple, unprincipled, troublesome cheat."[31] To Aristophanes, Socrates was a subversive who caused Athenians to repudiate civil morality and to speculate about nonsense questions. Clearly, Aristophanes admired the Athens that had bested the Persians at the battle of Marathon and feared the rationalism that Euripides, the Sophists, and Socrates had injected into Athenian intellectual life.

*Fine linen dress

History

The Mesopotamians and the Egyptians kept annals that purported to narrate the deeds of gods and their human agents, the priest-kings or god-kings. These chronicles, filled with religious sayings, royal records, and boastful accounts of military campaigns, are devoid of critical analysis and interpretation. The Hebrews valued history, but believing that God acted in human affairs, they did not remove historical events from the realm of religious-mythical thought. The Greeks initiated a different approach to the study of history. For the Greeks, history was not the record of God's wrath or benevolence—as it was for the Hebrews—but the actions solely of human beings. As the gods were eliminated from the nature philosophers' explanations for the origins of things in the natural world, mythical elements were also removed from the writing of history.

Greek historians asked themselves questions about the deeds of people, based their answers on available evidence, and wrote in prose, the language of rational thought. They not only narrated events but also examined them, says Italian historian Arnaldo Momigliano, with a "critical attitude . . . enabling [them] to distinguish between facts and fancies. To the best of my knowledge no historiography earlier than the Greek or independent of it developed these critical methods."[32] In the same spirit, British philosopher and historian R. G. Collingwood states:

> *The Greeks quite clearly and consciously recognized both that history is, or can be, a science, and that it has to do with human actions. Greek history is not legend, it is research; it is an attempt to get answers to definite questions about matters of which one recognizes oneself as ignorant. It is not theocratic, it is humanistic; the matters inquired into are not of gods, they are of men. Moreover, it is not mythical. The events inquired into are not events in a dateless past, at the beginning of things; they are events in a dated past, a certain number of years ago. This is not to say that legend, either in the form of theocratic history or in the form of myth, was a thing foreign to the Greek mind. . . . But what is remarkable about the Greeks was not*

> *the fact that their historical thought contained a certain residue of elements which we should call non-historical, but the fact that side by side with these, it contained elements of what we call history.*[33]

In several respects, however, the Greeks were unhistorical. To them, history moved in cycles; events and periods repeated themselves. Unlike the Hebrews, they had little awareness of historical uniqueness and progression. Nor was history as vital to the Greeks as it was to the Hebrews. Greek philosophers preferred fixing their minds on eternal and changeless truths rather than on the vicissitudes of history. Aristotle said that poetry (which also included drama) is "more philosophic and of greater import than history, since its statements are of the nature of universals," whereas histories deal only with particular events.[34]

Herodotus

Often called the "father of history," Herodotus (c. 484–c. 424 B.C.) wrote a history of the Persian Wars. Herodotus valued the present and recognized that it is not timeless but has been shaped by earlier happenings. To understand the conflict between Persia and Greece, the most important event during his lifetime, he first inquired into the histories of these societies. Much of his information was derived from posing questions to natives of the lands he visited. Interested in everything, Herodotus frequently interlaced his historical narrative with a marvelous assortment of stories and anecdotes.

The central theme of Herodotus' *Histories* is the contrast between Near Eastern despotism and Greek freedom and the subsequent clash of these two world-views in the Persian Wars. Certain of their superiority, the Greeks considered the non-Hellenic world to be steeped in ignorance and darkness. But Herodotus was generally free of this arrogance. A fair-minded, sympathetic, and tolerant observer, he took joy in examining the wide range of human character and experience.

Though Herodotus found much to praise in the Persian Empire, he was struck by a lack of freedom and by what he considered barbarity. Herodotus emphasized that the mentality of the free citizen was foreign to the East, where men were trained to obey the ruler's commands absolutely. Not the rule of law but the whim of despots prevailed in the East. When a Persian official urged some Greeks to submit to Xerxes, Herodotus wrote that the Greeks said: "You understand well enough what slavery is, but freedom you have never experienced, so you do not know if it tastes sweet or bitter. If you ever did come to experience it, you would advise us to fight for it not with spears only, but with axes too."[35] Of all the Greek city-states, Herodotus admired Athens most. Freedom had enabled Athens to achieve greatness, said Herodotus, and it was this illustrious city that had rescued the Greek world from Persia.

Another theme evident in Herodotus' work was punishment for hubris. In seeking to become king of both Asia and Europe, Xerxes had acted arrogantly; although he behaved as if he were superhuman, "he too was human, and was sure to be disappointed of his great expectations."[36] Like the Greek tragedians, Herodotus drew universal moral principles from human behavior.

In several ways, Herodotus was a historian rather than a teller of tales. First, he recognized that there is value in studying and preserving the past. Second, he asked questions about the past, instead of merely repeating ancient legends; he tried to discover what had happened, analyzed the motivations behind actions, and searched for cause and effect connections. Third, he demonstrated at times a cautious and critical attitude toward his sources, refusing to rely on legends based on little or no objective evidence:

> *The course of my story now leads me to Cyrus: who was this man who destroyed the empire of Croesus, and how did the Persians win their predominant position in Asia? I could, if I wished, give three versions of Cyrus' history, all different from what follows; but I propose to base my account on those Persian authorities who seem to tell the simple truth about him without trying to exaggerate his exploits.*[37]

Fourth, rising above inherited prejudices and a narrow parochialism, he attempted to examine disinterestedly and critically the histories of both Greeks and Persians. Fifth, although the gods appeared in Herodotus' narrative, they played a far less important role than they did in Greek popular mythology. Still, by retaining a belief in the significance of dreams, omens, and oracles and by allowing divine intervention, Herodotus fell short of being a thoroughgoing rationalist. Herodotus' writings contain the embryo of rational history; Thucydides brought it to maturity.

Thucydides

Thucydides (c. 460–c. 400 B.C.) also concentrated on a great political crisis confronting the Hellenic world: the Peloponnesian War. Living in Periclean Athens, whose lifeblood was politics, Thucydides regarded the motives of statesmen and the acts of government as the essence of history. He did not just catalogue facts, but sought those general concepts and principles that the facts illustrated. His history was the work of an intelligent mind trying to make sense of his times.

Thucydides applied to the sphere of political history a rationalist empiricism worthy of the Ionian natural philosophers. He strove for factual accuracy and drew conclusions based on a critical analysis of events and motives. He searched for the truth underlying historical events and attempted to present it objectively. From the Sophists, Thucydides learned that the motives and reactions of human beings follow patterns. Therefore, a proper analysis of the events of the Peloponnesian War would reveal general principles that govern human behavior. He intended his history to be a source of enlightenment for future ages, a possession for all time, because the kinds of behavior that caused the conflict between Sparta and Athens would recur regularly throughout history:

> *Of the events of the war I have not ventured to speak from any chance information, nor according to any notion of my own; I have described nothing but what I either saw myself, or learned from others of whom I made the most careful and particular inquiry. The task was a laborious one, because eyewitnesses of the same occurrences gave different accounts of them, as they remembered or were [partial to] one side or the other. And very likely the strictly historical character of my narrative may be disappointing to the ear. But if he who desires to have before his eyes a true picture of the events which have happened, and of the like events which may be expected to happen hereafter in the order of human things shall pronounce what I have written to be useful, then I shall be satisfied. My history is an everlasting possession, not a prize composition which is heard and forgotten.*[38]

In Thucydides' history, there was no place for myths, for legends, for the fabulous—all hindrances to historical truth. He recognized that a work of history was a creation of the rational mind and not an expression of the poetic imagination. The historian seeks to learn and to enlighten, not to entertain.

Rejecting the notion that the gods interfere in history, Thucydides looked for the social forces and human decisions behind events. Undoubtedly, he was influenced by Hippocratic doctors, who frowned on divine explanations for disease and distinguished between the symptoms of a disease and its causes. Where Herodotus occasionally lapsed into supernatural explanations, Thucydides wrote history in which the gods were absent, and he denied their intervention in human affairs. For Thucydides, history was the work of human beings. And the driving force in history was men's will to power and domination.

In addition to being a historian, Thucydides was also an astute and innovative political thinker with a specific view of government, statesmen, and international relations. He warned against the dangers of extremism unleashed by the strains of war, and he believed that when reason was forsaken, the state's plight would worsen. He had contempt for statesmen who waged war lightly, acting from impulse, reckless daring, and an insatiable appetite for territory. Consequently, he regarded the decision to attack Syracuse in Sicily, which cost so many lives, as a gross political blunder. Although Thucydides admired Athens for its democratic institutions, rule of law, sense of civic duty, and cultural achievements, he recognized an inherent danger in democracy: the emergence of demagogues, who rise to power by stirring up the populace. He extended to international relations the Sophists' insight that people tend to act out of self-interest; national interest, he maintained, was the motivating force in relations between states. And he explicitly formulated the principle of balance of power as a basic formula governing international relations. What caused the Peloponnesian War, he said, was the sudden and spectacular increase of Athenian power and the Spartans' fear that this would upset the balance.

Political scientists, historians, and statesmen still turn to Thucydides for insights into the realities of power politics, the dangers of political fanaticism, the nature of imperialism, the methods of demagogues, and the effects of war on democratic politics.

The Greek Achievement: Reason, Freedom, Humanism

Like other ancient peoples, the Greeks warred, massacred, and enslaved; they could be cruel, arrogant, contentious, and superstitious; and they often violated their ideals. But their achievement was unquestionably of profound historical significance. Western thought essentially begins with the Greeks, who first defined the individual by the capacity to reason. It was the great achievement of the Greek spirit to rise above magic, miracles, mystery, authority, and custom and to discover the procedures and terminology that permit a rational understanding of nature and society. Every aspect of Greek civilization—science, philosophy, art, literature, politics, historical writing—showed a growing reliance on human reason and a diminishing dependence on the gods.

In Mesopotamia and Egypt, people had no clear conception of their individual worth and no understanding of political liberty. They were not citizens but subjects who marched to the command of a ruler whose power originated with the gods. Such royal power was not imposed on an unwilling population but was religiously accepted and obeyed.

In contrast, the Greeks created both civic politics and political freedom. They saw the state as a community of free and equal citizens who made laws in their own interest, and disputes between citizens were decided by a jury of one's peers, not by the whims of a ruler or his officials. The citizens had no other masters but themselves. Denouncing arbitrary rule, they argued that power should be regulated by law and justice. The Greeks held that men are capable of governing themselves, and they valued active citizenship. For the Greeks, the state was a civilizing agent that permitted people to live the good life. Greek political thinkers arrived at a conception of the rational or legal state, in which law was an expression of reason, not of whim or divine commands; of justice, not of might; of the general good of the community, not of self-interest. At the beginning of the fourth century B.C., an Athenian orator eloquently captured the meaning of his city's political achievement. The Athenians, he said, "deemed that it was the way of wild beasts to be held subject to one another by force, but the duty of men to delimit justice by law, to convince by reason, and to serve these two in act by submitting to the sovereignty of law and the instruction of reason."[39] The ideas and terminology of this statement were totally alien to the political experience of the ancient Near East and remain an integral component of the Western democratic tradition. An offshoot of the Greek democratic experience was the emergence of political thought. Greek thinkers' discussions of justice, power, freedom, and the strengths and weaknesses of democracy are the foundation of Western political theory.

The Greeks also gave to Western civilization a conception of inner, or ethical, freedom. People were free to choose between shame and honor, cowardice and duty, moderation and excess. The heroes of Greek tragedy suffered not because they were puppets manipulated by higher powers but because they possessed the freedom of decision. The idea of ethical freedom reached its highest point with Socrates, who shifted the focus of thought from cosmology to the moral life. To shape oneself according to ideals known to the mind, to develop into an autonomous and self-directed person, became for the Greeks the highest form of freedom.

Underlying everything accomplished by the Greeks was a humanist attitude toward life. The Greeks expressed a belief in the worth, significance, and dignity of the individual. They called for the maximum cultivation of human talent, the full development of human personality, and the deliberate pursuit of excellence. In valuing human personality, the Greek humanists did not approve of living without restraints; they aimed at creating a higher type of man. Such a man would mold himself according to worthy standards; he would make his life as harmonious and flawless as a work of art. This aspiration required effort, discipline, and intelligence. Fundamental to the Greek humanist outlook was the belief that human beings could master themselves. Although people could not alter the course of nature, for there was an order to the universe over which neither human beings nor gods had control, Greek humanists believed that people could control their own lives. Contemporary humanists continue to derive inspiration and guidelines from the literary, artistic, and philosophical creations of ancient Greece.

Despite their lauding of the human being's creative capacities, the Greeks were not naive about human nature. Rather, intensely aware of the individual's inherent capacity for evil, Greek thinkers repeatedly warned that without the restraining forces of law, civic institutions, moral norms, and character training, society would be torn apart by the savage elements within human nature.

By discovering theoretical reason, defining political freedom, and affirming the worth and potential of human personality, the Greeks broke with the past and founded the rational and humanist tradition of the West. "Had Greek civilization never existed," wrote poet W. H. Auden, "we would never have become fully conscious, which is to say that we would never have become, for better or worse, fully human."[40]

❖ ❖ ❖

Online Study Center **ACE the Test**

Notes

1. John N. Theodorakopoulos, "The Origins of Science and Philosophy," in *History of the Hellenic World: The Archaic Period* (University Park: Pennsylvania State University Press, 1975), p. 438.
2. Quoted in George Sarton, *A History of Science,* vol. 1 (Cambridge, Mass.: Harvard University Press, 1952), pp. 355–356.
3. Euripides, *Iphigenia at Aulis,* in *Ten Plays by Euripides*, trans. Moses Hadas and John McClean (New York: Bantam Books, 1960), p. 348 (lines 1400–1401).
4. Excerpted in Kathleen Freeman, *Ancilla to the Pre-Socratic Philosophers* (Cambridge, Mass.: Harvard University Press, 1957), pp. 157–158.
5. Plato, *Apology,* trans. F. J. Church, rev. R. D. Cummings (Indianapolis: Bobbs-Merrill, 1956), sec. 28.
6. Ibid., secs. 16–17.
7. Plato, *The Republic,* trans. F. M. Cornford (New York: Oxford University Press, 1945), p. 289.
8. Ibid.
9. Ibid., p. 293.
10. Ibid., pp. 178–179.
11. *Historia Animalium,* in *Works of Aristotle,* vol. 4, trans. D'Arcy Wentworth Thompson (New York: Oxford University Press, 1962), p. 561.
12. *Nicomachean Ethics,* in *Basic Works of Aristotle,* ed. Richard McKeon (New York: Random House, 1941), p. 996.
13. Ibid., p. 1104.
14. *Politics,* in *Basic Works of Aristotle,* ed. McKeon, pp. 1144–45.
15. Ibid., p. 1164.
16. Ibid., pp. 1246, 1251.
17. Ibid., pp. 1220–21.
18. Cited in Werner Jaeger, *Paideia: The Ideals of Greek Culture,* trans. Gilbert Highet (New York: Oxford University Press, 1945), 1:135.
19. Sappho, "A Girl," in *The Oxford Book of Greek Verse in Translation,* ed. T. F. Higham and C. M. Bowra (Oxford: Clarendon Press, 1938), p. 211.
20. Lyn Hatherly Wilson, *Sappho's Sweet Bitter Songs* (London and New York: Routledge, 1966), p. 70.
21. Cited in H. D. F. Kitto, *The Greeks* (Baltimore: Penguin Books, 1957), pp. 174–175.

22. Sophocles, *Oedipus the King,* trans. Bernard M. W. Knox (New York: Washington Square Press, 1959), p. 61.
23. Aeschylus, *The Persians,* trans. Anthony J. Podlecki (Englewood Cliffs, N.J.: Prentice-Hall, 1970), p. 49, lines 250–251.
24. Ibid., pp. 96–97, lines 818–822, 829–831.
25. Euripides, *Medea,* trans. Rex Warner (London: The Bodley Head, 1944), p. 18.
26. *Medea,* trans. Rex Warner, in *Euripides*, vol. 3 of *The Complete Greek Tragedies*, ed. David Grene and Richmond Lattimore (Chicago: University of Chicago Press, 1959–1960), p. 101, line 1260.
27. Ibid., p. 96, lines 1078–80.
28. Euripides, *The Trojan Women,* trans. Gilbert Murray (New York: Oxford University Press, 1915), p. 16, lines 95–97.
29. *Lysistrata*, in *Five Comedies of Aristophanes,* trans. Benjamin Bickley Rogers (Garden City, N.Y.: Doubleday Anchor Books, 1955), p. 292.
30. Ibid., p. 320.
31. *The Clouds,* in *Five Comedies of Aristophanes,* trans. Rogers, pp. 156–157, 169–170.
32. Arnaldo Momigliano, *The Classical Foundations of Modern Historiography* (Berkeley: University of California Press, 1990), p. 30.
33. R. G. Collingwood, *The Idea of History* (New York: Oxford University Press, 1956), pp. 17–18.
34. *Poetics,* in *Basic Works of Aristotle,* ed. McKeon, p. 1464.
35. Herodotus, *The Histories,* trans. Aubrey de Sélincourt (Baltimore: Penguin Books, 1954), p. 458.
36. Ibid., p. 485.
37. Ibid., p. 53.
38. Thucydides, *The Peloponnesian War,* trans. B. Jowett (Oxford: Clarendon Press, 1881), bk. 1, chap. 22.
39. Quoted in Jennifer Tolbert Roberts, *Athens on Trial: The Antidemocratic Tradition in Western Thought* (Princeton, N.J.: Princeton University Press, 1994), p. 46.
40. W. H. Auden, ed., *The Portable Greek Reader* (New York: Viking, 1952), p. 38.

Suggested Reading

Brunschwig, Jacques, and Geoffrey E. R. Lloyd, eds., *Greek Thought* (2000). Essays dealing with many areas of Greek thought.

Gottlieb, Anthony, *The Dream of Reason* (2000). Superb chapters on Greek philosophy.

Guthrie, W. K. C., *The Greek Philosophers from Thales to Aristotle* (1960). A short, reliable survey of Greek philosophy.

Jaeger, Werner, *Paideia: The Ideals of Greek Culture* (1939–1944). A three-volume work on Greek culture by a distinguished classicist. The treatment of Homer, the early Greek philosophers, and the Sophists in volume 1 is masterful.

Jones, W. T., *A History of Western Philosophy,* vol. 1 (1962). Clearly written; contains useful passages from original sources.

Kitto, H. D. F., *Greek Tragedy* (1954). A valuable introduction to Greek drama.

Levi, Peter, *The Pelican History of Greek Literature* (1985). Sound insights into Greek writers.

Chapter 5

The Hellenistic Age: Cultural Diffusion

Battle of Issus, Roman mosaic. The subject of the mosaic is believed to be Alexander's victory over the Persian king, Darius III, in 333 B.C. at the battle of Issus. On the right side of the mosaic, we see a realistic battle scene filled with both commotion and emotion. (Scala/Art Resource, NY.)

- Alexander the Great
- Hellenistic Society
- Hellenistic Culture
- The Hellenistic Legacy

Focus Questions

1. What are the basic differences between the Hellenic and Hellenistic Ages?
2. How did Alexander the Great contribute to the shaping of the Hellenistic Age?
3. Why are the terms *individualism, universalism,* and *cosmopolitanism* used to characterize the Hellenistic Age?
4. What prescriptions did each of the Hellenistic philosophies offer for achieving happiness?
5. What is the enduring significance of Stoicism for the modern world?

Online Study Center

This icon will direct you to interactive map and primary source activities on the website http://college.hmco.com/pic/perrywc8e.

Greek civilization, or Hellenism, passed through three distinct stages: the Hellenic Age, the Hellenistic Age, and the Greco-Roman Age. The **Hellenic Age** began about 800 B.C. with the early city-states, reached its height in the fifth century B.C., and endured until the death of Alexander the Great in 323 B.C. At that time, the ancient world entered the **Hellenistic Age,** which ended in 30 B.C., when Egypt, the last major Hellenistic state, fell to Rome. The **Greco-Roman Age** lasted five hundred years, encompassing the period of the Roman Empire up to the collapse of the Empire's western half in the last part of the fifth century A.D.

Although the Hellenistic Age absorbed the heritage of classical (Hellenic) Greece, its style of civilization changed. During the first phase of Hellenism, the polis was the center of political life. The polis gave Greeks an identity, and only within the polis could Greeks live a good and civilized life. With the coming of the Hellenistic Age, this situation changed. Kingdoms and empires eclipsed the city-state in power and importance. Cities retained a large measure of autonomy in domestic affairs but lost their freedom of action in foreign affairs. Dominated by monarchs, cities were no longer self-sufficient and independent communities as they had been in the Hellenic period. Monarchy—the essential form of government in the Hellenistic world—had not been admired by the Greeks of the Hellenic Age. They agreed with Aristotle that monarchy was suitable only for non-Greeks, who lacked the capacity to govern themselves.

As a result of Alexander the Great's conquests of the lands between Greece and India, tens of thousands of Greek soldiers, merchants, and administrators settled in eastern lands. Their encounters with the different peoples and cultures of the Near East widened the Greeks' horizon and weakened their ties to their native cities. Because of these changes, the individual had to define a relationship not to the narrow, parochial society of the polis, but to the larger world. The Greeks had to examine their place in a world more complex, foreign, and threatening than the polis. They had to fashion a conception of a community that would be more comprehensive than the city-state.

Hellenistic philosophers struggled with these problems of alienation and community. They sought to give people the inner strength to endure

ALEXANDER THE GREAT ON HORSEBACK. In conquering the lands from Greece to India, Alexander the Great displayed a military genius that would fascinate commanders from Caesar to Napoleon. *(Museo Nazionale, Naples/Art Resource, NY.)*

in a world where the polis no longer provided security. In this new situation, philosophers no longer assumed that the good life was tied to the affairs of the city. Freedom from emotional stress—not active citizenship and social responsibility—was the avenue to the good life. This pronounced tendency of people to withdraw into themselves and seek emotional comfort helped shape a cultural environment that contributed to the spread and triumph of Christianity in the Greco-Roman Age.

In the Hellenic Age, Greek philosophers had a limited conception of humanity, dividing the world into Greek and barbarian. In the Hellenistic Age, the intermingling of Greeks and peoples of the Near East caused a shift in focus from the city to the **oikoumene** (the inhabited world); parochialism gave way to **cosmopolitanism** and **universalism** as people began to think of themselves as members of a world community. Philosophers came to regard the civilized world as one city, the city of humanity. This new concept was their response to the decline of the city-state and the quest for an alternative form of community.

By uniting the diverse nationalities of the Mediterranean world under one rule, Rome gave political expression to the Hellenistic philosophers' longing for a world community. But the vast and impersonal Roman Empire could not rekindle the sense of belonging, the certainty of identity, that came with being a citizen of a small polis. In time, a resurgence of the religious spirit, particularly in the form of Christianity, helped to overcome the feeling of alienation by offering an image of community that stirred the heart.

Alexander the Great

After the assassination of Philip of Macedon in 336 B.C., his twenty-year-old son, Alexander, succeeded to the throne. Alexander inherited a proud and fiery temperament from his mother. From his tutor Aristotle, Alexander gained an appreciation for Greek culture, particularly the Homeric epics. Undoubtedly, the young Alexander was excited by these stories of legendary heroes, particularly of Achilles, and their striving for personal glory. Alexander acquired military skills and qualities of leadership from his father.

Alexander also inherited from Philip an overriding policy of state: the invasion of Persia. Such an exploit attracted the adventurous spirit of the young Alexander. A war of revenge against the Persians, who were masters of the Greek city-states of Asia Minor, also appealed to his Pan-Hellenic sentiments. Alexander was heir to the teachings of the fourth-century orator Isocrates, who urged a crusade against Persia to unite the Greeks in a common cause. Philip had intended to protect his hold on Greece by driving the Persians from Asia Minor. But Alexander, whose ambition knew no bounds, aspired to conquer the entire Persian Empire. Daring, brave, and intelligent, Alexander possessed the irrepressible energy of a romantic adventurer.

With an army of thirty-five thousand men, Alexander crossed into Asia Minor in 334 B.C. After capturing the coast of Asia Minor, he marched into Syria and defeated the Persian army at the battle of Issus. Rather than pursuing the fleeing Persian king, Darius III, Alexander stayed with his master plan, which included the capture of coastal ports in order to crush the Persian navy. He captured Tyre, thought to be an impregnable city, and advanced into Egypt. Grateful to Alexander for having liberated them from Persian rule, the Egyptians made him pharaoh. Alexander appointed officials to administer the country and founded a new city, Alexandria.

Having destroyed or captured the Persian fleet, Alexander, in 331 B.C., moved into Mesopotamia in pursuit of Darius and his army. The Macedonians defeated the numerically superior Persians at Gaugamela, just east of the Tigris River, but Darius escaped. After a stopover at Babylon and at Persepolis, which Alexander burned, perhaps in revenge for Xerxes' destruction of Athens more than 150 years earlier, he resumed the chase. When he finally caught up with Darius, the Persian king was dead, killed by Persian conspirators.

Alexander relentlessly pushed deeper into Asia, crossing from Afghanistan (then called Bactria) into northern India, where he defeated King Porus in a costly battle. When Alexander announced plans to push deeper into India, his troops, exhausted and far from home in a strange land, resisted. Alexander yielded to their wishes and returned to Babylon in 324 B.C. In these campaigns, which covered about ten thousand miles, Alexander proved himself to be a superb strategist and leader of men. Winning every battle, Alexander's army had carved an empire that stretched from Greece to India. Future conquerors, including Caesar and Napoleon, would read of Alexander's career with fascination and longing.

The world after Alexander differed sharply from that existing before he took up the sword. His conquests brought West and East closer together, marking a new epoch. Alexander himself helped implement this transformation. He took a Persian bride, arranged for eighty of his officers and ten thousand of his soldiers to marry oriental women, and planned to incorporate thirty thousand Persian youths into his army. Alexander founded Greek-style cities in Asia, where Greek settlers mixed with the native population.

As Greeks acquired greater knowledge of the Near East, the parochial-mindedness of the polis gave way to a world outlook. As trade and travel between West and East expanded, as Greek merchants and soldiers settled in Asiatic lands, and as Greek culture spread to non-Greeks, the distinctions between barbarian and Greek lessened. Although Alexander never united all the peoples in a world-state, his career pushed the world in a new direction, toward a fusion of disparate peoples and the intermingling of cultural traditions.

Online Study Center **Improve Your Grade**
Interactive Map: The Conquests of Alexander the Great

Hellenistic Society

Competing Dynasties

In 323 B.C., Alexander, not yet thirty-three years old, died after a sickness that followed a drinking party. He had built an empire that stretched from Greece to the Punjab of India, but he was denied the time needed to organize effective institutions to govern these vast territories. After Alexander's premature death, his generals engaged in a long and bitter struggle to see who would succeed the conqueror. Since none of the generals or their heirs had enough power to hold together Alexander's vast empire, the wars of succession ended in a stalemate. By 275 B.C., the empire was fractured into three dynasties: the Ptolemies in Egypt, the Seleucids in western Asia, and the Antigonids in Macedonia. Macedonia—Alexander's native country—continued to dominate the Greek cities, which periodically tried to break its hold. Later, the kingdom of Pergamum, in western Asia Minor, emerged as the fourth Hellenistic monarchy. These Hellenistic kings were not native rulers enjoying local support (except in Macedonia), but were foreign conquerors. Consequently, they had to depend on mercenary armies and loyal administrators.

In the third century B.C., Ptolemaic Egypt was the foremost power in the Hellenistic world. The Seleucid Empire, which stretched from the Mediterranean to the frontiers of India and encompassed many different peoples, attempted to extend its power in the west but was resisted by the Ptolemies. Finally, the Seleucid ruler Antiochus III (223–187 B.C.) defeated the Ptolemaic forces and established Seleucid control over Phoenicia and Palestine. Taking advantage of Egypt's defeat, Macedonia seized several of Egypt's territories.

Rome, a new power, became increasingly drawn into the affairs of the quarrelsome Hellenistic kingdoms. By the middle of the second century B.C., it had imposed its will upon them. From that time on, the political fortunes of the western and eastern Mediterranean were inextricably linked.

Cosmopolitanism

Hellenistic society was characterized by a mingling of peoples and an interchange of cultures. Greek traditions spread to the Near East, while Mesopotamian, Egyptian, Hebrew, and Persian traditions—particularly religious beliefs—moved westward. A growing cosmopolitanism replaced the parochialism of the city-state. Although the rulers of the Hellenistic kingdoms were Macedonians and their high officials and generals were Greeks, the style of government was modeled after that of the ancient oriental kingdoms. In the Hellenic Age, the law had expressed the will of the community, but in this new age of monarchy, the kings laid down the law. The Macedonian rulers encouraged the oriental practice of worshiping the king as a god or as a representative of the gods. In Egypt, for example, the priests conferred on the Macedonian king the same divine powers and titles traditionally held by Egyptian pharaohs. In accordance with ancient tradition, statues of the divine king were installed in Egyptian temples.

Following Alexander's lead, the Seleucids founded cities in the east patterned after the city-states of Greece. The cities, which were often founded to protect trade routes and as fortresses against hostile tribes, adopted the political institutions of Hellenic Greece, including a popular assembly and a council. Hellenistic kings generally did not intervene in the cities' local affairs. Thousands of Greeks settled in these cities, which were Greek in architecture and contained Greek schools, temples, theaters, where performances of classical plays were staged, and gymnasia. Gymnasia were essentially places to exercise, train in sports, and converse, but some had libraries and halls where public lectures and competitions of orators and poets were held. Hellenistic kings brought books, paintings, and statues to their cities from Greece. Hellenistic cities, inhabited by tens of thousands of people from many lands and dominated by a Hellenized upper class, served as centers and agents of Hellenism, which non-

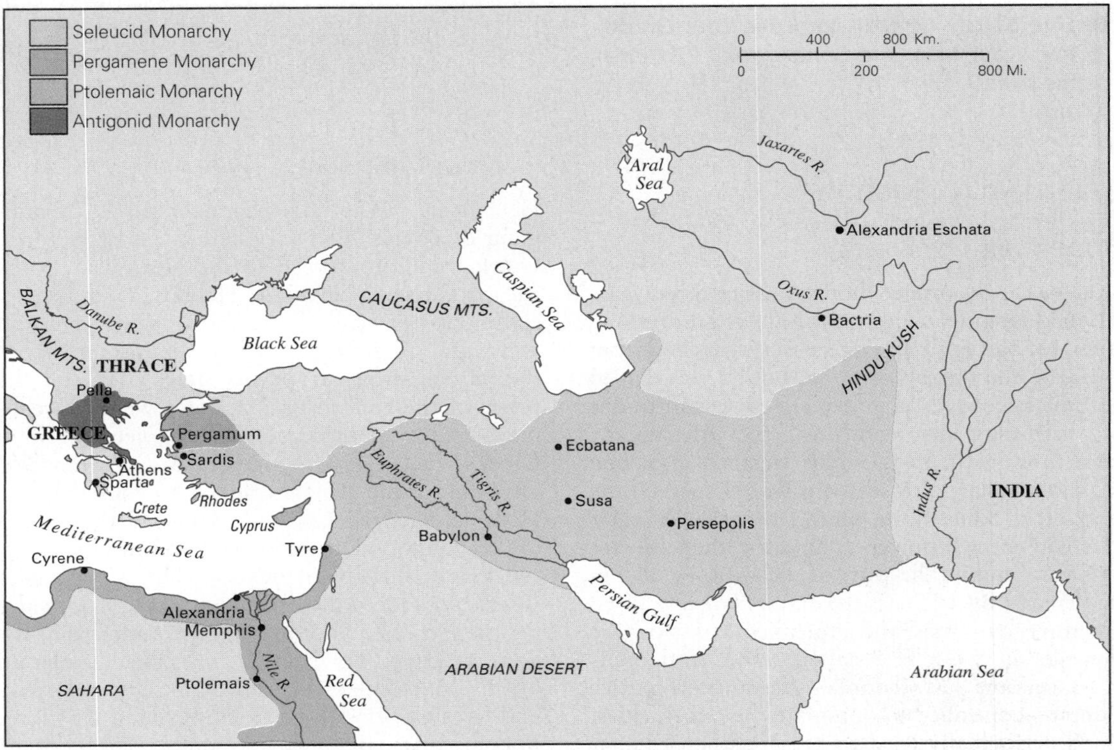

Map 5.1 **The Division of Alexander's Empire and the Spread of Hellenism** None of Alexander's generals could hold together the vast empire, which fractured into competing dynasties.

Greeks adopted. The ruling class in each Hellenistic city was united by a common Hellenism, which overcame national, linguistic, and racial distinctions. *Koine* (or shared language), a form of spoken Greek spread by soldiers, administrators, merchants, teachers, and others, became a common tongue throughout much of the Mediterranean world.

Hellenistic cities engaged in economic activity on a much greater scale than the classical Greek city-states. Increased trade integrated the Near East and Greece into a market economy, and business methods became more developed and refined. The middle and upper classes enjoyed homes, furniture, and jewelry more elegant than those of Periclean Athenians, and some people amassed great fortunes. In contrast to the ideal of citizenship, which distinguished the fifth-century polis, many Greeks who settled in Egypt, Syria, and other eastern lands ran roughshod over civil law and moral values and engaged in competitive struggles for wealth and power.

The greatest city of the time and the one most representative of the Hellenistic Age was Alexandria, in Egypt, founded by Alexander. Strategically located at one of the mouths of the Nile, it became a hub of commerce and culture. The most populous city of the Mediterranean world, Alexandria had about 300,000 inhabitants fifty years after its founding. At the beginning of the Christian era, it contained perhaps a million people: Macedonians, Greeks, Romans, Jews, Syrians, Ethiopians, and Arabs.

Alexandria was an unrivaled commercial center; goods from the Mediterranean world, eastern

Nike, the Goddess of Victory, on a Gold Earring, Hellenistic Period. The calm, timeless, idealized forms of classical period sculpture gave way to a new style—the Hellenistic, marked by more dynamic, emotion-laden realism. This new aesthetic form reflected the cosmopolitan character of the Greek culture that emerged from Alexander's conquests. (*H. L. Pierce Fund. Courtesy Museum of Fine Arts, Boston.*)

Africa, Arabia, and India circulated in its marketplaces. Two handsome boulevards, squares, fountains, and great temples added to the city's beauty. Its library, created by the first two Ptolemies, had some half a million books. The library was part of a larger complex, the museum, which contained an astronomical observatory and botanical and zoological gardens. Some of the greatest poets, philosophers, physicians, and scientists of the Mediterranean world utilized these facilities.

Aside from the proliferation of Greek urban institutions and ideas, Hellenistic cosmopolitanism expressed itself in an increased movement of peoples, the adoption of common currency standards, and an expansion of trade. International trade was made easier by improvements in navigation techniques, better port facilities, the extension of the monetary economy at the expense of barter, and the rapid development of banking. The makeup of Hellenistic armies also reflected the cosmopolitanism of the age. Serving the Hellenistic kings were men from lands stretching from India to the little-known areas north of the Danube. In Egyptian and Syrian cities, a native elite emerged who spoke Greek, wore Greek-style clothes, and adopted Greek customs.

Cultural exchange permeated all phases of cultural life. Sculpture showed the influence of many lands. Historians wrote world histories, not just local ones. Greek astronomers worked with data collected over the centuries by the Babylonians. Like other Near Eastern people, the Jews—both those in Judea and the **Diaspora** (Jews who lived outside Palestine)—came under the influence of Hellenism. Some Jewish scholars, admiring Greek learning, expressed Jewish religious ideas in philosophical terms; God was identified with reason, and Moses' Law with the rational order of the universe. They wanted to show that their faith was not incompatible with reason, that there was no insurmountable gulf separating Mosaic religion from Greek philosophy. The Hebrew Scriptures were translated into Greek—the *Septuagint*—for use by Greek-speaking Jews living in Alexandria and other areas outside of Judea. Greek words entered the Hebrew language, and newly constructed synagogues employed Hellenistic architectural styles.

Greeks increasingly demonstrated a fascination with Near Eastern religious cults. Philosophers helped to break down the barriers between peoples by asserting that all inhabit a single fatherland. As the philosopher Crates said, "My fatherland has no single tower, no single roof. The whole earth is my citadel, a home ready for us all to live in."[1]

The spread of Greek civilization from the Aegean to the Indus River gave the Hellenistic world a cultural common denominator, but **Hellenization** did not transform the East and make it one with the West. Hellenization was limited almost entirely to the cities, and in many urban centers it was often only a thin veneer. Many Egyptians in Alexandria learned Greek, generally a necessity for advancement in the state bureaucracy, and some assumed Greek names. But for most, Hellenization did not go much deeper. The countryside lacked even the veneer of Greek culture. Retaining traditional attitudes, the country-

OLD MARKET WOMAN, C. 2ND CENTURY B.C. Hellenistic genre sculpture depicted people in everyday situations, as individuals, rather than as types. Her stooped shoulders, weighed down by her groceries, also suggest the harsh physical conditions that have worn her down over the years. (*The Metropolitan Museum of Art, New York.*)

side in the East resisted Greek ways. In the villages, local and traditional law, local languages, and family customs remained unchanged; religion, the most important ingredient of the civilizations of the Near East, also kept its traditional character, even if ancestral gods were given Greek names.

HELLENISTIC CULTURE

Literature, History, and Art

The Hellenistic Age saw a great outpouring of literary works. Callimachus (c. 305–240 B.C.), an Alexandrian scholar-poet, felt that no one could duplicate the great epics of Homer or the plays of the fifth-century B.C. dramatists. He urged poets to write short, finely crafted poems instead of composing on a grand scale. A student of his, Apollonius of Rhodes, took issue with him and wrote the *Argonautica*. This Homeric-style epic tells the story of Jason's search for the Golden Fleece.

The poet Theocritus (c. 315–250 B.C.), who lived on the island of Sicily, wrote pastorals that showed great sensitivity to natural beauty. He responded with uncommon feeling to the sky and wind, to the hills, trees, and flowers, and to the wildlife of the countryside.

The Athenian playwright Menander (c. 342–291 B.C.) depicted Athenian life at the end of the fourth century. Menander's plays, unlike Aristophanes' lampoons of inept politicians, dealt little with politics. Apparently, Menander reflected the attitude of his fellow Athenians, who, bored with public affairs, had accepted their loss of freedom to Macedonia and were preoccupied with their private lives. Menander dealt sympathetically with human weakness and wrote about stock characters: the clever slave, the young playboy, bragging soldiers, compassionate prostitutes, the elderly seducer, the heroine in trouble. Menander also expressed a warm concern for people, urging them to recognize the humanity of their fellows—whether Greeks, barbarians, or slaves—and to treat each other with kindness and respect.

The leading historian of the Hellenistic Age was Polybius (c. 200–118 B.C.), a Greek, whose history of the rise of Rome is one of the great works of historical literature. Reflecting the universal tendencies of the Hellenistic Age, Polybius endeavored to explain how Rome had progressed from a city-state to a world conqueror.

Hellenistic art, like Hellenistic philosophy, expressed a heightened awareness of the individual. Whereas Hellenic sculpture aimed to depict ideal beauty—the perfect body and face—Hellenistic sculpture, moving from idealism to realism, captured individual character and expression, often of ordinary people—an old fisherman, a crippled man, a drunken lady, a dwarf. Scenes of daily life were realistically portrayed. Wealthy merchants commissioned artists to embellish their private homes. Monarchs, eager to glorify their reigns, sought the services of eminent artists to produce royal portraits, victory monuments, paintings of great battles, temples, and tombs. Continuing a practice initiated during the Hellenic Age, Hellenistic cities commissioned artists. What was new, however, was the proliferation of portrait statues honoring prominent civic leaders, orators, poets, philosophers, and playwrights.

Science

During the Hellenistic Age, Greek scientific achievement reached its height. When Alexander invaded Asia Minor, the former student of Aristotle brought along surveyors, engineers, scientists, and historians, who continued with him into Asia. The vast amount of data in botany, zoology, geography, and astronomy collected by Alexander's staff stimulated an outburst of activity. To integrate so much information, scientists had to specialize in the various disciplines. Hellenistic scientists preserved and expanded the tradition of science developed in the Hellenic Age. They attempted a rational analysis of nature; they engaged in research, organized knowledge in logical fashion, devised procedures for mathematical proof, separated medicine from magic, grasped the theory of experiment, and applied scientific principles to mechanical devices. Hellenistic science, says historian Benjamin Farrington, stood "on the threshold of the modern world. When modern science began in the sixteenth century, it took up where the Greeks left off."[2]

Although Alexandria was the principal center of scientific research, Athens still retained some of its former luster in this area. After Aristotle died in 322 B.C., he was succeeded as head of the Lyceum by Theophrastus and then by Strato. Both wrote treatises on many subjects—logic, ethics, politics, physics, and botany. Theophrastus systematized knowledge of botany in a manner similar to Aristotle's treatment of animals. Strato is most famous for his study of physics. It is likely that Strato, in his investigation of physical problems, did not rely on logic alone but performed a series of experiments to test his investigations.

Because of its library, the finest in the ancient world, and its state-supported museum, Alexandria attracted leading scholars and superseded Athens in scientific investigation. The museum was really a research institute—the first institution in history specifically established for the purpose of scientific research—in which some of the best minds of the day studied and worked.

Alexandrian doctors advanced medical skills. They improved surgical instruments and techniques and, by dissecting bodies, added to anatomical knowledge. Through their research, they discovered organs of the body not known until then, made the distinction between arteries and veins, divided nerves into those comprising the motor and the sensory system, and identified the brain as the source of intelligence. Their investigations advanced knowledge of anatomy and physiology to a level that was not significantly improved until the sixteenth century A.D.

Knowledge in the fields of astronomy and mathematics also increased. Eighteen centuries before Copernicus, Alexandrian astronomer Aristarchus (310–230 B.C.) said that the sun was the center of the universe, that the planets revolved around it, and that the stars were situated at great distances from the earth. But these revolutionary ideas were not accepted, and the belief in an earth-centered universe persisted. In geometry, Euclid, an Alexandrian mathematician who lived around 300 B.C., creatively synthesized earlier developments. Euclid's hundreds of geometric proofs, derived from reasoning alone—his conclusions flowed logically and flawlessly from given assumptions—are a profound witness to the power of the rational mind.

Alexander's expeditions had opened the eyes of Mediterranean peoples to the breadth of the earth and had stimulated explorations and geographic research. Eratosthenes (c. 275–194 B.C.), an Alexandrian geographer, sought a scientific understanding of this enlarged world. He divided the planet into climatic zones, declared that the oceans are joined, and with extraordinary ingenuity and accuracy measured the earth's circumference.

Archimedes of Syracuse (c. 287–212 B.C.), who studied at Alexandria, was a mathematician, a physicist, and an ingenious inventor. His mechan-

Profile

Polybius

Rome's expansion from a city-state to a world empire that embraced many different nationalities and the extension of citizenship to non-Romans exemplified the universalism and cosmopolitanism of the Hellenistic Age. So too did Polybius' *Histories,* which sought to account for Rome's unprecedented accomplishment.

In 168 B.C. at the battle of Pynda, the Romans defeated Macedonia, which ruled Greece, ending its independence. After the battle, Polybius, along with a thousand other Greeks who had shown sympathy for Macedonia, was deported to Rome to be questioned. Protected by an influential Roman family, no harm came to him.

In the tradition of Thucydides, Polybius believed that a historian had a duty to teach moral lessons and to enlighten by pointing to general principles governing the course of historical events. Like Thucydides he believed that there

Jose F. Poblete/Corbis.

ical inventions, including war engines, dazzled his contemporaries. However, Archimedes dismissed his practical inventions, preferring to be remembered as a theoretician. In one treatise, he established the general principles of hydrostatics, a branch of physics that deals with the pressure and equilibrium of liquids at rest.

Philosophy

Hellenistic thinkers preserved the rational tradition of Greek philosophy. Like their Hellenic predecessors, they regarded the cosmos as governed by universal principles intelligible to the rational mind. For the philosophers of both ages, a crucial problem was the achievement of the good life. Also, both Hellenic and Hellenistic thinkers sought rules for human conduct that accorded with rational standards; both believed that individuals attain happiness through their own efforts, unaided by the gods. In the tradition of Socrates, Hellenistic thinkers taught a morality of self-mastery. But although they retained the inheritance of the classical age, they also transformed it, for they had to adapt thought to the requirements of a cosmopolitan society.

In the Hellenic Age, the starting point of philosophy was the citizen's relationship to the city; in the Hellenistic Age, the point of departure was the solitary individual's relationship to humanity and the individual's personal destiny in a larger and more complex world. Philosophy tried to deal with the feeling of alienation—of not belonging—resulting from the weakening of the individual's attachment to the polis and to arrive at a conception of community that corresponded to the social realities of a world grown larger. Unlike Plato and Aristotle, Hellenistic philosophers were moralists, not great speculators and theorists. The Hellenistic schools of philosophy, in contrast to their predecessors, were far less concerned with the scientific understanding of nature. Also in contrast to earlier Greek thinkers, they were less concerned with po-are lessons to be learned from a study of history and that his work would instruct current and future officials regarding the proper course of action under given circumstances. But whereas Thucydides wrote about the Peloponnesian War, which involved the Greek city-states, Polybius, reflecting the spirit of the Hellenistic Age, took the entire Mediterranean world as his subject. His aim was to recount how "the Romans succeeded in less than fifty-three years in bringing under their rule the whole inhabited world, an achievement which is without parallel in human history."* No question was of greater importance, he said, than to understand how Rome acquired this supremacy. Polybius stated explicitly that, unlike his predecessors who wrote specialized narrow studies dealing with aspects of Greek or Persian history, he was attempting a unique project—a systematic world history that "examine[s] the general and comprehensive scheme of events."† Such a study, he held, was an avenue to a wisdom closed to historians who write monographs on parochial, insignificant, and obsure topics.

Among the reasons Polybius gave for Rome's success was its political system, which balanced aristocratic and democratic elements: the Senate, representing the aristocracy, wielded great power, but the Assembly, representing the commoners, also played an important role in political life. Polybius held that such a political balance promoted loyalty and effective government. Polybius was greatly impressed with the Roman army. The discipline and dedication of citizen soldiers, he said, help explain Rome's success in creating a world empire.

*Polybius, *The Rise of the Roman Empire,* trans. Ian Scott-Kilvert (New York: Penguin Classics, 1979), pp. 41.
†Ibid., p. 44.

litical organization. Philosophy was now chiefly preoccupied with the life of the individual, and it tried to alleviate spiritual uneasiness and loss of security. It aspired to make people ethically independent so that they could achieve happiness in a hostile and competitive world. As the philosopher Epicurus said: "Empty are the words of that philosopher who offers no therapy for human suffering. For just as there is no use in medical expertise if it does not give therapy for bodily disease, so too there is no use in philosophy if it does not expel the suffering of the soul."[3] To "expel the suffering of the soul"—to conquer fear and anxiety and to achieve happiness—said Hellenistic philosophers, people must not allow themselves to be troubled by cares and concerns that are ultimately trivial.

In striving for tranquillity of mind and relief from conflict, Hellenistic thinkers reflected the general anxiety that pervaded their society. They retained respect for reason and aspired to the rational life, but by stressing peace of mind and the effort to overcome anxiety, they were performing a quasi-religious function. Philosophy was trying to provide comfort for the individual suffering from feelings of loneliness and insignificance. This attempt indicated that Greek civilization was undergoing a spiritual transformation. (We examine the full meaning of this transformation in Chapters 7 and 8). The gravitation toward religion in an effort to relieve despair gathered momentum in the centuries that followed. Thus, Hellenistic philosophies helped prepare people to accept Christianity, which promised personal salvation. Ultimately, the Christian answer to the problems of alienation and the need for community would predominate over the Greco-Roman attempt at resolution.

The Hellenistic world gave rise to four principal schools of philosophy: Epicureanism, Stoicism, Skepticism, and Cynicism.

Epicureanism. In the tradition of Plato and Aristotle, Epicurus (342–270 B.C.) founded a

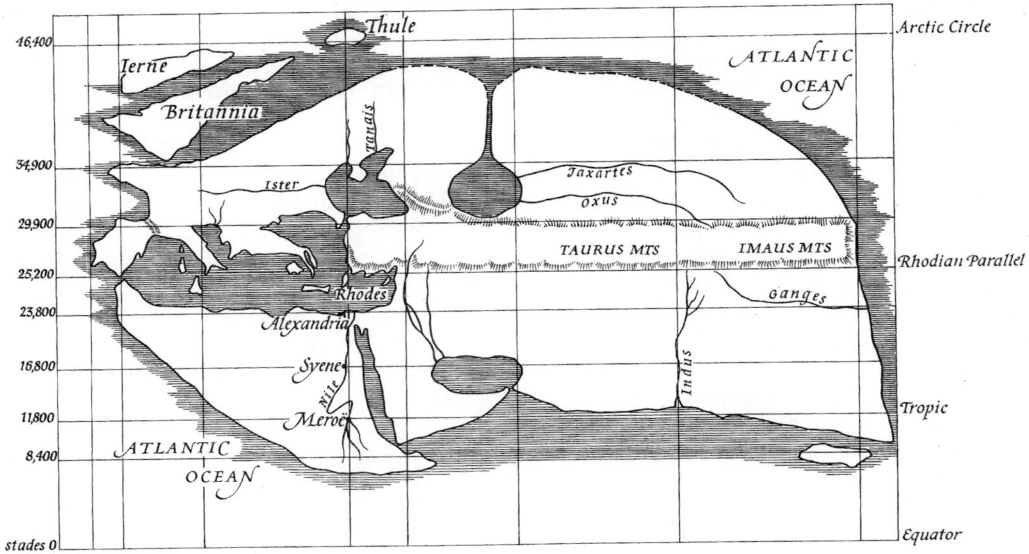

Reconstruction of the Map of the World by Eratosthenes (c. 275–194 b.c.). Geographic knowledge expanded enormously among the Hellenistic Greeks. The first systematic scientific books on geography were credited to Eratosthenes, head of the Alexandrian Library, the greatest scientific and humanistic research center in the Hellenistic world. Eratosthenes estimated the circumference of the earth with remarkable accuracy for his time. His map illustrates the limits of the world known to the Greeks. (*From John Onians,* Art and Thought in the Hellenistic Age [*Thames and Hudson, 1979*]. *Reprinted by permission of Thames and Hudson Ltd.*)

school in Athens at the end of the fourth century B.C. He broke with the attitude of the Hellenic Age in significant ways. Unlike classical Greek philosophers, Epicurus, reflecting the Greeks' changing relationship to the city, taught the value of passivity and withdrawal from civic life. To him, citizenship was not a prerequisite for individual happiness. Wise persons, said Epicurus, would refrain from engaging in public affairs, for politics is marred by clashing factions and treachery that deprive individuals of their self-sufficiency, their freedom to choose and to act. Nor would wise individuals pursue wealth, power, or fame, as the pursuit would only provoke anxiety. For the same reason, wise persons would not surrender to hate or love, desires that distress the soul. A wise person would also try to live justly, for one who behaves unjustly is burdened with troubles. Nor could there be happiness when one worried about dying or pleasing the gods.

To Epicurus, dread that the gods interfered in human life and could inflict suffering after death was the principal cause of anxiety. To remove this source of human anguish, he favored a theory of nature that had no place for supernatural intervention in nature or in people's lives. Therefore, he adopted the physics of Democritus, which taught that all things consist of atoms in motion. In a universe of colliding atoms, there could be no higher intelligence ordering things; there was no room for divine activity. Epicurus taught that the gods probably did exist but that they could not influence human affairs; hence, it was pointless to worry about them. Individuals should order their lives without considering the gods. Epicurus embraced atomism, not as a disinterested scientist aspiring to truth, but as a moral philosopher seeking to liberate emotional life from fear of the gods.

People could achieve happiness, said Epicurus, when their bodies were "free from pain" and

Marble Portrait of Epicurus. The direct gaze and inner calm of the philosopher suggest the essence of his teachings. Epicurus believed that happiness came from a rationally ordered life. He urged his followers to disengage from the uncertainties and stress of politics, business, family, and religion. (*The Metropolitan Museum of Art, Rogers Fund, 1911 [11.90].*)

their minds "released from worry and fear." Although Epicurus wanted to increase pleasure for the individual, he rejected unbridled hedonism. Because he believed that happiness must be pursued rationally, he thought that the merely sensuous pleasures with unpleasant aftereffects (such as overeating and excessive drinking) should be avoided. In general, Epicurus espoused the traditional Greek view of moderation and prudence. Most important for achieving the good life, said Epicurus, was the company of friends.

By opening his philosophy to men and women, slave and free, Greek and barbarian, and by separating ethics from politics, Epicurus fashioned a philosophy adapted to the post-Alexandrian world of kingdoms and universal culture.

Online Study Center

Improve Your Grade
Primary Source: A Materialist Ethic: The Principal Doctrines of Epicureanism

Stoicism. Around the time of the founding of Epicurus' school, Zeno (335–263 B.C.) also opened a school in Athens. Zeno's teachings, called Stoicism, became the most important philosophy in the Hellenistic world. By teaching that the world constituted a single society, Stoicism gave theoretical expression to the world-mindedness of the age. By arriving at the concept of a world-state, the city of humanity, Stoicism offered an answer to the problem of community and alienation posed by the decline of the city-state. By stressing inner strength in dealing with life's misfortunes, Stoicism offered an avenue to individual happiness in a world fraught with uncertainty.

At the core of Stoicism was the belief that the universe contained a principle of order, variously called the Divine Fire, God—more the fundamental force of the universe than a living person—and Divine Reason (*Logos*). This ruling force underlay reality and permeated all things; it ordered the cosmos according to law. The Stoics reasoned that, being part of the universe, people too shared in the **Logos** that operated throughout the cosmos. The Logos was implanted in every human soul; it enabled people to act virtuously and intelligently and to comprehend the principles of order that governed nature. This **natural law** provides human beings with an awareness of what is and is not correct behavior, especially when dealing with other human beings. Living in accordance with natural law is the avenue to both virtue and happiness. Natural law alone commands our ultimate obedience.

Since reason was common to all, human beings were essentially brothers and fundamentally equal. Reason gave individuals dignity and enabled them to recognize and respect the dignity of others. To the Stoics, all people, Greek and barbarian, free and slave, rich and poor, were fellow human beings, and one law, the law of nature, applied to all of them. What people had in common as fellow human beings far outweighed differences based on culture. All rational human beings were fellow citizens of a cosmopolis, a world community. Thus, the Stoics, like the Hebrews, arrived at the idea of a common humanity subject to the same moral obligations.

Pericles had spoken of the Athenians' obligation to abide by the laws and traditions of their city; Stoics, viewing people as citizens of the world, emphasized the individual's duty to understand and obey the natural law that governed the cosmos and applied to all. Socrates had taught a morality of self-mastery—reason exercising control over feelings; the Stoics spread Socrates' philosophy beyond Athens, beyond Greece, and enlarged it, offering it as a way of life for all. Like Socrates, the Stoics believed that a person's distinctive quality was the ability to reason and that happiness came from the disciplining of emotions by the rational part of the soul. Also like Socrates, the Stoics maintained that individuals should progress morally, should perfect their character.

In the Stoic view, wise persons ordered their lives according to the natural law—the Logos, or law of reason—that underlay the cosmos. To live in agreement with nature—that is, to follow the dictates of reason—was the aim of moral activity. This harmony with the Logos would give these individuals the inner strength to resist the torments inflicted by others, by fate, and by their own passionate natures. Self-mastery and inner peace, or happiness, would follow. Such individuals would remain undisturbed by life's misfortunes, for their souls would be their own. Even slaves were not denied this inner freedom; although their bodies were subjected to the power of their masters, their minds still remained independent and free.

Stoicism had an enduring influence on the Western mind. To some Roman political and legal thinkers, the Empire fulfilled the Stoic ideal of a world community, in which people of different nationalities held citizenship and were governed by a worldwide law that accorded with the law of reason, or natural law—a moral order operating throughout the universe. Stoic beliefs—that by nature we are all members of one family, that each person is significant, that distinctions of rank and race are of no account, and that human law should not conflict with natural law—were incorporated into Roman jurisprudence, Christian thought, and modern liberalism. There is continuity between the Stoic idea of natural law and the principle of inalienable rights, rights to which all are entitled by nature, stated in the American Declaration of Independence. In the modern age, the principle of natural law provided theoretical justification for human rights that are the birthright of each individual.

Skepticism. The Epicureans tried to withdraw from the evils of this world and to attain personal happiness by reducing physical pain and mental anguish. The Stoics sought happiness by actively entering into harmony with universal reason, that is, with nature. Both philosophies sought peace of mind, but the Stoics did not disengage themselves from political life and often exerted influence over Hellenistic rulers. Skepticism, another school of philosophy, attacked the Epicurean and Stoic belief that there is a definite avenue to happiness. Skeptics held that one could achieve spiritual comfort by recognizing that none of the beliefs by which people lived were true or could bring happiness. For the Skeptic, nothing can be known with certainty. Therefore, suspending judgment—that is, recognizing the existence of alternative viewpoints and disdaining a commitment to dogmatic beliefs—calms the mind and brings contentment.

Some Skeptics taught indifference to all theory and urged conformity to accepted views whether or not they were true. This attitude would avoid arguments and explanations. Gods might not exist, said the Skeptics, but to refuse to worship or to deny their existence would only cause trouble; therefore, individuals should follow the crowd. The life of the mind—metaphysical speculation inquiring into the origin of things, and clever reasoning—did not bring truth or happiness, so why should one bother with it? Suspending judgment, recognizing the inability to understand, not committing oneself to a system of belief—by these means one could achieve peace of mind. Instead of embracing doctrines, said the Greek writer Lucian, individuals should go their way "with ever a smile and never a passion."[4] This was the position of those Skeptics who were suspicious of ideas, particularly all-encompassing rational systems, and hostile to intellectuals.

The more sophisticated Skeptics did not run away from ideas but pointed out their limitations; they did not avoid theories but refuted them. In doing so, they did not reject reason. Rather, they focused on a problem of reason: whether indeed it could arrive at truth. Thus, Carneades of Cyrene (213–129 B.C.) insisted that all ideas, even mathematical principles, must be regarded as hypotheses and assumptions, not as absolutes. Just because the universe showed signs of order, Carneades argued, one could not assume that it had been created by God. Since there was never any certainty, only probability, morality should derive from practical experience rather than from dogma.

Cynicism. The Cynics were not theoretical philosophers but supreme individualists who rebelled against established values and conventions—against every barrier of society that restrained individuals from following their own natures. Cynics regarded laws and public opinion, private property and employment, and wives and children as hindrances to the free life. Extreme individualists, the Cynics had no loyalty to family, city, or kingdom and ridiculed religion, philosophy, and literature. They renounced possessions and showed no respect for authority. When Diogenes, a fourth-century B.C. Cynic, met Alexander the Great, he is supposed to have asked only that the great conqueror get out of his light.

Cynics put their philosophy into practice. They cultivated indifference and apathy and scorned wealth, fame, and noble birth. To harden themselves against life's misfortunes, they engaged in strenuous exercise, endured cold and hunger, and lived ascetically. Not tied down by property or employment, Cynics wandered shoeless from place to place, wearing dirty and ragged clothes and carrying staffs. To show their disdain for society's customs, Cynics grew long scraggly beards, used foul language, and cultivated bad manners. Diogenes supposedly said: "Look at me, . . . I am without a home, without a city, without property, without a slave; I sleep on the ground; I have neither wife nor children, no miserable governor's mansion, but only earth, and sky, and one rough cloak. Yet what do I lack? Am I not free from pain and fear, am I not free?"[5]

In their attack on inherited conventions, Cynics strove for self-sufficiency and spiritual security. Theirs was the most radical philosophical quest for meaning and peace of soul during the Hellenistic Age.

The Hellenistic Legacy

The Hellenistic Age encompassed the period from the death of Alexander to the formation of the Roman Empire. During these three centuries, Greek civilization spread eastward as far as India and westward to Rome. As Greeks settled in the Near East and intermingled with Egyptians, Syrians, Persians, and others, the parochialism of the Greek polis gave way to a new cosmopolitanism, an interest in the culture of other ethnic groups, and to universalism, an awareness that people were members of a world community that transcended citizenship in one's native city. Both philosophy and the arts reflected these new concerns.

Rome, conqueror of the Mediterranean world and transmitter of Hellenism, inherited the universalist tendencies of the Hellenistic Age and embodied them in its law, institutions, and art. So too did Christianity, which welcomed converts from every ethnic background and held that God loved all people, that Christ died for all humanity. The Stoic idea of natural law that applies to all human beings and its corollary that human beings are fundamentally equal were crucial to the formulation of the modern idea that the individual is endowed with **natural rights** that no government can violate. A parallel can be drawn between the Hellenistic Age, in which Greek civilization spread to the Near East, and our own age, in which the ideas, institutions, and technology of Western civilization have been exported throughout the globe.

❖ ❖ ❖

Online Study Center **ACE the Test**

Notes

1. Quoted in John Ferguson, *The Heritage of Hellenism* (New York: Science History Publications, 1973), p. 30.
2. Benjamin Farrington, *Greek Science* (Baltimore: Penguin Books, 1961), p. 301.
3. Quoted in Anthony Gottlieb, *The Dream of Reason* (New York: W. W. Norton, 2000), pp. 283–284.
4. Quoted in J. H. Randall, Jr., *Hellenistic Ways of Deliverance and the Making of the Christian Synthesis* (New York: Columbia University Press, 1970), p. 74.
5. Epictetus, *The Discourses as Reported by Arrian, the Manual and Fragments,* trans. W. A. Oldfather (Cambridge, Mass.: Harvard University Press, 1966), 2:147.

Suggested Reading

Bonnard, André, *Greek Civilization,* vol. 3 (1961). Self-contained chapters on various phases of late classical and Hellenistic periods.

Cartledge, Paul, *Alexander the Great* (2004). A recent biography.

Ferguson, John, *The Heritage of Hellenism* (1973). A good introduction to Hellenistic culture.

Grant, Michael, *From Alexander to Cleopatra* (1982). A fine survey of all phases of Hellenistic society and culture.

Koester, Helmut, *Introduction to the New Testament, Volume One: History, Culture and Religion of the Hellenistic Age* (1982). An intelligent guide.

Wallbank, F. W., *The Hellenistic World* (1982). A survey of the Hellenistic world that makes judicious use of quotations from original sources.

Chapter 6

The Roman Republic: City-State to World Empire

Roman Relief: Praetorian Soldiers (Louvre, Paris/Giraudon/Art Resource, NY.)

- **Evolution of the Roman Constitution**
- **Roman Expansion to 146 B.C.**
- **Culture in the Republic**
- **Collapse of the Republic**

Focus Questions

1. What was the significance of the conflict between plebeians and patricians?
2. What factors enabled the city-state of Rome to conquer Italy and the Mediterranean world?
3. What was the significance of Roman expansion?
4. What were the reasons for the collapse of the Roman republic?

Online Study Center

This icon will direct you to interactive map and primary source activities on the website http://college.hmco.com/pic/perrywc8e.

Rome's great achievement was to transcend the narrow political orientation of the city-state and to create a world-state that unified the different nations of the Mediterranean world. Regarding the polis as the only means to the good life, the Greeks had not desired a larger political unit and had almost totally excluded foreigners from citizenship. Although Hellenistic philosophers had conceived the possibility of a world community, Hellenistic politics could not shape one. Rome overcame the limitations of the city-state mentality and developed an empirewide system of law and citizenship. The Hebrews were distinguished by their prophets and the Greeks by their philosophers. The Romans produced no Amos or Isaiah, and no Plato or Aristotle; their genius found expression in law and government, the practical, not the theoretical.

Historians divide Roman history into two broad periods: the period of the **Republic** began in 509 B.C., with the overthrow of the Etruscan monarchy; the period of the **Empire** began in 27 B.C., when Octavian (Augustus) became in effect the first Roman emperor, ending almost five hundred years of republican self-government. By conquering the Mediterranean world and extending Roman law and, in some instances, citizenship to different nationalities, the Roman Republic transcended the parochialism typical of the city-state. The Republic initiated the trend toward political and legal universalism, which reached fruition in the second period of Roman history, the Empire.

Evolution of the Roman Constitution

By the eighth century B.C., peasant communities existed on some of Rome's seven hills near the Tiber River in central Italy. To the north stood Etruscan cities and to the south Greek cities. The more advanced civilizations of both Etruscans and Greeks were gradually absorbed by the Romans.

The origin of the Etruscans remains a mystery, although some scholars believe that they came from Asia Minor and settled in north-central Italy. From them, Romans acquired architectural styles and skills in road construction, sanitation,

Chronology 6.1 ❖ The Roman Republic

509 B.C.	Expulsion of the Etruscan monarch
450	Law of Twelve Tables
287	End of the Struggle of the Orders
264–241	First Punic War: Rome acquires provinces
218–201	Second Punic War: Hannibal is defeated
149–146	Third Punic War: destruction of Carthage
133–122	Land reforms by the Gracchi brothers; they are murdered by the Senate
88–83	Conflict between Sulla and the forces of Marius; Sulla emerges as dictator
79	After restoring rule by Senate, Sulla retires
73–71	Slave revolt is led by Spartacus
58–51	Caesar campaigns in Gaul
49–44	Caesar is dictator of Rome
31 B.C.	Antony and Cleopatra are defeated at Actium by Octavian

hydraulic engineering (including underground conduits), metallurgy, ceramics, and portrait sculpture. Symbols of authority and rule were also borrowed from the Etruscans: purple robes, ivory-veneer chariots, thrones for state officials, and a bundle of rods and an ax held by attendants. Etruscan words and names entered into the Latin language, and Roman religion absorbed Etruscan gods.

The Etruscans had expanded their territory in Italy during the seventh and sixth centuries B.C., and they controlled the monarchy in Rome. But the Etruscan city-states failed to establish a federal union with a centralized government. Defeated by Celts, Greeks, and finally Romans, by the third century B.C., the Etruscans had ceased to exercise any political power in Italy.

Rome became a republic at the end of the sixth century B.C.—the traditional date is 509 B.C.—when the landowning aristocrats, or patricians, overthrew the Etruscan king. As in the Greek cities, the transition from theocratic monarchy to republic offered possibilities for political and legal growth. In the opening phase of republican history, religion governed the people, dictated the law, and legitimized the rule of the **patricians**—aristocrats by birth who regarded themselves as the preservers of sacred traditions. Gradually, the Romans loosened the ties between religion and politics and hammered out a constitutional system that paralleled the Greek achievement of rationalizing and secularizing politics and law. In time, the Romans, like the Greeks, came to view law as an expression of the public will and not as the creation of god-kings, priest-kings, or a priestly caste.

The impetus for the growth of the Roman constitution came from a conflict—known as the Struggle of the Orders—between the patricians and the commoners, or **plebeians.** At the beginning of the fifth century B.C., the patrician-dominated government consisted of two annually elected executives called consuls, the Centuriate Assembly, and the Senate. Patricians owned most of the land and controlled the army. The two consuls, who came from the nobility, commanded the army, served as judges, and initiated legislation. To prevent either consul from becoming an autocrat, decisions had to be approved by both of them. In times of crisis, the consuls were authorized by the Senate to nominate a dictator; he would possess absolute powers during the emergency, but these powers would expire after six months. The consuls were aided by other annually elected magistrates and administrators. The Centuriate Assembly was a popular assembly but, because of voting procedures, was controlled by the nobility. The Assembly elected consuls and other magistrates and made the laws, which also needed Senate approval. The Senate advised the Assembly but did not itself enact laws; it controlled public finances and foreign policy. Senators either were appointed for life terms by the consuls or were former magistrates. The Senate was the principal organ of patrician power.

The tension between patricians and commoners stemmed from plebeian grievances, which included enslavement for debt, discrimination in the courts, prevention of intermarriage with patricians, lack of political representation, and the absence of a written code of laws. Resenting their inferior status and eager for economic relief, the plebeians organized and waged a struggle for political, legal, and social equality. They were resisted every step of the way by patricians, who wanted to preserve their own dominance. The plebeians had one decisive weapon: their threat to secede from Rome, that is, not to pay taxes, work, or serve in the army. Realizing that Rome, which was constantly involved in warfare on the Italian peninsula, could not endure without plebeian help, the pragmatic patricians begrudgingly made concessions. Thus, the plebeians slowly gained legal equality.

Early in the fifth century, the plebeians won the right to form their own assembly (the Plebeian Assembly, which was later enlarged and called the Tribal Assembly). This Assembly could elect tribunes, officials who were empowered to protect plebeian rights. As a result of plebeian pressure, in about 450 B.C., the first Roman code of laws was written. Called the Twelve Tables, the code gave plebeians some degree of protection against unfair and oppressive patrician officials, who could interpret customary law in an arbitrary way. Other concessions gained later by the plebeians included the right to intermarry with patricians; access to the highest political, judicial, and religious offices in the state; and the elimination of slavery as payment for debt. In 287 B.C., a date generally recognized as the termination of the plebeian-patrician struggle, laws passed by the Tribal Assembly no longer required Senate approval. Now the plebeians had full civil equality and legal protection and their assembly full power to enact legislation.

Although the plebeians had gained legal equality and the right to sit in the Senate and to hold high offices, Rome was still ruled by an upper class. True, the Tribal Assembly and the tribunes constituted democratic elements and, in theory, seemed to balance the power of the patrician-dominated Senate. Actually, though, power was still concentrated in a ruling oligarchy of wealthy landowners, this time consisting of patricians and influential plebeians who had joined forces with the old nobility. Marriages between patricians and politically powerful plebeians strengthened this alliance. Generally only wealthy plebeians became tribunes, and they tended to side with the old nobility rather than defend the interests of poor plebeians. By using bribes, the ruling oligarchy of patricians and wealthy plebeians maintained control over the Assembly, and the Senate remained a bastion of aristocratic power.

A patron-client relationship extending back to the days of the monarchy reinforced upper-class rule. In early Rome, a plebeian seeking protection for himself and his family in the courts looked to a patrician for assistance. In return, the plebeian gave his patrician patron both military and political support. Enduring over the centuries, the patron-client relationship assured powerful nobles of their commoner clients' support in the Assembly, and it provided clients with food, money, and protection.

Thus, from beginning to end, an upper class—sometimes expanded to allow entry of new talent—governed the Roman Republic. This aristocracy's view of liberty always remained elitist: freedom for Rome's best men to achieve virtue (*virtus*), dignity (*dignitas*), and fame (*fama*) by competing with each other for political power and privilege. Cicero (see below), himself a member of the ruling elite, aptly summed up its outlook: "the safety of the State depends upon the wisdom of its best men, especially since Nature has provided not only that those men who are superior in virtue and in spirit should rule the weaker, but also that the weaker should be willing to obey the stronger."[1] Like others of the upper class, Cicero held that "the perversity and rashness of popular assemblies" precluded them

STATUE PORTRAIT, FIRST CENTURY A.D. The Romans valued family, city, and tradition. Here a noble proudly exhibits the busts of his ancestors. (*Scala/Art Resource, NY.*)

from governing effectively.[2] In the Greek cities, tyrants had succeeded in breaking aristocratic dominance, thereby clearing a pathway for democratic government. But in the Roman Republic, the nobility maintained its tight grip on the reins of power until the civil wars of the first century B.C.

Deeming themselves Rome's finest citizens, the ruling oligarchy led Rome during its period of expansion and demonstrated a sense of responsibility and a talent for statesmanship. In noble families, parents and elders prepared the young for public service. They recounted the glorious deeds of ancestors who had served Rome, and they reminded youngsters of their responsibility to bring additional honors to the family by winning distinction as a commander, orator, or jurist. In this way, a son would prove his worth as a man and as a Roman.

During their two-hundred-year class struggle, the Romans forged a constitutional system based on civic needs rather than on religious mystery. The essential duty of government ceased to be the regular performance of religious rituals and became the maintenance of order at home and the preservation of Roman might and dignity in international relations. Although the Romans retained the ceremonies and practices of their ancestral religion—correct observance was a way of showing respect for tradition—public interest, not religious tradition, determined the content of law and was the standard by which all the important acts of the city were judged. When Romans chose a course of action in public life, they rarely took into consideration the fear of displeasing the gods. By the late Republic, Romans did not seem concerned about divine intervention in their daily lives; the prospect of divine punishment seemed quite remote. In the opening stage of republican history, law was priestly and sacred, spoken only by priests and known only to men of religious families. Gradually, as law was written, debated, and altered, it became disentangled from religion. Another step in this process of secularization and rationalization occurred when the study and interpretation of law passed from the hands of priests to a class of professional jurists, who analyzed, classified, systematized, and sought commonsense solutions to legal problems.

The Roman constitution was not a product of abstract thought, nor was it the gift of a great lawmaker, such as the Athenian Solon. Rather, like the unwritten British constitution, the Roman constitution evolved gradually and empirically in response to specific needs. The Romans, unlike the Greeks, were distinguished by practicality and common sense, not by a love of abstract thought. In their pragmatic and empirical fashion, they gradually developed the procedures of public politics and the legal state.

Undoubtedly, the commoners' struggle for rights and power did arouse hatred on both sides. But in contrast to the domestic strife in Greek cities, Rome's class conflict did not end in civil war. This peaceful solution testifies to the political good sense of the Romans. Fear of foreign powers and the tradition of civic patriotism prevented the patrician-plebeian conflict from turning into a fight to the death. At the time of the class struggle, Rome was also engaged in the extension of its power over the Italian peninsula. Without civic harmony and stability, Rome could not have achieved expansion.

Online Study Center

Improve Your Grade
Primary Source: Law in Early Roman Society: The Regulation of Women and Family

Roman Expansion to 146 B.C.

By 146 B.C., Rome was the dominant state in the Mediterranean world. Roman expansion occurred in three main stages: the uniting of the Italian peninsula, which gave Rome the forces that transformed it from a city-state into a great power; the collision with Carthage, from which Rome emerged as ruler of the western Mediterranean; and the subjugation of the Hellenistic states, which brought Romans in close contact with Greek civilization. As Rome expanded territorially, its leaders enlarged their vision. Instead of restricting citizenship to people having ethnic kinship, Rome assimilated other peoples into its political community. Just as Roman law had grown to cope with the earlier grievances of the plebeians, so it adjusted to the new situations resulting from the creation of a multinational empire. The city of Rome was evolving into the city of humanity—the cosmopolis envisioned by the Stoics.

The Uniting of Italy

Frequent conflicts with hostile neighbors had forced the Romans to develop militarily and to strengthen their commitment to Rome—circumstances that fostered expansion. During the first stage of this expansion, Rome extended its hegemony over Italy, subduing in the process neighboring Latin kinsmen, semicivilized Italian tribes, the once-dominant Etruscans, and Greek city-states in southern Italy. At the beginning, Roman warfare was principally motivated by the hunger for more farmland. As Rome expanded and its territory and responsibilities increased, it was often drawn into conflict to protect its widened boundaries and its allies. Also fueling Roman expansion was an aristocratic ethos, which placed the highest value on glory and reputation. Demonstrating prowess in war, aristocrats believed, was the finest way to win the esteem of fellow Romans, bring honor to their families, and enhance their own political careers.

Rome's conquest of Italy stemmed in part from superior military organization, training, and iron discipline. From the Greeks they acquired the most advanced methods of siegecraft. Also copying the Greeks, the Romans organized their soldiers into battle formations; in contrast, their opponents often fought as disorganized hordes, which were prone to panic and flight. Fighting as part of a unit strengthened the courage and confidence of the Roman soldier, for he knew that his comrades would stand with him. Roman soldiers who deserted their posts or fled from battle were punished and disgraced, an ordeal more terrible than facing up to the enemy. The promise of glory and rewards also impelled the Roman soldier to distinguish himself in battle.

Ultimately, Rome's success was due to the character of its people and the quality of its statesmanship. The Roman farmer-soldier was dedicated, rugged, persevering, and self-reliant. He could march thirty miles a day laden with arms, armor, and equipment weighing sixty pounds. In the face of danger, he remained resolute and tenacious, obedient to the poet Virgil's maxim: "Yield you not to ill fortune, but go against it with more daring." Romans willingly made sacrifices so that Rome might endure. In conquering Italy, they were united by a moral and religious devotion to their city strong enough to overcome social conflict, factional disputes, and personal ambition.

Despite its army's might, Rome could not have mastered Italy without the cooperation of other Italian peoples. Like other ancient peoples, Rome plundered, enslaved, and brutalized, at times with great ferocity. But it also endeavored, through generous treatment, to gain the loyalty of those it had conquered. Some defeated Italian communities retained a measure of self-government but turned the conduct of foreign affairs over to Rome and contributed contingents to the army when Rome went to war. Other conquered people received partial or full citizenship. In extending its dominion over Italy, Rome displayed a remarkable talent for converting former enemies into allies and eventually into Roman citizens. No Greek city had ever envisaged integrating nonnatives into its political community.

The Italian Confederation formed by Rome was a unique and creative organization that conferred on Italians a measure of security and order previously unknown. Rome prevented internecine wars within the peninsula, suppressed internal revolutions within city-states, and protected the Italians from barbarians (Gallic invaders from the north). In the wars of conquest outside Italy, a share of the glory and plunder fell to all Italians, another benefit of the confederation.

By 264 B.C., Rome had achieved two striking successes. First, it had secured social cohesion by redressing the grievances of the plebeians. Second, it had increased its military might by conquering Italy, thus obtaining the human resources with which it would conquer the Mediterranean world.

Conquest of the Mediterranean World

When Rome finished unifying Italy, there were five great powers in the Mediterranean area: the Seleucid monarchy in the Near East, the Ptolemaic monarchy in Egypt, the kingdom of Macedonia, Carthage in the western Mediterranean, and the Roman-dominated Italian Confederation. One hundred twenty years later, by 146 B.C., Rome had subjected these states to its dominion—"an event for which the past affords no precedent," said the contemporary Greek historian Polybius.

Roman expansion beyond Italy did not proceed according to predetermined design. Indeed, some Roman leaders considered involvement in foreign adventures a threat to both Rome's security and its traditional way of life. But it is difficult for a great power not to get drawn into conflicts as its interests grow, and, without planning it, Rome acquired an overseas empire.

Shortly after asserting supremacy in Italy, Rome engaged Carthage, the other great power in the western Mediterranean, in a prolonged conflict. Founded about 800 B.C. by Phoenicians, the North African city of Carthage had become a prosperous commercial center. Its wealth was derived from a virtual monopoly of trade in the western Mediterranean and along the western coasts of Africa and Europe. The Carthaginians (*Poeni* in Latin) had acquired an empire comprising North Africa and coastal regions of southern Spain, Sardinia, Corsica, and western Sicily.

War between the two great powers began because Rome feared Carthage's designs on the northern Sicilian city of Messana. Rome was apprehensive about the southern Italian city-states that were its allies, fearing that Carthage would use Messana either to attack them or to interfere with their trade. Rome decided that the security of its allies required intervention in Sicily.

The two powers had stumbled into a collision, the First Punic War, 264–241 B.C., that neither had deliberately sought. Although Rome suffered severe losses—including the annihilation of an army that had invaded North Africa and the destruction of hundreds of ships in battle and storms—the Romans never considered anything but a victor's peace. Drawing manpower from loyal allies throughout Italy, Rome finally prevailed over Carthage, which had to surrender Sicily to Rome. Three years later, Rome seized the islands of Corsica and Sardinia from a weakened Carthage. With the acquisition of these territories beyond Italy, which were made

CAST MADE FROM TRAJAN'S COLUMN. Emperor Trajan (A.D. 98–117) constructed a column to commemorate his campaigns. One of the reliefs depicts a Roman fleet landing at the port of Acona. During the First Punic War, Rome had become a naval power able to counter Carthage's fleet. (*Alinari/Art Resource, NY.*)

into provinces, Rome had the beginnings of an empire.

Carthaginian expansion in Spain in order to recoup wealth—Spain was rich in metals—and to obtain manpower for the depleted Carthaginian forces precipitated the Second Punic War (218–201 B.C.). Coming from Spain, the Carthaginian army was commanded by Hannibal (247–183 B.C.), whose military genius astounded the ancients. Hannibal led a seasoned army, complete with war elephants for charging enemy lines, through passes in the Alps so steep and icy that men and animals sometimes lost their footing and fell to their deaths. Some twenty-six thousand men survived the crossing into Italy; fifteen thousand more were recruited from Gallic tribesmen of the Po valley. At the battle of Cannae (216 B.C.), the Carthaginian forces, brilliantly deployed by Hannibal, completely destroyed a Roman army of sixty thousand soldiers, the largest single force Rome had ever put into the field.

Romans were in a state of shock. Mixed with grief for the dead was the fear that Hannibal would crown his victory with an attack on Rome itself. To prevent panic, the Senate ordered women and children indoors, limited mourning to thirty days, and prepared to raise a new army. Adding to Rome's distress was the defection of many southern Italian allies to Hannibal.

These were the Republic's worst days. Nevertheless, says the Roman historian Livy, the Romans did not breathe a word of peace. Hannibal could not follow up his victory at Cannae with a finishing blow, for Rome wisely would not allow its army to be lured into another major engagement. Nor did Hannibal possess the manpower to capture the city itself, with its formidable fortifications. In addition, most of Rome's Italian allies remained loyal. Rome invaded North Africa, threatening Carthage and forcing Hannibal to withdraw his troops from Italy in order to defend his homeland. Hannibal, who had won every battle in Italy, was defeated by Scipio Africanus at the battle of Zama in North Africa in 202 B.C., ending the Second Punic War. Carthage was compelled to surrender Spain and to give up its elephants and its navy.

The Second Punic War left Rome as the sole great power in the western Mediterranean; it also hastened Rome's entry into the politics of the Hellenistic world. In the year after Cannae, during Rome's darkest ordeal, Philip V of Macedonia formed an alliance with Hannibal. Fearing that the Macedonian ruler might have intentions of invading Italy, Rome initiated the First Macedonian War and won it in 205 B.C. To end Macedonian influence in Greece, which Rome increasingly viewed as a Roman protectorate, the Romans fought two other wars with Macedonia. Finally, in 148 B.C., Rome created the province of Macedonia.

Intervention in Greece led to Roman involvement in the Hellenistic kingdoms of the Near East and Asia Minor—Seleucia, Egypt, and Pergamum. The Hellenistic states became client kingdoms of Rome and consequently lost their freedom of action in foreign affairs.

Roman imperialism is a classic example of a great power being snared into overseas adventures. To achieve security, Rome protected its allies, prevented endemic warfare, and thwarted any would-be conquerors of Italy. In the course of these actions came considerable spoils of war, but Rome's principal motives for expansion were strategic and political, not economic.

In 146 B.C., the same year that Rome's hegemony over the Hellenistic world was assured, Rome concluded an unnecessary Third Punic War with Carthage. Although Carthage was by then a second-rate power and no longer a threat to Rome's security, Rome had launched this war of annihilation against Carthage in 149 B.C. The Romans were driven by old hatreds and the traumatic memory of Hannibal's near-conquest. Rome sold Carthaginian survivors into slavery, obliterated the city, and turned the territory into the Roman province of Africa. Rome's savage and irrational behavior toward a helpless Carthage was an early sign of the deterioration of senatorial leadership; there would be others.

Rome had not yet reached the limits of its expansion, but there was no doubt that by 146 B.C. the Mediterranean world had been subjected to its will. No power could stand up to Rome.

Online Study Center **Improve Your Grade**
Interactive Map: The Roman World in the Republic and Early Empire

Consequences of Expansion

As a result of Rome's eastern conquests, thousands of Greeks came to Rome; many were educated persons who had been enslaved because of the conquests. This influx accelerated the process of Hellenization begun earlier with Rome's contact with the Greek cities of southern Italy.

A crucial consequence of expansion was Roman contact with the legal experience of other peoples, including the Greeks. Roman jurists, demonstrating the Roman virtues of pragmatism and common sense, selectively incorporated into Roman law

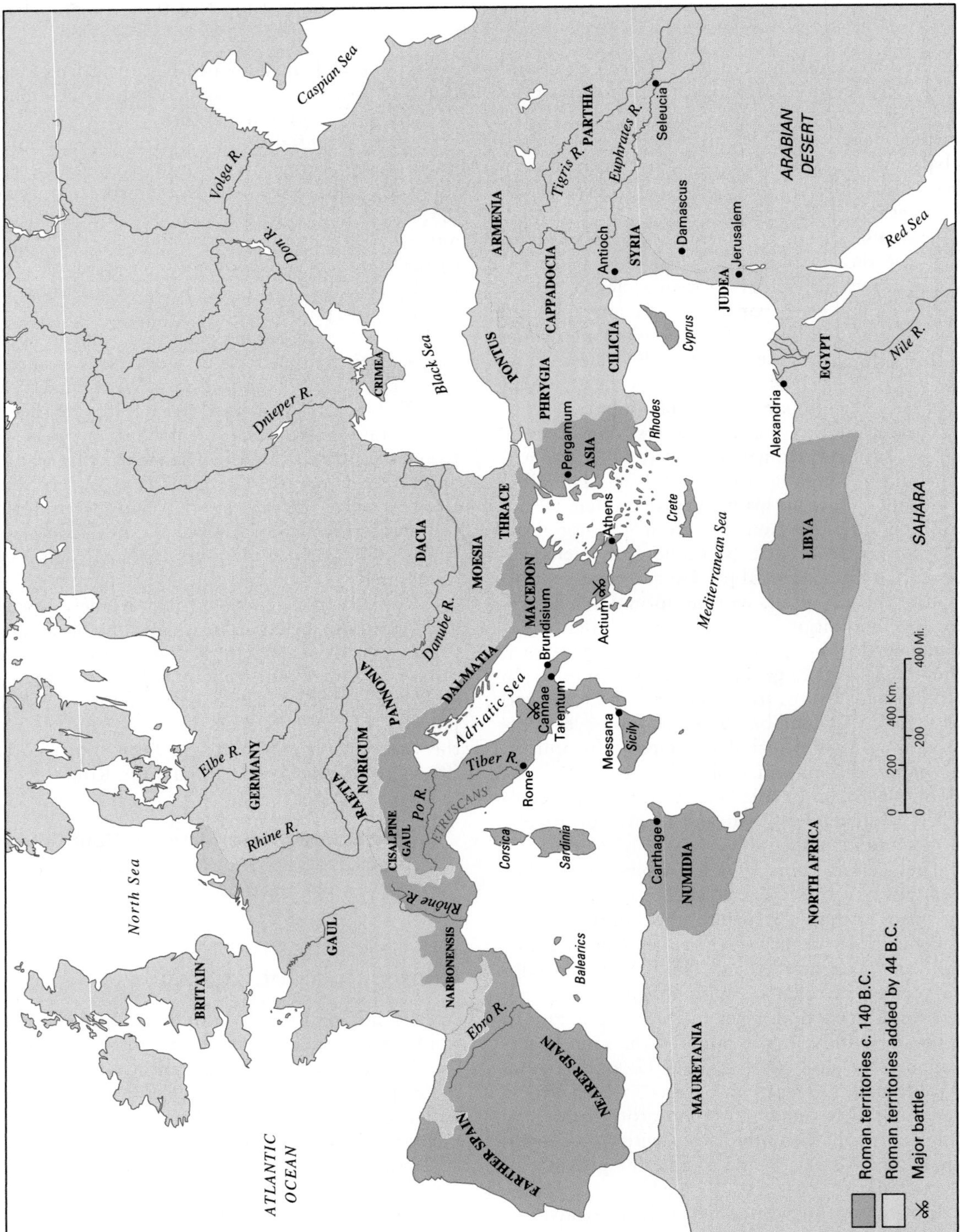

Roman territories c. 140 B.C.
Roman territories added by 44 B.C.
Major battle
0 200 400 Mi.
0 200 400 Km.
ATLANTIC OCEAN
North Sea
BRITAIN
GAUL
NARBONENSIS
Rhône R.
Ebro R.
FARTHER SPAIN
NEARER SPAIN
Balearics
Corsica
Sardinia
CISALPINE GAUL
Po R.
ETRUSCANS
Rhine R.
GERMANY
Elbe R.
RAETIA
NORICUM
PANNONIA
DALMATIA
Adriatic Sea
Tiber R.
Rome
Cannae
Tarentum
Brundisium
Messana
Sicily
Danube R.
DACIA
MOESIA
MACEDON
Actium
Athens
THRACE
Crete
Mediterranean Sea
Dnieper R.
CRIMEA
Black Sea
Don R.
Volga R.
Caspian Sea
Pergamum
ASIA
Rhodes
PHRYGIA
PONTUS
CILICIA
CAPPADOCIA
Cyprus
ARMENIA
Antioch
SYRIA
Tigris R.
PARTHIA
Euphrates R.
Seleucia
Damascus
Jerusalem
JUDEA
ARABIAN DESERT
Red Sea
Nile R.
EGYPT
Alexandria
LIBYA
SAHARA
Carthage
NUMIDIA
NORTH AFRICA
MAURETANIA

RUINS IN SPAIN. This Roman aqueduct in Spain stands as an impressive reminder of the ancient Romans' engineering skills. (*Robert Frerck/Woodfin Camp.*)

elements of the legal codes and traditions of these nations. Thus, Roman jurists empirically fashioned the *jus gentium,* the law of nations, or peoples, which gradually was applied throughout the Empire (see "Law," in Chapter 7).

Rome's conquests also contributed to the rise of a business class, whose wealth was derived from trade, army supply contracts, construction, and tax collecting in the provinces. Rome had no professional civil service, and the collection of public revenues was open to bidding—the highest bidder receiving a contract to collect customs duties, rents on public lands, and tribute in the provinces. The collector's profit came from milking as much tax money as he could from the provincials. These financiers belonged to a group called the Equites, which also included prosperous landowners. Generally, the interests of the Equites paralleled those of the ruling oligarchy. At times, however, they did support generals—notably Julius Caesar—who challenged senatorial rule.

The immense wealth brought to Rome from the East gave the upper classes a taste for luxury. The rich built elaborate homes, which they decorated with fine furniture and works of art and

◀ *Map 6.1* ROMAN CONQUESTS DURING THE REPUBLIC The conquest of Italy gave Rome the manpower to expand throughout the Mediterranean world. In the Second Punic War, Rome defeated its greatest rival, Carthage.

staffed with servants, cooks, and tutors. They delighted in sumptuous banquets, which contained all types of delicacies. Wealthy matrons wore fancy gowns and elaborate hairstyles. These excesses prompted Roman moralists to castigate the people for violating traditional values. Moralists lamented that the new prosperity produced a deterioration in the Roman character.

Roman conquerors had transported to Italy hundreds of thousands of war captives, including Greeks, from all over the Empire. The enslavement and deportations would continue in the first century B.C. (Julius Caesar, for example, enslaved some one million Gauls.) It is estimated that between 80 and 8 B.C. more than two million enslaved aliens were transported to Italy. By the middle of that century, slaves constituted about one-third of Italy's population, compared with about 10 percent before the Second Punic War. The wars of conquest (and piracy) had made the slave trade a vast and lucrative commercial venture. Like the Greeks, Romans considered slavery indispensable for the preservation of civilized life. Roman jurists and intellectuals regarded the division of humanity into masters and slaves as a rule of nature and viewed the slave as an animate tool, an object that produced and served; like other forms of property, slaves could be sold or rented out by their masters. The more fortunate or more capable slaves worked as domestic servants, artisans, bookkeepers, scribes, and administrators; the luckless and more numerous toiled on the growing number of plantations or died early laboring in mines under inhuman conditions. Except for the very poor, every free Roman owned at least one slave. Roman masters often treated their slaves brutally: torture was common, and masters sexually exploited both male and female slaves for their own pleasure or compelled them to work as prostitutes. But strong personal bonds between master and slave also existed—for example, there are accounts of slaves enduring torture and death to protect their masters from enemies.

Although slave uprisings were not common, their ferocity terrified the Romans. In 135 B.C., slaves in Sicily revolted and captured some key towns, defeating Roman forces before being subdued. In 73 B.C., gladiators led by Spartacus broke out of their barracks and were joined by tens of thousands of runaways. Spartacus aimed to escape from Italy to Gaul and Thrace, the homelands of many slaves. The slave army, which grew to some 150,000, defeated Roman armies and devastated southern Italy before the superior might of Rome prevailed. Some 6,000 of the defeated slaves were tortured and crucified on the road from Capua to Rome.

Republican Rome treated the people in overseas lands differently from its Italian allies. Italians were drafted into the Roman army, but provincials as a rule served only in emergencies, for Rome was not certain of their loyalty or of their readiness to meet Roman standards of discipline. Whereas Rome had been somewhat generous in extending citizenship to Italians, provincials were granted citizenship only in exceptional cases. All but some favored communities were required to pay taxes to Rome. Roman governors, lesser officials, and businessmen found the provinces a source of quick wealth; they were generally unrestrained by the Senate, which was responsible for administering the overseas territories. Exploitation, corruption, looting, and extortion soon ran rampant. "No administration in history has ever devoted itself so whole-heartedly to fleecing its subjects for the private benefit of its ruling class as Rome of the last age of the Republic," concludes E. Badian.[3] The Roman nobility proved unfit to manage a world empire.

Despite numerous examples of misrule in the provinces, Roman administration had many positive features. Rome generally allowed its subjects a large measure of self-government and did not interfere with religion and local customs. Usually, the Roman taxes worked out to be no higher, and in some instances lower, than those under previous regimes. Most important, Rome reduced the endemic warfare that had plagued these regions.

Essentially, Rome used its power for constructive ends: to establish order; to build roads, aqueducts, and public buildings; and to promote Hellenism. When Rome destroyed, it rebuilt creatively; when it conquered, it spread civilization and maintained peace. But no doubt its hundreds of thousands of prisoners of war, uprooted, enslaved, and degraded, did not view Roman conquest as beneficial; nor did the butchered Spanish tribesmen or the massacred Carthaginians. To these hapless victims, Rome appeared as an evil oppressor, not as the creator of a cosmopolis that brought order and security.

Culture in the Republic

One of the chief consequences of expansion was increased contact with Greek culture. During the third century B.C., Greek civilization started to exercise an increasing and fruitful influence on the Roman mind. Greek teachers, both slave and free, came to Rome and introduced Romans to Hellenic cultural achievements. As they conquered the eastern Mediterranean, Roman generals began to ship libraries and works of art from Greek cities to Rome. Roman sculpture and painting imitated Greek prototypes. In time, Romans acquired from Greece knowledge of scientific thought, philosophy, medicine, and geography. Roman writers and orators used Greek history, poetry, drama, and oratory as models. The Elder Pliny (A.D. 23–79), who wrote on many topics but is most famous for *Natural History,* refers to Homer's poetry as "the most valuable work of the human mind"[4] Cicero, Rome's greatest orator, tells us that ambitious young men eager to learn the art of oratory but unaware of the existence of any "course of training or any rules of art . . . attain[ed] what skill they could by means of their natural ability. . . . But later, having heard the Greek orators, gained acquaintance with their literature and called in Greek teachers, our people were fired with a really incredible enthusiasm for eloquence."[5]

Adopting the humanist outlook of the Greeks, the Romans came to value human intelligence and eloquent and graceful prose and poetry. Wealthy Romans retained Greek tutors, poets, and philosophers in their households and sent their sons to Athens to study. By the late Republic, educated Romans could speak and read Greek. Thus, Rome creatively assimilated the Greek achievement and transmitted it to others, thereby extending the orbit of Hellenism. To be sure, some conservative Romans were hostile to the Greek influence, which they felt threatened traditional Roman values that had accounted for Roman greatness. Cato the Censor (234–149 B.C.), and other Roman moralists, denounced Socrates for undermining respect for Athenian law and warned that Greek philosophy might lure Roman youth into similar subversive behavior. Moreover, said these moralists, Greek philosophy, with its endless discussions of abstract themes, contrasted with the virtue most cherished by Romans—*gravitas,* or seriousness, which enabled Romans to conduct public affairs effectively. Philosophy seemed designed for a life of leisure and inaction whereas a virtuous Roman was actively involved in practical civic matters. But the tide of Hellenism could not be stemmed.

Plautus (c. 254–184 B.C.), Rome's greatest playwright, adopted features of fourth- and third-century Greek comedy. His plays had Greek characters and took place in Greek settings; the actors wore the Greek style of dress. His characters resembled those found in Menander's New Comedy: a cunning slave, a lovesick youth, a foolish old man, a braggart soldier. The plots often consisted of a struggle between two antagonists over a woman or money, or both. The plays usually had the ending desired by the audience: the "good guy" won and the "bad guy" received a fitting punishment. The pains of love were a common theme:

> *Not the throes of all mankind*
> *Equal my distracted mind.*
> *I strain and I toss*
> *On a passionate cross;*
> *Love's goad makes me reel,*
> *I whirl on Love's wheel,*
> *In a swoon of despair*
> *Hurried here, hurried there—*
> *Torn asunder, I am blind*
> *With a cloud upon my mind.*[6]

Another playwright, Terence (c. 185–159 B.C.), was originally from North Africa and was brought to Rome as a slave. His owner, a Roman senator, provided the talented youth with an education and freed him. Like Plautus, Terence was influenced by Menander, the fourth-century Athenian comic playwright. Terence's Latin style, graceful and polished, was technically superior to that of Plautus. But Terence's humor, restrained and refined, lacked the boisterousness of Plautus, which appealed to the Roman audience. For this reason, Terence's plays were less popular. Terence demonstrated more humaneness than

Plautus, a quality that can be seen in his attitude toward child rearing:

> *I give—I overlook; I do not judge it necessary to exert my authority in everything. . . . I think it better to restrain children through a sense of shame and liberal treatment than through fear. . . . This is the duty of a parent to accustom a son to do what is right rather of his own choice, than through fear of another.*[7]

Catullus (c. 84–c. 54 B.C.) is generally regarded as one of the greatest lyric poets in world literature. He was a native of northern Italy whose father had provided him with a gentleman's education. In his early twenties, Catullus came to Rome and fell in love with Clodia; she was the wife of the governor of Cisalpine Gaul, who was away at the time. For the older Clodia, Catullus was a refreshing diversion from her many other lovers. Tormented by Clodia's numerous affairs, Catullus struggled to break away from passion's grip:

> *I look no more for her to be my lover*
> *As I love her. That thing could never be.*
> *Nor pray I for her purity—that's over.*
> *Only this much I pray, that I be free.*
> *Free from insane desire myself, and guarded*
> *In peace at last. O heaven, grant that yet*
> *The faith by which I've lived may be*
> *rewarded.*
> *Let me forget.*[8]

Lucretius (c. 96–c. 55 B.C.), the leading Roman Epicurean philosopher, was influenced by the civil war fostered by two generals, Marius and Sulla, which is discussed later in this chapter. Distraught by the seemingly endless strife, Lucretius yearned for philosophical tranquillity. Like Epicurus, he believed that religion prompted people to perform evil deeds and caused them to experience terrible anxiety about death and eternal punishment. In his work, *On the Nature of Things,* Lucretius expressed his appreciation of Epicurus. Like his mentor, Lucretius denounced superstition and religion for fostering psychological distress and advanced a materialistic conception of nature, one that left no room for the activity of gods—mechanical laws, not the gods, governed all physical happenings. To dispel the fear of punishment after death, Lucretius marshaled arguments to prove that the soul perishes with the body. He proposed that the simple life, devoid of political involvement and excessive passion, was the highest good and the path that would lead from emotional turmoil to peace of mind. Epicurus' hostility to traditional religion, disparagement of politics and public service, and rejection of the goals of power and glory ran counter to the accepted Roman ideal of virtue. On the other hand, his glorification of the quiet life amid a community of friends and his advice on how to deal with life's misfortunes with serenity had great appeal to first-century Romans like Lucretius, who were disgusted with civil strife.

Rome's finest orator, as well as a leading statesman, Cicero (106–43 B.C.) was an unsurpassed Latin stylist and a student of Greek philosophy. His letters, more than eight hundred of which have survived, provide modern historians with valuable insights into the politics of the late Republic. His Senate speeches have been models of refined rhetoric for all students of the Latin language. Cicero's discussion of such topics as republicanism, citizenship, friendship, virtue, duty, and justice had an enduring influence on Western moral and political thought. Dedicated to republicanism and public-spiritedness, Cicero sought to prevent one-man rule and in his writings exhorted fellow Romans to serve their city.

Cicero was drawn to Stoicism, the most influential philosophy in Rome. Stoicism's stress on virtuous conduct and performance of duty coincided with Roman ideals, and its doctrine of natural law that applies to all nations harmonized with the requirements of a world empire. Cicero admired the Stoic goal of the self-sufficient sage who sought to accord his life with standards of virtue inherent in nature. Natural law commands people to do what is right and deters them from doing what is wrong, and our gift of reason enables us to abide by its commands. Thus, knowledge and virtue are closely linked. Cicero adopted the Stoic belief that the law of the state should conform with the rational and moral norms embodied in natural law, for adherence to such rationally formulated law creates a moral bond among citizens.

He also shared the Stoic view that because natural law applies to all, we are all citizens of a single commonwealth and belong to a society of humanity. As he expressed it,

> *there is no difference in kind between man and man; for Reason, which alone raises us above the level of the beasts and enables us to draw inferences, to prove and disprove, to discuss and solve problems, and to come to conclusions, is certainly common to us all, and though varying in what it learns, at least in the capacity to learn it is invariable. . . . In fact, there is no human being of any race who, if he finds a guide, cannot attain virtue.*[9]

In the eighteenth century, the Founding Fathers of the United States praised Cicero's natural law philosophy; his condemnation of tyranny; and his advocacy of liberty, republicanism, and constitutional government.

Collapse of the Republic

In 146 B.C., Roman might spanned the Mediterranean world. After that year, the principal concerns of the Republic were no longer foreign invasions but adjusting city-state institutions to the demands of empire and overcoming critical social and political problems at home. The Republic was unequal to either challenge. Instead of developing a professional civil service to administer the conquered lands, Roman leaders attempted to govern an empire with city-state institutions that had evolved for a different purpose. The established Roman administration proved unable to govern the Mediterranean world. In addition, Rome's ruling elites showed little concern for the welfare of their subjects, and provincial rule worsened as governors, tax collectors, and soldiers shamelessly exploited the provincials.

During Rome's march to empire, all its classes had demonstrated a magnificent civic spirit in fighting foreign wars. With Carthage and Macedonia no longer threatening Rome, this cooperation deteriorated, as Cato the Elder (234–149 B.C.) had forewarned: "What was to become of Rome, when she should no longer have any state to fear?"[10] Internal dissension tore Rome apart as the drive for domination formerly directed against foreign enemies turned inward against fellow Romans. Civil war replaced foreign war.

The Romans had prevailed over their opponents partly because of their traditional virtues: resoluteness, simplicity of manners, and willingness to sacrifice personal interests for the good of Rome. But the riches flowing into Rome from the plundered provinces caused these virtues to decay, and rivalry for status and a frenzied pursuit of wealth overrode civic patriotism. This "perverted greed" and "lack of principle," said the poet Horace (65–8 B.C.), has caused "impious slaughter, . . . intestine [domestic] fury, . . . and lawless licence."[11] And the masses, landless and afflicted with poverty and idleness, withdrew their allegiance from the state.

In this time of agony, both great and self-seeking individuals emerged. Some struggled to restore the social harmony and political unity that had prevailed in the period of expansion. Others, political adventurers, attacked the authority of the Senate to gain personal power. The Senate, which had previously exercised leadership creatively and responsibly, degenerated into a self-serving oligarchy that resisted reform and fought to preserve its power and privilege.

Neither the Senate nor its opponents could rejuvenate the Republic. Eventually it collapsed, a victim of class tensions, poor leadership, power-hungry demagogues, and civil war. Underlying all these conditions was the breakdown of social harmony and the deterioration of civic patriotism. The Republic had conquered an empire only to see the character of its citizens decay. In a high moral tone, the historian Sallust (c. 86–34 B.C.) condemned the breakdown of republican values:

> *Growing love of money, and the lust for power which followed it, engendered every kind of evil. Avarice destroyed honor, integrity, and every other virtue, and instead taught men to be proud and cruel, to neglect religion, and to hold nothing too sacred to sell. Ambition tempted many to be false. . . . At first these vices grew slowly and sometimes met with punishments; later on, when the disease had spread like a plague, Rome changed: her government, once so just and admirable, became harsh and unendurable.*[12]

ROMAN FORUM. In the central part of a city the Romans set aside a large rectangular space that served first as a marketplace and then as as political center. The Forum in Rome was surrounded by prominent public buildings including the *curia,* the place where the Senate met. (*Alex Segre/Alamy Images.*)

Crisis in Agriculture

The downhill slide of the Republic began with an agricultural crisis. During the long war with Hannibal in Italy, each side had tried to deprive the other of food supplies; in the process, they ruined farmland, destroyed farmhouses and farm equipment, and slaughtered animals. With many Roman soldier-farmers serving in the army for long stretches of time, fields lay neglected. Returning veterans with small holdings lacked the money to restore their land. They were forced to sell their farms to wealthy landowners at low prices.

Another factor that helped to squeeze out the owners of small farms was the importation of hundreds of thousands of slaves to work on large plantations called **latifundia.** This massive use of slaves was unprecedented in Roman history. Farmers who had formerly increased their meager incomes by working for wages on neighboring large estates were no longer needed. Sinking ever deeper into poverty and debt, farmers gave up their lands and went to Rome, seeking work. The dispossessed peasantry found little to do in Rome, where there was not enough industry to provide them with employment and where much of the work was done by slaves. Congregated in rundown, crime-ridden slums, and chronically unemployed, the urban poor faced a daily struggle for survival. The once sturdy and independent Roman farmer, who had done all that his country had asked of him, was becoming part of a vast urban underclass—destitute, embittered, and alienated. The uprooting of a formerly self-reliant peasantry was Hannibal's posthumous revenge on Rome; severing the civic bond, it would prove even more deadly than Cannae.

The Gracchan Revolution

In 133 B.C., Tiberius Gracchus (163–133 B.C.), who came from one of Rome's most honored families, was elected tribune. Distressed by the injustice done to the peasantry and recognizing that the Roman army depended on the loyalty of small landowners, Tiberius made himself the spokesman for land reform. He proposed a simple and moderate solution for the problem of the landless peasants: implementing an old law barring any Roman from using more than 312 acres of the state-owned land obtained in the process of uniting Italy. For many years, the upper class had ignored this law, occupying vast tracts of public land. By reenacting the law, Tiberius hoped to free land for distribution to landless citizens.

Rome's leading families viewed Tiberius as a revolutionary threatening their property and political authority. They thought him a dangerous democrat who would undermine the Senate, the seat of aristocratic power, in favor of the Assembly, which represented the commoners. When Tiberius sought reelection as a tribune, a violation of constitutional tradition, the senators were convinced that he was a rabble-rouser who aimed to destroy the republican constitution and become a one-man ruler. To preserve the status quo, with wealth and power concentrated in the hands of a few hundred families, senatorial extremists killed Tiberius and some three hundred of his followers, dumping their bodies into the Tiber.

The cause of land reform was next taken up by Gaius Gracchus (153–121 B.C.), a younger brother of Tiberius. An emotional and gifted speaker, Gaius won the support of the city poor and was elected tribune in 123 B.C. A more astute politician than his brother, Gaius increased his following by favoring the Equites, the new class of plebeian businessmen, and by promising full citizenship to all Italians. He aided the poor by reintroducing his brother's plan for land distribution and by enabling them to buy grain from the state at less than half the market price. But like his brother, Gaius aroused the anger of the senatorial class. A brief civil war raged in Rome, during which Gaius Gracchus (who may have committed suicide) and three thousand of his followers perished.

By killing the Gracchi, the Senate had substituted violence for reason and made murder a means of coping with troublesome opposition. Soon the club and the dagger became common weapons in Roman politics, hurling Rome into an era of political violence that ended with the destruction of the Republic. Though the Senate considered itself the guardian of republican liberty, in reality it was expressing the determination of a few hundred families to retain their control over the state. This is a classic example of a once-creative minority clinging tenaciously to power long after it has ceased to govern effectively or to inspire allegiance. The Senate, which had led Rome to world dominance, became a self-seeking, unimaginative, entrenched oligarchy that was dragging the Republic and the Mediterranean world into disaster.

Rome in the first century B.C. was very different from the Rome that had defeated Hannibal. Entranced by luxuries flowing into Rome from its eastern conquests and determined to retain oligarchic rule, the senatorial families neglected their responsibility to the state. Many upper-class Romans, burning to achieve the dignity that would mark them as great men, tried to climb onto the crowded stage of Roman politics, but the best roles were already reserved for members of the senatorial families. With so few opportunities, aspirants to political power stopped at nothing.

Roman politics in the century after the Gracchi was bedeviled by intrigues, rivalries, personal ambition, and violence. Political adventurers exploited the issue of cheap grain and free land in order to benefit their careers. Whereas the Gracchi were sincere reformers, these later champions of social reform were unscrupulous demagogues who cleverly charmed and manipulated the city poor with bread and circuses: low-cost food and free admission to games. These demagogues aspired to the tribunate of the plebes, an office possessing powers formidable enough to challenge the Senate and not too difficult to obtain since ten tribunes were elected each year. By riding a wave of popular enthusiasm, these political adventurers hoped to sweep aside the Senate and

Profile

Cleopatra

Cleopatra (69–30 B.C.), the Greek queen of Egypt, belonged to the Ptolemaic family, the Macedonian Greeks who ruled Egypt during the Hellenistic Age. Cleopatra spoke Greek, received a Greek education, and viewed herself as Greek, but in contrast to her Ptolemaic predecessors, she also learned to speak the Egyptian tongue. Aspiring to revive Ptolemaic power, which had once extended into Palestine and Lebanon, she had the political good sense to realize that this could not be accomplished by antagonizing Rome, which dominated the Mediterranean world.

Cleopatra became Julius Caesar's mistress when the Roman leader stopped at Alexandria. In 47 B.C., she bore a son, declaring that Caesar was the father, and in the next year she followed Caesar to Rome. Three years after Caesar's assassination, she became Mark Antony's lover and bore him twins. She worked closely with Antony, who competed with Octavian for control of the Roman world. After their defeat

Antikenmuseum Berlin, Staatliche Museum, Preussischer Kulturbesitz.

concentrate power in their own hands. The poor, denied land and employment, demoralized, alienated, and lulled into political ignorance by decades of idleness, food handouts, and free entertainment, were ready to back whomever made the most glittering promises. The Senate behaved like a decadent oligarchy, and the Tribal Assembly, which had become the voice of the urban mob, demonstrated a weakness for demagogues, an openness to bribery, and an abundance of deceit and incompetence. The Roman Republic had passed the peak of its greatness.

Rival Generals

Marius (157–86 B.C.), who became consul in 107 B.C., adopted a military policy that eventually contributed to the wrecking of the Republic. Until about 100 B.C., soldiers served essentially at their own expense, paying for their arms, armor, and food. This meant that only men of some substance could serve. Short of troops for a campaign in Numidia in North Africa, Marius disposed of the traditional property requirement for entrance into the army and filled his legions with volunteers from the urban poor, a dangerous precedent. These new soldiers, disillusioned with Rome, served only because Marius held out the promise of pay, loot, and land grants after discharge. In effect, they were Marius's clients. Their loyalty was not to Rome but to Marius, and they remained loyal to their commander only as long as he fulfilled his promises.

Marius set an example that other ambitious commanders followed. They saw that a general

in the naval battle of Actium in 31 B.C., Antony and Cleopatra escaped to Egypt, where Octavian pursued them. When Antony's forces either surrendered to Octavian without a fight or fled, Cleopatra barricaded herself inside her mausoleum. Thinking that she had killed herself, Antony plunged a sword into his body. A messenger told the dying Antony that Cleopatra was still alive and wished to see him. Slaves carried him to her. Since the mausoleum's doors were sealed, he had to be hoisted with great difficulty to an opening in the wall by Cleopatra and her female servants. Plutarch, the ancient biographer, described the scene:

> *Those that were present say that nothing was ever more sad than this spectacle, to see Antony, covered all over with blood and just expiring, thus drawn up, still holding up his hands to her, and lifting up his body with the little force he had left. . . . When she had got him up, she laid him on the bed, tearing all her clothes, which she spread upon him; and beating her breast with her hands, lacerating herself, and disfiguring her own face with the blood from his wounds, she called him her lord, her husband, her emperor.**

Antony died shortly afterward. Captured by the Romans, Cleopatra feared that Octavian would parade her in a victory celebration at Rome. To avoid such a humiliation, the proud Cleopatra poisoned herself, ending the Ptolemaic dynasty in Egypt. In a last letter, she requested to be buried beside Antony.

Cleopatra's life and death have intrigued historians; writers, including Shakespeare; and Hollywood producers. Her true character remains elusive. She had sufficient allure to attract both Caesar and Antony and sufficient ruthlessness to murder her younger brother, and coruler, in order to make her son coruler. No doubt her determination and ambition made her an equal partner with Antony in their political quest.

*Plutarch, *The Lives of Noble Grecians and Romans,* trans. John Dryden, rev. A. H. Clough (New York: The Modern Library, n.d.), p. 1148.

could use his army to advance his political career, that by retaining the confidence of his soldiers he could cow the Senate and dictate Roman policy. The army, no longer an instrument of government, became a private possession of generals. Seeing its authority undermined by generals appointed by the Assembly, the Senate was forced to seek army commanders who would champion the cause of senatorial rule. In time, Rome would be engulfed in civil wars as rival generals used their troops to strengthen their political affiliations and to further their own ambitions.

Meanwhile, the Senate continued to deal ineffectively with Rome's problems. When Rome's Italian allies pressed for citizenship, the Senate refused to make concessions. The Senate's shortsightedness plunged Italy into a terrible war known as the Social War. As it ravaged the peninsula, the Romans reversed their policy and conferred citizenship on the Italians. The unnecessary and ruinous rebellion petered out.

While Rome was fighting its Italian allies, Mithridates, king of Pontus in northern Asia Minor, invaded the Roman province of Asia. In 88 B.C., he incited the local population to massacre eighty thousand Italian residents of the province. Mithridates and his forces crossed into Greece and occupied Athens and other cities. Faced with this crisis, the Senate entrusted command to Sulla (138–78 B.C.), who had distinguished himself in the Social War. But supporters of Marius, through intrigue and violence, had the order rescinded and the command given to Marius.

Sulla refused to accept his loss of command and, with his loyal troops, proceeded to the capital. This was a fateful moment in Roman history:

the first march on Rome, the first prolonged civil war, and the first time a commander and his troops defied the government. Sulla won the first round. But when Sulla left Rome to fight Mithridates in Greece, Marius and his troops retook the city and, in a frenzy, lashed out at Sulla's supporters. The killing lasted for five days and nights.

Marius died shortly afterward. Sulla, on his return, quickly subdued Marius's supporters and became dictator of Rome. He instituted a terror that far surpassed Marius's violence. Without legal sanction and with cold-blooded cruelty, Sulla marked his opponents for death; the state seized their property and declared their children and grandchildren ineligible for public office.

Sulla resolved to use his absolute power to revive the Senate's rule and make it permanent. He believed that only rule by an aristocratic oligarchy could protect Rome from future military adventurers and assure domestic peace. Therefore, he restored the Senate's right to veto acts of the Assembly, limited the power of the tribunes and the Assembly, and, to prevent any march on Rome, reduced the military authority of provincial governors. To make the Senate less oligarchic, he increased its membership to six hundred. Having put through these reforms, Sulla retired.

Bust of Caesar. Julius Caesar tried to rescue a dying Roman world by imposing strong rule. He paved the way for the transition from republican to imperial rule. (*Vatican Museum.*)

Julius Caesar

The Senate failed to wield its restored authority effectively. The Republic was still menaced by military commanders who used their troops for their own political advantage, and underlying problems remained unsolved. In 60 B.C., a triumvirate, a ruling group of three, consisting of Julius Caesar (c. 100–44 B.C.), a politician; Pompey, a general; and Crassus, a wealthy banker; conspired to take over Rome. The ablest of the three was Caesar.

Recognizing the importance of a military command as a prerequisite for political prominence, Caesar gained command of the legions in Gaul in 59 B.C. The following year he began the conquest of the part of Gaul outside of Roman control, bringing the future France into the orbit of Greco-Roman civilization. The campaign was brilliantly described in his *Commentaries*. The successful Gallic campaigns and the invasion of Britain revealed Caesar's exceptional talent for generalship: he acted decisively, moved troops rapidly, and had excellent rapport with his men. Indeed, Caesar's victories alarmed the Senate, which feared that Caesar would use his devoted troops and soaring reputation to seize control of the state.

Meanwhile, the triumvirate had fallen apart. In 53 B.C., Crassus had perished with his army in a disastrous campaign against the Parthians in the East. The bonds between Pompey and Caesar were weak, consisting essentially of Pompey's marriage to Caesar's daughter Julia. After her death in 54 B.C., Pompey and Caesar grew apart. Pompey, who was jealous of Caesar's success and eager to expand his own power, drew closer to the Senate. Supported by Pompey, the Senate ordered Caesar to relinquish his command. Caesar realized that without his troops he would be defenseless; he decided instead to march on Rome. After Caesar crossed the Rubicon River into Italy in 49 B.C., civil war again ravaged the Republic. Pompey proved no match for so talented a general; the Senate acknowledged Caesar's victory and appointed him to be dictator, a legal office, for ten years.

Caesar realized that republican institutions no longer operated effectively and that only strong and enlightened leadership could permanently end the civil warfare destroying Rome. His reforms were designed to create order out of chaos. Caesar responded to the grievances of the provincial subjects by lowering taxes, making the governors responsible to him, restraining Roman businessmen from ruthlessly draining the provinces' wealth, and generously extending citizenship. To aid the poor in Rome, he began a public works program, which provided employment and beautified the city. He also relocated more than a hundred thousand veterans and members of Rome's lower class to the provinces, where he gave them land. To improve administration, he reorganized town governments in Italy, reformed the courts, and planned to codify the law. He attempted to conciliate the senatorial class by treating former enemies with moderation and generosity.

In February 44 B.C., Rome's ruling class—jealous of Caesar's success and power and afraid of his ambition—became thoroughly alarmed when his temporary dictatorship was converted into a lifelong office. The aristocracy saw this event as the end of senatorial government and their rule, which they equated with liberty, and as the beginning of a Hellenistic type of monarchy. On March 15 of that year, a group of aristocrats, regarding themselves as defenders of republican traditions more than four and a half centuries old, assassinated Caesar. The group included the general and orator Marcus Junius Brutus. Cicero expressed the feeling that motivated the conspirators:

> *Our tyrant deserves his death, [for his] was the blackest crime of all. [Caesar was] a man who was ambitious to be king of the Roman people and master of the whole world. . . . The man who maintains that such an ambition is morally right is a madman, for he justifies the destruction of law and liberty.*[13]

The Republic's Last Years

The assassination of Julius Caesar did not restore republican liberty but plunged Rome into renewed civil war. Thousands more died in battle or were killed in the proscriptions—lists of Roman citizens declared by their political enemies to be outlaws. Those proscribed had their property confiscated and could be executed. Two of Caesar's trusted lieutenants, Mark Antony and Lepidus, joined with Octavian, Caesar's adopted son, and defeated the armies of Brutus and Cassius, two conspirators in the plot against Caesar. After Lepidus was forced into political obscurity, Antony and Octavian fought each other, with control of Rome as the prize. In 31 B.C., at the naval battle of Actium in western Greece, Octavian crushed the forces of Antony and his wife, Egypt's Queen Cleopatra (who had earlier borne Julius Caesar's son). Octavian emerged as master of Rome and four years later became, in effect, the first Roman emperor. The Roman Republic, whose death throes had lasted for decades and kept the Mediterranean world in turmoil, had finally perished.

The Roman Republic, which had amassed power to a degree hitherto unknown in the ancient world, was wrecked not by foreign invasion but by internal weaknesses: the personal ambitions of power seekers; the degeneration of senatorial leadership and the willingness of politicians to use violence; the formation of private armies, in which soldiers gave their loyalty to their commander rather than to Rome; the transformation of a self-reliant peasantry into an impoverished and demoralized city rabble; and the deterioration of the ancient virtues that had been the source of the state's vitality. Before 146

B.C., the threat posed by foreign enemies, particularly Carthage, had forced Romans to work together for the benefit of the state, and the equilibrium achieved during the patrician-plebeian struggle was maintained. This social cohesion broke down when foreign danger diminished. In the ensuing century of turmoil, the apparatus of city-state government failed to function effectively.

Thus, the high point of Roman rule was not achieved under the Republic. The city-state constitution of the Republic was too limited to govern an immense empire. Rome first had to surpass the narrow framework of city-state government before it could unite the Mediterranean world in peace and law. The genius of Augustus (Octavian), the first emperor, made this development possible.

❖ ❖ ❖

Online Study Center **ACE the Test**

Notes

1. Cicero, *De Republica*, trans. Clinton Walker Keyes (Cambridge, Mass.: Harvard University Press, Loeb Classical Library, 1994), p. 79.
2. Ibid., p. 81.
3. E. Badian, *Roman Imperialism in the Late Republic* (Ithaca, N.Y.: Cornell University Press, 1971), p. 87.
4. Quoted in Alan Wardman, *Rome's Debt to Greece* (New York: St. Martin's Press, 1976), p. 62.
5. Cicero, *De Oratore*, trans. E. W. Sutton (Cambridge, Mass.: Harvard University Press, Loeb Classical Library, 1967), p. 14.
6. Quoted in J. Wright Duff, *A Literary History of Rome* (New York: Barnes & Noble, 1960), pp. 136–137.
7. Terence, *The Brothers,* trans. H. T. Riley (London: Henry G. Bohn, 1853), pp. 202–203.
8. Catullus, quoted in E. A. Havelock, *The Lyric Genius of Catullus* (New York: Russell and Russell, 1929), p. 63.
9. Cicero, *De Legibus,* trans. C. W. Keyes (Cambridge, Mass.: Harvard University Press, Loeb Classical Library, 1928), pp. 329–330.
10. Quoted in Eli Sagan, *The Honey and the Hemlock* (New York: Basic Books, 1991), p. 25.
11. Horace, *The Odes and Epodes*, trans. C. E. Bennett (Cambridge, Mass.: Harvard University Press, 1988), ode 24, pp. 255–256.
12. Sallust, *The Conspiracy of Catiline,* trans. S. A. Handford (Baltimore: Penguin Books, 1963), pp. 181–182.
13. Cicero, *De Officiis,* trans. Walter Miller (Cambridge, Mass.: Harvard University Press, Loeb Classical Library, 1913), p. 357.

Suggested Reading

Boren, H. C., *Roman Society* (1977). A social, economic, and cultural history of the Republic and the Empire, written with the student in mind.

Christ, Karl, *The Romans* (1984). A good survey.

Crawford, M., *The Roman Republic* (1982). A reliable survey, with many quotations from original sources.

Dupont, Florence, *Daily Life in Ancient Rome* (1989). Everyday private and public lives of Roman citizens.

Errington, R. M., *The Dawn of Empire: Rome's Rise to World Power* (1972). A study of Rome, the reluctant imperialist.

Grant, Michael, *History of Rome* (1978). A synthesis of Roman history by a leading classical scholar; valuable in regard to both the Republic and the Empire.

Ogilvie, R. M., *Roman Literature and Society* (1980). An introductory survey of Latin literature.

Chapter 7

The Roman Empire: A World-State

The Roman Colosseum. (Art Resource, NY.)

- **Augustus and the Foundations of the Roman Empire**
- **The Pax Romana**
- **Signs of Trouble**
- **The Decline of Rome**
- **The Roman Legacy**

Focus Questions

1. What is the historical significance of Augustus?
2. Why is the Pax Romana regarded as one of the finest periods in world history? What continuity is there between the Pax Romana and the Hellenistic Age?
3. How did Roman law evolve? How did it incorporate Stoic principles?
4. Why is the third century regarded as an age of crisis?
5. What are the reasons for the decline of the Roman Empire?
6. What is Rome's legacy to Western civilization?

Online Study Center

This icon will direct you to interactive map and primary source activities on the website http://college.hmco.com/pic/perrywc8e.

Rome's republican institutions, designed for a city-state, proved incapable of coping with the problems created by the conquest of a world empire. Invincible against foreign enemies, the Republic collapsed from within. But after Octavian's brilliant statesmanship brought order out of chaos, Rome entered its golden age under the rule of emperors. For more than two hundred years, from 27 B.C. to A.D. 180, the Mediterranean world enjoyed unparalleled peace and stability. The Roman world-state, erected on a Hellenic cultural foundation and cemented with empirewide civil service, laws, and citizenship, gave practical expression to Stoic cosmopolitanism and universalism. Yet even this impressive monument had structural defects, and in the third century A.D., the Empire was wracked by crises from which it never fully recovered. In the fifth century, German tribesmen overran the western half of the Empire, which had by then become a shadow of its former self.

During its time of trouble, Rome also experienced an intellectual crisis. Forsaking the rational and secular values of classical humanism, many Romans sought spiritual comfort in Near Eastern religions. One of these religions, Christianity, won out over its competitors and was made the official religion of the Empire. With the triumph of Christianity in the Late Roman Empire, Western civilization took a new direction. Christianity would become the principal shaper of the European civilization that emerged from the ruins of Rome.

Augustus and the Foundations of the Roman Empire

After Octavian's forces defeated those of Antony and Cleopatra at the battle of Actium in 31 B.C., no opponents could stand up to him. The century of civil war, political murder, corruption, and mismanagement had exhausted the Mediterranean world, which longed for order. Like Caesar before him, Octavian recognized that only a strong monarchy could rescue Rome from civil war and anarchy. But learning from Caesar's assassination, he also knew that republican ideals were far from dead. To exercise autocratic power openly, like a Hellenistic monarch, would have

Chronology 7.1 ❖ The Roman Empire

27 B.C.	Senate grants Octavian the title Augustus, and he becomes, in effect, the first Roman emperor; start of the principate and the Pax Romana
A.D. 14	Death of Augustus; Tiberius gains the throne
66–70	Jewish revolt: Romans capture Jerusalem and destroy the second temple
79	Eruption of Mount Vesuvius and destruction of Pompeii and Herculaneum
132–135	Hadrian crushes another Hebrew revolt
180	Marcus Aurelius dies: end of the Pax Romana
212	Roman citizenship is granted to virtually all free inhabitants of Roman provinces
235–285	Military anarchy; Germanic incursions
285–305	Diocletian tries to deal with the crisis by creating a regimented state
378	Battle of Adrianople: Visigoths defeat the Roman legions
406	Imperial borders collapse, and Germanic tribes move into the Empire
410	Rome is plundered by Visigoths
455	Rome is sacked by Vandals
476	End of the Roman Empire in the West

aroused the hostility of the Roman ruling class, whose assistance and good will Octavian desired.

Octavian demonstrated his political genius by reconciling his military monarchy with republican institutions: he held absolute power without abruptly breaking with a republican past. Magistrates were still elected and assemblies still met; the Senate administered certain provinces, retained its treasury, and was invited to advise Octavian. With some truth, Octavian could claim that he ruled in partnership with the Senate. By maintaining the facade of the Republic, Octavian camouflaged his absolute power and contained senatorial opposition, already weakened by the deaths of leading nobles in battle or in the purges that Octavian had instituted against his enemies. Moreover, Octavian's control over the armed forces made resistance futile, and the terrible violence that followed Caesar's assassination made senators amenable to change.

In 27 B.C., Octavian shrewdly offered to surrender his power, knowing that the Senate, purged of opposition, would demand that he continue to lead the state. By this act, Octavian could claim to be a legitimate constitutional ruler leading a government of law, not one of lawless despotism so hateful to the Roman mentality. In keeping with his policy of maintaining the appearance of traditional republican government, Octavian refused to be called king or even, like Caesar, dictator; instead, he cleverly disguised his autocratic rule by taking the inoffensive title *princeps* (first citizen). The Senate also honored Octavian by conferring on him the semireligious and revered name of *Augustus.* (The rule of Augustus and his successors is referred to as the *principate.*)

The reign of Augustus signified the end of the Roman Republic and the beginning of the Roman Empire—the termination of senatorial rule and aristocratic politics and the emergence of one-man rule. The old Roman aristocracy, decimated by war and the proscriptions employed by Antony, Lepidus, and Octavian, had to adjust to a political situation in which they no longer predominated. As the historian Tacitus recognized, Augustus accomplished a profound revolution in Roman political life: "The country had been transformed, and there was nothing left of the

THE PANTHEON, C. A.D. 125. The Pantheon, the most complete surviving building of Roman antiquity, was built by Emperor Hadrian in the second century A.D. In the temple, Greek forms of ornamentation are combined with Roman building techniques. The vast hemispherical dome was constructed by pouring concrete into great wooden forms; then the interior was faced with marble. In contrast to a Greek temple, where the exterior is paramount, the Roman temple emphasizes interior space. (*Anderson/Art Resource.*)

fine old Roman character. Political equality was a thing of the past; all eyes watched for imperial commands."[1] Under Augustus, who ruled from 27 B.C. to A.D. 14, the power of the ruler was disguised; in ensuing generations, however, emperors would wield absolute power openly. As Rome became more autocratic and centralized, it took on the appearance of an oriental monarchy.

MAP 7.1 THE ROMAN EMPIRE UNDER AUGUSTUS AND HADRIAN ▶ During the Pax Romana, the Roman Empire expanded beyond the Rhine-Danube Rivers, the imperial boundary during the reign of Augustus.

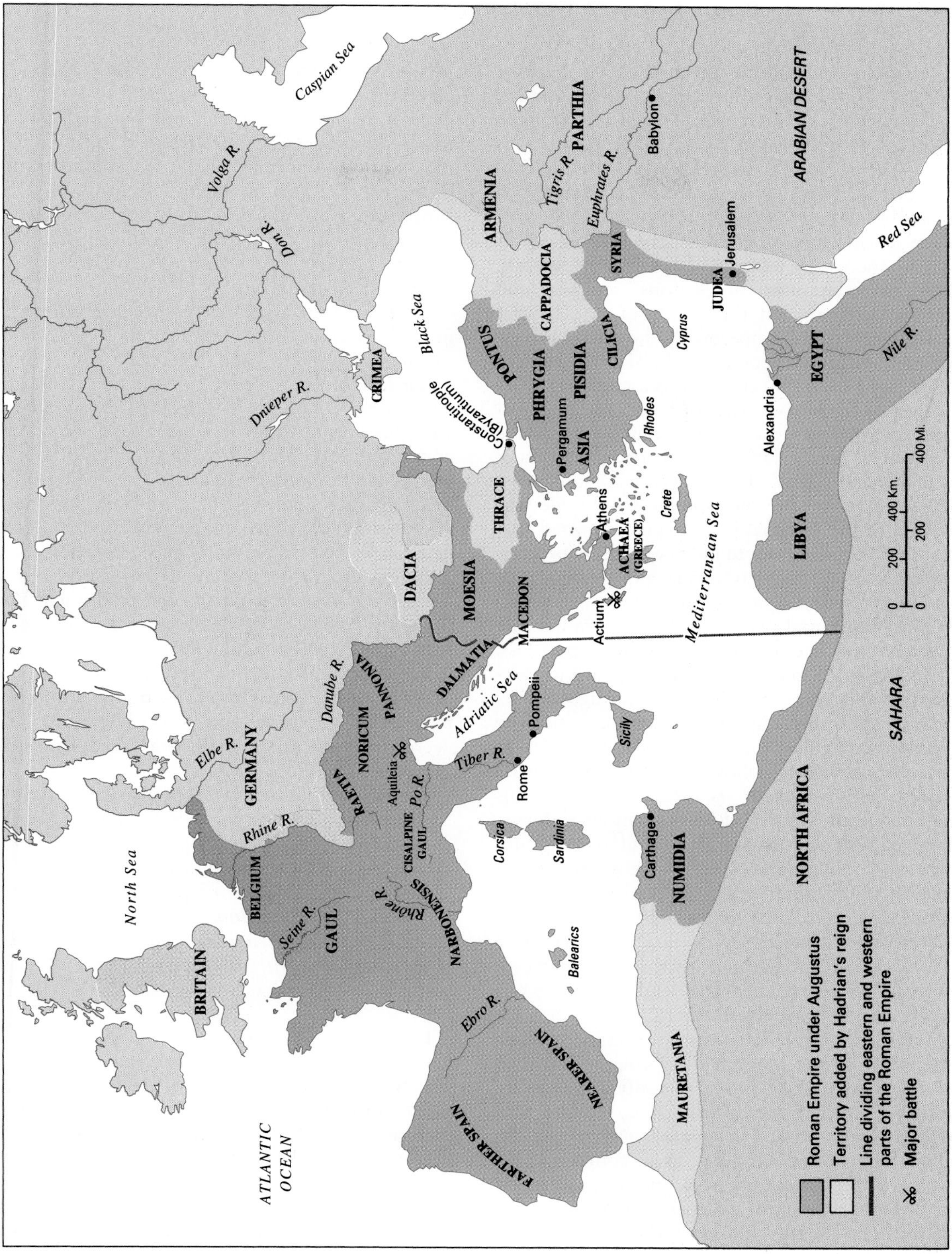
ATLANTIC OCEAN
North Sea
BRITAIN
BELGIUM
GAUL
Seine R.
Rhône R.
NARBONENSIS
CISALPINE GAUL
Rhine R.
GERMANY
Elbe R.
RAETIA
NORICUM
Aquileia
Po R.
Danube R.
PANNONIA
DALMATIA
Adriatic Sea
Tiber R.
Rome
Pompeii
Corsica
Sardinia
Sicily
Balearics
Ebro R.
NEARER SPAIN
FARTHER SPAIN
MAURETANIA
NUMIDIA
Carthage
NORTH AFRICA
SAHARA
DACIA
MOESIA
MACEDON
THRACE
Actium
ACHAEA (GREECE)
Athens
Crete
Mediterranean Sea
LIBYA
Dnieper R.
CRIMEA
Black Sea
Constantinople (Byzantium)
Pergamum
ASIA
PHRYGIA
PONTUS
PISIDIA
CILICIA
Rhodes
Cyprus
CAPPADOCIA
ARMENIA
SYRIA
JUDEA
Jerusalem
Alexandria
EGYPT
Nile R.
Red Sea
Don R.
Volga R.
Caspian Sea
Tigris R.
Euphrates R.
PARTHIA
Babylon
ARABIAN DESERT
0 200 400 Km.
0 200 400 Mi.
Roman Empire under Augustus
Territory added by Hadrian's reign
Line dividing eastern and western parts of the Roman Empire
Major battle

Augustus introduced the practice of emperor worship. In the eastern provinces, where oriental and Hellenistic monarchs had been traditionally regarded as divine, the person of Augustus was worshiped as a god. In Italy, where the deification of leaders was alien to the republican spirit, divine honors were granted to Augustus's genius, or spirit of leadership; once deceased, Augustus and his successors were deified. The imperial cult, with its ceremonies, processions, temples, and statues, strengthened the bonds of loyalty that tied subjects to the emperor. By the third century, Italians and other peoples in the western territories viewed the living emperor as a god-king.

Despite his introduction of autocratic rule, Augustus was by no means a self-seeking tyrant, but a creative statesman. Heir to the Roman tradition of civic duty, he regarded his power as a public trust delegated to him by the Roman people. He was faithful to the classical ideal, which required that the state should promote the good life by protecting civilization from barbarism and ignorance; he sought to rescue a dying Roman world by restoring political order and reviving the moral values and civic spirit that had contributed to Rome's greatness.

To prevent a renewal of civil war and to safeguard the borders of the Empire, Augustus reformed the army. As commander in chief, he could guard against the reemergence of ambitious generals like those whose rivalries and private armies had wrecked the Republic. Augustus maintained the loyalty of his soldiers by ensuring that veterans, on discharge, would receive substantial bonuses and land in Italy or in the provinces. By organizing a professional standing army made up mostly of volunteers who generally served for twenty-five years, Augustus was assured a well-trained and loyal force capable of maintaining internal order, extending Roman territory, and securing the frontier.

For the city of Rome, Augustus had aqueducts and water mains built, which brought water to most Roman homes, and he beautified the city by restoring ancient monuments and temples and building new ones. He created a fire brigade, which reduced the danger of great conflagrations in crowded tenement districts, and he organized a police force to contain violence. He improved the distribution of free grain to the impoverished urban masses and financed the popular gladiatorial combats out of his own funds.

In Italy, Augustus had roads repaired, and he fostered public works. He arranged for Italians to play a more important role in the administration of the Empire. For the Italians' security, his army suppressed brigandage, which had proliferated in the countryside during the preceding century of agony, and he guarded the northern borders from barbarian incursions.

By ending the civil wars and their accompanying devastation and by ruling out forced requisition of supplies and extortion of money, Augustus earned the gratitude of the provincials. Also contributing to his empirewide popularity were his efforts to correct tax abuse and to end corruption through improving the quality of governors and enabling aggrieved provincials to bring charges against Roman officials. An imperial bureaucracy, which enabled talented and dedicated men to serve the state, gradually evolved. In addition, Augustus continued the sensible practice of not interfering with the traditional customs and religions of the provinces. During his forty-year reign—the longevity itself was a stabilizing factor—Rome overcame the chaos of the years of revolution. The praise bestowed on him by grateful provincials was not undeserved. One decree from the province of Asia called Augustus

> *the savior of all mankind in common whose provident care has not only fulfilled but even surpassed the hopes of all: for both land and sea are at peace, the cities are teeming with the blessings of concord, plenty, and respect for law, and the culmination and harvest of all good things bring fair hopes for the future and contentment with the present.*[2]

The Pax Romana

The brilliant statesmanship of Augustus inaugurated Rome's greatest age. For the next two hundred years, the Mediterranean world enjoyed the blessings of the **Pax Romana**, the Roman peace. The ancient world had never experienced such a long period of peace, order, efficient administration, and prosperity. Although both proficient and inept rulers succeeded Augustus, the essential features of the Pax Romana persisted.

Online Study Center **Improve Your Grade**
Interactive Map: The Economic Aspect of the Pax Romana

The Successors of Augustus

The first four emperors who succeeded Augustus were related either to him or to his third wife, Livia. They constituted the Julio-Claudian dynasty, which ruled from A.D. 14 to 68. Although their reigns were marked by conspiracies, summary executions, and assassinations, the great achievements of Augustus were preserved and strengthened. The Senate did not seek to restore republicanism and continued to assist the princeps; the imperial bureaucracy grew larger and more professional; the army, with some exceptions, remained a loyal and disciplined force.

The Julio-Claudian dynasty came to an end in A.D. 68, when the emperor Nero committed suicide. Nero had grown increasingly tyrannical and had lost the confidence of the people, the senatorial class, and the generals, who rose in revolt. In the year following his death, anarchy reigned as military leaders competed for the throne. After a bloody civil war, the execution of two emperors, and the suicide of another, Vespasian gained the principate. Vespasian's reign (A.D. 69–79) marked the beginning of the Flavian dynasty. By rotating commanding officers and stationing native troops far from their homelands, Vespasian improved discipline and discouraged mutiny. By having the great Colosseum of Rome constructed for gladiatorial contests, he earned the gratitude of the city's inhabitants. Vespasian also had nationalist uprisings put down in Gaul and Judea.

In Judea, Roman rule clashed with Jewish religious-national sentiments. Recognizing the tenaciousness with which Jews clung to their faith, the Roman leaders deliberately refrained from interfering with Hebraic religious beliefs and practices. Numerous privileges, such as exemption from emperor worship because it conflicted with the requirements of strict monotheism, were extended to Jews not only in Judea but throughout the Empire. Sometimes, however, the Romans engaged in activities that outraged the Jews. For example, Pontius Pilate, the Roman procurator in Judea from A.D. 26 to 36, at one point ordered a Roman army unit into Jerusalem with banners bearing the image of the emperor. The entire Jewish nation was aroused. To the Jews, this display of a pagan idol in their holy city was an abomination. Realizing that the Jews would die rather than permit this act of sacrilege, Pilate ordered the banners removed. Another explosive situation emerged when the emperor Caligula (A.D. 37–41) ordered that a golden statue of himself be placed in Jerusalem's temple. Again, the order was rescinded when the Jews demonstrated their readiness to resist.

Relations between the Jews of Judea and the Roman authorities deteriorated progressively in succeeding decades. Militant Jews, who rejected Roman rule as a threat to the purity of Jewish life, urged their people to take up arms. Feeling a religious obligation to reestablish an independent kingdom in their ancient homeland and unable to reconcile themselves to Roman rule, the Jews launched a full-scale war of liberation in A.D. 66. In A.D. 70, after a five-month siege had inflicted terrible punishment on the Jews, Roman armies captured Jerusalem and destroyed the temple, the central site and focus of Jewish religious life. After the conquest of Jerusalem, some fortresses, including Masada on the western side of the Dead Sea, continued to resist. The defenders of Masada withstood a Roman siege until A.D. 73; refusing to become Roman captives, they took their own lives.

Vespasian was succeeded by his sons Titus (A.D. 79–81) and Domitian (A.D. 81–96). The reign of Titus was made memorable by the eruption of Mount Vesuvius, which devastated the towns of Pompeii and Herculaneum. After Titus's brief time as emperor, his younger brother Domitian became ruler. Upon crushing a revolt led by the Roman commander in Upper Germany, a frightened Domitian executed many leading Romans. These actions led to his assassination in A.D. 96, ending the Flavian dynasty. The Flavians, however, had succeeded in preserving internal peace and in consolidating and extending the borders of the Empire.

Profile

Epictetus

Born a slave, Epictetus (c. A.D. 55–135) belonged to an official (himself a former slave) who served the emperors Nero and Domitian. Even before he was given his freedom, Epictetus received a good education from his master. In A.D. 89, Domitian, fearful that philosophers would cast doubt on the emperor's divinity, banished all philosophers from Rome and Italy. Epictetus moved to Epirus in Greece, where he attracted students. One student recorded and organized Epictetus's thoughts into eight books, four of which were lost. Epictetus presented his views in the form of maxims: admonitions from a teacher to his students to pursue the moral life. His ideas greatly influenced Marcus Aurelius, the Roman emperor and Stoic philosopher.

Like other Stoic philosophers, Epictetus was concerned with attaining peace of mind—an inner contentment that produces happiness. For Epictetus, happiness did not depend on material possessions, status, reputation, or the affection others have for us. By pursuing these externals, he said, we become subject to the people who are needed to procure them for us: "If you are absorbed in externals, you must necessarily be tossed up and down, according to the inclination of your master. Who is your master? Whosoever controls those things which you seek."*

The Granger Collection.

*Epictetus, *Discourses,* based on translation of Thomas Wentworth Higginson (Roslyn, N.Y.: Walter J. Black, Classics Club, 1944), bk. 2, chap. 2, p. 92.

The Senate selected one of its own, Nerva, to succeed the murdered Domitian. Nerva's reign (A.D. 96–98) was brief and uneventful. But he introduced a wise practice that would endure until A.D. 180: he adopted as his son and designated as his heir a man with proven ability, Trajan, the governor of Upper Germany. This adoptive system assured a succession of competent rulers.

During his rule (A.D. 98–117), Trajan eased the burden of taxation in the provinces, provided for the needs of poor children, and had public works built. With his enlarged army, he conquered Dacia (parts of Romania and Hungary), where he seized vast quantities of gold and silver. He made the territory into a Roman province, adding to the large frontier Rome had to protect. The settlement of the region by many of Trajan's veterans led to its Romanization. Trajan also waged war against Parthia (a kingdom southeast of the Caspian Sea that had once been part of the Hellenistic kingdom of Seleucia), capturing Armenia and advancing to the Persian Gulf. However, overextended lines of communication, revolts by Jews in several eastern provinces, and counterattacks by the Parthians forced his armies to return to Rome.

Trajan's successor, Hadrian (A.D. 117–138), abandoned what remained of Trajan's eastern conquests. He strengthened border defenses in

Epictetus maintained that to achieve happiness we must reduce desires, shun things that are beyond our power to control, and deliberately strive for inner dignity and moral integrity. Human beings, said Epictetus, can shield themselves from life's uncertainties and misfortunes, even slavery, by taking control of the part of themselves that belongs to no one else: their minds. Epictetus defined man as a rational being. It is reason that distinguishes man from wild beasts and cattle. He wrote:

> *Take care, then to do nothing like a wild beast; otherwise you have destroyed the man; you have not fulfilled what your nature promises. Take care too, to do nothing like cattle; for thus likewise the man is destroyed. In what do we act like cattle? When we act gluttonously, lewdly, rashly, sordidly, inconsiderately, into what are we sunk? Into cattle. What have we destroyed? The rational being. When we behave contentiously, injuriously, passionately, and violently, into what we have sunk? Into wild beasts. . . . By all these means the nature of man is destroyed.*[†]

[†]Ibid., bk. 2, chap. 9, pp. 106–107.

Britain and fought the second Hebrew revolt in Judea (A.D. 132–135). After initial successes, including the capture of Jerusalem, the Jews were again defeated by superior Roman might. The majority of Palestinian Jews were killed, sold as slaves, or forced to seek refuge in other lands. The Romans renamed the province Syria Palestina; they forbade Jews to enter Jerusalem, except once a year, and encouraged non-Jews to settle the land. Although the Jews continued to maintain a presence in Palestine, they had become a dispossessed and dispersed people.

After Hadrian came another ruler who had a long reign, Antoninus Pius (A.D. 138–161). He introduced humane and just reforms. He set limits on the right of masters to torture their slaves to obtain evidence, and he established the principle that an accused person be considered innocent until proven guilty. During the reign of Antoninus, the Empire remained peaceful and prosperous.

Marcus Aurelius (A.D. 161–180), the next emperor, was also a philosopher; his *Meditations* eloquently expressed Stoic thought. Frequent strife marked his reign. Roman forces had to fight Parthians, who had seized Armenia, a traditional bone of contention between Rome and Parthia. The Roman legions were victorious in this campaign but brought back from the East an epidemic that decimated the population of the Empire. Marcus Aurelius also had to deal with German incursions into Italy and the Balkan peninsula—incursions far more serious than any faced by previous emperors. Roman legions gradually repulsed the Germans, but the wars forced Marcus Aurelius to resort to a desperate financial measure: devaluation of the coinage.

From the accession of Nerva in A.D. 96 to the death of Marcus Aurelius in A.D. 180, the Roman Empire was ruled by the "Five Good Emperors." During this period, the Empire was at the height of its power and prosperity, and nearly all its peoples benefited. The four emperors preceding Marcus Aurelius had no living sons, so they had resorted to the adoptive system in selecting successors, which served Rome effectively. But Marcus Aurelius chose his own son, Commodus, to succeed him. With the accession of Commodus—a misfit and a megalomaniac—in A.D. 180, the Pax Romana came to an end.

The "Time of Happiness"

The Romans called the Pax Romana the "Time of Happiness." They saw it as the fulfillment of Rome's mission: the creation of a world-state that provided peace, security, ordered civilization, and the rule of law. Roman legions defended the Rhine-Danube river frontiers from incursions by German tribesmen, held the Parthians at bay in the east, and subdued the few uprisings that occurred. Nerva's adoptive system of selecting emperors provided Rome with internal stability and a succession of emperors with exceptional ability. These Roman emperors did not use military force needlessly but fought for sensible political goals; generals did not wage war recklessly but tried to

Aqueduct at Pont du Gard, Nîmes, France, 19 b.c. The discovery and use of concrete allowed the Romans to carry out a vast program of public works—roads, bridges, aqueducts, harbor facilities, and fortifications. Without such aqueducts to bring clean water from distant sources, the Roman style of urban life would have been impossible. (*Foto Marburg/Art Resource.*)

limit casualties, avoid risks, and deter conflicts by a show of force.

Constructive Rule. Roman rule was constructive. The Romans built roads—some fifty-three thousand miles of roads, from Scotland to the Euphrates—improved harbors, cleared forests, drained swamps, irrigated deserts, and cultivated undeveloped lands. The aqueducts they constructed brought fresh water for drinking and bathing to large numbers of people, and the effective sewage systems enhanced the quality of life. Goods were transported over roads made safe by Roman soldiers and across a Mediterranean Sea swept clear of pirates.

A wide variety of goods circulated throughout the Empire. From Spain came gold, silver, copper, tin, fruit, and salt; from Gaul, wool, cheese, ham, and glass products; and from Britain, iron, hides, and tin. Greece and Macedonia supplied wine, honey, and marble; and Asia Minor, textiles, olive oil, carpets, and jewels. Syria, Judea, and Arabia offered leather goods, perfume, drugs, and timber; and Egypt, grain. From Parthia, China, and India—lands beyond the eastern borders of the Empire—came silk, spices, pearls and other jewels, cotton, perfumes, and drugs. African lands south of the Sahara yielded gold, ivory, and wild animals. A stable currency, generally not subject to depreciation, contributed to the economic well-being of the Mediterranean world.

Scores of new cities sprang up, and old ones grew larger and wealthier. Although these municipalities had lost their power to wage war and had to bow to the will of the emperors, they retained considerable freedom of action in local matters. Imperial troops guarded against civil wars within the cities and prevented warfare between cities—two traditional weaknesses of city life in the ancient world. Some two thousand municipalities served as centers of Greco-Roman civilization, which spread to the farthest reaches of the Mediterranean, continuing a process initiated during the Hellenistic Age. Regions of North Africa, Gaul, Britain, and South Germany, hitherto untouched by Hellenism, were brought into the orbit of Greco-Roman civilization. Barriers between Italians and provincials broke down as Spaniards, Gauls, Africans, and other provincials rose to high positions in the army and in the imperial administration, and even became emperors. Citizenship, generously granted, was finally extended to virtually all free people by an edict of A.D. 212.

Improved Conditions for Both Slaves and Women. Conditions improved for those at the bottom of society, the slaves. At the time of Augustus, slaves may have accounted for a quarter of the population of Italy. But their numbers declined as Rome engaged in fewer wars of conquest. The freeing of slaves also became more common during the Empire. Urban slaves, who were often skilled artisans, could be induced to work more effectively if there was the hope of **manumission.** Often, nobles liberated and set up in business skilled and enterprising slaves in return for a share of the profits. Freed slaves became citizens, with most of the rights and privileges of other citizens; their children suffered no legal disabilities. (The poet Terence, the Stoic philosopher Epictetus, and the father of the poet Horace were all freed slaves.)

During the Republic, slaves had been terribly abused; they were often mutilated, thrown to wild beasts, crucified, or burned alive. Several emperors issued decrees protecting slaves from cruel masters. Claudius forbade masters to kill sick slaves; Vespasian forbade masters to sell slaves into prostitution. Domitian prohibited the castration of slaves, and Hadrian barred the execution of slaves without a judicial sentence.

BASALT BUST OF LIVIA. Octavian's third wife, Livia (58 B.C.–A.D. 29), was admired for her wisdom and dignity, and the emperor valued her counsel. (*Alinari/Art Resource, NY.*)

The status of women had been gradually improving during the Republic. In the early days of the Republic, a woman lived under the absolute authority first of her father and then of her husband. By the time of the Empire, a woman could own property and, if divorced, keep her dowry. A father could no longer force his daughter to marry against her will, although upper-class marriages were usually based on political and social considerations. Women could make business arrangements and draw up wills without the consent of their husbands. Roman women, unlike their Greek counterparts, were not secluded in their homes but could come and go as they pleased. Upper-class women of Rome had far greater opportunities for education than did those of Greece, and some formed groups that read and discussed poetry.

Supervising the household remained the principal responsibility of Roman women. The Romans regarded marriage as a sacred civic duty. Seeking to restore traditional values, Augustus issued decrees encouraging Romans to marry. Romans greatly admired the woman who loved only one man and had only one husband, but in reality promiscuity, adultery, divorce, and remarriage were quite common. A wife could obtain a divorce just as easily as her husband, but as a rule children remained with their father. Despite the frequency of divorce, husbands and wives did demonstrate genuine affection for each other. In a eulogy to his recently deceased wife, a grieving Roman noble declared:

> *Why recall your inestimable qualities, your modesty, deference [respectful obedience], affability [courteousness], your amiable disposition, your faithful attention to the household duties, your enlightened religion, your unassuming elegance, the modest simplicity and refinement of your manners? Need I speak of your attachment to your kindred, your affection for your family? . . . These qualities which I claim for you are your own, equalled or excelled by but few; for the experience of men teaches us how rare they are.*[3]

The history of the Empire, indeed Roman history in general, was filled with talented and influential women. Cornelia, the mother of Tiberius and Gaius Gracchus, influenced Roman politics through her sons. The historian Sallust said that Sempronia, the wife of a consul and the mother of Brutus, one of the assassins of Julius Caesar, was "well-educated in Greek and Latin literature. . . . She could write poetry, crack a joke, and converse at will . . . she was in fact a woman of ready wit and considerable charm."[4] Livia, the dynamic wife of Augustus, was often consulted on important government matters, and during the third century there were times when women controlled the throne.

An Orderly World Community. From Britain to the Arabian Desert, from the Danube River to the sands of the Sahara, some fifty to sixty million people with differing native languages, customs, and histories were united by Roman rule into a world community. Unlike officials of the Republic, when corruption and exploitation in the provinces were notorious, officials of the Empire felt a strong sense of responsibility to preserve the Roman peace, institute Roman justice, and spread Roman civilization.

In creating a stable and orderly political community with an expansive conception of citizenship, Rome resolved the problems posed by the limitations of the Greek city-state: civil war, intercity warfare, and a parochial attitude that divided people into Greek and non-Greek. Rome also brought to fruition an ideal of the Greek city-state—the protection and promotion of civilized life. By constructing a world community that broke down barriers between nations, by preserving and spreading Greco-Roman civilization, and by developing a rational system of law that applied to all humanity, Rome completed the trend toward universalism and cosmopolitanism that had emerged in the Hellenistic Age. The Roman world-state was the classical mind's response to the problem of community posed by the decline of the city-state in the era of Alexander the Great. Aelius Aristides, a second-century rhetorician, although Greek, proudly considered himself a Roman and glowingly extolled the Roman achievement:

> *Neither sea nor any intervening distance on land excludes one from citizenship. No distinction is made between Asia and Europe in this respect. Everything lies open to everybody; and no one fit for office or a position of trust is an alien. . . . You have made the word "Roman" apply not to a city but to a universal people. . . . You no longer classify peoples as Greek or barbarian. . . . You have redivided mankind into Romans and non-Romans. . . . Under this classification there are many in each city who are no less fellow*

Bas-Relief from Constantine's Arch. Emperor Marcus Aurelius dispenses aid to needy citizens. (*Alinari/Art Resource, NY.*)

> *citizens of yours than those of their own stock, though some of them have never seen this city.*[5]

Roman Culture and Law During the Pax Romana

During the late Roman Republic, Rome had creatively assimilated the Greek achievement (see Chapter 6) and transmitted it to others who had little or no contact with Hellenism. Rome had acquired Greek scientific thought, philosophy, medicine, and geography. Roman writers used Greek models; sharing in the humanist outlook of the Greeks, they valued human achievement and expressed themselves in a graceful and eloquent style. Roman cultural life reached its high point during the reign of Augustus, when Rome experienced the golden age of Latin literature.

Literature and History. At the request of Augustus, who wanted a literary **epic** to glorify the Empire and his role in founding it, Virgil (70–19 B.C.) wrote the *Aeneid*, a masterpiece in world literature. The *Aeneid* is a long poem that recounts the tale of Aeneas and the founding of Rome. The first six books, which describe the wanderings of Aeneas, a survivor of Troy, show the influence of Homer's *Odyssey*; the last six, dealing with the wars in Italy, show the *Iliad*'s imprint. Whereas Homer's epics focused on the deeds and misdeeds of heroic warriors, the *Aeneid* is a literary epic of national glory. The profoundest ideas and feelings expressed in the *Aeneid* are Roman virtues—patriotism, devotion to the family, duty to the state, and a strong sense of religion. Intensely patriotic, Virgil ascribed to Rome a divine mission to bring peace and civilized life to the world, and he praised Augustus as a divinely appointed ruler who had fulfilled Rome's mission. The Greeks might be better sculptors, orators, and thinkers, said Virgil, but only the Romans knew how to govern an empire:

> *For other peoples will, I do not doubt,*
> *still cast their bronze to breathe with softer features,*
> *or draw out of the marble living lines, plead causes better,*
> *trace the ways of heaven with wands and tell the rising*
> *constellations; but yours will be the rulership of nations,*
> *remember, Roman, these will be your arts:*
> *to teach the ways of peace to those you conquer, to spare*
> *defeated peoples, to tame the proud.*[6]

In his *History of Rome,* the historian Livy (59 B.C.–A.D. 17) also glorified Roman virtues, customs, and deeds. He praised Augustus for attempting to revive traditional Roman morality, to which Livy felt a strong attachment. Modern historians criticize Livy for failing to utilize important sources of information in this work, for relying on biased authorities, and for allowing fierce patriotism to warp his judgment. Although Livy was a lesser historian than Thucydides or Polybius, his work was still a major achievement, particularly in its depiction of the Roman character, which helped make Rome great.

An outstanding poet, Horace (65–8 B.C.) was the son of a freed slave. He broadened his education by studying literature and philosophy in Athens, and Greek ideals are reflected in his writings. Horace enjoyed the luxury of country estates, banquets, fine clothes, and courtesans, along with the simple pleasures of mountain streams and clear skies. His poetry touched on many themes—the joy of good wine, the value of moderation, and the beauty of friendship. Desiring to blend reason and emotion, Horace urged men to seek pleasurable experiences but to avoid extremes and to keep desire under rational control. He also reminded Romans of the terrible civil wars that had ruined the Republic:

> *What plain is not enriched with Latin blood, to bear witness with its graves to our unholy strife. . . . What pool or stream has failed to taste the dismal war! What sea has Italian slaughter not discolored! What coast knows not our blood!*[7]

Unlike Virgil, Livy, or Horace, Ovid (43 B.C.–A.D. 17) did not experience the civil wars during his adult years. Consequently, he was less inclined to praise the Augustan peace. His poetry showed a preference for romance and humor, and he is best remembered for his advice to lovers contained in his most famous work, *The Art of Love*. Written when Ovid was fifty years old, the work deals with the art of seduction. Book I tells how to attact a woman who is the object of a man's desire; Book II explains how a man can keep a woman's love; Book III advises women about men. To the man who wants to win a woman, Ovid gave this counsel:

> *First of all, be quite sure that there isn't a woman who cannot be won, and make up your mind that you will win her. Only you must prepare the ground.*
>
> *You must play the lover for all you're worth. Tell her how you are pining for her.*
>
> *Never cease to sing the praises of her face, her hair, her taper fingers, and her dainty foot.*
>
> *Tears too are a mighty useful resource in the matter of love. They would melt a diamond. Make a point, therefore, of letting your mistress see your face all wet with tears.*
>
> *Women are things of many moods. You must adapt your treatment to the special case.*[8]

The writers who lived after the Augustan age were of a lesser quality than their predecessors, although the historian Tacitus (A.D. 55–c. 118) was an exception. Sympathetic to republican institutions, Tacitus denounced Roman emperors and the imperial system in his *Histories* and *Annals*. In *Germania*, he turned his sights on the habits of the Germanic peoples. He described the Germans as undisciplined but heroic, with a strong love of freedom.

The satirist Juvenal (A.D. c. 55–138) attacked the evils of Roman society, such as the misconduct of emperors, the haughtiness of the wealthy, the barbaric tastes of commoners, and the failures of parents. He also described the noise, congestion, and poverty of the capital, as well as its dangers:

> *. . . a piece of pot*
> *Falls down on my head, how often a broken vessel is shot*
> *From the upper windows, with what force it strikes and dints*
> *The cobblestones! . . .*
>
> *But these aren't your only terrors. For you can never restrain*
> *The criminal element. Lock up your house, put bolt and chain*
> *On your shop, but when all's quiet, someone will rob you or he'll*
> *Be a cutthroat perhaps and do you in quickly with cold steel.*[9]

In addition, Juvenal expressed venomous views toward women. He describes the humiliations husbands must face—infidelity, poisonings, public harlotry, and being ignored, intimidated, and dominated. All of this, says Juvenal, is a consequence of a wife's failure to live up to the obligations of the married state—being silent, loyal, obedient, respectful of her husband, and caring for the children.

Philosophy. Stoicism was the principal philosophy of the Pax Romana, and its leading exponents were Seneca, Epictetus (A.D. c. 60–c. 117), and Marcus Aurelius. Perpetuating the rational tradition of Greek philosophy, Roman Stoics saw the universe as governed by reason, and they esteemed the human intellect. Like Socrates, they sought the highest good in this world, not in an afterlife, and envisioned no power above human reason. Moral values were obtained from reason alone. The individual was self-sufficient and depended entirely on rational faculties for knowing and doing good. Stoics valued self-sufficient persons who attained virtue and wisdom by exercising rational control over their lives. Roman thinkers also embraced the Stoic doctrine that all people, because of their capacity to reason, belong to a common humanity.

Lucius Annaeus Seneca (4 B.C.–A.D. 65), a student of rhetoric and philosophy, served the emperor Nero. After Nero accused him of participating in a conspiracy against the throne, Seneca was forced to commit suicide. Seneca's Stoic humanitarianism was expressed in his denunciation of the gladiatorial combats and in his concern for slaves.

> *Were you to consider, that he whom you call your slave, is sprung from the same origin, enjoys the same climate, breathes the same air, and is subject to the same condition of life and death as yourself, you will think it possible to see him as a free-born person, as he is free to see you as a slave. . . .*
>
> *I will not discuss at length the treatment of slaves towards whom we behave cruelly and arrogantly. But this is the essence of what I would prescribe: treat your inferiors as you would have a superior treat you. As often as you think of the power that you have over a slave, reflect on the power that your master has over you. But you say, "I have no master." Be it so. The world goes well with you at present; it may not do so always. You may one day be a slave yourself.*[10]

The emperor Marcus Aurelius, the last of the great Stoics, also had to deal with serious problems confronting the Empire. While commanding troops engaged in fighting plundering tribesmen in the Balkans, he wrote in Greek the *Meditations,* a classic work of Stoic thought. In Stoicism, he sought the strength to overcome the burdens of ruling an empire, the fear of death, and the injustices and misdeeds committed by his fellows.

> *Hour by hour resolve firmly, like a Roman and a man, to do what comes to hand with correct and natural dignity, and with humanity, independence, and justice. Allow your mind freedom from all other considerations. This you can do, if you will approach each action as though it were your last, dismissing the wayward thought, the emotional recoil from the commands of reason, the desire to create an impression, the admiration of self, the discontent with your lot. See how little a man needs to master, for his days to flow on in quietness and piety: he has but to observe these few counsels, and the gods will ask nothing more.*[11]

Science. The two most prominent scientists during the Greco-Roman age were Ptolemy, the mathematician, geographer, and astronomer, who worked at Alexandria in the second century A.D., and Galen (A.D. c. 130–c. 201), who investigated medicine and anatomy. Ptolemy's thirteen-volume work, *Mathematical Composition*—more commonly known as the *Almagest,* a Greek-Arabic term meaning "the greatest"—summed up antiquity's knowledge of astronomy and became the authoritative text during the Middle Ages. In the Ptolemaic system, a motionless, round earth stood in the center of the universe, and the moon, sun, and planets moved about the earth in circles, or in combinations of circles. The Ptolemaic system was built on a faulty premise, as modern astronomy eventually showed. However, it did work—that is, it did provide a model of the universe that adequately accounted for most observed phenomena. The Ptolemaic system would not be challenged until the middle of the sixteenth century.

As Ptolemy's system dominated astronomy, so the theories of Galen dominated medicine down to

THE COLOSSEUM, ROME, A.D. 70–80 The joint work of the emperors Vespasian and his sons Titus and Domitian, this huge amphitheater was the largest in the ancient world. It was the site of innumerable spectacles, sham sea battles, gladiatorial games, wild beast hunts, and the deaths of Christian martyrs. (*Art Resource, NY.*)

modern times. By dissecting both dead and living animals, Galen attempted a rational investigation of the body's working parts. Although his work contains many errors, he made essential contributions to the knowledge of anatomy. Thanks to Arab physicians who preserved his writings during the Middle Ages, Galen's influence continued in the West into early modern times.

Art, Architecture, and Engineering. Romans borrowed art forms from other peoples, particularly the Greeks, but they borrowed creatively, transforming and enhancing their inheritance. Roman portraiture continued trends initiated during the Hellenistic Age. Imitating Hellenistic models, Roman sculptors realistically carved every detail of a subject's face: unruly hair, prominent nose, lines and wrinkles, a jaw that showed weakness or strength. Sculpture also gave expression to the imperial ideal. Statues of emperors conveyed nobility and authority; reliefs commemorating victories glorified Roman might and grandeur.

The Romans most creatively transformed the Greek inheritance in architecture. The Greek temple was intended to be viewed from the outside; the focus was exclusively on the superbly balanced exterior. By using arches, vaults, and domes, the Romans built structures with large, magnificent interiors. The vast interior, massive walls, and overarching dome of the famous Pantheon, a temple built in the early second century, during the reign of Hadrian, symbolizes the power and majesty of the Roman world-state.

The Romans excelled at engineering. They built amphitheaters, public baths, and aqueducts that carried water to Roman cities—some still survive. Roman engineers with an eye for natural barriers and drainage problems carefully selected routes and designed great embanked roads, the finest in the ancient world.

Law. Expressing the Roman yearning for order and justice, law was Rome's great legacy to Western civilization. Roman law passed through two essential stages: the formation of civil law (*jus civile*) and the formation of the law of nations (*jus gentium*). The basic features of the civil law evolved during the two-hundred-year Struggle of the Orders, at the same time that Rome was extending its dominion over Italy. The Twelve Tables, drawn up in the early days of the patrician-plebeian struggle (described at the beginning of the previous chapter), established for the Roman state written rules of criminal and civil law that applied to all citizens. Over the centuries, the civil law was expanded by statutes enacted by the assemblies, by the legal decisions of jurisdictional magistrates, by the rulings of emperors, and by the commentaries of professional jurists, who, aided by familiarity with Greek logic, engaged in systematic legal analysis.

During the period of the Republic's expansion outside Italy, contact with the Greeks and other peoples led to the development of the second branch of Roman law, jus gentium, which combined Roman civil law with principles selectively drawn from the legal tradition of Greeks and other peoples. Roman jurists identified the jus gentium with the natural law (jus naturale) of the Stoics. The jurists said that a law should accord with rational principles inherent in nature: uniform and universally valid standards that can be discerned by rational people. Serving to bind different peoples together, the law of nations harmonized with the requirements of a world empire and with Stoic ideals, as Cicero pointed out:

> *True law is right reason in agreement with nature; it is of universal application, unchanging and ever lasting. . . . And there will not be different laws at Rome and at Athens or different laws now and in the future, but one eternal and unchangeable law will be valid for all nations and all times.*[12]

The law of nations came to be applied throughout the Empire, although it never entirely supplanted local law. In the eyes of the law, a citizen was not a Syrian or a Briton or a Spaniard but a Roman. In effect, through jus gentium, an international law, Rome transformed what was a theoretical principle for the Stoics into a political reality.

After the fall of the western Roman Empire, Roman law fell into disuse in western Europe. Gradually reintroduced in the twelfth century, it came to form the basis of the common law in all Western lands except Britain and its dependencies. Some provisions of Roman law are readily recognizable in modern legal systems, as the following excerpts illustrate:

> *Justice is a constant, unfailing disposition to give everyone his legal due.*
> *No one is compelled to defend a cause against his will.*
> *No one suffers a penalty for what he thinks.*
> *In the case of major offenses it makes a difference whether something is committed purposefully or accidentally.*
> *The guilt or punishment of a father can impose no stigma upon the son, for every individual is subjected to treatment in accordance with his own action, and no one is made the inheritor of the guilt of another.*
> *In inflicting penalties, the age . . . of the guilty party must be taken into account.*[13]

Entertainment. Despite its many achievements, Roman civilization presents a paradox. On the one hand, Roman culture and law evidence high standards of civilization. On the other, the Romans institutionalized barbaric practices: battles to the death between armed gladiators and the tormenting and slaughtering of wild beasts.

The major forms of entertainment in both the Republic and the Empire were chariot races, wild animal shows, and gladiatorial combat. Chariot races were gala events in which the most skillful riders and the finest and best-trained stallions raced in an atmosphere of incredible excitement. The charioteers, many of them slaves hoping that victory would bring them freedom, became popular heroes. The rich staked fortunes on the races, and the poor bet their last coins.

The Romans craved brutal spectacles. One form of entertainment pitted wild beasts against each other or against men armed with spears. Another consisted of battles, sometimes to the death, between highly trained gladiators. The gladiators, mainly prisoners of war and condemned criminals, learned their craft at schools run by professional trainers. Some gladiators entered the arena armed with a sword, others with a trident and a net. The spectators were transformed into a frenzied mob that lusted for blood. If they were displeased with a losing gladiator's performance, they would call for his immediate execution.

Over the centuries, these spectacles grew more bizarre and brutal. Hundreds of tigers were set against elephants and bulls; wild bulls tore apart men dressed in animal skins; women battled in the arena; dwarfs fought each other. One day in the Colosseum, which could seat fifty thousand people, three thousand men fought each other; on the day the Colosseum opened in A.D. 80, nine thousand beasts were slaughtered. In fact, much of the African trade was devoted to supplying animals for the contests.

Few Romans questioned these barbarities, which became a routine part of daily life. Occasionally, however, thoughtful Romans had strong doubts. After watching a public spectacle, the Stoic philosopher Seneca wrote in disgust: "There is nothing more harmful to one's character than attendance at some spectacle, because vices more easily creep into your soul while you are being entertained. When I return from some spectacle, I am greedier, more aggressive and . . . more cruel and inhuman."[14]

Signs of Trouble

The Pax Romana was one of the finest periods in ancient history. But even during the Time of Happiness, signs of trouble appeared that would grow to crisis proportions in the third century.

Internal Unrest

The Empire's internal stability was always subject to question. Were the economic foundations of the Empire strong and elastic enough to endure hard blows? Could the Roman Empire retain the loyalty of so many diverse nationalities, each with its own religious and cultural traditions? Were the mass of people committed to the values of Greco-Roman civilization, or would they withdraw their allegiance and revert to their native traditions if imperial authority weakened?

During the Pax Romana, dissident elements did surface, particularly in Gaul, Judea, and Egypt. The Jews fought two terrible and futile wars to try to liberate their land from Roman rule. Separatist movements in Gaul were also crushed by Roman forces. To provide free bread for Rome's poor, Roman emperors exploited the Egyptian peasantry. Weighed down by forced labor, heavy taxes, requisitions, and confiscations, Egyptian peasants frequently sought to escape from farmwork.

The unrest in Egypt, Gaul, and Judea demonstrated that not all people at all times welcomed the grand majesty of the Roman peace and that localist and separatist tendencies persisted in a universal empire. In the centuries that followed, as Rome staggered under the weight of economic, political, and military difficulties, these native loyalties reasserted themselves. Increasingly, the masses, and even the Romanized elite of the cities, withdrew their support from the Roman world-state.

Social and Economic Weaknesses

A healthy world-state required empirewide trade to serve as an economic base for political unity, expanding agricultural production to feed the cities, and growing internal mass markets to stimulate industrial production. But the economy of the Empire during the Pax Romana had serious defects. The means of communication and transportation were slow, which hindered long-distance commerce. Roman roads, built for military rather than commercial purposes, were often too narrow for large carts and in places were too steep for any vehicles. Consequently, transporting goods by land, even short distances, necessitated huge price increases that hampered trade. Many nobles, considering it unworthy for a gentleman to engage in business, chose to squander their wealth rather than invest it in commercial or industrial enterprises. Lacking the stimulus of capital investment, the economy could not expand.

Limited employment opportunities resulted from the Greco-Roman civilization's failure to improve its technology substantially and from reliance on slave labor. Also, because manual labor was considered degrading, fit only for a slave, there was little incentive for innovation that might have triggered economic growth and expanded employment opportunities. Because of these factors, millions of people simply did not engage in productive labor. Moreover, scarce employment left the masses with little purchasing power; this too adversely affected business and industry. Many unemployed inhabitants of Italian towns lived on free or cheap grain provided by the state. To feed this unemployed underclass, the government kept the price of grain artificially low. This practice discouraged farmers from planting more crops and expanding grain production and forced many of them to seek other livelihoods. As more farmers left the countryside, the towns became increasingly swollen with an impoverished proletariat. Rural areas eventually faced a serious shortage of laborers due to this population migration.

Ultimately, only a small portion of the urban population—landlords, whose estates were outside the city, merchants, and administrators—reaped the benefits of the Roman peace. They basked in luxury, leisure, and culture. The urban poor, on the other hand, derived few of the economic gains and shared little in the political and cultural life of the city. The privileged classes bought off the urban poor with bread and circuses, but occasionally mass discontent expressed itself in mob violence. Outside the cities, the peasantry—still the great bulk of the population—was exploited to provide cheap food for the city dwellers.

Such a parasitical, exploitative, and elitist social system might function in periods of peace and tranquillity, but could it survive crises? Would the impoverished people of town and country—the overwhelming majority of the population—remain loyal to a state whose benefits barely extended to them and whose sophisticated culture, which they hardly comprehended, virtually excluded them?

Cultural Stagnation and Transformation

Perhaps the most dangerous sign for the future was the spiritual paralysis that crept over the ordered world of Pax Romana. A weary and sterile Hellenism underlay the Roman peace. The ancient world was undergoing a transformation of values that foreshadowed the end of Greco-Roman civilization.

During the second century A.D., Greco-Roman civilization lost its creative energies, and the values of classical humanism were challenged by mythic-religious movements. No longer regarding reason as a satisfying guide to life, the educated elite subordinated the intellect to feelings and an unregulated imagination. No longer finding the affairs of this world to have purpose, people placed their hope in life after death. The Roman world was undergoing a religious revolution and seeking a new vision of the divine.

The application of reason to nature and society, as we have seen, was the great achievement of the Greek mind. Yet despite its many triumphs, Greek rationalism never entirely subdued the mythic-religious mentality, which draws its strength from human emotion. The masses of peasants and slaves remained attracted to religious forms. **Ritual**, mystery, magic, and ecstasy never lost their hold on the ancient world—nor, indeed, have they on our own scientific and technological society. During the Hellenistic Age, the tide of rationalism gradually receded, and the nonrational, an ever-present undercurrent, showed renewed vigor. This resurgence of the mythical mentality could be seen in the popularity of the occult, magic, alchemy, and astrology. Feeling themselves controlled by heavenly powers, burdened by danger and emotional stress, and fearing fate as fixed in the stars, people turned for deliverance to magicians, astrologers, and exorcists.

They also became devotees of the many Near Eastern religious cults that promised personal salvation. More and more people felt that the good life could not be achieved by individuals through their own efforts; they needed outside help. Philosophers eventually sought escape from this world through union with a divine presence greater than human power. Increasingly, the masses, and then even the educated elite, came to believe that the good life could be found not on earth but only in a world beyond the grave. Seeing themselves as isolated souls wandering aimlessly in a social desert, people sought refuge in religion. Reason had been found wanting; the time for faith and salvation was at hand.

The Roman Empire had imposed peace and stability, but it could not alleviate the feelings of loneliness, anxiety, impotence, alienation, and boredom that had been gaining ground in the Mediterranean world since the fourth century B.C. A spiritual malaise descended on the Greco-Roman world. Among the upper classes, the philosophical and scientific spirit withered; rational and secular values were in retreat. Deprived of the excitement of politics and bored by idleness and pleasure, the best minds, says historian Michael Rostovtzeff,

> *lost faith in the power of reason. . . . Creative genius dwindled; science repeated its previous results. The textbook took the place of research; no new artistic discoveries were made, but echoes of the past were heard . . . [writers] amuse[d] the mind but [were] incapable of elevating and inspiring it.*[15]

The Spread of Mystery Religions

The proliferation of Eastern mystery religions was a clear expression of this transformation of classical values. During the Hellenistic era, slaves, merchants, and soldiers brought many religious cults westward from Persia, Babylon, Syria, Egypt, and Asia Minor. The various mystery cults possessed many common features. Converts underwent initiation rites and were bound by oath to secrecy. The initiates, in a state of rapture, attempted to unite with the deity after first purifying themselves through baptism (sometimes with the blood of a bull), fasting, having their heads shaved, or drinking from a sacred vessel. Communion was achieved by donning the god's robe, eating a sacred meal, or visiting the god's sanctuary. This sacramental drama propelled initiates through an intense mystical experience of exaltation and rebirth. Cultists were certain that their particular savior-god would protect them from misfortune and ensure their soul's immortality.

Of special significance was the cult of Mithras, which had certain parallels with early Christianity and was its principal competitor. Originating in Persia, Mithraism spread westward into the Roman Empire. Because it stressed respect for the masculine virtues of bravery and camaraderie, it became particularly popular with the army. The god Mithras, whose birth date was celebrated on December 25, had as his mission the rescuing of humanity from evil. He was said to demand high standards of morality, to judge souls after death, and to grant eternal life to his faithful followers.

The popularity of magic and mystery demonstrates that many people in Roman society either did not comprehend or had lost faith in the rational and secular values of classical humanism. Religion proved more comforting to the spirit. People felt that the gods could provide what reason, natural law, and civic affairs could not: a sure way of overcoming life's misfortunes and discouragements, a guarantee of immortality, a sense of belonging to a community of brethren who cared, an exciting outlet for bottled-up emotions, and a sedative for anxiety at a time when dissatisfaction with the human condition showed itself in all phases of society and life.

The Spiritualization of Philosophy

The religious orientation also found expression in philosophy, which demonstrated attitudes markedly at odds with classical humanism. These attitudes, commonly associated with religion, included indifference to the world, withdrawal, and pessimism about the earthly state. From trying to understand nature and individuals' relationships to one another, the philosophers more and more aspired to a communion with a higher reality. Like the mystery religions, philosophy reached for something beyond this world in order to comfort the individual. In Neo-Platonism, which replaced Stoicism as the dominant school of philosophy in the Late Roman Empire, religious yearnings were transformed into a religious system that transcended reason.

Plotinus (A.D. c. 205–c. 270), the most influential spokesman of Neo-Platonism, went far beyond Marcus Aurelius's natural religion; in aspiring to the ecstatic union of the soul with God, he subordinated philosophy to mysticism and the occult. Plato's philosophy, we have seen, contained both a major and a minor key. The major key stressed a rational interpretation of the human community and called for reforming the polis on

Stone Relief of Mithras Sacrificing a Bull. The spread and popularity of Near Eastern mystery cults in the western Roman Empire was a sign of the Hellenistic cosmopolitanism that dominated Roman imperial society. Among the most popular mystery cults, especially among soldiers, was that of Mithras, a Persian warrior-deity also associated with the sun and justice. Mithras promised immortality to those who upheld high ethical standards of conduct and underwent cultic initiation rites. (*Cincinnati Art Museum, Gift of Mr. and Mrs. Fletcher E. Nyce, 1968.*)

the basis of knowledge whereas the minor key urged the soul to rise to a higher world of reality. Although Plotinus retained elements of Platonic rationalism (he viewed the individual as a reasoning being and used rational argument to explain his religious orientation), he was intrigued by Plato's otherworldliness.

What Plotinus desired was union with the One, or the Good, sometimes called God—the source of all existence. Plotinus felt that the intellect could neither describe nor understand the One, which transcended all knowing, and that joining with the One required a mystical leap, a purification of the soul that dispensed with logic, evidence, and proof. This vision, which intended the soul to return to its true home, was for Plotinus something greater and more compelling than reason. For Plotinus, philosophy became a religious experience, a contemplation of the eternal. His successors held that through acts of magic the soul can unite with the One. Compared with this union with the divine One, of what value was knowledge of the sensible world or a concern for human affairs? For Plotinus, this world was a sea of tears and troubles from which the individual yearned to escape. Reality was not in this world but beyond it, and the principal goal of life was not comprehension of the natural world or fulfillment of human potential or betterment of the human community but attaining spiritual truth—knowledge of the One—through a transrational experience. Thus, his philosophy broke with the essential meaning of classical humanism.

Neo-Platonism, concludes historian of philosophy W. T. Stace, "is founded upon . . . the despair of reason." It seeks to reach the Absolute not through reason but through "spiritual intoxication." This marks a radical transformation of philosophical thinking:

> *For philosophy is founded upon reason. It is the effort to comprehend, to understand, to grasp the reality of things intellectually. Therefore it cannot admit anything higher than reason. To exalt intuition, ecstasy, or rapture, above thought—this is the death of philosophy. . . . In Neo-Platonism, therefore, ancient philosophy commits suicide. This is the end. The place of philosophy is taken henceforth by religion.*[16]

By the time of the Late Roman Empire, mystery religions intoxicated the masses, and mystical philosophy beguiled the educated elite. Classical civilization was being transformed. Philosophy had become subordinate to religious belief; secular values seemed inferior to religious experience. The earthly city had raised its eyes toward heaven. The culture of the Roman world was moving in a direction in which the quest for the divine was to predominate over all human enterprises.

The Decline of Rome

Third-Century Crisis

At the death of Marcus Aurelius in A.D. 180, the Empire was politically stable, economically prosperous, and militarily secure. In the third century, the ordered civilization of the Pax Romana ended. Several elements caused this disruption. The Roman Empire was plunged into military anarchy, raided by Germanic tribes, and burdened by economic dislocations. In addition, Eastern religions, which undermined the rational foundations of Greco-Roman civilization, pervaded the Roman world. During these critical times, effective leadership was lacking, for the adoptive system abandoned by Marcus Aurelius was not restored.

The degeneration of the army was a prime reason for the third-century crisis. During the great peace, the army had remained an excellent fighting force, renowned for its discipline, organization, and loyalty. In the third century A.D., however, there was a marked deterioration in the quality of Roman soldiers. Lacking loyalty to Rome and greedy for spoils, soldiers used their weapons to prey on civilians and to make and unmake emperors. Fearful of being killed by their unruly troops who wanted spoils or of being murdered by a suspicious emperor, generals were driven to seize the throne. Once in power, they had to buy the loyalty of their soldiers and guard against assassination by other generals. From A.D. 235 to 285, military mutiny and civil war raged as legion fought legion. During this period, there were twenty-six soldier-emperors, twenty-five of whom died violently. The once stalwart army neglected its duty of defending the borders and disrupted the internal life of the Empire.

Perhaps this change in attitude can be explained by the liberal granting of citizenship. In A.D. 212, citizenship was extended to virtually all freeborn inhabitants of the Empire. Previously, many army recruits had been drawn from among provincials, who were attracted by the promise of citizenship and its advantages. These recruits generally were men of a high caliber who were interested in bettering themselves and their families' lot. With citizenship no longer an inducement for enlistment, says Edward T. Salmon,

> *recruits were now only too likely to be drawn from the lowest and most primitive elements . . . men of the rough and reckless type, who were joining the army chiefly in order to get weapons in their hands with which they would be able to extort for themselves an even greater share of the Empire's collective wealth . . . men who knew little and cared less about Rome's mission and who, when not preying upon the civilians, had not the slightest compunction about preying upon one another.*[17]

Taking advantage of the military anarchy, Germanic tribesmen crossed the Rhine-Danube frontier to loot and destroy. The Goths raided coastal cities of Asia Minor and Greece and even burned much of Athens. In the West, other Germanic tribes penetrated Gaul, Spain, and Italy and engaged the Romans in a full-scale battle near Milan. At the same time that the European defense lines were being breached, a reborn Persian Empire, led by the Sassanid dynasty, attacked and for a while conquered Roman lands in the East. Some sections of the Empire, notably in Gaul, attempted to break away; these moves reflected an assertion of local patriotism over Roman universalism. The "city of mankind" was crumbling.

These eruptions had severe economic repercussions. Cities were pillaged and destroyed, farmland ruined, and trade disrupted. To obtain funds and supplies for the military, emperors confiscated goods, exacted forced labor, and devalued the currency by reducing the gold and silver content of coins and adding base metals: zinc, tin, and lead. Cheap money caused a ruinous inflation, causing many people to turn to barter as a medium of exchange. These measures led many citizens to withdraw their loyalty from Rome.

Repeated invasions, civil war, pillage by Germans and by Roman soldiers, soaring prices, a debased coinage, declining agricultural production, disrupted transportation, and the excessive demands of the state caused economic havoc and famine in the cities. Compounding the problem was a great plague that spread across North Africa and the Balkans in midcentury. Driven to desperation by famine and plague, by invading barbarians and plundering Roman soldiers, and by the extortions and requisitions of government officials, many people fled the cities. The urban centers of the ancient world, creators and disseminators of high civilization, were caught in a rhythm of breakdown. As cities decayed, the center of life gravitated back to the countryside. Large, fortified estates, or villas, owned by the emperor or wealthy aristocrats, provided refuge for the uprooted and destitute of town and country. In the countryside, people had no deep commitment to classical civilization, which had made little headway against native languages, religions, and manners.

During the third century A.D., the spiritual crisis intensified as the rational foundations of Greco-Roman civilization eroded further. People turned increasingly to the mystery cults, which offered relief from earthly misery, a sense of belonging, and a promise of immortality. In philosophy, creative energies were directed not toward a greater understanding of nature or society but toward a knowledge of the divine, which, taught the philosophers, was the path to happiness. Hellenism was breaking down.

Diocletian and Constantine: The Regimented State

The emperors Diocletian (A.D. 285–305) and Constantine (A.D. 306–337) tried to contain the awesome forces of disintegration. At a time when agricultural production was steadily declining, they had to feed the city poor and an expanded army of more than 500,000, strung out over the Empire. They also had to prevent renewed outbreaks of military anarchy, drive the Germans back across the Danube frontier, and secure the eastern region against renewed aggression from Persia. Their solution was to tighten the reins of government and to extort more taxes and requisitions from the citizens. In the process, they transformed Rome into a bureaucratic, regimented, and militarized state, which some historians refer to as "a vast prison."

Ruling like an oriental despot, Diocletian completed a trend that had been developing for generations. He imitated the pomp of the East, wore magnificent robes and jewels, and demanded that subjects prostrate themselves in his presence. Cities lost their traditional right of local self-government—a loss that also culminated an earlier trend. To increase the size of the army, Diocletian drafted prisoners of war and hired German mercenaries. He also established, on vacant or deserted Roman lands, colonies of Germans from which soldiers could be recruited. To ensure continuous production of food and goods, as well as the collection of taxes, the state forced unskilled workers and artisans to hold their jobs for life and to pass them on to their children. For the same reasons, peasants were turned into virtual serfs, bound to the land that they cultivated. An army of government agents was formed to hunt down peasants who fled the land to escape crushing taxes and poverty.

Also frozen into their positions were city officials, or *curiales*. They often found it necessary to furnish from their own pockets the difference between the state's tax demands and the amount that they could collect from an already overtaxed population. This system of a hereditary class of tax collectors and of crippling taxes to pay for a vastly expanded bureaucracy and military establishment enfeebled urban trade and industry. Such conditions killed the civic spirit of townspeople, who desperately sought escape. By overburdening urban dwellers with taxes and regulations, Diocletian and Constantine helped to shatter the vitality of city life, on which Roman prosperity and civilization depended. During the Pax Romana, municipal authorities had enjoyed considerable autonomy; now the state bureaucracy extended its often onerous and rapacious power everywhere.

Rome was governed by an oriental despotism, a highly centralized monarchy regimenting the lives of its subjects. Whereas Augustus had upheld the classical ideal that the commonwealth was a means of fostering the good life for the individual, Diocletian adopted the Eastern attitude that the individual lives for the state. The absolutism inherent in the concept of the principate had eclipsed the republican elements that had endured in the Augustan political settlement.

To guard against military insurrection, Diocletian appointed a loyal general as emperor to govern the western provinces of the Empire while he ruled the eastern regions; although both emperors bore the title Augustus, Diocletian remained superior. (Each emperor then chose an heir-designate, who received his own territory to govern. For a time, the Empire was a tetrarchy—a government by four.) By building an imperial capital, Constantinople, at the Bosporus, a strait where Asia meets Europe, Constantine furthered this trend of dividing the Empire into eastern and western halves.

Tribal Migrations and Invasions

Nearly two centuries after Diocletian's reign, the Roman historian Zosimus described the emperor's accomplishment:

> *By the foresight of Diocletian the frontiers were everywhere studded with cities and forts and towers, and the whole army stationed along them. It was thus impossible for the barbarians to break through, since at every point they encountered an opposing force strong enough to repel them.*[18]

By imposing some order on what had been approaching chaos, Diocletian and Constantine prevented the Empire from collapsing. Rome was given a reprieve. A long period of peace might have brought economic recovery, but misfortune continued to burden Rome, and the process of breakdown and disintegration resumed.

In the last part of the fourth century, the problem of guarding the frontier grew more acute. The Huns, a nomadic people from central Asia, swept across the plains of Russia. With their formidible cavalry—the Huns were expert riders and archers—they subdued the Ostrogoths, a Germanic tribe that had established itself in the Ukraine, and forced the Germanic Visigoths, who had migrated along the Danube in what is now Romania, to seek refuge within the eastern Roman Empire. Enraged by their mistreatment at the hands of Roman officials, the Visigoths took up arms. In 378, Goths and Romans fought each other in a historic battle at Adrianople. The Visigoths routed the Roman forces, largely tribal mercenaries, killing and capturing perhaps as many as two-thirds of the Roman army. Emperor Valens perished in what was Rome's worst defeat since Cannae in the war with Hannibal. The Visigoths were on Roman territory to stay. The battle of Adrianople signified that Rome could no longer defend its borders. Since it was the Visigoth cavalry that prevailed over a Roman army comprised mainly of foot soldiers, the battle also signified that cavalry had begun to supersede infantry as a principal instrument of warfare.

Other Germanic tribes increased their pressure on the Empire's borders. Attracted by the warmer climate, riches, and advanced civilization of the Roman Empire, they were also looking for new lands to farm and were frightened by the advent of the Huns. The borders finally collapsed at the very end of 406 as Vandals, Alans, Suebi, and other tribes joined the Goths in devastating and overrunning the Empire's western provinces. In 408–409, the Visigoths, led by Alaric, besieged Rome itself, extorting huge sums in return for permitting food to enter the city. Then in 410, they rampaged

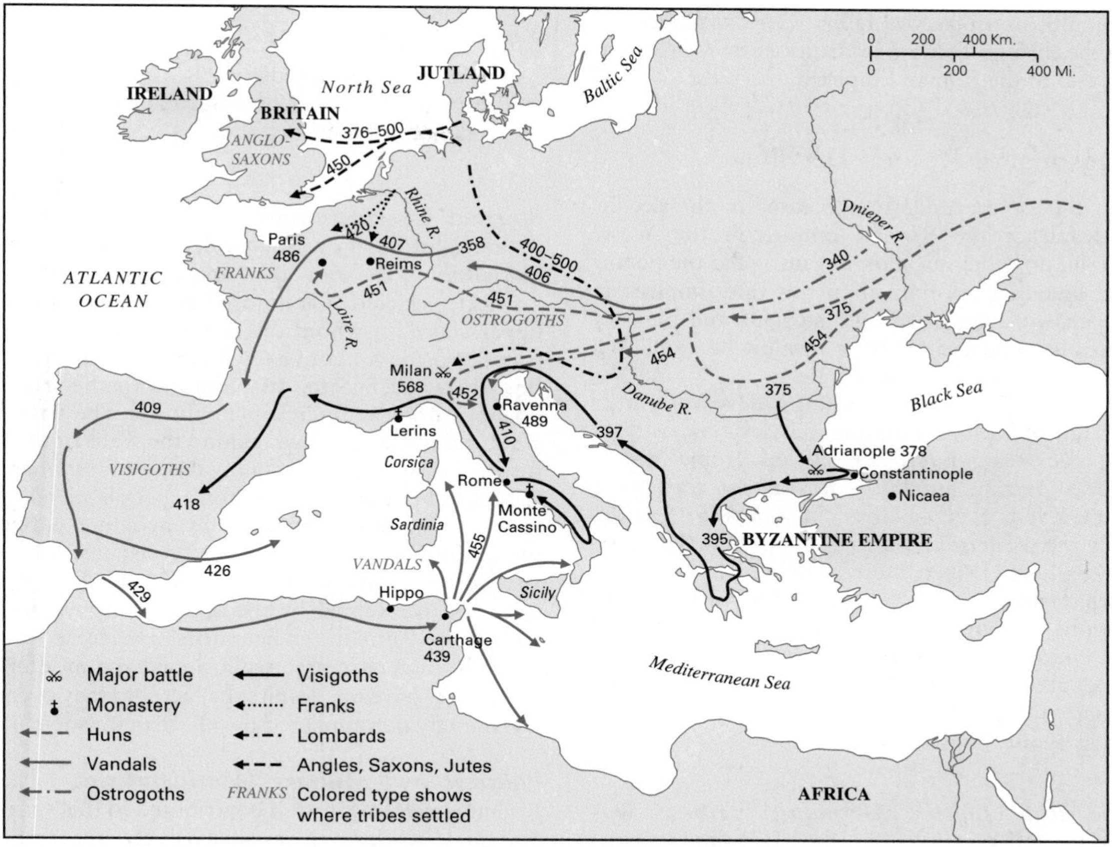

Map 7.2 Incursions and Migrations, c. a.d. 300–500 In the fifth century, German tribes, seeking land and desperate to escape the Huns, overran the weakened Roman borders.

through the city, which for eight hundred years had remained free of foreign attack, slaughtering, destroying, and plundering. Saint Jerome lamented: "Who could believe that Rome, built upon the conquest of the whole world, would fall to the ground? that the mother herself would become the tomb of her peoples?"[19]

Economic conditions continued to deteriorate. Cities in Britain, Gaul, Germany, and Spain lay abandoned. Other metropolises saw their populations dwindle and production stagnate. The great network of Roman roads was not maintained, and trade in the West almost disappeared or passed into the hands of Greeks, Syrians, and Jews from the East. Everywhere famine, the extortion of taxes by government officials, and murderous warfare added to the misery of the Roman populace.

In 451, Attila (c. 406–453), who had united Mongol tribes, led his Huns into Gaul, where he suffered his only defeat at the hands of a coalition of Germans and the remnants of the Roman army. He died two years later, having come within a hairsbreadth of turning Europe into a province of a Mongolian empire. But Rome's misfortunes persisted. In 455, Rome was again pillaged, this time by the Vandals. Additional regions fell under the control of Germanic chieftains. Germanic soldiers in the pay of Rome gained control of the government and dictated the choice of emperor. In 476, German officers overthrew the Roman emperor

Romulus and placed a fellow German, Odoacer, on the throne. This act is traditionally regarded as the end of the Roman Empire in the West.

Reasons for Rome's Decline

What were the underlying causes of the decline and fall of the Roman Empire in the West? Surely, no other question has intrigued the historical imagination more than this one. Implicit in the answers suggested by historians and philosophers is a concern for their own civilization. Will it suffer the same fate as Rome?

To analyze so monumental a development as the fall of Rome, some preliminary observations are necessary. First, the fall of Rome was a process lasting hundreds of years; it was not a single event that occurred in A.D. 476. Second, only the western half of the Empire fell. The eastern half—wealthier, more populous, less afflicted with civil wars, and less exposed to barbarian invasions—survived as the Byzantine Empire until the middle of the fifteenth century. Third, no single explanation suffices to account for Rome's decline; multiple forces operated concurrently to bring about the fall.

The Role of the Germanic Tribes. Was Rome's fall suicide or murder? Did the Germans walk over a corpse, or did they contribute substantially to Rome's decline and fall? Undoubtedly, an empire enfeebled by internal rot succumbed to the Germanic migrations. Perhaps a stronger Rome might have secured its borders, as it had done during the Pax Romana. But the Germanic attacks occurred mainly in the West, and the western Empire, poorer and less populated than the eastern portion, reeled under these increasingly more numerous and more severe barbarian onslaughts. The pressures exerted by the Germans along an immense frontier also aggravated Rome's internal problems. The barbarian attacks left border regions impoverished and depopulated. The Empire imposed high taxes and labor services on its citizens in order to strengthen the armed forces, causing the overburdened middle and lower classes to hate the imperial government that took so much from them.

Online Study Center

Improve Your Grade
Primary Sources: Noble Savages: Rome Encounters the Germans

Spiritual Considerations. The classical mentality, once brimming with confidence about the potentialities of the individual and the power of the intellect, suffered a failure of nerve. The urban upper class, on whom the responsibility for preserving cosmopolitan Greco-Roman culture traditionally rested, became dissolute and apathetic and no longer took an interest in public life. The aristocrats secluded themselves behind the walls of their fortified country estates; many did not lift a finger to help the Empire. The townspeople demonstrated their disenchantment by avoiding public service and by rarely organizing resistance forces against the barbarian invaders. Hounded by the state and persecuted by the army, many farmers viewed the Germans as liberators. The great bulk of the Roman citizenry, disillusioned and indifferent, simply gave up, despite the fact that they overwhelmingly outnumbered the German invaders.

Political and Military Considerations. The Roman government itself contributed to this spiritual malaise through its increasingly autocratic tendencies, which culminated in the regimented rule of Diocletian and Constantine. The insatiable demands and regulations of the state in the Late Roman Empire sapped the initiative and civic spirit of its citizens. The ruined middle and lower classes withdrew their loyalty. For many, the state had become the enemy, and its administration was hated and feared more than the barbarians. Salvianus of Marseilles (c. A.D. 400–470), a monk from Gaul, described the disaffection toward Rome that led many to welcome the barbarians as liberators:

> *Meanwhile the poor are being robbed, widows groan, orphans are trodden down, so that many, even persons of good birth, who have enjoyed a liberal education, seek refuge with the enemy to escape death under the trials of general persecution. They seek among the barbarians the Roman mercy, since they cannot endure the barbarous mercilessness they*

> *find among the Romans. . . . So you find men passing over everywhere, now to the Goths . . . , or whatever other barbarians have established their power anywhere. . . . Hence the name of Roman citizen, once . . . much valued. . . , is now voluntarily repudiated and shunned, and is thought not merely valueless, but even almost abhorrent.*[20]

Related to the political decline was the government's inability to retain the allegiance of its armies and to control ambitious military commanders, who used their troops to seize the throne and its immense power. The internal security and stability of the Empire was thus constantly imperiled by army leaders more concerned with grandiose personal dreams than with defending the Empire's borders. These civil wars imposed terrible financial burdens on the Empire and gravely weakened the frontier defenses—an invitation to the Germans to increase their pressure.

During the Pax Romana, superior training and organization, rigorous discipline, a professional system of command, and a network of walls and forts enabled the Roman legions to protect the frontiers against incursions. The Roman soldier, for whom discipline was a deeply ingrained tradition, knew that his comrades would not desert the field, no matter how hard the fighting—an attitude that usually meant certain victory against untrained barbarian hordes. However, in the Late Roman Empire, the quality of Roman soldiers deteriorated and the legions failed to defend the borders, even though the German invaders were fewer numerically. During the third century, the army consisted predominantly of the provincial peasantry. These nonurban, non-Italian, semicivilized soldiers, often the dregs of society, were not committed to Greco-Roman civilization. They had little comprehension of Rome's mission and at times used their power to attack the cities and towns and to prey on hapless citizens. The emperors also recruited large numbers of Germans into the army to fill depleted ranks. Ultimately, the army consisted predominantly of barbarians, as both legionnaires and officers. Although these Germans made brave soldiers, they too had little loyalty to Greco-Roman civilization and to the Roman state. This deterioration of the Roman army occurred in part because many young citizens evaded conscription. No longer imbued with patriotism, they considered military service a servitude to be shunned.

The deterioration of the Roman army is seen also on the level of tactics. Roman soldiers continued to fight in organized units, but the training and discipline required for fighting in close-order formations had lapsed. Barbarian units serving with the Roman army under their own commanders did not easily submit to traditional discipline. Thus, Rome lost the tactical superiority that it had once enjoyed over the barbarians.

Economic Considerations. Contributing to the decline of the Roman Empire in the West were population decline, the lack of technological advance, the heavy burden of taxation, and economic decentralization, which abetted political decentralization.

During the Late Roman Empire, the population shrank. The epidemic during the reign of Marcus Aurelius, which might have been the bubonic plague, lasted fifteen years. A second plague struck the Empire during the reign of Commodus, Marcus Aurelius's son. Other plagues, in the middle of the third century, and constant warfare further reduced the population. The birthrate did not rise to compensate for these losses. Worsening economic conditions and lack of hope in the future apparently discouraged people from increasing the size of their families.

The decline in population adversely affected the Empire in at least three important ways. First, at the same time that the population was declining, the costs of running the Empire were spiraling, which created a terrible burden for taxpayers. Second, fewer workers were available for agriculture, the most important economic activity of the Empire. Third, population decline reduced the manpower available for the army, forcing emperors to permit the establishment of Germanic colonies within the Empire's borders to serve as feeders for the army. This situation led to the barbarization of the army.

The Roman peace brought stability, but it failed to discover new and better ways of producing goods and agricultural products. To be sure, some advances in technology did take place during the Hellenistic Age and the Pax Romana: rotary mills for grain, screw-presses, and improvements in glass-blowing and field-drainage methods. But the high intellectual culture of Greece and Rome rested on a meager economic and technological foundation. The widespread use of slave labor probably precluded a breakthrough in technology, for slaves had little incentive to invent more efficient ways of producing. The upper classes, identifying manual labor with slavery, would not condescend to engage in the mechanical arts. This failure to improve the level of technology limited employment opportunities for the masses. Because the masses could not increase their purchasing power, business and industry were without a mass internal market that might have acted as a continual stimulus for the accumulation of capital and for economic expansion.

Instead of expanding industry and trade, towns maintained their wealth by exploiting the countryside. The Roman cities, centers of civilized life and opulence, lacked industries. They spent but did not produce. Provided with food and entertainment—"bread and circuses"—the unproductive city dwellers, driven out of the labor force by slavery and economic stagnation, were a heavy burden for the state. The towns were dominated by landlords whose estates lay beyond the city and whose income derived from grain, oil, and wine. Manufacturing was rudimentary, confined essentially to textiles, pottery, furniture, and glassware. The methods of production rarely improved; the market was limited; the cost of transportation, particularly by land, was high; and agricultural productivity was low—the labor of perhaps nineteen peasants was required to support one townsman. Such a fundamentally unhealthy economy could not weather the dislocations caused by uninterrupted warfare and the demands of a mushrooming bureaucracy and the military.

With the barbarians pressing on the borders, the increased military expenditures overstrained the Empire's resources. To pay for the food, uniforms, arms, and armor of the soldiers, taxes were raised, growing too heavy for peasants and townspeople, particularly since the large landowners did not pay their fair share. The state also requisitioned wood and grain and demanded that citizens maintain roads and bridges. The government often resorted to force to collect taxes and exact services. Crushed by these demands, many peasants simply abandoned their farms and sought the protection of large landowners or turned to banditry.

Making the situation worse was the administrative separation of the Empire into eastern and western parts, undertaken by Diocletian and Constantine. As a result, western emperors could no longer rely on financial aid from the wealthier East to pay for the defense of the borders. Slow communications and costly transport continued to hamper the empirewide trade, which was required to sustain political unity. Meanwhile, industries gravitated outward, to search for new markets in the frontier army camps and for new sources of slaves in border regions. This dispersion further weakened the bonds of economic unity. Gradually, trade became less international and more local, and provincial regions grew more self-sufficient. The strife of the third century intensified the drift toward economic self-sufficiency in the provinces, a condition that promoted localism and separatism.

Contributing to the economic decentralization was the growth of industries on latifundia, the large, fortified estates owned by wealthy aristocrats. Producing exclusively for the local market, these estates contributed to the impoverishment of urban centers by reducing the number of customers available to buy goods made in the cities. As life grew more desperate, urban craftsmen and small farmers, made destitute by the state, sought the protection of these large landlords, whose estates grew in size and importance. The growth of latifundia was accompanied by the decline of cities and the transformation of independent peasants into virtual serfs.

These great estates were also new centers of political power, which the imperial government could not curb. A new society was taking shape in the Late Roman Empire. The center of gravity shifted from the city to the landed estate, from the imperial bureaucrat to the local aristocrat. These developments epitomized the decay of ancient civilization and presaged a new era, the Middle Ages.

The Roman Legacy

Rome left the West a rich heritage, which endured for centuries. The idea of a world empire united by a common law and effective government never died. In the centuries following the collapse of Rome, people continued to be attracted to the idea of a unified and peaceful world-state. By preserving and adding to the philosophy, literature, science, and the arts of ancient Greece, Rome strengthened the basic foundations of the Western cultural tradition. Latin, the language of Rome, lived on long after Rome perished. The Western church fathers wrote in Latin, and during the Middle Ages, Latin was the language of learning, literature, and law. From Latin came Italian, French, Spanish, Portuguese, and Romanian. Roman law, the quintessential expression of Roman genius, influenced church law and formed the basis of the legal codes of most European states. Finally, Christianity, the core religion of the West, was born within the Roman Empire and was greatly influenced by Roman law (the church's **canon law** owed much to Roman jurisprudence) and organization (the pope, head of the church and ruling from Rome, was the counterpart of the Roman emperor). The ideal of a single Christian society embracing many different nationalities, so dear to medieval thinkers, was superimposed on the model of the Roman Empire.

❖ ❖ ❖

Online Study Center **ACE the Test**

Notes

1. Tacitus, *The Annals of Imperial Rome,* trans. Michael Grant (Baltimore: Penguin Books, 1959), p. 31.
2. Cited in David Magie, *Roman Rule in Asia Minor* (Princeton, N.J.: Princeton University Press, 1950), p. 490.
3. Excerpted in Dana C. Munro, ed., *A Source Book of Roman History* (Boston: D. C. Heath, 1904), p. 201.
4. Sallust, *The Conspiracy of Cataline,* trans. S. A. Handford (Baltimore: Penguin Books, 1963), p. 193.
5. Excerpted in Naphtali Lewis and Meyer Reinhold, eds., *Roman Civilization, Sourcebook II: The Empire* (New York: Harper & Row, 1966), p. 136.
6. *The Aeneid of Virgil,* trans. Allen Mandelbaum (Berkeley: University of California Press, 1971), pp. 160–161.
7. *The Odes and Epodes of Horace,* trans. C. E. Bennett (Cambridge, Mass.: Harvard University Press, Loeb Classical Library, 1914), p. 109.
8. *The Art of Love and Other Love Books of Ovid* (New York: Grosset & Dunlap, The Universal Library, 1959), pp. 117–118, 130–132, 135.
9. *The Satires of Juvenal,* trans. Hubert Creekmore (New York: Mentor Books, 1963), pp. 58–61, lines 242–248, 269–272, 302–305.
10. Adapted from Seneca, *The Epistles,* trans. Thomas Morell (London: W. Woodfall, 1786), vol. 1, epistle 47.
11. Marcus Aurelius, *Meditations,* trans. Maxwell Staniforth (Baltimore: Penguin Classics, 1964), bk. 2.
12. Cicero, *De Republica,* trans. Clinton Walker Keyes (Cambridge, Mass.: Harvard University Press, Loeb Classical Library, 1994), p. 211.
13. Excerpted in Lewis and Reinhold, eds., *Roman Civilization, Sourcebook II: The Empire,* pp. 535, 539, 540, 547, 548.
14. Seneca, *The Epistles,* vol. 1, epistle 7.
15. Michael Rostovtzeff, *Rome* (New York: Oxford University Press, 1960), p. 322.
16. W. T. Stace, *A Critical History of Greek Philosophy* (London: Macmillan, 1924), p. 377.
17. Excerpted in Mortimer Chambers, ed., *The Fall of Rome* (New York: Holt, Rinehart & Winston, 1963), pp. 45–46.

18. Quoted in Stephen Williams, *Diocletian and the Roman Recovery* (New York: Methuen, 1985), p. 101.
19. Excerpted in James Harvey Robinson, ed., *Readings in European History* (Boston: Ginn, 1904), p. 24.
20. Salvian, *On the Government of God*, trans. Eva M. Sanford (New York: Octagon, 1966), pp. 141–142.

Suggested Reading

Boardman, John, et al., eds., *The Oxford History of the Classical World* (1986). Essays on all facets of Roman culture.

Christ, Karl, *The Romans* (1984). Good chapters on social and cultural life in the Empire.

Clarke, M. L., *The Roman Mind* (1968). Studies in the history of thought from Cicero to Marcus Aurelius.

Grant, Michael, *The Fall of the Roman Empire* (1990). A clearly written synthesis.

Southern, Pat, *Augustus* (1998). A recent biography.

White, Lynn, ed., *The Transformation of the Roman World* (1973). A useful collection of essays on the transformation of the ancient world and the emergence of the Middle Ages.

Chapter 8

Early Christianity: A World Religion

Christ Gives the Law to Saints Peter and Paul. 5th century, Santa Costanza, Rome. This mosaic portrays a haloed, beardless Christ bestowing the law in the manner of an emperor delivering an edict. (Scala/Art Resource, NY.)

- Origins of Christianity
- The Spread and Triumph of Christianity
- The Growth of Christian Organization, Doctrine, and Attitudes
- Saint Augustine: The Christian World-View
- Christianity and Classical Humanism: Alternative World-Views

Focus Questions

1. How did Saint Paul transform a Jewish sect into a world religion?
2. What factors contributed to the triumph of Christianity in the Roman Empire?
3. How was early Christianity influenced by Judaism, Greek philosophy, and Hellenistic mystery religions?
4. What factors contributed to Christian anti-Judaism? What is the historical significance of the negative image of Jews and Judaism taught by early Christians?
5. What are the core features of Saint Augustine's theology?
6. What do the world-views of Christianity and Greco-Roman humanism have in common? Why are they essentially different?

Online Study Center

This icon will direct you to interactive map and primary source activities on the website http://college.hmco.com/pic/perrywc8e.

As confidence in human reason and hope for happiness in this world waned in the last centuries of the Roman Empire, a new outlook began to take hold. Evident in philosophy and in the popularity of oriental religions, this viewpoint stressed escape from an oppressive world and communion with a higher reality. Christianity evolved and expanded within this setting of declining classicism and heightening otherworldliness. As one response to a declining Hellenism, Christianity offered a spiritually disillusioned Greco-Roman world a reason for living: the hope of personal immortality. The triumph of Christianity marked a break with classical antiquity and a new stage in the evolution of the West, for there was a fundamental difference between the classical and the Christian concepts of God, the individual, and the purpose of life.

Origins of Christianity

A Palestinian Jew named Jesus was executed by the Roman authorities during the reign of Tiberius (A.D. 14–37), who succeeded Augustus. At the time, few people paid much attention to what proved to be one of the most pivotal events in world history. In the quest for the historical Jesus, scholars have stressed the importance of both his Jewishness and the religious ferment that prevailed in Palestine in the first century B.C. Jesus' ethical teachings are rooted in the moral outlook of the Old Testament prophets. Jesus, who prayed as a Jew, taught as a Jew to fellow Jews, and valued Jewish law and prophetic teachings, could only conceive of himself as a Jew. Hans Küng, the prominent Swiss student of religion, elaborates on this point:

> *Jesus was a Jew, a member of a small, poor, politically powerless nation living at the periphery of the Roman Empire. He was active among Jews and for Jews. His mother Mary, his father Joseph, his family, his followers were Jews. His name was Jewish (Hebrew Yeshu'a). . . . His Bible, his worship, his prayers were Jewish. In the situation at that time he could not have thought of any proclamation among the gentiles. His message was for the Jewish people, but for this people in its*

Chronology 8.1 ❖ Early Christianity

c. A.D. 29	Crucifixion of Jesus
c. 34–64	Missionary activity of Saint Paul
c. 66–70	The Gospel According to Mark is written
250–260	A decade of brutal persecution of Christians by the Romans
313	Constantine grants toleration of Christianity
c. 320	First convent is founded
325	Council of Nicaea rules that God and Christ are of the same substance, coequal and coeternal
391–392	Theodosius I prohibits public acts of pagan worship and the public profession of pagan religion; during his reign, Christianity becomes the state religion
430	Death of Saint Augustine
451	Council of Chalcedon rules that Christ is truly God and truly man
529	Saint Benedict founds monastery at Monte Cassino

> *entirety without any exception. From this basic fact it follows irrevocably that without Judaism there would be no Christianity. The Bible of the early Christians was the "Old Testament." The New Testament Scriptures became part of the Bible only by being appended to the Old. The gospel of Jesus Christ everywhere quite consciously presupposes the Torah and the Prophets.*[1]

Judaism in the First Century B.C.

In the first century B.C., four principal social-religious parties, or sects, existed among the Palestinian Jews: Sadducees, Pharisees, Essenes, and Zealots. Composed of the upper stratum of Jewish society—influential landed gentry and hereditary priests, who controlled the temple in Jerusalem—the religiously conservative Sadducees insisted on a strict interpretation of **Mosaic Law** (Torah) and the perpetuation of temple ceremonies. Claiming to be the descendants of Sadok, the high priest of Solomon, Sadducees believed that they were maintaining the ancient Hebrew teachings concerning the Torah, which they interpreted literally. Rejecting the concepts of the resurrection of the dead and of an afterlife, they held that God meted out rewards and punishments on earth. Challenging the aristocratic Sadducees, the Pharisees adopted a more liberal attitude toward Mosaic Law. They allowed discussion on varying interpretations of the Law and granted authority to oral tradition—an "oral Torah," which was communicated from one generation to another—as well as to written Scripture. Unlike the Sadducees, the Pharisees believed in life after death. The concept of personal immortality is barely mentioned in the Hebrew Scriptures. A later addition to Hebrew religious thought, probably acquired from Persia, the idea had gained wide acceptance by the first century A.D. The Pharisees had the support of most of the Jewish people. All later forms of Judaism developed from the Pharisees.

The third religious party, the Essenes, established a semimonastic community near the Dead Sea. Like the Sadducees, they considered themselves to be the true descendants of Sadok, but they rejected the temple priests as corrupt. Only those priests affiliated with their sect were deemed pure. In 1947, leather scrolls in hermetically sealed cylinders were found near the Essene community of Qumran, about fourteen miles from Jerusalem, close to the Dead Sea. Dated from between c. 200 B.C. and A.D. 66–70, the *Wady Qumran Manu-*

SARCOPHAGUS OF BAEBIA HERTOFILA, LATE 3RD CENTURY, MUSEO DELLE TERME, ROME. Symbolizing the Christian Eucharist, Jesus distributes the bread and the wine of the Last Supper to his disciples. (*Museo delle Terme, Rome Scala/Art Resource, NY.*)

scripts, commonly called "The Dead Sea Scrolls," contain the oldest extant Hebrew manuscripts and also documents that are unique to the sect of the Essenes, founded by a man they refer to as the "Teacher of Righteousness." The Essenes believed in the physical resurrection of the body, like the Pharisees, but gave this doctrine a more compelling meaning by tying it to the immediate coming of God's kingdom. Certain that the Messiah was about to come, the Essenes saw themselves as the first generation of God's people.

By adding to our knowledge of Palestinian Judaism in the first century, the scrolls shed light on the period in which Christianity arose and the New Testament was written. Because of the similarity between many of the teachings of Jesus, particularly in the Sermon on the Mount, and the teachings of the Essenes' "Teacher of Righteousness," some modern scholars have suggested that Jesus may have been a member of the Essene community. These scholars argue that the teachings of Jesus concerning the imminent coming of the kingdom of God parallel the messianic expectations of the Essenes.

The fourth sect, the Zealots, demanded that the Jews neither pay taxes to Rome nor acknowledge the authority of the Roman emperor. Devoted patriots, the Zealots engaged in acts of resistance to Rome, which culminated in the great revolt of A.D. 66–70, discussed in Chapter 7.

Besides the afterlife, another widely recognized idea in the first century B.C. was the belief in a Messiah, a redeemer chosen by God to liberate Israel from foreign rule. In the days of the Messiah, it was predicted, Israel would be free, the exiles would return, and the Jews would be blessed with peace, unity, and prosperity. The Messiah, in contrast to wicked Roman rulers, would govern justly and righteously.

Jesus (c. 4 B.C.–c. A.D. 29) practiced his ministry within this context of Jewish religious-national expectations and longings. The hopes of Jesus' early followers encompassed a lower-class dissatisfaction with the aristocratic Sadducees; a Pharisee emphasis on prophetic ideals and the afterlife; an Essene preoccupation with the end-of-days, the nearness of God, and the need for repentance; and a conquered people's yearning for a **Messiah** who would liberate their land from Roman rule and establish God's reign.

Jesus: The Inner Person

Historians are able to speak with greater certainty about social-religious developments in Judea at the time of Jesus than they can about Jesus himself. In reconstructing what Jesus did and believed, the historian labors under a handicap for the sources are few. Jesus himself wrote nothing, and nothing was written about him during his lifetime. In the generations following his death, both Roman and Jewish historians paid him scant attention. Consequently, virtually everything known about Jesus derives from the Bible's New Testament, which was written decades after Jesus' death by devotees seeking to convey a religious truth and to propagate a faith.

Modern historians in quest of the historical Jesus have rigorously and critically analyzed the New Testament; their analyses have provided some insights into Jesus and his beliefs. Nevertheless, much about Jesus remains obscure. Very little is known about his childhood. Like other Jewish youths, he was taught Hebrew religious-ethical thought and the many rules that governed daily life. At about the age of thirty, no doubt influenced by John the Baptist, who likely was once part of the Essene community, Jesus began to preach the coming of the reign of God and the need for people to repent—undergo moral transformation—so that they could enter God's kingdom. "Now after John was arrested, Jesus came into Galilee, preaching the gospel of God, and saying, 'The time is fulfilled, and the kingdom of God is at hand; repent, and believe in the gospel' [good news]" (Mark 1:14–15).[2]* This apocalyptic vision that the existing world was coming to an end and would be replaced by God's perfect kingdom had been preached by John the Baptist and other religious thinkers before him.

For Jesus, the coming of the kingdom was imminent; the process leading to the establishment of God's kingdom on earth had already begun. A new order would soon be established in which God would govern his people righteously and mercifully. Hence the present moment became critical for him—a time for spiritual preparedness and repentance—because an individual's thoughts, goals, and actions would determine whether he or she would gain entrance into the kingdom. People had to radically change their lives. They had to eliminate base, lustful, hostile, and selfish feelings; stop pursuing wealth and power; purify their hearts; and show their love for God and their fellow human beings.

Like the Hebrew prophets, Jesus saw ethics as the core of Mosaic Law: "So whatever you wish that men would do to you, do so to them; for this is the law and the prophets" (Matthew 7:12). Like the prophets, he denounced injustice and oppression, urged mercy and compassion, and expressed a special concern for the poor and downtrodden.

Jesus did not intend to lead his fellow Jews, who called him rabbi, away from their ancestral religion: "'Think not that I have come to abolish the law and the prophets; I have come not to abolish them but to fulfil them'" (Matthew 5:17). Although Jesus did not negate the Law, some of his interpretations offended Jewish leaders.

While not seeking to break with his past or to reject Jewish law, Jesus was distressed by the Judaism of his day. Following the prophets, the rabbis taught the Golden Rule, as well as God's love and mercy for his children, but it seemed to Jesus that these ethical considerations were being undermined by an exaggerated rabbinical concern with ritual, restrictions, and the fine points of the Law. Jesus believed that the center of Judaism had shifted from prophetic values to obedience to rules and prohibitions regulating the smallest details of daily life. (To Jewish leaders, of course, these detailed regulations governing eating, washing, Sabbath observance, family relations, and so forth were God's commands intended to sanctify all human activities.) To Jesus, such a rigid view of the Law distorted the meaning of prophetic teachings. Rules dealt only with an individual's visible behavior; they did not engage the person's inner being and lead to a moral transformation based on love, compassion, and selflessness. Observing the Lord's command to rest on the Sabbath—for example, by not eating an egg laid on Saturday or by not lifting a chair on that day—did not purify a person's heart.

For Jesus, the best way to realize the true meaning of Jewish law was through moral purity, which

*The biblical quotations in this chapter are taken from the Revised Standard Version of the Holy Bible.

finds expression in a love for one's fellows. The inner person concerned Jesus, and it was an inner change that he sought: "'For from within, out of the heart of man, come evil thoughts, fornication, theft, murder, adultery, coveting, wickedness, deceit, licentiousness, envy, slander, pride, foolishness. All these evil things come from within, and they defile a man'" (Mark 7:21–23). To Jesus, the spirit of Mosaic Law was more important than the letter of the Law; for him, right living and a pure loving heart were Judaism's true essence. With the fervor of a prophet, he urged a moral transformation of human character through a direct encounter between the individual and God. Jesus also acquired a reputation as a miracle worker who cured the sick and drove demons from the insane.

By preaching active love for others and genuine compassion for sufferers and by stressing a personal and intimate connection between the individual and God, Jesus associated himself more with the Hebrew prophetic tradition than with the Hebrew rituals, rules, and prohibitions that served to perpetuate a national and cultural tradition of a distinct people. Jewish history reveals both universal and parochial components; Jesus' teachings embody the universalism inherent in the concept of the one God and in the prophets' teachings.

It was inevitable that Jewish scribes and priests, guardians of the faith, would regard Jesus, who had become a popular preacher, as a threat to ancient traditions. To Jewish leaders, he was a troublemaker and a subversive. They accused him of associating with social outcasts, sinners, and imperial tax collectors; undermining respect for the Sabbath by violating God's strict command prohibiting any form of labor on this holy day; proclaiming spiritual truth in his own name and on his own authority; and claiming that he, above all other men, had a special and intimate relationship with God and could forgive sins. Stated succinctly, Jewish leaders believed that Jesus was setting the authority of his person over Mosaic Law—an unpardonable blasphemy in their eyes.

The Romans, who ruled Palestine, had little interest in Jewish intrareligious disputes. They feared Jesus as a political agitator, as a charismatic leader who could ignite Jewish messianic expectations into a revolt against Rome. After Jewish leaders turned Jesus over to the Roman authorities, the Roman procurator, Pontius Pilate, sentenced him to death by crucifixion, a customary punishment for someone guilty of high treason. Jesus' execution was consistent with Roman policy in Judea, for the Romans routinely arrested and executed Jews suspected of inciting unrest against Roman rule.

Some Jews, believing that Jesus was an inspired prophet or even the long-awaited Messiah, had become his followers; the chief of these were the Twelve Disciples. At the time of Jesus' death, Christianity was not a separate religion but a small Hebrew sect with dim prospects for survival. What established the Christian movement and gave it strength was the belief of Jesus' followers that he was raised from the dead on the third day after he was buried. The doctrine of the resurrection enabled people to regard Jesus as more than a superb ethical soul, more than a righteous rabbi, more than a prophet, more than the Messiah; it made possible belief in Jesus as a divine **savior-god** who had come to earth to show people the way to heaven. For early Christians, Jesus' death and belief in his resurrection took on greater importance than his life.

It is the nature of the prophet to propose a new religious-moral vision or to reinterpret an older conception in a profoundly novel way. That is what the charismatic Jesus did. There is no evidence that he intended to establish a new church; this was accomplished by his followers. In the years immediately following the crucifixion, the religion of Jesus was confined almost exclusively to Jews, who could more appropriately be called Jewish-Christians. The word *Christian* came from a name given Jesus: *Christ* (the Lord's Anointed, the Messiah). Missionaries of this dissenting Christian movement within Judaism were called Apostles—those sent out to preach the gospel about Christ. They addressed themselves to Jews and to converts to Judaism who, because they did not adhere fully to Mosaic Law, were not wholly accepted by the Jewish community.

Before this new Jewish messianic movement could realize the universal implications of Jesus' teachings and become a world religion, as distinct from a Jewish sect, it had to extricate itself from Jewish ritual, politics, culture, and history. Gradually, the Jewish messianic sect would separate itself both ideologically and socially from the corporate body of Judaism. Instrumental in this

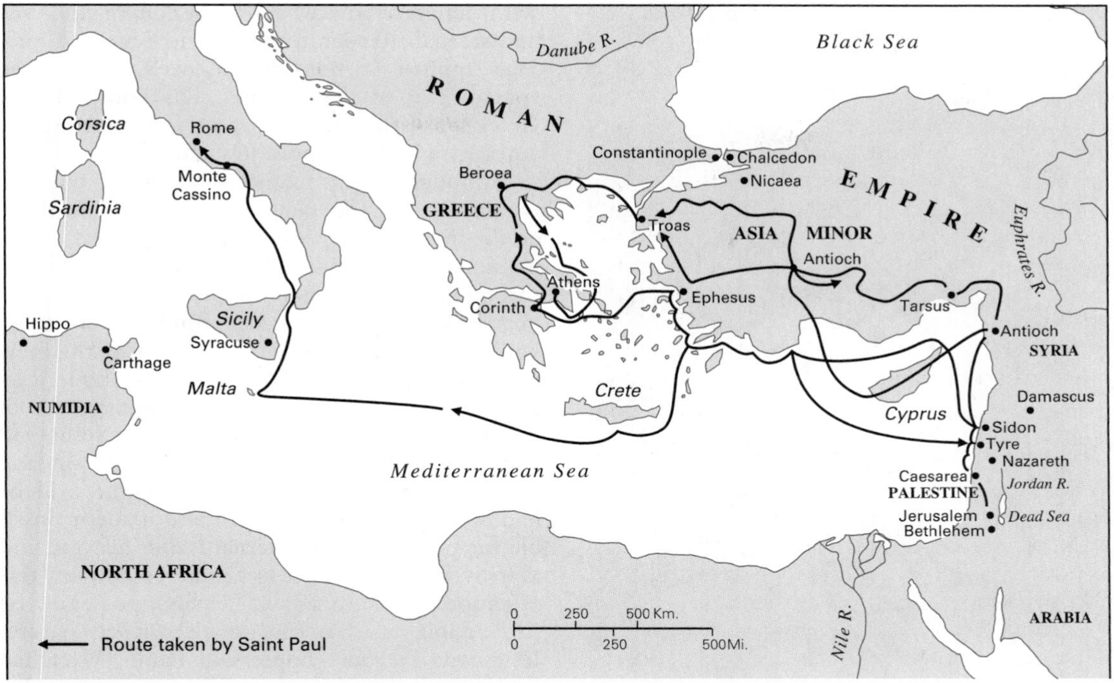

Map 8.1 THE JOURNEYS OF SAINT PAUL Paul, a Greek-speaking citizen of Rome and thus free to travel throughtout the Empire, won converts to the new religion.

development was the work of a Hellenized Jew named Saul, known to the world as Saint Paul.

Saint Paul: From a Jewish Sect to a World Religion

Saint Paul (A.D. c. 5–c. 67) came from the Greek city of Tarsus in southeastern Asia Minor. Originally called Saul, he belonged to the Diaspora, or the "Dispersion"—the millions of Jews living outside Palestine. Though the Jews of the Diaspora retained their ancient faith, they were also influenced by Greek culture. An example is the Alexandrian Jew Philo (c. 20 B.C.–c. A.D. 50), who tried to demonstrate that Hebrew Scriptures could be explained and justified in terms of Greek philosophy.

Non-Jews, or *Gentiles* (from Latin *gens,* or "nation"), coming into contact with Jews of the Diaspora were often favorably impressed by Hebrew monotheism, ethics, and family life. Some Gentiles embraced Hebrew monotheism but refused to adhere to provisions of the Law requiring circumcision and dietary regulations. Among these Gentiles and non-Palestinian Jews who were greatly influenced by the Greco-Roman milieu, Jesus' Apostles would find receptive listeners.

Reared in Tarsus, a stronghold of Greek culture, Saul knew Greek well, but it is unlikely, despite a respectable writing style, that he had great knowledge of Greek literature, philosophy, and science. Trained in the outlook of the Pharisees, the young Saul went to Jerusalem to study with Rabban Gamaliel, an outstanding Pharisee teacher. In Jerusalem, Saul persecuted Jesus' followers in the time after his crucifixion, but then Saul underwent a spiritual transformation and became a convert. Serving as a zealous missionary of Jewish Christianity in the Diaspora, Saul, now called by his Roman name, Paul, preached to his fellow Jews in synagogues throughout the Roman Empire and

ST. PAUL MOSAIC FROM THE BAPTISTRY OF THE ARIANS, RAVENNA, ITALY. Inspired by Jesus' life and death, Paul taught that Jesus was a resurrected redeemer who held the promise of salvation for both Jews and Gentiles. *(Scala/Art Resource, NY.)*

wrote letters of advice back to the congregations he had started. Recognizing that the Christian message applied to non-Jews as well, Paul urged spreading it to the Gentiles. His knowledge of Greek was of inestimable value in his missionary work with both Diaspora Jews and Gentiles.

Although he was neither the first nor the only missionary to the Gentiles, Paul was without doubt the most important. In the process of his missionary activity—and he traveled extensively throughout the Roman Empire—he formulated doctrines that represented a fundamental break with Judaism and became the heart of this new religion. Paul taught that all people, both Jews and Gentiles, were sinners as a consequence of Adam's original defiance of God; that Jesus had come to earth to save all people from sin and death; that by suffering and dying on the cross he had atoned for the sins of all and made it possible for people to have eternal life in heaven; and that by believing in Jesus people could gain this salvation. Alone, one was helpless, possessed by sin, unable to overcome one's wicked nature. Jesus was the only hope, said Paul. "Wretched man that I am! Who will deliver me from this body of death? Thanks be to God through Jesus Christ our Lord!" (Romans 7:24–25).

Christ: A Savior-God. To the first members of the Christian movement, Jesus was both a prophet who proclaimed the power and purpose of God and the Messiah whose coming heralded a new age. To Paul, Jesus was a resurrected redeemer who offered salvation to all peoples. He taught that the crucified Messiah had suffered and died for the sins of human beings, that through Jesus God had shown his love of humanity and revealed himself to all people, both Jews and Gentiles, and that this revelation supplanted the earlier one to the Jewish people.

Increasingly Jesus' followers came to view the sacrificial Messiah as a **savior-god,** indeed, as God incarnate. The idea of a slain savior-god was well known in the mystery religions of the eastern Mediterranean. Like these religions, Christianity initiated converts into the mysteries of the faith, featured a sacramental meal, and in time developed a priesthood. But the similarities between Christianity and the mystery cults should not be overstressed since the differences are more profound.

Unlike the cultic gods, Jesus had actually lived in history. Hence people could identify with him, which enormously increased the appeal of this new religion. Moreover, the deities of the mystery religions were killed against their will by evil powers. In Jesus, it was said, God had become a man and suffered pain and death out of compassion for human beings, to show a floundering humanity the way that would lead from sin to eternal life. This suffering Savior evoked from distressed human beings deep feelings of love and loyalty. Adherents of the mystery cults were not required to undergo a profound moral transformation. Christian converts, however, felt a compelling obligation to make their behavior, in the words of Paul, "worthy of the God who calls you" (Thessalonians 2:12) and to obey Jesus' command: "Be perfect as your heavenly Father is perfect" (Matthew 5:48). Finally, Christians, with their Jewish heritage, would tolerate no other divinity but God. Pagans, on the other hand, often belonged to more than one cult, or at least recognized the divinity of gods in other cults.

The Break with Judaism. In attempting to reach the Gentiles, Paul had to disentangle Christianity from a Jewish sociocultural context. Thus, he held that neither Gentile nor Jewish followers of Jesus were bound by the hundreds of rituals and rules that constitute Mosaic Law. Paul saw no distinctive difference between Jew and Gentile; in his view, the ministry of Jesus was intended for all. As a consequence of Jesus' coming, Paul insisted, Mosaic regulations were obsolete and hindered missionary activity among the Gentiles. For Paul, not the Law of Moses but love of and faith in Christ was the avenue to God and salvation.

To Paul, the new Christian community was the true fulfillment of Judaism; it was granted the promise of a Messiah that God had earlier bestowed on Israel; it was the means to moral transformation and eternal life. The Jews regarded their faith as a national religion, bound inseparably with the history of their people. Paul saw the new Christian community not as a nation but as an oikoumene, a world community. Jesus fulfilled not only the messianic aspirations of the Jews but also the spiritual needs and expectations of all peoples. To this extent, Christianity shared in the universalism of the Hellenistic Age.

In preaching the doctrine of a risen Savior and insisting that Mosaic Law had been superseded, Paul (whatever his intentions) was breaking with his Jewish roots and transforming a Jewish sect into a new religion. Separating Christianity from Judaism enormously increased its appeal for non-Jews, who were attracted to Hebrew ethical monotheism but repelled by practices like circumcision, dietary regulations, and other strict requirements of Mosaic Law. Paul built on Jesus's appeal for individual spiritual renewal and his empathy for all humanity (both also concerns of the ancient Hebrew prophets) to create a religion intended not for a people with its own particular history, culture, and land, but for all humankind.

The Spread and Triumph of Christianity

By establishing Christianity's independence from Judaism and its practices, Paul made the new religion attractive to the Greco-Roman world. Originating in the first century, Christianity took firm root in the second, grew extensively in the third, and became the official religion of the Roman Empire at the end of the fourth century.

Online Study Center **Improve Your Grade**
Interactive Map: The Expansion of Christianity to 600

The Appeal of Christianity

The triumph of Christianity was related to a corresponding decline in the vitality of Hellenism and a shift in cultural emphasis—a movement from reason to emotion and revelation. Offering comforting solutions to the existential problems of life and death, religion demonstrated a greater capacity than reason to stir human hearts. Hellenism had invented the tools of rational thought, but the power of mythical thought was never entirely subdued. By the Late Roman Empire, science and philosophy were unable to compete with mysticism, myth, and the divine.

This deterioration of the classical outlook was demonstrated by the growing popularity of Eastern religions and the transformation of philosophy. Mystery cults, which promised personal

Profile

Blandina

During the reign of Marcus Aurelius, a number of Christians in Lyons, Gaul, including Blandina, a frail young slave, were imprisoned, accused of engaging in cannibalism and incest. The Roman authorities tortured Blandina, hoping that she would implicate the Christian community in these abhorrent crimes. Despite the torments inflicted on her, Blandina would not speak falsely against her fellow Christians. The historian Eusebius described her terrible ordeal:

> *Blandina was filled with such power that those who took it in turns to subject her to every kind of torture from morning to night were exhausted by their efforts and confessed themselves beaten—they could think of nothing else to do to her. They were amazed that she was still breathing, for her whole body was mangled and her wounds gaped; they declared that torment of any one kind was enough to part soul and body, let alone a succession of torments of*

Alinari/Art Resource, NY.

salvation, were spreading and gaining followers. Astrology and magic, which offered supernatural explanations for the operations of nature, were also popular. Stoicism and Epicureanism were performing a religious function by trying to help individuals overcome emotional stress, while Neo-Platonists yearned for a mystical union with the One. This recoil from rational and worldly values helped prepare the way for Christianity. In a culturally stagnating and spiritually troubled Greco-Roman world, Christianity gave new meaning to life and offered new hope to disillusioned men and women.

During the Hellenistic Age, the individual had struggled with the problems of alienation and lack of community. With the decline of the independent city-state, the individual searched for a new frame of reference, a new form of attachment. The Roman Empire represented one possible allegiance. But for many people, it was not a satisfying relationship; the individual found it difficult to be devoted to a political organization so vast, remote, and impersonal. The Christian message of a divine Savior and a concerned Father, as well as of brotherly love, inspired men and women who were dissatisfied with the world of the here and now—who felt no attachment to city or empire, derived no inspiration from philosophy, and suffered from a profound sense of loneliness. Christianity offered the individual what the city and the Roman world-state could not: an intensely personal relationship with God, an intimate connection with a higher world, and membership in a community of the faithful who cared for one another.

Stressing the intellect and self-reliance, Greco-Roman thought did not provide for the emotional needs of many people. Christianity addressed itself to this defect in the Greco-Roman outlook. Particularly those who were poor, oppressed, or enslaved were attracted to the personality, life, death, and resurrection of Jesus, his love for all,

such extreme severity. But the blessed woman, wrestling magnificently, grew in strength as she proclaimed her faith, and found refreshment, rest, and insensibility to her sufferings in uttering the words: "I am a Christian: we do nothing to be ashamed of."

*For several days Blandina had to watch other Christians being whipped, roasted, and set upon by wild beasts in the amphitheater. Finally, after surviving similar torments, she was "dropped into a basket and thrown to a bull. Time after time the animal tossed her, but she was indifferent now to all that happened to her, because of her hope and sure hold on all that her faith meant, and of her communing with Christ. Then she, too, was sacrificed, while the heathen themselves admitted that never yet had they known a woman suffer so much or so long."**

*Eusebius, *The History of the Church from Christ to Constantine,* trans. G. A. Williamson (New York: New York University Press, 1966), pp. 196, 202.

and his concern for suffering humanity. They found spiritual sustenance in a religion that offered a hand in love and taught that a person need not be wellborn, rich, educated, or talented to be worthy, that God draws no distinction between the lowly poor and slave and the mightiest aristocrats. To people burdened with misfortune and terrified by death, Christianity held the promise of eternal life, a kingdom of heaven where they would be comforted by God the Father. Thus, Christianity gave to the common person what the aristocratic values of Greco-Roman civilization generally did not: hope, a sense of dignity, and inner strength. By and large, classical philosophy offered little compassion for the sufferer, but the cardinal principle of Christianity was that Jesus had endured earthly torments because of his love for all human beings and even the lowliest could be redeemed.

Christianity succeeded not only through the appeal of its message but also through the power of its organization. To retain the devotion of the faithful, win new converts, protect itself from opponents, and administer its services, Christianity developed an organized body of followers. This body became the Christian church, which grew into a strong organization uniting the faithful. To city dwellers—lonely, alienated, disillusioned with public affairs, stranded mortals groping for a sense of community—the church that called its members "brother" and "sister" filled an elemental need of human beings to belong. Another attraction for Christian converts was the absence of painful or expensive initiation rites, such as those required for entrance into Mithraism, a leading rival (see "The Spread of Mystery Religions" in Chapter 7). Unlike Mithraism, the church also welcomed women converts, who were often the first to join and who brought their menfolk after them. Among the reasons that the church drew women was its command to husbands to treat their wives kindly, remain faithful, and provide for the children. Moreover, in the eyes of God, women were spiritually equal with men. The church also won new converts and retained the loyalty of its members by furnishing social services for the poor and infirm; welcoming slaves and criminals, sinners, and other outcasts; and offering community and comfort during difficult times.

The ability of an evolving Christianity to assimilate elements from Greek philosophy and even from the mystery religions also contributed in no small measure to its growth. By becoming infused with Greek philosophy, Christianity could present itself in terms intelligible to those versed in Greek learning and thus attract educated people. Philosophers who converted to Christianity proved to be able defenders of their newly adopted faith. Because some Christian doctrines (the risen Savior-God, the Virgin and her child, life after death, communion with the divine), practices (purification through baptism), and holy days (December 25 was the birth date of the god Mithras) either paralleled or were adopted from the mystery religions, it became relatively easy to win converts from these rivals.

Christianity and Rome

Generally tolerant of religions, at first the Roman government did not interfere much with the Christian movement. In fact, Christianity benefited in many ways from its association with the Roman

Empire. Christian missionaries, among them some of the Twelve Disciples, who were the original followers of Christ, traveled throughout the Empire over roads and across seas made safe by Roman arms. The common Greek dialect, Koine, spoken in most parts of the Empire, facilitated the missionaries' task. Had the Mediterranean world been fractured into separate and competing states, the spread of Christianity might well have faced an insurmountable obstacle. The universalism of the Roman Empire, which made citizenship available to peoples of many nationalities, prepared the way for the universalism of Christianity, which welcomed membership from all nations. Early Christians grafted onto Rome's imperial mission a spiritual evangelical cause: "Go ye therefore and teach all nations" (Matthew 28:19).

As the number of Christians increased, Roman officials began to fear the Christians as subversives, preaching allegiance to God and not to Rome, and as a self-absorbed sect that did not want to fit into the Empire. To many Romans, Christians were disloyal citizens, strange people who would not accept the state gods, would not engage in sacrifices to Roman divinities, scorned gladiatorial contests, stayed away from public baths, glorified nonviolence, refused to honor deceased emperors as gods, and worshiped a crucified criminal as Lord. Romans ultimately found in Christians a scapegoat for the ills burdening the Empire, such as famines, plagues, and military reverses. In an effort to stamp out Christianity, emperors occasionally resorted to persecution. Christians were imprisoned, beaten, starved, beheaded, burned alive, torn apart by wild beasts in the arena for the amusement of the Romans, and crucified. The authorities freed accused Christians who agreed to renounce their faith.

However, the early persecutions, beginning with those incited under Emperor Nero in A.D. 64, were local and did not cause much loss of life; they were too sporadic to impede the growth of Christianity. The persecutions in the mid third century and during Diocletian's rule caused the brutal deaths of many Christians. Some, fearful of torture and death, abandoned their faith. However, the persecutions did not last long enough to seriously threaten the new religion. Actually, they strengthened the determination of most of the faithful and won new converts, who were awed by the extraordinary courage of the martyrs willingly dying for their faith.

Unable to crush Christianity by persecution, Roman emperors decided to gain the support of the growing number of Christians within the Empire. In A.D. 313, Constantine, probably genuinely attracted to Christianity, issued the Edict of Milan, granting toleration to Christians. By allowing the free flow of Christian teachings and instituting legislation favorable to the church, Constantine and his successors accelerated the growth of Christianity and the Christianization of the Empire. By A.D. 392, Theodosius I had made Christianity the state religion of the Empire and declared the worship of pagan gods illegal. With Christian in power, persecution did not end, but its target shifted to pagans, Jews, and Christians with unorthodox views. The polytheistic religions of the Roman world did not claim to possess an exhaustive truth—did not assert that a particular god or a particular form of worship should prevail over all others and that wrongful religious expressions should be rooted out. People were relatively free to select their own credo and engage in their own acts of worship. Christianity, in contrast, possessing an exclusive attitude toward truth, felt compelled to cleanse society of false gods and beliefs. Such an outlook often led Christians to view nonbelievers as enemies of God deserving of punishment. Thus mobs, often driven by fanatic clergy, hurled non-Christian writings into bonfires, destroyed pagan altars and sacred images, and squelched pagan rites and festivals. Emperors, often pushed by the clergy, passed decrees calling for fining, imprisoning, torturing, and executing adherents of pagan cults.

Christianity and Greek Philosophy

Christianity synthesized both the Hebrew and the Greco-Roman traditions. Having emerged from Judaism, Christianity assimilated Hebrew monotheism and prophetic morality and retained the Old Testament as the Word of God. Without this Hebraic foundation, Christianity cannot be understood. As the new religion evolved, it also assimilated elements of Greek philosophy. The ability to combine a historic Judaic monotheism, which had many admirers in the Gentile world,

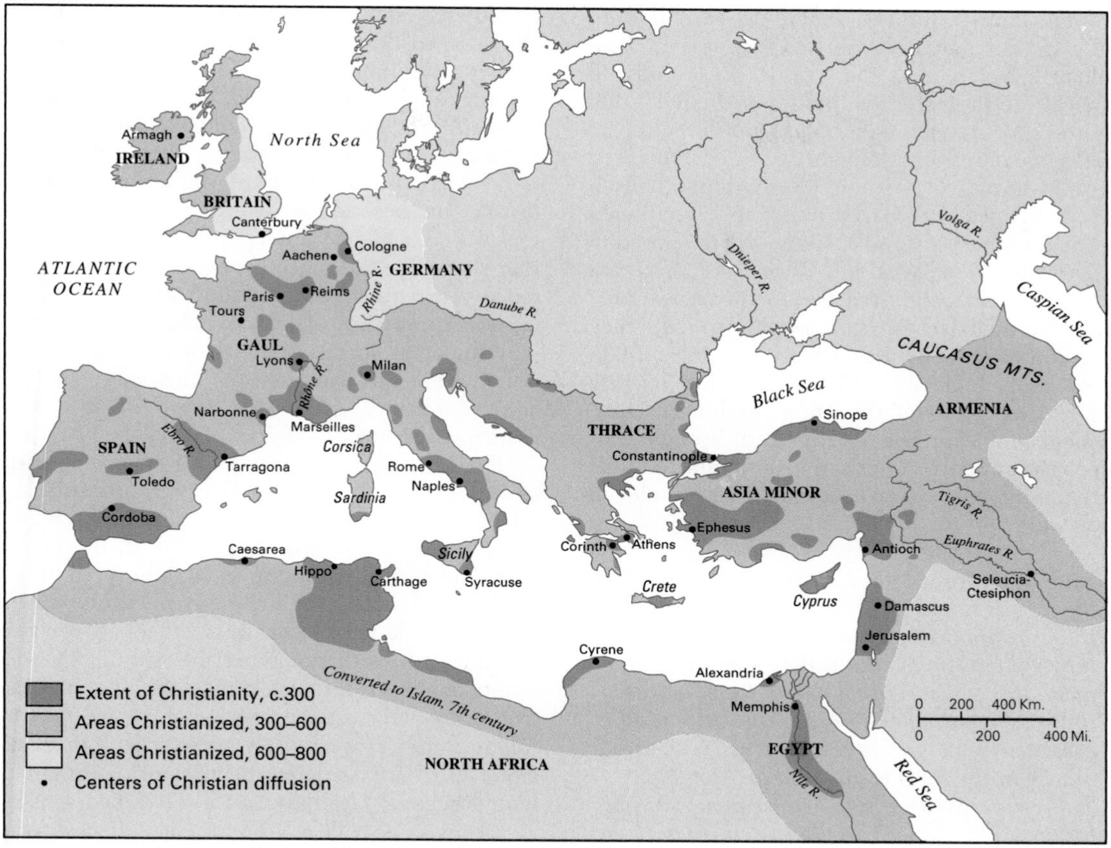

Map 8.2 The Spread of Christianity Aided by dedicated missionaries, Christianity expanded throughout the Mediterranean world and later into Germanic lands.

with Greek rational philosophy was a crucial reason for Christianity's triumph in the Roman Empire. But there was a struggle between conservatives, who wanted no dealings with pagan philosophy, and those believers who recognized the value of Greek thought to Christianity.

To conservative church fathers—early Christian writers whose works are accepted as authoritative by the church—classical philosophy erred completely because it did not derive from divine revelation. As the final statement of God's truth, Christianity superseded both pagan philosophy and pagan religions. According to the church fathers, the simple peasant who accepted Christ possessed more knowledge than the most learned philosopher who did not. These conservatives feared that studying classical authors would contaminate Christian morality (did not Plato propose a community of wives, and did not the dramatists treat violent passions?) and promote heresy (was not classical literature replete with references to pagan gods?). For these church fathers, there could be no compromise between Greek philosophy and Christian revelation. For them, faith was more reliable than all the demonstrations of human reason. "What indeed has Athens to do with Jerusalem?" asked Tertullian (A.D. 150–225). "With our faith, we desire no further belief. For this is our faith that there is nothing which we ought to believe besides."[3]

Some church fathers, including several who had a Greek education, resisted this anti-intellectualism. Defending the value of studying classical literature, they maintained that such literature, properly taught, could aid in the moral development of children because it presented many examples of virtuous deeds. Some church fathers claimed that Greek philosophy contained a dim glimmer of God's truth, a pre-Christian insight into divine wisdom. Christ had corrected and fulfilled an insight reached by the philosophic mind. Knowledge of Greek philosophy, they also contended, helped Christians to explain their beliefs logically and to argue intelligently with pagan critics of Christian teachings. Thus, Clement of Alexandria (c. 150–220) brought reason to the support of faith in his attempt to make Christianity more intellectually respectable in his world:

> *Rather, philosophy is a clear image of truth, a divine gift to the Greeks. Before the advent of the Lord, philosophy helped the Greeks to attain righteousness, and is now conducive to piety, it supplies a preparatory teaching for those who will later embrace the faith. God is the cause of all good things: some given primarily in the form of the Old and the New Testament; others are the consequence of philosophy. Perchance too philosophy was given to the Greeks primarily till the Lord should call the Greeks to serve him. Thus philosophy acted as a schoolmaster to the Greeks, preparing them for Christ, as the laws of the Jews prepared them for Christ.*[4]

Utilizing the language and categories of Greek philosophy, Christian intellectuals transformed Christianity from a simple ethical creed into a theoretical system, a theology. Greek philosophy enabled Christians to explain rationally God's existence and revelation to show that Christian teachings did not violate the laws of logic. Christ was depicted as the divine or incarnate Logos (reason) in human form. Educated believers could argue that the fundamental principles that Greek philosophers maintained operated in the universe were established by God the Father. The Stoic teaching that all people are fundamentally equal because they share in universal reason could be formulated in Christian terms: all are united in Christ. Christians could interpret the church to be the true fulfillment of the Stoic idea of a polity embracing the entire world. Stoic ethics, which stressed moderation, self-control, and brotherhood, could be assimilated by Christian revelation. Particularly in Platonism, which drew a distinction between a world perceived by the senses and a higher order—a transcendent world that should be the central concern of human existence—Christian thinkers found a congenial vehicle for expressing Christian beliefs. The perfect and universal Forms, or Ideas, which Plato maintained were the true goal of knowledge and the source of ethical standards, were held by Christians to exist in God's mind.

That Greek philosophy had a strong hold on church doctrine was immensely important, for it meant that rational thought, the priceless achievement of the Greek mind, was not lost. But Greek philosophy had to sacrifice its ability to think freely to the needs of Christian revelation: reason had to serve faith. And in any conflict between reason and faith, faith would prevail. Although Christianity made use of Greek philosophy, Christian truth ultimately rested on faith, not reason. As Tertullian stated, it is precisely because faith in a crucified Lord contradicted all human logic that he would believe: "And the Son of God died; it is by all means to be believed, because it is absurd. And He was buried, and rose again; the fact is certain because it is impossible."[5]

The Growth of Christian Organization, Doctrine, and Attitudes

Early in its history, the church gradually developed along hierarchical lines. Those members of the Christian community who had the authority to preside over the celebration of the Mass—breaking bread and offering wine as Christ had done in the Last Supper—were called either priests or bishops. Gradually, the designation *bishop* was reserved for the one clergyman in the community with the authority to resolve disputes over doctrines and practices. Regarded as the successors to Jesus' Twelve Disciples, bishops supervised religious activities within their regions. The most influential bishops ministered to the leading cities of the Empire: Rome, Alexandria, Antioch, and Milan. In creating a diocese that was supervised by a bishop and had its center in a leading city, the church adapted Roman administrative techniques.

The Primacy of the Bishop of Rome

The bishop of Rome, later called the *pope* ("father"), claimed primacy over the other bishops, maintaining that the Apostle Peter founded the Roman see (official seat of authority) and that both Peter and Paul were martyred in Rome. Moreover, as the traditional capital of the Empire, Rome seemed the logical choice to serve as the center of the church.

In developing the case for their supremacy over the church organization, bishops of Rome increasingly referred to the famous New Testament passage in which Jesus says to his disciple Simon (also called Peter): "'And I tell you, you are Peter, and on this rock I will build my church'" (Matthew 16:18). Because *Peter* in Greek means "rock" (petra), it was argued that Christ had chosen Peter to succeed him as ruler of the universal church. It was commonly accepted that Saint Peter had established a church in Rome and was martyred there, so it was argued further that the Roman bishop inherited the power that Christ had passed on to Peter. Thus, the argument continued, the bishop of Rome held a unique office: of all the bishops, only he had inherited the powers originally granted by Christ to Peter. Because the Apostles had been subordinate to Peter, so too must the bishops defer to Peter's successor. In the fourth and fifth centuries, popes took a leading part in doctrinal disputes, which threatened to divide the church. More and more Christians came to esteem Rome as the champion of true Christianity.

The Rise of Monasticism

Some devout Christians committed to living a perfect Christian life were distressed by the wickedness of the world about them, including the moral laxity of those clergy who chased after wealth and pomp. Seeking to escape from the agonies and corruptions of this world, some ardent Christians withdrew to deserts and mountains in search of solitude and spiritual renewal; they were inspired by Jesus' words: "If any man would come after me, let him deny himself and take up his cross and follow me" (Mark 8:34). In their zeal to emulate Jesus' self-denial, they sometimes practiced extreme forms of asceticism: self-flogging, wearing spiked corsets, eating only herbs, or living for years atop a column high above the ground.

Gradually, colonies of these hermits sprang up, particularly in Egypt and Syria; in time, the leaders of these monastic communities drew up written rules for prayer and work. Saint Basil (c. 329–c. 379), a Greek who was bishop of Caesarea in Cappadocia (eastern Asia Minor), established the rules that became the standard for monasteries in the East. Basil required monks to refrain from bodily abuses and to engage in manual labor. Through farming, weaving, and construction, monks could make a monastery self-supporting and have the means to assist the needy. Aware of the lure of materialism and selfishness, Basil forbade his monks to own personal property other than clothing and insisted that they spend much of their time in silence.

The monastic ideal spread from east to west. The principal figure in the shaping of **monasticism** in the West was Saint Benedict (c. 480–c. 543), who founded a monastery at Monte Cassino, Italy, in 529. The Rule of Saint Benedict required the monks to live in poverty and to study, labor, and obey the abbot, the head of the monastery. They had to pray often, work hard, talk little, and surrender private property. In imposing discipline and regulations, Benedict eliminated the excessive and eccentric individualism of the early monks. Benedict demonstrated the same genius for administration that the Romans had shown in organizing and governing their Empire. Benedict's rule became the standard for monasteries throughout western Europe.

Scriptural Tradition and Doctrinal Disputes

The earliest surviving Christian writings are Paul's Epistles, written some twenty-five to thirty years after the death of Jesus. Jesus' sayings were preserved by word of mouth. Sometime around

A.D. 66–70, about forty years after the crucifixion, Saint Mark formulated the Christian message from this oral tradition and perhaps from some material that had been put in writing earlier. Later, Saint Matthew and Saint Luke, relying heavily on Mark's account, wrote somewhat longer Gospels. The Gospels of Mark, Matthew, and Luke are called *synoptic* because their approach to Jesus is very similar. The remaining Gospel, written by Saint John around A.D. 110, varies significantly from the synoptic Gospels. The Gospel of John uses the Stoic concept of Logos to present Jesus as the divine being. John identifies Jesus with the eternal word, or Logos, which became the incarnate Son of God: "In the beginning was the Word and the Word was with God, and the Word was God. . . . And the Word became Flesh and dwelt among us" (John 1:1, 14). The synoptic Gospels; the Gospel According to Saint John; Acts of the Apostles; the twenty-one Epistles, including those written by Saint Paul; and Revelation constitute the twenty-seven books of the Christian New Testament. Christians also accepted the Old Testament of the Hebrews as God's Word. The New Testament was written not by historians with the critical spirit of a Thucydides or a Polybius but by men moved by the fervor of faith. Under these circumstances, it is understandable that it contains discrepancies, some nonhistorical legends, and polemics.

The early Christians had a Bible and a clergy to teach it. But the Holy Writ could be interpreted differently by equally sincere believers, and controversies over doctrine threatened the loose unity of the early church. The most important controversy concerned how people viewed the relationship between God and Christ. Arius (A.D. 250–336), a Greek priest in Alexandria, led one faction; he denied the complete divinity of Christ, one of the basic tenets of the church. To Arius, Christ was more than man but less than God; the Father and the Son did not possess the same nature, or essence. Arius said that there was no permanent union between God and Christ; the Father alone is eternal and truly God.

The Council of Nicaea (A.D. 325), the first assembly, or ecumenical council, of bishops from all parts of the Roman world, was called to settle the controversy. The council condemned Arius and ruled that God and Christ were of the same substance, coequal and coeternal. The position adopted at Nicaea became the basis of the Nicene Creed, which remains the official doctrine of the church. Although Arianism, the name given the heresy of Arius, won converts for a time, it eventually died out, helped along by persecution. The death toll of Arians killed by fellow Christians was far greater than the number of Christan victims of Roman persecution.

Christianity and Society

Although salvation was their ultimate aim, Christians still had to dwell within the world and deal with its imperfections. In the process, Christian thinkers challenged some of the mores of Greco-Roman society and formulated attitudes that would endure for centuries.

Influenced by passages in the New Testament that condemned acts of revenge and the shedding of blood, and concerned only with the heavenly kingdom, some early Christians refused military service. Others, however, held that in a sinful world, defense of the state was necessary, and without concealment or apology, they served in the army. With the barbarians menacing the borders, Christian officials could not advocate nonviolence. Christian theorists began to argue that under certain circumstances—to punish injustice or to restore peace—war was just. But even such wars must not entail unnecessary violence.

Christians denounced the gladiatorial combats and contests between men and beasts as blood lust and murder. Nevertheless, these spectacles persisted even after the majority of the population had converted to Christianity. When the games finally ended, it was probably due more to the growing poverty of the western Empire than to the Christian conscience.

The early Christian view of women was rooted in the patriarchal tradition of Jewish society. Paul subjected the wife to her husband's authority. "Wives, be subject to your husbands, as to the Lord. For the husband is the head of the wife as Christ is the head of the church" (Ephesians 5:22–23). Paul wanted women to remain quiet at church meetings. "If there is anything they desire to know, let them ask their husbands at home. For it is shameful for a woman to speak in church" (I Corinthians 14:35). But Paul also held that all are baptized in Christ: "There is neither Jew nor Greek, there is neither slave nor free, there is neither male nor female; for you are all one in Christ Jesus" (Galatians 3:28). Consequently, both sexes were subject to divine law, and both possessed moral autonomy. The early church held to strict standards on sexual matters. It condemned adultery and esteemed virginity pledged for spiritual reasons.

Christians waged no war against slavery, which was widely practiced and universally accepted in the ancient world. Paul commanded slaves to obey their masters, and many Christians, including leaders of local churches, were slave owners. While Christians did not try to alter the legal status of slaves, they did teach that slaves, too, were children of God, they sought their conversion, they urged owners not to treat slaves harshly, and they considered it a virtue for owners to free slaves. In the modern world, the Christian teaching that all persons are spiritually equal before God would arouse some Christians to fight for the abolition of slavery.

Christianity and the Jews

Increasingly, Christians identified opponents—Jews, pagans, and heretics—with Satan, the fallen angel, and viewed conflicts in a moral context: a struggle between God's faithful and Satan's servants. Over the centuries, the view that they were participants in a cosmic struggle between good and evil led Christians to demonize adversaries, a practice that exacerbated hatred and justified mistreatment, even massacre. Christian attitudes and behavior toward Jews poignantly illustrate this point.

Numerous links connect early Christianity and Judaism. Jesus himself and his earliest followers, including the Twelve Disciples, were Jews who were faithful to Jewish law. Jesus frequently quoted the Hebrew Scriptures, which both to him and to his disciples was the authoritative word of God, to support a particular viewpoint. Jesus' message was first spread in synagogues throughout the Roman Empire. Early Christianity's affirmation of the preciousness of the human being, created in God's image; its belief that God rules history; its awareness of human sinfulness; its call for repentance; and its appeal to God for forgiveness are rooted in Judaism. The Christian reference to God as a "merciful Father" derives from Jewish prayer. Also rooted in Judaism are the moral norms proclaimed by Jesus in the Sermon on the Mount and on other occasions. For example, "Thou shalt love thy neighbor as thyself" was the motto of the Jewish sage Hillel, a contemporary of Jesus, who founded a school. The great value that the Torah gives to charity was inherited by Christianity. Jesus' use of parables to convey his teachings, the concept of the Messiah, respect for the Sabbath, and congregational worship also stem from Judaism. And, of course, Christians viewed the Hebrew Scriptures as God's word.

However, over the years, particularly after more and more non-Jews became followers of Christ, Christians forgot or devalued this relationship to Judaism, and some thinkers began to show hostility toward Judaism and Jews that had tragic consequences in later centuries. Several factors fueled this anti-Judaism: resentment against Jews for their refusal to embrace Jesus; the polemics of the Jewish establishment against followers of Jesus; the role in Jesus' death ascribed to Jews by the New Testament; resentment against those Christians who Judaized, that is, continued to observe Jewish festivals and the Jewish Sabbath, regard the synagogue as holy, and practice circumcision; and anger that Judaism remained a vital religion, for this undermined the conviction that Christianity was the fulfillment of Judaism and the one true faith.

What made Christian anti-Judaism particularly ominous was the effort of some theologians to **demonize** the Jewish people. The myth emerged that the Jews, murderers of the incarnate God who embodied all that was good, were a cursed people, children of the Devil, whose suffering was intended by God. Thus Origen (c. 185–c. 251) maintained that "the blood of Jesus [falls] not only upon those who lived then but also upon all generations of the Jewish people following afterwards until the end of the world."[6] In the late fourth century, John Chrysostom described Jews as "inveterate murderers, destroyers, men possessed by the Devil." "[T]hey murder their offspring and immolate them to the devil." The synagogue, he said, was "the domicile of the devil as is also the soul of the Jews."

Their rites are "criminal and impure," their religion is "a disease." For the "odious assassination of Christ," there is "no expiation possible, . . . no pardon." Jews will live "under the yoke of servitude without end."[7] Since the Devil was very real to early and medieval Christians, the Jew became identified with evil. Christians developed a mindset, concludes the Rev. Robert A. Everett, that was "unable to see anything positive in Judaism. . . . Judaism and the Jewish people came to have no real value for Christians except as a negative contrast to Christianity."[8] Because of this "teaching of contempt" and the "diabolization of the Jew," the Christian ethic of love did not extend to Jews:

> *[O]nce it is established that God has cursed the Jews, how can one argue that Christians should love them? If Jews have been fated by God to have . . . a long history of suffering, who are Christians to alter their history by doing anything to relieve Jewish suffering? The theology of victimization thus precludes Christian love as a basis of relating to Jews.*[9]

The diabolization of the Jew, which bore no relationship to the actual behavior of Jews or to their highly ethical religion, and the "theology of victimization," which held that the Jews were collectively and eternally cursed for denying Christ, became powerful myths, which, over the centuries, poisoned Christians' hearts and minds against Jews, spurring innumerable humiliations, persecutions, and massacres by Christians who believed that their actions were pleasing to God. Alongside this hatred of Jews and antipathy to their suffering, there also evolved the belief that the Jews, faithless and perfidious though they were, should be permitted to survive, for one day they would see the light and convert to the true faith.

Saint Augustine: The Christian World-View

During the early history of Christianity, learned fathers of the church explained and defended church teachings. Most of the leading early fathers wrote in Greek, but in the middle of the fourth century, three great Latin writers—Saint Jerome, Saint Ambrose, and Saint Augustine—profoundly influenced the course of Christianity in the West.

As a youth, Saint Jerome (A.D. c. 340–420) studied Latin literature in Rome. Throughout his life, he remained an admirer of Cicero, Virgil, Lucretius, and other great Latin writers, and he defended the study of classical literature by Christians. Criticized for attacking the luxurious living and laxness of the clergy, he left Rome and established a monastery near Bethlehem, where he devoted himself to prayer and study. His greatest achievement was the translation of the Old and New Testaments from Hebrew and Greek into Latin. Jerome's text, the common, or Vulgate, version of the Bible, became the official edition of the Bible for the Western church.

Saint Ambrose (A.D. 340–397), bishop of Milan, Italy, urged clerics not to pursue wealth but to practice humility and avoid favoring the rich over the poor. Ambrose sought to defend the autonomy of the church against the power of the state. Emperors are not the judges of bishops, he wrote. His dictum that "the Emperor is within the church, not above it" became a cardinal principle of the medieval church.

The most important Christian theoretician in the Late Roman Empire was Saint Augustine (A.D. 354–430), bishop of Hippo, in North Africa. Born in the North African province of Numidia, Augustine attended school at Carthage, where he studied the Latin classics. Struggling to find meaning in a world that abounded with evil, Augustine turned to Manichaeism, an Eastern religious philosophy whose central doctrine was the struggle of the universal forces of light and good against those of darkness and evil. But Augustine still felt spiritually restless. In Milan, inspired by the sermons of Ambrose, he abandoned Manichaeism and devoted his life to following Christ's teachings. After serving as a priest, he was appointed bishop of Hippo in 395.

In his autobiography, the *Confessions,* Augustine described his spiritual quest and appealed to devotees of Manichaeism and to adherents of pagan philosophy to embrace Christianity. At the turn of the fifth century, when the Greco-Roman world-view was disintegrating and the Roman world-state was collapsing, Augustine wrote his greatest and most influential work, *The City of God.* He became the chief architect of the

CHRIST ENTHRONED. Detail from the funerary sarcophagus of Junius Bassus, A.D. 359. (*Hirmer Fotoarchiv, München.*)

Christian outlook that succeeded a dying classicism.

Online Study Center
Improve Your Grade
Primary Source: St. Augustine's Search for Truth: Divination and Manichaeism

In 410, when Augustine was in his fifties, Visigoths sacked Rome—a disaster for which the classical consciousness was unprepared. Throughout the Empire, people panicked. Non-Christians blamed the tragedy on Christianity, saying that the Christians had predicted the end of the world and by refusing to offer sacrifices to ancient gods had turned those deities against Rome. Even Christians expressed anxiety. Why were the righteous also suffering? Where was the kingdom of God on earth that had been prophesied in the Scriptures?

Augustine's *City of God* was a response to the crisis of the Roman Empire, just as Plato's *The Republic* had been a reaction to the crisis of the Athenian polis. Whereas Plato expressed hope that a state founded on rational principles could remedy the abuses of Athenian society, Augustine maintained that the worldly city could never be the central concern of a Christian. The ideal state, he wrote, could not be realized on earth; it existed only in heaven. The misfortunes of Rome, therefore, should not distress a Christian unduly for Christianity belonged to the realm of the spirit and could not be identified with any state. The collapse of Rome did not diminish the greatness of Christianity because the true Christian was a citizen of a heavenly city that could not be pillaged by ungodly barbarians but would endure forever. Compared with God's heavenly city, Rome and its decline were unimportant. What really mattered in history, Augustine said, was not the coming to be or the passing away of cities and empires, but the individual's spiritual destiny, his or her entrance into heaven or hell.

Yet Augustine remained a man of this world. Although the earthly city was the very opposite of the heavenly city, he insisted that people must still deal with this earthly abode. Christians could not reject their city entirely but must bend it to fit a Christian pattern. The city that someday would rise from the ruins of Rome must be based on Christian principles. Warfare, economic activity, education, and the rearing of children should all be conducted in a Christian spirit. The church could not neglect the state but must guide it to protect human beings from their own sinful natures. The state must employ repression and punishment to restrain people, who were inherently sinful, from destroying each other. But the earthly city would never know tranquillity, said Augustine, for it would always be inhabited predominantly by wretched sinners. People should be under no illusion that it could be transformed into the City of God. Because human beings are infected with sin, everywhere in human society we see

> *love for all those things that prove so vain and . . . breed so many heartaches, troubles, griefs, and fears; such insane joys in discord, strife, and war; such wrath and plots of enemies . . . such fraud and theft and robbery; such perfidy . . . homicide and murder, cruelty and savagery, lawlessness and lust; all the shameless passions of the impure—fornication and adultery . . . and countless other uncleannesses too nasty to be mentioned; the sins against religion—sacrilege and heresy . . . the iniquities against our neighbors—calumnies and cheating, lies and false witness, violence to persons and property . . . and the innumerable other miseries and maladies that fill the world, yet escape attention.*[10]

Augustine did not hold that Christ, by his sacrificial death, had opened the door to heaven for all. Most of humanity remained condemned to eternal punishment, said Augustine; only a handful had the gift of faith and the promise of heaven. Whereas the vast majority of people, said Augustine, were citizens of a doomed earthly city, the small number endowed with God's grace constituted the City of God. These people lived on earth as visitors only, for they awaited deliverance to the Kingdom of Christ, where together with the good angels and God they would know perfect happiness. But the permanent inhabitants of the earthly city were destined for eternal punishment in hell. A perpetual conflict existed between the two cities and between their inhabitants; one city stood for sin and corruption, the other for God's truth and perfection. For Augustine, the highest good was not of this world but consisted of eternal life with God.

Augustine's distinction between this higher world of perfection and a lower world of corruption remained influential throughout the Middle Ages. But the church, rejecting Augustine's doctrine that only a limited number of people are predestined for heaven, emphasized that Christ had made possible the salvation of all who would embrace the precepts and injunctions of the church. The Protestant reformers of the sixteenth century, however, accepted Augustine's position.

Augustine repudiated the distinguishing feature of classical humanism: the autonomy of reason. For him, ultimate wisdom could not be achieved through rational thought alone. Reason had to be guided by faith. Without faith, there could be no true knowledge, no understanding. Philosophy had no validity if it did not first accept as absolutely true the existence of God and the authority of his revelation. Valid ethical standards could not be formulated by reason alone but were revealed to people by the living God. Christian truth did not rest on theoretical excellence or logical consistency; it was true because its source was God.

Augustine's belief contrasts with that of Socrates, who insisted that through rational reflection each individual could arrive at standards of good and evil. For the humanist Socrates, ultimate values were something that the individual could grasp through thought alone and could defend rationally. For Augustine, reason alone could not serve as a proper guide to life. He maintained that individuals, without divine guidance, lacked the capacity to comprehend ultimate truth or to regenerate themselves morally. Without God, they could not attain wisdom or liberate themselves from a wicked and sinful human nature: "the happiness of man can come not from himself but only from God, and . . . to live according to oneself is sin."[11]

Thus, against the classical view that asserted the primacy of reason, Augustine opposed the primacy of faith. He denied the classical view that reason *alone* could attain wisdom, could instruct people how to live. The wisdom that Augustine sought was Christian wisdom, God's revelation to humanity. The starting point for this wisdom, he said, was belief in God and the Scriptures. For Augustine, secular knowledge for its own sake had little value; the true significance of knowledge lay in its role as a tool for comprehending God's will. Let us utilize truths useful to the faith that pagan philosophers might have chanced upon, he said. Augustine adapted the classical intellectual tradition to the requirements of Christian revelation.

With Augustine, the human-centered outlook of classical humanism, which for centuries had been undergoing transformation, gave way to a God-centered world-view. The fulfillment of God's will, not the full development of human talent, became the chief concern of life.

Augustinian Christianity is a living philosophy because it still has something vital to say about the human condition. To those who believe that people have the intelligence and goodwill to transform their earthly city into a rational and just community that promotes human betterment, Augustine offers a reminder of human sinfulness, weakness, and failure. Nor will new and ingenious political and social arrangements alter a defective human nature. He cautions the optimist that progress is not certain; that people, weak and ever prone to wickedness, are their

Saint Augustine in His Studio. Saint Augustine was the most influential Christian theoretician in the Late Roman Empire. (*Corbis-Bettmann.*)

own worst enemies; that success is illusory; and that misery is the essential human reality.

Christianity and Classical Humanism: Alternative World-Views

Christianity and classical humanism are the two principal components of the Western tradition. The value that modern Western civilization places on the individual derives ultimately from classical humanism and the Judeo-Christian tradition. Classical humanists believed that human worth came from the capacity of individuals to reason and to shape their character and life according to rational standards. Christianity also places great stress on the individual. In the Christian view, God cares for each person; he wants people to behave righteously and to enter heaven; Christ died for all because he loves humanity. Christianity espouses active love and genuine concern for fellow human beings. Without God, people are as Augustine described them: "foul, crooked, sordid, . . . vicious." With God, the human personality can undergo a moral transformation and become loving, good, and free. The idea of a Christian conscience, prompted by God and transcending all other loyalties, reinforces respect for all human beings regardless of cultural and national differences. Also promoting respect for each person is the presupposition of natural equality stemming from the Christian belief that each individual, regardless of birth, wealth, or talent, is precious to God.

There are striking parallels between Christian and Stoic ethics. Both Stoics and Christians believed that there is an essential "brotherhood of man," that all human beings are related and possess a fundamental dignity. Both urged suppressing wild passions, expressing concern for others, and living simply and heeding the inner voice of conscience that commands human beings to do what is right.

But Christianity and classical humanism also represent two essentially different world-views. The triumph of the Christian outlook signified a break with the essential meaning of classical humanism; it pointed to the end of the world of antiquity and the beginning of an age of faith, the Middle Ages. With the victory of Christianity, the ultimate goal of life shifted. Life's purpose was no longer to achieve excellence in this world through the full and creative development of human capacities, but to attain salvation in a heavenly city. A person's worldly accomplishments amounted to very little if he or she did not accept God and his revelation. The Christian ideal of the isolated and contemplative monk, who rejected the world in order to serve God, was alien to the spirit of classical humanism, which valued active citizenship and active participation in worldly activities. Equally foreign to the Greco-Roman mind was another idea introduced by Christianity: the need to escape from a sinful human nature, a consequence of Adam and Eve's defiance of God. This view of a corrupt human nature and an unclean human body, particularly in Augustine's formulation, became deeply embedded in the European mind during the Christian centuries—the Middle Ages.

In the classical view, history had no ultimate end, no ultimate meaning; periods of happiness and misery repeated themselves endlessly. In the Christian view, history is filled with spiritual meaning. It is the profound drama of individuals struggling to overcome their original sin in order to gain eternal happiness in heaven. History began with Adam and Eve's fall and would end when Christ returns to earth, evil is eradicated, and God's will prevails. For the Christian, Christ on the cross was both the central event and a turning point in world history.

Classicism held that there was no authority higher than reason, that individuals had within themselves, through unaided reason, the ability to understand the world and life. Christianity teaches that, without God as the starting point, knowledge is formless, purposeless, and prone to error. Classicism, unlike Judaism or Christianity, possessed no truths or moral precepts revealed by a divine power. Rather, classicism held that ethical standards were expressions of universal reason, laws of nature, which reason could discover. Through reason, individuals could discern the norms by which they should regulate their lives. Reason would enable them to govern desires and will; it would show where their behavior was wrong and teach them how to correct it. Because individuals sought what was best for themselves, they would obey the voice of reason. Christianity, on the other hand, maintains that ethical standards emanate from the personal will of God. Without submission to God's commands, people remain wicked forever; the human will, essentially sinful, cannot be transformed by the promptings of reason. Only when individuals turn to God for forgiveness and guidance can they find the inner strength to overcome their sinful nature. People cannot perfect themselves through scientific knowledge; it is spiritual insight and belief in God that they require and that must serve as the first principle of their lives. For classicism, the ultimate good was sought through independent thought and action; for Christianity, the ultimate good comes through knowing, obeying, and loving God.

Although some Christian thinkers dismissed Greek philosophy as erroneous and useless, others respected the Greek intellectual tradition and rejected attempts to eradicate it. Rather, they sought to fit it into a Christian framework—that is, rational inquiry must be guided by and never conflict with Christian teachings. By holding that the mind is limited in its capacity to think for itself and must be guided by faith and clerical authority, Christianity contributed to the waning of the classical tradition in the Late Roman Empire. For centuries articles of faith would predominate over empirical observation and logic. Nevertheless, by preserving the Greek philosophical tradition—even if it remained subordinate to the Christian outlook—Christian thinkers performed a task of immense historical significance.

Christianity inherited the Hebrew view of the overriding importance of God for humanity: God, who is both Lawgiver and Judge, makes life intelligible and purposeful. For the Christian, God is a living being, loving and compassionate, in whose company one seeks to spend eternity; one knows God essentially through faith and feeling. Although the Greek philosophers had a conception of God, it was not comparable to the God of Hebrews and Christians. For the Greeks, God was a logical abstraction, a principle of order, the prime mover, the first cause, the mind of the universe, pure thought, the supreme good, the highest truth; God was a concept, impersonal, unfeeling, and uninvolved with human concerns. The Greeks approached God through the intellect, not the heart; they neither loved nor worshiped God. In addition, because religion was at the periphery, not the center, of classical humanism, the idea of God did not carry the same significance as it did for Christianity.

The Ascension of Jesus into Heaven: A Miniature Painting c. a.d. 586. In this illustration contained in a manuscript produced by a monk at Saint John's Abbey, Zagba, Mesopotamia, the upper zone of the painting reflects a vision of the prophet Ezekiel (1:3–28). The lower zone shows Jesus' Disciples and his mother Mary with two angels as witnesses to Jesus' ascension into heaven. (Acts 1:7–14). (*Courtesy Biblioteca Medicea Laurenziana, Florence. Photo by Donato Pineides.*)

From the Hebrews, Christianity also inherited the beliefs that there was a prescribed way to worship the one true God, that belief in other gods was an abomination, and that nonbelievers (or infidels) and heretics were wicked sinners hated by God. Over the centuries, this outlook sanctioned fanaticism, persecution, and holy war with accompanying massacres—a terrible legacy that constitues the dark side of monotheism. Unlike the monotheistic faiths—Judaism, Christianity, and Islam—Greek and Roman polytheism had no concepts of **martyrdom** for the true faith and holy war against the infidel and consistently tolerated many different religious beliefs and practices as long as they did not threaten the state.

In the classical world, the political community was the avenue to justice, happiness, and self-realization. In Christianity, the good life was identified not with worldly achievement but with life eternal, and the ideal commonwealth could only be one that was founded and ruled by Christ. It was entrance into God's kingdom that each person must make the central aim of life. For the next thousand years, this distinction between heaven and earth, this otherworldly, theocentric outlook, would define the Western mentality.

In the Late Roman Empire, when classical values were in decay, Christianity was a dynamic and creative movement. Possessing both institutional and spiritual strength, Christianity survived the fall of Rome. Because it retained elements of Greco-Roman civilization and taught a high morality, Christianity served as a civilizing agent in the centuries that followed Rome's collapse. Indeed, Christianity was the essential shaper of the European civilization that emerged in the Middle Ages.

❖ ❖ ❖

Online Study Center **ACE the Test**

Notes

1. Hans Küng, "Christianity and Judaism," in *Jesus' Jewishness,* ed. James H. Charlesworth (New York: Crossroad, 1991), p. 259.
2. The biblical quotations, used with permission, are from the Holy Bible, Revised Standard Version (New York: Thomas Nelson & Sons, 1952). The Revised Standard Version is the text used for biblical quotations throughout, except where noted otherwise.
3. Tertullian, "On Prescription Against Heretics," chap. 7, in Alexander Roberts and James Donaldson, eds., *The Ante-Nicene Fathers* (New York: Charles Scribner's Sons, 1918), 3:246.
4. Clement of Alexandria, *Stromata (Miscellanies),* trans. William Wilson, in Alexander Roberts and James Donaldson, *Ante-Nicene Christian Library* (Edinburgh: T & T Clark, 1867–1872), vol. 4, *The Writings of Clement of Alexandria,* pp. 303–304.
5. Tertullian, "On the Flesh of Christ," in Roberts and Donaldson, *The Ante-Nicene Fathers,* p. 525.
6. *Origenis, Commentariorum in Evangelium Secundum Matthaeum* in *Patrologiae Cursus Completus,* Series Graeca Prior, ed. J. P. Migne (Paris: Parisiorum, 1862), vol. 13, cols. 1494–1495, pars. 775–776; trans. J. Castora for this volume.
7. Quoted in Edward H. Flannery, *The Anguish of the Jews* (London: Macmillan, 1965), p. 48.
8. Randolph Braham, ed., *The Origins of the Holocaust: Christian Anti-Semitism* (Boulder, Colo: Social Science Monographs and Institute for Holocaust Studies of the City University of New York, 1986), p. 36.
9. Ibid., p. 37.
10. Saint Augustine, *The City of God,* trans. Gerald G. Walsh et al., abridged (Garden City, N.Y.: Doubleday Image Books, 1958), p. 519.
11. Ibid., p. 300.

Suggested Reading

Armstrong, Karen, *A History of God* (1994). Good material on early Christianity.

Benko, Stephen, *Pagan Rome and the Early Christians* (1984). How Romans and Greeks viewed early Christianity.

Chadwick, Henry, *The Early Church* (1967). A survey of early Christianity in its social and ideological context.

Charlesworth, James, ed., *Jesus' Jewishness* (1991). Essays by prominent scholars exploring the Jewish context of early Christianity.

Ferguson, Everett, ed., *Encyclopedia of Early Christianity* (1990). Entries on all aspects of early Christianity.

———, *Backgrounds of Early Christianity* (1993). A clear and thorough examination of the milieu in which Christianity was born.

Perkins, Pheme, *Reading the New Testament* (1978). Introduces the beginning student to the New Testament.

Perry, Marvin, and Frederick M. Schweitzer, eds., *Jewish-Christian Encounters over the Centuries* (1994). Useful essays on Jesus, Paul, the Dead Sea Scrolls, and early Christian anti-Judaism.

Part Two

The Middle Ages: The Christian Centuries

500–1400

500
600
700
800
900
1000
1100
1200
1300

Politics and Society	Thought and Culture
Germanic kingdoms established on former Roman lands (5th and 6th cent.) Saint Benedict founds monastery at Monte Cassino (529) Pope Gregory I sends missionaries to convert Anglo-Saxons (596)	Boethius, *Consolation of Philosophy* (523) Law code of Justinian (529) Byzantine church Hagia Sophia (532–537) Cassiodorus establishes a monastic library at Vivarium (540)
Spread of Islam (622–732)	The Koran
Charles Martel defeats Muslims at Tours (732)	Bede, *Ecclesiastical History of the English People* (c. 700) Muslim Golden Age (700s and 800s)
Charlemagne crowned emperor of Romans Alfred the Great, ruler of Saxon kingdom of Wessex (871–899) Muslim, Magyar, and Viking invasions of Latin Christendom (9th and early 10th cent.) Growth of feudalism (800–1100)	Carolingian Renaissance (768–814) Alfred the Great promotes learning in England (871–899)
German king Otto I becomes first Holy Roman Emperor (962)	
Split between the Byzantine and Roman churches (1054) Norman conquest of England (1066) Start of First Crusade (1096)	Romanesque style in architecture (1000s and 1100s)
Philip Augustus expands central authority in France (1180–1223) Development of common law and jury system in England (1100s) Pontificate of Innocent III: height of papal power (1198–1216)	Flowering of medieval culture (12th and 13th cent.): universities, Gothic architecture, scholastic philosophy, revival of Roman law
Magna Carta (1215) Destruction of Baghdad by Mongols (1258)	Aquinas, *Summa Theologica* (1267–1273)
Hundred Years' War (1337–1453) Black Death (1347–1351) Great Schism of papacy (1378–1417)	Dante, *Divine Comedy* (c. 1307–1321) Chaucer, *Canterbury Tales* (c. 1388–1400)

Chapter 9

The Heirs of Rome: Byzantium, Islam, and Latin Christendom

Coronation of Charlemagne. (Scala/Art Resource, NY.)

- **Byzantine Civilization: The Medieval Christian East**
- **Islamic Civilization: Its Development and Dissemination**
- **Latin Christendom: The Rise of Europe**
- **The Church: Shaper of Medieval Civilization**
- **The Kingdom of the Franks**
- **Medieval Society**

Focus Questions

1. How did Latin Christendom blend Christian, Greco-Roman, and Germanic traditions?
2. In what ways were Greco-Roman ideas and institutions alien to Germanic traditions?
3. What was Byzantium's long-term influence on world history?
4. What does Islam have in common with Christianity? How do they differ?
5. What was the significance of medieval Muslim intellectual life?
6. What conditions led to the rise of feudalism and manorialism?

Online Study Center

This icon will direct you to interactive map and primary source activities on the website http://college.hmco.com/pic/perrywc8e.

The triumph of Christianity, the decay of the Roman Empire, and the establishment of Germanic kingdoms on once Roman lands constituted a new phase in Western history: the end of the ancient world and the beginning of the Middle Ages, a period that spanned a thousand years. In the ancient world, the locus of Greco-Roman civilization had been the Mediterranean Sea; the heartland of Western medieval civilization gradually shifted to the north, to regions of Europe that Greco-Roman civilization had barely penetrated. **Latin Christendom** (western and central Europe) was only one of three new civilizations based on religion that emerged after the decline of the Roman Empire; Byzantium and Islam were the other two. Both of these Eastern civilizations influenced the emerging Europe in important ways.

Byzantine Civilization: The Medieval Christian East

Although the Roman Empire in the West fell to the German tribes, the eastern provinces of the Empire survived. They did so because they were richer, more urbanized, and more populous and because the main thrust of the Germanic and Hunnish invaders had been directed at the western regions. In the eastern parts, Byzantine civilization took shape. Its religion was Christianity, its culture Greek, and its machinery of administration Roman. The capital, Constantinople, was built on the site of the ancient Greek city of Byzantium, on a peninsula in the Straits of Bosporus—the dividing line between Asia and Europe. Constantinople was a fortress city perfectly situated to resist attacks from land and sea.

During the Early Middle Ages (500–1050), Byzantine civilization was economically and culturally far more advanced than the Latin West. At a time when few westerners (Latin Christians) could read or write, Byzantine scholars studied the literature, philosophy, science, and law of ancient Greece and Rome. Whereas trade and urban life had greatly declined in the West, Constantinople was a magnificent Byzantine city of

Chronology 9.1 ❖ The Rise of Europe

496	Clovis adopts Roman Christianity
523	Boethius writes *Consolation of Philosophy*
540	Cassiodorus establishes a monastic library at Vivarium
596	Pope Gregory I sends missionaries to convert the Anglo-Saxons
717	Charles Martel becomes mayor of the palace under a weak Merovingian king
732	Charles Martel defeats the Muslims at Tours
751	Pepin the Short, with papal support, deposes the Merovingian ruler and becomes king of the Franks
755	Pepin donates to the papacy lands taken from the Lombards
768	Charlemagne becomes king of the Franks
774	Charlemagne defeats the Lombards
782	Alcuin of York heads Charlemagne's palace school
c. 799	Charlemagne subdues the Saxons
800	Charlemagne is crowned emperor of the Romans by Pope Leo III
814	Charlemagne dies and is succeeded by his son, Louis the Pious
840	Death of Louis the Pious: the empire is divided among his sons
c. 840s	Height of Viking attacks
c. 890	Magyars invade central Europe

schools, libraries, open squares, and bustling markets.

Conflict with the Roman Church

Over the centuries, many differences developed between the Eastern church and the Roman church. The pope in Rome resisted domination by the Byzantine emperor, and the Byzantines denied the pope's claim to authority over all Christians. The two churches quarreled over ceremonies, holy days, the display of images, and the rights of the clergy. The final break came in 1054. The Christian church split into the Roman Catholic in the West and the Eastern (Greek) Orthodox in the East, a division that still persists.

Political and cultural differences widened the rift between Latin Christendom and Byzantium. Latin Christians refused to recognize that the Byzantine emperors were, as they claimed, successors to the Roman emperors. In the Byzantine Empire, Greek was the language of religion and intellectual life; in the West, it was Latin.

Imperial Growth and Decline

Byzantine emperors were absolute rulers who held that God had chosen them to rule and to institute divine will on earth. As successors to the Roman emperors, they claimed to rule all the lands once part of the Roman Empire. The first great Byzantine ruler was Justinian, who reigned nearly forty years, from 527 to 565. Justinian often relied on the advice of his wife, Theodora. Theodora's background was unusual for an empress; she was not from the nobility but was the daughter of a bear trainer in the circus and had been an actress, a profession most people considered degrading. In a number of crises, the strong-

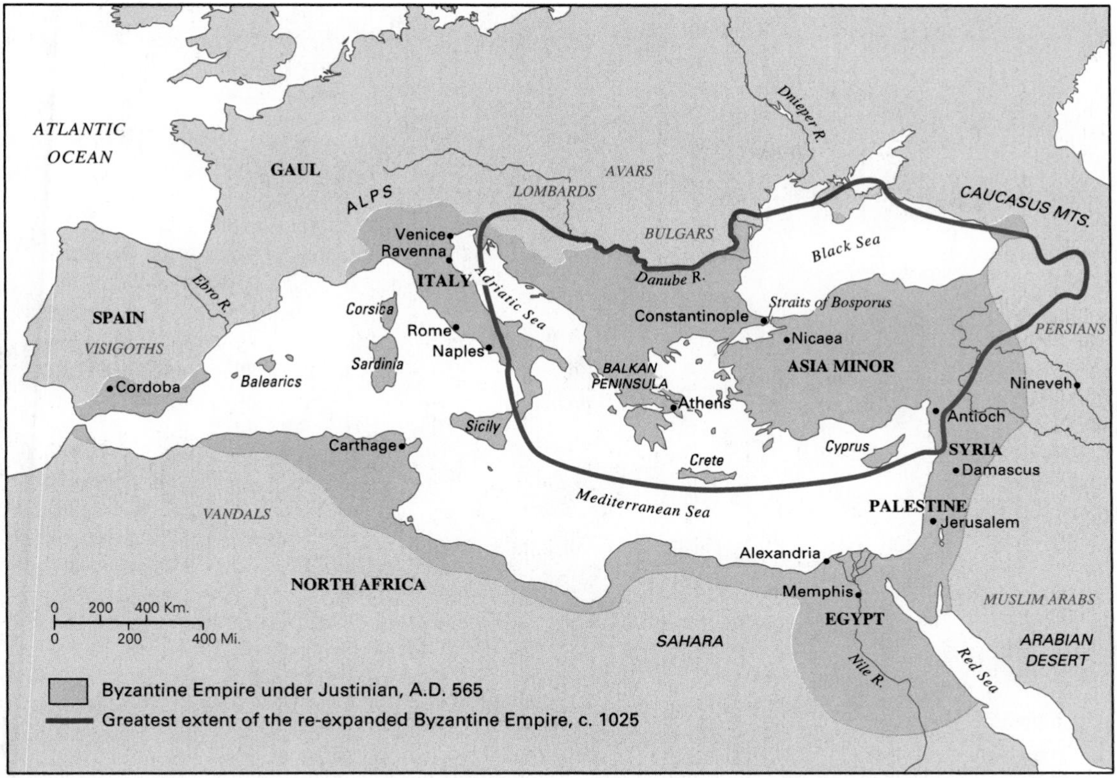

Map 9.1 **The Byzantine Empire** In the centuries after Justinian regained lands in the western Mediterranean that had been lost to Germanic invaders, the Byzantines faced attacks from Avars, Bulgars, Lombards, Persians, Arabs, Latin Christians, Seljuk Turks, and the Ottoman Turks, who captured Constantinople in 1453.

willed and astute Theodora gave Justinian the courage to act decisively.

Justinian's most lasting achievement was the appointment of a commission of scholars to collect and codify Rome's ancient laws and the commentaries of learned jurists. The result was the *Corpus Juris Civilis,* which became the official body of law of the Byzantine Empire. In the twelfth century, it was gradually reintroduced into western Europe, where it became the basis of common law in many European lands.

Justinian sought to regain the lands in the western Mediterranean that had been conquered by Germanic invaders. During his reign, Byzantine forces retook North Africa from the Vandals, part of southern Spain from the Visigoths, and Italy from the Ostrogoths, establishing a western capital at Ravenna.

Besides draining the treasury, the long and costly wars led to the neglect of defenses in the Balkan Peninsula and the Near East. The Balkans were invaded by Slavic tribes from the Black Sea region and by Avars and Bulgars, originally from central Asia; Syria was ravaged by the Persians. Nor were the conquered territories in the west secure. The Germanic Lombards, who had moved into northern Italy in the late sixth century, conquered much Byzantine territory that had been recently recovered from the Ostrogoths. By 629, the Visigoths had driven the Byzantines from Spain.

In the early seventh century, the Byzantines faced a renewed threat from the Persians, who

RAVENNA MOSAICS. Theodora, emperor Justinian's wife, was a strong-willed woman who exercised considerable authority and often advised her husband on matters of state. (*AKG London.*)

seized the Byzantine provinces of Syria, Palestine, and Egypt. In an all-out effort, however, Emperor Heraclius (610–641) regained the provinces and in 627 crushed the Persians near the ruins of the ancient city of Nineveh. But the exhausted Byzantine Empire had become vulnerable to the Muslim Arabs, who had moved swiftly out of the Arabian Desert seeking to propagate Islam, their new faith (discussed later in this chapter).

By 642, the Arabs had stripped the Byzantine Empire of Syria, Palestine, and Egypt, and by the beginning of the eighth century, they had taken North Africa. Near the end of the seventh century and again in 717, the Muslims besieged Constantinople. But the Byzantine fleet was armed with a new weapon, "Greek fire"—a fiery explosive liquid shot from tubes—which set enemy ships aflame and made blazing pools on the water's surface. Thus, the light Byzantine ships were able to repulse the better-built Arabian ships.

The Arabs' failure to take Constantinople was crucial not only for the Byzantine Empire but also for the history of Christianity. Had this Christian fortress fallen in the eighth century, the Arabs would have been able to overrun the Balkan Peninsula and sail up the Danube River into the European heartland. After this defeat, however, Islamic armies largely concentrated their conquests outside Europe.

From the late ninth to the early eleventh century, the Byzantine forces grew stronger and even took the offensive against the Muslims. But soon

CHURCH OF THE HOLY WISDOM (HAGIA SOPHIA), CONSTANTINOPLE, A.D. 532–537. The largest church ever built in the Byzantine world, Hagia Sophia was constructed by Emperor Justinian. The interior of its immense dome was decorated with golden mosaics simulating the light of heaven. After the Turkish conquest of Constantinople in A.D. 1453, the mosaics were painted white, the church was converted into a mosque, and minarets (towers from which the faithful were summoned for prayer five times a day) were constructed. (*Gary Yeowell/Tony Stone.*)

new enemies threatened. By 1071, the Normans from France had driven the Byzantines from Italy. In the same year, the Seljuk Turks, a people from central Asia who had adopted Islam, defeated the Byzantines in Asia Minor and subjugated most of the peninsula, the heart of the Byzantine Empire. Internal dissension, however, led to the breakup of the Seljuk Empire.

Seeking to exploit Seljuk weakness and to regain lost territories, the Byzantines appealed to Latin Christians for help. Although European Christians had little love for the Byzantines, they did want to free Christian holy places from the Muslims. For this purpose, they undertook a series of Crusades, beginning in the late eleventh century (see Chapter 10). In 1204, during the Fourth Crusade, Latin Christian knights (greedy for riches) and Venetian merchants (eager to gain control of the rich Byzantine trade) decided to take Constantinople rather than fight the Muslims.

The Latin Christians looted the city, destroying sacred books, vandalizing churches, and carrying huge amounts of gold, jewels, Christian relics, and works of art back to western Europe. They also seized islands along Constantinople's major trade routes, set up kingdoms on Byzantine lands, and tried to force Latin forms of Christianity on the Byzantine Greeks. The Orthodox Greeks resisted, and for nearly sixty years Latin and Greek Christians fought one another. Not until 1261 were the westerners driven from Constantinople. The Byzantine Empire regained its independence, but its power was disastrously weakened. Crushing taxes, decreasing agricultural production, declining trade, and civil war continued to sap the tottering empire.

The deathblow to the empire was dealt by another group of Turks from central Asia. The Ottoman Turks had accepted Islam and had begun to build an empire. They drove the Byzantines from Asia Minor and conquered much of the Balkans. By the beginning of the fifteenth century, the Byzantine Empire consisted of only two small territories in Greece and the city of Constantinople. In 1453, the Ottoman Turks broke through Constantinople's great walls and plundered the city. After more than ten centuries, the Byzantine Empire came to an end.

The Bequest of Byzantium

During its thousand years, Byzantium made a significant impact on world history. First, it prevented the Muslim Arabs from advancing into eastern Europe. Had the Arabs broken through Byzantine defenses, much of Europe might have been converted to the new faith of Islam. A far-reaching accomplishment was the codification of the laws of ancient Rome under Justinian. This monumental achievement preserved Roman law's principles of reason and justice. Today's legal codes in much of Europe and Latin America trace their roots to the Roman law recorded by Justinian's lawyers. The Byzantines also preserved the philosophy, science, mathematics, and literature of ancient Greece.

Contacts with Byzantine civilization stimulated learning in both the Islamic world to the east and Latin Christendom to the west. Speros Vryonis, a student of Byzantine civilization, states: "The Byzantines carried the torch of civilization unextinguished at a time when the barbarous Germanic and Slav tribes had reduced much of Europe to near chaos: and they maintained this high degree of civilization until Western Europe gradually emerged and began to take form."[1] Byzantium exerted an important religious, cultural, and linguistic influence on Latin Romanians, eastern Slavs (Russians and Ukrainians), and southern Slavs (Serbs and Bulgars). From Byzantium, the Slavs acquired legal principles, art forms, and an alphabet (the Cyrillic, based on the Greek) for writing their languages. (On the other hand, the western Slavs—Poles, Czechs, and Slovaks—came under the influence of Latin Christianity and Latin culture.)

Islamic Civilization: Its Development and Dissemination

The Prophet: The Founding of a New Religion

The second eastern civilization to arise after Rome's fall was based on the vital new religion of Islam, which emerged in the seventh century among the Arabs of Arabia. Its founder was Muhammad (c. 570–632), a prosperous merchant in Mecca, a trading city near the Red Sea. When Muhammad was about forty, he believed that he was visited in his sleep by the angel Gabriel, who ordered him to "recite in the name of the Lord!" Transformed by this experience, Muhammad came to believe that he had been chosen as a prophet.

Although most desert Arabs worshiped tribal gods, in the towns and trading centers many Arabs were familiar with Judaism and Christianity, and some had accepted the idea of one God. Rejecting the many deities of the tribal religions, Muhammad offered the Arabs a new monotheistic faith, Islam, which means "surrender to Allah (God)."

Islamic standards of morality and rules governing daily life are set by the Koran, the book that Muslims believe contains the words of Allah as revealed to Muhammad. For Muslims, the Koran is both God's final word and infallible. Muslims see their religion as the completion and perfection of Judaism and Christianity; they believe both of those monotheistic predecessors were superseded by Allah's revelation to Muhammad. Muslims regard the ancient Hebrew prophets as sent from God and value their messages about compassion and the oneness of humanity. They also regard Jesus as a great prophet but do not consider him di-

MOSQUE OF MOHAMMED ALI, CAIRO, TWELFTH CENTURY A.D. This mosque was a gathering place for prayer, preaching, and study of the Koran. Mosques were usually rectangular buildings, with arcaded porticos surrounding an open court. Inside, the focal point was an apse facing Mecca from which the local *Imam* (holy man) led the congregation in prayer. Nearby was a pulpit for preaching and a copy of the Koran on a lectern. In the outer court were pools or fountains for ritual purification. At the Cairo mosque, the fountains were covered by a domed building. Attached to the mosque were minarets for calling the faithful to daily prayers. (*Courtesy Trans World Airlines.*)

vine. They see Muhammad as the last and greatest of the prophets and believe that he was entirely human, not divine. Muslims worship only Allah, the creator and ruler of heaven and earth, a single, all-powerful God who is merciful, compassionate, and just. According to the Koran, on the Day of Judgment, unbelievers and the wicked "shall dwell amidst scorching winds and seething water: in the shade of pitch-black smoke . . . sinners that deny the truth . . . shall eat . . . [bitter] fruit . . . [and] drink boiling water."[2] Faithful Muslims who have lived virtuously are promised paradise, which they believe to be a garden where they will experience bodily pleasures and spiritual delights.

An essential feature of Islam is the obligation of the faithful to obey the Five Pillars of the faith:

SHI'A MANUSCRIPT, C. 1307. The Shi'ites give their loyalty to the house of Ali, cousin and son-in-law of Muhammad. In this picture, Muhammad, on the left, declares Ali his successor. (*Special Collections, Edinburgh University Library.*)

(1) A Muslim must accept and repeat the statement of faith: "There is no God but Allah, and Muhammad is his Prophet." (2) At least five times a day, a believer must face the holy city of Mecca and pray. (3) Muslims have a religious duty to be generous to the poor. (4) During the holy month of Ramadan, believers should not eat or drink between sunrise and sunset. (5) Muslims are expected to make at least one pilgrimage to the holy city of Mecca.

Muhammad's religion began to win followers, but the ruling elite of Mecca would not accept this new faith. To escape persecution, Muhammad and his small band of followers left Mecca in 622 for Medina, a town about two hundred miles away. Their flight, known as the *Hegira,* or "emigration," is one of the most important events in Muslim history and is commemorated by yearly pilgrimages. The date of the Hegira became year one of the Muslim calendar.

In Medina, Muhammad gained converts and won respect as a judge, rendering decisions on such matters as family relations, property inheritance, and criminal behavior. Preaching a holy war against unbelievers, Muhammad urged followers to raid the trading caravans from Mecca and to subdue unfriendly Bedouin tribes. He tried to convert the Jews of Medina, but they would not accept him as a prophet and mocked his unfamiliarity with the Hebrew Scriptures and the learned writings of the rabbis. To a large extent, political considerations determined Muhammad's attitude toward Jews, who sided with his Meccan enemies. He expelled several thousand Jews from Medina, seized Jewish property, beheaded some six hundred Jewish men, and enslaved women and children. Later, he permitted the Arabian Jews the free exercise of their religion and guaranteed the security of their property. In 630, Mecca surrendered to a Muslim army without a fight. Soon Bedouin tribes all over Arabia embraced Islam and recognized the authority of the Prophet Muhammad.

In a little more than two decades, Muhammad united the often feuding Arabian tribes into a powerful force dedicated to Allah and the spreading of the Islamic faith. After Muhammad's death in 632, his friend and father-in-law, Abu Bakr, became his successor, or caliph. Regarded as the defender of the faith, whose power derived from Allah, the caliph governed in accordance with Muslim law as defined in the Koran.

Islam gave the many Arab tribes the unity, discipline, and organization to succeed in their wars of conquest. Under the first four caliphs, who ruled from 632 to 661, the Arabs, with breathtaking speed, overran the Persian Empire, seized some of Byzantium's provinces, and invaded Europe. Muslim warriors believed that they were engaged in a holy war, **jihad**—literally, striving in the path of God—to spread Islam to nonbelievers and that those who died in the jihad were assured a place in paradise. A desire to escape from the barren Arabian Desert and to exploit the rich Byzantine and Persian lands was another compelling reason for expansion. In the east, Islam's territory eventually extended into India and to the borders of China; in the west, it encompassed North Africa and most of Spain. The Muslims' northward push lost momentum and was halted in 717 by the Byzantines at Constantinople and in 732 by the Franks at the battle of Tours, in central France.

Online Study Center **Improve Your Grade**
Interactive Map: The Expansion of Islam to 732

The Muslim State and Society

After the death of Muhammad, Muslims sought authoritative guidance on religious, social, and moral questions that the Koran did not specifically address. The most important source for such guidance was *Hadith*—a collection of sayings, stories, and actions of the Prophet on a wide range of topics. The Koran coupled with the Hadith provided directions for a complete way of life for Muslims.

The Islamic state was a theocracy: government and religion were inseparable; there could be no distinction between secular and spiritual authority. Muslims viewed God as the source of all law and political authority and the caliph as his earthly deputy. Divine law regulated all aspects of human relations. The ruler who did not enforce Koranic law failed in his duties. Thus, Islam was more than a religion; it was also a system of government, society, law, and thought that bound its adherents into an all-encompassing community. The idea of a single society governed by the Koran remained in the Muslim mind over the centuries and is a principal aim of Muslim fundamentalists today. The separation of church and state, which became firmly rooted in the West in modern times, still remains an alien concept in much of the Muslim world.

Christians and Jews who lived in Islamic lands had fewer rights than Muslims—they could not bear arms, were assessed a special tax, and, at times, were barred from testifying in court against a Muslim. Nevertheless, as "people of the book," Jews and Christians were protected communities, and despite instances of loss of property or life, or both, the two groups generally went about their business and practiced their religions free of persecution. In fact, Jews were physically safer in Muslim than in Christian lands, and unlike medieval Christians, Muslims generally did not demonize Jews as a hateful and cursed people deserving divine punishment.

Muslims perceived themselves as members of a single community of the faithful, but the emergence of sects ruptured the unity of Islam. In the Muslim world, dissent from the established social and political order was expressed through religious movements that challenged orthodoxy. The principal division—one that still incites bitter animosity—was between the Sunnis and the Shi'ites. The Sunnis, who were in the majority, followed traditional teachings and established practices as defined by the consensus of the Muslim community. The Shi'ites (*Shi'a* means "Party") maintained that not the existing caliphs but the descendants of Muhammad, starting with Ali, cousin and son-in-law of Muhammad and the fourth caliph, were the rightful rulers of the Islamic community.

Ali had been murdered in 661, his older son in 669. The massacre in 680 of Ali's younger son, Husayn, and some of Husayn's followers and relatives gave rise to passionate devotion to the house of Ali, which is still expressed in processions, poetry, and self-mortification. To Shi'ites, the anniversary of Husayn's death remains the most important religious holiday in the Muslim calendar. Suffering and martyrdom are central to Shi'a.

Shi'ites viewed Ali and his descendants as *Imams,* holy men, innocent of all sin, the most excellent of beings, selected by God to inherit Muhammad's spiritual and political powers. The Imams linked the new generation with Muhammad's original inspiration. Shi'ites believed that without the Imams' guidance, the true meaning of Islam could not be grasped.

The Muslim Golden Age

In the eighth and ninth centuries, under the Abbasid caliphs, based in Baghdad, Muslim civilization entered its golden age. Islamic civilization creatively integrated Arabic, Byzantine, Persian, and Indian cultural traditions. During the Early Middle Ages, when learning was at a low point in western Europe, the Muslims forged a high civilization.

Muslim science, philosophy, and mathematics, based largely on the achievements of the ancient Greeks, made brilliant contributions to the sum of knowledge at a time when Latin Christendom had lost much of Greco-Roman thought and culture. The Muslims had acquired Greek learning from the older Persian and Byzantine civilizations, which had kept alive the Greek inheritance. By translating Greek works into Arabic and commenting on them, Muslim scholars performed the great historical task of preserving the philosophical and scientific heritage of ancient Greece.

Ancient Medicine. For much of the Middle Ages, Muslim physicians were more skilled than their counterparts in the West. Here an Arab doctor performs a type of cataract operation. (*World Health Organization.*)

Muslim scholars also creatively interpreted these Greek works and in some areas, particularly mathematics, pushed the frontiers of knowledge beyond what the Greeks had achieved. This intellectual heritage was passed on to Christian Europe, a transmission of immense historical significance, as the historian W. Montgomery Watt explains:

> *When one becomes aware of the full extent of Arab experimenting, Arab thinking and Arab writing, one sees that without the Arabs European science and philosophy would not have developed when they did. The Arabs were no mere transmitters of Greek thought, but genuine bearers, who both kept alive the disciplines they had been taught and extended their range. When about 1100 Europeans became seriously interested in . . . science and philosophy . . . [they] had to learn all they could from the Arabs before they themselves could make further advances.*[3]

There are numerous examples of Muslim brilliance in mathematics, medicine, science, and philosophy. From India the Muslims acquired the concept of the zero and "Arabic" numerals, passing these ideas on to the West. Muslim mathematicians did original work in algebra and trigonometry; Muslim astronomers corrected the observations made by ancient astronomers, particularly Ptolemy. In physics, the Muslim Arabs' most significant contribution was in the field of optics. Rejecting Euclid's and Ptolemy's explanation that the eye emits visual rays, they recognized that vision is a consequence of rays of light. Building on the medical knowledge of the Greeks, Muslim physicians became the best-trained and most skillful doctors of the time. Surgeons performed amputations, removed cancerous tissue, devised new medicines, and used anesthetics when performing operations. The best Muslim hospitals had separate wards for fevers, surgical cases, eye diseases, and dysentery. Well ahead of their time were those Muslim doctors who recommended humane treatment for the mentally ill. The Persian al-Razi, or Rhazes, who headed the hospital in Baghdad in the ninth century, wrote a medical encyclopedia, in which he discussed measles, kidney stones, poisons, skin diseases, and ways of maintaining one's health. The works of Rhazes, translated into Latin, were widely consulted in Latin Christendom.

Muslim thinkers employed the categories of Greek philosophy to explain Islamic doctrine. Al-Farabi (c. 870–950), who wrote commentaries on Aristotle, offered proofs for God's existence based on Aristotelian logic that were later studied by medieval Christian philosophers. The most eminent Muslim thinker, Ibn-Sina, known to the West as Avicenna (980–1037), was a poet, doctor, scientist, and philosopher who wrote on every field of knowledge. His philosophical works, which relied heavily on Aristotle, had an important influence on medieval Christian thinkers. Another giant of Muslim learning was Ibn-Rushd, whom westerners call Averroës (1126–1198). Averroës insisted that the Koran did not oppose the study of philosophy and held that the ancient Greeks—even though they were not Muslims—had discovered truth. His commentaries on Aristotle were studied in western universities, where they sparked an important controversy (see page 261).

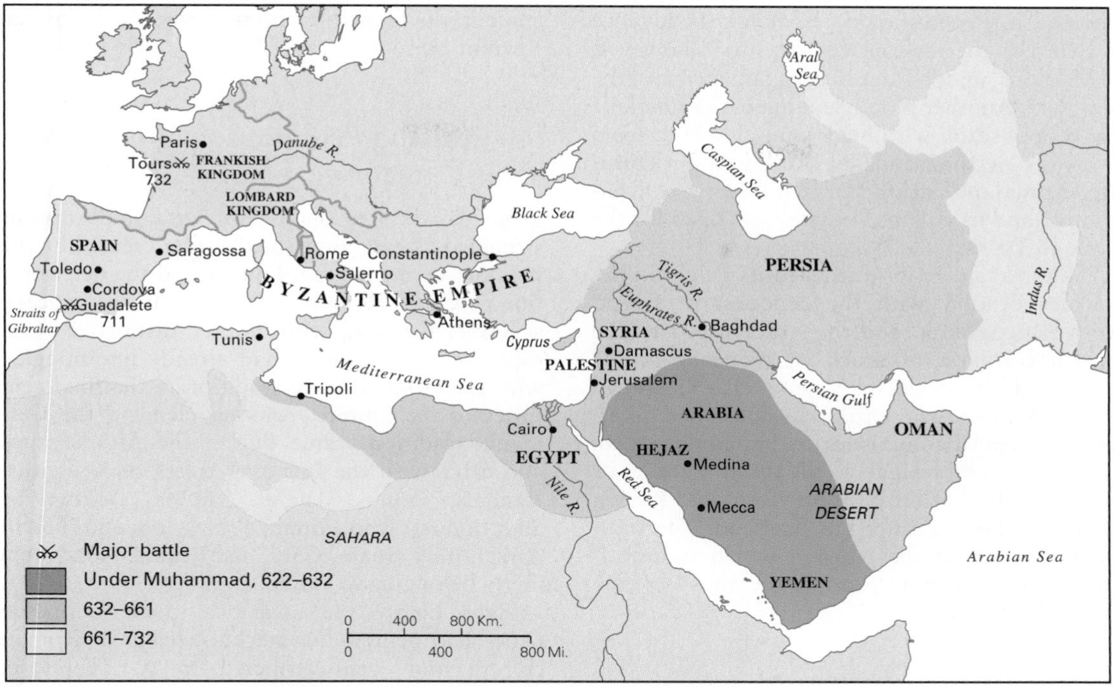

Map 9.2 **The Expansion of Islam, 622–732** From 632 to 661, the Arabs, with breathtaking speed, overran the Persian Empire, seized some of Byzantium's provinces, and invaded southern Europe. Their northward momentum was halted in 717 by the Byzantines at Constantinople and in 732 by the Franks at the battle of Tours in central France.

Mongol Invasions and Ottoman Dominance

The Arab empire, stretching from Spain to India, was unified by a common language (Arabic), a common faith, and a common culture. By the eleventh century, however, the Arabs began losing their dominance in the Islamic world. The Seljuk Turks, who had taken Asia Minor from the Byzantines, also conquered the Arabic lands of Syria, Palestine, and much of Persia. Although the Abbasid caliphs remained the religious and cultural leaders of Islam, political power was exercised by Seljuk sultans. In the eleventh and twelfth centuries, the Muslims lost Sicily and most of Spain to Christian knights, and European Crusaders carved out kingdoms in the Near East.

In the thirteenth century came a new wave of invaders, the Mongols from central Asia. Led by Genghis Khan, Mongolian archers, mounted on fast-moving ponies, poured across Asia into Muslim lands. By 1227, when Genghis Khan died, the eastern part of the Muslim world had fallen to the Mongols. After the death of Genghis Khan, some Mongol forces swept across Russia and threatened central Europe; others continued to advance on Muslim lands in the Near East. Storming Baghdad in 1258, the Mongols burned, plundered, and killed with savage fury; among the fifty thousand people slaughtered was the last Abbasid caliph. The Mongols devastated the palaces, libraries, and schools that had made Baghdad the cultural capital of the Islamic world. A year later, they marched into Syria, again killing and looting. Their brutal advance westward was finally stopped in 1260 in Palestine by Egyptian forces.

By the beginning of the fourteenth century, the Mongols, who had by this time converted to Islam, remained in Persia and were unable to advance westward. In the late fourteenth century, however, the Mongols, under Tamerlane, again menaced the Near East. Another bloody conqueror, Tamerlane cowed opposition with huge pyramids built from the skulls of thousands of slaughtered victims. After Tamerlane's death in 1404, his empire disintegrated, and its collapse left the way open for the Ottoman Turks.

The Ottoman Empire reached its height in the sixteenth century with the conquest of Egypt, North Africa, Syria, and the Arabian coast. The Turkish conquest of much of Hungary in the 1520s and the siege of Vienna (1529) spread panic in Europe. The Ottomans developed an effective system of administration but could not restore the cultural brilliance, the thriving trade, or the prosperity that the Muslim world had known under the Abbasid caliphs of Baghdad. The vitality that had kept the Muslim world more advanced than western Europe for most of the Middle Ages dissipated.

Latin Christendom: The Rise of Europe

The centuries of cultural greatness of the Islamic and the Byzantine civilizations enriched the Western world. They did not, however, produce the major breakthroughs in science, technology, philosophy, economics, and political thought that gave rise to the modern world. That process was the singular achievement of Europe. During the Middle Ages, a common European civilization—Latin Christendom—evolved. It integrated Christian, Greco-Roman, and German elements. Christianity was at the center of medieval civilization, Rome was the spiritual capital and Latin the language of intellectual life, and Germanic customs pervaded social and legal relationships.

During the Early Middle Ages (500–1050), Latin Christendom was culturally far behind the two Eastern civilizations and did not catch up until the twelfth century. In succeeding centuries, however, it produced the movements that ushered in the modern age: the Renaissance, the Reformation, the Scientific Revolution, the Age of Enlightenment, the French Revolution, and the Industrial Revolution.

Political and Economic Transformation

From the sixth to the eighth century, Europeans struggled to overcome the disorder created by the breakup of the Roman Empire and the deterioration of Greco-Roman civilization. In the process, a new civilization, with its own distinctive style, took root. Christianity had already intermingled with the Greco-Roman tradition in the final centuries of the Empire. Another element, the Germanic tradition, came during the fifth century and after with the invading tribes of Visigoths, Vandals, Franks, Angles, Saxons, Ostrogoths, and others, who founded kingdoms in North Africa, Italy, Spain, Gaul, and Britain—lands formerly belonging to Rome.

Even before the invasions, these Germanic tribes had acquired some knowledge of Roman culture and were attracted to it. Therefore, the new rulers sought not to destroy Roman civilization but to share in its advantages. For example, Theodoric the Great (474–526), the Ostrogoth ruler of Italy, retained the Roman Senate, civil service, and schools; and rich aristocratic Roman families continued to hold high government offices. The Burgundians in Gaul and the Visigoths in Spain maintained Roman law for their conquered subjects; and the Frankish ruler Clovis (c. 466–511) wore Roman imperial colors and took Roman titles. All the Germanic kingdoms tried to maintain Roman systems of taxation; furthermore, Latin remained the official language of administration.

However, torn by warfare, internal rebellion, and assassination, the Germanic kingdoms provided a poor political base on which to revive a decadent and dying classical civilization. Most of the kingdoms survived for only a short time and had no enduring impact. An exception to this trend occurred in Gaul and south-central Germany, where the most successful of the Germanic kingdoms was established by the Franks—the founders of the new Europe.

The Roman world was probably too far gone to be rescued, but even if it had not been, the Germans were culturally unprepared to play the role of restorer. By the end of the seventh century, the old Roman lands in western Europe showed a marked decline in central government, town life, commerce, and learning. Though vigorous and brave, the German invaders were essentially a rural and warrior people, tribal in organization and outlook. Their native culture, without cities or written literature, was primitive compared with the literary, philosophical, scientific, and artistic achievements of the Greco-Roman world. The Germans were not equipped to reform the decaying Roman system of administration and taxation or cope with the economic problems that had burdened the Empire. Nor could they maintain roads and irrigation systems, preserve skills in the arts of stoneworking and glassmaking, or breathe new life into the dying humanist culture.

Roman ideas of citizenship and the legal state were totally alien to Germanic tradition. The Germans gave loyalty to their kin and to a tribal chief, not to an impersonal state that governed citizens of many nationalities. The king viewed the land he controlled as a private possession that could be divided among his sons after his death—a custom that produced numerous and devastating civil wars and partitions. Unlike the Romans, the Germanic invaders had no trained civil servants to administer the state and no organized system of taxation to provide a secure financial base for government.

The Germans also found Roman law strange. Roman law incorporated elements of Greek philosophy and was written, whereas German law at the time of the invasions consisted of unwritten tribal customs. Roman law applied to all people throughout the Empire, regardless of nationality; a German could be judged only by the law of his own tribe. Roman judges investigated evidence and demanded proof; German courts, in the absence of clear evidence, relied on trial by ordeal. In a typical ordeal, a bound defendant was thrown into a river. Sinking meant innocence; floating was interpreted as divine proof of guilt, because the pure water had "rejected" the evildoer. Although primitive by Roman standards, Germanic law did help to lessen blood feuds between families. Before long, the Germanic kingdoms began to put customary tribal law, which had absorbed and continued to absorb elements from Roman law, into writing. Replacing Roman law and spreading throughout Europe, Germanic law became an essential element of medieval society.

The distinguishing feature of classical civilization, its vital urban institutions, had deteriorated in the Late Roman Empire. The shift from an urban to a rural economy accelerated under the kingdoms created by Germanic chieftains. Although the German kings retained Roman cities as capitals, they did not halt the process of decay that had overtaken urban centers. These rulers settled their people in the countryside, not in towns; they did not significantly utilize cities as instruments of local government; and they failed to maintain Roman roads. Although towns did not vanish altogether, they continued to lose control over the surrounding countryside and to decline in wealth and importance. They were the episcopal seats (sees) of bishops, rather than centers of commerce and intellectual life. Italy remained an exception to this general trend. There, Roman urban institutions persisted, even during the crudest period of the Early Middle Ages. Italian cities kept some metal currency in circulation and traded with one another and with Byzantium.

Shrinking commerce during the Early Middle Ages was part of the process of decline begun in the Late Roman Empire. Although commerce never wholly disappeared, it was predominantly localized. Furthermore, it was controlled by colonies of Jews, Syrians, and Greeks—a sign of the economic inertia of Latin Christians. From the last decade of the fifth century to the middle of the seventh century, Byzantine merchants established themselves in the western lands and exchanged papyrus, spices, and textiles for European slaves. Then, in the second half of the seventh century, this trade dropped off greatly; as Muslim power expanded to control the Mediterranean, Byzantine merchants had to turn eastward for markets. Thus, the bonds between East and West weakened, and Europe shifted its axis northward, away from the Mediterranean. Few goods exchanged hands and few coins circulated; people produced for themselves what they needed.

The Waning of Classical Culture

Greco-Roman humanism, in retreat since the Late Roman Empire, continued its decline in the centuries immediately following Rome's demise. The old Roman upper classes abandoned their heritage and absorbed the ways of their Germanic conquerors, the Roman schools closed, and Roman law faded into disuse. Aside from clerics, few people could read and write Latin, and even learned clerics were rare. Europeans' knowledge of the Greek language was almost totally lost, and the Latin rhetorical style deteriorated. Many literary works of classical antiquity were either lost or unread. Raids by Germanic tribes and later by Muslims, Magyars, and Vikings (see below) devastated libraries. Many works by great authors were lost forever. For example, only seven of the one hundred dramas written by Sophocles have survived. European culture was much poorer than the high civilizations of Byzantium, Islam, and ancient Rome.

During this period of cultural poverty, the few persons who were learned generally did not engage in original thought but salvaged and transmitted remnants of classical civilization. Given the context of the times, this was a considerable achievement. These individuals retained respect for the inheritance of Greece and Rome while remaining devoted to Christianity. In a rudimentary way, they were struggling to create a Christian culture that combined the intellectual tradition of Greece and Rome with the religious teachings of the Christian church.

An important figure in the intellectual life of this transitional period was Boethius (480–c. 525), a descendant of a noble family. Boethius had received a classical education at the Platonic Academy at Athens before Emperor Justinian closed it in 529. He was the last Latin-speaking scholar of the Roman world to have mastered the Greek language and to have intimate knowledge of Greek philosophy. Later, Boethius served the Ostrogoth Theodoric I, who ruled Italy. Recognizing that Greco-Roman civilization was dying, Boethius tried to rescue the intellectual heritage of antiquity. He translated into Latin some of Aristotle's treatises on logic and wrote commentaries on Aristotle, Cicero, and Porphyry (a Neo-Platonist philosopher). He also wrote treatises on theology and textbooks on arithmetic, astronomy, and music. A sudden turn of fortune deprived him of power, prestige, and possessions and confronted him with imminent death when Theodoric ordered him executed in 524 or 525 for allegedly participating in a plot against the throne.

While in prison awaiting execution, Boethius wrote *The Consolation of Philosophy,* which is regarded as one of the masterpieces of world literature. In it, Boethius pondered life's meaning: "Think you that there is any certainty in the affairs of mankind when you know that often one swift hour can utterly destroy a man?"[4] Alone in his dungeon, he turned for guidance and consolation not to Christ but to the philosophical training of his youth. He derived comfort from Lady Philosophy, who reassured him, in the tradition of Socrates and the Stoics, that "if then you are master of yourself, you will be in possession of that which you will never wish to lose, and which Fortune will never be able to take from you."[5] No tyrant can "ever disturb the peculiar restfulness which is the property of a mind that hangs together upon the firm basis of its reason."[6] In the life and thought of Boethius, the classical tradition lived on. He was a bridge between a classical civilization too weakened to be revived and a Christian civilization still in embryo.

Until the twelfth century, virtually all that Latin Christendom knew of Aristotle came from Boethius's translations and commentaries. Similarly, his work in mathematics, which contains fragments from Euclid, was the principal source for the study of that discipline in the Early Middle Ages. Boethius also bequeathed to future generations basic philosophical definitions and terms. In his theological writings, he strove to demonstrate that reason did not conflict with orthodoxy—an early attempt to attain a rational comprehension of belief, or, as he expressed it, to join faith to reason. Boethius's effort to examine Christian doctrines rationally, a principal feature of medieval philosophy, would grow to maturity in the twelfth and thirteenth centuries. Writing in the sixth century, Boethius was a forerunner of this movement.

Cassiodorus (c. 490–575), a contemporary of Boethius, was born in southern Italy of a good family; he served three Ostrogoth kings. Although Cassiodorus wrote the twelve-volume *History of the Goths* and some theological treatises, his prime legacies were the establishment of a monastic library containing Greek and Latin manuscripts and his advocacy of higher education to improve the quality of the clergy. In his educational writings, he justified the importance of studying secular litera-

The Art of the Ancient World and the Middle Ages

1. Praxiteles. *Hermes with Young Dionysus*, c. 350 B.C. *(Olympia Museum/Bridgeman Art Library.)*

The art of the classical period (c. fifth century B.C.) was important not only to the ancient Greeks but also to the Romans and to later generations, from the Renaissance to the postmodern period of the late twentieth century. Through the ages, classical art has been kept alive—adopted, adapted, altered, and appreciated—by artists and craftspeople. Why has the classical style remained at the forefront of artistic endeavor?

The classical period has given us the first works of the Western world to represent the human form with accuracy. The body itself was the sculptors' subject. Their aim was to shape their marble so as to make a general and schematic figure lifelike. Classical sculpture has been a powerful learning device for aspiring artisans from Michelangelo to nineteenth-century artists such as Auguste Rodin. Ancient sculptures—and plaster casts made from them—have been used as teaching tools by educators since the Renaissance. Learning to draw from casts of ancient works was the traditional first step in an artist's education; even many abstract artists of the twentieth century had a solid grounding in works of the classical period.

2. Venus de Milo. Greek statue from the first century B.C., probably an imitation of a fourth-century work. *(Louvre/Giraudon/Art Resource, NY.)*

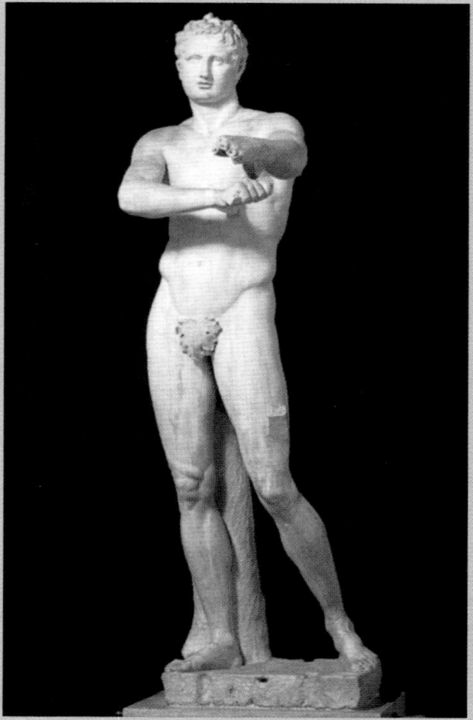

3. Lysippos. Roman copy of *Apoxyomenos,* original c. 325–300 B.C. *(Museo Pio Clementino, Vatican Museums, Vatican State/Scala/Art Resource, NY.)*

The balanced, rhythmical composition of classical sculpture and architecture is another element that has influenced later artists. Earlier works—from the Greek Archaic period (sixth century B.C.) as well as works from ancient Egypt and Mesopotamia—are solid, blocklike, and devoid of any sense of movement. Classical sculptors, by contrast, were able to bring the stone alive with innovative poses, luxuriant drapery, and a careful balancing between relaxation and tension.

The works of Praxiteles embody the ideal of classical sculpture and offer visual proof that the Greeks' search for beauty and truth extended beyond their literature and philosophy.

Praxiteles (fl. 375–330 B.C.) is renowned for the quality of his marble sculpture, such as the *Hermes with Young Dionysus* (Figure 1), considered one of his finest works. Little is known of Praxiteles himself, but much has been written about his art.

The Hermes statue has many of the attributes that distinguish the best classical sculpture. The stance is relaxed: an S-curve takes the weight off one leg and shifts it to the opposite hip. This *contrapposto,* or counterbalanced, pose draws attention to every part of the god's body. The turned and slightly tilted head is a departure from the fully frontal works of earlier periods. The drapery is a careful, three-dimensional rendering of drapery in vase painting from the same period. It is realistic and so fluid that viewers might forget they are looking at marble.

A roughly contemporary work, the *Venus de Milo* (Figure 2), by an unidentified artist, embodies many of the same principles as the Hermes figure. Venus puts her weight on one leg, tensing some muscles and relaxing others. Drapery loosely covers her waist and has the look of soft cotton.

A contemporary of Praxiteles, Lysippos (fl. fourth century B.C.), is credited with changing the "Canon of Proportions" established by his predecessor Polyclitus. The "Canon of Proportions," rules that earlier sculptors followed in carving their masterpieces, assured a certain uniformity in the rendering of the human form. Heads were always a certain proportion of the whole, eyes were placed at a certain level within the face, and so on. But the work of Lysippos is notably different.

One of Lysippos's best-known works, the *Apoxyomenos* (*Scraper*) (Figure 3), shows a youthful athlete cleaning himself with a *strigyl* (scraper) after exercising. What distinguishes this work from the works of other artists are the proportions. Lysippos's youth has a smaller head and a more slender body. Although he stands with his weight on one foot, his hips are not as sharply angled as the hips of other classical figures, in whom the S-curve is more clearly pronounced. Even the face of the athlete foretells a new era in art. Unlike the serene, perfect faces of other classical figures, the Apoxyomenos' expression seems thoughtful and dreamy, not remote and dispassionate.

Distinguished by its portrayal of emotion and drama, *The Laocoön Group* (Figure 4) is one of the most famous works of Western art. Dated to the second century B.C., the work depicts the death of Laocoön, a priest of the god Apollo, and his twin sons, killed by sea serpents because they tried to prevent the entry into Troy of the huge wooden horse in which Greek warriors were concealed. The sculptors, Agesander, Atheodorou, and Polydoros of Rhodes, convey the violence and intensity of events through the exaggeration of facial features, musculature, and pose.

4. Hellenistic sculpture. *The Laocoön Group*, second century B.C. *(Museo Pio Clementino, Vatican Museums, Vatican State/Scala/Art Resource, NY.)*

This work from the Hellenistic period differs from its classical predecessors in its emotionality and exaggeration of the human form. Laocoön's face shows anguish over the loss of his sons, and his muscles bulge as he strains to wrest himself from the serpent's grasp. Laocoön's children are depicted as smaller than their father yet as fully mature men.

Many historians have described the art of Rome as unoriginal and deriving from classical Greek works. The Romans did make multiple copies of many Greek prototypes, but they also excelled in areas of the decorative arts in which we have no evidence of Greek virtuosity. The Romans developed distinctive styles in wall painting (fresco), mosaic, and minor metal arts; their contributions to architecture are also noteworthy.

Frescoes are made by painting directly on wet or damp plaster. Some fresco painters limit their work to small scenes; others cover entire walls with landscapes, people, and architectural elements. Roman fresco painters were adept at reproducing the look of marble and

5. Detail of a Pompeian wall fresco. *Lady Playing the Cithera,* first century B.C.
(Metropolitan Museum of Art, NY.)

other materials. The *trompe l'oeil* (literally "fool the eye") style of Roman fresco painters demonstrates their skill at reproducing the world around them.

As can be seen in Figure 5, Roman painters were able to convincingly present three-dimensional objects on a two-dimensional surface. This first-century B.C. fresco, *Lady Playing the Cithera* (a harplike musical instrument), from a villa at Boscoreale, near Pompeii, is an excellent example of the fresco painter's art. Though painted on a flat surface, the chair is set at an angle and projects outward toward the viewer. The chair's three-dimensionality is further emphasized by the placement of the young attendant, who stands behind it, holding on to its back.

Roman sculptors tended to follow closely the classical Greek and Hellenistic traditions. Some art historians assert that originality in Roman sculpture is evident only in lifelike portrait busts of the emperors, often planted firmly on the necks of copies of Greek or Hellenistic gods and heroes. To an extent, this is the case with the life-size *Augustus of the Prima Porta* (Figure 6), a work probably completed during the reign of Augustus (27 B.C.–A.D. 14) or shortly after his death and deification. Many elements of this work are direct borrowings from classical and Hellenistic prototypes. It is the head, however, that sets this work apart from its forebears. The face of Augustus is a lifelike representation of the emperor, if we assume that the great number of coins bearing Augustus's image offer an accurate likeness. Unlike Greek sculpture, which idealized the human form, this Roman work presents an image that would be recognized by all who viewed it.

Roman works such as the Augustus statue also served as illustrations of contemporary events. Carvings on the breastplate in *Augustus of the Prima Porta* portray the Romans' victory over the Parthians. Pictorial narratives of other Roman achievements were sculpted on free-standing columns and triumphal arches, as well as on the walls of buildings. In this way, Roman rulers were able to transmit news and information throughout their vast empire to people who could not read or who did not speak Latin.

The art and architecture of the Byzantine era and the Middle Ages show a transformation in subject matter. Christianity, with its theme of resurrection and salvation, dominated the period. Both Latin and Greek churches used art to spread Christian teachings and to buttress their authority. Because few people could read or write, both churches relied on sculpture, painting, and drawing to convey the essence of Christianity.

Figure 7, the mosaic *The Court of Justinian,* from the Church of San Vitale in the Italian city of Ravenna, shows the emperor Justinian and his attendants and dates to c. A.D. 547. The emperor stands in the center of the scene and is flanked by officials and local clergy. The contrast between this work and the Boscoreale fresco (Figure 5) is noteworthy. Here, the emphasis is on two-dimensionality and the vertical. All of the figures face front; there is little attempt to show depth or three-dimensionality, except for the somewhat unsuccessful overlapping of figures. These Byzantine figures, with small heads, tiny feet, and disproportionate arms, are elongated and slender, unlike the figures of the Roman painting or the Greek sculptures shown earlier.

As political and spiritual ruler of the Byzantine Empire, Justinian is flanked by twelve companions, drawing a parallel between him and Jesus Christ. His golden halo brings to mind the one usually shown around Christ's head; the attributes of Christianity, including a cross, a censer (incense burner), and a shield bearing a symbolic version of Jesus' name, remind viewers of Justinian's dual roles.

Easily recognized symbols such as the halo became common devices for transmitting the message of Christ and the church. To understand the extent to which symbols and images became the common language, consider two representations of the Madonna and Child: *Enthroned Madonna and Child,* from the Byzantine school (Figure 8), and *Madonna Enthroned Between Saints Peter and Leonard,* by the Magdalen Master of the Tuscan school (Figure 9). Both date from the thirteenth century. The similarities between them are noteworthy. The Madonna is shown in what now seems to be a conventional pose—seated on an elaborate chair or throne, facing front, holding the child on her left knee, and supporting him with her left hand. The Madonna is heavily robed, although in neither work was the artist able to depict the clothes with the fluidity of the painter responsible for the Boscoreale fresco (Figure 5).

The *Enthroned Madonna and Child*'s origins are Eastern—the Byzantine school having developed in Byzantium, the capital of the eastern Roman Empire. Byzantium (renamed Constantinople in A.D. 330) had a certain sphere of influence in the West, attested to by the Ravenna mosaic (Figure 7), and as a result, a fusion of Eastern and Western styles is evident in works such as the *Enthroned Madonna.* What is typically Byzantine about this work is the richness of color and the use of gold—in the background and in the Madonna's robes. The faces of the figures owe more to Western art, however. Soft modeling and careful shading make them look almost as if they were superimposed by another artist at another time.

6. *Augustus of the Prima Porta. (Vatican Museums, Vatican State/Scala/Art Resource, NY.)*

The *Madonna Enthroned Between Saints Peter and Leonard* is from Italy. The artist, a conservative painter, used many elements familiar to us from the Byzantine work. Such characteristics as the smaller narrative elements that surround the central figures, the poses, the facial expressions, and the stylized painting of the drapery are all standard for the Middle Ages.

At this point, Western art begins to undergo another transformation. Styles and subject matter change, paralleling developments in

7. Mosaic. *The Court of Justinian,* c. A.D. 547. *(Church of San Vitale, Ravenna/Scala/Art Resource, NY.)*

politics and society. Artists working at the end of the Middle Ages and on the verge of the Renaissance include the brothers Jan and Hubert Van Eyck. Figure 10 shows *The Last Judgement* (c. 1420–1425), one panel of a diptych (a two-paneled work) painted by one or both of them (the other panel portrays the Crucifixion). *The Last Judgement* illustrates some of the stylistic elements that distinguish these artists. The image is divided in two horizontally. In the upper half, which represents heaven, the mood is one of calm and order; below, on earth and in hell, pandemonium reigns. This suggestion of the promise of heaven and the threat of hell was intended to motivate people to heed Christian teachings and clerical authority.

The Van Eycks portrayed this idea with a clarity and realistic feeling unseen in other works. Their virtuosity is paralleled by the work of a slightly earlier Italian artist, Giotto di Bondone (1267–1337), whose style also marked a definite break with his peers, and whose work stands on the cusp between the Renaissance and what preceded it.

Giotto's *Kiss of Judas*, in the Scrovengi Chapel in Padua, dates from 1305 (Figure 11). A work of the Late Middle Ages, or Gothic period, it represents a major shift in artistic direction; its lifelike depiction of the human figures seen in the lower foreground anticipates later perspectival painting. To understand this change in representational art in the fourteenth century, it is necessary to remember what was

8. Byzantine school. *Enthroned Madonna and Child,* thirteenth century. *(National Gallery of Art, Washington, D.C. Gift of Mrs. Otto H. Kahn, 1940.)*

9. Magdalen Master, Tuscan school. *Madonna Enthroned Between Saints Peter and Leonard,* c. 1270. *(Yale University Art Gallery, New Haven, Connecticut. University purchase from James Jackson Jarves.)*

happening in Italy at the time. Although the art was meant to reflect the kingdom of heaven, actual events in the kingdom on earth played a great role.

As noted earlier, Byzantium and Byzantine art influenced Italian art and society in the medieval period. Images, symbols, and techniques that flourished in Eastern workshops took root in Italy, culminating in what art historians call a "neo-Byzantine style" in the early thirteenth century, soon after the Crusaders conquered Constantinople in 1204. Italian artists adopted the Byzantine style, which had its roots in classical Greek prototypes. The combination of Byzantine, Greek, and native Italian styles produced the new way of seeing epitomized by Giotto.

10. Hubert or Jan Van Eyck. *The Last Judgement,* c. 1420–1425. *(Metropolitan Museum of Art, NY.)*

11. Giotto di Bondone. *Kiss of Judas,* c. 1305. Scrovengi Chapel, Padua, Italy. *(Alinari/Art Resource, NY.)*

ture as an aid to understanding sacred writings. Even though his works were not original, they did rescue some ideas of the ancients from oblivion; these ideas would bear fruit again in later centuries. Cassiodorus's plans for founding a university in Rome modeled after the one in Alexandria did not materialize; in fact, six hundred years would elapse before universities would arise in Latin Christendom. Leaving political office, Cassiodorus retired to a monastery, where he helped initiate the monastic practice of copying ancient texts. Without this tradition, many key Christian and Greco-Roman works would undoubtedly have perished.

In Spain, Isidore of Seville (c. 576–636) compiled an encyclopedia, *Etymologiae,* covering a diversity of topics from arithmetic and God to furniture. Isidore derived his information from many secular and religious sources. Quite understandably, his work contained many errors, particularly in its references to nature. For centuries, though, the *Etymologiae* served as a standard reference work and was found in every monastic library of note.

The translations and compilations made by Boethius, Cassiodorus, and Isidore, the books collected and copied by monks and nuns, and schools established in monasteries (particularly those in Ireland, England, and Italy) kept intellectual life from dying out completely in the Early Middle Ages. Amid the deterioration of political authority, the stagnation of economic life, and the decline in learning, a new civilization was emerging. German and Roman peoples intermarried, and Roman, German, and Christian traditions intermingled. But it was the church more than anything else that gave form and direction to the emerging civilization.

The Church: Shaper of Medieval Civilization

The Church as Unifier

Christianity was the integrating principle and the church was the dominant institution of the Middle Ages. During the Late Roman Empire, as the Roman state and its institutions decayed, the church gained power and importance; its organization grew stronger and its membership increased. Unlike the Roman state, the church was a healthy and vital institution. The elite of the Roman Empire had severed their commitment to the values of classical civilization, whereas church leaders were intensely devoted to their faith.

During the invasions of the fifth and sixth centuries, the church, retaining an effective administrative system, assumed many political functions formerly performed by the Roman state and continued to convert the Germanic tribes. By teaching a higher morality, the church tamed the warrior habits of the German peoples. By preserving some of the high culture of Greece and Rome, it opened German minds to new ideas. A unifying and civilizing agent, the church provided people with an intelligible and purposeful conception of life and death. In a dying world, the church was the only institution capable of reconstructing civilized life.

Thus, the Christian outlook, rather than the traditions of the German tribes, was the foundation of medieval civilization. During the course of the Middle Ages, people came to see themselves as participants in a great drama of salvation. There was only one truth: God's revelation to humanity. There was only one avenue to heaven, and it passed through the church. God had established the church to administer the rites through which his love was bestowed on people. The church had the awesome responsibility of caring for human souls. Without the church, it was believed, people would remain doomed sinners. To the medieval mind, society without the church was inconceivable. Membership in a universal church replaced citizenship in a universal empire. Across Europe, from Italy to Ireland, a new society centered on Christianity was forming.

Monks and the Papacy

Monks helped construct the foundations of medieval civilization. During the seventh century, intellectual life on the European continent continued its steady decline. In the monasteries of Ireland and England, however, a tradition of learning persisted. Early in the fifth century, Saint Patrick began the conversion of the Irish to

MONASTERY OF MONT ST. MICHEL. The monastic institutions throughout western Europe stood firm amid the intellectual and cultural confusion of the Early Middle Ages. By copying ancient manuscripts and studying Latin, monks preserved elements of classical civilizations. (©*Paul Almasy/CORBIS.*)

Christianity. In Ireland, Latin became firmly entrenched as the language of both the church and scholars at a time when it was in danger of disappearing in many parts of Europe. Irish monks preserved and cultivated Latin and even kept some knowledge of Greek alive. Irish scholars engaged in biblical analysis, and, besides copying manuscripts, they decorated them, with an exquisite eye for detail. In England, the Anglo-Saxons, both women and men, who converted to Christianity mainly in the seventh century, also established monasteries that kept learning alive. Double monasteries existed, in which monks and nuns obeyed a common rule and one superior, sometimes an abbess. The Venerable Bede (673–735) wrote commentaries on Scripture and translated the fourth Gospel (Saint John's) into Anglo-Saxon. Bede is best known for his *Ecclesiastical History of the English People,* one of the finest medieval historical works.

In the sixth and seventh centuries, Irish and Anglo-Saxon monks and nuns built monasteries in continental Europe and converted people in the surrounding areas. They became the chief agents in Christianizing people in northern Europe. Thus, monks and nuns made possible a unitary European civilization based on a Christian foundation. By copying and preserving ancient texts, they also kept alive elements of ancient civilization.

Book of Kells. The beauty of the Book of Kells lies in the intricate richness of its interlacing and abstract design. The Virgin and Child on this manuscript page illustrate a more primitive representation of the human form than that found in classical art; the barbarian kingdoms had brought artistic activity to a virtual standstill. (*The Board of Trinity College, Dublin/Art Resource, NY.*)

During the Early Middle Ages, when cities were in decay, monasteries, whose libraries contained theological works and ancient Latin classics, were the main cultural centers; they would remain so until the rebirth of towns in the High Middle Ages. By instructing peasants in superior methods of farming, monks were partly responsible for the reclamation of lands that had been neglected or devastated during the great invasions. Monasteries also offered succor to the sick and the destitute and served as places of refuge for travelers. To the medieval mind, the monks' and nuns' selfless devotion to God, adoption of apostolic poverty, and dedication to prayer and contemplation represented the highest expression of the Christian way of life; it was the finest and most certain path to salvation. It was not uncommon for both men and women, with old age or even death approaching, to take the vows so they might die as monks or nuns. Regarding the monks as soldiers in the war against paganism, unorthodoxy, and heresy, the popes protected monasteries and encouraged their spread.

The Early Middle Ages was a formative period for the **papacy**, as well as for society in general. The status of the papacy was closely tied to events in Italy. In the late sixth century, the papacy was compelled to protect Rome and the surrounding territory from the Lombards, the last Germanic people to settle in once-Roman lands. At this critical stage, Gregory I, the Great (590–604), became pope. A descendant of a prominent Roman family and a monk, Gregory turned out to be one of the ablest medieval popes. He used Roman methods of administration effectively to organize and administer papal property in Italy, Sicily, Sardinia, Gaul, and other regions. The papacy owned huge estates worked by serfs. It also owned timberlands and mines, which provided the income for maintaining the clergy, churches, monasteries, hospitals, and orphanages in Rome and other places. Because of Gregory's efforts, the papacy became the leading financial institution of the day.

Gregory tried to strengthen the pope's authority within the church, insisting that all bishops and the Byzantine church in Constantinople were subject to papal authority. Establishing monasteries, he tightened the bonds between the monks and the papacy, and it was he who dispatched Benedictine monks to England to win over the Anglo-Saxons. The newly established Anglo-Saxon church looked to Rome for leadership. Gregory realized that to lead Christendom effectively the papacy must exercise authority over churches outside Italy—a policy adopted by popes who succeeded him.

He was also an intellectual who wrote commentaries on the books of the Bible and authored many works dealing with Christian themes: the

Map 9.3 **The Carolingian World** Resting more on the personal qualities of Charlemagne than on any firm economic or political foundation, the Carolingian empire did not survive the emperor's death in 814.

duties of bishops, the lives of saints and monks, miracles, and purgatory. Because of his many writings, Gregory is regarded as a father of the Latin church. An astute diplomat, he knew that the papacy required the political and military support of a powerful kingdom to protect it from its enemies, especially the Lombards. Accordingly, he set his sights on an alliance with the Franks. Finally materializing 150 years later, this alliance between the papacy and Frankish kings helped shape medieval history.

The Kingdom of the Franks

From their homeland in the Rhine River valley, the Frankish tribes had expanded into Roman territory during the fourth and fifth centuries.

The ruler Clovis united the various Frankish tribes and conquered most of Gaul. In 496, he converted to Roman Christianity. Clovis's conversion to Catholicism was an event of great significance. A number of other German kings had adopted the Arian form of Christianity, which the church had declared heretical. By embracing Roman Christianity, the Franks became a potential ally of the papacy.

Clovis's successors could not maintain control over their lands, and power passed to the mayor of the palace, the king's chief officer. Serving as mayor of the palace from 717 to 741, Charles Martel subjected all Frankish lands to his rule. In addition, at the battle of Tours in 732, he defeated the Muslims. Although the Muslims continued to occupy the Iberian Peninsula, they would advance no further north into Europe.

Charles Martel was succeeded by his son, Pepin the Short, who in 751 deposed the king. With the approval of the papacy and his nobles, Pepin was crowned king by Boniface, a prominent bishop. Two years later, Pope Stephen II anointed Pepin again as king of the Franks and appealed to him to protect the papacy from the Lombards, the last German tribe to invade formerly Roman territory. Pepin crossed into Italy, defeated the Lombards, and turned over captured lands to the papacy. This famous Donation of Pepin made the pope ruler of the territory between Rome and Ravenna, which became known as the Papal States.

The Era of Charlemagne

The alliance between the Franks and the papacy was continued by Pepin's successor, Charlemagne (Charles the Great), who ruled from 768 to 814. Charlemagne continued the Carolingian policy of expanding the Frankish kingdom. He destroyed the Lombard kingdom and declared himself king of the Lombards. He added Bavaria to his kingdom, and after long, terrible wars, he compelled the Saxons to submit to his rule and convert to Christianity—thousands were beheaded when they were slow to choose between baptism or execution. He also conquered a region in northern Spain, the Spanish March, which served as a buffer between the Christian Franks and the Muslims in Spain.

Immense difficulties arose in governing the expanded territories. Size seemed an insuperable obstacle to effective government, particularly since Charlemagne's administrative structure, lacking trained personnel, was primitive by Islamic, Byzantine, or Roman standards. The empire was divided into about 250 counties administered by counts—nobles personally loyal to the ruler. Men from powerful families, the counts served as generals, judges, and administrators, implementing the king's decisions. To supervise the counts, Charlemagne created *missi dominici* (royal messengers)—generally two laymen and a bishop or abbot—who made annual journeys to the different counties. The purpose of the missi dominici was to prevent counts and their subordinates from abusing their power and undermining Charlemagne's authority.

On Christmas Day in Rome in the year 800, Pope Leo III crowned Charlemagne emperor of the Romans. The initiative for the coronation probably came from the papacy, not from Charlemagne. The meaning of this event has aroused conflicting opinions among historians, but certain conclusions seem justified. The title signified that the tradition of a world empire still survived despite the demise of the western Roman Empire three hundred years earlier. But because it was the pope who crowned Charlemagne, this meant that the emperor had a spiritual responsibility to spread and defend the faith. Thus, Roman universalism was fused with Christian universalism.

The Frankish empire, of course, was only a dim shadow of the Roman Empire. The Franks had no Roman law or Roman legions; there were no cities that were centers of economic and cultural activity; and officials were not trained civil servants with a world outlook, but uneducated war chieftains with a tribal viewpoint. Yet Charlemagne's empire did embody the concept of a universal Christian empire, an ideal that would endure throughout the Middle Ages.

The crowning of a German ruler as emperor of the Romans by the head of the church represented the merging of German, Christian, and Roman traditions, which is the essential characteristic of medieval civilization. This blending

Profile

Saint Boniface

Of the many English monks and nuns who converted inhabitants of the Netherlands and Germany, none was more important than Saint Boniface (c. 680–754). In 716, Boniface, then a monk called Wynfrid who had earned a reputation as a Latin scholar, left England for Frisia in order to restore the churches that had been destroyed when the Frisians revolted against Frankish rule and Christian proselytizing. Consecrated bishop in 722, he extended his missionary activity into Bavaria and Thuringia. Working closely with the papacy, he founded monasteries, including the famous Abbey of Fulda, converted pagans, and imposed Christian standards of behavior on both clergy and laypeople. For example, he prohibited idol worship and the selling of slaves to heathens for sacrifices. In a letter to Pope Zacharias, he expressed his displeasure with deacons who "have four or five concubines in their beds, still read

Alinari/Art Resource, NY.

of traditions was also evident on a cultural plane, for Charlemagne, a German warrior-king, showed respect for classical learning and Christianity, both non-Germanic traditions.

Online Study Center

Improve Your Grade
Primary Source: The Life of Charlemagne: The Emperor Himself

Carolingian Renaissance

Charlemagne felt that it was his religious duty to raise the educational level of the clergy so that they understood and could properly teach the faith. To do so required overcoming the illiteracy or semiliteracy of clergymen and preparing sacred Scriptures that were uniform, complete, and free of errors. Charlemagne also fostered education to train administrators who would be capable of overseeing his empire and the royal estates; such men had to be literate.

To achieve his purpose, Charlemagne gathered some of the finest scholars in Europe. Alcuin of York, England (735–804), was given charge of the palace school attended by Charlemagne and his sons and daughters, high lords, and youths training to serve the emperor. Throughout France, Alcuin expanded schools and libraries, promoted the copying of ancient manuscripts, and imposed basic literary standards on the clergy.

The focus of the Carolingian Renaissance was predominantly Christian: an effort to train clergymen and improve their understanding of the Bible and the writings of the church fathers. This process raised the level of literacy and improved the Latin style. Most important, monastic copyists continued to preserve ancient texts, which otherwise might never have survived; the oldest

the Gospel and are not ashamed or afraid to call themselves deacons—nay rather, entering upon the priesthood, they continue in the same vices, add sin to sin, declare that they also have a right . . . to celebrate mass."* He also denounced "any layman, be he emperor, king, official, or count [who] may capture a monastery from the power of a bishop, an abbot, or an abbess and begin to hold property bought by the blood of Christ—the ancient fathers called such a man a robber, sacrilegious, a murderer of the poor, a devil's wolf entering the sheepfold of Christ, to be condemned with the ultimate anathema before the judgment of Christ."†

Boniface maintained a correspondence with his cousin Lioba, an English-born nun, who became abbess of the convent Boniface founded at Tauberbischofsheim, near the Main River. Shortly before his death, Boniface visited with Lioba at her convent. He urged her not to "forsake the land of your pilgrimage. . . . Hold bravely to your course, carry on the good work day by day, and heed not the body's weakness. Time is not long, suffering is not hard, if your eyes are set upon eternity."‡

When Boniface died, Archbishop Cuthbert of Canterbury praised him for bringing "savage peoples from their long and devious wanderings in the wide abyss of eternal perdition into the glorious pathways of the heavenly fatherland by the inspiration of his holy words and by the example of his pious and gentle life."§ When Lioba died in 780, she was buried at Fulda to be joined with Boniface.

---

*_The Letters of Saint Boniface,_ trans. Ephraim Emerton (New York: Columbia University Press, 1940), p. 80.

†Ibid., p. 140.

‡Quoted in Eleanor Duckett, _The Wandering Saints of the Early Middle Ages_ (New York: Norton, 1959), p. 227.

§_The Letters of Saint Boniface,_ p. 184.

surviving manuscripts of many ancient Greek and Roman are Carolingian copies. Carolingian scholars thus helped to fertilize the cultural flowering known as the Twelfth-Century Awakening—the high point of medieval civilization.

Compared with the Greco-Roman past, with the cultural explosion of the twelfth and thirteenth centuries, or with the great Italian Renaissance of the fifteenth century, the Carolingian Renaissance seems slight indeed. Although it did rediscover and revive ancient Roman works and adopt Roman architecture and artistic forms, it did not recapture the worldly spirit of Greece and Rome. Carolingian scholars did not engage in independent philosophical speculation or search for new knowledge, nor did they achieve that synthesis of faith and reason that would be constructed by the great theologians of the twelfth and thirteenth centuries. The Carolingian Renaissance did, however, reverse the process of cultural decay, which had characterized much of the Early Middle Ages. Learning would never again fall to the low level it had reached during the centuries following the decline of Rome.

During the era of Charlemagne, a distinct European civilization took root. It blended the Roman heritage of a world empire, the intellectual achievement of the Greco-Roman mind, Christian otherworldliness, and the customs of the Germanic peoples. This nascent western European civilization differed from Byzantine and Islamic civilizations, and Europeans were growing conscious of the difference. But the new medieval civilization was still centuries away from its high point, which would be reached in the twelfth and thirteenth centuries.

Charlemagne's empire also engendered the ideal of a unified Latin Christendom: a single Christian community under one government; this new collectivity would supersede the separate German tribal units. Over the centuries, the pursuit of this ideal of a Christian world-state,

Christendom, would inspire many people, both clergy and laity.

The Breakup of Charlemagne's Empire

After Charlemagne's death in 814, his son, Louis the Pious, inherited the throne. Louis aimed to preserve the empire, but the task was virtually impossible. The empire's strength rested more on the personal qualities of Charlemagne than on any firm economic or political foundation. Moreover, the empire was simply too large and consisted of too many diverse peoples to be governed effectively. Besides Frankish nobles, who sought to increase their own power at the emperor's expense, Louis had to deal with his own rebellious sons. After Louis died in 840, the empire was divided among the three surviving sons.

The Treaty of Verdun in 843 gave Louis the German the eastern part of the empire, which marked the beginning of Germany; to Charles the Bald went the western part, which was the start of France; and Lothair received the Middle Kingdom, which extended from Rome to the North Sea. This Middle Kingdom would become a source of conflict between France and Germany into the twentieth century. As central authority waned, large landowners increasingly exercised authority in their own regions. Simultaneous invasions from all directions furthered this movement toward localism and decentralization.

In the ninth and tenth centuries, Latin Christendom was attacked on all sides. From bases in North Africa, Spain, and Sicily, Muslims ravaged regions of southern Europe, even as far as the suburbs of Rome. The Magyars, originally from western Asia and linguistically related to Finns and Turks, crossed the Carpathian Mountains in the ninth century and established themselves on the plains of the Danube; their horsemen launched lightning raids into northern Italy, western Germany, and parts of France. Defeated in Germany in 933 and again in 955, the Magyars withdrew to what is now Hungary; they ceased their raids and adopted Christianity.

Still another group of invaders, the Northmen, or Vikings, sailed from Scandinavia in their long, open, wooden ships to raid the coasts and river valleys of western Europe. Superb seamen, the Vikings crossed the North Atlantic and settled in Iceland and Greenland; from there, they almost certainly traveled to and landed on the coast of North America. In addition to their conquests and explorations, the Vikings also produced rich poetry, excelled at crafts, and contributed greatly to the revival of trade in the High Middle Ages.

In pursuit of slaves, jewels, and precious metals hoarded in monasteries, the Viking invaders plundered, destroyed, raped, and murdered. Villages were devastated, ports were ruined, and the population was decimated. Trade was at a standstill, coins no longer circulated, and farms were turned into wastelands. The European economy, already gravely weak, collapsed; the political authority of kings disappeared; and cultural life and learning withered.

These terrible attacks heightened political insecurity and accelerated anew the process of decentralization that had begun with the decline of Rome. During these chaotic times, counts came to regard as their own the land that they administered and defended for their king. At a time when monarchs could no longer guarantee the safety of their subjects, the inhabitants of a district looked on the count or local lord as their ruler, for his men and fortresses protected them. In their regions, nobles exercised public power formerly held by kings, an arrangement later designated as *feudalism.*

In instances where great lords failed to protect their territories from neighboring counts or from invaders, political power was further fragmented. In other areas, local nobles chipped away at a count's authority in his county. In his region, the local lord, aided by warrior knights, exercised virtually supreme authority; people turned to him for protection and for the administration of justice. Europe had entered an age of feudalism, in which the essential unit of government was not a kingdom but a local region, and political power lay in the hands of local lords.

Medieval Society

Arising during a period of collapsing central authority, invasion, scanty public revenues, and declining commerce and town life, feudalism attempted to provide some order and security. Feudalism was not a planned system devised logically from general principles but rather an improvised response to the challenge posed by ineffectual central authority. Feudal practices differed from locality to locality and in some regions barely took root. Although it was only a stopgap means of government, feudalism did bring some order, justice, and law during an era of breakdown, localism, and transition. It would remain the predominant political arrangement until kings reasserted their authority in the High and Late Middle Ages.

Feudalism made an enduring impact on Western civilization. It contributed to Western notions about honor, gentlemen, and romantic love (see Chapter 11). Most important, feudal traditions laid the groundwork for the principle of limiting a king's power and for the practice of parliamentary government (see Chapters 10 and 12).

Feudalism was built on an economic foundation known as *manorialism.* Although pockets of free peasantry remained, a village community, or manor, consisting of serfs bound to the land became the essential agricultural arrangement for much of the Middle Ages. The manorial village was the means of organizing an agricultural society with limited markets and money. Neither lords nor priests performed economically productive work. Their ways of life were made possible by the toil of serfs.

Manorialism and feudalism presupposed a stable social order: clergy who prayed, lords who warred, and serfs who toiled. People believed that society functioned smoothly when individuals accepted their status and performed their proper role. In the words of an eleventh-century cleric,

> *Mankind, since the beginning of time has been divided in three, those who pray, those who cultivate, those who fight, and each of the three is comforted on either side by the two others. He who, forsaking the world, gives himself to a life of prayer owes it to the warriors that he is able to carry out his holy task in safety, while he owes his bodily nourishment to the farmers. Similarly, the farmers ascend to God through the prayers of the ecclesiastics and are defended by the weapons of the warriors. So also, the warriors are fed by the produce of the fields and benefit from the income therefrom, while the holy prayers of the pious whom they protect will expiate the crimes which they commit in battle.*[7]

A person's rights, duties, and relationship to law depended on his or her ranking in the social order. To change position was to upset the organic unity of society. And no one, serfs included, should be deprived of the traditional rights associated with his or her rank. This arrangement was justified by the clergy:

> *God himself has willed that among men, some must be lords and some serfs, in such a fashion that the lords venerate and love God, and that the serfs love and venerate their lord following the word of the Apostle; serfs obey your temporal lords with fear and trembling; lords treat your serfs according to justice and equity . . .* [8]

Vassalage

Feudal relationships enabled lords to increase their military strength. The need for military support was the principal reason for the condition of vassalage. A vassal was a knight who in a solemn ceremony pledged loyalty to a lord. This feature of feudalism derived from an ancient German ceremony during which warriors swore personal allegiance to the head of the war-band. Among other things, the vassal gave military service to his lord and received in return a *fief,* which was usually land sufficient to support his needs. This fief was inhabited by peasants, and the crops that they raised provided the vassal with his means of support.

Besides rendering military assistance and supplying knights, the vassal owed several other obligations to his lord in return for the fief and the lord's protection. These duties included sitting in the lord's court and judging cases, such as the breach of feudal agreements between the lord and his other vassals; providing lodgings when the lord traveled through the vassal's territory; offering a gift when the lord's son was knighted or when his eldest daughter married; and raising a ransom should the lord be captured by an enemy.

Both lord and vassal felt honor-bound to abide by the oath of loyalty. It became an accepted custom for a vassal to renounce his loyalty to his lord if the latter failed to protect him from enemies, mistreated him, or increased the vassal's obligations as fixed by the feudal contract. Similarly, if a vassal did not live up to his obligations, the lord would summon him to his court, where he would be tried for treachery. If found guilty, the vassal could lose his fief and perhaps his life. Sometimes disputes between vassals and lords erupted into warfare. Because a vassal often held land from more than one lord and sometimes was himself a lord to vassals, situations frequently became awkward, complex, and confusing. On occasion, a vassal had to decide to which lord he owed *liege homage* (prime loyalty).

As feudalism evolved, the king came to be regarded as the chief lord, who had granted fiefs to the great lords, who in turn had divided them into smaller units and regranted them to vassals. Thus, all members of the ruling class, from the lowliest knights to the king, occupied a place in the feudal hierarchy. In theory, the king was the highest political authority and the source of land tenure, but in actual fact he was often less powerful than other nobles of the realm.

Feudalism would decline when kings converted their theoretical powers into actual powers. The decline of feudalism was a gradual process; conflict between the crown and the aristocracy would persist, with varying degrees of intensity, for several centuries, but the future belonged to the centralized state being shaped by kings, not to feudal fragmentation.

Feudal Law

Feudal law, which incorporated many features of traditional German law, differed markedly from Roman law. Roman law was universal, having been enacted by a central government for a world empire. It was also rational, for it sought to be in accord with natural law that applied to all; and it was systematic, for it offered a framework of standards that applied to individual cases. Feudal law, in contrast, was local, covering only a small region. Moreover, it was personal. In the Roman view, the individual as a citizen owed obligations to the state, whereas under feudalism, a vassal owed loyalty and service to a lord according to the terms of a personal agreement made between them.

In the feudal view, lords and kings did not make law; rather, they were guided by tradition and precedent. They discovered and confirmed law by examining ancient customs. Therefore, feudal patterns of landownership, military service, and wardship came to be regarded an expression of ancient, unchanging, and inviolable custom. Consequently, if the vassal believed that his lord had violated the feudal agreement, that is, had broken faith with him and had transgressed tradition, the vassal would demand restoration of customary rights before an audience of his fellow vassals. Often lords battled each other, believing that they were defending their rights. Similarly, lords claimed the right to resist kings who did not honor their feudal agreements.

Feudal Warriors

Feudal lords viewed manual labor and commerce as degrading for men of their rank. They considered only one vocation worthy: that of warrior. Through combat, the lord demonstrated his valor, earned his reputation, measured his individual worth, derived excitement, added to his wealth, and defended his rights. Warfare was his whole purpose in life. During the twelfth century, to relieve the boredom of peacetime, nobles staged gala tournaments in which knights, fighting singly or in teams, engaged each other in battle to prove their skill and courage. The victors in these pageants gained prestige in the eyes of fellow nobles and admiring ladies and received prizes—falcons, crowns, and substantial amounts of money. The feudal glorification of combat became deeply ingrained in Western society and endured into the twentieth century. Over the centuries, a code of behavior, called *chivalry,* evolved for the feudal nobility. A true knight was expected to fight bravely, demonstrate loyalty to his lord, and treat other knights with respect and courtesy.

In time, the church interjected a religious element into the warrior culture of the feudal knight. It sought to use the fighting spirit of the feudal class for Christian ends: knights could assist the clergy in enforcing God's will. Thus, to the Germanic tradition of loyalty and courage was added a Christian component. As a Christian gentleman, a knight was expected to honor the laws of the church and to wield his sword in the service of God. He was supposed to protect women, children, and the weak and to defend the church against heretics and infidels. The very ceremony of knighthood was placed within a Christian framework. A priest blessed the future knight's arms and prayed that the knight would always "defend the Just and Right."

Regarding the private warfare of lords as lawless violence that menaced social life, the church, in the eleventh century, imposed strictures called the Peace of God and the Truce of God. These restrictions limited feudal warfare to certain days of the week and certain times of the year. Thus, the church tried to regulate warfare according to moral principles. Although only partially effective, the Peace of God did offer Christian society some respite from plundering and incessant warfare.

Noblewomen

Feudal society was very much a man's world. In theory, women were deemed to be physically, morally, and intellectually inferior to men; in practice, they were subjected to male authority. Fathers arranged the marriages of their daughters. Girls from aristocratic families were generally married at age sixteen or younger to a man often twice as old. The wife of a lord was at the mercy of her husband; if she angered him, she might expect a beating. A French law code of the thirteenth century stated: "In a number of cases men may be excused for the injuries they inflict on their wives, nor should the law intervene. Provided he neither kills nor maims her, it is legal for a man to beat his wife when she wrongs him."[9] Although the church taught that both men and women were precious to God and spiritual equals, church tradition also regarded women as agents of the devil—evil temptresses who, like the biblical Eve, used their sexuality to lure men into sin—and church law also permitted wife beating.

In Mary, the mother of Jesus, however, Christians had an alternative image of women to the image suggested by Eve, one that placed women in a position of honor. Devotion to the Virgin Mary reached its high point in the twelfth and thirteenth centuries with the growing belief in the Immaculate Conception (the idea, which later became a doctrine, that Mary was conceived free of original sin and remained free of sin throughout her life*). Moreover, medieval Christians believed that Mary, by dedicating her entire life to Jesus in his work of redemption, cooperated with him in his ministry and could intercede with him in behalf of individual Christians. The numerous artistic depictions of Mary as the Mother of God and the Queen of Heaven, as well as the multitude of churches named after the Virgin, are evidence of the popular piety the cult of Mary generated throughout the Middle Ages.

NOBLEWOMEN. At times, medieval ladies joined their husband's hunting party. (*Universitat Bibliothek, Heidelberg, cod. Pal. Germ.048 fol, 64r/AKG London.*)

Aristocratic girls who did not marry often entered a convent. (Peasant daughters, because they were needed on the farm—they probably worked as hard and as well as men—rarely became nuns. Moreover, their parents could not afford the dowry, payable in land, cash, or goods, required by the convent for admission.) The nunneries provided

*The Immaculate Conception did not become Roman Catholic dogma until 1854, when Pope Pius IX promulgated the bull *Ineffabilis Deus*.

an outlet for the talents of unmarried noblewomen. Abbesses demonstrated organizational skills in supervising the convent's affairs. Some nuns acquired an education and, like their male counterparts, copied manuscripts and thus preserved knowledge and ideas of the past. The nun Hroswitha (c. 935–c. 1001) of Gandersheim, in Saxony, Germany, produced poetry, history, and plays. Inspired by the Roman poet Terence, she wrote six dramas—the first since Roman times—along with a history of German rulers and one of her own convent.

As the lady of the castle, the lord's wife performed important duties. She assigned tasks to the servants, made medicines, preserved food, taught young girls how to sew, spin, and weave—she was responsible for providing the lord and his companions with most of the clothes they required—and, despite her subordinate position, took charge of the castle when her husband was away. If the lord was taken prisoner in war, she raised the ransom to pay for his release. Sometimes she put on armor and went to war. For amusement, noblewomen enjoyed chess and other board games, played musical instruments, or embroidered tapestries to cover castle walls. A lady might also join her husband on the hunt, a favorite recreation of the medieval nobility.

Agrarian Life

The origins of manorialism can be traced in part to the Late Roman Empire, when peasants depended on the owners of large estates for protection and security. This dependence increased during the Early Middle Ages, especially during the invasions of Northmen, Magyars, and Muslims in the ninth and tenth centuries. Peasants continued to sacrifice their freedom in exchange for protection, or, in some cases, they were too weak to resist the encroachments of local magnates. Like feudalism, manorialism was not an orderly system but consisted of improvised relationships and practices that varied from region to region.

A lord controlled at least one manorial village; great lords might control hundreds. A small manor included a dozen families; a large one, as many as fifty or sixty. The manorial village was never completely self-sufficient because salt, millstones, and metalware were generally obtained from outside sources; it did, however, constitute a balanced economic setting. Peasants grew grain and raised cattle, sheep, goats, and hogs; blacksmiths, carpenters, and stonemasons built and repaired dwellings and implements; the village priest cared for the souls of the inhabitants; and the lord defended the manor and administered the customary law.

The serf and his family lived in a dismal, one-room cottage that they shared with chickens and pigs. In the center burned a small fire, the smoke escaping through a hole in the roof. In cold weather when the fire was strong, the room filled with smoke. When it rained, water came through the thatched roof and turned the earth floor into mud. The odor from animal excrement was ever present.

Poor roads, few bridges, and dense forests made travel difficult; thieves and warring knights made it unsafe. Peasants generally lived, worked, and died on the lord's estate and were buried in the village churchyard. Few had any contact with the world beyond the village of their birth. When a manor was attacked by another lord, the peasants found protection inside the walls of their lord's house. In many places, by the twelfth century, this building had become a well-fortified stone castle.

In return for protection and the right to cultivate fields and to pass these holdings on to their children, serfs owed obligations to their lord, and their personal freedom was restricted in a variety of ways. Bound to the land, they could not leave the manor without the lord's consent. Before a serf could marry, he had to obtain the lord's permission and pay a fee. The lord could select a wife for his serf and force him to marry her. Sometimes a serf, objecting to the lord's choice, preferred to pay a fine: "Thomas of Oldbury came on summons and was commanded to take Agatha of Halesowen to wife; he said he would rather be fined."[10] These rules also applied to serfs' children, who inherited their parents' obligations. In addition to working their allotted land, the serfs had to tend the fields reserved for the lord. Other services exacted by the lord included digging ditches, gathering firewood, building fences, repairing roads and bridges, and sewing clothes. Probably somewhat more than half of a serf's workweek was devoted to these labor obligations. Serfs also paid a variety of dues to the lord, most notably for using the lord's mill, bake-oven, and winepress.

Serfs did derive some benefits from manorial relationships. They received protection from roving brigands and warring nobles, and they possessed customary rights, which the lord generally respected, to cottages and farmland. But in a world periodically threatened with famine and epidemics, serfs faced an unrelenting struggle to survive, a struggle made all the more difficult by the contempt lords had for them. Medieval literature often depicted peasants as repulsive creatures—ugly, dirty, cowardly, and uncouth.

If a lord demanded more services or dues than were customary, or if he interfered with their right to cottages or strips of farmland, the peasants might demonstrate their discontent by refusing to work for the lord. Up to the fourteenth century, however, open rebellion was rare because lords possessed considerable military and legal power. The manorial system promoted attitudes of dependency and servility among the serfs; their hopes for a better life were directed toward heaven.

Medieval agriculture suffered from several deficiencies. Among them was the short supply of fertilizer; farmers depended solely on animal manure. Inadequate wooden plows and primitive methods of harnessing draft animals resulted in low yields. Yet as the Middle Ages progressed, important improvements in agriculture (discussed in Chapter 10) took place and had wide ramifications for medieval economic and social life. In the High Middle Ages, the revival of an urban economy and the reemergence of central authority would undermine manorial (and feudal) relationships.

❖ ❖ ❖

Online Study Center **ACE the Test**

Notes

1. Speros Vryonis, Jr., *Byzantium and Europe* (New York: Harcourt, Brace & World, 1967), p. 193.
2. *The Koran,* tr. N. J. Dawood (Baltimore: Penguin Books, 1961), pp. 108–109.
3. W. Montgomery Watt, *The Influence of Islam on Medieval Europe* (Edinburgh: Edinburgh University Press, 1972), p. 43.
4. Boethius, *The Consolation of Philosophy,* trans. W. V. Cooper (New York: Modern Library, 1943), p. 26.
5. Ibid., p. 29.
6. Ibid., p. 34.
7. Quoted in Jean-Pierre Poly and Eric Bournazel, *The Feudal Transformation 900–1200,* trans. Caroline Higgitt (New York: Holmes & Meier, 1991), p. 149.
8. Quoted in V. H. H. Green, *Medieval Civilization in Western Europe* (New York: St. Martin's Press, 1971), p. 35.
9. Cited in Frances Gies and Joseph Gies, *Women in the Middle Ages* (New York: Thomas Y. Crowell, 1978), p. 46.
10. Quoted in G. G. Coulton, *Medieval Village, Manor, and Monastery* (New York: Harper Torchbooks, 1960), p. 82.

Suggested Reading

Gies, Frances, and Joseph Gies, *Life in a Medieval Castle* (1974). The castle as the center of medieval life; passages from journals, songs, and account books.

Holmes, George, ed., *The Oxford History of Medieval Europe* (1988). Essays by several scholars; good opening essay on transformation of the Roman world.

Lewis, A. R., *Emerging Medieval Europe* (1967). Good discussions of both economic and social changes.

Lucas, Angela M., *Women in the Middle Ages* (1983). Women and religion, marriage, and letters.

Rowling, Marjorie, *Life in Medieval Times* (1973). All phases of medieval daily life.

Tierney, Brian, *Western Europe in the Middle Ages* (1970). An outstanding text.

Zacour, Norman, *An Introduction to Medieval Institutions* (1969). Comprehensive essays on all phases of medieval society.

Chapter 10

The High Middle Ages: Vitality and Renewal

Miniature Painting of Flemish Citizens Receiving a City Charter, Chronique de Hainout, Fifteenth Century. (Koninklijke Bibliotheek Albert 1st, Brussels.)

- **Economic Expansion**
- **The Rise of States**
- **The Growth of Papal Power**
- **Christians and Jews**

Focus Questions

1. What were the signs of vitality and recovery in European economic, political, and religious life during the High Middle Ages?
2. What factors contributed to the rise of towns? What was the significance of the medieval town?
3. Why was there a conflict between church and state during the Middle Ages?
4. What prompted lords and commoners to heed the papacy's call for a crusade?
5. What conditions led to the rise of states? What were the essential differences characterizing the development of medieval England, France, and Germany?
6. What factors led to the rise of anti-Semitism during the Middle Ages? How does anti-Semitism demonstrate the power of mythical thinking?

Online Study Center

This icon will direct you to interactive map and primary source activities on the website http://college.hmco.com/pic/perrywc8e.

By the end of the eleventh century, Europe showed many signs of recovery and vitality. The invasions of Magyars and Vikings had ended, and powerful lords and kings imposed greater order on their territories. Improvements in technology and the clearing of new lands increased agricultural production. More food, the fortunate absence of plagues, and the limited nature of feudal warfare contributed to a population increase. The revival of long-distance trade and the emergence of towns were other visible signs of economic expansion. Offensives against the Muslims—in Spain, in Sicily, and (at the end of the century) in the Holy Land—demonstrated Europe's growing might and self-confidence. So too did the German conquest and colonization of lands on the northeastern frontier of Latin Christendom.

Reform movements strengthened the bonds between the church and the people and increased the power of the papacy. During the High Middle Ages (1050–1300), the pope, as Christ's deputy, sought to direct, if not rule, all Christendom. European economic and religious vitality was paralleled by a cultural flowering in philosophy, literature, and the visual arts. The civilization of Latin Christendom had entered its golden age.

Online Study Center **Improve Your Grade**
Interactive Map: Europe, ca. 1230

Economic Expansion

A period of economic expansion, the High Middle Ages witnessed an agricultural revolution, a commercial revolution, the rebirth of towns, and the rise of an enterprising and dynamic middle class.

Agricultural Revolution

During the Middle Ages, important advances were made in agriculture. Many of these innovations occurred in the Early Middle Ages but were adopted only gradually and were not used everywhere. In time, however, they markedly increased production. By the end of the thirteenth century,

Chronology 10.1 ❖ The High Middle Ages

910	Founding of the Abbey of Cluny
962	Otto I crowned emperor of the Romans, beginning the Holy Roman Empire
987	Hugh Capet becomes king of France
1054	Split between the Byzantine and the Roman churches
1061–1091	Norman conquest of Sicily
1066	Norman conquest of England
1075	Start of the Investiture Controversy
1096	First Crusade begins
c. 1100	Revival of the study of Roman law at Bologna
1163	Start of the construction of the Cathedral of Notre Dame
1198–1216	Pontificate of Innocent III: height of the church's power
1267–1273	Saint Thomas Aquinas writes *Summa Theologica*
c. 1321	Dante completes *Divine Comedy*

medieval agriculture had reached a technical level far superior to that of the ancient world.

One innovation was a heavy plow that cut deeply into the soil. This new plow enabled farmers to work more quickly and effectively. As a result, they could cultivate more land, including the heavy, moist soils of northern Europe, which had offered too much resistance to the light plow. Another important advance in agricultural technology was the invention of the collar harness. The old yoke harness worked well with oxen but tended to choke horses, which, because they move faster and have greater stamina than oxen, are more valuable for agricultural work. The introduction of the horseshoe to protect the soft hoofs of horses added to their ability to work on difficult terrain.

Two other developments were the widening use of the water mill by the tenth century and the introduction of windmills, which came into use in the twelfth century. Replacing ancient hand-worked mills, both inventions saved labor in grinding grain.

The gradual emergence of the three-field system of managing agricultural land, particularly in northern Europe, increased production. In the old, widely used two-field system, half the land was planted in autumn with winter wheat, while the other half was left fallow to restore its fertility. In the new three-field system, one-third of the land was planted in autumn with winter wheat, a second third was planted the following spring with oats and vegetables, and the last third remained fallow. The advantages of the three-field system were that two-thirds of the land were farmed and only one-third was left unused and that the diversification of crops made more vegetable protein available.

Higher agricultural production reduced the number of deaths caused by starvation and dietary disease and thus contributed to a population increase. Grain surpluses also meant that draft animals and livestock could survive the winter. The growing numbers of animals provided a steady source of fresh meat and milk and increased the quantity of manure for fertilizer.

Soon the farmland of a manorial village could not support the growing village population. Consequently, peasants had to look beyond their immediate surroundings and colonize trackless wasteland. Lords vigorously promoted this conversion of uncultivated soil into agricultural land because it increased their incomes. Monastic

Agricultural Improvements. The invention of the heavy plow and the horse collar and the switch to a three-field system greatly expanded agricultural production. The increase in the food supply was a principal reason for the growth of towns. (*Bibliothèque Nationale de France, Paris.*)

communities also actively engaged in this enterprise. Almost everywhere peasants were draining swamps, clearing forests, and establishing new villages. Their endeavors during the eleventh and twelfth centuries brought vast areas of Europe under cultivation for the first time. New agricultural land was also acquired through expansion, the most notable example being the organized settlement of lands toward the east by German colonists.

The colonizing and cultivation of virgin lands contributed to the decline of serfdom. Lords owned vast tracts of forests and swamps that would substantially increase their incomes if cleared, drained, and farmed. But serfs were often unwilling to move from their customary homes and fields to do the hard labor needed to cultivate these new lands. To lure serfs away from their villages, lords promised them freedom from most or all personal services. In many cases, the settlers fulfilled their obligations to the lord by paying rent rather than by performing services or providing foodstuffs, thus making the transition from serfs to freemen. In time, they came to regard the land as their own. As a result of these changing economic conditions, the percentage of French peasants who were serfs fell from 90 percent in 1050 to about 10 percent in 1350.

The improvement in agricultural technology and the colonization of new lands altered the conditions of life in Europe. Surplus food and the increase in population freed people to work at nonfarming occupations, making possible the expansion of trade and the revival of town life.

Revival of Trade

Expanding agricultural production, the end of Viking attacks, greater political stability, and an increasing population produced a revival of commerce. During the Early Middle Ages, Italians and Jews kept alive a small amount of long-distance trade between Catholic Europe and the Byzantine and Islamic worlds. In the eleventh century, sea forces of Italian trading cities cleared the Mediterranean of Muslim fleets, which had blocked trade. As in Roman times, goods could circulate once again from one end of the sea to the other. The cities of Venice, Amalfi, Genoa, and Pisa grew prosperous from the lucrative Mediterranean trade. The expanding population of northern Europe provided a market for Eastern silks, sugar, spices, and dyes, and Italian merchants were quick to exploit this demand.

By the start of the eleventh century, the European economy showed unmistakable signs of recovery from the disorders of the previous century. During the next two centuries, local, regional, and long-distance trade gained such momentum that some historians describe the period as a commercial revolution that surpassed the commercial activity of the Roman Empire during the Pax Romana. A class of traders emerged, many of them former serfs who had started trading by taking to the road as humble peddlers. Gradually they acquired business contacts in other lands, know-how, and ambition.

Crucial to the growth of trade were international fairs, where merchants and craftspeople set up stalls and booths to display their wares: swords, leather saddles, tools, rugs, shoes, silks, spices, furs, fine furniture, and other goods. Because of ever-present robbers, lords provided protection for merchants carrying their wares to and from fairs. Each fair lasted about three to six weeks; then the merchants would move on to another site. The Champagne region in northeastern France was the great center for fairs because the count of Champagne provided protection for merchants both on route to and at the fair, judges to guarantee the enforcement of contracts, and the necessary equipment, including covered stalls and accurate scales.

The principal arteries of trade flowed between the eastern Mediterranean and the Italian cities; between Scandinavia and the Atlantic coast; between northern France, Flanders, and England; and from the Baltic Sea in the north to the Black Sea and Constantinople via Russian rivers. The fine woolen cloth manufactured in Flanders provided the main stimulus for commerce along the Atlantic coast, and Flemish merchants prospered. In exchange for Flemish cloth, Scandinavians traded hunting hawks and fur; the English traded raw wools; and the Germans traded iron and timber. A wine trade also flourished between French vineyards and English wine merchants. Progress in navigation, including the compass borrowed from the Arabs, and improvements in sails greatly aided long-distance commerce.

Because of their strategic position, Italian towns acted as intermediaries between the trade centers of the eastern Mediterranean and those of Latin Christendom. Luxury goods from as far away as India and China were transported to Italy by Italian ships and then taken overland to parts of Germany and France. In addition, the Italians extended their trade and increased their profits by sailing westward into the Atlantic Ocean and then north to the markets of Spain, the Netherlands, and England. On return voyages, they brought back wool and unfinished cloth, which in turn stimulated the Italian textile industry. Since individual merchants often lacked sufficient capital for these large-scale enterprises, groups of merchants formed partnerships. By enabling merchants to pool their capital, reduce their risks, and expand their knowledge of profit-making opportunities, these arrangements furthered commerce.

Increased economic activity led to other advances in business techniques. Underwriters insured cargoes; the development of banking and credit instruments made it unnecessary for merchants to carry large amounts of cash. The international fairs not only were centers of international trade but also served as capital markets for international credit transactions. The arrangements made by fair-going merchants to settle their debts

Local Market in Florence. The birth of towns in the eleventh and twelfth century was a revolutionary development. Towns gave rise to a middle class that moved away from the outlook of traditional medieval society—clergy, lords, and peasants. This picture depicts the commercial vitality of a market in Florence. (*Bibliothèque Municipale, Rouen/Art Resource, NY.*)

were the origin of the bill of exchange, which allowed one currency to be converted into another. The invention of double-entry bookkeeping gave merchants an overview of their financial situation: the value of their goods and their ready cash. Without such knowledge, no large-scale commercial activity could be conducted on a continuous basis. Another improvement in business techniques was the formation of commercial law, which defined the rules of conduct for debts and contracts.

Rebirth of Towns

In the eleventh century, towns emerged anew throughout Europe, and in the next century, they became active centers of commercial and intellectual life. Towns were a revolutionary force—socially, economically, and culturally. Because they provided new opportunities, other than food production, for commoners, towns contributed to the decline of manorialism. A new class of merchants and craftspeople came into being. This new class—the middle class—comprised those who, unlike the lords and serfs, were not affiliated with the land. The townsman was a new man, with a value system different from that of the lord, the serf, or the cleric.

What spurred town growth was the increased food supply resulting from advances in agricultural technology. Surplus farm production meant that the countryside could support an urban population of artisans and professionals. Expanding trade, too, fostered urbanization. Towns emerged in places that were natural for trade: seacoasts, riverbanks, crossroads, and market sites. They also sprang up outside fortified castles and monasteries and on surviving Roman sites. The colonies of merchants who gathered at these locations were joined by peasants skilled in crafts or willing to work as laborers. From a medieval record comes this description of a town taking shape:

> *After this castle was built, certain traders began to flock to the place in front of the gate to the bridge of the castle, that is merchants, tavernkeepers, then other outsiders drifted in for the sake of food and shelter of those who might have business transactions with the count, who often came there. Houses and inns were erected for their accommodation, since there was not room for them within the chateau. These habitations increased so rapidly that soon a large ville came into being.*[1]

Medieval towns were protected from outside attack by thick, high walls, towers, and drawbridges. Most towns had a small population. The largest ones—Florence, Ghent, and Paris—had between fifty thousand and a hundred thousand inhabitants by the start of the fourteenth century; Venice and Milan had somewhat more than a hundred thousand. Covering only small areas, these walled towns were crowded with people. Booths and wares of merchants and artisans lined the narrow and crooked streets, which were strewn with refuse—animal blood and bones dumped by butchers, rotten fish discarded by fishmongers, and human waste thrown from windows. Such unsanitary conditions were a breeding ground for contagious disease.

During the day, the streets were jammed with merchants hawking their goods, women carrying baskets, men carting produce and merchandise, beggars pleading, children playing, and thieves lurking. A festive occasion, such as a procession honoring a patron saint, sometimes brought traffic to a standstill. A hanging—in Paris decomposing corpses on gallows were a permanent fixture—a beheading, or the burning of a heretic was looked upon as another festive occasion and always attracted a huge crowd. At night, the streets were deserted; few people ventured forth because the few elderly watchmen were no match for the numerous thieves. Even greater danger came from fires, which raged through overcrowded streets lined with wooden houses. And quarrels between individuals or groups were often settled violently.

Merchants and craftspeople organized guilds to protect themselves from outside competition. The merchant guild in a town prevented outsiders from doing much business. A craftsman new to a town had to be admitted to the guild of his trade before he could open a shop. Competition between members of the same guild was discouraged. To prevent any one member from making significantly more money than another, a guild required its members to work the same number of hours, pay employees the same wages, produce goods of equal quality, and charge customers a just price. These rules were strictly enforced. Guilds also performed social and religious functions. Guild members attended meetings in the guildhall, celebrated holidays together, and marched in processions. The guilds cared for members who were ill or needy and extended help to widows and children of deceased members.

Women took an active part in the economic life of towns, working with men, usually their husbands, in the various crafts—as cobblers, tailors, hatters, bakers, goldsmiths, and so forth. Women brewed beer; made and sold charcoal; sold vegetables, fish, and poultry; and ran inns. In many towns, the wives and widows of master craftsmen were admitted to guilds. These guildswomen had many of the privileges of a master, including the right to train apprentices.

Because many towns were situated on land belonging to lords or on the sites of old Roman towns ruled by bishops, these communities at first came under feudal authority. In some instances, lords encouraged the founding of towns, for urban industry and commerce brought wealth to the region. However, tensions soon developed between merchants, who sought freedom from feudal restrictions that interfered with their pursuit of financial gain, and lords and bishops, who wanted to preserve their authority over the towns. Townspeople, or burghers (a *burg* is a fortified town), refused to be treated as serfs bound to a lord and liable for personal services and customary dues. The burghers wanted to travel, trade, marry, and dispose of their property as they pleased; they wanted to make their own laws and levy their own taxes. Sometimes by fighting, but more often by payments of money, townspeople obtained charters from the lords giving them the right to set up their own councils. These assemblies passed laws, collected taxes, and formed courts, which enforced the laws. Towns became more or less self-governing municipalities, the first since Greco-Roman days.

The leading citizens of the towns, the patricians, were members of the merchant guilds who engaged in commerce, industry, and banking. Some patricians in the prosperous Italian towns enjoyed great wealth, owned considerable real estate, and conducted business transactions involving large sums. These people generally dominated town politics; often they obtained country estates and intermarried with the feudal aristocracy. Successful doctors and lawyers also belonged to the urban elite. Below them on the social scale were master craftsmen in the more lucrative crafts (goldsmiths, for example) and large retailers. Then came small retailers, masters in the less profitable crafts, and journeymen training to be masters. At the bottom were the laboring poor—the bulk of the population—who had no special skills and were subject to unemployment.

In virtually every medieval city, the church was the largest property owner. Because the church frowned on the pursuit of wealth, many businessmen had guilt pangs, particularly in old age, about the way they had earned their livelihood. Compounding their guilt and fear of hellfire was an awareness of having violated the church's strict prohibitions against practicing usury. To allay these concerns about the destiny of their souls, business people often bequeathed money and property to the church. These bequests helped to finance hospitals and schools, which were the church's responsibility.

In a number of ways, towns loosened the hold of lords on serfs. "City air makes a man free," went a medieval proverb. Seeking freedom and fortune, serfs fled to the new towns, where, according to custom, lords could no longer reclaim them after a year and a day. Enterprising serfs earned money by selling food to townspeople. When the serfs acquired a sufficient sum of money, they bought their freedom from lords, who needed cash to pay for goods bought from merchants. Lords increasingly began to accept fixed cash payments from serfs in place of labor services or foodstuffs. As serfs met their obligations to lords with money, they gradually became rent-paying tenants and, in time, were no longer bound to the lord's land. The manorial system of personal relations and mutual obligations was disintegrating.

The activities of townspeople made them a new breed; they engaged in business and had money and freedom. Their world was the market rather than the church, the castle, or the manor. Townspeople were freeing themselves from the prejudices both of feudal aristocrats, who considered trade and manual work degrading, and of the clergy, who cursed the pursuit of riches as sordid and shameful and an obstacle to salvation. They revived the Greco-Roman ideal of active citizens devoted to their city. Processions, celebrations, and feasts commemorating holy days or memorable events in the town's history strengthened civic bonds. An emerging secular civic life, combined with the new value given to business and the need for some secular education in order to handle business transactions, produced a spiritual counterforce to Christian otherworldliness that would gain momentum in succeeding centuries. The townspeople were critical, dynamic, and progressive—a force for change. Medieval towns nurtured the origins of the **bourgeoisie** (literally, "citizens of the burg," the walled town), the urban middle class, which would play a crucial role in modern European history.

The Rise of States

The revival of trade and the burgeoning of towns signaled a growing vitality in Latin Christendom. Another sign of strength was the greater order and security provided by the emergence of states. While feudalism fostered a Europe that was split into many local regions, each ruled by a lord, the church envisioned a vast Christian commonwealth, **Respublica Christiana,** governed by an emperor who was guided by the pope. During the High Middle Ages, the ideal of a universal Christian community seemed close to fruition. Never again would Europe possess such spiritual unity.

But other forces were propelling Europe in a different direction. Aided by educated and trained officials who enforced royal law, tried people in royal courts, and collected royal taxes—all of which served to reduce the power of local lords—

kings expanded their territory and slowly fashioned strong central governments. Gradually, subjects began to transfer their prime loyalty from the church and the lords to the person of the king. These developments laid the foundations of European states. Not all regions followed the same pattern. Whereas England and France achieved a large measure of unity during the Middle Ages, the areas that later became Germany and Italy remained divided, with numerous independent territories.

England

After the Roman legions abandoned England in the fifth century, the Germanic Angles and Saxons invaded the island and established several small kingdoms. In the ninth century, the Danes—one group of the Northmen who raided western Europe—conquered most of Anglo-Saxon England. But the Saxon kingdom of Wessex, ruled by Alfred the Great (871–899), survived. To resist the Danes, Alfred strengthened his army and built a fleet. To stem the decline of learning that accompanied the Danish invasions, Alfred, like Charlemagne, founded a palace school, bringing to it scholars from other areas. Alfred himself studied Latin and translated a work of Pope Gregory I into Anglo-Saxon. He also had other works translated into Anglo-Saxon, including Boethius's *Consolation of Philosophy.* Alfred's descendants gradually regained land from the Danes and reestablished Anglo-Saxon control over the island.

In 1066, the Normans—those Northmen who had first raided and then settled in France—defeated the Anglo-Saxons in the battle of Hastings and became masters of England. Determined to establish effective control over his new kingdom, William the Conqueror (1027–1087), duke of Normandy (in western France), kept one-sixth of conquered England for himself. In accordance with feudal practice, he distributed the rest among his Norman nobles, who swore an oath of loyalty to him and provided him with military assistance. But William made certain that no feudal baron had enough land or soldiers to threaten his power. The Norman conquest led to the replacement of an Anglo-Saxon aristocracy with a Norman one, and it strengthened the king's position as never before.

To tighten royal control, William retained some Anglo-Saxon administrative practices. The land remained divided into *shires* (counties) administered by *sheriffs* (royal agents). This structure gave the king control over local government. To determine how much money he could demand, William ordered a vast census taken of people and property in every village. Census data, compiled in the *Domesday Book,* indicated the number of tenants, cattle, sheep, and pigs and the quantities of farm equipment throughout the realm. Thus, better than any other monarch of his day, William knew what the assets of his kingdom were. Because William conquered England in one stroke, his successors did not have to travel the long, painful road to national unity that French monarchs had to take.

Crucial to shaping national unity was the development of common law. When Henry I became king in 1100, England had conflicting baronial claims and legal traditions, which were a barrier to unity. These legal traditions included Anglo-Saxon law, feudal law introduced by the Normans from France, church law, and the commercial law emerging among the town businesspeople. During the reigns of Henry I (1100–1135) and Henry II (1154–1189), royal judges traveled to different parts of the kingdom. Throughout England, important cases began to be tried in the king's court rather than in local courts, thereby increasing royal power. The decisions of royal judges were recorded and used as guides for future cases. In this way, a law common to the whole land gradually came to prevail over the customary law of a specific locality. Because common law applied to all England, it served as a force for unity. It also provided a fairer system of justice. Common law remains the foundation of the English legal system and the legal systems of lands settled by English people, including the United States.

Henry II made an early form of trial by jury a regular procedure for many cases heard in the king's court, laying the foundations of the modern judicial system. Twelve men familiar with the facts of the case appeared before the king's justices and were asked under oath if the plaintiff's statement was true. The justices based their decisions on the answers. Henry II also ordered representatives of a given locality to report under oath to visiting royal judges any local persons who were suspected of murder or robbery. This indictment jury was the ancestor of the modern grand jury.

The growth of an efficient financial administration paralleled the development of a strong judicial system. The Exchequer, the royal accounting office, was formed during the early years of Henry I's reign. Its officials saw to the collection of all revenues owed the king. Like the judges, these officials formed a class of professional administrators who were personally loyal to the king.

King John (1199–1216) inadvertently precipitated a situation that led to another step in the political development of England. Fighting a costly and losing war with the king of France, John had coerced his vassals into giving him more and more revenue; he had also punished some vassals without a proper trial. In 1215, the angry barons rebelled and compelled John to fix his seal to a document called Magna Carta, or Great Charter. Magna Carta is celebrated as the root of the uniquely English respect for basic rights and liberties. Although essentially a feudal document directed against a king who had violated rights of feudal barons, Magna Carta stated certain principles that eventually could be interpreted more widely.

Over the centuries, these principles were expanded to protect the liberties of the English against governmental oppression. Magna Carta stated that no unusual feudal dues "shall be imposed in our kingdom except by the common consent of our kingdom." In time, this right came to mean that the king could not levy taxes without the consent of Parliament, the governmental body that represents the English people. Magna Carta also provided that "no freeman shall be taken or imprisoned . . . save by the lawful judgment of his peers or by the law of the land." The barons who drew up the document had intended it to mean that they must be tried by fellow barons. As time passed, these words were regarded as a guarantee of trial by jury for all men, a prohibition against arbitrary arrest, and a command to dispense justice fully, freely, and equally. Implied in Magna Carta is the idea that the king cannot rule as he pleases but must govern according to the law: not even the king can violate the law of the nation. Centuries afterward, when the English sought to limit the king's power, they would interpret Magna Carta in this way.

Women Workers. At times noble ladies fought side by side with men when their castle was attacked. Here women hurl rocks and shoot arrows at the attackers. (*Bibliothèque royale Albert 1er, Brussels.*)

Anglo-Saxon England retained the Germanic tradition that the king should consider the advice of the leading men in the land. William the Conqueror continued this practice by seeking the opinions of leading nobles and bishops. In the thirteenth century, it became accepted custom that the king should not decide major issues without consulting these advisers, who assembled together as the Great Council. Lesser nobility and townspeople also began to be summoned to meet with the king. These two groups were eventually called the House of Lords (bishops and nobles) and the House of Commons (knights and burghers). Thus did the English Parliament evolve, and by the mid-fourteenth century, it was a permanent institution of government.

Frequently in need of money but unable to levy new taxes without the approval of Parliament, the king had to turn to that body for help. Parliament used this control over money matters to enhance its power. The tradition grew that the

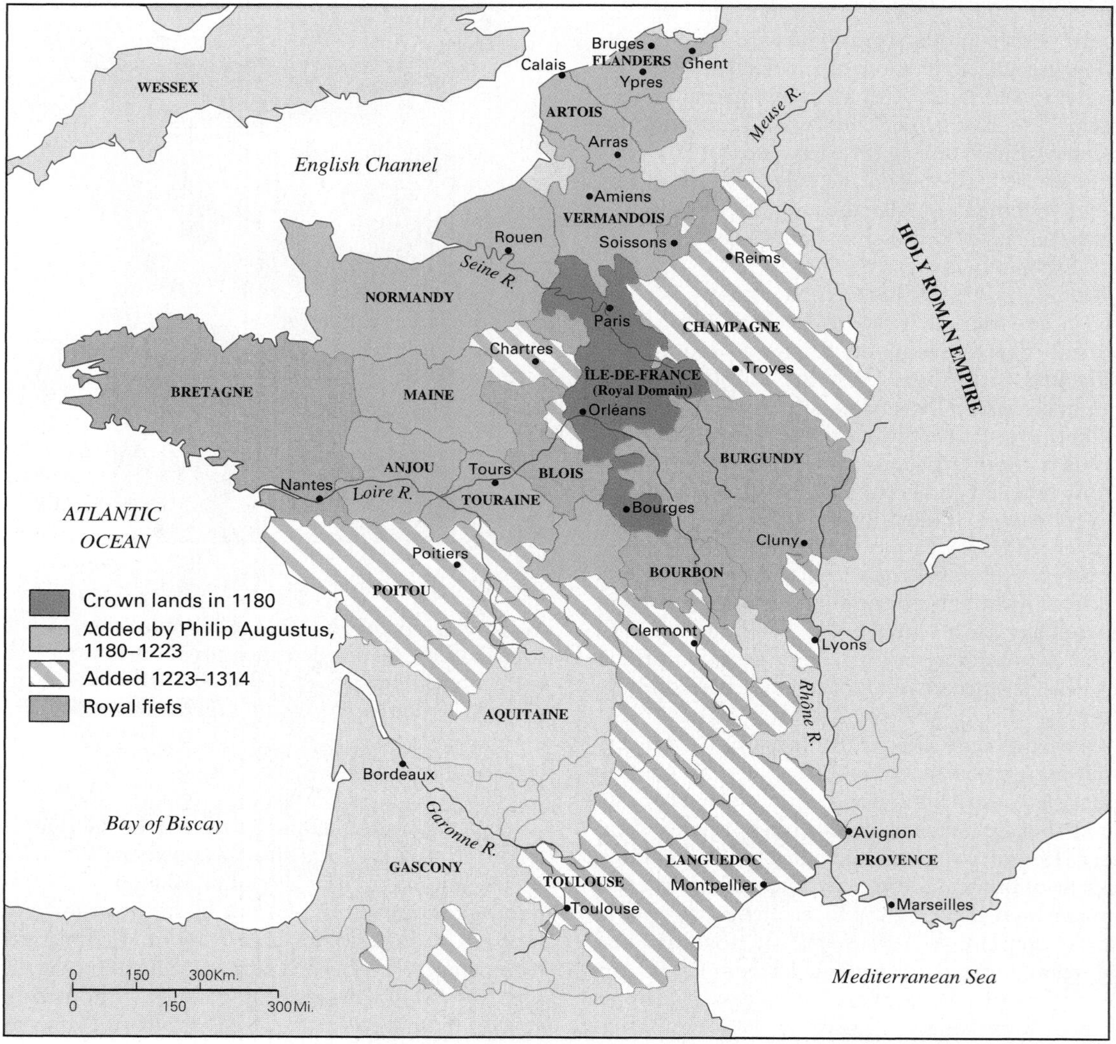

Map 10.1 **The Kingdom of France, 1180–1314** Through wars, alliances, and marriages, French kings expanded their territory.

power to govern rested not with the king alone but with the king and Parliament together.

During the Middle Ages, England became a centralized and unified state. But the king did not have unlimited power; he was not above the law. The rights of the people were protected by certain principles implicit in the common law and in Magna Carta and by the power of Parliament.

France

In the 150 years after Charlemagne's death, the western part of his empire, which was destined to become France, faced terrible ordeals. Charlemagne's heirs fought one another for the crown; the Vikings raided everywhere their ships would carry them; Muslims from Spain plundered the southern coast; and strong lords usurped power for themselves. With the Carolingian family unable to maintain the throne, the great lords bestowed the title of king on one of their own. In 987, they chose Hugh Capet (987–996), the count of Paris. Because many great lords held territories far larger than those of Hugh, the French king did not seem a threat to noble power. But Hugh strengthened the French monarchy by having the lords also elect his son as his coruler. This practice continued until it became understood that the crown would remain with the Capetian family.

With the accession of Louis VI (1108–1137), a two-hundred-year period of steadily increasing royal power began. Louis started this trend by successfully subduing the barons in his own duchy. A decisive figure in the expansion of French royal sway was Philip Augustus (1180–1223). Philip struck successfully at King John of England (of Magna Carta fame), who held more territory as feudal lord in France than Philip did. By stripping John of most of his French lands (Normandy, Anjou, and much of Aquitaine), Philip tripled the size of his kingdom and became stronger than any French lord.

How the king of England came to hold so much of France is a convoluted tale. It began when William, duke of Normandy, conquered England in 1066, becoming ruler of both territories. Later, William's great-grandson, Henry, acquired much of southern France through his marriage to Eleanor of Aquitaine (c. 1122–1204), perhaps the most powerful queen of the medieval era. First married to Louis VII, she had reigned as queen of France for fifteen years and had even gone with Louis on the Second Crusade. This marriage was annulled in 1152, and shortly afterward Eleanor married Henry Plantagenet, who became King Henry II of England in 1154. She bore Henry eight children, among them Richard the Lion-Hearted and John (whom Philip Augustus defeated), both of whom became kings of England. Thus, as a result of the Norman Conquest and intermarriage, the destinies of France and England were closely intertwined until the end of the Middle Ages.

Louis IX (1226–1270)—pious, compassionate, and conscientious and a genuine lover of peace—was perhaps the best-loved French monarch of the Middle Ages. Departing from feudal precedent, Louis issued ordinances for the entire realm without seeking the consent of his vassals. One ordinance prohibited private warfare among the nobility. Another promoted the nationwide circulation of coins produced by royal mints. These ordinances furthered royal power and promoted order.

Under Louis IX and his successors, the power of the French monarch continued to grow. Kings added to their lands by warfare and marriage; they devised new ways of raising money, including taxing the clergy. A particularly effective way of increasing the monarch's power was by extending royal justice. In the thirteenth century, the king's court, the *parlement,* became the highest court in France. Quarrels between the king and his vassals were resolved in the parlement, and many cases previously tried in lords' courts were transferred to the king's court. Moreover, because the decision of feudal courts could be appealed to the parlement, lords no longer had the last say on legal questions.

At the beginning of the fourteenth century, Philip IV (the Fair) engaged in a struggle with the papacy (see page 274). Seeking to demonstrate that he had the support of his subjects, Philip summoned representatives of the church (First Estate), the nobility (Second Estate), and the townspeople (Third Estate) to meet in a national assembly known as the Estates General. This assembly would be called again to vote funds for the crown. Unlike the English Parliament, the Estates General never became an important body in French political life, and it never succeeded in controlling the monarch. Whereas the basis for limited monarchy had been established in England, no comparable checks on the king's power developed in France. By the end of the Middle Ages, French kings had succeeded in creating a unified state. But regional and local loyalties remained strong and persisted for centuries.

Germany

After the destruction of Charlemagne's empire, its German territories were broken into large duchies. Following traditional Germanic practice, the ruling dukes elected one of their own as king. The German king, however, had little authority outside his own duchy. Some German kings tried not to antagonize the dukes, but Otto the Great (936–973) was determined to control them. He entered into an alliance with German bishops and archbishops, who could provide him with fighting men and trained administrators—a policy continued by his successors.

In 951, Otto marched into northern Italy in an attempt to assert his influence. Ten years later, he returned to protect the pope from his Italian enemies. In 962, emulating the coronation of Charlemagne, the pope crowned Otto "Emperor of the Romans" (later the title would be changed to "Holy Roman Emperor").

The revival of the empire meant that the history of medieval Germany was closely tied to that of Italy and the papacy. Otto and his successors wanted to dominate both Italy, which had been part of Charlemagne's empire, and the pope—an ambition that embroiled the Holy Roman Emperor in a life-and-death struggle with the papacy. The papacy allied itself with the German dukes and the Italian cities, enemies of the emperor. German intervention in papal and Italian politics was the principal reason why German territories did not achieve unity in the Middle Ages.

Thirteenth-Century Politics. The representative assembly, antecedent of the modern parliament, was an original achievement of the Middle Ages. Here the king of Aragon presides over the *cortes*, an assembly representing clergy, nobles, and townspeople. (*MAS Barcelona.*)

The Emergence of Representative Institutions

One great contribution of the Middle Ages to the modern world was the representative institution. Representative assemblies, or parliaments, had their beginnings at the end of the twelfth century in the Spanish kingdom of León. In the thirteenth century, they developed in other Spanish kingdoms—Castile, Aragon, Catalonia, and Valencia—as well as in Portugal, England, and the Holy Roman Empire. In the fourteenth century, parliaments formed in France and the Netherlands.

Kings generally came to accept the principles that parliamentary consent was required for levying taxes and that the king should consult parliament about important laws and obtain its approval. By and large, the parliaments had grown out of royal dependence on the nobility for military support. Because of this dependence, monarchs considered it wise to listen to the opinions of the lords. Consequently, it became customary for the king to summon councils to discuss matters of war and peace and other vital questions. Since the high clergy constituted an important group in the realm, they too were consulted. As towns gained in wealth and significance, townspeople were also asked to royal councils. Leading nobles came to represent the nobility as an order of society; members of the upper clergy—archbishops, bishops, and abbots—represented the entire clergy; and deputies from the towns represented the townspeople. An important tradition had been established: the duty of the monarch to seek advice and consent on issues of concern to his subjects. Perhaps the practice of representative government was influenced by those church lawyers who held that the pope should seek the guidance of the Christian community as expressed in church councils—meetings of representatives of the clergy.

To be sure, in succeeding centuries, parliaments would be either ignored or dominated by kings. Nevertheless, the principle of constitutional government—government by consent—was woven into the fabric of Western society. The representative parliament is unique to Western civilization; it has no parallel in the political systems of the non-European world. Originating in the Middle Ages, the representative assembly is a distinct achievement and contribution of Western civilization.

The Growth of Papal Power

In the High Middle Ages, a growing spiritual vitality accompanied economic recovery and increasing political stability. It was marked by several developments. The common people were showing greater devotion to the church. Within the church, reform movements were attacking clerical abuses, and the papacy was becoming more powerful. A holy war against the Muslims was drawing the Christian community closer together. During this period, the church tried with great determination to make society follow divine standards: it tried to shape institutions and cultural expressions according to a comprehensive Christian outlook.

The Sacraments

As the sole interpreters of God's revelation and the sole ministers of his sacraments—sacred rites—the clergy imposed and supervised the moral outlook of Christendom. Divine grace was channeled through seven sacraments, which could be administered only by the clergy, the indispensable intermediary between individuals and God. On persons who resisted its authority, the church could impose the penalty of excommunication (expulsion from the church and denial of the sacraments, without which there could be no salvation).

The seven sacraments involved the church in the lives of individuals from birth to death. Baptism cleansed individuals—usually infants—of the stain of original sin. Confirmation granted additional **grace** to previously baptized young adults. Matrimony made marriage a holy union. Extreme unction, administered to the dying, was intended to remove the remains of sin. The sacrament of the Eucharist, derived from Gospel accounts of Christ's Last Supper, took place within a liturgical service, the Mass. In a solemn ceremony, bread and wine were miraculously transformed into the substance of the body and blood of Christ, which the priest administered, allowing believers to partake of Christ's saving grace. The sacrament of penance required sinners to show sorrow for their sins, to confess them to a priest, and to perform an act of contrition: prayer, fasting, almsgiving, or a pilgrimage to a holy shrine. Through the priest, the sinner could receive absolution and be rescued from spending eternity in hell. This sacrament enabled the church to enforce its moral standards throughout Latin Christendom. The final sacrament, ordination, consecrated men to serve as clergy.

Gregorian Reform

By the tenth century, the church was western Europe's leading landowner, owning perhaps a third of the land in Italy and vast properties in other lands. However, the papacy was in no position to exercise commanding leadership over Latin Christendom. The office of pope had fallen under the domination of aristocratic families; they conspired and on occasion murdered in order to place one of their own on the wealthy and powerful throne of Saint Peter. As the papacy became a prize for Rome's leading families, it was not at all unusual for popes themselves to be involved in conspiracies and assassinations. Also weakening the authority of the papacy were local lords, who dominated churches and monasteries by appointing bishops and abbots and by collecting the income from church taxes. These bishops and abbots, appointed by lords for political reasons, lacked the spiritual devotion to maintain high standards of discipline among the priests and monks.

What raised the power of the papacy to unprecedented heights was the emergence of a reform movement, particularly in French and German monasteries. High-minded monks called for a reawakening of spiritual fervor and the elimination of moral laxity among the clergy. They particularly denounced the concern for worldly goods, the taking of mistresses, and the diminishing commitment to the Benedictine rule. Of the many monasteries that took part in this reform movement, the Benedictine monks of Cluny, in Burgundy, France, were the most influential.

In the middle of the eleventh century, popes came under the influence of the monastic reformers. In 1059, a special synod, convened by the reform-minded Pope Nicholas II, moved to end the interference of Roman nobles and German Holy Roman emperors in choosing the pope. Henceforth, a select group of clergymen in Rome, called *cardinals,* would be responsible for picking a new pontiff.

The reform movement found its most zealous exponent in the person of Hildebrand, who became Pope Gregory VII in 1073. Gregory insisted that human society was part of a divinely ordered universe, governed by God's universal law, and as the supreme spiritual leader of Christendom, the pope was charged with the mission of establishing a Christian society on earth. As successor to Saint Peter, the pope had the final word on matters of faith and doctrine. All bishops came under his authority; so did kings, whose powers should be used for Christian ends. Disobeying the pope, God's viceroy on earth, constituted disobedience to God himself. The pope was responsible for instructing rulers in the proper use of their God-given powers, and kings had the solemn duty to obey these instructions. If the king failed in his Christian duty, the pope could deny him his right to rule. Responsible for implementing God's law, the pope could never take a subordinate position to kings.

Like no other pope before him, Gregory VII made a determined effort to assert the preeminence of the papacy over both the church hierarchy and secular rulers. This determination led to a bitter struggle between the papacy and the German monarch and future Holy Roman Emperor Henry IV. The dispute was a dramatic confrontation between two competing versions of the relationship between secular and spiritual authority.

Through his reforms, Gregory VII intended to improve the moral quality of the clergy and to liberate the church from all control by secular authorities. He forbade priests who had wives or concubines to celebrate Mass, deposed clergy who had bought their offices, excommunicated bishops and abbots who had received their estates from a lay lord, and expelled from the church lay lords who invested bishops with their office. The appointment of bishops, Pope Gregory insisted, should be controlled entirely by the church.

This last point touched off the conflict, called the Investiture Controversy, between King Henry and Pope Gregory. Bishops served a dual function. On the one hand, they belonged to the spiritual community of the church; on the other, as members of the nobility and holders of estates, they were also integrated into the feudal order. Traditionally, emperors had both granted bishops their feudal authority and invested them with their spiritual authority. In maintaining that no lay rulers could confer ecclesiastical offices on their appointees, Pope Gregory threatened Henry's authority.

In earlier times, seeking allies in the conflict with feudal nobility, German kings had made vassals of the upper clergy. In return for a fief, bishops had agreed to provide troops for a monarch in his struggle against the lords. But if kings had no control over the appointment of bishops—in accordance with Pope Gregory's view—they would lose the allegiance, military support, and financial assistance of their most important allies. To German monarchs, bishops were officers of the state who served the throne. Moreover, if they agreed to Gregory's demands, German kings would lose their freedom of action and be dominated by the Roman pontiff. Henry IV regarded Gregory VII as a fanatic who trampled on custom, meddled in German state affairs, and challenged legitimate rulers established by God, thereby threatening to subordinate kingship to the papacy.

With the approval of the German bishops, Henry called for Pope Gregory to descend from the throne of Saint Peter. Gregory in turn excommunicated Henry and deposed him as king. German lands were soon embroiled in a civil war as German lords used the quarrel to strike at Henry's power. Finally, Henry's troops crossed the Alps, successfully attacked Rome, and installed a new pope, who crowned Henry emperor of the Romans. Gregory died in exile in 1085.

In 1122, the papacy and Emperor Henry V reached a compromise. Bishops were to be elected exclusively by the church and invested with the staff and the ring—symbols of spiritual power—by the archbishop, not the king. This change signified that a bishop owed his role as spiritual leader to the church only. But the king would grant the bishop the scepter, to indicate that the bishop was also the recipient of a fief and the king's vassal, owing feudal obligations to the crown. This compromise, called the Concordat of Worms, recognized the dual function of the bishop as a spiritual leader in the church and a feudal landowner. Similar settlements had been reached with the kings of France and England several years earlier.

The conflict between the papacy and the German rulers continued after the Concordat of Worms—a contest for supremacy between the heir of Saint Peter and the heir of Charlemagne. German monarchs wanted to control the papacy and the prosperous northern Italian cities. When Frederick I (1152–1190), known as Frederick Barbarossa (Red Beard), tried to assert authority over these cities, they resisted. In 1176, the armies of an alliance of Italian cities, supported by the pope, trounced Frederick's forces at the battle of Legnano. The Italian infantry showed that it could defeat knights on horseback, and Frederick was compelled to recognize the independence of the Italian cities. His numerous expeditions to Italy weakened his authority. German princes strengthened themselves at the expense of the monarchy, thereby continuing to preclude German unity.

The Struggle between the Papacy and the Empire: A Painting of Pope Gregory VII, Emperor Henry IV, and Countess Matilda of Tuscany, twelfth century. Matilda, a strong ally of the Gregorian reform movement, tried unsuccessfully to mediate the dispute between the German king and the pope over the issue of lay investiture. Both Germany and Italy were plunged into civil war by partisans of each faction. Some fifty years later, in 1122, a compromise was reached, but enmity and suspicion between popes and emperors continued for centuries. (*Coll. Biblioteca Vaticana, Madeline Grimaldi Archives.*)

The Crusades

Like the movement for spiritual renewal associated with the Cluniac reformers, the Crusades—wars to regain the Holy Land from the Muslims—were an outpouring of Christian zeal and an attempt by the papacy to assert its preeminence. Along with the renewal of commerce and the growth of towns, the Crusades were a sign of vitality and self-confidence in western Europe. The victims of earlier Muslim attacks, Latin Christians now took the offensive. Furthermore, the Crusades were part of a general movement of European expansion during the High Middle Ages. Latin Christians were venturing forth as pioneers to open new lands to cultivation and as conquerors to expand the borders of Christendom.

By the middle of the eleventh century, forces from the cities of Genoa and Pisa had driven the Muslims from Sardinia. In 1087, these northern Italians successfully attacked the North African port of Tunis, a leading base for Muslim pirates, and forced the emir of Tunis to free Christian captives and to favor Genoese and Pisan merchants. By 1091, Normans had taken Sicily from the Muslims and southern Italy from Byzantium. With the support of the papacy, Christian knights engaged in the long struggle to drive the Muslims from Spain; by 1248, after more than two centuries of conflict, only the small southern kingdom of Granada remained in Muslim hands. Germans conquered and colonized lands south of the Baltic coast inhabited by non-Christian Slavs, Balts, and Prussians. German settlers brought with them Christianity and German language and culture. They cleared vast tracts of virgin land for farming and established towns, bishoprics, and monasteries in a region where urban life had been virtually unknown.

In the eleventh century, the Seljuk Turks, who had earlier embraced Islam, conquered vast regions of the Near East, including Anatolia, a province of the Byzantine Empire. With the death of the Turkish sultan in 1092, the Seljuk Empire broke up, which reduced the pressure on Byzantium. Seeking to strengthen his army in preparation for the reconquest of Anatolia, Byzantine emperor Alexius appealed to Western rulers for mercenaries.

Pope Urban II, at the Council of Clermont (in France) in 1095, exaggerated the danger confronting Eastern Christianity. He called for a holy crusade against the heathen Turks, whom he accused of defiling and destroying Christian churches. Several months later, he expanded his objectives to include the conquest of Jerusalem. A Christian army, mobilized by the papacy to defend the faith and to regain the Holy Land from nonbelievers, accorded with the papal concept of a just war; it would channel the endemic violence of Europe's warrior class in a Christian direction. A crusade against the Muslims also held the promise of bringing the Eastern church, which had formally broken with Rome in 1054, under papal leadership. In organizing a crusade for Christian ends, Urban II, like Gregory VII in his struggle with Henry IV, sought to demonstrate the supremacy of the pope.

What motivated the knights and others who responded to Urban's appeal? To some younger sons with no hope of inheriting land at home, a crusade offered an opportunity to gain land by conquest. No doubt the Crusaders regarded themselves as armed pilgrims dedicated to rescuing holy places from the hated Muslims. Through the years, Christian pilgrims had made the journey to Jerusalem to do penance for crimes against the church and to demonstrate their piety. These pilgrims and other devout Christians found it deplorable that Christian holy places were controlled by heathen Muslims. Moreover, Urban declared that participation in a crusade was itself an act of penance, an acceptable way of demonstrating sorrow for sin. In their eagerness to recruit warriors, popular preachers went even further: they promised cancellation of penalties for sin. To a knight, a crusade was no doubt a great adventure that promised land, glory, and plunder, but it was also an opportunity to remit sins by engaging in a holy war. The enthusiasm with which knights became Christian warriors demonstrated the extent to which the warrior mentality of the nobles had become permeated by Christian principles.

Stirred by popular preachers, the common people also became gripped by the crusading spirit. The most remarkable of the evangelists was Peter the Hermit. Small and thin, with a long gray beard caked with mud, Peter rode his donkey through the French countryside arousing the religious zeal of plain folk. Swayed by the old man's eloquence, thousands of poor people abandoned their villages and joined Peter's march to Jerusalem. As this army of the poor crossed Germany, the credulous peasants expected to find Jerusalem just beyond the horizon; some thought that Peter was leading them straight to heaven. While Peter's army made its way to Constantinople, another army of commoners recruited in Germany began their crusade by massacring the Jews of the Rhineland despite the efforts of bishops to protect them. Unlike Peter's army, these commoners never reached Constantinople; after plundering Hungary, they were slaughtered by Hungarians (Magyars). Camped in the suburbs of Constantinople, Peter's restless recruits crossed from Byzantine-controlled land into Turkish ter-

Map 10.2 **The Holy Roman Empire, c. 1200** ▶
Unable to overcome the German princes, Holy Roman Emperors, unlike French and English rulers, could not build a unified state during the Middle Ages. Germany did not achieve unity until the late nineteenth century.

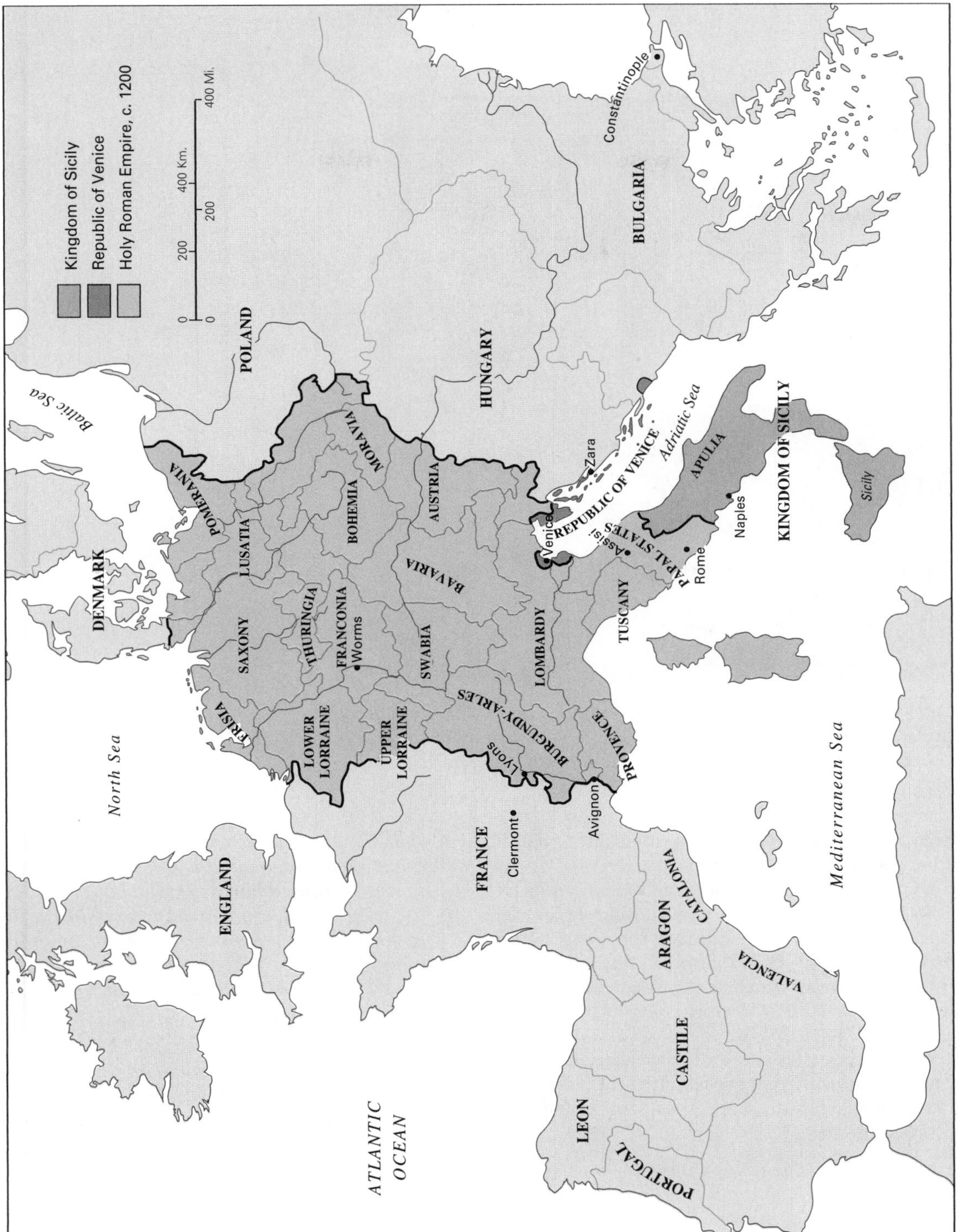
Kingdom of Sicily
Republic of Venice
Holy Roman Empire, c. 1200
0 200 400 Km.
0 200 400 Mi.
Baltic Sea
North Sea
ATLANTIC OCEAN
Mediterranean Sea
Adriatic Sea
POLAND
HUNGARY
BULGARIA
Constantinople
DENMARK
POMERANIA
LUSATIA
MORAVIA
BOHEMIA
AUSTRIA
SAXONY
THURINGIA
FRANCONIA
Worms
BAVARIA
SWABIA
FRISIA
LOWER LORRAINE
UPPER LORRAINE
BURGUNDY-ARLES
Lyons
LOMBARDY
PROVENCE
Avignon
Venice
Zara
REPUBLIC OF VENICE
TUSCANY
PAPAL STATES
Assisi
Rome
Naples
APULIA
KINGDOM OF SICILY
Sicily
ENGLAND
FRANCE
Clermont
ARAGON
CATALONIA
VALENCIA
CASTILE
LEON
PORTUGAL

CAPTURE OF JERUSALEM. Gripped by religious frenzy, the crusaders, "dripping with blood," massacred the Muslim and Jewish inhabitants of Jerusalem. (*Bibliothèque Nationale, Paris/Snark/Art Resource, NY.*)

ritory, where they too were massacred. Faith alone could not win Jerusalem.

Departing later than the commoners, an army of knights assembled at Constantinople in the spring of 1097. After enduring the long march through Anatolia, the Christian army arrived at Antioch in Syria, which it captured after a long siege. In June 1099, three years after Urban's appeal, the soldiers of the First Crusade (1096–1099) stood outside the walls of Jerusalem. Using siege weapons, they broke into the city and slaughtered Muslims and Jews. An eyewitness recorded the scene:

> *It was impossible to look upon the vast numbers of the slain without horror; everywhere lay fragments of human bodies, and the very ground was covered with the blood of the slain. It was not alone the spectacle of headless bodies and mutilated limbs strewn in all directions that roused horror in all who looked upon them. Still more dreadful was it to gaze upon the victors themselves, dripping with blood from head to foot, an ominous sight which brought terror to all who met them. . . .*
>
> *When at last the city had been set in order in this way, arms were laid aside. Then, clad in fresh garments, with clean hands and bare feet, in humility and contrition, [the victors] began to make the rounds of the venerable places which the Saviour had deigned to sanctify and make glorious with His bodily presence. With tearful sighs and heartfelt emotion they pressed kisses upon these revered spots.*[2]

Weakened by local rivalries and religious quarrels, the Muslim world failed to unite against the Christian invaders, who, besides capturing Jerusalem, carved out four small states in Syria and Palestine. How long could these Christian states, islands in a Muslim sea, endure against a Muslim counteroffensive?

Never resigned to the establishment of Christian states in their midst, Muslim leaders called for a jihad, or holy war. In 1144, one of the Crusader states, the County of Edessa, in Syria, fell to the resurgent forces of Islam. Alarmed by the loss of Edessa, Pope Eugenius II called for the Second Crusade (1147–1149), which was a complete failure.

Online Study Center

Improve Your Grade
Primary Source: The Call for a Second Crusade

After 1174, Saladin, a brilliant commander, became the most powerful leader in the Muslim Near East. In 1187, he invaded Palestine, annihilated a Christian army near Nazareth, and recaptured Jerusalem. In contrast to Christian knights of the First Crusade, who filled Jerusalem with blood and corpses, Saladin permitted no slaughter. The capture of Jerusalem led to the Third Crusade (1189–1192), in which some of Europe's most prominent rulers participated—Richard I, the Lion-Hearted, of England; Philip Augustus of France; and Frederick Barbarossa of Germany. The Crusaders captured Acre and Jaffa, but Jerusalem remained in Muslim hands.

Pope Innocent III who called the Fourth Crusade (1202–1204), was enraged by the actions of the Crusaders. They had first attacked the Christian port of Zara, controlled by the king of Hungary, and then looted and defiled churches and massacred Byzantines in Constantinople. This shameful behavior, along with the belief that the papacy was exploiting the crusading ideal to extend its own power, weakened both the crusading zeal of Christendom and the moral authority of the papacy. It also left a legacy of bitterness and distrust that still taints relations between the two principal branches of Christianity.

Other Crusades followed, including even the Children's Crusade in 1212. Stirred by Stephen of Cloyes, a young shepherd boy who claimed that Christ had communicated with him, thousands of French peasant children, accompanied by priests, marched to Marseilles, where they expected the Mediterranean Sea to part, permitting them to continue their march to the Holy Land. When the miracle did not occur, the children boarded seven ships offered to them by William the Pig and Hugo the Iron, two seemingly pious townsmen. Two of the ships were lost in a terrible storm, and the other five were captured by Muslim pirates, with whom William and Hugo had worked out a deal. The children were sold into slavery in North Africa, and as far as is known none ever returned (one priest eventually did).

Despite other crusades, the position of the Christian states in the Near East continued to deteriorate. In 1291, almost two centuries after Pope Urban's appeal, the last Christian strongholds in the Near East fell.

The Crusades had some immediate effects on Latin Christendom. They may have contributed to the decline of feudalism and the strengthening of monarchy because many lords were killed in battle or squandered their wealth financing expeditions to the Holy Land. The Crusades did foster trade between Latin Christendom and the East, but the revival of trade had already begun and would have proceeded without the Crusades. The Crusades sparked an interest in geography and travel; introduced Westerners to new foods, clothing, and architecture; and became a theme in literature. Nevertheless, they did not significantly influence European intellectual progress. The Crusaders had no contact with Muslim centers of learning in the Near East; it was through Spain and Sicily that Muslim learning penetrated Latin Christendom and helped stimulate the cultural awakening of the twelfth and thirteenth centuries. Over the centuries, some have praised the Crusades for inspiring idealism and heroism. Others, however, have castigated the movement for corrupting the Christian spirit and unleashing religious intolerance and fanaticism—including the massacre of Jews in the Rhineland and of Muslims and Jews in Jerusalem—which would lead to strife in future centuries.

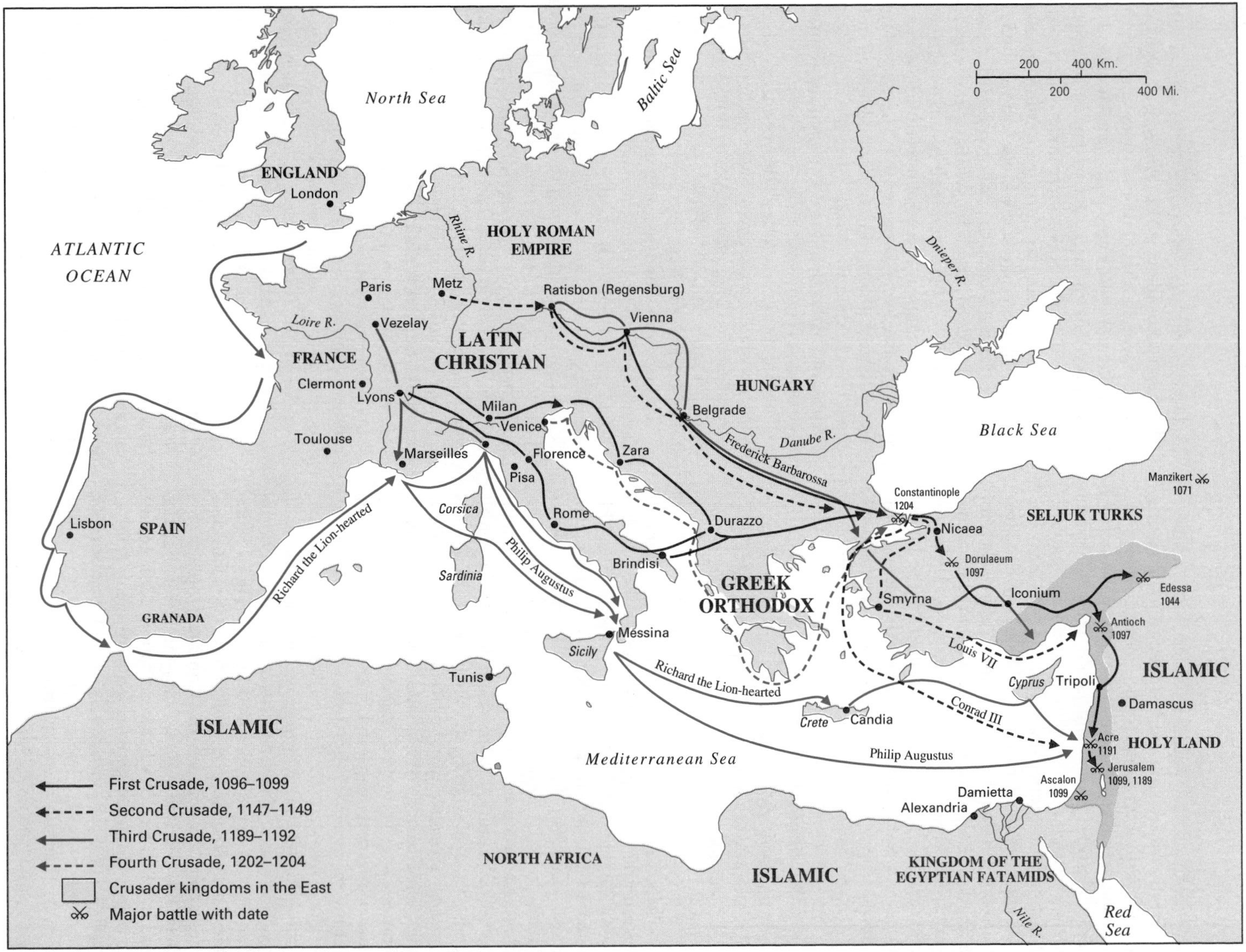
0 200 400 Km.
0 200 400 Mi.
North Sea
Baltic Sea
ATLANTIC OCEAN
ENGLAND
London
HOLY ROMAN EMPIRE
Rhine R.
Dnieper R.
Paris
Metz
Ratisbon (Regensburg)
Loire R.
Vezelay
Vienna
LATIN CHRISTIAN
FRANCE
Clermont
Lyons
HUNGARY
Milan
Venice
Belgrade
Danube R.
Black Sea
Toulouse
Marseilles
Florence
Pisa
Zara
Frederick Barbarossa
Manzikert 1071
Constantinople 1204
SELJUK TURKS
Lisbon
SPAIN
Corsica
Rome
Durazzo
Nicaea
Dorulaeum 1097
Brindisi
Sardinia
Richard the Lion-hearted
Philip Augustus
GREEK ORTHODOX
Iconium
Edessa 1044
Smyrna
GRANADA
Messina
Antioch 1097
Sicily
Louis VII
Tunis
Cyprus
Tripoli
ISLAMIC
Damascus
Richard the Lion-hearted
Conrad III
Crete
Candia
ISLAMIC
Acre 1191
HOLY LAND
Mediterranean Sea
Philip Augustus
Jerusalem 1099, 1189
Ascalon 1099
Damietta
Alexandria
First Crusade, 1096–1099
Second Crusade, 1147–1149
Third Crusade, 1189–1192
Fourth Crusade, 1202–1204
Crusader kingdoms in the East
Major battle with date
NORTH AFRICA
ISLAMIC
KINGDOM OF THE EGYPTIAN FATAMIDS
Nile R.
Red Sea

Dissenters and Reformers

Freedom of religion is a modern concept; it was totally alien to the medieval outlook. Regarding itself as the possessor and guardian of divine, and therefore ultimate, truth, the church felt a profound obligation to purge Christendom of **heresy**—beliefs that challenged Christian orthodoxy. To the church, heretics had committed treason against God and were carriers of a deadly infection. Heresy was the work of Satan; lured by false ideas, people might abandon the true faith and deny themselves salvation. The church could never create a Christian world community if heretics rebelled against clerical authority and created divisions among the faithful. In the eyes of the church, heretics not only obstructed individual salvation but also undermined the foundations of society. The church believed that it had a sacred duty to eradicate this moral defect.

To compel obedience, the church used its power of excommunication. An excommunicated person could not receive the sacraments or attend church services—fearful punishments in an age of faith. In dealing with a recalcitrant ruler, the church could declare an interdict on his territory, which in effect denied the ruler's subjects the sacraments (although exceptions could be made). The church hoped that the pressure exerted by an aroused populace would compel the offending ruler to mend his ways.

The church also conducted heresy trials. Before the thirteenth century, local bishops were responsible for locating heretics and putting them on trial. Gregory IX (1227–1241) started to use Franciscans and Dominicans (see page 245) as official investigators, in effect creating a permanent tribunal, the Inquisition, directly under the pope's authority. An inquisitor and his staff established themselves in a region suspected of heresy. After taking testimony, often in secret, the inquisitors summoned suspects to answer accusations made against them. The accused were not told the names of their accusers, nor could they have legal defense or examine evidence of witnesses. They were tortured (torture had been sanctioned by Roman law), and those who persisted in their beliefs might be turned over to the civil authorities to be burned at the stake.

Dissent in the Middle Ages was often reformist in character. Inspired by the Gospels, reformers criticized the church for its wealth and involvement in worldly affairs. They called for a return to the simpler, purer life of Jesus and the Apostles. Reform movements drew support from the new class of town dwellers; the church often rebuked the way of life in towns and only slowly adjusted to the townsmen's spiritual needs.

The Waldensians. In their zeal to emulate the moral purity and material poverty of the first followers of Jesus, reform-minded dissenters attacked ecclesiastical authority. The Waldensians, followers of Peter Waldo, a rich merchant of Lyons, were a case in point. Peter was greatly moved by a passage in Matthew: "If thou wilt be perfect go sell what thou hast and give to the poor and thou shalt have treasure in heaven" (19:22). In the 1170s, Peter distributed his property to the poor and attracted both male and female supporters. Like their leader, they committed themselves to poverty and to preaching the Gospel in the vernacular, or native tongue, rather than in the church's Latin, which many Christians did not understand. The Waldensians considered themselves true Christians, faithful to the spirit of the apostolic church. Repelled by Waldensian attacks against the immorality of the clergy and by the fact that these laymen were preaching the Gospel without the permission of ecclesiastical authorities, the church condemned the movement as heretical. Despite persecution, however, the Waldensians continued to survive as a group in northern Italy.

The Cathari. Catharism was the most radical heresy to confront the medieval church. This belief represented a curious mixture of Gnosticism and Manichaeism—Eastern religious movements that had competed with Christianity in the days of the Roman Empire—and of doctrines condemned as heretical by the early church. Carried to Italy and southern France by Bulgarian missionaries, Catharism gained followers in regions

◀ *Map 10.3* **The Routes of the Crusades**
In 1291, almost two hundred years after Pope Urban II's appeal for a crusade, the last Christian stronghold in the Near East had fallen.

Profile

Saladin

Salah al-Din Yusuf (1137–1193), known to the Western world as Saladin, recaptured Jerusalem from the Franks in 1187. Born into a prominent Kurdish family, Saladin served the emir of Syria, whose troops invaded Egypt in 1167. Rising quickly, Saladin was appointed vizier of Egypt and then confirmed as sultan of Egypt and Syria. After extending his authority over Muslim-controlled territories of Egypt, Syria, and Palestine, Saladin, deeply committed to the jihad, turned against the Franks. In particular, he vowed to liberate Islamic holy places in Jerusalem from Christian control.

In 1187, Saladin lured the Franks into an engagement at Hittin, near Tiberias, in northern Palestine. Marching all day, the exhausted and thirst-crazed Franks suffered terrible losses

Ann Ronan Picture Library/Heritage Image Partnership.

where opposition to the worldliness and wealth of the clergy was already strong.

Cathari tenets differed considerably from those of the church. The Cathari believed in an eternal conflict between the forces of the god of good and those of the god of evil. Because the evil god, whom they identified with the God of the Old Testament, created the world, this earthly home was evil. The soul, spiritual in nature, was good but was trapped in wicked flesh. Because sexual activity was responsible for imprisoning the spirit in the flesh, the Cathari urged abstinence to avoid the birth of still another wicked human being. They also abstained from eggs, cheese, milk, and meat because these foods were the products of sexual activity. (This rigorous asceticism was demanded only of a select few, the *perfecti* [perfect ones]; simple believers could marry and their diets were not restricted.) The Cathari taught that, since the flesh is evil, Christ would not have taken a human form; hence he could not have suffered on the cross or have been resurrected. Nor could God have issued forth from the evil flesh of the Virgin. According to Catharism, Jesus was not God but an angel. In order to enslave people, the evil god created the church, which demonstrated its wickedness by pursuing power and wealth. Repudiating the church, the Cathari organized their own ecclesiastical hierarchy.

The center for the Catharist heresy was southern France, where a strong tradition of protest existed against the moral laxity and materialism of the clergy. When the Cathari did not submit to peaceful persuasion, Innocent III called on kings and lords to exterminate Catharism with the sword. Lasting from 1208 to 1229, the war against the Cathari was marked by brutality and fanati-

when, in desperation, they threw themselves at the prepared Muslim lines, which blocked the Franks from reaching Lake Tiberias and its life-giving water. After the victory at Hittin, Saladin's forces took several Christian strongholds, most of them surrendering without a fight. Then Saladin turned on Jerusalem.

Living up to his reputation as a man of honor and magnanimity, Saladin made the Christian inhabitants of Jerusalem a generous proposal. If the Franks surrendered, Christians would be free to leave the city with their property, and Christian pilgrims would not be harmed. But the Frankish lords would not surrender without a fight the city where Jesus was crucified. On September 20, 1187, Saladin's soldiers besieged Jerusalem and began battering its walls. A Muslim historian noted: "Then began the fiercest struggle imaginable; each side looked on the fight as an absolute religious obligation. There was no need for a superior authority to drive them on."* On October 2, the Muslims rushed through the breached walls and captured the city. In stark contrast to the Christian conquest of Jerusalem in 1099, Saladin permitted no massacre and no plundering. The Franks could escape enslavement by paying a moderate ransom, and in an extraordinary display of tolerance, Saladin guarded Christian holy places from Muslims seeking revenge for earlier Frankish brutalities.

*Excerpted in Francesco Gabriel, ed., *Arab Historians of the Crusades* (Berkeley: University of California Press, 1969), p. 130.

cism. An army of crusading knights led by a papal legate assembled in northern France; it headed south, massacring heretics. Soon command of the crusading army passed to Simon de Montfort, a minor baron with great ambition. De Montfort slaughtered suspected heretics throughout the county of Toulouse, and for a short time he held the title of count of Toulouse. The crusading knights had effectively broken the power of the nobles who had protected the heretics. Innocent III sent legates to the region to arrest and try the Cathari. Under his successor, Dominican and Franciscan inquisitors completed the task of exterminating them.

The Franciscans and the Dominicans. Driven by a zeal for reform, devout laypeople condemned the clergy for moral abuses. Sometimes their piety and resentment exploded into heresy; at other times it was channeled into movements that served the church. Such was the case with the two great orders of friars, the Franciscans and the Dominicans.

Like Peter Waldo, Saint Francis of Assisi (c. 1181–1226) came from a wealthy merchant family. After undergoing an intense religious experience, Francis abandoned his possessions and devoted his life to imitating Christ. Dressed as a beggar, he wandered into villages and towns preaching, healing, and befriending. Unlike the monks who withdrew into walled fortresses, Francis proclaimed Christ's message to the poor of the towns. Like Peter Waldo, he preached a religion of personal feeling; like Jesus, he stretched out a hand of love to the poor, to the helpless, to the sick, and even to lepers, whom everyone feared to approach. The saintly Francis soon attracted disciples, called Little Brothers, who followed in the footsteps of their leader.

To suspicious churchmen, the Little Brothers seemed to be another heretical movement protesting against a wealthy and worldly church. However, Francis respected the authority of the priesthood and the validity of the sacraments. Recognizing that such a popular movement could be useful to the church, Innocent III allowed Francis to continue his mission. Innocent hoped that the Franciscans would help keep within the church those members of the laity who had deep religious feelings but were dissatisfied with the leadership of the traditional hierarchy.

As the Franciscans grew in popularity, the papacy exercised greater control over their activities; in time, the order was transformed from a spontaneous movement of inspired laymen into an organized agent of papal policy. The Franciscans served the church as teachers and missionaries in eastern Europe, North Africa, the Near East, and China. The papacy set aside Francis's prohibition against the Brothers owning churches, houses, and lands corporately. His desire to keep the movement a lay order was abandoned when the papacy granted the Brothers the right to hear confession. Francis's opposition to formal learning as irrelevant to preaching Gospel love was rejected when the movement began to urge university education for its members. Those who protested against these changes as a repudiation of Francis's spirit were persecuted, and a few were even burned at the stake as heretics.

The Dominican order was founded by Saint Dominic (c. 1170–1221), a Spanish nobleman who had preached against the Cathari in southern France. Believing that those well versed in Christian teaching could best combat heresy, Dominic, unlike Francis, insisted that his followers engage in study. In time, the Dominicans became some of the leading theologians in the universities. Like the Franciscans, they went out into the world to preach the Gospel and to proselytize. Dominican friars became the chief operators of the Inquisition. For their zeal in fighting heresy, they were known as "hounds of the Lord."

Innocent III: The Apex of Papal Power

During the pontificate of Innocent III (1198–1216), papal theocracy reached its zenith. More than any earlier pope, Innocent made the papacy the center of European political life. In the tradition of Gregory VII, he forcefully asserted the theory of papal monarchy. As head of the church, Vicar of Christ, and successor of Saint Peter, Innocent claimed the authority to intervene in the internal affairs of secular rulers when they threatened the good order of Christendom. According to Innocent, the pope, "lower than God but higher than man . . . judges all and is judged by no one."[3]

Innocent applied these principles of papal supremacy in his dealings with the princes of Europe. When King Philip Augustus of France repudiated Ingeborg of Denmark the day after their wedding and later divorced her to marry someone else, Innocent placed an interdict on France to compel Philip to take Ingeborg back. For two decades, Innocent III championed Ingeborg's cause until she finally became the French queen. When King John of England rejected the papal candidate for archbishop of Canterbury, Stephen Langton, Innocent first laid an interdict on the country. Then he excommunicated John, who expressed his defiance by confiscating church property and by forcing many bishops into exile. However, when Innocent urged Philip Augustus of France to invade England, John backed down. He accepted Innocent's nominee for archbishop, returned the property to the church, welcomed the exiles back, and, as a sign of complete capitulation, turned his kingdom over to Innocent to receive it back as a fief. Thus, as vassals of the papacy, John and his successors were obligated to do homage to the pope and to pay him a feudal tribute. Innocent also laid interdicts on the Spanish kingdoms of Castile and León and on Norway and strove to make the Holy Roman Emperor subservient to the papacy.

Innocent called the Fourth Crusade against the Muslims and a crusade against the heretical Cathari. The culminating expression of Innocent's supremacy was the Fourth Lateran Council, summoned in 1215. Comprising some twelve hundred clergy and representatives of secular rulers, the council issued several far-reaching decrees. It maintained that the Eastern Orthodox church was subordinate to the Roman Catholic church, prohibited the state from taxing the clergy, and declared laws detrimental to the church null and void. The council made bishops responsible for ferreting out heretics in their dioceses and ordered secular authorities to punish convicted heretics. Insisting on high standards of behavior for the clergy, it also required each Catholic to confess his or her sins to a priest at least once a year and to perform the prescribed penance. Through this directive, the church tightened its control over the conscience of Europe. The council also decreed that in the sacrament of the Eucharist the body and blood of Christ are actually present in the bread and wine used in the sacrament. This meant that the priest at the altar was God's agent in the performance of a wondrous miracle.

Christians and Jews

In their relations with heretics, pagans, and Muslims, medieval Christians demonstrated a narrow and hostile attitude that ran counter to the Gospel message that all human beings were children of God and that Christ had suffered for all humanity. Muslims were seen, in the words of Pope Urban II, as a "vile breed," "infidels," and "enemies of God." While the clergy denounced war among Christians, they considered it a duty to wage holy war against non-Christians, and knights regarded fighting the Muslims in Spain or the Holy Land as the highest expression of the chivalric ideal.

Medieval Christians also showed hatred for Jews—a visibly alien group in a society dominated by the Christian world-view. The First Crusade was a turning point for medieval Jews. Until then there were few instances of organized violence against Jewish communities. If we are warring against God's enemies, reasoned zealous crusaders, why not annihilate the Lord's enemies living in our midst? In 1096, bands of crusaders, proclaiming that they were seeking vengeance against "Christ-killers," slaughtered Jews in French and German towns. The crusaders were often aided by townspeople driven by hateful images of Jews and eager to seize Jewish property. In the German city of Mainz, more than a thousand Jews lost their lives. Some, in an act of martyrdom, chose to kill themselves and their children rather than submit to forced baptism or face a crueler death at the hands of the Crusaders. One contemporary wrote:

> *I know not whether by a judgment of the Lord, or by some error of mind, they rose in a spirit of cruelty against the Jewish people scattered throughout these cities and slaughtered them without mercy, . . . asserting it to be their duty against the enemies of the Christian faith. . . . The Jews of [Mainz], knowing of the slaughter of their brethren, . . . fled in hope of safety to Bishop Rothard. . . . He placed the Jews in the very spacious hall of his own house, [but the crusaders] attacked the Jews in the hall with arrows and lances. Breaking the bolts and doors, they killed the Jews, about seven hundred in number, who in vain resisted the force and attack of so many thousands. They killed the women, also, and with their swords pierced tender children of whatever age and sex.*[4]

This venomous hatred of Jews unleashed by the First Crusade triggered other massacres during the Middle Ages, at times fomented by clergy.

Viewing the Jews as possessions to be exploited, kings and lords taxed and fined them relentlessly and periodically expelled Jews from their territories in order to confiscate their property. In 1290, Jews were expelled from England, and in 1306, from France. Between 1290 and 1293, expulsions, massacres, and forced conversions led to the virtual disappearance of a centuries-old Jewish community life in southern Italy. In Germany, savage riots periodically led to the torture and murder of Jews. In 1348–49, when the Black Death (see page 271) raged across Europe, Jews were accused of spreading the plague by poisoning well water; thousands of them were burned alive in Basel, Freiburg, Strasbourg, Mainz, and other towns.

Several factors contributed to anti-Jewish feelings during the Middle Ages. To medieval Christians, the refusal of the Jews to embrace Christianity was an act of wickedness, particularly since the church taught that the coming of Christ had been prophesied by the Old Testament. Related to this prejudice was the portrayal of the Crucifixion in the Gospels. In the minds of medieval Christians, the crime of deicide—the killing of God—eternally stained the Jews as a people; medieval Christians saw Jews as danger-

Anti-Semitism. Holding the Jews responsible for the Black Death, Christians committed mass murder. In Basel several hundred Jews were herded into a wooden house and burned to death. Some six thousand Jews were burned alive in Mainz. Flames consumed another two thousand in a huge pyre outside Strasbourg, and their property was distributed to the local townspeople. In this picture depicting the slaughter of the Jews of Strasbourg, the townspeople evidently enjoy the spectacle. (*Koninklijke Bibliotheek Albert 1st, Brussels.*)

ous, criminal people rejected by God and deserving of ceaseless punishment. Christian theologians taught that they were to remain forever in subjection to Christians. It was just such a view that led town magistrates and princes periodically to confiscate Jewish property, at times after burning the helpless Jews alive in a public spectacle. The flames of hatred were fanned by the absurd allegation that Jews, made bloodthirsty by the spilling of Christ's blood, tortured and murdered Christians, particularly children, to obtain blood for ritual purposes. Although some popes condemned the charges as groundless, this blood libel was widely believed by the credulous masses and incited numerous riots, which led to the torture, burning alive, pillaging of property, and expulsion of countless Jews.

The role of Jews as moneylenders also provoked animosity toward them. Jews were increasingly excluded from international trade and most professions and were barred from the guilds and in some areas from landholding as well. Hence virtually the only means of livelihood open to them was moneylending—in reality an important activity in an expanding economy. This activity, which was in theory forbidden to Christians, aroused the hatred of the individual peasants, clergy, lords, and kings who did the borrowing.

The policy of the church toward the Jews was that they should not be harmed and several medieval popes sought to protect Jewish life and property from wanton violence. But the church also wanted Jews to live in humiliation, a fitting punishment for their act of deicide and continued refusal to embrace Christianity. Thus, the Fourth Lateran Council barred Jews from public office, ordered them to remain off the streets during Christian festivals, and required them to wear a distinguishing badge on their clothing, a symbol of their degradation. Christian art, literature, and religious instruction depicted the Jews in a derogatory manner, often identifying them with the Devil, who was very real and very terrifying to medieval Christians. Such people deserved no mercy, reasoned medieval Christians. Indeed, nothing was too bad for them. Because Jews were seen as evil allies of Satan engaged in a diabolical plot against God and Christendom, Jew-hatred was regarded as an expression of Christian virtue, a message routinely spread by preachers. Deeply etched into the minds and hearts of Christians, the distorted image of the Jew as a contemptible creature persisted in the European mentality into the twentieth century.

Despite their precarious position, medieval Jews maintained their faith, expanded their tradition of biblical and legal scholarship, and developed a flourishing Hebrew literature. The work of Jewish translators, doctors, and philosophers contributed substantially to the flowering of medieval culture in the High Middle Ages. The foremost Jewish scholar of the Middle Ages was Moses ben Maimon (1135–1204), also called by the Greek name Maimonides. He was born in Córdoba, Spain, then under Muslim rule. After his family emigrated from Spain, Maimonides went to Egypt, where he became physician to the sultan. During his lifetime, Maimonides achieved fame as a philosopher, theologian, mathematician, and physician. He was recognized as the leading Jewish sage of his day, and his writings were respected by Christian and Muslim thinkers as well. Like Christian and Muslim philosophers, Maimonides tried to harmonize faith with reason, to reconcile the Hebrew Scriptures and the Talmud (Jewish biblical commentary) with Greek philosophy. In his writings on ethical themes, Maimonides demonstrated piety, wisdom, and humanity.

❖ ❖ ❖

Online Study Center **ACE the Test**

Notes

1. Quoted in J. W. Thompson, *Social and Economic History of the Middle Ages* (New York: Frederick Ungar, 1959), 2:772.
2. William of Tyre, *A History of Deeds Done Beyond the Sea,* trans. Emily Atwater Babcock and A. C. Krey (New York: Columbia University Press, 1943), p. 372, 373.
3. Excerpted in Brian Tierney, ed., *The Crisis of Church and State, 1050–1300* (Englewood Cliffs, N.J.: Prentice-Hall, 1964), p. 132.
4. Excerpted in A. C. Krey, ed., *The First Crusade: The Accounts of Eye-Witnesses and Participants* (Princeton, N.J.: Princeton University Press, 1921), pp. 54–55.

Suggested Reading

Chazan, Robert, *Medieval Stereotypes and Modern Antisemitism* (1997). The deterioration of the image of the Jew in the High Middle Ages.

Duby, Georges, ed., *A History of Private Life, vol. 2, Revelations of the Medieval World* (1988). Among the topics discussed are sex, child-rearing, old age, and aristocratic households.

Gimpel, Jean, *The Medieval Machine* (1977). Technological advances in the Middle Ages.

Lopez, R. S., *The Commercial Revolution of the Middle Ages, 950–1350* (1976). How an undeveloped society succeeded in developing itself.

Madden, Thomas E., ed., *Crusades* (2004). Essays by specialists on medieval crusading movements.

Pernoud, Regine, ed., *The Crusades* (1964). A compilation of original sources.

Pounds, N. J. G., *An Economic History of Medieval Europe* (1974). A lucid survey.

Chapter 11

The Flowering of Medieval Culture: The Christian Synthesis

School of Bologna Manuscript Illumination. (Staatliche Museen zu Berlin/Bildarchiv Preussischer Kulturbesitz/Art Resource, NY.)

- Revival of Learning
- The Medieval World-View
- Philosophy-Theology
- Science
- The Recovery of Roman Law
- Literature
- Architecture

Focus Questions

1. What conditions contributed to the revival of learning during the High Middle Ages?
2. What were scholastic philosophers trying to accomplish?
3. How does the medieval view of the universe differ from the modern view?
4. How did religion pervade much of medieval philosophy, science, literature, art, and architecture?

Online Study Center

This icon will direct you to interactive map and primary source activities on the website http://college.hmco.com/pic/perrywc8e.

Europe in the High Middle Ages showed considerable vitality. The population grew, long-distance trade revived, new towns emerged, states started to take shape, and papal power increased. The culminating expression of this recovery and resurgence was the cultural flowering in philosophy, the visual arts, and literature. Creative intellects achieved on a cultural level what the papacy accomplished on an institutional level: the integration of life around a Christian viewpoint. The High Middle Ages saw the restoration of some of the learning of the ancient world, the rise of universities, the emergence of an original form of architecture (the Gothic), and the erection of an imposing system of thought, called **scholasticism.** Medieval theologian-philosophers fashioned Christian teachings into an all-embracing philosophy, which represented the spiritual character of medieval civilization. They perfected what Christian thinkers in the Roman Empire had initiated and what the learned men of the Early Middle Ages were groping for: a synthesis of Greek philosophy and Christian **revelation.**

Revival of Learning

In the late eleventh century, Latin Christendom began to experience a cultural revival; all areas of life showed vitality and creativeness. In the twelfth and thirteenth centuries, a rich civilization with a distinctive style united the educated elite in the lands from England to Sicily. Gothic cathedrals, an enduring testament to the creativeness of the religious impulse, were erected throughout Europe. Universities sprang up in several cities. Roman authors were again read, and their style was imitated. The quality of written Latin—the language of the church, learning, and education—improved, and secular and religious poetry, both in Latin and in the vernacular, abounded. Roman law emerged anew in Italy, spread to northern Europe, and regained its importance (lost since Roman times) as worthy of study. Some key works of ancient Greece were translated into Latin and studied in universities. Employing the rational tradition of Greece, men of genius harmonized Christian doctrines and Greek philoso-

MAP 11.1 **MEDIEVAL CENTERS OF LEARNING** Medieval universities established in the West a tradition of learning that never died. There is direct continuity between the universities of our own day and the medieval centers of learning.

phy. During this period, the status and influence of learned men grew considerably.

Several conditions contributed to this cultural explosion, known as the Twelfth-Century Awakening. As attacks of Vikings, Muslims, and Magyars ended and kings and great lords imposed more order and stability, people found greater opportunities for travel and communication. The revival of trade and the growth of towns created a need for literacy and provided the wealth required to support learning. Increasing contact with Islamic and Byzantine cultures in Spain and Sicily led to the translation into Latin of ancient Greek works preserved by these Eastern civilizations. By preserving Greek philosophy and science—and by commenting creatively on these classical works—Islamic civilization acted as a bridge between antiquity and the cultural revival of the High Middle Ages. The Twelfth-Century Awakening was also kindled by the legacy of the Carolingian Renaissance, whose cultural lights had dimmed but never wholly vanished in the period of disorder after the dissolution of Charlemagne's empire.

In the Early Middle Ages, the principal educational centers were the monastic schools. During the twelfth century, cathedral schools in towns gained importance. Paid a stipend by a local church, their teachers taught grammar, rhetoric, and logic. But the chief expression of expanding intellectual life was the university, a distinct creation of the Middle Ages.

The origins of the medieval university are obscure and varied. The first universities were not planned but grew spontaneously. They developed as students eager for knowledge and skills needed for high positions in government gathered around prominent teachers. The renewed importance of Roman law for business and politics, for example, drew students to Bologna to study with acknowledged masters.

The university was really a guild or corporation of masters or students who joined together to defend their interests against church or town authorities or the townspeople. A university might emerge when students united because of common needs, such as protection against townspeople who overcharged them for rooms and necessities. Organized into a body, students could also make demands on their instructors. At Bologna, professors faced fines for being absent or for giving lectures that drew fewer than five students; they were required to leave behind a deposit as security to ensure their return if they took a journey. A corporation of students formed the University at Bologna. The University of Paris, which evolved from the Cathedral School of Notre Dame, was the creation of a corporation of masters.

University students attended lectures, prepared for examinations, and earned degrees. They studied grammar, rhetoric, logic, arithmetic, geometry, astronomy, music, medicine, and, when ready, church law and theology, which was considered queen of the sciences. The curriculum relied heavily on Latin translations of ancient texts, chiefly the works of Aristotle. In mathematics and astronomy, students read Latin translations of Euclid and Ptolemy, while students of medicine studied the works of two great medical men of the ancient world, Hippocrates and Galen.

But sometimes students followed other pursuits. Instead of studying, they turned to drinking, gambling, and fighting. At Oxford University, it was reported that students "went through the streets with swords and bows and arrows and assaulted all who passed by."[1] Fathers complained that their sons preferred "play to work and strumming a guitar while the others are at their studies."[2] Students often faced financial problems, and they knew whom to ask for help: "Well-beloved father, to ease my debts . . . at the tavern, at the baker's, with the doctor . . . and to pay . . . the laundress and the barber, I send you word of greetings and of money."[3]

Universities performed a crucial function in the Middle Ages. Students learned the habit of reasoned argument. Universities trained professional secretaries and lawyers, who administered the affairs of church and state and of the growing cities; these institutions of learning also produced theologians and philosophers, who shaped the climate of public opinion. Since the curriculum and the texts studied were essentially the same in all lands, the learning disseminated by universities tightened the cultural bonds that united Christian Europe. Medieval universities established in the West a tradition of learning that has never died; there is direct continuity between the universities of our own day and the medieval ones.

Online Study Center **Improve Your Grade**
Interactive Map: Intellectual Centers of Medieval Europe

THE MEDIEVAL WORLD-VIEW

A distinctive world-view, based essentially on Christianity, evolved during the Middle Ages. This outlook differed from both the Greco-Roman and the modern scientific and secular views of the world. In the Christian view, not the individual but the Creator determined what constituted the good life. Thus, reason that was not illuminated by revelation was either wrong or inadequate, for God had revealed the proper rules for the regulation of individual and social life. Ultimately, the good life was not of this world but came from a union with God in a higher world. This Christian belief as formulated by the church made life and death purposeful and intelligible; it dominated the thought of the Middle Ages.

The Universe: Higher and Lower Worlds

Medieval thinkers sharply differentiated between spirit and matter, between a realm of grace and an earthly realm, between a higher world of perfection and a lower world of imperfection. Moral values derived from the higher world, which was also the final destination for the faithful. Two sets of laws operated in the medieval universe, one for the heavens and one for the earth. The cosmos was a giant ladder, with God at the summit; earth, composed of base matter, stood at the bottom, just above hell, where, farthest from God, dwelled Satan, his evil spirits, and the souls of the damned.

From Aristotle and Ptolemy, medieval thinkers inherited the theory of an earth-centered universe—the *geocentric theory*—which they imbued with Christian symbolism. The geocentric theory held that revolving around the motionless earth at uniform speeds were seven transparent spheres, in which were embedded each of the seven "planets"—the moon, Mercury, Venus, the sun, Mars, Jupiter, and Saturn. A sphere of fixed stars (that is, the stars, like chandeliers in a ceiling, stayed in a constant relationship to each other) enclosed this planetary system. Above the firmament of the stars were the three heavenly spheres. The outermost, the Empyrean Heaven, was the abode of God and the Elect. Through the sphere below—the Prime Mover—God transmitted motion to the planetary spheres. Underneath this was the lowermost sphere, the Crystalline Heaven, composed of a clear transparent substance.

An earth-centered universe accorded with the Christian idea that God created the universe for men and women and that salvation was the primary aim of life. Because God had created people in his image, they deserved this central position. Though they might be at the bottom of the cosmic ladder, only they, of all living things, had the capacity to ascend to heaven, the realm of perfection.

GOD AS ARCHITECT OF THE UNIVERSE, FRENCH OLD TESTAMENT MINIATURE PAINTING, THIRTEENTH CENTURY. To the medieval Christian, God was the creator of the world. The universe had a known hierarchical order, a "great chain of being" extending from God downward to the lowest form of being. (*Osterreichische Nationalbibliothek, Vienna.*)

Also acceptable to the Christian mentality was the sharp distinction drawn by Aristotle between the world above the moon and the one below it. Aristotle held that terrestrial bodies were made of four elements: earth, water, air, fire. Celestial bodies, which occupied the region encompassing the moon and the area above, were composed of a fifth element, the ether—too clear, too pure, and too perfect to be found on earth. The planets and stars existed in a world apart; they were made of the divine ether and followed celestial laws, which did not apply to earthly objects. Whereas earthly bodies underwent change—ice converting to water, a burning log converting to ashes—heavenly objects were incorruptible, immune to all change. Unlike earthly objects, they were indestructible.

Heavenly bodies also followed different laws of motion than earthly objects. Aristotle said that it was natural for celestial bodies to move eternally in uniform circles, such motion being considered a sign of perfection. According to Aristotle, it was also natural for heavy bodies (stone) to fall downward and for light objects (fire, smoke) to move upward toward the celestial world; the falling stone and the rising smoke were finding their natural place in the universe. This view of the universe would be shattered by the Scientific Revolution of the sixteenth and seventeenth centuries.

The Individual: Sinful but Redeemable

At the center of medieval belief was the idea of a perfect God, who had conceived and created the universe, and wretched and sinful human beings. God had given Adam and Eve freedom to choose; rebellious and presumptuous, they had used their freedom to disobey God. In doing so, they made evil an intrinsic part of the human personality. But God, who had not stopped loving human beings, showed them the way out of sin. God became man and died so that human beings might be saved. Men and women were weak, egocentric, and sinful. With God's grace, they could overcome their sinful nature and gain salvation; without grace, they were utterly helpless.

The medieval individual's understanding of self stemmed from a comprehension of the universe as a **hierarchy** instituted by and culminating in God. On earth, the basest objects were lifeless stones devoid of souls; higher than stones were plants, endowed with a primitive type of soul, which allowed for reproduction and growth. Still higher were animals, which had the capacity for motion and sensation. The highest of the animals were human beings; unlike other animals, they could grasp some part of universal truth. Far superior to them were the angels, for they apprehended God's truth without difficulty. At the summit of this graduated universe was God, who was pure Being, without limitation, and the source of all existence. God's revelation reached down to humanity through the hierarchical order. From God, revelation passed to the angels, who were also arranged hierarchically. From the angels, the truth reached men and women, grasped first by prophets and apostles and then by the multitudes. Thus, all things in the universe, from angels, men, and women to the lowest earthly objects, occupied a place peculiar to their nature and were linked by God in a great, unbroken chain.

Medieval individuals derived a sense of security from this hierarchical universe, in which the human position was clearly defined. Although they were sinners who dwelt on a corruptible earth, at the bottom of the cosmic hierarchy, they *could* ascend to the higher world of perfection above the moon. As children of God, they enjoyed the unique distinction that each human soul was precious; all Christians commanded respect, unless they were heretics. (A heretic forfeited dignity and could be justly executed.)

Medieval thinkers also arranged knowledge in a hierarchical order: knowledge of the spiritual surpassed all worldly knowledge, all the sciences. Therefore, the true Christian understood that the pursuit of worldly knowledge could not proceed properly unless guided by divine revelation. To know what God wanted of the individual was the summit of self-knowledge and permitted entry into heaven. Thus, God was both the source and the end of knowledge. The human capacity to think and to act freely constituted the image of God within each individual; it ennobled man and woman and offered them the promise of associating with God in heaven.

True, human nobility derived from intelligence and free will. But if individuals disobeyed God, they brought misery on themselves. To challenge the divine will with human will constituted the sin of pride, contempt for God, and a violation of the divine order. Such sinful behavior invited self-destruction.

In the medieval view, neither nature nor the human being could be understood apart from God and his revelation. All reality emanated from God and was purposefully arranged in a spiritual hierarchy. Three great expressions of this view of life were scholastic philosophy, *The Divine Comedy* of Dante, and the Gothic cathedral.

Philosophy-Theology

Medieval philosophy, or scholasticism, applied reason to revelation. It explained and clarified Christian teachings by means of concepts and principles of logic derived from Greek philosophy. Scholastics tried to show that the teachings of faith, though not derived from reason, were not contrary to reason, that logic could confirm church dogma. They tried to prove through reason what they already held to be true through faith. For example, the existence of God and the immortality of the soul, which every Christian accepted as articles of faith, could also, they thought, be demonstrated by reason. In struggling to harmonize faith with reason, medieval thinkers constructed an extraordinary synthesis of Christian revelation and Greek thought.

The scholastic masters used reason not to challenge but to serve faith: to elucidate, clarify, and buttress it. They did not break with the central concern of Christianity, that of earning God's grace and achieving salvation. Although this goal could be realized solely through faith, scholastic thinkers insisted that a science of nature did not obstruct the pursuit of grace and that philosophy could assist the devout in the contemplation of God. They did not reject those Christian beliefs that were beyond the grasp of human reason and therefore could not be deduced by rational argument. Instead, they held that such truths rested entirely on revelation and were to be accepted on faith. To medieval thinkers, reason did not have an independent existence but ultimately had to acknowledge a suprarational, superhuman standard of truth. They wanted rational thought to be directed by faith for Christian ends and guided by scriptural and ecclesiastical authority. Ultimately, faith had the final word.

Not all Christian thinkers welcomed the use of reason. Regarding Greek philosophy as an enemy of faith (would not reason lead people to question belief in miracles?), a fabricator of heresies (would not reason encourage disbelief in essential church teachings?), and an obstacle to achieving communion of the soul with God (would not a deviation from church teachings, under the influence of pagan philosophy, deprive people of salvation?), conservative theologians opposed the use of reason to elucidate Christian revelation. For if reason could demonstrate the proof of Christian teachings, as its advocates insisted, it could also be used, warned conservatives, to challenge and reject those teachings. In a sense, the conservatives were right. By revitalizing Greek thought, medieval philosophy nurtured a powerful force that eventually would shatter the medieval concepts of nature and society and weaken Christianity. Modern Western thought was created by thinkers who refused to subordinate reason to religious authority. Reason proved to be a double-edged sword: it both ennobled and undermined the medieval world-view.

Saint Anselm and Abelard

An early scholastic, Saint Anselm (1033–1109) was abbot of the Benedictine monastery of Bec in Normandy. He used rational argument to serve the interests of faith. Like Augustine before him and other thinkers who followed him, Anselm said that faith was a precondition for understanding. Without belief there could be no proper knowledge. He developed philosophical proof for the existence of God. Anselm argued as follows: We can conceive of no being greater than God. But if God were to exist only in thought and not in actuality, his greatness would be limited; he would be less than perfect. Hence he exists. Anselm's motive and method reveal something about the essence of medieval philosophy. He does not begin as a modern might: "If it can be proven that God exists, I will adopt the creed of Christianity; if not, I will either deny God's existence (atheism) or reserve judgment (agnosticism)." Rather, Anselm accepts God's existence as an established fact because he believes what Holy Scripture says and what the church teaches. He then proceeds to employ logical argument to demonstrate that God can be known not only through faith but also through reason. He would never use reason to subvert what he knows to be true by faith. In general, this attitude would characterize later medieval thinkers, who also applied reason to faith.

As a young teacher of theology at the Cathedral School of Notre Dame, Peter Abelard (1079–1142) acquired a reputation for brilliance and combativeness. His tragic affair with Héloise, whom he tutored and seduced, has become one of the great romances in Western literature. Héloise had a child and entered a nunnery; Abelard was castrated on orders of Canon Fulbert, Héloise's guardian, and sought temporary refuge in a monastery. After resuming his career as a teacher in Paris, Abelard again had to seek refuge, this time for writing an essay on the **Trinity** that church officials found offensive. After further difficulties and flights, he again returned to Paris to teach dialectics. Not long afterward, his most determined opponent, Bernard of Clairvaux, accused Abelard of using the method of dialectical argument to attack faith. To Bernard, a monk and **mystic,** subjecting revealed truth to critical analysis was fraught with danger:

> *[T]he deepest matters become the subject of undignified wrangling. . . . Virtues and vices are discussed with no trace of moral feelings, the sacraments of the Church with no evidence of faith, the mystery of the Holy Trinity with no spirit of humility or sobriety: all is presented in a distorted form, introduced in a way different from the one we learned and are used to.*[4]

Hearkening to Bernard's powerful voice, the church condemned Abelard and confined him to a monastery for the rest of his days.

Abelard believed that it was important to apply reason to faith and that careful and constant questioning led to wisdom. Since all knowledge derives from God, said Abelard, it is good to pursue learning. In *Sic et Non* (Yes and No), he took 150 theological issues and, by presenting passages from the Bible and the church fathers, showed that there were conflicting opinions. He suggested that the divergent opinions of authorities could be reconciled through proper use of dialectics. But like Anselm before him, Abelard did not intend to refute traditional church doctrines. Reason would buttress, not weaken, the authority of faith. Abelard wrote after his condemnation in 1141:

> *I will never be a philosopher, if this is to speak against St. Paul, I would not be an Aristotle if this were to separate me from Christ. . . . I have set my building on the cornerstone on which Christ has built his Church. . . . I rest upon the rock that cannot be moved.*[5]

The Recovery of Aristotle

During the Early Middle Ages, scholars in the Muslim world translated the works of Aristotle into Arabic and wrote commentaries on them. The preservation of ancient Greek thought was a major contribution of Islamic civilization. During the High Middle Ages, these works were translated into Latin by learned Europeans.

The introduction into Latin Christendom of the major works of Aristotle created a dilemma for religious authorities. Aristotle's comprehensive philosophy of nature and man, a product of human reason alone, conflicted in many instances with essential Christian doctrine. For Aristotle, God was an impersonal principle that accounted for order and motion in the universe, the unmoved mover. For Christianity, not only was God responsible for order in the physical universe, but he was also a personal being—a loving Father concerned about the deeds of his children. Whereas Christianity taught that God created the universe at a specific point in time, Aristotle held that the universe was eternal. Nor did Aristotle believe in the personal immortality of the soul, another cardinal principle of Christianity. For Aristotle, it was impossible for the soul to exist independently of the body.

Some church officials feared that the dissemination of Aristotle's natural philosophy would endanger faith. Would the teachings of Christ and the church fathers have to answer to pagan philosophy? Would Athens prevail over Jerusalem? At various times in the first half of the thirteenth century, the teaching of Aristole's scientific works was forbidden at the University of Paris. However, because the ban did not apply throughout Christen-

Profile

Abelard and Héloise

Our knowledge of the love affair of Abelard and Héloise derives essentially from the candid autobiography Abelard wrote—something highly unusual for medieval scholars—and the exchange of letters between the two lovers. Abelard was nearly forty when Fulbert, the canon of Notre Dame, asked the famous scholar to tutor his bright and attractive seventeen-year-old niece. In *The Story of My Misfortunes,* Abelard described the tutorial:

> *Under a pretence of study, we gave ourselves up wholly to love. The lessons furnished us with the means to those mysterious communings dictated by vows of love. The books were open, but our words were more of love than of philosophy, and there were more kisses than explanations. My hands wandered more often to her breast than to our books and our eyes turned lovingly on one another more often than on the texts before us.**

When Héloise gave birth to a son, Abelard proposed marriage. Sharing the widely accepted view that married life was a barrier to scholarly pursuits, Héloise at first resisted but then relented. The couple tried to hide their marriage by living apart, but the news of their betrothal spread quickly. Canon Fulbert was

Scala/Art Resource, NY.

dom and was not consistently enforced in Paris, Aristotle's philosophy continued to be studied.

Saint Thomas Aquinas: Synthesis of Christian Belief and Reason

Rejecting the position of conservatives, who insisted that philosophy would contaminate faith, Saint Thomas Aquinas (c. 1225–1274) upheld the value of human reason and natural knowledge. He set about reconciling Aristotelianism with Christianity. Aquinas taught at Paris and at various institutions in Italy. His greatest work, *Summa Theologica,* is a systematic exposition of Christian thought and the crowning expression of the medieval attempt to integrate Aristotle with Christianity. As a devout Catholic and member of the Dominican order, he of course accepted the truth of revelation. He never used reason to undermine faith.

Online Study Center

Improve Your Grade

Primary Source: Summa Theologica: On Free Will

pleased with the marriage, which salvaged his niece's honor. However, when Héloise, always concerned with the best interests of her beloved, swore that no marriage had taken place, Fulbert placed her in a convent and subjected Abelard "to the most barbarous and shameful revenge."

The castrated Abelard retreated to the Abbey of Saint Denis, but soon resumed his teaching at a school near the monastery. His talents undiminished, Abelard continued to attract many students. But his misfortunes persisted. In 1121, a church council ruled that his *Treatise on the Unity and Trinity of God* be burned and that its author retire to Saint Denis.

More than a decade after their romance, Abelard was the reform-minded abbot of Saint Gildas and Héloise the abbess of the Paraclete, a newly established convent. Still in love, Héloise wrote to Abelard:

> *Those lovers' delights we enjoyed together were so sweet to me that I cannot find it in my heart to condemn them, or even wipe out the memory of them without pain. Whichever way I turn, they are always in my sight, they and their desires. Even while I sleep, their illusions pursue me. Always, even in the most solemn moments of the mass, when prayer should be most pure, the obscene images of these pleasures still enthrall my poor soul so that I give myself up to this depravity rather than to prayer. I, who should bemoan what I have done, sigh instead after that which I have lost. And not only those things we have done, but the very times and places in which we did them together are so graven in my heart that I see them all again with you and am not free from them even in my sleep. Sometimes even the movements of my body reveal the thoughts that are in my soul, and they betray themselves by involuntary words. I am so unhappy and with what justice I repeat the lament of a soul in torment: "Wretched that I am, who will deliver me from this living death?"*

In a gentle rebuke, Abelard replied that their sexual encounter, in which he "slaked my miserable desires [did] not deserve the name of love," and beseeched her to direct all her love to Christ. Abelard died in 1142 at the age of sixty-three. When Héloise died twenty-two years later, also at the age of sixty-three, she was buried at his side. Their remains are still together, though not in the original gravesite.

---

*The passages from Abelard's *The Story of My Misfortunes* and from his correspondence with Héloise are taken from the admirable translations of selected passages from these works found in Philippe Wolf, *The Cultural Awakening,* trans. Anne Carter (New York: Pantheon, 1968), pt. 1, chap. 3.

Aquinas divided revealed truth into two categories: beliefs whose truth can be demonstrated by reason and beliefs that reason cannot prove to be either true or false. For example, he believed that philosophical speculation could prove the existence of God and the immortality of the human soul but could not prove or disprove the doctrines of the Trinity, the **Incarnation,** and the **Redemption** because those articles of faith wholly surpassed the capacity of human reason. This fact, however, did not detract from their certainty. Doctrines of faith did not require rational proof to be valid. They were true because they originated with God, whose authority is unshakable.

Can the teachings of faith conflict with the evidence of reason? For Aquinas, the answer was emphatically no. He said that revelation could not be the enemy of reason because revelation did not contradict reason and reason did not corrupt the purity of faith. Revelation supplemented and perfected reason. If there appeared to be a conflict between philosophy and faith, it was certain that reason had erred somewhere, for the doctrines of faith were infallible. Since *both* faith and reason came from God, they were not in competition with each

THE TRIUMPH OF SAINT THOMAS AQUINAS: WALL PAINTING, THE SPANISH CHAPEL, CHURCH OF SANTA MARIA NOVELLA, FLORENCE, FOURTEENTH CENTURY. In a church built by his fellow Dominican friars, the saint, theologian, and philosopher Thomas Aquinas sits enthroned, expounding Christian theology illuminated by the principles of Aristotle. This painting is by Taddeo Gaddi, a pupil of the master painter Giotto. (*Photo Alinari-Giraudon.*)

other but, properly understood, supported each other and formed an organic unity. Consequently, reason should not be feared, for it was another avenue to God. Because there was an inherent agreement between true faith and correct reason—they both ultimately stemmed from God—contradictions between the two were only a misleading appearance. Although philosophy had not yet been able to resolve the dilemma, for God no such contradictions existed. In heaven, human beings would attain complete knowledge, as well as complete happiness. While on earth, however, they must allow faith to guide reason; they must not permit reason to oppose or undermine faith.

Because reason was no enemy of faith, applying it to revelation need not be feared. As human reasoning became more proficient, said Aquinas, it also became more Christian, and apparent incompatibilities between faith and reason disappeared. Recognizing that both faith and reason point to the same truth, the wise person accepts the guidance of religion in all questions that relate directly to knowledge needed for salvation. There also existed a wide range of knowledge that God had not revealed and that was not required for salvation. Into this category fell much knowledge about the natural world of things and creatures, which human beings had perfect liberty to explore.

Thus, in exalting God, Aquinas also paid homage to human intelligence, proclaimed the value of rational activity, and asserted the importance of physical reality revealed through human senses. Consequently, he valued the natural philosophy of Aristotle. Correctly used, Aristotelian thought would assist faith. Aquinas's great effort was to synthesize Aristotelianism with the divine revelation of Christianity. That the two could be harmonized he had no doubt. He made use of Aristotelian categories in his five proofs of God's existence. In his first proof, for example, Aquinas argued that a thing cannot move itself. Whatever is moved must be moved by something else, and that by something else again. "Therefore, it is necessary to arrive at a first mover, moved by no other; and this everyone understands to be God."[6]

Aquinas upheld the value of reason. To love the intellect was to honor God and not to diminish the truth of faith. He had confidence in the power of the rational mind to comprehend most of the truths of revelation, and he insisted that in nontheological questions about specific things in nature—those questions not affecting salvation—people should trust only to reason and experience.

Aquinas gave new importance to the empirical world and to scientific speculation and human knowledge. The traditional medieval view, based largely on Saint Augustine, drew a sharp distinction between the higher world of grace and the lower world of nature, between the world of spirit and the world of sense experience. Knowledge derived from the natural world was often seen as an obstacle to true knowledge. Aquinas altered this tradition by affirming the importance of knowledge of the social order and the physical world. He gave human reason and worldly knowledge a new dignity. Thus, the City of Man was not merely a sinful place from which people tried to escape in order to enter God's city; it was worthy of investigation and understanding. But Aquinas remained a medieval thinker, for he always maintained that secular knowledge should be supervised and corrected by revealed truth, and he never questioned the truth of the medieval Christian view of the world and the individual. As historian Steven Ozment explains,

> *Aquinas brought reason and revelation together, but strictly as unequals. . . . In this union, reason, philosophy, nature, secular man and the state ultimately had value only in subservience to the higher goals of revelation, theology, grace, religious man, and the church. . . . Thomist theology was the most sophisticated statement of the medieval belief in the secondary significance of the lay and secular world, a congenial ideology for a church besieged by independent and aggressive secular political powers.*[7]

Strict Aristotelianism: The Challenge to Orthodoxy

Some teachers in the Faculty of Arts at Paris, relying heavily on the commentaries of Averroës, the great Muslim thinker (see page 204), found Aquinas's approach of Christianizing or explaining away Aristotle unacceptable. Unlike Aquinas, they did not seek to reconcile Aristotle's philosophy with Christian dogma. They held that certain Aristotelian propositions contradicting faith were philosophically true, or at least could not be proven false. These teachers maintained that it was impossible to refute these propositions by natural reason alone—that is, without recourse to faith. For example, by reason alone Aristotle had demonstrated that the world was eternal and that the processes of nature were unalterable. The first doctrine conflicted with the Christian belief that God created the universe at a point in time; the second conflicted with the belief that God could work miracles.

But these teachers did not take the next step and argue that Aristotle was correct and faith wrong. They maintained only that Aristotle's arguments could not be refuted by natural reason, and that philosophers—as philosophers, not as Christians—should base their judgments on rational arguments only, not on miracles and revelation. These strict Aristotelians did not deny the truths of faith, but they did assert that natural reason could construct conclusive proofs for propositions that the church had explicitly stated to be false.

In 1277, the bishop of Paris condemned 219 propositions, many of them taught by these expositors of Aristotle at the University of Paris. Included in the condemnation were some propositions held by the great Aquinas. This move attempted to prevent Aristotle's philosophical naturalism from undermining Christian beliefs. Consequently, the condemnation was a triumph for conservative theologians, who had grown increasingly worried about the inroads made by Aristotelianism. To them, even the Christian Aristotelianism of Aquinas was suspect.

Condemnations generally hinder the pursuit of knowledge, but, ironically, the condemnation of 1277 may have had the opposite effect. It led some thinkers to examine critically and reject elements of Aristotle's natural philosophy. This development may have served as a prelude to modern science, which, born in the sixteenth and seventeenth centuries, grew out of a rejection of Aristotelian physics.

Science

During the Early Middle Ages, few scientific works from the ancient world were available to western Europeans. Scientific thought was at its lowest ebb since its origination more than a thousand years earlier in Greece. By contrast, both Islamic and Byzantine civilizations preserved and, in some instances, added to the legacy of Greek science. In the High Middle Ages, however, many ancient texts were translated from Greek and Arabic into Latin and entered Latin Christendom for the first time. The principal centers of translation were Spain, where Christian and Muslim civilizations met, and Sicily, which had been controlled by Byzantium up to the last part of the ninth century and then by Islam until Christian Normans completed the conquest of the island by 1091. Often learned Jews, who knew both Arabic and Latin, served as translators. These translations of ancient Greek scientific works and of Arabic commentaries stimulated interest in nature.

In the thirteenth and fourteenth centuries, a genuine scientific movement did occur. Impressed with the naturalistic and empirical approach of Aristotle, some medieval schoolmen spent time examining physical nature. Among them was the Dominican Albert the Great (Albertus Magnus). Born in Germany, Albert (c. 1206–1280) studied at Padua and taught at the University of Paris, where Thomas Aquinas was his student. To Albert, philosophy meant more than employing Greek reason to contemplate divine wisdom: it also meant making sense of nature. Albert devoted himself to mastering, editing, and commenting on the vast body of Aristotle's works.

While retaining the Christian stress on God, revelation, the supernatural, and the afterlife, Albert (unlike many earlier Christian thinkers) considered nature a valid field for investigation. In his writings on geology, chemistry, botany, and zoology, Albert, like Aristotle, displayed respect for the concrete details of nature, utilizing them as empirical evidence:

> *I have examined the anatomy of different species of bees. In the rear, i.e. behind the waist, I discovered a transparent, shining bladder. If you test this with your tongue, you find that it has a slight taste of honey. In the body there is only an insignificant spiral-shaped intestine and nerve fibers which are connected with the sting. All this is surrounded with a sticky fluid.*[8]

Showing a modern-day approach, Albert approved of inquiry into the material world, stressed the value of knowledge derived from experience with nature, sought rational explanations for natural occurrences, and held that theological debates should not stop scientific investigations. He pointed to a new direction in medieval thought.

Robert Grosseteste (c. 1175–1253), chancellor of Oxford University, was also a scholar of the scientific movement. He declared that the roundness of the earth could be demonstrated by reason. In addition, he insisted that mathematics was necessary in order to understand the physical world, and he carried out experiments on the refraction of light.

Another Englishman, the monk and philosopher Roger Bacon (c. 1214–1294), foreshadowed the modern attitude of using science to gain mastery over nature. He recognized the practical advantages that might come and predicted these great changes:

> *Machines for navigation can be made without rowers so that the largest ships on rivers or seas will be moved by a single man in charge with greater velocity than if they were full of men. Also oars can be made so that without animals they will move with unbelievable rapidity. . . . Also flying machines can be constructed so that a man sits in the midst of the machine revolving some engine by which artificial wings are made to beat the air like a flying bird. Also a machine small in size can be made for walking in the sea and rivers, even to the bottom without danger.*[9]

Bacon valued the study of mathematics and read Arabic works on the reflection and refraction of light. Among his achievements were experiments in optics and the observation that light travels much faster than sound. His description of the anatomy of the vertebrate eye and optic nerves was the finest of that era, and he recommended dissecting the eyes of pigs and cows to obtain greater knowledge of the subject.

The study of the ancient texts of Hippocrates and Galen and their Islamic commentators, particularly Avicenna's *Canon of Medicine,* which synthesized Greek and Arabic medicine, elevated medicine to a formal discipline. Although these texts contained numerous errors and contradictions, they had to be mastered, if only to be challenged, before modern medicine could emerge. In addition, medieval doctors dissected animals and, in the late fourteenth century, human bodies. From practical experience, medieval doctors, monks, and laypersons added to the list of plants and herbs that would ease pain and heal.

Medieval scholars did not make the breakthrough to modern science. They kept the belief that the earth was at the center of the universe and that different sets of laws operated on earth and in the heavens. They did not invent analytic geometry or calculus or arrive at the modern concept of inertia. Although some medieval thinkers explicitly urged seeking natural explanations to account for physical occurrences, medieval science was never wholly removed from a theological setting. Modern science self-consciously seeks the advancement of specifically scientific knowledge, but in the Middle Ages, many questions involving nature were raised merely to clarify a religious problem.

Medieval scholars and philosophers, however, did advance knowledge about optics, the tides, and mechanics. They saw the importance of mathematics for interpreting nature, and they performed some experiments. By translating and commenting on ancient Greek and Arabic works, medieval scholars provided future ages with ideas to reflect on and to reject and surpass, a necessary precondition for the emergence of modern science.

Medieval thinkers also developed an anti-Aristotelian physics, which some historians of science believe influenced Galileo, the creator of modern mechanics, more than two centuries later. To explain why heavy objects do not always fall downward—why an arrow released by a bow moves in a straight line before it falls—Aristotle said that when the arrow leaves the bow, it separates the air, which then moves behind the arrow and pushes it along. Aristotle, of course, had no comprehension of the law of inertia, which, as formulated by Isaac Newton in the seventeenth century, states that a body in motion will continue in a straight line unless interfered with. Unable to imagine that being in motion is as natural a condition as being at rest, Aristotle concluded that an outside force must maintain continual contact with the moving object. Hence, the flying arrow requires the "air-engine" to keep it in motion.

In the fourteenth century, Jean Buridan, a professor at the University of Paris, rejected Aristotle's theory. Buridan argued that the bowstring transmits to the arrow a force called impetus, which keeps the arrow in motion. Whereas Aristotle attributed the arrow's motion to the air, which was external to the arrow, Buridan found the motive force to be an agent imparted to the arrow by the bowstring. Though still far from the modern theory of inertia, Buridan's impetus theory was an advance over Aristotle's air-engine. In the impetus theory, a moving body requires a cause to keep it in motion. In the theory of inertia, as noted above, once a body is in motion, no force is required to keep it moving in a straight line.

Late medieval physics went beyond Aristotle in other ways as well, particularly in the importance given to expressing motion mathematically. The extent to which late medieval thinkers influenced the thinkers of the Scientific Revolution is a matter of debate. Some historians view modern science as a child of the Middle Ages. Other historians believe that the achievements of medieval science were slim and that modern science owes very little to the Middle Ages.

The Recovery of Roman Law

During the Early Middle Ages, western European law essentially consisted of Germanic customs, some of which had been written down. Although some elements of Roman law endured as custom, the formal study of Roman law disappeared. The late eleventh and the twelfth centuries saw the revival of Roman law, particularly in Bologna, Italy. Irnerius lectured on the *Corpus Juris Civilis*, Roman laws and judicial commentaries codified by Byzantine jurists in the sixth century by order of the emperor Justinian. He made Bologna the leading center for the study of Roman law. Irnerius and his students applied to the study of law the methods of organization and logical analysis that scholastic theologians used in studying philosophical texts.

Unlike traditional Germanic law, which was essentially tribal law, Roman law assumed the existence of universal principles, which could be grasped by the human intellect and expressed in the law of the state. Roman jurists had systematically and rationally structured the legal experience of the Roman people. The example of Roman law stimulated medieval jurists to organize their own legal tradition. Intellectuals increasingly came to insist on both a rational analysis of evidence and judicial decisions based on rational procedures. Law codes compiled in parts of France and Germany and in the kingdom of Castile were influenced by the recovery of Roman law.

Roman law also influenced church law, which was derived from the Bible, the church fathers, church councils, and the decisions of popes. In the last part of the eleventh century, church scholars began to codify church (or canon) law and were helped by the Roman legal tradition.

Literature

Medieval literature was written both in Latin and in the vernacular—the normal spoken language, as distinct from the language of learning. Much of medieval Latin literature consisted of religious hymns and dramas depicting the life of Christ and saints.

Medieval university students, like their modern counterparts, lampooned their elders and social conventions, engaged in drinking bouts, and rebelled against the rigors of study. They put their feelings into poetry written in Latin. For them, youth and study did not mix:

> *Let's away with study,*
> *Folly's sweet.*
> *Treasure all the pleasure of our youth:*
> *Time enough for age*
> *To think of Truth.*
>
> *So short a day,*
> *And life so quickly hasting*
> *And is study wasting*
> *Youth that would be gay!*[10]

And, of course, their thoughts turned to romance:

> *All I care for is to play,*
> *Gaze upon my treasure,*
> *Now and then to touch her hand,*
> *Kiss in modest measure;*
> *But the fifth act of love's game,*
> *Dream not of that pleasure!*[11]

Poor or errant students who had given up their studies roamed the roads as free spirits. These vagabonds sometimes composed poetry that ridiculed clerics and sang the praises of wine, gambling, and women:

> *Down the highway-broad I walk,*
> *Like a youth in mind,*
> *Implicate myself in vice,*
> *Virtue stays behind,*
> *Avid for the world's delight*
> *More than for salvation,*
> *Dead in soul, I care but for*
> *Body's exultation.*[12]

Vernacular literature emerged in the High Middle Ages. The French *chansons de geste*—epic poems of heroic deeds that had first been told orally—were written in the vernacular of northern France. The poems dealt with Charlemagne's battles against the Muslims, with rebellious nobles, and with feudal warfare. The finest of these epic poems, *The Song of Roland,* expressed the feudal ethic—loyalty to one's lord and devotion to Christianity were the highest virtues and treachery an impardonable crime. Roland, Charlemagne's nephew, who was killed in a battle with the Muslims, is idealized as the brave Christian knight who battles God's enemies, a warrior of heroic proportions with great physical prowess, who is loyal to God, king, and his knightly entourage.

The *Nibelungenlied,* the best expression of the heroic epic in Germany, is often called "the *Iliad* of the Germans." Like its French counterpart, it dealt with heroic feats:

> *In stories of our fathers, high marvels we are told*
> *Of champions well-approved in perils manifold.*
> *Of feasts and merry meetings, of weeping and of wail,*
> *And deeds of gallant daring I'll tell you in my tale.*[13]

The *roman*—a blending of old legends, chivalric ideals, and Christian concepts—combined love with adventure, war, and the miraculous. Among the romans were the tales of King Arthur and his Round Table. Circulating by word of mouth for centuries, these tales spread from the British Isles to France and Germany. In the twelfth century, they were put into French verse.

Another form of medieval poetry, which flourished particularly in Provence, in southern France,

Millefleurs Tapestry: Two Musicians, School of the Loire, France, c. 1500. The courtly love tradition, in which women were worshiped and untouchable, inspired poetry. Troubadours sang this poetry, which expressed a changing attitude toward women. By inviting poets to their courts and writing poetry themselves, noblewomen actively influenced the rituals and literature of courtly love. (*Frick Museum, Pittsburg, PA.*)

dealt with the romantic glorification of women. Sung by *troubadours,* many of them nobles, the courtly love poetry expressed a changing attitude toward women. Although medieval men generally regarded women as inferior and subordinate, courtly love poetry ascribed to noble ladies superior qualities of virtue. To the nobleman, the lady became a goddess worthy of devotion, loyalty, and worship. He would honor her and serve her as he did his lord; for her love, he would undergo any sacrifice. Troubadours sang love songs that praised ladies for their beauty and charm and expressed both the joys and the pains of love:

I sing of her, yet her beauty
is greater than I can tell,
with her fresh color, lively eyes,
and white skin, untanned
and untainted by rouge.
She is so pure and noble
that no one can speak ill of her.
But above all, one must praise,
it seems to me, her truthfulness,
her manners and her gracious speech
for she never would betray a friend. . . .[14]

Noblewomen actively influenced the rituals and literature of courtly love. They often invited poets to their courts and wrote poetry themselves. Sometimes a lady troubadour expressed disdain for her husband and desire for the knight whom she truly loved:

I should like to hold my knight
Naked in my arms at eve,
That he might be in ecstasy
As I cushioned his head against my breast,
For I am happier far with him
Than Floris with Blancheflor;
I grant him my heart, my love,
My mind, my eyes, my life.

Fair friend, charming and good,
When shall I hold you in my power?
And lie beside you for an hour
And amorous kisses give to you;
Know that I would give almost anything
To have you in my husband's place,
But only if you swear
To do everything I desire.[15]

Ladies demanded that knights treat them with gentleness and consideration and that knights dress neatly, bathe often, play instruments, and compose (or at least recite) poetry. To prove worthy of his lady's love, a knight had to demonstrate patience, charm, bravery, and loyalty. It was believed that a knight would ennoble his character by devoting himself to a lady.

Courtly love involved not a husband-wife relationship but a noble's admiration and yearning for another woman of his class. Among nobles, marriages were arranged for political and economic reasons. The rituals of courtly love, it has been suggested, provided an outlet for erotic feelings condemned by the church. They also enhanced the skills and refined the tastes of the noble. The rough warrior acquired wit, manners,

Virgil and Dante Watch Lucifer: A Miniature Painting in an Early Manuscript of *The Divine Comedy*. Dante reserved the lowest depth of hell for those guilty of treason. Lucifer, the angel who betrayed God, is depicted as a monster with three mouths. With these he perpetually chews on Judas Iscariot, Brutus, and Cassius. (*Trivulzian Library, Milan.*)

The Visitation, West Portal, Reims Cathedral, c. 1225–1245. The reflection of Roman art exhibited by these statues of the expectant mothers (Mary and Elizabeth) of Jesus and John the Baptist suggests that the sculptor was well versed in the classical tradition. The carving of the draperies and the poses of the figures reveal classical traits, but instead of being idealizations, the figures display human warmth. (*Bildarchiv Foto Marburg/Art Resource, NY.*)

charm, and a facility with words. He was becoming a courtier and a gentleman.

The greatest literary figure of the Middle Ages was Dante Alighieri (1265–1321) of Florence. Dante appreciated the Roman classics and wrote not just in Latin, the traditional language of intellectual life, but also in Italian, his native tongue. In this respect, he anticipated the Renaissance. In the tradition of the troubadours, Dante wrote poems to his beloved Beatrice.

In *The Divine Comedy,* Dante synthesized the various elements of the medieval outlook and summed up, with immense feeling, the medieval understanding of the purpose of life. Written while Dante was in exile, *The Divine Comedy* describes the poet's journey through hell, purgatory, and paradise. Dante arranges hell into nine concentric circles; in each region, sinners are punished in proportion to their earthly sins. The poet experiences all of hell's torments—burning sand, violent storms, darkness, and fearful monsters that whip, claw, bite, and tear sinners apart. The ninth circle, the lowest, is reserved for Lucifer and traitors. Lucifer has three faces, each a different color, and two batlike wings. In each mouth he gnaws on the greatest traitors in history: Judas Iscariot, who betrayed Jesus, and Brutus and Cassius, who assassinated Caesar. Those condemned to hell are told: "All hope abandon, ye who enter in."

In purgatory, Dante meets sinners who, although they undergo punishment, will eventually enter paradise. He and Beatrice ascend to the highest heaven, a realm of light that radiates truth, goodness, and gentleness. In paradise, the poet meets the great saints and the Virgin Mary. He glimpses the Vision of God. In this mystical experience, the aim of life is realized.

Architecture

Two styles of architecture evolved during the Middle Ages: Romanesque and Gothic. The **Romanesque** style dominated the eleventh century and the greater part of the twelfth. In imitation of ancient Roman structures, Romanesque buildings used massive walls to support stone barrel and groin vaults with rounded arches. Thick walls were needed to hold up the great weight of the roofs. Because the walls had few spaces for windows, little light entered the interior of Romanesque buildings.

The development of the pointed arch permitted supports that lessened the bearing pressure of the roof on the walls. This new style, called **Gothic,** allowed buildings to have lofty, vaulted ceilings and huge windows. Whereas Romanesque buildings produced an impression of massive solidity, Gothic buildings created an illusion of lightness and upward motion. The Gothic cathedral gave visual expression to the medieval conception of a hierarchical universe. As the historian Joan Gadol puts it, "Inside and out, the Gothic cathedral is one great movement upward through a mounting series of grades, one ascent through horizontal levels marked by arches, galleries, niches, and towers . . . the material ascends to the spiritual, the natural is assumed into the supernatural—all in a graduated rise."[16] This illusion is created by the tall and narrow proportions of the interior spaces, the springing pointed arches, and the marching patterns of closely spaced columns and colonnettes.

The magnificently designed stained-glass windows and complex sculptural decoration of Gothic cathedrals depicted scenes from the Bible and the lives of saints, as well as scenes from daily life, for the worshipers, many of whom were illiterate. The reduction of wall space, which allowed these massive glass illustrations, was made possible by the flying buttresses on the buildings' exteriors. These great arcs of masonry carry the weight and thrust of the stone vaults out to the exterior walls. The light cage of buttresses surrounding the cathedral makes the exterior silhouette appear as airy and diffuse as the interior spaces.

Gothic cathedrals took many decades to complete and required donations from the devout. Only in an age of intense religious faith could such energy have been spent to glorify God. These vast building projects, many of them in northern France, were made possible by economic prosperity. Funds were raised from a variety of sources. Cathedrals owned income-producing properties, such as farmland, mills, and forests, and received donations from pilgrims visiting the relics of famous saints. Clerics also collected tolls and taxes on goods shipped to fairs through their region.

The Gothic style was to remain vigorous until the fifteenth century, spreading from France to England, Germany, Spain, and beyond. Revived from time to time thereafter, it has proved to be one of the most enduring styles in Western art and architecture.

Not too long ago, some intellectuals viewed the Middle Ages as a period of ignorance and superstition, an era of cultural sterility that stood between the high civilizations of ancient Greece and Rome and the modern West. This view of the Middle Ages as a dark age has been abandoned, and quite properly so, for the High Middle Ages saw the crystallizing of a rich and creative civilization. To be sure, its religious orientation sets it apart both from classical civilization and from our own modern secular and scientific civilization. But the *Summa Theologica* of Aquinas, *The Divine Comedy* of Dante, and the Gothic cathedral all attest to the creativeness and genius of the medieval religious spirit.

❖ ❖ ❖

Online Study Center **ACE the Test**

NOTES

1. Quoted in G. G. Coulton, *Life in the Middle Ages* (New York: Macmillan, 1928), 1:74.
2. Quoted in Charles Homer Haskins, *The Rise of Universities* (Ithaca, N.Y.: Cornell University Press, 1957), p. 79.
3. Quoted in Coulton, *Life in the Middle Ages,* 3:113.
4. Quoted in Anders Piltz, *The World of Medieval Learning* (Oxford: Blackwell, 1981), p. 83.
5. Quoted in David Knowles, *The Evolution of Medieval Thought* (New York: Vintage Books, 1964), p. 123.
6. *Summa Theologica,* excerpted in Anton C. Pegis, ed., *Introduction to Saint Thomas Aquinas* (New York: Modern Library, 1948), p. 25.
7. Steven Ozment, *The Age of Reform* (New Haven, Conn.: Yale University Press, 1980), p. 20.
8. Quoted in Piltz, *The World of Medieval Learning,* p. 176.
9. Quoted in A. C. Crombie, *Medieval and Early Modern Science* (Garden City, N.Y.: Doubleday Anchor Books, 1959), 1:55–56.
10. Quoted in Marcia L. Colish, *Medieval Foundations of the Western Intellectual Tradition, 400–1400* (New Haven, Conn.: Yale University Press, 1997), p. 202.
11. Excerpted in David C. Riede and J. Wayne Baker, eds., *The Western Intellectual Tradition,* vol. 1 (Dubuque, Ia.: Kendall/Hunt, 1980), p. 62.
12. Excerpted in E. H. Zeydel, ed., *Vagabond Verse: Secular Latin Poems in the Middle Ages* (Detroit: Wayne State University Press, 1966) p. 61.
13. *The Fall of the Nibelungers,* trans. William Nanson Lettsom (London: Williams & Norgate, 1890), p. 1.
14. Excerpted in Anthony Bonner, ed., *Songs of the Troubadours* (New York: Schocken Books, 1972), pp. 42–43.
15. Quoted in Frances Gies and Joseph Gies, *Women in the Middle Ages* (New York: T. Y. Crowell, 1978), p. 45.
16. Joan Gadol, *Leon Battista Alberti, Universal Man of the Early Renaissance* (Chicago: The University of Chicago Press, 1969), pp. 149–150.

SUGGESTED READING

Bonner, Anthony, ed., *Songs of the Troubadours* (1972). Collection of troubadour poetry.

Colish, Marcia L., *Medieval Foundations of the Western Intellectual Tradition,* 400–1400 (1997). A lucid account; highly recommended.

Copleston, F. C., *A History of Medieval Philosophy* (1974). A lucid, comprehensive survey of medieval philosophy.

Gilson, Etienne, *Reason and Revelation in the Middle Ages* (1966). A superb brief exposition of the medieval philosophical tradition.

Gimpel, Jean, *The Cathedral Builders* (1984). The financial, political, and spiritual forces behind the building of cathedrals.

Pieper, Josef, *Scholasticism* (1964). Written with intelligence and grace.

Wieruszowski, Helene, *The Medieval University* (1966). A good survey, followed by documents.

Chapter 12

The Late Middle Ages: Crisis and Dissolution

The Jacquerie: Enraged French Peasants Attack the Castle of a Lord. (Bibliothèque Nationale, Paris.)

- **An Age of Adversity**
- **The Decline of the Papacy**
- **Breakup of the Thomistic Synthesis**
- **The Middle Ages and the Modern World: Continuity and Discontinuity**

Focus Questions

1. Why is the fourteenth century described as an age of adversity?
2. What led to the decline of the medieval papacy? What is the historical significance of this development?
3. What is the significance of thinkers who challenged the Thomistic synthesis?
4. What is the legacy of the Middle Ages to the modern world?
5. How does the characteristic outlook of the Middle Ages differ from that of the Modern Age?

Online Study Center

This icon will direct you to interactive map and primary source activities on the website http://college.hmco.com/pic/perrywc8e.

By the start of the fourteenth century, Latin Christendom had experienced more than 250 years of growth. On an economic level, agricultural production had expanded, commerce and town life had revived, and the population had increased. On a political level, kings had become more powerful, bringing greater order and security to large areas. On a religious level, the papacy had demonstrated its strength as the spiritual leader of Christendom, and the clergy had been reformed. On a cultural level, a unified world-view, blending faith and reason, had been forged.

During the Late Middle Ages, roughly the fourteenth and early fifteenth centuries, medieval civilization was in decline. The fourteenth century, an age of adversity, was marked by crop failures, famine, population decline, plagues, stagnating production, unemployment, inflation, devastating warfare, and abandoned villages. Violent rebellions by the poor of the towns and countryside were ruthlessly suppressed by the upper classes. The century witnessed flights into mysticism, outbreaks of mass hysteria, and massacres of Jews; it was an age of pessimism and general insecurity. The papacy declined in power, heresy proliferated, and the synthesis of faith and reason, erected by Christian thinkers during the High Middle Ages, began to disintegrate. These developments were signs that the stable and coherent civilization of the thirteenth century was drawing to a close.

But all was not decline and gloom. On the positive side, representative institutions developed, and thinkers showed a greater interest in the world of nature. And in Italy, the dynamic forces of urbanism and secularism were producing a period of cultural and humanistic flowering known as the Renaissance.

An Age of Adversity

Economic Problems, Black Death, and Social Tension

In the Late Middle Ages, Latin Christendom was afflicted with severe economic problems. The earlier increases in agricultural production did not continue. Limited use of fertilizers and limited

Chronology 12.1 ❖ The Late Middle Ages

1303	The French attack papal summer palace at Anagni
1309–1377	Babylonian Captivity: the popes, all French, reside at Avignon and are influenced by the French monarchy
1323–1328	Peasants revolt in Flanders
1328	End of France's Capetian dynasty; Edward III of England tries to gain the French throne
1337–1453	Hundred Years' War between England and France
1346	Battle of Crécy: the English defeat the French
1347–1351	Black Death reaches Italian ports and ravages Europe
1356	Battle of Poitiers: the English defeat the French
1358	Jacquerie, the French peasants' revolt
1377	Pope Gregory XI returns papacy to Rome
1378	Florentine laborers revolt
1378–1417	Great Schism: Christendom has two and then three popes
1381	English peasants revolt
1382	Weavers revolt in Ghent
1415	Battle of Agincourt: Henry V of England defeats the French; Jan Hus, a Bohemian religious reformer, is burned at the stake
1429	Joan of Arc liberates Orléans
1431	Joan of Arc is condemned as a witch
1453	The English are driven from France, except Calais: end of the Hundred Years' War
1460	Pope Pius II condemns the Conciliar Movement as heretical

knowledge of conservation exhausted the topsoil. As more grazing land was converted to the cultivation of cereals, animal husbandry decreased, causing a serious shortage of manure needed for arable land. Intermittent bouts of prolonged heavy rains and frost also hampered agriculture. From 1301 to 1314, there was a general shortage of food, and from 1315 to 1317, famine struck Europe. People subsisted by scavenging. On roads and in villages people died of starvation, and the dead remained unattended. Throughout the century, starvation and malnutrition were widespread. In Bruges, for example, two thousand of the town's thirty-five thousand inhabitants died of starvation.

Other economic problems abounded. A shortage of silver, caused by technical problems in sinking deeper shafts in mines, led to the debasement of coins and spiraling inflation, which hurt the feudal nobility in particular. Prices for manufactured luxury goods, which the nobility craved, rose rapidly. At the same time, the dues that the nobility collected from peasants diminished. To replace their revenues, lords and knights turned to plunder and warfare.

Compounding the economic crisis was the Black Death, or bubonic plague. This disease was carried by fleas on black rats and probably first struck Mongolia in 1331–32. From there, it crossed into Russia. Carried back from Black Sea

GREAT PLAGUE. The Black Death, or bubonic plague, devastated Europe, carrying off entire villages. A new piety swept through European art in the plague's aftermath. The elegant French courtly love style was replaced by tightly swaddled infants and suffering saints. (*Bibliothèque Royale Albert I, Brussels/Art Resource, NY.*)

ports, the plague reached Sicily in 1347. Spreading swiftly throughout much of Europe through human contact, the plague attacked an already declining and undernourished population. The first crisis lasted until 1351, and other serious outbreaks occurred in later decades. The crowded cities and towns had the highest mortalities. Perhaps twenty million people—about one-quarter to one-third of the European population—perished in the worst disaster in recorded history caused by natural forces. Contemporaries viewed the disaster as divine punishment for humanity's sins.

Online Study Center **Improve Your Grade**
Interactive Map: Bubonic Plague and Social Upheaval in Fourteenth Century Europe

Overwhelmed by terror, people abandoned their sick children, spouses, and parents. Panic-stricken people drifted into debauchery, lawlessness, and frenzied forms of religious life. Organized bands of flagellants marched from region to region beating themselves and each other with sticks and whips in a desperate effort to appease God, who, they believed, had cursed them with the plague. Art concentrated on morbid scenes of decaying flesh, open graves laden with worm-eaten corpses, dances of death, and the torments of hell. Sometimes this hysteria was directed against Jews, who were accused of causing the plague by poisoning wells. Terrible massacres of Jews, often by mass burnings, occurred despite the pleas of the papacy.

The millions of deaths caused production of food and goods to plummet and some prices to soar. Nobles tried to make peasants bear the brunt of the crisis, as the value of land decreased and agricultural income lessened. A law decreed in England in 1349 required peasants to work for lords at fixed wages. Similar regulations of wages in German, Spanish, and Portuguese principalities aggravated tensions between peasants and nobles.

Economic and social tensions, some of them antedating the Black Death, escalated into rebellions. Each rebellion had its own specific causes, but a general pattern characterized the uprisings in the countryside. When kings and lords, breaking with customary social relationships, imposed new and onerous regulations, the peasants rose in defense of their traditional rights. No doubt their revolt was also fueled by an instinctive hatred for the haughty lords, who, for centuries, had treated peasants with contempt. In 1323, the lords' attempt to reimpose old manorial obligations infuriated the free peasants of Flanders, whose condition had improved in earlier decades. The Peasants' Revolt lasted five bloody years. In 1358, French peasants took up arms in protest against the plundering of the countryside by soldiers. Perhaps twenty thousand peasants died in the uprising known as the Jacquerie. In 1381, English peasants revolted, angered over legislation that tied them to the land and imposed new taxes. John Ball, who claimed to be a priest, expressed egalitarian sentiments:

> *My good friends, things cannot go on well in England, nor ever will until everything shall be in common; when there shall neither be vassal nor lord, and all distinctions leveled;*

> *when the lords shall be no more masters than ourselves. But ill have they used us! and for what reason do they thus hold us in bondage? Are we not all descended from the same parents, Adam and Eve? and what can they show, or what reasons give, why they should be more the masters than ourselves? except, perhaps, in making us labor and work, for them to spend. . . . They have handsome manors, when we must brave the wind and rain in our labors in the field; but it is from our labor they have wherewith to support their pomp.*[1]

Like the revolts in Flanders and France, the uprising in England failed. To the landed aristocracy, the peasants were sinners attacking a social system ordained by God. Possessing superior might, the nobility suppressed the peasants, sometimes with savage cruelty.

Social unrest afflicted the towns as well as the countryside. The wage earners of Florence (1378), the weavers of Ghent (1382), and the poor of Paris (1382) rose up against the ruling oligarchy. These revolts were generally initiated not by the poorest and most downtrodden but by those who had made some gains and were eager for more. The rebellions of the urban poor were crushed just like the peasant uprisings.

Fourteenth-century Europeans suffered because of the numerous long wars, which devastated towns and farmland and seriously hampered economic life. To deprive an invading army of food, fields were laid waste. Invaders, too, decimated farms to destroy the enemy's morale, and discharged soldiers plundered the countryside.

Online Study Center

Improve Your Grade
Primary Source: The Great Revolt of 1381: Provocation from Both Sides

The Hundred Years' War

In earlier centuries, wars had generally been short and small in scale, sparing noncombatants the worst effects. In the fourteenth century, this trend changed. The most destructive war was the series of conflicts between France and England known as the Hundred Years' War (1337–1453). Because English kings had ruled parts of France, conflicts between the two monarchies had been common.

In the opening phase of the war, the English inflicted terrible defeats on French knights at the battles of Crécy (1346) and Poitiers (1356). Using longbows, which allowed them to shoot arrows rapidly, English archers cut down wave after wave of charging French cavalry. The war continued on and off throughout the fourteenth century. During periods of truce, gangs of unemployed soldiers roamed the French countryside killing and stealing, actions that precipitated the Jacquerie, the peasant uprising.

After the battle of Agincourt (1415), won by the English under Henry V, the English controlled most of northern France. It appeared that England would shortly conquer France and join the two lands under one crown. At this crucial moment in French history, a young and illiterate peasant girl, Joan of Arc (1412–1431), helped rescue France. Believing that God commanded her to drive the English out of France, Joan rallied the demoralized French troops, leading them in battle. In 1429, she liberated the besieged city of Orléans. Imprisoned by the English, Joan was condemned as a heretic and a witch in 1431 by a handpicked church court and was burned at the stake. The English intended to undermine the French cause by demonstrating that Joan was not divinely chosen. But Joan's life and death inspired the French people with a sense of devotion to their country. The reorganized and aroused French army recaptured Paris. By 1453, the English were driven from all French territory except the port of Calais.

During the Hundred Years' War, French kings introduced new taxes, which added substantially to their incomes. These monies furnished them with the means to organize a professional army of well-paid and loyal troops. By evoking a sense of pride and oneness in the French people, the war also contributed to a growing, but still incomplete, national unity. The English, too, emerged from the war with a greater sense of solidarity, and Parliament, because it had to finance the war, gained in stature.

However, the war had terrible consequences for the French peasants. Thousands of farmers were killed, and valuable farmland was destroyed by English armies and marauding bands of mercenaries. In another portentous development, the later stages of the Hundred Years' War saw the use of gunpowder and heavy artillery.

The Decline of the Papacy

The principal sign of breakdown in the Late Middle Ages was the waning authority and prestige of the papacy. In the High Middle Ages, the papacy had been the dominant institution in Christendom, but in the Late Middle Ages, its power disintegrated. The medieval ideal of a unified Christian commonwealth guided by the papacy was shattered. Papal authority declined in the face of the growing power of kings, who championed the parochial interests of states. The papacy's prestige and its capacity to lead diminished as it became more embroiled in European politics. Many pious Christians felt that the pope behaved more like a secular ruler than like an Apostle of Christ. Political theorists and church reformers further undermined papal authority.

Conflict with France

Pope Boniface VIII (1294–1303) vigorously upheld papal claims to supremacy over secular rulers. In the famous bull *Unam Sanctam* (1302), he declared:

> *. . . if the earthly power errs, it shall be judged by the spiritual power . . . but [the pope] can be judged only by God not by man. . . . Whoever therefore resists this power so ordained by God resists the ordinance of God. . . . Therefore, we declare, state, define, and pronounce that it is altogether necessary to salvation for every human creature to be subject to the Roman Pontiff.*[2]

But in trying to enforce this idea of papal supremacy on proud and increasingly more powerful kings, Boniface suffered defeat and humiliation.

Philip IV of France (1285–1314) taxed the church in his land to raise revenue for war. In doing so, he disregarded the church prohibition against the taxing of its property without papal permission. In 1296, in the bull *Clericis Laicos,* Pope Boniface VIII decreed that kings and lords who imposed taxes on the clergy and the clergy who paid them would be excommunicated. Far from bowing to the pope's threat, Philip acted forcefully to assert authority over the church in his kingdom. Boniface backed down from his position, declaring that the French king could tax the clergy in times of national emergency. Thus, the matter was resolved to the advantage of the state.

A second dispute had more disastrous consequences for Boniface. Philip tried and imprisoned a French bishop despite Boniface's warning that this was an illegal act and a violation of church law and tradition, which held that the church, not the state, must judge the clergy. Philip summoned the first meeting of the Estates General to gain the backing of the nation. Shortly afterward, Boniface threatened to excommunicate Philip. The outraged monarch raided the papal summer palace at Anagni in September 1303 and captured the pope. Although Boniface was released, this shocking event proved too much for him, and a month later he died.

Boniface's two successors, Benedict XI (1303–1304) and Clement V (1305–1314), tried to conciliate Philip. In particular, Clement decided to remain at Avignon, a town on the southeastern French frontier, where he had set up a temporary residence.

From 1309 to 1377, a period known as the Babylonian Captivity, the popes were all French and resided in Avignon, not Rome. During this time, the papacy, removed from Rome and deprived of revenues from the Papal States in Italy, was often forced to pursue policies favorable to France. The growing antipapalism among the laity further damaged the papal image. Laypeople were repelled by the luxurious style of living at Avignon and by the appointment of high churchmen to lands where they did not know the language and showed little concern for the local population. Criticism of the papacy increased.

The conflict between Boniface and Philip provoked a battle of words between proponents of papal supremacy and defenders of royal rights. In his treatise *On Ecclesiastical Power,* Giles of

THE BATTLE OF CRÉCY, 1346. English claims to the French throne led to the Hundred Years' War between the French and the English monarchies. The English victory at Crécy was catastrophic for the French mounted knights, who fell in droves under the withering fire of English longbowmen. In the end, however, the English effort was unsuccessful; although France was devastated by invading armies and internal revolts, the English kings lost almost all their French possessions. (*Photo Hachette.*)

Rome (c. 1245–1316) vigorously supported the doctrine of papal power. Because the spiritual is inherently superior to the temporal, he argued, the pope has the authority to judge temporal rulers. All temporal lords ought to be governed by spiritual and ecclesiastical authority, and especially by the pope, who heads the church.

Defenders of royal prerogatives challenged the pope's claim to primacy over both secular rulers and the clergy. They argued that the church was primarily a spiritual body charged with administering the sacraments; as such, its authority did not extend to temporal affairs. The most important critique of clerical intrusion into worldly affairs was *The Defender of the Peace* (1324) by Marsiglio of Padua (c. 1290–c. 1343). Marsiglio held that the state ran according to principles that had nothing to do with religious commands originating in a higher realm. Religion dealt with a supernatural world and with principles of faith that could not be proved by reason, wrote Marsiglio. Politics, in contrast, dealt with a natural world and with the affairs of the human community. Political thinkers should not try to make the earthly realm conform to articles of faith. According to Marsiglio, the state was self-sufficient; it needed no instruction from a higher authority. Thus, Marsiglio denied the essential premises of medieval papal political theory: that kings received their power from God; that the pope, as God's vicar, was empowered to guide kings; that the state, as part of a divinely ordered world, must conform to and fulfill supranatural ends; and that the clergy were above the laws of the state. Marsiglio viewed the church as a spiritual institution with no temporal power. "Christ himself," said Marsiglio, "refuse[d] rulership in this world . . . and taught that all men, both priests and nonpriests, should be subject . . . to the coercive judgment of the rulers of this world."[3] Marsiglio even went so far as to suggest that the church should be subordinate to the state; his concept of an autonomous state that did not answer to clerical authority anticipates modern political thought.

The Baptism of Christ. Depicting the baptism of Jesus by John the Baptist, this painting by Pico della Francesca, an early Italian Renaissance artist, expresses the power and persistence of the medieval religions impluse. (*National Gallery, London/Erich Lessing/Art Resource, NY.*)

The Great Schism and the Conciliar Movement

The Avignon popes were often competent men who, despite the hard times that had overtaken the papacy, tried to bolster papal power. They tightened their hold over church administration by reserving for themselves certain appointments and collections of fees formerly handled by local bishops. Through a deliberate effort at financial centralization, including the imposition of new taxes and the more efficient collection of old ones, the Avignon popes substantially increased papal income.

Although Pope Gregory XI returned the papacy to Rome in 1377, the papacy was to suffer another humiliation: the Great Schism. Elected pope in 1378, Urban VI immediately displayed tactlessness, if not mental imbalance, by abusing and even imprisoning cardinals. Fleeing from Rome, the cardinals declared that the election of Urban had been invalid and elected Clement VII as the new pope. Refusing to step down, Urban excommunicated Clement, who responded in kind. To the utter confusion and anguish of Christians throughout Europe, there were now two popes: Urban ruling from Rome and Clement from Avignon.

Prominent churchmen urged the convening of a general council to end the disgraceful schism, which obstructed the papacy from performing its sacred duties. Held in 1409 and attended by hundreds of churchmen, the Council of Pisa deposed both Urban and Clement and elected a new pope. Since neither deposed pope recognized the council's decision, Christendom then had three popes. A new council was called at Constance in 1414. In the struggle that ensued, each of the three popes either abdicated or was deposed in favor of an appointment by the council. In 1417, the Great Schism ended.

During the first half of the fifteenth century, church councils met at Pisa (1409), Constance (1414–1418), and Basel (1431–1449) in order to end the schism, combat heresy, and reform the church. The Conciliar Movement attempted to transform the papal monarchy into a constitutional system in which the pope's power would be regulated by a general council. Supporters of the movement held that the papacy could not reform the church as effectively as a general council representing the clergy. But the Conciliar Movement ended in failure. As the Holy Roman Emperor and then the French monarch withdrew their support from the councils, the papacy regained its authority over the higher clergy. In 1460, Pope Pius II condemned the Conciliar Movement as heretical.

Deeply embroiled in European power politics and the worldly life of Renaissance Italy, the papacy often neglected its spiritual and moral responsibilities. Many devout Christians longed for religious renewal, a return to simple piety; the papacy did not hear this cry for reform. The papacy's failure to provide creative leadership for reform made possible the Protestant Reformation of the sixteenth century. By splitting Christendom into Catholic and Protestant, the Reformation destroyed forever the vision of a Christian world commonwealth guided by God's vicar, the pope.

Fourteenth-Century Heresies

Another threat to papal power and to the medieval ideal of a universal Christian community guided by the church came from radical reformers who questioned the function and authority of the entire church hierarchy. These heretics in the Late Middle Ages were forerunners of the Protestant Reformation. The two principal dissenters were the Englishman John Wycliffe (c. 1320–1384) and the Czech Jan Hus (c. 1369–1415).

By stressing a personal relationship between the individual and God and by claiming that the Bible itself, rather than church teachings, is the ultimate Christian authority, Wycliffe, a respected English theologian teaching at the University of Oxford, challenged the fundamental position of the medieval church: that the avenue to salvation passed through the church alone. He argued that Scripture, which was the final authority, needed no further development by church authorities and that the sacraments are not necessary for salvation. He denounced the wealth of the higher clergy and sought a return to the spiritual purity and material poverty of the early church. To Wycliffe, the wealthy, elaborately organized hierarchy of the church was unnecessary and wrong. The splendidly dressed and propertied bishops bore no resemblance to the simple people who first followed Christ. Indeed, these worldly bishops, headed by a princely and tyrannical pope, were really anti-Christians, the "fiends of Hell." Wycliffe wanted the state to confiscate church property and the clergy to embrace poverty. By denying that priests changed the bread and wine of communion into the substance of the body and blood of Christ, Wycliffe rejected the special powers of the clergy.

In Bohemia, Wycliffe's ideas were enthusiastically received by Czech reformers led by Jan Hus. Like Wycliffe, Hus advocated vernacular translations of the Bible, which would be accessible to common people, and he upbraided the upper clergy for their luxury and immorality.

Both movements were declared heretical. The church deprived the Lollards—an order of poor priests that spread Wycliffe's teachings—of their priestly functions. In the early fifteenth century, some of Wycliffe's followers were burned at the stake, as was Jan Hus. Nevertheless, the church could not crush the dissenters' followers or eradicate their teachings. To some extent, the doctrines of the Reformation would parallel the teachings of Wycliffe.

Breakup of the Thomistic Synthesis

In the Late Middle Ages, the papacy lost power, as kings, political theorists, and religious dissenters challenged papal claims to supreme leadership. The great theological synthesis constructed by the scholastic theologians of the twelfth and thirteenth centuries was also breaking down. The process of fragmentation evident in the history of the church took place in philosophy as well.

Saint Thomas Aquinas's system culminated the scholastic attempt to show the basic agreement of philosophy and religion. In the fourteenth century, a number of thinkers cast doubt on the possibility of synthesizing Aristotelianism and Christianity, that is, reason and faith. Consequently, philosophy grew more analytical and critical. Denying that reason could demonstrate the truth of Christian doctrines with certainty, philosophers tried to separate reason from faith. Whereas Aquinas had said that reason proved or clarified much of revelation, fourteenth-century thinkers asserted that the basic propositions of Christianity were not open to rational proof. Whereas Aquinas had held that faith supplemented and perfected reason, some philosophers were now proclaiming that reason often contradicted faith.

Duns Scotus (1265–1308), a Scottish Franciscan, held that human reason cannot prove that God is omnipotent, that he forgives sins, that he rewards the righteous and punishes the wicked, or that the soul is immortal. These Christian doctrines, which scholastic philosophers believed could be proven by reason, were for Scotus the province of revelation and faith, not reason.

To be sure, this new outlook did not urge abandoning faith in favor of reason. Faith had to prevail in any conflict with reason because faith rested on God, the highest authority in the universe. But the relationship between reason and revelation was altered. Articles of faith, it was now held, had nothing to do with reason; they were to be believed, not proved. Reason was not an aid to theology but a separate sphere of activity. This new attitude snapped the link between reason and faith that Aquinas had so skillfully forged. The scholastic synthesis was disintegrating.

The chief proponent of the new outlook was William of Ockham (c. 1285–1349). In contrast to Aquinas, Ockham insisted that natural reason could not prove God's existence, the soul's immortality, or any other essential Christian doctrine. Reason could say only that God probably exists and that he probably endowed humankind with an immortal soul. But it could not prove these propositions with certainty. The tenets of faith were beyond the reach of reason, said Ockham; there was no rational foundation to Christianity. For Ockham, reason and faith did not necessarily complement each other as they did for Aquinas; it was neither possible nor helpful to join reason to faith. Ockham, however, sought not to undermine faith—only to disengage it from reason.

In the process of proclaiming the authority of theology, Ockham furthered the use of reason to comprehend nature. His approach, separating natural knowledge from religious dogma, made it easier to explore the natural world empirically without fitting it into a religious framework. Ockham, thus, is a forerunner of the modern mentality, which is characterized by a separation of reason from religion and an interest in the empirical investigation of nature.

The Middle Ages and the Modern World: Continuity and Discontinuity

Medieval civilization began to decline in the fourteenth century, but no dark age comparable to the three centuries following Rome's fall descended on Europe; its economic and political institutions and technological skills had grown too strong. Instead, the waning of the Middle Ages opened up possibilities for another stage in Western civilization: the modern age.

The modern world is linked to the Middle Ages in innumerable ways. European cities, the middle class, the state system, English common law, universities—all had their origins in the Middle Ages. During medieval times, important advances were made in business practices, including partnerships, systematic bookkeeping, and the bill of exchange, which paved the way for modern banking. By translating and commenting on the writings of Greek and Arabic thinkers, medieval scholars preserved a priceless intellectual heritage without which the modern mind could never have evolved. In addition, numerous strands connect the thought of the scholastics and that of early modern philosophers.

Feudal traditions lasted long after the Middle Ages. Up to the French Revolution, for instance, French aristocrats enjoyed special privileges and exercised power over local government. In England, the aristocracy controlled local government until the Industrial Revolution transformed English society in the nineteenth century. Retaining the medieval ideal of the noble warrior, aristocrats continued to dominate the officer corps of European armies through the nineteenth century and even into the twentieth. Aristocratic notions of duty, honor, loyalty, and courtly love have endured into our own day.

During the Middle Ages, Europeans began to take the lead over the Muslims, the Byzantines, the Chinese, and all the other peoples in the use of technology. Medieval technology and inventiveness stemmed in part from Christianity, which taught that God had created the world specifically for human beings to subdue and exploit. Consequently, medieval people tried to employ animal power and laborsaving machinery to relieve human drudgery. Moreover, Christianity taught that God was above nature, not within it, so the Christians faced no spiritual obstacle to exploiting nature—unlike, for instance, the Hindus. In contrast to classical humanism, the Christian outlook did not consider manual work degrading; even monks combined it with study.

The Christian stress on the sacred worth of the individual (each person had an immortal soul that was God's concern), on human equality (differences in rank and birth were of no account to God on **Judgment Day**), and on the higher law of God (divine precepts had a greater pull on conscience than did the state's laws) has never ceased to influence Western civilization. Even though in modern times the various Christian churches have not often taken the lead in political and social reform, the ideals identified with the Judeo-Christian tradition have become part of the Western heritage. As such, they have inspired social reformers who may no longer identify with their ancestral religion.

Believing that God's law was superior to state or national decrees, medieval philosophers provided a theoretical basis for opposing tyrannical kings who violated Christian principles. The idea that both the ruler and the ruled are bound by a higher law would, in a secularized form, become a principal element of modern liberal thought.

Feudalism also contributed to the history of liberty. According to feudal custom, the king, as a member of the feudal community, was duty-bound to honor agreements made with his vassals. Lords possessed personal rights, which the king was obliged to respect. Resentful of a king who ran roughshod over customary feudal rights, lords also negotiated contracts with the crown, such as Magna Carta (1215), to define and guard their customary liberties. To protect themselves from the arbitrary behavior of a king, feudal lords initiated what came to be called *government by consent* and the *rule of law*.

During the Middle Ages, then, there gradually emerged the idea that law was not imposed on inferiors by an absolute monarch but required the collaboration of the king and his subjects; that the king, too, was bound by the law; and that lords had the right to resist a monarch who violated agreements. A related phenomenon was the rise of representative institutions, with which the king was expected to consult on the realm's affairs. The most notable of such institutions was the British Parliament; though subordinate to the king, it became a permanent part of the state. Later, in the seventeenth century, Parliament would successfully challenge royal authority. Thus, continuity exists between the feudal tradition of a king bound by law and the modern practice of limiting the authority of the head of state.

Although the elements of continuity are clear, the characteristic outlook of the Middle Ages is as different from that of the modern age as it was from the outlook of the ancient world. Religion—often expressing a disdain of earthly pursuits and a preoccupation with the world to come—was the integrating feature of the Middle Ages, whereas science and secularism—a preoccupation with worldly life—determine the modern outlook. The period from the Italian Renaissance of the fifteenth century through the eighteenth-century Age of Enlightenment saw a gradual breaking away from the medieval world-view—a rejection of the medieval conception of nature, the individual, and the purpose of life. The transition from medieval to modern was neither sudden nor complete, for there are no sharp demarcation lines separating historical periods. While many distinctively medieval ways endured in the sixteenth, seventeenth, and even eighteenth centuries, these centuries saw as well the rise of new intellectual, political, and economic forms, which marked the emergence of **modernity.**

Medieval thought began with the existence of God and the truth of his revelation as interpreted by the church, which set the standards and defined the purposes for human endeavor. The medieval mind rejected the fundamental principle of Greek philosophy: the autonomy of reason. Without the guidance of revealed truth, reason was seen as feeble. Philosophical inquiry was permissible only if the mind arrived at clerically approved conclusions.

Scholastics engaged in genuine philosophical speculation, but they did not allow philosophy to challenge the basic premises of their faith. Unlike either ancient or modern thinkers, medieval schoolmen ultimately believed that reason alone could not provide a unified view of nature or society. A rational soul had to be guided by a divine light. For all medieval philosophers, the natural order depended on a supernatural order for its origin and purpose. To understand the natural world properly, it was necessary to know its relationship to the higher world. The discoveries of reason had to accord with Scripture as interpreted by the church. In medieval thought, says the historian-philosopher Ernst Cassirer,

> *neither science nor morality, neither law nor state, can be erected on its own foundations. Supernatural assistance is always needed to bring them to true perfection. . . . Reason is and remains the servant of revelation; within the sphere of natural intellectual and psychological forces, reason leads toward, and prepares the ground for, revelation.*[4]

In the modern view, both nature and the human intellect are self-sufficient. Nature is a mathematical system that operates without miracles or any other form of divine intervention. To comprehend nature and society, the mind needs no divine assistance; it accepts no authority above reason. The modern mentality finds it unacceptable to reject the conclusions of science on the basis of clerical authority and revelation or to ground politics, law, or economics on religious dogma. It refuses to settle public issues by appeals to religious belief, which is now seen as a strictly private conern.

The medieval philosopher understood both nature and society to be a hierarchical order. God was the source of moral values, and the church was responsible for teaching and upholding these ethical norms. Kings acquired their right to rule from God. The entire social structure constituted a hierarchy: the clergy, the highest order, guided society according to Christian standards; lords defended Christian society from its enemies; and serfs, lowest in the social order, toiled for the good of all. In the hierarchy of knowledge, a lower form of knowledge derived from the senses, and the highest type of knowledge, theology, dealt with God's revelation. To the medieval mind, this hierarchical ordering of nature, society, and knowledge had a divine sanction.

Rejecting the medieval division of the universe into higher and lower realms and superior and inferior substances, the modern view postulated the uniformity of nature and of nature's laws: the cosmos knows no privilege of rank; heavenly bodies follow the same laws of nature as earthly objects. Space is geometric and homogeneous, not hierarchical, heterogeneous, and qualitative. The universe was no longer conceived as finite and closed but as infinite, and the operations of nature were explained mathematically. The modern thinker studies mathematical law and chemical composition, not grades of perfection. Spiritual meaning is not sought in an examination of the material world. Roger Bacon, for example, described seven coverings of the eye and then concluded that God had fashioned the eye in this manner in order to express the seven gifts of the Spirit. This way of thinking is alien to the modern outlook. So, too, is the medieval belief that natural disasters, such as plagues and famines, are God's punishments for people's sins.

The outlook of the modern West also broke with the rigid division of medieval society into three orders: clergy, nobles, and commoners. The intellectual justification for this arrangement, as expressed by the English prelate John of Salisbury (c. 1115–1180), has been rejected by modern westerners: "For inferiors owe it to their superiors to provide them with service, just as the superiors in their turn owe it to their inferiors to provide them with all things needful for their protection and succor."[5] To be sure, Christian theorists also maintained that as God's children, all human beings are in principle equal in God's eyes. Opposing the feudal principle that an individual's obligations and rights are a function of his or her rank in society, the modern view stressed equality of opportunity and equal treatment under the law. It rejected the idea that society should be guided by clergy who were deemed to possess a special wisdom, by nobles who were entitled to special privileges, and by monarchs who were thought to receive their power from God.

The modern West also rejected the personal and customary character of feudal law. As the modern state developed, law assumed an impersonal and objective character. For example, if the lord demanded more than the customary forty days of military service, the vassal might refuse to comply because he would see the lord's request as an unpardonable violation of custom and agreement, as well as an infringement on his liberties. In the modern state, with a constitution and a representative assembly, if a new law increasing the length of military service is passed, it merely

Wisdom Urges Medieval Scholars Forward. During the Middle Ages, Europeans made considerable advances in technology. The astrolabe, quadrant, sundials, and mechanical clocks shown here exemplify medieval technical skills. (*Bibliothèque Royale Albert 1er, Brussels.*)

replaces the old law. People do not refuse to obey it because the government has broken faith or violated custom.

In the modern world, the individual's relationship to the universe has been radically transformed. Medieval people lived in a geocentric universe that was finite in space and time. The universe was small, enclosed by a sphere of stars, beyond which were the heavens. The universe, it was believed, was some four thousand years old, and, in the not-too-distant future, Christ would return and human history would end. People in the Middle Ages knew why they were on earth and what was expected of them; they never doubted that heaven would be their reward for living a Christian life. Preparation for heaven was the ultimate aim of life. J. H. Randall, Jr., a historian of ideas, eloquently sums up the medieval view of a purposeful universe in which the human being's position was clearly defined:

> *The world was governed throughout by the omnipotent will and omniscient mind of God, whose sole interests were centered in man, his trial, his fall, his suffering and his glory. Worm of the dust as he was, man was yet the central object in the whole universe. . . . And when his destiny was completed, the heavens would be rolled up as a scroll and he would dwell with the Lord forever. Only those who rejected God's freely offered grace and with*

Profile

Joan of Arc

A crucial phase in the Hundred Years War occurred in 1415 when England inflicted an overwhelming defeat on the French at Agincourt. The victorious English imposed on the French the Treaty of Troyes (1420). Its terms stipulated that the daughter of Charles VI, the French monarch, would marry the English ruler, Henry V, and that their future son would reign over the dual monarchy of England and France. This provision deprived Charles VI's only living son, the dauphin Charles, from succeeding to the throne. From Bourges in central France, the dauphin continued the struggle against the English invaders and three Burgundian allies. In 1428, the English besieged Orléans in preparation for an attack on Bourges. The dauphin's position seemed hopeless.

At this critical moment, Joan of Arc appeared on the scene. Born to a peasant family in northern France, Joan very early demonstrated extreme piety. At age thirteen, she experienced revelations—voices from angels and saints who guided her behavior. When she was about sixteen, her voices instructed her to raise the siege of Orléans and have Charles anointed king of France at Rheims. Joan the maid, as she was called, attracted followers who believed that Joan was sent by God to rescue Orléans from the English.

Demonstrating great resolve, Joan, dressed in men's clothing and accompanied by believers in her mission, made the arduous journey to the dauphin's castle. Charles reluctantly granted an audience to Joan, whom some of his counselors considered mad. After listening to Joan detail her divine mission, Charles had her examined by his clerks and sages, who reported that the uneducated, but devout, peasant girl was neither a heretic nor a sorceress. With the military position worsening, the desperate dauphin provided Joan with an army—perhaps this religiously inspired maid had indeed been sent by God. Wearing a full set of armor and wielding a lance,

The Art Archive.

Joan demonstrated remarkable leadership and courage that inspired her troops. She also showed a facility for military planning. To the inhabitants of Orléans, it seemed that God had provided them with a deliverer. When she entered the city, crowds pressed to touch her. Aided by the citizens of Orléans, Joan's army attacked the English fortifications. Hit by an arrow above the breast, Joan had the wound dressed and immediately returned to the fray. In a decisive encounter, the maid grabbed her standard from a squire and led a successful assault on an English fortress. Soon after, the English abandoned the siege: the maid's forces had liberated the city. Several months later Joan achieved her greatest victory, an open field battle at Patay, which caught the English by surprise. Following the battle, the dauphin was crowned Charles VII at Rheims.

Meanwhile in the ongoing conflict with the English and Burgundians, Joan could not escape a Burgundian siege and was taken prisoner. Charles VII made no effort to ransom Joan; he simply abandoned her. Purchasing the now-famous prisoner from the Burgundians, the English organized a show trial in Rouen, conducted by learned but hostile French clerics, to prove that the despised Joan was a heretic and a witch. The proceedings took about five months. During that time Joan wore leg irons; at night in her dungeon, her jailers chained the leg irons to the foot of the bed. During the interrogation Joan displayed remarkable self-control, dignity, cleverness, and even eloquence and humor that often exasperated the inquisitors. In a particular revealing interchange, the inquisitors tried to show that Joan was placing her voices above the church, a rebellious act which amounted to heresy:

> *"If the Church Militant tells you that your revelations are illusions or somehow diabolic, would you defer to the church?"*
>
> *"In that case, I would defer as always to God, whose command I have always obeyed, and I know well that what is contained in this trial comes through God's command, and what I have affirmed in this process that I have done by God's command. It would be impossible for me to do the contrary. And should the Church Militant command me to do otherwise, I would not defer to any man of the world, other than our Lord, whose good command I have always done."*
>
> *"Do you believe that you are subject to the church of God that is on earth, that is to say, to our lord the pope, to the cardinals, archbishops, bishops, and other prelates of the church?"*
>
> *"Yes, so long as Our Lord is first served."*
>
> *"Have you received the command from your voices not to submit to the Church Militant, which is on earth, nor to her judgment?"*
>
> *"I shall not answer anything that comes into my head, but what I do answer is at the command of my voices; they do not command me not to obey the church, God being first served."**

When the judges accused her of lying and threatened to inflict torture unless she altered her statements, Joan replied: "Truly, though you were to have my limbs torn off and send the soul out of my body, I should not say otherwise; and if I did tell you otherwise, I should always thereafter say that you had made me speak so by force."**

Ruling that she had been doing the work of the Devil, Joan was declared a heretic and condemed to burn at the stake. The sentence was carried out on May 30, 1431, and her ashes were thrown into the Seine. In 1456, the church nullified the condemnation, and in 1920 Joan was declared a saint.

---

*Régine Pernoud and Marie-Véronique Clin, *Joan of Arc: Her Story,* translated and revised by Jeremy Du Quesnay Adams and edited by Bonnie Wheeler (New York: St. Martin's Press, 1998), p. 124.

**Quoted in Régine Pernoud, *Joan of Arc: By Herself and Her Witnesses,* translated by Edward Hyans (Lanham, MD: Scarborough House, 1994), p. 206.

> *hardened hearts refused repentance would be cut off from this eternal life.*[6]

This comforting medieval vision is alien to the modern outlook. Today, in a universe some twelve to fifteen billion years old, in which the earth is a tiny speck floating in an endless cosmic ocean, where life evolved over tens of millions of years, many westerners no longer believe that human beings are special children of God; that heaven is their ultimate goal; that under their feet is hell, where grotesque demons torment sinners; and that God is an active agent in human history. To many intellectuals, the universe seems unresponsive to the religious supplications of people, and life's purpose is sought within the limits of earthly existence. Science and secularism have driven Christianity and faith from their central position to the periphery of human concerns.

In the nineteenth and twentieth centuries, Christian thinkers lamented the waning of faith. Distressed by all-consuming secularism, crude materialism, and vicious class and national antagonisms, these thinkers attributed the ills of the modern West to a diminishing commitment to Christianity and called for spiritual renewal. Some of them, looking back nostalgically to the Middle Ages when life had an overriding religious purpose and few doubted the truth of Christian teachings, contended that the modern West would benefit from a reaffirmation of those Christian concerns and values that had energized medieval society.

The modern outlook developed gradually in the period from the Renaissance to the eighteenth-century Age of Enlightenment. Mathematics rendered the universe comprehensible. Economic and political thought broke free of the religious frame of reference. Science became the great hope of the future. The thinkers of the Enlightenment wanted to liberate humanity from superstition, ignorance, and traditions that could not pass the test of reason. They saw themselves as emancipating culture from theological dogma and clerical authority. Rejecting the Christian idea of a person's inherent sinfulness, they held that the individual was basically good and that evil resulted from faulty institutions, poor education, and bad leadership. Thus, the concept of a rational and free society in which individuals could realize their potential slowly emerged.

❖ ❖ ❖

Online Study Center **ACE the Test**

Notes

1. Jean Froissart, *Chronicles of England, France, Spain* (London: Henry G. Bohn, 1849), p. 653.
2. Excerpted in Brian Tierney, ed., *The Crisis of Church and State, 1050–1300* (Englewood Cliffs, N.J.: Prentice-Hall, 1964), p. 189.
3. Marsilius of Padua, *Marsilius of Padua: The Defender of the Peace,* Vol. 2, trans. Alan Gewirth (New York: Columbia University Press, 1956), p. 119.
4. Ernst Cassirer, *The Philosophy of the Enlightenment* (Boston: Beacon Press, 1955), p. 40.
5. John of Salisbury, *Policraticus,* trans. John Dickinson (New York: Russell & Russell, 1963), pp. 243–244.
6. J. H. Randall, Jr., *The Making of the Modern Mind* (Boston: Houghton Mifflin, 1940), p. 34.

Suggested Reading

Bowsky, W. M., ed., *The Black Death* (1971). Readings on the impact of the plague.

Holmes, George, *Europe: Hierarchy and Revolt, 1320–1450* (1975). A good survey of the period.

Lerner, Robert E., *The Age of Adversity* (1968). A short, readable survey of the fourteenth century.

Ozment, Steven E., *The Age of Reform, 1250–1550* (1980). An intellectual and religious history of late medieval and Reformation Europe.

Russell, Burton Jeffrey, *Witchcraft in the Middle Ages* (1972). Describes the development of a phenomenon that is deeply rooted in the nonrational.

Spinka, M., *John Hus and the Czech Reform* (1941). A reliable work on Hus and the Hussite wars.

Ziegler, Philip, *The Black Death* (1969). The spread and impact of the great plague.

Part Three

Early Modern Europe: From Renaissance to Enlightenment

1350–1789

1300

1400

1500

1600

1700

Politics and Society	Thought and Culture
Hundred Years' War (1337–1453)	Italian Renaissance begins (c. 1350)
War of Roses in England (1455–1485) Rule of Ferdinand and Isabella in Spain (1469–1516) Charles VIII of France (1483–1498) Henry VII; beginning of Tudor dynasty in England (1485–1509) French invasion of Italy (1494) Columbus reaches America (1492)	Early Renaissance artists: Brunelleschi, Masaccio, van Eyck Printing with movable type (c. 1445) Humanists: Valla, Pico della Mirandola Late Renaissance artists: Botticelli, Leonardo da Vinci, Michelangelo, Raphael, Bellini, Giorgione, Titian Renaissance spreads to northern Europe (late 15th–early 16th cent.)
Henry VIII of England (1509–1547) Francis I of France (1515–1547) Charles V, Holy Roman Emperor (1519–1556) Henry VIII of England breaks with Rome (1529–1536) Council of Trent (1545–1563) Treaty of Augsburg in Germany (1555) Philip II of Spain (1556–1598) Elizabeth I of England (1558–1603) Religious wars in France (1562–1598) Revolt of the Netherlands from Spain (1566–1609) Defeat of Spanish Armada (1588)	Humanists: Castiglione, Erasmus, Montaigne, Rabelais, More, Machiavelli, Cervantes, Shakespeare Luther writes Ninety-five Theses (1517) Calvin, *The Institutes of the Christian Religion* (1536) Copernicus, *On the Revolution of the Heavenly Spheres* (1543)
Thirty Years' War (1618–1648) English Revolutions (1640–1660, 1688–1689) Louis XIV of France (1643–1715) Peter the Great of Russia (1682–1725)	Scientists: Kepler, Galileo, Newton Philosophers: Bacon, Descartes, Spinoza, Hobbes, Bayle, Locke
War of Spanish Succession (1702–1714) War of Austrian Succession (1740–1748) Frederick the Great of Prussia (1740–1786) Maria Theresa of Austria (1740–1780) Seven Years' War (1756–1763) Catherine the Great of Russia (1762–1796) American Declaration of Independence (1776) American Revolution (1776–1783) Beginning of French Revolution (1789)	Enlightenment thinkers: Voltaire, Montesquieu, Rousseau, Diderot, Hume, Adam Smith, Thomas Jefferson, Kant

Chapter 13

The Renaissance: Transition to the Modern Age

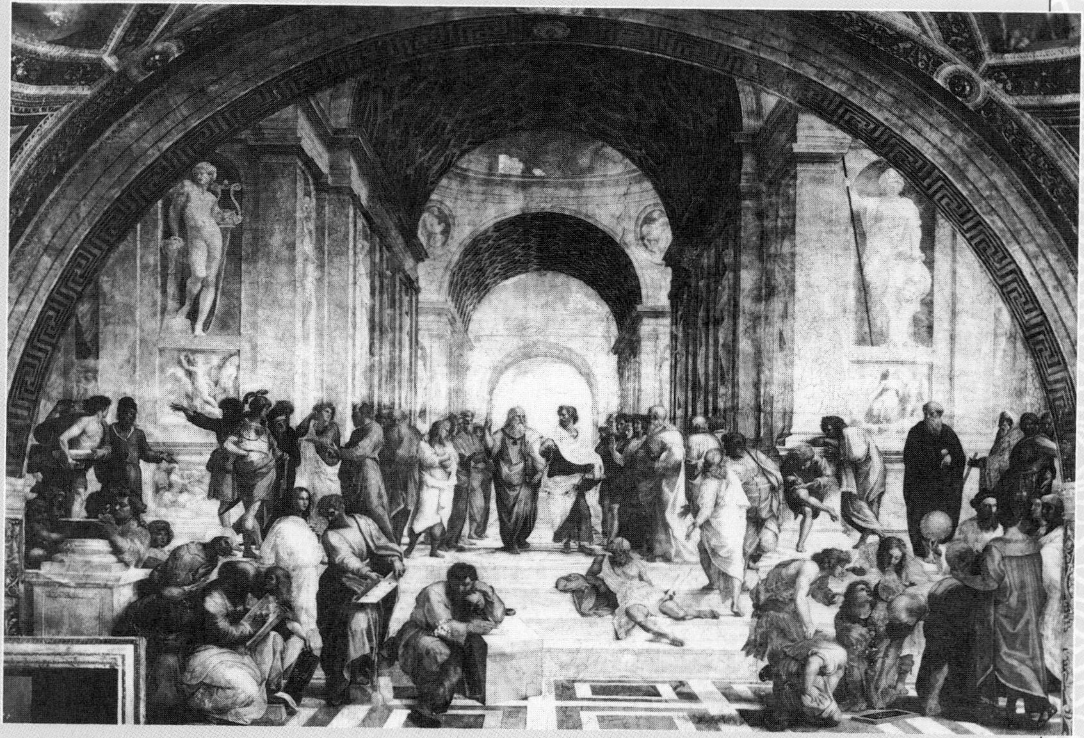

The School of Athens by Raphael (1483–1520). The ancient Greek philosophers, with Plato and Aristotle at the center, are depicted here, assembled in classical grandeur. Painted to decorate the Vatican, the papal palace in Rome, the picture exudes the Renaissance reverence for classical antiquity and reflects the widely held view that ancient philosophy represented a foreshadowing of Christianity and was essentially in harmony with it. (Stanza della segnaturna, Vatican Palace, Vatican State/Art Resource, NY.)

- **Italy: Birthplace of the Renaissance**
- **The Renaissance Outlook: Humanism and Secular Politics**
- **The Spread of the Renaissance**
- **The Renaissance and the Modern Age**

Focus Questions

1. What conditions gave rise to the Italian Renaissance?
2. What is the historical significance of Renaissance humanism?
3. How did Machiavelli's political thought mark a break with the medieval outlook?
4. What were the effects of the printing press on European civilization?

Online Study Center

This icon will direct you to interactive map and primary source activities on the website http://college.hmco.com/pic/perrywc8e.

From the Italian Renaissance of the fifteenth century through the Age of Enlightenment of the eighteenth century, the outlook and institutions of the Middle Ages disintegrated and distinctly modern forms emerged. The radical change in European civilization could be seen on every level of society. On the economic level, commerce and industry expanded greatly, and capitalism in some countries largely replaced medieval forms of economic organization. On the political level, central government grew stronger at the expense of feudalism. On the religious level, the rise of Protestantism fragmented the unity of Christendom. On the social level, middle-class townspeople, increasing in number and wealth, were playing a more important role in economic and cultural life. On the cultural level, the clergy lost its monopoly over learning, and the otherworldly orientation of the Middle Ages gave way to a secular outlook in literature and the arts. Theology, the queen of knowledge in the Middle Ages, surrendered her crown to science. Reason, which in the Middle Ages had been subordinate to revelation, asserted its independence.

Many of these tendencies manifested themselves dramatically during the Renaissance. The word *renaissance* means "rebirth," and it is used to refer to the attempt by artists and thinkers to recover and apply the ancient learning and standards of Greece and Rome. In historical terms, the Renaissance is both a cultural movement and a period. As a movement, it was born in the city-states of northern Italy and spread to the rest of Europe. As a period, it runs from 1350 to 1600. Until the late fifteenth century, the Renaissance was restricted to Italy. What happened there in the fourteenth and fifteenth centuries sharply contrasts with civilization in the rest of Europe, which, until the end of the fifteenth century, still belonged to the Late Middle Ages.

The nineteenth-century historian Jacob Burckhardt in his classic study, *The Civilization of the Renaissance in Italy* (1860), held that the Renaissance is the point of departure for the modern world. During the Renaissance, said Burckhardt, individuals showed increasing concern with worldly life and self-consciously aspired to shape their destinies—attitudes that are the key to modernity.

Chronology 13.1 ❖ The Renaissance

1200–1300	Bologna, Padua, and Ravenna become centers of legal studies
1300–1450	Republicanism reigns in northern Italian city-states
1304–1374	Petrarch, "father of humanism"
1378	Ciompi revolt in Florence
c. 1407–1457	Lorenzo Valla, author of *Declamation Concerning the False Decretals of Constantine*
c. 1445	Johann Gutenberg invents movable metal type
1454	Peace of Lodi is signed
1494	Charles VIII of France invades northern Italy; Pope Julius II commissions frescoes by Michelangelo for the Vatican's Sistine Chapel
1513	Machiavelli writes *The Prince*
1528	*The Book of the Courtier,* by Baldesar Castiglione, is published
1535	Sir Thomas More, English humanist and author of *Utopia,* is executed for treason

Burckhardt's thesis has been challenged, particularly by medievalists, who view the Renaissance as an extension of the Middle Ages, not as a sudden break with the past. These critics argue that Burckhardt neglected important links between medieval and Renaissance culture. One distinguishing feature of the Renaissance, the revival of classical learning, had already emerged in the High Middle Ages to such an extent that historians speak of "the renaissance of the twelfth century" and the "Twelfth-Century Awakening." The Renaissance owes much to the legal and scholastic studies that flourished in the Italian universities of Padua and Bologna before 1300. Town life and trade, hallmarks of Renaissance society, were also a heritage from the Middle Ages.

To be sure, the Renaissance was not a complete and sudden break with the Middle Ages. Many medieval ways and attitudes persisted. Nevertheless, Burckhardt's thesis that the Renaissance represents the birth of modernity has much to recommend it. Renaissance writers and artists themselves were aware of their age's novelty. They looked back on the medieval centuries as the "Dark Ages" that followed the grandeur of ancient Greece and Rome, and they believed that they were experiencing a rebirth of cultural greatness. Renaissance artists and writers were fascinated by the cultural forms of Greece and Rome; they sought to imitate **classical** style and to capture the secular spirit of antiquity. In the process, they broke with medieval artistic and literary forms. They valued the full development of human talent and expressed fresh excitement about the possibilities of life in this world. This outlook represents a new trend in European civilization.

The Renaissance, then, was an age of transition that saw the rejection of certain elements of the medieval outlook, the revival of classical cultural forms, and the emergence of distinctly **modern** attitudes. As mentioned earlier, this rebirth began in Italy during the fourteenth century. It gradually spread north and west to Germany, France, England, and Spain during the late fifteenth and sixteenth centuries.

Italy: Birthplace of the Renaissance

The city-states of northern Italy that spawned the Renaissance were developed urban centers where the elite had the wealth, freedom, and inclination to cultivate the arts and to enjoy the fruits of worldly life. In Italy, moreover, reminders of ancient Rome's grandeur were visible everywhere. Roman roads, monuments, and manuscripts intensified Italians' links to their Roman past.

Political Evolution of the City-States

During the Middle Ages, the feudal states of northern Italy had been absorbed into the Holy Roman Empire. They continued to owe nominal allegiance to the German emperor during the early Renaissance. But protracted wars with the papacy had sapped the empire's vitality. Its consequent weakness allowed the states of northern Italy to develop as autonomous political entities. The weakening of the papacy in the fourteenth century also promoted this development.

In their size and their varied types of governments, the city-states in northern Italy resembled those of ancient Greece. Among the more important were Rome, Milan, Florence, Venice, Mantua, Ferrara, Padua, Bologna, and Genoa. They differed markedly from most of Europe in two fundamental respects.

First, by the late eleventh and twelfth centuries, these city-states were flourishing commercial and banking centers and monopolized trade in Mediterranean areas, including trade between the Orient and the West. Merchant fleets, especially those of Venice and Genoa, carried goods from ports in the eastern Mediterranean westward into the Atlantic and from there north to the Baltic Sea. In contrast to the rest of Europe, the wealth of these cities lay not in land but in commerce and industry. When popes, monarchs, and feudal magnates of Europe needed money, they borrowed it from Italian, especially Florentine, merchant-bankers.

Second, the predominance of business and commerce within these city-states meant that the feudal nobility, which held the land beyond the city walls, played a much lesser role in government than they did elsewhere in Europe. By the end of the twelfth century the city-states no longer were dominated by the feudal nobility, or landed aristocracy. The aristocracy and the rich merchants had to share power, and when their alliances broke down, as they often did, the two groups struggled for power based on their opposing interests and outlooks. The interests of the smaller merchants and the artisans in the towns also had to be catered to. When they were not, those groups rioted and rebelled, as they did, for instance, in 1378, during the revolt of the *Ciompi* (wool-workers) in Florence.

Politically, the city-states in Northern Italy were inherently unstable. The instability had two sources: internal conflicts between merchants and nobles and external rivalries among the city-states themselves. The city-states managed to keep both the papacy and the Holy Roman Empire at bay, sometimes by playing one giant against the other, as Third World nations do today. But the price of this continued independence was that the city-states, without any externally imposed power structure, had to seek their own solutions to their instability. Out of this situation came experiments in the form and technique of government. The origins of modern political thought and practice can be discerned in this experimentation, which is an important link between the Renaissance and the modern age.

The political experimentation in the northern Italian city-states can usefully, if only roughly, be divided into two periods: the first (1300–1450) marked by the defense of **republicanism;** the second (1450–1550), by the triumph of **despotism.** By the end of the twelfth century, the city-states had adopted a fairly uniform pattern of republican self-government built around the office of a chief magistrate. Elected by the citizens on the basis of a broad franchise, he ruled with the advice of two councils—a large public one and a small secret one. His powers were tightly circumscribed by the **constitution;** with his term of office restricted ordinarily to six months, he could be removed from government or punished at the end of his tenure.

The city-states not only developed republican institutions; they also devised important theories to defend and justify their liberty and self-government in the face of their external enemies, the papacy and the empire. With the emperor, they argued that their customary feudal subjection to imperial authority must be radically adjusted to fit the changed reality that they were in fact self-governing. With the papacy, they contended that Christ had denied all political jurisdiction to the clergy, including the pope, and that this fact

LUDOVICO GONZAGA, HIS FAMILY AND COURT: A FRESCO PAINTED BY ANDREA MANTEGNA, 1465–1474. The Gonzaga family came to power as princes of Mantua, selling their services as condottieri to the Venetians, Milanese, and others as their interests dictated. Ludovico (1414–1478) presided over Mantua at a time of great prosperity. He commissioned the famous painter Andrea Mantegna to decorate his palace, and the architect Leon Battista Alberti to build several churches. His patronage of humanistic scholars, poets, and philosophers enhanced the prestige of both the city and its princely ruler. (*Scala/Art Resource, NY.*)

undercut the papal claim to political control in Italy and elsewhere.

However, given the city-states' internal instability and rivalry, their republicanism proved precarious. During the fourteenth and early fifteenth centuries, the republican institutions in one city after another toppled in favor of despotic rule. Three conditions were responsible for this development. First, class war between rich merchants and nobles caused one group or the other, or both, to seek a resolution of the crisis by turning to one-man rule. Second, the economic disasters, famine, and disease of the period from 1350 to 1450 encouraged the drift toward despotism. Northern Italy was particularly hard hit by the bubonic plague. The citizenry lost faith in the ability of short-term republican governments to cope with such emergencies and put its trust in long-term, one-man rule. Third, and perhaps most important, the city-states, in wars with their rivals, had come to rely on mercenary troops. The

MAP 13.1 ITALIAN CITY-STATES, C. 1494 ▶
During the Renaissance, Italy was divided between large kingdoms in the south, dominated by the Spanish monarchy, and smaller city-states in the north, each with its own government and army and often hostile to one another. The French king Charles VIII took advantage of these divisions by invading and occupying much of northern Italy beginning in 1494.

0 50 100 Km.
0 50 100 Mi.
OTTOMAN EMPIRE
DUCHY OF SAVOY
DUCHY OF MILAN
Milan
Turin
Pavia
Lodi
SALUZZO
Po R.
M. OF MANTUA
Mantua
Padua
Venice
REPUBLIC OF VENICE
REP. OF GENOA
Genoa
Ferrara
D. OF FERRERA
D. OF MODENA
Bologna
Ravenna
REP. OF LUCCA
Pisa
Arno R.
REP. OF FLORENCE
Florence
Urbino
Siena
Tiber R.
Assisi
REP. OF SIENA
PAPAL STATES
CORSICA
DALMATIA
Adriatic Sea
Rome
KINGDOM OF NAPLES
SARDINIA
Naples
Bari
Salerno
Palermo
Mediterranean Sea
KINGDOM OF SICILY

leaders of those troops, the notorious *condottieri*—unschooled in and owing no loyalty to the republican tradition—simply seized power during emergencies.

Some city-states held out for a long time against the trend toward despotism. Among those that did, Florence was by far the most successful. In the process, the Florentines developed new arguments and theories for the maintenance of republicanism and liberty (see below). But by the middle of the fifteenth century, even Florentine republicanism was giving way before the intrigues of a rich banking family, the Medicis. They had installed themselves in power in the 1430s, with the return of Cosimo de Medicis from exile. Cosimo's grandson, Lorenzo the Magnificent, completed the destruction of the republican constitution in 1480, when he managed to set up a government staffed by his own supporters.

The one city-state where republicanism survived until the advent of Napoleon was Venice. Protected from the rest of Italy by lagoons, Venice, during the Middle Ages, controlled a far-flung and exceptionally lucrative seagoing trade and a maritime empire stretching along the Adriatic and the eastern Mediterranean Seas. Venetian maritime commercial successes were matched by political ones at home. For centuries, Venice managed to govern itself without a major upheaval; its republican constitution made this stability possible. Its chief executive offices, the Council of Ten, were elective, but after 1297, both these offices and the electorate were narrowly restricted by law to old patrician families. Venice was an aristocratic **republic.** The government proved remarkably effective because the ruling elite was able to instill in its young a sense of public duty that was passed on from one generation, and one century, to the next. Because Venetian government was at once stable and republican, it served as a model to republican theorists in seventeenth- and eighteenth-century Europe.

Aside from Venice, the city-states in Northern Italy were not only internally unstable but also constantly warring with each other. By the middle of the fifteenth century, however, five major powers had emerged from the fighting: the kingdom of Naples and Sicily in the south; the Papal States, a papacy-controlled territory running across the center of the Italian peninsula; and the city-states of Florence, Venice, and Milan in the north. In 1454, these five powers, largely through the efforts of Cosimo de Medicis, concluded the Peace of Lodi. For the next forty years, they were relatively peaceful, until the French king Charles VIII invaded northern Italy in 1494.

The Peace of Lodi endured so long thanks to diplomacy. The essential techniques of modern diplomacy were worked out and applied in the second half of the fifteenth century in Italy. The practices of establishing embassies with ambassadors, sending and analyzing intelligence reports, consulting and negotiating during emergencies, and forming alliances all developed during this period. Some historians also see this time in Italian history as the seedbed for the notion of balance of power, which eventually became fundamental to the diplomacy of all Europe. Later, in the early modern period, European governments formed alliances so that no single state or group of allied states could dominate the Continent. Some elements of this balance of power were anticipated in the struggles among the Italian city-states.

Renaissance Society

The new way of life in the city-states paralleled developments in relations among them. Prosperous merchants played a leading role in the political and cultural life of the city. With the growth of commerce and industry, the feudal values of birth, military prowess, and a fixed hierarchy of lords and vassals decayed in favor of ambition and individual achievement, whether at court, in the countinghouse, or inside the artist's studio. The old feudal chivalric code was not destroyed but transformed to serve different purposes.

The new urban, commercial **oligarchies** could not justify their power in the old way, through heredity. Moreover, they had to function within the inherently unstable political climate of the city-states. Faced with this dual problem, the oligarchs fell back on the feudal idea of honor and developed elaborate codes. These codes differed in significant ways from their medieval antecedents. First came a depreciation (though never a complete elimination) of birth as a basis of merit, and a corresponding emphasis on effort, talent, and (in the case of the artist) creative genius. Second, honor was no longer defined in narrow, largely military terms; it was expanded to include both the civic and courtly virtues of the worthy citizen and courtier and the artistic achievement of the painter, sculptor, architect, and poet.

The new code, however, did remain elitist and even aristocratic. Indeed, the new oligarchs of the Renaissance, because of their newness and insecurity, were all the more anxious to adopt the aristocratic outlook of the old nobility. The *nouveaux riches* (newly rich) aped the feudal aristocracy in dress and manners, even as they accommodated the code of knightly chivalry to the demands of a new urban and commercial culture. Renaissance society was a highly unstable compound of old and new.

Marriage and Family Life. City life profoundly altered family structure, marriage patterns, and relations between the sexes. Elsewhere in Europe, most people still lived on the land and tended to marry early in order to produce large families to work the fields. But in cities, early marriage could be a liability for a man who was attempting to make his fortune. The results were that older men married young brides and that wives usually outlived their husbands. Because a widow inherited her husband's property, she was not pressed to remarry and was likely to bring up her children in a single-parent household. According to the historian David Herlihy, the fact that so many women were responsible for nurturing their children may have encouraged the development of the Renaissance ideal of a gentleman, which emphasized civility, courtliness, and an appreciation of art, literature, and the feminine graces.

The large number of single, relatively prosperous, and leisured adults probably explains why Renaissance cities were notorious for sodomy, prostitution, and triangles involving an older husband, a young wife, and a young lover. Such sexual behavior was encouraged by the relative anonymity of the large cities and by the constant influx of young men of talent from the country districts.

Whatever the effect on their sons, upper-class women enjoyed greater freedom in greater numbers than they had since the fall of Rome. If they were married, they had the income to pursue pleasure in the form of clothes, conversation, and romance. If a well-to-do husband died while his wife was still young, she had no financial reasons to remarry and was free, to a degree previously unknown, to go her own way.

Patronage of the Arts. Members of the urban upper class became patrons of the arts, providing funds to support promising artists and writers. Urban patricians, whose wealth was based on commerce and banking, not land, had become dominant in both republican Florence and despotic Milan. Unable to claim power by birth or to rely on traditional loyalties, they looked to culture to provide the trappings and justification of power.

For the newly rich, art could serve a political function. In its sheer magnificence, art could manifest power. Art, like literature, could also serve as a focus of civic pride and patriotism. Just as insecure rulers contended on the battlefield, they competed for art and artists to bolster their egos. Art became a desirable political investment, especially when, in the fifteenth century, economic investments were not offering as much return as they had a century or two before. The popes invested in art as well. Having lost the battle for temporal dominion in Europe, the papacy concentrated on increasing its direct dominion in Italy by consolidating and expanding the Papal States. As an adjunct to this policy, the popes heaped wealth on artists to enhance papal prestige. Indeed, the popes became the most lavish patrons of all, as the works of Michelangelo, Botticelli, and Raphael testify.

The result of this new patronage by popes and patricians was an explosion of creativity. The amount, and especially the nature, of this patronage also helped to shape both art and the artist. For the first time since antiquity, portraiture became a separate genre and was developed much further than ever before. Patrician rivalry and insecurity of status, fed by the Renaissance ethic of achievement and reward, produced a scramble for honor and reputation. This fostered the desire to be memorialized in a painting, if not in a sculpture. A painter like Titian was in great demand.

Secularism. Renaissance society was marked by a growing **secular** outlook. Intrigued by the active life of the city and eager to enjoy the worldly pleasures that their money could obtain, wealthy merchants and bankers moved away from the medieval preoccupation with salvation. Although they were neither nonbelievers nor atheists, for them religion increasingly had to compete with worldly concerns. Consequently, members of the urban upper class paid religion less heed or at least did not allow it to interfere with their quest for a full life. The challenge and pleasure of living well in this world seemed more exciting than the promise of heaven. This outlook found expression in Renaissance art and literature.

Individualism. Individualism was another hallmark of Renaissance society. Urban life released people of wealth and talent from the old constraints of manor and church. The urban elite sought to assert their own personalities, discover and express their individual feelings, and demonstrate their unique talents. They strove to win fame and glory and to fulfill their ambitions. This Renaissance ideal was explicitly elitist. It applied only to the few, entirely disregarding the masses, and it valued what was distinctive and superior in an individual, not what was common to all. Concerned with the distinctions of the few, it did not consider the needs or rights of the many. Individualism became deeply embedded in the Western soul and was expressed by artists who sought to capture individual character, by explorers who ventured into uncharted seas, by conquerors who carved out empires in the New World, and by merchant-capitalists who amassed fortunes.

The Renaissance Outlook: Humanism and Secular Politics

Humanism

The most characteristic intellectual movement of the Renaissance was *humanism,* an educational and cultural program based on the study of ancient Greek and Roman literature. The humanist attitude toward antiquity differed from the attitude of medieval scholars, who had taken pains to fit classical learning into a Christian worldview. Renaissance humanists did not subordinate the classics to the requirements of Christian doctrines; rather, they valued ancient literature for its own sake—for its clear and graceful style and its insights into human nature. From the ancient classics, humanists expected to learn much that could not be provided by medieval writing: for instance, how to live well in this world and how to perform one's civic duties. For the humanists the classics were a guide to the good life, the active life. To achieve self-cultivation, to write well, to speak well, and to live well, it was necessary to know the classics. In contrast to scholastic philosophers, who used Greek philosophy to prove the truth of Christian doctrines, Italian humanists used classical learning to nourish their new interest in a worldly life.

Whereas medieval scholars were familiar with only some ancient Latin writers, Renaissance humanists restored to circulation every Roman work that could be found. Similarly, knowledge of Greek was very rare in Latin Christendom during the Middle Ages, but Renaissance humanists increasingly cultivated the study of Greek in order to read Homer, Demosthenes, Plato, and other ancients in the original.

Although predominantly a secular movement, Italian humanism was not un-Christian. True, humanists often treated moral problems in a purely secular manner. Yet in dealing with religious and theological questions, they did not challenge Christian belief or question the validity of the Bible. They did, however, attack scholasticism for its hairsplitting arguments and preoccupation with trivial questions. They stressed instead a purer form of Christianity, based on direct study of the Bible and writings by the church fathers.

The early humanists, sometimes called the fathers of humanism, were Petrarch (1304–1374) and Boccaccio (1313–1375). Petrarch, Boccaccio, and their followers carried the recovery of the classics further by making a systematic attempt to discover the classical roots of medieval Italian rhetoric. Petrarch's own efforts to learn Greek were largely unsuccessful, but by encouraging his students to master the ancient tongue, he advanced humanist learning. Petrarch was particularly drawn to Cicero, the ancient Roman orator. Following the example of Cicero, Petrarch insisted that education should consist not only of learning and knowing things but also of learning how to communicate one's knowledge and how to use it for the public good. Therefore, the emphasis in education should be on rhetoric and moral philosophy, wisdom combined with eloquence. As Bartolommeo della Fonte (1446–1513), professor of rhetoric at Florence, said, such a program of instruction would fit a man for effective rule: that is, "to punish the wicked, to care for the good, to embellish his native land and to benefit all mankind."[1] Thus, Petrarch helped make Ciceronian values dominant among the humanists. His followers set up schools to inculcate the new Ciceronian educational ideal.

Implicit in the humanist educational ideal was a radical transformation of the medieval (Augustinian) view of men and women. According to this view, since human beings were completely subject to divine will, not only were they incapable of attaining excellence through their own efforts and talents, but it was also wrong and sinful for them even to try. In contrast, the humanists, recalling the classical Greek concept of *arête,* made the achievement of excellence through individual striving the end not only of education but also of life itself. Moreover, because individuals were capable of this goal, it was their duty to pursue it as the end of life, although the pursuit was not effortless and indeed demanded extraordinary energy and skill.

People were deemed capable of excellence in every sphere and duty-bound to make the effort. This emphasis on human creative powers was one of the most characteristic and influential doctrines of the Renaissance. A classic expression of it is found in the *Oration on the Dignity of Man* (1486) by Giovanni Pico della Mirandola (1463–1494). Man, said Pico, has the freedom to shape his own life. Pico has God say to man: "We have made you a creature" such that "you may, as the free and proud shaper of your own being, fashion yourself in the form you may prefer."[2]

Pico also spelled out another implication of man's duty to realize his potential: through his own exertions, man can come to understand and control nature. One of the new and powerful Renaissance images of man was as the *magus,* the magician. The vision of the mastery of nature would continue to inspire experimentalists, like Francis Bacon, and natural philosophers, like Robert Boyle and Isaac Newton, until at least the early eighteenth century. A major psychological driving force of the Scientific Revolution, this vision stemmed in large part from the philosophy of Italian humanists like Pico.

The attack on the medieval scholastics was implicit in the humanist educational ideal. From the humanist perspective, scholasticism failed not only because its terms and Latin usage were barbarous but also because it did not provide useful knowledge. This humanist emphasis on the uses of knowledge offered an additional stimulus to science and art.

So hostile were the humanists to all things scholastic and medieval that they reversed the prevailing view of history. The Christian view saw history as a simple unfolding of God's will and **providence.** The humanists stressed the importance of human actions and human will in history—of people as active participants in the shaping of events. The humanists rejected the providentialist scheme in favor of a cyclical view deriving from the ancients, particularly Aristotle, Polybius, and Cicero. History alternated between times of darkness and times of light, of ignorance and illumination, of decline and rebirth.

This cyclical view allowed the humanists to characterize the preceding epoch as a period of decline from classical heights. It also let them see their own time as a period of rebirth, the recovery of classical wisdom and ideals. On the basis of this cyclical view, the humanists invented the notion of the Middle Ages as a gulf of darkness separating the ancient world from their own. To the humanists, then, we owe the current periodization of history into ancient, medieval, and modern. The humanists' view also contained an element of today's idea of progress: they dared to think that they, "the moderns," might even surpass the ancient glories of Greece and Rome.

The humanist emphasis on historical scholarship yielded a method of critical inquiry that, in the right hands, could help undermine traditional loyalties and institutions. The work of Lorenzo Valla (c. 1407–1457) provides the clearest example of this trend. Educated as a classicist, Valla trained the guns of critical scholarship on the papacy in his most famous work, *Declamation Concerning the False Decretals of Constantine.* The papal claim to temporal authority rested on a document that purported to verify the so-called Donation of Constantine, whereby the emperor Constantine, when moving the capital of the Roman Empire to Constantinople in the fourth century, bestowed on the pope dominion over all of the western Empire. Valla proved that the document was based on an eighth-century forgery because some of the language it contained was unknown in Constantine's time and did not come into use until much later.

Also embedded in the humanist reevaluation of individual potential was new appreciation of the moral significance of work. For the humanist, the honor, fame, and even glory bestowed by one's city or patron for meritorious deeds were the ultimate rewards for effort. The humanist pursuit of praise and reputation became something of a Renaissance cult.

In fourteenth- and fifteenth-century republican Florence, at least until the Medicis took control, Petrarchan humanism was not meant for a court elite. Humanism was a civic idea: to educate and inform citizens so that they could contribute to the common good to the greatest possible extent. In this sense, humanism was put in the service of republican values and the republican cause, and the mixture of the two is what has come to be called *civic humanism* by recent historians. This civic ideal developed furthest in the Florentine republic.

By the second half of the fifteenth century, as the Medicis gained increasing control, the civic ideal was being replaced by an ideal more fitting to the times, the ideal of princely rule. This ideal borrowed much from civic humanism even though it was directed toward princes and courtiers and not toward citizens. The emphasis on the pursuit of virtue and honor continued. Like the ideal gentleman, the ideal prince would evolve through humanistic education, which would so prepare him for the struggle between virtue and fortune that virtue would prove victorious.

The similarities between the civic and princely ideals, however, were not as important as the differences. The aim of princely rule was not liberty but peace and security, and the best means to this end was not a republic but hereditary monarchy. This new princely ideal was reflected in a new spate of advice books, the most influential of which was *The Book of the Courtier,* written between 1513 and 1518 by Baldesar Castiglione (1478–1529). These books promoted the notion that the ideal ruler should be universally talented and skillful, equally commanding on the battlefield, at court, and in the state, and virtuous throughout. These advice books, especially Castiglione's, were to serve as indispensable handbooks for courtiers and would-be gentlemen not only in Renaissance Italy but throughout Europe for centuries.

A Revolution in Political Thought

One advice book transcended all the others: *The Prince,* written in 1513 by the Florentine Niccolò Machiavelli (1469–1527). It offered an indictment of the humanist ideal of princely rule and in so doing made some fundamental contributions to political theory. Indeed, Machiavelli may be called the first major modern political thinker. To Machiavelli, the humanist ideal was naive in its insistence on the prince's virtues and eloquence to the exclusion of all other considerations. He attacked the medieval and humanist tradition of theoretical politics:

> *Since my intention is to say something that will prove of practical use to the inquirer, I have thought it proper to represent things as they are in real truth, rather than as they are imagined. Many have dreamed up republics and principalities which have never in truth been known to exist; the gulf between how one should live and how one does live is so wide that a man who neglects what is actually done for what should be done learns the way to self-destruction.*[3]

Politics, Machiavelli argued, requires the rational deployment of force, as well as, and even prior to, the exercise of virtue.

On this point, Machiavelli's advice is quite specific. He wrote *The Prince* in part as a plea. Since 1494, Italy had fallen prey to France and Spain. Their great royal armies overpowered the mercenary armies of the city-states and proceeded to lay waste to Italy in their struggle for domination of the peninsula. To prevent this, Machiavelli said, the Italians should unite behind a leader—the prince—whose first act would be to

NICCOLÒ MACHIAVELLI (1469–1527). Machiavelli looked back to the ancient Roman republic for his ideals and spent his life serving the city-state of Florence, but as the author of *The Prince,* his name became a byword for atheism and deceit. "Machiavellian" is still used to describe an unscrupulous politician. (*Palazzo Vecchio, Florence, Italy/Erich Lessing/Art Resource, NY.*)

disband the mercenaries and forge a new citizen army worthy of the glorious Roman past and capable of repelling the "barbarian" invasion. "Mercenaries," Machiavelli claimed, "are useless and dangerous." They are useless because "there is no . . . inducement to keep them on the field apart from the little they are paid, and this is not enough to make them want to die for you." And they are dangerous because their leaders, the infamous *condottieri,* "are anxious to advance their own greatness" at the expense of the city-state. Reliance on mercenaries was the sole cause of "the present ruin of Italy," and the cure lay in the creation of a national militia, led by a prince.[4]

This prince had to be both wily and virtuous, not just virtuous (as humanists had said): "The fact is that a man who wants to act virtuously in every way necessarily comes to grief among so many who are not virtuous." So Machiavelli scandalized Christian Europe by asserting that "if a prince wants to maintain his rule he must learn how not to be virtuous, and to make use of this or not according to his need."[5] Even more shocking, the prince must know how to dissemble, that is, to make all his actions appear virtuous, whether they are so or not. In ironic parody of conventional advice-book wisdom, Machiavelli argued that a ruler must cultivate a *reputation* for virtue rather than virtue itself. In this connection, Machiavelli arrived at a fundamental political truth: politics (and especially the relationship between the ruler and the ruled) being what it is, the road to success for the prince lies in dissimulation (the art of appearance and cover-up). As he put it, "Everyone sees what you appear to be, few experience what you really are. And those few dare not [contradict] the many who are backed by the majesty of the state."[6] Here again the Renaissance arrived at modernity.

Machiavelli broke with both the medieval and the humanist traditions of political thought. He was a secularist who tried to understand and explain the state without recourse to Christian teachings. Influenced by classical thought, especially the works of Livy, he rejected the prevailing view that the state is God's creation and the ruler should base his policies on Christian moral principles. For Machiavelli, religion was not the foundation for politics but merely a useful tool in the prince's struggle for success. The prince might even dissemble, if he thought he had to, in matters of the faith, by appearing pious, whether he was or not, and by playing on and exploiting the piety of his subjects.

Online Study Center

Improve Your Grade

Primary Source: A Model for Judas: Leonardo Paints The Last Supper

THE SPREAD OF THE RENAISSANCE

The Renaissance spread to Germany, France, England, and Spain in the late fifteenth and the sixteenth centuries. In its migration northward,

Profile

A Renaissance Man

Uffizi Gallery/Dagli Orti/The Art Archive

Leonardo da Vinci (1452–1519) is a supreme example of the so-called "universal man," someone wonderfully gifted who could excel in any number of fields. Because he was born illegitimate, he was disqualified from being trained in a learned profession like law or medicine. But recognizing his immense talent, his father saw to it that he was apprenticed to Andrea del Verrocchio (1435–1488), the esteemed Florentine painter and sculptor, who carefully developed Leonardo's skills in the visual arts. Once Leonardo had been fully trained, it is said, Verrocchio was so struck by the beauty of his pupil's work that he decided never to paint again.

Given Leonardo's restless energy and insatiable curiosity, his genius could not be channeled in only one or a few directions. He quickly gained a reputation for tremendous skill in both science and art, and was highly sought after. Florence was ruled by the Medicis, and Milan was ruled by the Sforzas. Leonardo worked for both, and briefly for the Medici pope Leo X (1513–1521) in Rome as well. He spent the last three years of his life in the pay of the French king Francis I (1515–1547), living in luxury at the French court and advising his patron on a variety of building projects.

Leonardo was a quick study and took advantage of opportunities for learning wherever he found them. At the Milanese court of the Sforzas, he met Luca Pacioli (1445–1517), the foremost Renaissance mathematician, who taught him geometry and the power of numbers to explain the world. Leonardo became committed to the view that mathematics provides the basis for true understanding in every field, not only in the physical and biological sciences but in painting and music as well. Leonardo had a large library and read widely, but he also believed that there was no substitute for studying nature firsthand and making experiments in order to obtain true and certain knowledge of things.

Leonardo was deeply interested in everything, and no subject was off limits. He studied human sexuality and, in his unpublished notebooks, made scientific drawings of a human fetus in the womb, male erections, and a couple having sex. One of his main fields of investigation was human anatomy, both for how it could inform his painting and for what it could tell him about the aging process. Once he discovered a one-hundred-year-old man in a hospital in Florence and waited expectantly for his death so that he could examine his blood vessels. By comparing the corpses of the very young and the very old, he was the first to describe the disease known as arteriosclerosis, the hardening of the arteries. At this time the church took a dim view of the carving up of human remains.

Much of Leonardo's effort was spent on practical design projects, large and small. In the prosperous and warring Italian city-states, there was always a need for industrial machinery, military fortifications, and weapons, and he received as many commissions for engineering work as he did for works of art. In 1502, he served as a military engineer to the commander of the papal army, the ruthless Cesare Borgia (d. 1507). The next year the Florentine government hired him to divert the course of the River Arno in order to cut off access to the sea by the city-state of Pisa, with which Florence was then at war. On this project, which was not successful, he collaborated with another famous Florentine, Machiavelli (pp. 298–299).

The list of Leonardo's ideas for new mechanical devices is staggering. He made some four hundred detailed drawings of machines. A shortlist of his proposals gives a hint of the range of his inventiveness. He came up with suggestions for a robot, a lifting fork, various cranes, machinery for making cloth, improvements on the printing press, a prototype of a car powered by springs and gears, a bicycle, and a flying machine. And then there were his ideas for weapons, including armored tanks, battering rams, scaling ladders, cannons, catapults, crossbows, and a submarine.

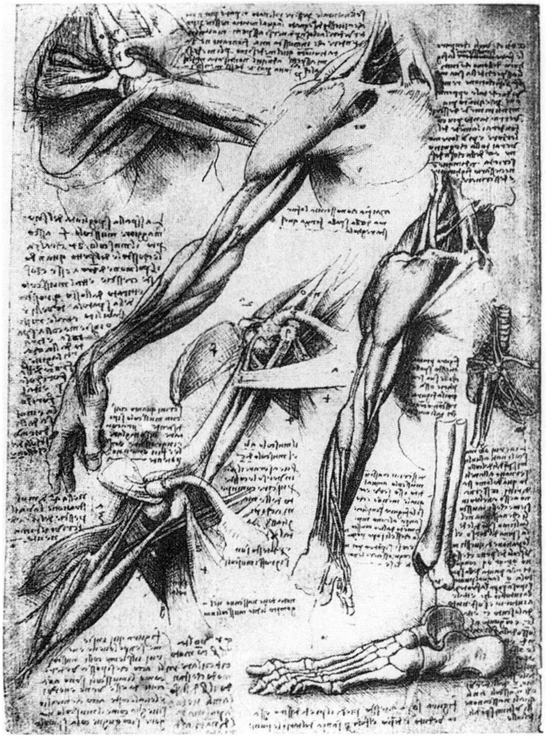

ANATOMICAL DRAWING BY LEONARDO DA VINCI (1452–1519). These drawings show the close connection between art and scientific anatomy and provide evidence of da Vinci's universal genius. (*Corbis-Bettmann.*)

For all his inventive energy, Leonardo was notorious for procrastinating and sometimes never finishing his commissions for artworks and building projects, so the number of his surviving paintings is very small. This meager output has always been looked on as a great loss because his finished work sets such a high standard, including such incomparable paintings, as *The Last Supper, Mona Lisa,* and *St. John the Baptist.*

GIOVANNI ARNOLFINI AND HIS BRIDE, BY JAN VAN EYCK (C. 1390–1441). The painting uses the new Renaissance technique of perspective and draws a careful, and idealized, portrait of a prosperous married couple in their bedroom. It depicts a world that values privacy, sober prosperity, and intimacy of a certain kind: he stares out at us, while she looks deferentially at him. (*Reproduced by courtesy of the Trustees, The National Gallery, London.*)

Renaissance culture adapted itself to conditions unknown in Italy, such as the growth of the monarchical state and the strength of **lay piety.** In England, France, and Spain, Renaissance culture tended to be court centered and hence antirepublican, as it was, for instance, under Francis I in France and Elizabeth I in England. In Germany and the Rhineland, no monarchical state existed, but a vital tradition of lay piety was present in the Low Countries. For example, the Brethren of the Common Life was a lay movement emphasizing education and practical piety. Intensely Christian and at the same time anticlerical, the people in such lay movements found in Renaissance culture tools for sharpening their wits against the clergy—not to undermine the faith but rather to restore it to its apostolic purity.

Thus, northern humanists were profoundly devoted to ancient learning, just as the humanists in Italy had been. But nothing in northern humanism compares to the paganizing trend associated with the Italian Renaissance. The northerners were chiefly interested in the problem of the ancient church and, in particular, the question of what constituted original Christianity. They sought a model in the light of which they might reform the corrupted church of their own time.

Everywhere, two factors operated to accelerate the spread of Renaissance culture after 1450: growing prosperity and the printing press. Prosperity, brought on by peace and the decline of famine and plague, led to the founding of schools and colleges. The sons (women were excluded) of gentlemen and merchants were sent to school to receive a humanistic education imported from Italy. The purpose of such education was to prepare men for a career in the church or the civil service of the expanding state and for acceptance into higher social spheres.

Printing with movable type, which was invented in the middle of the fifteenth century, quickened the spread of Renaissance ideas. Back in the Late Middle Ages, the West had learned, through the Muslims from the Chinese, of printing, paper, and ink. However, in this block printing process, a new block had to be carved from wood for each new impression, and the block was discarded as unusable as soon as a slightly different impression was needed. About 1445, Johann Gutenberg (c. 1398–1468) and other printers in Mainz in the Rhineland invented movable metal type to replace the cumbersome blocks. It was possible to use and reuse the separate pieces of type—as long as the metal in which they were cast did not wear down—simply by arranging them in the desired order.

With the advent of the printing press, the book-publishing industry began to develop. The first printed books were religious: Bibles, sermons, and prayer books. But other kinds soon followed because there was a ready market for books on a great variety of secular subjects. The market was enormous and continued to expand during the sixteenth century. Printed books were

Map 13.2 **The Growth of Printing in Europe** The printing press was invented in the mid-fifteenth century, and its use had spread across Europe in less than a century. Even by 1500, some twenty million books had already been printed using the new technology.

much cheaper than the earlier hand-copied ones, and many more people could now afford to buy them. Publishers catered to every taste in reading—learned and popular, technical and imaginative, serious and light. Books became big business, driven by both consumer demand and the profit motive. Fifteen or twenty million books had already been published by 1500, and another 150 million more a century later.

Not only were books cheaper and more numerous, but printing also made it easier to learn to read. Literacy rates were still very low, especially among women and the poor, but the clerical and gentry monopoly on reading had been broken. More and more books were also published in the **vernacular** (rather than Latin), which helped standardize written language and stimulated the development of national literatures all across Europe. Printing, moreover, provided a surer basis for scholarship and prevented the further corruption of texts through hand copying. By giving all scholars the same text to work from, it made progress in critical scholarship and science faster and more reliable.

But in early modern Europe printing was not an unmixed blessing. Elite opinion was often divided, or at least ambivalent, on the issue. Printing was an obvious boon; the authorities, however, saw the need for censorship, for imposing controls on what was published. Today, ours is a **pluralistic** society that values new ideas and a variety of opinions, even differences of opinion, at least up to a point. Early modern Europeans were not so tolerant; in fact, they were suspicious of intellectual novelty and variety and sometimes downright hostile to **heterodox** thinking. For centuries, leaders in church and state had tried to build unity by enforcing Christian **orthodoxy** and punishing heresy. The motto of the French monarchy aptly sums up the point: "One king, one law, one faith." The Catholic church established an *Index of Prohibited Books* in the mid-sixteenth century, and books like Machiavelli's *The Prince* were put on the list. Protestant authorities also set up machinery for regulating the book trade. Printers of "dangerous" books were punished, sometimes executed, and their book stocks confiscated. All intellectual life would be affected by this atmosphere: the tension between the power of print and the desire to control opinion.

ERASMUS, BY QUENTIN MASSYS, 1517. Erasmus (c. 1466–1536) was a great biblical scholar and Christian humanist who hoped to purify the Catholic church by calling for moral reform and criticizing clerical wealth and corruption. (*The Royal Collection © Her Majesty Queen Elizabeth II.*)

Online Study Center **Improve Your Grade**
Interactive Map: The Growth of Printing

Erasmian Humanism

To Desiderius Erasmus (c. 1466–1536) belongs the credit for making Renaissance humanism an international movement. He was educated in the Netherlands by the Brethren of the Common Life, which was one of the most advanced religious movements of the age, combining mystical piety with rigorous humanist pedagogy. Erasmus traveled throughout Europe as a humanist educator and biblical scholar. Like other Christian humanists, he trusted the power of words and used his pen to attack scholastic theology and clerical abuses and to promote his philosophy of Christ. His weapon was satire, and his *Praise of Folly* and *Colloquies* won him a reputation for acid wit vented at the expense of conventional religion.

True religion, Erasmus argued, does not depend on dogma, ritual, or clerical power. Rather, it is revealed clearly and simply in the Bible and therefore is directly accessible to all people, from the wise and great to the poor and humble. Nor is true religion opposed to nature. Rather, people are naturally capable of both apprehending what is good as set forth in the Scriptures and living in accordance with it. Perfect harmony between human nature and true religion allows humanity to attain, if not perfection, at least the next best thing, peace and happiness in this life.

This clear but quiet voice was drowned out by the storms of the Reformation (see Chapter 14), and the weight Erasmus gave to the individual's natural capacities could not hold its own before the renewed emphasis on human sinfulness and dogmatic theology. Erasmus was caught in the middle and condemned by both sides; for him, the Reformation was both a personal and a historical tragedy. He had worked for peace and unity and was treated to a spectacle of war and fragmentation. Erasmian humanism, however, survived these horrors as an ideal, and during the

The Renaissance

1. Filippo Brunelleschi. Church of San Lorenzo. Interior, looking toward the apse. Florence, Italy. *(Erich Lessing/Art Resource, NY.)*

The most vivid image of the Renaissance is conveyed through its architecture, sculpture, and painting. Renaissance examples of all three art forms display a style that stressed proportion, balance, and harmony. These artistic values were achieved through a new, revolutionary conceptualization of space and spatial relations. To a considerable extent, Renaissance art also reflects the values of Renaissance humanism, in the use of classical models in architecture, in the rendering of the nude human figure, and in the heroic vision of human beings.

Medieval art sought to represent spiritual aspiration; the world was a veil merely hinting at the other perfect eternal world. Renaissance art expresses spiritual aspiration, but its setting and character differ altogether. This world is no longer a veil but the *place* where people live, act, and worship. The reference is less to the other world and more to this world, and people are treated as creatures who find their spiritual destiny as they fulfill their human one.

Renaissance artists produced revolutionary discoveries which served as the foundation of Western art up to the twentieth century. In art, as in philosophy, the Florentines played a leading role in this esthetic transformation. The first major contributor to Renaissance painting was the Florentine painter Giotto (c. 1276–1337). Giotto developed several techniques of perspective, representing three-

2. Donatello. *David,* c. 1425–1430. *(Museo Nazionale del Bargello, Florence/Scala/Art Resource, NY.)*

dimentional figures and objects on two-dimensional surfaces so that they appear to stand in space. Giotto's figures look remarkably alive. They are drawn and arranged in space to tell a story, and the expressions they wear and the illusion of movement they convey heighten the dramatic effect. The dramatic work of Giotto marked the end of the stiff, other-worldly style of the Middle Ages. The artists who followed Giotto diverged from his style and subject matter. Although Christianity was still an important theme, Renaissance artists also depicted subjects from Greek and Roman mythology as well as scenes from everyday life.

Painting, sculpture, architecture, and the minor arts evolved at a different pace throughout this period. It was not as if all artists declared themselves to be Renaissance figures simultaneously. Instead, styles changed with new artistic sensibilities, technological advances, and the requests of new patrons.

Rarely can one ascribe the development of an entire period of art to a single individual. Such is the case of Renaissance architecture, however. Filippo Brunelleschi (c. 1377–1446) began his career as a sculptor in Florence. He turned to architecture sometime after 1402 and traveled to Rome, where he studied the remains of imperial Roman buildings and monuments. Brunelleschi learned the theory of scientific perspective, perhaps while trying to draw on paper three-dimensional images of the monuments. He also developed a method of building double domes linked to reinforce each other. This lightened the weight of the dome, allowing the structure beneath to be built with fewer supporting elements.

One of the earliest expressions of his architectural skill can be seen in the Church of San Lorenzo in Florence (1421–1469) (Figure 1). Thanks to the benevolence of the Medici family, Brunelleschi was granted license to design an entire building himself. The Church of San Lorenzo was a new structure, not an adaptation of or an addition to an older, medieval building. Although some of its elements may have derived from earlier prototypes, the new building was distinct in its symmetry and regu-

3. Sassetta. *Saint Anthony Tempted by the Devil in the Form of a Woman*, c. 1430. *(Yale University Art Gallery, New Haven, Connecticut. University Purchase from James Jackson Jarves.)*

larity. Its floor plan shows a markedly regular repetition of equal-size squares to establish the nave, transept, and aisles. The centrally planned chapel, with its strict adherence to mathematical proportion, distinguishes the Church of San Lorenzo from the medieval Gothic cathedral. Brunelleschi's ability to grasp the concept of perspective in two dimensions is translated into three dimensions by the strong use of line and rhythmical arches that draw the eye to the altar.

Brunelleschi effected the same fusion of antique and Christian as his contemporaries did in other fields. Poets and writers experimented with classical and Christian styles; so, too, did Brunelleschi. Note, for example, the Corinthian capitals topping the San Lorenzo columns, whereas the floor plan is in the shape of a cross.

Architecture was not the only medium that combined experimentation and echoes of the past; sculpture did as well. Whereas Brunelleschi can be viewed as the father of Renaissance architecture, a host of sculptors advanced the Renaissance style in their medium. Prominent among them in the early Renaissance was

4. Pietro Perugino. *The Delivery of the Keys,* 1481. *(Sistine Chapel, Vatican Palace, Vatican State/Scala/Art Resource, NY.)*

Donatello (1386–1466), whose works distinguished him as a master even in his own time. The bronze *David* (c. 1425–1430) is perhaps the most controversial of his best-known sculptures (Figure 2). The first life-size, free-standing nude sculpture since antiquity, this work is still something of an enigma.

Art historians assume that the statue was to have been exhibited outdoors, or at least in a central location, because it was meant to be viewed from all sides. The young David is wearing only a hat and high boots. Unlike the well-muscled athletes of the classical period, however, he is slender and slight, an adolescent instead of a developed adult. Donatello does pay homage to classical prototypes in the stance of his David—a *contrapposto*, or counterbalanced, pose, in which the weight on the legs is uneven (compare David's stance with Hermes' stance in Figure 1 of the first art essay).

Symbolic devices provide the key to the significance of the sculpture. David represents the city of Florence itself, and the helmet of Goliath under his feet represents the duchy of Milan, which at the time was at war with Florence. David's nudity may allude to the city's classical past, and the wreathed hat may suggest victory.

In painting, experiments in depth and linear perspective stand out as the major developments. Artists were seeking ways of making two-dimensional surfaces seem three-dimensional. Brunelleschi was the first to develop a system in which all parallel lines of a scene converge in one central point on the horizon; other artists adopted his scheme and carried it further.

An early Renaissance work from Siena, *Saint Anthony Tempted by the Devil in the Form of a Woman* (c. 1430) (Figure 3), foreshadows developments that distinguish later paintings. The artist is on the brink of discovering the mechanics of perspective. The path taken by Saint Anthony leads back into the hills, which are shown on a curved horizon.

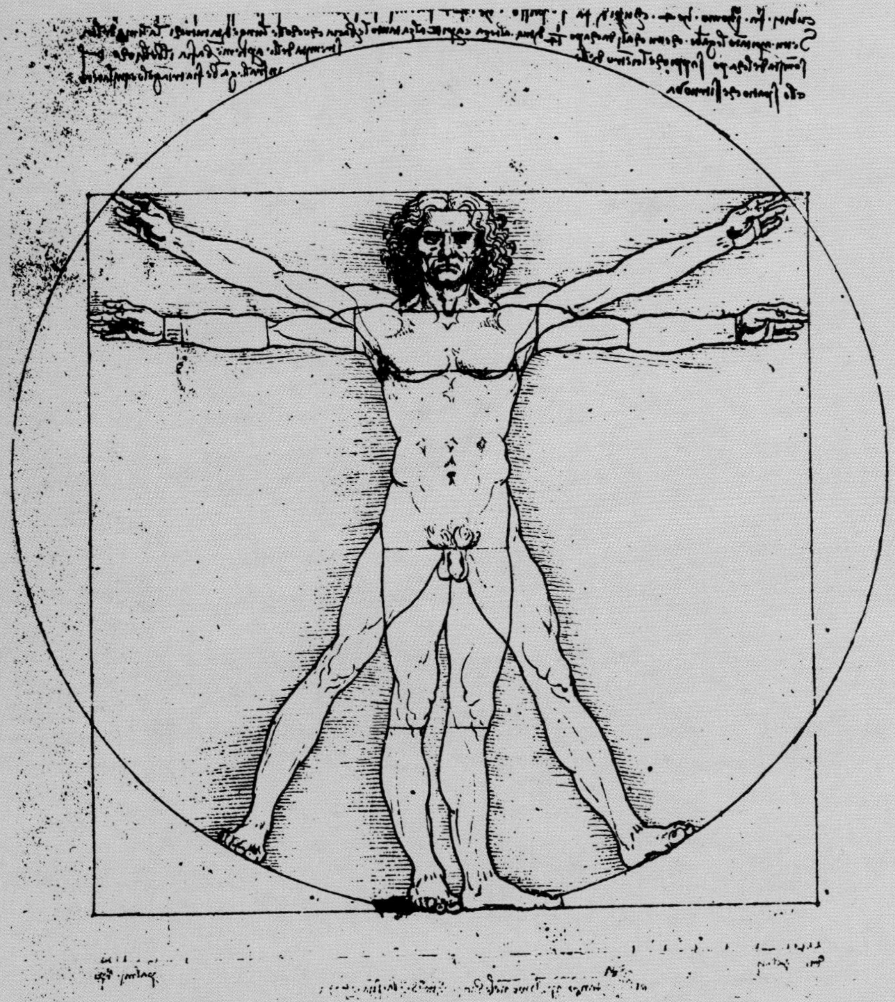

5. Leonardo da Vinci, *The Proportions of Man,* from his notebooks. *(Hulton Archive/ Getty Images.)*

The work, which is more than five hundred years old, is strangely modern in its abstraction, stripped of many of the decorative elements that mark both earlier and later works.

Pietro Perugino's *The Delivery of the Keys*, a fresco from the Sistine Chapel in the Vatican (1481) (Figure 4), illustrates the enthusiasm with which other artists achieved perspective. Note that all the parallel lines in the foreground converge at the church in the center of the background. The viewer's eye is drawn into the painting, and figures seem real, not flat. Compare this portrayal with the flat and linear rendering of Justinian and his retinue in the mosaic from Ravenna. There, the effect is two-dimensional, and the viewer does not expect to see beyond the layer of figures. In the Perugino, by contrast, the figures are full and exist in a three-dimensional space.

The works of Leonardo da Vinci—his drawings, paintings, sculpture, innumerable inventions, and copious writings—exemplify the Renaissance spirit. He expands the idea of three-dimensional, perspectival space to include the

6. Michelangelo Buonarroti. *Creation of Adam*, 1510. *(Vatican Museum and Galleries, Rome/Bridgeman Art Library.)*

living form of things, their mathematical proportions. He announced a new way of looking at nature and the individual. For Leonardo, visual art offered a means of arriving at nature's truths. Truth was attained when the artist brought both human reason and creative capacity to bear on the direct experience of the senses. Leonardo examined objects in all their diversity and represented them realistically. He visually delineated the natural world with unprecedented scientific precision, and he asserted his spiritual and intellectual freedom to do so. Through his art, Leonardo helped lay the foundations for modern science.

In his notebooks, Leonardo sketched an infinite variety of objects—inorganic, organic, human—and recorded fragmentary thoughts about them. Everywhere, he demonstrated concern for the concrete specificity of things, which he depicted in minute detail. He was perpetually engaged in a quest for the essential living form of a thing, the relationship of its parts to the whole, the numerical ratios subsisting among the parts, and the laws operative in the ratios. He found such ratios and laws everywhere, in both animate and inanimate objects. He was particularly fascinated by the human body, and in his notebook his written observations are accompanied by a marvelous sketch of the body, *The Proportions of Man* (Figure 5), conceived and framed with realism and mathematical proportion.

By the end of the fifteenth century, Renaissance art in Italy had reached its height. The so-called High Renaissance flowered in the visual arts as well as in other areas of culture. Michelangelo, Titian, and Giorgione are among the best-known artists of this era.

The works of Michelangelo Buonarroti (1475–1564)—paintings, sculpture, literature,

7. Titian. *Bacchus and Ariadne*, 1523. *(Erich Lessing/Art Resource, NY.)*

and architecture—epitomize the Renaissance. Looking at his paintings—for instance, *Creation of Adam* on the ceiling of the Vatican's Sistine Chapel (1510) (Figure 6)—a viewer is struck by the extent to which he learned from the art of the ancient world. Nevertheless, Michelangelo's reliance on the classical is subordinate to his Renaissance vantage point. Here, the figures float freely through a celestial landscape and depict the biblical story of creation.

But the artists of the Renaissance looked to the classical past not only for technique; they also borrowed and adapted subject matter. Unlike the art of the Middle Ages, which concentrated on Christian themes, Renaissance paintings also illustrated the myths of ancient Greece and Rome.

The Venetian artist Titian (1488/90–1576) was well known for his use of both mythology and biblical themes. His *Bacchus and Ariadne* (1523) (Figure 7) illustrates his independence from the stylistic conventions of other High Renaissance schools. Titian offers a sensual rendering of the classical tale, in which the young Ariadne marries Bacchus (Dionysus), the god of wine, after being abandoned by the Greek king Theseus. Titian's use of *chiaroscuro* (alternating areas of light and dark) is pronounced. The general feeling of the work is much looser and freer than the feelings of the carefully constructed canvases produced by his contemporaries. The painting also has a roughness, as though it were unfinished—a quality that marks a departure from the meticulously realistic works of other High Renaissance artists.

As the artistic styles of the Italian Renaissance spread northward, they were adapted and superimposed on a different set of political

8. Pieter Brueghel the Elder. *Hunters in the Show*, 1565. *(Erich Lessing/Kunsthistoriches, Vienna/Art Resource, NY.)*

and religious circumstances, resulting in a fusion of Renaissance method and local themes. Pieter Brueghel the Elder's (1525/30–1569) *Hunters in the Snow* (1565) (Figure 8) exemplifies this trend. The artist uses line and motion as Titian did. But the image he presents, while it contains many elements of the old style, looks ahead to the future.

Brueghel had spent almost two years studying in Italy, during which he had developed a technique for dealing with the problem of landscape. In his treatment of objects in three-dimensional space, he created a recessional movement that dominates the painting. The viewer's eye is drawn inwardly into the painting at an angle from the foreground to the background through myriad intermediate, diminishing shapes—dogs, human figures, trees, houses, a flying bird—all unified by one sweeping, sloping, downward motion. Brueghel thus achieves a perspectival depth that is entirely new, not relying on the correlation of stratified forms from left to right, but on the recession of foreshortened forms. In this painting, the artist has surpassed the medieval representation of space in two dimensions and has produced a boundless three-dimensional space that belongs to the modern age.

By the late fifteenth and sixteenth centuries, the styles of the Renaissance spread from Italy to the Low Countries (the Netherlands, Belgium, and Luxembourg), Germany, France, England, and Spain. These styles were not exported wholesale; rather, elements of the Renaissance fused with local traditions to produce new styles and variants of the Italian themes. What is consistent from one country to the next, however, is the extent to which Renaissance art really was a rebirth—a departure from the style of the medieval period.

next two centuries, whenever thinkers sought toleration and rational religion (Rabelais and Montaigne, for instance), they looked back to Erasmus for inspiration.

French Humanism

German and French humanists pursued Christian humanist aims. They used humanist scholarship and language to satirize and vilify medieval scholastic Christianity and to build a purer, more scriptural Christianity. These northern humanists had great faith in the power of words. The discovery of accurate biblical texts, it was hoped, would lead to a great religious awakening. Protestant reformers, including Martin Luther, relied on humanist scholarship.

French thinkers of the next generation exploited and carried the humanist legacy in more radical directions. Among them, two were outstanding: Michel de Montaigne (1533–1592) and François Rabelais (c. 1494–1553). Both thought and wrote in reaction to the religious wars resulting from the Reformation. In the face of competing religious dogmatisms—Catholic, Protestant, and sectarian—Montaigne advanced a skepticism in which he maintained that one can know little or nothing with certainty. He therefore advocated political quietism and acceptance of Christianity on faith. This skepticism also entailed tolerance. An individual was not fully responsible for his or her beliefs since they were the product of frail reason and force of circumstance. Thus, Montaigne argued, people should not be punished for their beliefs, and the only ones who deserved to be severely dealt with were the dogmatists in religion. These people deserved to be punished because their certainty and self-righteousness flew in the face of a fundamental epistemological fact: that reason cannot be relied on, especially in matters of religion.

Montaigne was not a systematic philosopher but devoted himself to what he could learn by Socratic self-examination, the results of which he set down in his *Essays*. In their urbane and caustic wit and their intense self-absorption, the *Essays* betray a crucial shift in humanist thought, which became more pronounced in the next century. Gone is the optimism and emphasis on civic virtue of the High Renaissance. In their place come skepticism and introspection, the attempt to base morality on the self rather than on public values. As Montaigne says, "Let us learn to be no more avid of glory than we are capable of it."[7] This shift, produced by the increasing scale and violence of religious war, represented a retreat from the idealism of Renaissance humanism.

Rabelais took a different route from Montaigne's. In response to religious dogmatism, he asserted the essential goodness of the individual and the right to be free to enjoy the world rather than being bound down, as John Calvin later would have it, by fear of a vengeful God. Rabelais's folk-epic, *Gargantua and Pantagruel,* in which he celebrates earthly and earthy life, is the greatest French work of its kind and perhaps the greatest in any literature. Rabelais said that, once freed from dogmatic religion, people could, by virtue of their native goodness, build a paradise on earth and disregard the one dreamed up by theologians. In *Gargantua and Pantagruel,* he imagined a monastery where men and women spend their lives "not in laws, statutes, or rules, but according to their own free will and pleasure." They sleep and eat when they desire and learn to "read, write, sing, play upon several musical instruments, and speak five or six . . . languages and compose in them all very quaintly." They observed one rule: "DO WHAT THOU WILT."[8]

Spanish Humanism

Spanish humanism represents a special case. The church hierarchy gained such a tight grip in Spain during the late fifteenth and early sixteenth centuries that it monopolized humanist learning and exploited it for its own repressive purposes. In contrast to Germany, France, or England, there was little or no room for a dissenting humanist voice. The mastermind behind this authoritarian Spanish humanism was Cardinal Francisco Jiménez de Cisneros (1436–1517). Jiménez founded the University of Alcalá, not far from Madrid, for the instruction of the clergy. He also sponsored and published the Complutensian Polyglot Bible, with Hebrew, Latin, and Greek texts in parallel columns. Jiménez, like Christian humanists elsewhere, sought to enlighten the clergy through a return to the pure sources of religion, and he saw his Polyglot Bible as one of the chief means of realizing that goal.

A century after Jiménez, Miguel de Cervantes Saavedra (1547–1616) produced his great novel, *Don Quixote,* in which he satirized the ideals of knighthood and chivalry. Don Quixote, the victim of his own illusions, roams the countryside looking for romance and an opportunity to prove his knightly worth. To Quixote's servant Sancho Panza, Cervantes assigned the role of pointing up the inanity of his master's quest by always acting prudently and judging according to common sense. Despite his earthy realism, however, Panza must share his master's misfortunes—so much for realism in a world run by men full of illusions. Cervantes's satire is very gentle. That knightly valor was still a valid subject for satire indicates how wedded Spain was even in the early seventeenth century to the conservative values of its crusading past.

English Humanism

Christian humanism in England sharply contrasted with that in Spain. It was developed by secular men in government as much as by clerics, and its objectives were often opposed to authority and tradition. Various Italian humanists came to England during the fifteenth century as bishops, merchants, court physicians, or artists. Englishmen also studied in Italy, especially in Florence, and introduced the serious humanistic study of the classics at Oxford University toward the end of the century.

The most influential humanist of the early English Renaissance was Sir Thomas More (1478–1535), who studied at Oxford. His impact arose from both his writing and his career. Trained as a lawyer, he became a successful civil servant and member of Parliament. His most famous book is *Utopia,* the major utopian treatise to be written in the West since Plato's *Republic* and one of the most original works of the entire Renaissance.

Many humanists had attacked private wealth as the source of pride, greed, and human cruelty. But in *Utopia,* More went further. He argued that an acquisitive society is by nature both unjust and unprosperous. "For, when everyone is entitled to get as much for himself as he can, all available property . . . is bound to fall into the hands of a small minority, which means that everyone else is poor." The unscrupulous few win out over the many who remain honest and decent. For More, the conclusion was inescapable: "I am quite convinced that you will never get a fair distribution of goods . . . until you abolish private property altogether."[9] But to balance things out, he stated the economic case against communism as well. In the absence of a profit motive, "there would always tend to be shortages because nobody would work hard enough. . . . Then when things really got short, the . . . result would be a series of murders and riots."[10] But More accused those who took this view of lacking the imagination to conceive of a truly just society. In *Utopia,* he set out to make up for this deficiency by inventing an ideal society in which private ownership was abolished and poverty eliminated because everyone had to work in order to eat. Such a system even produced surpluses, which allowed people the leisure for instruction and recreation.

More succeeded Cardinal Wolsey as lord chancellor under Henry VIII. But when the king broke with the Roman Catholic church, More resigned, unable to reconcile his conscience with the king's rejection of papal supremacy. Three years later, in July 1535, More was executed for treason for refusing to swear an oath acknowledging the king's ecclesiastical supremacy.

William Shakespeare (1564–1616), widely considered the greatest playwright the world has ever produced, gave expression to conventional Renaissance values: honor, heroism, and the struggle against fate and fortune. But there is nothing conventional about Shakespeare's treatment of characters possessing these virtues. His greatest plays, the tragedies (*King Lear, Julius Caesar,* and others), explore a common theme: men, even heroic men, despite virtue, are able only with the greatest difficulty, if at all, to overcome their human weaknesses. What fascinated Shakespeare was the contradiction between the Renaissance image of nobility, which is often the self-image of Shakespeare's heroes, and man's capacity for evil and self-destruction. Thus, Ophelia says of Hamlet, her lover, in the play of the same name:

> *O, what a noble mind is here o'erthrown!*
> *The courtier's, soldier's, scholar's, eye,*
> *tongue, sword;*

> *The expectancy and rose of the fair state,*
> *The glass of fashion and the mould of form,*
> *The observ'd of all observers, quite, quite*
> *down!*
> *[And] I, of ladies most deject and wretched,*
> *That suck'd the honey of his music vows,*
> *Now see that noble and most sovereign*
> *reason,*
> *Like sweet bells jangled, out of tune and*
> *harsh;*
> *That unmatch'd form and feature of blown*
> *youth*
> *Blasted with ecstasy. O, woe is me,*
> *T' have seen what I have seen, see what I*
> *see!*[11]

The plays are intensely human—so much so that humanism fades into the background. Thus, art transcends doctrine to represent life itself.

The Renaissance and the Modern Age

The Renaissance, then, marks the birth of modernity—in art, in the idea of the individual's role in history and nature, and in society, politics, war, and diplomacy. Central to this birth is a bold new view of human nature: individuals in all endeavors are free of a given destiny imposed by God from the outside—free to make their own destiny, guided only by the example of the past, the force of present circumstances, and the drives of their own inner nature. Individuals, set free from theology, are seen to be the products, and in turn the shapers, of history. Their future is not wholly determined by Providence but is partly the work of their own free will.

Within the Italian city-states, where the Renaissance was born, rich merchants were at least as important as the church hierarchy and the old nobility. The city-states were almost completely independent because of the weakness of church and empire. So the northern Italians were left free to invent new forms of government, in which merchant-oligarchs, humanists, and condottieri played a more important part than priests and nobles, who dominated politics in the rest of Europe. Along with the inventiveness, however, this newness and lack of tradition produced disorder and violence. Condottieri grabbed power from hapless citizens, and republics gave way to despotism.

But the problems created by novelty and instability demanded solutions, and the wealth of the cities called forth the talent to find them. Commercial wealth and the new politics produced a new culture: Renaissance art and humanism. Talented individuals—scholars, poets, artists, and government officials—returned to classical antiquity, which in any case lay near at hand in Italy and Greece. Ancient models in art, architecture, literature, and philosophy provided answers to their questions. This return to antiquity also entailed a rejection of the Middle Ages as dark, barbarous, and rude. The humanists clearly preferred the secular learning of ancient Greece and Rome to the clerical learning of the more recent past. The reason for this was obvious: the ancients had the same worldly concerns as the humanists; the scholastics did not.

The revival of antiquity by the humanists did not mean, however, that they identified completely with it. The revival itself was done too self-consciously for that. In the very act of looking back, the humanists differentiated themselves from the past and recognized that they were different. They were in this sense the first modern historians because they could study and appreciate the past for its own sake and, to some degree, on its own terms.

In the works of Renaissance artists and thinkers, the world was, to a large extent, depicted and explained without reference to a higher supernatural realm of meaning and authority. This is clearly seen in Machiavelli's analysis of politics. Closely associated with this secular element in Renaissance culture was a new realism that beckoned toward the modern outlook. What else is Machiavelli's new politics but a politics of realism, dealing with the world as he found it rather than as it ought to be? This realism also manifests itself in the realm of art, where mathematical perspective renders the world in its spatial dimension and gives it the solidity and drama that constitute a modern visual and esthetic realism. The sources for both the esthetic and the political realism were the cultural forms of ancient Greece and Rome.

Renaissance humanism exuded deep confidence in the capacities of able people, instructed in the wisdom of the ancients, to understand and change the world. Renaissance realism, then, was mixed with idealism, and this potent combination departed sharply from the medieval outlook. In place of Christian resignation there grew a willingness to confront life directly and a belief that able human beings can succeed even against great odds.

This new confidence is closely related to another distinctive feature of the Renaissance: the cult of the individual. Both prince and painter were motivated in part by the desire to display their talents and to satisfy their ambitions. Such individual striving was rewarded and encouraged by the larger society of rich patrons and calculating princes, who valued ability. Gone was the medieval Christian emphasis on the virtue of self-denial and the sin of pride. Instead, the Renaissance placed the highest value on self-expression and self-fulfillment, on the realization of individual potential, especially of the gifted few. The Renaissance fostered an atmosphere in which talent, even genius, was allowed to flourish. The ideal, at least, was meritocracy.

To be sure, the Renaissance image of the individual and the world, bold and novel, was the exclusive prerogative of a small, well-educated urban elite and did not reach down to include the masses. Nevertheless, the Renaissance set an example of what people might achieve in art and architecture, taste and refinement, education, and urban culture. In many fields, the Renaissance set the cultural standards of the modern age.

❖ ❖ ❖

Online Study Center **ACE the Test**

Notes

1. Quoted in Quentin Skinner, *The Foundations of Modern Political Thought,* 2 vols. (Cambridge: Cambridge University Press, 1978), 1:89.
2. Giovanni Pico della Mirandola, *Oration on the Dignity of Man,* trans. A. Robert Caponigri (Chicago: Henry Regnery, 1956), p. 7.
3. Niccolò Machiavelli, *The Prince,* trans. George Bull (Harmondsworth, England: Penguin Books, 1961), pp. 90–91.
4. Ibid., pp. 77–78.
5. Ibid., p. 91.
6. Ibid., p. 101.
7. Quoted in Eugen Weber, ed., *The Western Tradition,* 2 vols., 4th ed. (Lexington, Mass., and Toronto: D. C. Heath, 1990), 1:395.
8. François Rabelais, *Gargantua and Pantagruel,* trans. Sir Thomas Urquhart (1883), bk. 1, chap. 57.
9. Thomas More, *Utopia,* trans. Paul Turner (Harmondsworth, England: Penguin Books, 1965), p. 66.
10. Ibid., p. 67.
11. From *Hamlet, Prince of Denmark,* in *The Complete Plays and Poems of William Shakespeare,* ed. William Allan Neilson and Charles Jarvis Hill (Boston: Houghton Mifflin, 1942), p. 1067.

Suggested Reading

Brucker, Gene A., *Renaissance Florence,* rev. ed. (1983). An excellent analysis of the city's economic and social structure, its political and religious life, and its cultureal achievements.

Febvre, Lucien, and Henri-Jean Martin, *The Coming of the Book: The Impact of Printing, 1450–1800* (1997). Covers all aspects of "the print revolution."

Hale, John, *The Civilization of Europe in the Renaissance* (1995). An informed and entertaining survey, full of interesting illustrations.

Kelley, Donald R., *Renaissance Humanism* (1991). A concise treatment of an important subject.

King, Margaret L., *Women of the Renaissance* (1991). A useful survey of a burgeoning field of scholarship.

Chapter 17

The Scientific Revolution: The Universe Seen as a Mechanism

When Galileo looked through his telescope, he saw shadows. But shadows meant depth and contour and that meant real, solid matter. The notion that the planets were ethereal globes of light gave way to their being just matter like the earth. (The Granger Collection.)

- **Medieval Cosmology**
- **A New View of Nature**
- **The Newtonian Synthesis: Experiment, Mathematics, and Theory**
- **Biology, Medicine, and Chemistry**
- **Bacon and Descartes: Prophets of the New Science**
- **Social Implications of the Scientific Revolution**
- **The Meaning of the Scientific Revolution**

Focus Questions

1. What were the basic features of the medieval view of the universe?
2. Who were the leading figures of the Scientific Revolution, and what were their accomplishments?
3. What was the relationship between science and magic during this period?
4. Why was the Scientific Revolution a decisive force in the shaping of the modern outlook?

Online Study Center

This icon will direct you to interactive map and primary source activities on the website http://college.hmco.com/pic/perrywc8e.

In the fifteenth century, the medieval view of the world began to disintegrate. By the late seventeenth century, educated Europeans no longer believed in it. Thus, the collapse of medieval institutions such as feudalism and serfdom had an intellectual parallel. No movement was as important in shaping the modern world-view as the Scientific Revolution of the seventeenth century. It made physical nature a valid object for experimental inquiry and mathematical calculation. For the new science to arise, a philosophical break with the medieval conception of nature had to occur. The medieval approach to nature sought to explain nature's appearances. To the naked eye, the earth seems to be in the center of our universe. Medieval philosophy explained how and why the earth was in the center; how and why heavy bodies fell toward it and light ones rose away from it. The philosophical revolution of the seventeenth century demolished such explanations. At the heart of the Scientific Revolution was the assumption that appearances could lie, that truth lay in conceptualizing the universe as an abstract entity: as matter in motion, as geometrical shapes, and as weight and number. The universe became a mechanism.

The Scientific Revolution brought a new, **mechanical conception of nature** that enabled westerners to discover and explain the laws of nature mathematically. They came to see nature as composed solely of matter, whose motion, occurring in space and measurable by time, is governed by the push and pull of bodies and by laws of force. This philosophically elegant construction rendered the physical world knowable and even possibly manageable. It also contributed decisively to the formulation of applied mechanics.

The Scientific Revolution also rested on a new, replicable methodology. Because of successful experiments performed by scientists and natural philosophers such as Galileo Galilei, William Harvey, Robert Boyle, and Isaac Newton, Western science acquired its still-characteristic methods of observation, experimentation, and replication. By the late seventeenth century, no one could entertain a serious interest in the physical order without actually doing—and recording—experiments or without observing, in a rigorous and systematic way, the behavior of physical phenomena. The mechanical concept of nature, coupled with a rigorous methodology, gave modern scientists the means to unlock and explain nature's secrets.

Mathematics increasingly became the language of the new science. For centuries, Europeans had used first geometry and then algebra to explain certain physical phenomena. With the Scientific Revolution came a new mathematics, the infinitesimal **calculus.** Even more important, philosophers became increasingly convinced that all nature—physical objects, as well as invisible forces—could be expressed mathematically. By the late seventeenth century, even geometry had become so complex that a gifted philosopher like John Locke (1632–1704), a friend and contemporary of Isaac Newton, could not understand the sophisticated mathematics used by Newton in the *Principia*. A new scientific culture had been born. During the eighteenth-century Enlightenment (Chapter 18), it provided the model for progress in the natural sciences and in the human sciences that were to imitate them.

Medieval Cosmology

The unique character of the modern scientific outlook is most easily grasped through contrast with the medieval understanding of the natural world and its physical properties. That understanding rested on a blend of Christian thought with theories derived from ancient Greek writers, such as Aristotle and Ptolemy.

Aristotle (384–322 B.C.) had argued simply that it was in the nature of things to move in certain ways. A stone falls because it is absolutely heavy; fire rises because it is absolutely light. Weight is an absolute property of a physical thing; therefore, motion results from the properties of bodies, and not from the forces that impinge on them. It follows (logically but incorrectly) that if the medium through which a body falls is taken as a constant, then the speed of its fall could be doubled if its weight were doubled. Only rigorous experimentation could refute this erroneous concept of motion; it was many centuries before such experimentation was undertaken.

Aristotle's physics fitted neatly into his *cosmology*, or world picture. The earth, being the heaviest object, lay stationary and suspended at the center of the universe. The sun, planets, and moon revolved in circles around the earth. Aristotle presumed that since the planets were round themselves, always in motion, and seemingly never altered, the most "natural" movement for them should be circular, for it is perfect motion.

Aristotle's physics and cosmology were unified. He could put the earth at the center of the universe and make it stationary because he presumed its absolute heaviness; all other heavy bodies that he had observed fall toward it. Aristotle believed that everything in motion had been moved by another object that was itself in motion—a continuing chain of movers and moved. By inference, this belief led back to some object or being that began the motion. Christian philosophers of the Middle Ages argued that Aristotle's Unmoved Mover must be the God of Christianity. For Aristotle, who had no conception of a personal God or an afterlife of rewards or punishments and who believed that the universe was eternal rather than created at a specific point in time, such an identification would have been meaningless.

Although Aristotle's cosmology never gained the status of orthodoxy among the ancient Greeks, by the second century A.D. in Alexandria, Greek astronomy became codified and then rigid. Ptolemy of Alexandria produced the *Almagest* (A.D. 150), a handbook of Greek astronomy based on the theories of Aristotle. The crucial assumption in the *Almagest* was that a motionless earth stood at the center of the universe and that the planets moved about it in a series of circular orbits, interrupted by smaller circular orbits, called epicycles. The epicycles explained why at certain times a planet was visibly closer to the earth. As Ptolemy put it, if the earth moved, "living things and individual heavy objects would be left behind . . . the earth itself would very soon have fallen completely out of the heavens."[1] By the Late Middle Ages, Ptolemy's handbook had come to represent standard astronomical wisdom. As late as the 1650s, more than a hundred years after the Polish astronomer Nicolaus Copernicus had argued mathematically that the sun was the center of the universe, educated Europeans in most universities still believed that the earth held the central position.

In the thirteenth century, mainly through the philosophical efforts of Thomas Aquinas (1225–1274), Aristotle's thought was adapted to Christian beliefs, often in ingenious ways. Aquinas emphasized that order pervaded nature and that every physical effect had a physical cause. The tendency in Aquinas's thought and that of his followers, who were called **scholastics,** was to search for these causes—again, to ask *why* things move, rather than *how* they move. Aquinas insisted that nature proves God's existence; God is the First Cause of all physical phenomena. The world picture taught by the scholastics affirmed the earth and humankind as the center of the Christian drama of birth, death, and salvation.

Medieval thinkers integrated the cosmology of Aristotle and Ptolemy into a Christian framework that drew a sharp distinction between the world beyond the moon and the earthly realm. Celestial bodies were composed of the divine ether, a substance too pure and too spiritual to be found on earth; heavenly bodies, unlike earthly bodies, were immune to all change and obeyed different laws of motion. The universe was not homogeneous but divided into a higher world of the heavens and a lower world of earth. Earth could not compare with the heavens in spiritual dignity, but God had nevertheless situated it in the center of the universe. Earth deserved this position of importance, for only here did Christ live and die for humankind. This vision of the universe was to be shattered by the Scientific Revolution.

Also shattered by the **natural philosophy** articulated in the seventeenth century was the belief that all reality, natural as well as human, could be described as consisting of *matter* and *form.* Following Aristotle, the scholastics argued that matter was inchoate, lifeless, and indistinguishable, and that form gave it shape and identity. A table, for instance, possessed a recognizable shape and could be identified as a table because it possessed the form of tableness. A human being existed only because the matter of the body was given life by the soul, by its form. This doctrine was central to both medieval philosophy and theology. Important beliefs were justified by it. For example, the church taught that the priest, when performing the sacrament of the **Eucharist,** had the power to transform bread and wine into the body and blood of Christ. This was possible because, theologians argued, the matter of the bread and wine remained the same (and hence looked the same), but its form was changed by the power of the priest. Consequently, the Mass could be explained without recourse to magic, which was highly suspect. Similarly, medieval people believed that the king's power resided within him; kingness was part of his essence. So, too, nobility was a quality said to adhere to the person of the nobleman or noblewoman. The mechanical philosophy of Galileo, Boyle, and Newton, which was central to the Scientific Revolution, denied the existence of form. Matter was simply composed of **tiny corpuscles, or atoms,** which were hard and impenetrable and were governed by the laws of impact or force. Such a conception of nature threatened whole aspects of medieval and even Christian doctrine; ultimately, for society its implications proved to be democratic.

A New View of Nature

Renaissance Neo-Platonism

Italian Renaissance thinkers rediscovered the importance of the ancient Greek philosopher Plato (c. 429–347 B.C.). Plato taught that the philosopher must look beyond the appearances of things to an invisible reality, which is abstract, simple, rational, and best expressed mathematically. For Plato, the greatest achievements of the human mind were mathematics and music; both revealed the inherent harmony and order within nature.

Renaissance Platonists interpreted Plato from a Christian perspective, and they believed that the Platonic search for truth about nature, about God's work, was but another aspect of the search for knowledge about God. The Italian universities and academies became centers where the revival of Plato flourished among teachers and translators, who came to be known as **Neo-Platonists.** Central to their humanist curriculum was the study of philosophy, mathematics, music, Greek and Latin, and in some cases Arabic. Those languages made available the world of pagan, pre-Christian learning and its many different philosophies of nature. The leading thinkers of the Scientific Revolution were all inspired by Renaissance Neo-Platonism. They revered Plato's search for a truth that was abstract and mathematically elegant, and they explored the ancient writers and their theories about nature. Some of the ancients had been atomists; a few had even argued that the sun might be at the center of the universe. They had also invented geometry.

With the impulse to mathematize nature came the desire to measure and experience it. The rediscovery of nature as mappable and quantifiable found expression in the study of human anatomy, as well as in the study of objects in motion. Renaissance art shows the fruits of this inquiry, for artists tried to depict the human body as exactly as possible yet to give it ideal form. The revival of artistic creativity associated with the Renaissance is linked to an interest in the natural world and to Neo-Platonism.

Magic and the Search for Nature

The thinkers of the Scientific Revolution also drew on a body of magical and mystical thought drawn from the first and second centuries A.D. Many of these anonymous students of magic believed that there had once been an ancient Egyptian priest, Hermes Trismegistus, who had possessed secret knowledge about nature's processes and the ultimate forces at work in the universe. Hermetic literature stated that true knowledge comes from a contemplation of the One, or the Whole—a spiritual reality higher than, yet embedded in, nature. Some of these ancient writings argued that the sun was the natural symbol of this Oneness, and such an argument seemed to give weight to a heliocentric picture of the universe. The Hermetic approach to nature also incorporated elements of the Pythagorean and Neo-Platonic traditions, which emphasized the inner mathematical harmony pervading nature. A follower of Hermeticism might approach nature mathematically as well as magically. For example, Johannes Kepler (see below) was both a fine mathematician and a believer in the magical power of nature. Though not directly influenced by Hermeticism as a system of belief, for much of his life Isaac Newton saw no contradiction in searching for the mathematical laws of nature while practicing alchemy—the illusive search for a way to transform ordinary metals into gold.

In early modern Europe, the practitioners of alchemy and astrology could also be mathematicians and astronomers, and the sharp distinction drawn today between magic and science—between the irrational and the rational—would not have been made by many of the leading natural philosophers who lived in the sixteenth and seventeenth centuries.

The Renaissance revival of ancient learning contributed a new approach to nature, one that was simultaneously mathematical, experimental, and magical. Although the achievements of modern science depend on experimentation and mathematics, the impulse to search for nature's secrets presumes a degree of self-confidence best exemplified and symbolized by the magician.

The Copernican Revolution

Nicolaus Copernicus was born in Poland in 1473. As a young man, he enrolled at the University of Kraków, where he may have come under the influence of Renaissance Platonism, which was spreading outward from the Italian city-states. Copernicus also journeyed to Italy, and in Bologna and Padua he may have become aware of ancient Greek texts containing arguments for the sun being the center of the universe. We know very little about his early education.

Copernicus's interest in mathematics and astronomy was stimulated by contemporary discussions of the need for calendar reform, which required a thorough understanding of Ptolemaic astronomy. The mathematical complexity of the Ptolemaic system troubled Copernicus, who believed that truth was the product of elegance and simplicity. In addition, Copernicus knew that Ptolemy had predecessors among the ancients who philosophized about a heliocentric universe or who held Aristotle's cosmology and physics in little regard. Thus, his Renaissance education gave Copernicus not a body of new scientific truth, but rather the courage to break with traditional truth taught in the universities.

Toward the end of his stay in Italy, Copernicus became convinced that the sun was at the center of the universe. So he began a lifelong task to work out mathematical explanations of how a heliocentric universe operated. Unwilling to engage in controversy with the followers of Aristotle, Coper-

COPERNICAN SYSTEM. In his *On the Revolutions of the Heavenly Spheres,* Copernicus proposed a heliocentric model in which the planets orbit around the sun. (*The Granger Collection.*)

nicus did not publish his findings until 1543, the year of his death, in a work titled *On the Revolutions of the Heavenly Spheres*. Legend says that his book, which in effect began the Scientific Revolution, was brought to him on his deathbed. Copernicus died a Catholic priest, hoping only that his book would be read sympathetically.

The treatise retained some elements of the Aristotelian-Ptolemaic system. Copernicus never doubted Aristotle's basic idea of the perfect circular motion of the planets or the existence of crystalline spheres within which the stars revolved, and he retained many of Ptolemy's epicycles—orbits within the circular orbits of the sun and planets. But Copernicus proposed a heliocentric model of the universe that was mathematically simpler than Ptolemy's earth-centered universe. Thus, he eliminated some of Ptolemy's epicycles and cleared up various problems that had troubled astronomers who had based their work on an earth-centered universe.

Copernicus's genius was expressed in his ability to pursue an idea—the concept of a sun-centered universe—and to bring to that pursuit lifelong dedication and brilliance in mathematics. By removing the earth from its central position and by giving it motion—that is, by making the earth just another planet—Copernicus undermined the system of medieval cosmology and made possible the birth of modern astronomy.

But because they were committed to the Aristotelian-Ptolemaic system and to biblical statements that they thought supported it, most thinkers of the time rejected Copernicus's conclusions. They also raised specific objections. The earth, they said, is too heavy to move. How, some of Copernicus's colleagues asked, can an object falling from a high tower land directly below the point from which it was dropped if the earth is moving so rapidly?

The Laws of Planetary Motion: Tycho and Kepler

Copernicus laid the foundation for the intellectual revolution that overturned the medieval conception of the universe and ushered in modern cosmology. But it fell to other observers to fill in the important details. Tycho Brahe (1546–1601) never accepted the Copernican system, but he saw that it presented a challenge to astronomers. Aided by the king of Denmark, Tycho built the finest observatory in Europe. In 1572, he observed a new star in the heavens. Its existence offered a direct and serious challenge to the Aristotelian and scholastic assumption of unalterable, fixed, and hence perfect heavens. To this discovery of what eventually proved to be an exploding star, Tycho added his observations on the comet of 1577. He demonstrated that it moved unimpeded through the areas between the planets and passed right through the crystalline spheres. This finding raised the question of whether such spheres existed, but Tycho himself remained an Aristotelian. Although his devotion to a literal reading of the Bible led Tycho to reject the Copernican sun-centered universe, he did propose an alternative system, in which the planets revolved around the sun but the sun moved about a motionless earth.

Ultimately, Tycho's fame rests on his skill as a practicing astronomer. He bequeathed to future generations precise calculations about the movements of heavenly bodies. These calculations proved invaluable. They were put to greatest use by Johannes Kepler (1571–1630), a German who collaborated with Tycho during the latter's final years. Tycho bequeathed his astronomical papers to Kepler, who brought to these data a scientific vision that was both experimental and mystical.

Kepler searched persistently for harmonious laws of planetary motion. He did so because he believed profoundly in the Platonic ideal. According to this ideal, a spiritual force infuses the physical order, beneath appearances are harmony and unity, and the human mind can begin to comprehend that unity only through *gnosis*—a direct and mystical realization of unity—and through mathematics. Kepler believed that both approaches were compatible, and he managed to combine them. He believed in and practiced astrology (as did Tycho) and throughout his lifetime tried to contact an ancient but lost and secret wisdom.

In the course of his observations of the heavens, Kepler discovered the three basic laws of planetary motion. First, the orbits of the planets are elliptical, not circular as Aristotle and Ptolemy had assumed, and the sun is one focus of the **ellipse.** Unlike Tycho, Kepler accepted Copernicus's theory and provided proof for it. Kepler's second law demonstrated that the velocity of a planet is not uniform, as had been believed, but increases as its distance from the sun decreases. Kepler's third law—that the squares of the times taken by any two planets in their revolutions around the sun are in the same ratio as the cubes of their average distances from the sun—brought the planets into a unified mathematical system.

The significance of Kepler's work was immense. He gave sound mathematical proof to Copernicus's theory, eliminated forever the use of epicycles, which had saved the appearance of circular motion, and demonstrated that mathematical relationships can describe the planetary system. But Kepler left a significant question unresolved: what kept the planets in their orbits? Why did they not fly out into space or crash into the sun? The answer would be supplied by Isaac Newton, who synthesized the astronomy of Copernicus and Kepler with the new physics developed by Galileo.

Galileo: Experimental Physics

At the same time that Kepler was developing a new astronomy, his contemporary, Galileo Galilei (1564–1642), was breaking with the older physics of Aristotle. A citizen of Pisa by birth, Galileo lived for many years in Padua, where he conducted some of his first experiments on the motion of bodies. Guided by the dominant philosophy of the Italian Renaissance—the revived doctrines of Plato—Galileo believed that beyond the visible world lay certain universal truths, subject to mathematical verification. Galileo insisted that the study of motion entails not only the use of logic (as Aristotle had believed) but also the

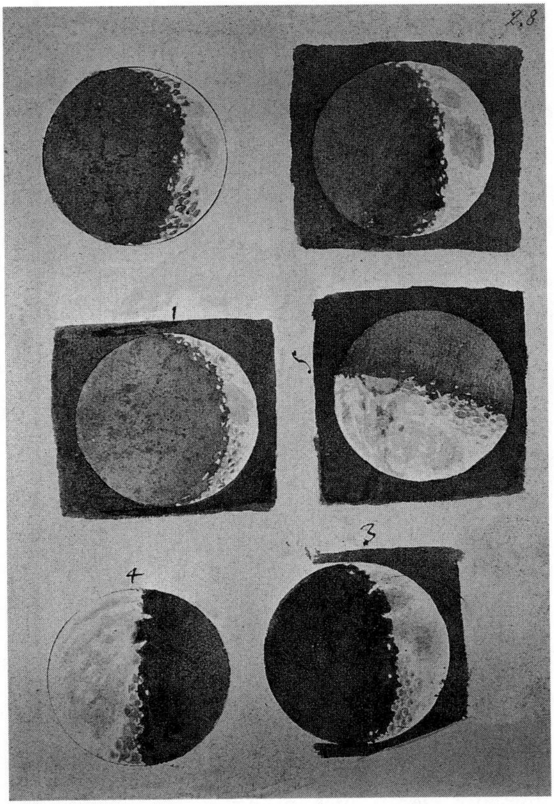

NOTEBOOK SKETCHES OF THE PHASES OF THE MOON BY GALILEO GALILEI, 1609–1610. Galileo saw only shadows when he looked into his telescope. But because he was trained as an artist in the principles of light and dark coloring to emphasize or shorten distance, he knew that what he saw represented real objects, in this case mountains and valleys. Somewhat satirically, he compared the moon to Bohemia. (*Biblioteca Nazionale Centrale, Florence.*)

application of mathematics. For this Late Renaissance natural philosopher, mathematics became the language of nature. Galileo also believed that only after experimenting with the operations of nature can the philosopher formulate harmonious laws and give them mathematical expression. Galileo was also trained in the practices of Renaissance art, in using shades to show depth and perspective. When he first looked at the moon through his telescope, that training became very important.

In his mechanical experiments, Galileo discovered that, all other things being equal, bodies of unequal weight will experience a uniform acceleration (due to gravity). He demonstrated that bodies fall with arithmetic regularity. Motion could, therefore, be treated mathematically.

Galileo established a fundamental principle of modern science: the order and uniformity of nature. There are no distinctions in rank or quality between the heavens and earth; heavenly bodies are not perfect and changeless as Aristotle had believed. In 1609, Galileo built a telescope through which he viewed the surface of the moon. The next year, in a treatise called *The Starry Messenger,* he proclaimed to the world that the moon "is not smooth, uniform, and precisely spherical as a great number of philosophers believe it and the other heavenly bodies to be, but is uneven, rough, and full of cavities . . . being not unlike the face of the earth, relieved by chains of mountains and deep valleys."[2] In addition, Galileo noticed spots on the sun, providing further evidence that heavenly objects, like earthly objects, undergo change. There are no higher and lower worlds; nature is the same throughout. When he saw shadows through his telescope, he assumed that actual bodies were casting them, just as they do on an earthly landscape. The art and science of his age were of a piece.

Through his telescope, Galileo also observed moons around Jupiter—a discovery that helped support the Copernican hypothesis. If Jupiter had moons, then all heavenly bodies did not orbit the earth. The moons of Jupiter removed a fundamental criticism of Copernicus and opened up the possibility that the earth, with its own moon, might be just like Jupiter and that both might in turn revolve around a central point—the sun.

With Galileo, the science of Copernicus and the assault on Aristotle entered a new phase. Scholastic priests began to attack Galileo from their pulpits in Florence. They saw a threat to their own power in Galileo's public notoriety and in his following among the laity. A secret group of priests and academics, named the Liga, formed with the express purpose of silencing Galileo; they used Aristotle and the Bible to attack him. But Galileo was also a courtier with friends in high places, so he dared to challenge the clergy and to offer his science directly to the laity. He argued publicly with the theologians. In the early seventeenth century, the Catholic church saw danger on every front: Protestants in Germany, Jews and Muslims in the East, and a laity demanding new schools that would provide practical education for their children. Now Galileo offered a view of the universe that conflicted with certain scriptural texts.

Historians used to believe that the church attacked Galileo solely because he was a Copernican, that is, because he believed the sun to be at the center of the universe. New evidence from the recently opened Vatican archives suggests that the church may also have worried about his theory of matter and his abandonment of the scholastics' view of the relationship between matter and form. That view went to the heart of the doctrine of the Eucharist, and the church saw, rightly, that the new science threatened the philosophical foundations of certain key doctrines.

In 1632, Galileo's teachings were condemned, and he was placed under house arrest. These actions cut short the open pursuit of science in many Catholic countries of the seventeenth century. Where the Inquisition was strong, the new science would be viewed as subversive. Censorship worked to stifle public intellectual inquiry. By the midcentury, science had become an increasingly Protestant and northern European phenomenon.

Online Study Center

Improve Your Grade

Primary Source: Galileo Discovers the Moons of Jupiter

The Newtonian Synthesis: Experiment, Mathematics, and Theory

By 1650, the works of Copernicus and especially of Galileo had dethroned the physics and astronomy of Aristotle and Ptolemy. A new philosophy of nature tied to observation and Neo-Platonism had come into existence; its essence lay in the mathematical expression of physical laws that describe matter in motion. Yet no single overriding law had been articulated that would bring together the experimental successes of the new science, its mathematical sophistication, and its philosophical revolution. This law was supplied by Isaac Newton.

Newton was born in 1642, in Lincolnshire, England, the son of a modest yeoman. Because of his intellectual promise, he obtained a place at Trinity College, Cambridge, and there he devoted himself to natural philosophy and mathematics. Newton's student notebooks survive and show him mastering philosophical texts while also trying to understand the fundamental truths of Protestant Christianity as taught at Cambridge. Combining Christian Neo-Platonism with a genius for mathematics, Newton produced a coherent synthesis of the science of Kepler and Galileo, which eventually captured the imagination of European intellectuals.

In 1666, Newton formulated the mathematics for the universal law of gravitation, and in the same year, after rigorous experimentation, he determined the nature of light. The sciences of physics and optics were transformed. However, for many years, Newton did not publish his discoveries, partly because even he did not grasp the immense significance of his work. Finally, another mathematician and friend, Edmund Halley, persuaded him to publish under the sponsorship of the Royal Society. The result was the *Principia Mathematica* of 1687. In 1704, Newton published his *Opticks* and revealed his theory that light was corpuscular or atomic in nature and that it emanated from luminous bodies in a way that scientists later described as waves.

Of the two books, both monumental achievements in the history of science, the *Principia* made the greater impact on contemporaries. Newton offered universal mathematical laws, as well as a philosophy of nature that sought to explain the essential structure of the universe: matter is always the same; it is atomic in structure, and in its essential nature it is dead or lifeless; and it is acted upon by immaterial forces that are placed in the universe by God. Newton said that the motion of matter could be explained by three laws: inertia, that a body remains in a state of rest or continues its motion in a straight line unless impelled to

Sir Isaac Newton (1642–1727). In 1666, Newton's mathematical formulation of the law of universal gravitation and his experiments in the nature of light opened a new stage in human understanding of the physical universe. The poet Alexander Pope expressed Newton's contemporaries' view of his achievements: "Nature, and Nature's Laws lay hid in Night. God said, 'Let Newton be!' and All was Light." (*The Granger Collection.*)

change by forces impressed on it; acceleration, that the change in the motion of a body is proportional to the force acting on it; and that for every action there is an equal and opposite reaction.

Newton argued that these laws apply not only to observable matter on earth but also to the motion of planets in their orbits. He showed that planets did not remain in their orbits because circular motion was "natural" or because crystalline spheres kept them in place. Rather, said Newton, planets keep to their orbits because every body in the universe exercises a force on every other body, a force that he called *universal gravitation.* Gravity is proportional to the product of the masses of two bodies and inversely proportional to the square of the distance between them. It is operative throughout the universe, whether on earth or in the heavens, and it is capable of mathematical expression. Newton built his theory on the work of other scientific giants, notably Kepler and Galileo. No one before him, however, had possessed the breadth of vision, mathematical skill, and dedication to rigorous observation to combine this knowledge into one grand synthesis.

The universe could now be described as matter in motion; it was governed by invisible forces that operated everywhere, both on earth and in the heavens, and these forces could be expressed mathematically. The medieval picture of the universe as closed, earthbound, and earth centered was replaced by a universe seen to be infinite and governed by universal laws. The earth was now regarded as simply another moving planet. Newtonian principles were taught by generations of

Newton's followers as, in effect, applied mechanics. A revolution in thought had changed Western ideas about nature forever.

But what was God's role in this new universe? Newton and his circle labored to create a mechanical world-view dependent on the will of God. At one time, Newton believed that gravity was simply the will of God operating on the universe. As he wrote in the *Opticks,* the physical order "can be the effect of nothing else than the wisdom and skill of a powerful ever-living agent."[3] Because of his strong religious convictions, Newton allowed his science to be used in the service of the established Anglican church, and his followers argued for social stability anchored in an ordered universe and an established church. Newton, a scientific genius, was also a deeply religious thinker committed to the maintenance of Protestantism in England. Among his contemporaries, however, were freethinkers who like John Toland (see "Skeptics, Freethinkers, and Deists" in Chapter 18) used his ideas to argue that nature can operate on its own, without the assistance of a providential God.

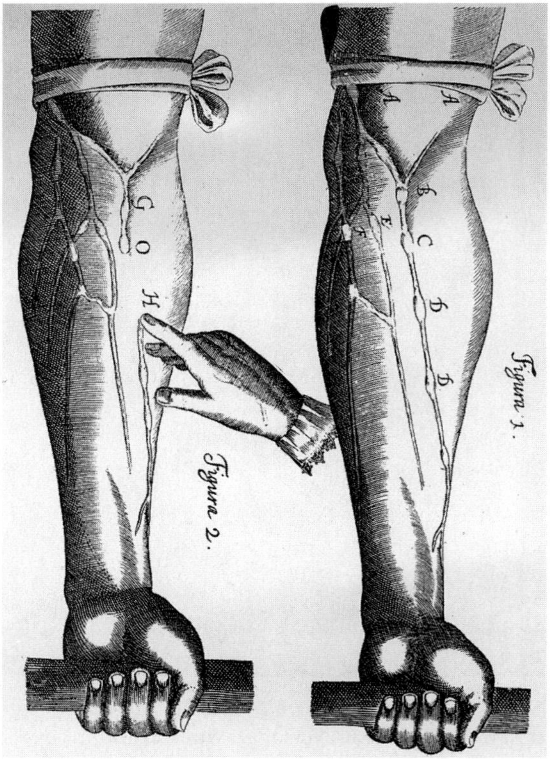

Science and Blood. For centuries it was believed that blood carried character traits as well as nobility. The English experimenter William Harvey viewed blood as simply a liquid that circulated in the body in a uniform way. Illustrations such as this one made the point graphically. (*Corbis.*)

Biology, Medicine, and Chemistry

The spectacular advances in physics and astronomy in the sixteenth and seventeenth centuries were not matched in the biological sciences. Indeed, the day-to-day practice of medicine throughout western Europe changed little in the period from 1600 to 1700, for much of medical practice relied, as it had since the Middle Ages, on astrology.

Doctors clung to the teachings of the ancient practitioners Galen and Hippocrates. In general, Galenic medicine paid little attention to the discovery of specific cures for particular diseases. As a follower of Aristotle, Galen emphasized the elements that make up the body; he called their manifestations *humors.* A person with an excess of blood was sanguine; a person with too much bile was choleric. Health consisted of a restoration of balances among these various elements, so Galenic doctors often prescribed purges of one sort or another. The most famous of these was bloodletting, but sweating was also a favorite remedy. Taught devotedly in the medical schools of Europe, these methods were often as dangerous as the diseases they sought to cure.

Despite the tenacity of Galenic medicine, sixteenth- and seventeenth-century innovators and reformers did try to challenge and overturn medical orthodoxy. With an almost missionary zeal, Paracelsus (1493–1541), a Swiss-German physician and Hermeticist, introduced the concept of diagnostic medicine. He argued that particular diseases can be differentiated and are related to chemical imbalances. His treatments relied on chemicals and not on bloodletting or the positions of the stars (although he did not discount such influences), and he proclaimed an almost ecstatic vision of human vitality and longevity. In most universities, the faculties of medicine bitterly opposed his views, but by 1650 in England and later in that century in France, Paracelsian ideas had many advocates. Support for Paracelsian medicine invariably accompanied an attack on the traditional medical establishment and its professional monopoly, and it often indicated support for the new science in general. The struggle between Galenists and Paracelsians quickly took on a social dimension; the innovators saw themselves pitted against a medical elite, which, in their opinion, had lost its commitment to medical research and existed solely to perpetuate itself. In the eighteenth century, Paracelsian ideas, stripped of their magical associations, became commonplace.

The medical reforms of the eighteenth century did not rest solely on the Paracelsian approach; they also relied heavily on the experimental breakthroughs made in the science of anatomy. A pioneer in this field was the Belgian surgeon Andreas Vesalius (1515–1564), who published *The Structure of the Human Body* in 1543. Opposing Galenic practice, Vesalius argued for observation and anatomical dissection as the keys to knowing how the human body works. By the late seventeenth century, doctors had learned a great deal about the human body, its structure, and its chemistry.

The study of anatomy yielded dramatic results. In 1628, William Harvey (1578–1657) announced that he had discovered the circulation of blood. Harvey compared the functioning of the heart to that of a mechanical pump, and once again the tendency to mechanize nature, so basic to the Scientific Revolution in physics, led to a significant discovery. Yet the acceptance of Harvey's work was very slow, and the practical uses of his discovery were not readily perceived.

The experimental method in medicine produced other innovations, among them systematic examination not only of corpses but also of patients. In the late 1600s, the finest doctor of the age, Herman Boerhaave, taught his students in Leiden, in the Netherlands, by taking them on house calls, arguing that nothing in medicine can be known without a careful and rigorous examination of the body. He proclaimed that he was trying to bring the methods and philosophy of the new science to medicine, and he pioneered hands-on medical techniques.

Just as Newton applied the theory and method of science to the heavens, his contemporaries on both sides of the English Channel sought to utilize science to illuminate every object we experience. Protestantism inspired them to be aggressive in their assault on scholasticism. Indeed, the most original experimenter of the age, who codified the experimental method as we know it, was a devout English Protestant. Robert Boyle (1627–1691) believed that Aristotle's physics and the philosophy that supported it promoted Catholic teachings and thus amounted to little more than magic. At a time when English Protestants feared a revival of Catholic and absolutist monarchy, Boyle wanted to abolish the invisible forces on which Catholic theology rested. He also wished to defeat the magic of what he called "the vulgar," that is, the beliefs of the populace, whose disorder and tendencies to rebellion he feared.

To accomplish these aims, Boyle urged scientists to adopt the zeal of the magicians, but without their secretive practices and their conjuring with spirits. As an alternative to spirits, Boyle advocated the atomic explanation of matter: that matter consists of small, hard, indestructible particles that behave with regularity. According to Boyle, the existence of these particles explained the changes in gases, fluids, and solids.

Boyle pioneered the experimental method with such exciting and accurate results that by the time of his death no serious scientist could attempt chemical experiments without following his guidelines. Thus, the science of chemistry acquired its characteristic experimentalism; it was also based on an atomic theory of matter. But not until late in the eighteenth century was this new discipline applied to medical research.

Bacon and Descartes: Prophets of the New Science

The new science needed prophets and social theorists to give it direction and to assess its implications. During the early modern period, two major reformers tried, in disparate ways, to channel science into the service of specific social programs:

Fontenelle, Portrait by Bernard Picart. Fontenelle understood the new science, but most important, he could make it understandable to those less learned than himself. He gave a eulogy on the death of Newton that was read throughout the century, and he also worked tirelessly for the French Academy of Sciences. *(The British Museum.)*

Francis Bacon (1561–1626) and René Descartes (1596–1650).

Bacon

The decidedly practical and empirical Francis Bacon stands as the most important English proponent of the new science, though not its most important practitioner. Bacon became profoundly suspicious of magic and the magical arts, not because they might not work but because he saw secrecy and arrogance as characteristic of their practitioners. Bacon was lord chancellor of England under James I, and he wrote about the usefulness of science partly in an effort to convince the crown of its advantages. He wanted science to serve the interests of strong monarchy.

Yet no philosopher of modern science has surpassed Bacon in elevating the study of nature to a humanistic discipline. In the *Advancement of Learning* (1605), Bacon argued that science must be open and all ideas must be allowed a hearing. Science must have human goals: the improvement of humanity's material condition and the advancement of trade and industry, but not the making of war or the taking of lives. Bacon also preached the need for science to possess an inductive methodology grounded in experience; the scientist should first of all be a collector of facts.

Although Bacon was rather vague about how the scientist as a theorist actually works, he knew that preconceived ideas imposed on nature seldom yield positive results. An opponent of Aristotle, Bacon argued that university education should move away from the ancient texts and toward the new learning. A powerful civil servant, he was not afraid to attack the guardians of tradition. The Baconian vision of progress in science leading to an improvement of the human condition and the security of the state inspired much scientific activity in the seventeenth century, particularly in England.

Descartes

René Descartes, a French philosopher of the first half of the seventeenth century, went to the best French schools and was trained by the Jesuits in mathematics and scholastic philosophy. Yet in his early twenties, he experienced a crisis of confidence. He felt that everything he had been taught was irrelevant and meaningless.

Descartes began to search within himself for what he could be sure was clear and distinct knowledge. All he could know with certainty was the fact of his existence, and even that he knew only because he experienced not his body but his mind: "I think, therefore I am." From this point of certitude, Descartes deduced God's existence.

Art of the Seventeenth and Eighteenth Centuries

1. Peter Paul Rubens. *The Betrothal of Saint Catherine,* sketch for a large altar painting, c. 1628. *(Staatliche Gemalde-Galerie, Berlin/Bridgeman Art Library.)*

The influence of political, economic, and social change permeates the visual arts of the seventeenth and eighteenth centuries. Perhaps most significant to the artists who made their living by providing paintings with religious themes for churches, as well as for private patrons, were the religious conflicts that split apart European society. Catholics and Protestants quarreled and openly fought over doctrine and dogma; as a result of the struggles, artists had to decide how best to please patrons whose religious sympathies may have changed or developed in new directions. Politically, the seventeenth and eighteenth centuries are also marked by the emergence of new sovereign states and by a change in the nature of artistic patronage.

Although a number of terms are used to describe the seventeenth and eighteenth centuries, the one most commonly applied by art historians is *baroque*. The word literally means irregularly shaped, whimsical, grotesque, or odd. Its origin is French, but it is generally agreed that the baroque style of art originated in Rome.

Baroque art is hard to explain within the context of the social and political changes that were sweeping over Europe. Some historians see it as illustrative of the Counter Reformation; others point out that the style was equally appealing to Catholics and Protestants. Nor

2. Giovanne Benedetto Castiglione. *Melancholia*, mid-seventeenth century. *(Philadelphia Museum of Art. Pennsylvania Academy Fine Arts Collection.)*

was baroque favored only by the absolute rulers of France or other monarchs; it was also a style of the bourgeois.

One of the most famous baroque painters was Peter Paul Rubens (1577–1640) of Flanders, which, prospering from its commercial connections, was home to many successful artists and patrons in this period. To study painting, Rubens traveled to Rome in 1600 and spent many years visiting other artistic centers in Italy. There he learned to paint on large-scale canvases and play with the size and weight of his subjects. Despite the influence of his southern contemporaries, however, his style remained essentially Flemish.

In his painting *The Betrothal of Saint Catherine* (Figure 1), we immediately sense the energy and fullness of the figures typical among Italian artists. But we also notice that Rubens's palette is much lighter than theirs, and consequently, the figures of Saint Catherine and the saints who surround her seem to move lightly as well.

Noteworthy, too, in this canvas is the depiction of the figures, whose hairstyles and mode of dress is contemporary rather than suggestive of biblical times. This juxtaposition of scenes from the Bible with the flavor of everyday life in the seventeenth century reveals much about the connection between the artist and his own surroundings.

The baroque style of highly finished, realistic works is very familiar to us. But we must also recall that baroque artists were skilled draftsmen. As an example, there is Giovanne Benedetto Castiglione's *Melancholia* (mid-seventeenth century) (Figure 2), a brush drawing in oil with added red chalk. Works on paper do not always survive as well as those on board or canvas. The drawings we do have attest to the artistic skill of seventeenth-century artists, who used line and shadow as well as did their Renaissance predecessors.

Melancholia is an allegory about the human dilemma of choosing among the worlds of art, religion, science, and learning. Symbols from each of these worlds—scientific tools, musical instruments, a globe, and the like—surround the figure of Genius, who sits in a contemplative pose.

Although by and large the artists of the baroque period were not well-rounded humanists like those of the Renaissance, some of them could work in two- and three-dimensional art forms. For example, Gian Lorenzo Bernini (1598–1680) distinguished himself as a sculptor as well as an architect.

Bernini was responsible for the sculptural program of Saint Peter's Basilica in the Vatican. He also completed sculptures in other Roman churches, including the Cornaro Chapel in the Church of Santa Maria della Vittoria. His *The Ecstasy of Saint Teresa* (1644–1647) (Figure 3) is a remarkable work that tells a dramatic story. The heart of Saint Teresa of Avila was said to have been pierced by an angel's golden arrow; the pain was exquisite, for not only was it the pain of death but also the pleasure of everlasting life in the arms of God. Bernini skillfully portrays the exact moment of Saint Teresa's ecstasy, in a theatrical setting using not only sculpture but also the architectural elements of the chapel.

3. Gian Lorenzo Bernini. *The Ecstasy of Saint Teresa,* 1644–1647. *(Church of Santa Maria della Vittoria, Rome/Scala/Art Resource, NY.)*

The saint and the angel are carved of white marble and seem to be floating on a cloud. The sculpted golden rays, which descend from a point above the figures, are bathed in light by a window hidden behind the frame that surrounds the two figures. Bernini decorated the entire chapel to follow the theme of Saint Teresa; ceiling frescoes show clouds of angels celebrating the event.

While Bernini was gaining fame in Italy, a French painter—one who spent almost his entire career in Rome—was winning an international reputation. Nicolas Poussin (1593/4–1665) relied strongly on the art of the classical and especially the Hellenistic periods for his inspiration. His *The Rape of the Sabine Women* (c. 1636–37) (Figure 4), a lavish and richly painted canvas, captures action like a carefully posed photograph. Indeed, if Bernini was theatrical in his portrayal of Saint Teresa, one could say that Poussin is cinematographic.

The story depicted in *The Rape of the Sabine Women* is derived from classical mythology; the poses of the figures hark back to the Hellenistic period. Compare the positioning of the arms of the women on the left of the canvas with the tortured stance of Laocoön, in the sculpture shown in Figure 4 of the first art

4. Nicolas Poussin. *The Rape of the Sabine Women,* c. 1636–37. *(Metropolitan Museum of Art, NY.)*

essay. Other groups in the Poussin canvas are also reminiscent of that sculpture. As another bow to the ancient past, Poussin paints in the background buildings that are faithful to Roman prototypes. Such reliance on archaeology and mythology are typical of his work.

While paintings depicting mythological, historical, or religious themes dominated the major art markets during the baroque era, patrons in Holland sought paintings that related more to their own experience. For that reason, the genre of the still life—paintings of flowers, fruit, dishes, food, and other familiar objects—reached its zenith in that country.

Willem Kalf (1622–1693), among the most skilled of Dutch still-life masters, was able to take a collection of objects and turn it into an object of art. His *Still Life* (Figure 5) showcases his meticulous, almost photo-realistic style. In particular, it focuses on the way in which glass reflects light and on the juxtaposition of different textures. Although modern art historians view some still lifes as merely ornamental displays of technical skill, there was a reason for them. The popularity of still lifes, and of landscapes, probably has to do with the human desire for reassurance that "things are as they should be," that the status quo is being maintained, regardless of the religious or political turmoil affecting other aspects of life. No matter what was going on politically, no matter what religious dispute was being negotiated, people could find a degree of comfort in being surrounded by familiar objects or scenes.

While Kalf distinguished himself as a still-life painter, another Dutch master, Rembrandt van Rijn (1606–1669) gained fame for his historical and religious canvases. Rembrandt was influenced in his early years by Italian painters, especially by their use of light. But that was not his only strength. His reputation as a portrait painter brought him renown and fortune in Amsterdam.

Even more impressive were his self-portraits, which he painted not for the commissions of patrons but entirely for himself in the pursuit of truth. For an artist to paint as many self-portaits as Rembrandt did in the seventeenth century was very unusual. Self-portraits are analogous to autobiographies: in both, the artist examines himself because he believes his own self is worthy of self-examination.

Rembrandt's quest for the meaning of the inner life is compatible with the growing introspectiveness of the seventeenth century, an age that also produced Descartes's dictum that to think is to be, the soliloquies of Shakespeare's Hamlet, and the hallucinations of Cervantes' Don Quixote.

Rembrandt produced a series of sixty-two self-portraits during the course of his lifetime, an exhaustive autobiography in pictures in which he seemed to engage in a dialogue with himself in a variety of atttitudes and poses: vigorous, youthful, heroic, flamboyant, melodramatic, enigmatic, aging, distraught, struggling with despair, grimly resolved, disdainful, strong, weak. Rembrandt completed *Self-Portrait at Old Age,* 1669 (Figure 6), the fifty-fifth in a corpus of sixty-two self-portraits, in the last year of his life. It is among a cluster of self-portraits in which he appears to have "pulled himself together" and defined his identity. In it, we find Rembrandt staring back at us with the calm assurance of a man who has mastered his art and life, and surpassed his time and place.

The later part of the eighteenth century marks the beginning of the rococo and neoclassical periods in art history. Especially popular in France, the rococo and neoclassical movements owed much to political and social forces. The term *rococo* describes a style that is frothy and frivolous and compatible with the peripheral concerns of royalty. In 1698, King Louis XIV ordered the redecoration of his palace at Versailles with works that were lighthearted and youthful instead of stodgy and serious. His dabbling with artistic matters led to quarrels and esthetic disagreements in the artistic community.

5. Willem Kalf. *Still Life,* c. 1660. *(Hermitage, St. Petersburg/Scala/Art Resource, NY.)*

An example of the rococo is François Boucher's (1703–1770) *The Toilet of Venus* (1751) (Figure 7). Although some art historians describe his work as slick and artificial, Boucher became the darling of the French court. In his *The Toilet of Venus*, the goddess is full figured and lush, surrounded by all the sensual accouterments that the goddess of love and erotic pleasure should have. Given her appearance and her surroundings, Boucher's Venus looks as though she would have been comfortable in period dress, supervising the decor of her boudoir at the palace at Versailles. Clearly, Boucher understood his audience well.

While Boucher exemplified the light and airy sentiment of the rococo, Jacques Louis David (1748–1825) typified the neoclassical.

6. Rembrandt van Rijn. *Self Portrait at Old Age*, 1669. *(Erich Lessing/National Gallery, London/Årt Resource, NY.)*

The neoclassical style represents a return to the rationality and harmony of the classical past; many of the works from this period also reflect contemporary political events.

Justice, honor for one's country, and the need to portray inspirational themes were the guideposts of the neoclassical artists. Their training ground was Italy, primarily because it was the source of the classical prototypes from which they could learn. Jacques Louis David's *The Death of Marat* (1793) (Figure 8) captures the essence of that event in a manner that combines the best of Poussin and Rubens.

The subject matter is important because it illuminates the neoclassical concept of virtue, represented by the martyrdom of Marat, a revolutionary. The style borrows from Poussin's ability to capture a scene with photographic stillness, rendering the figures in an almost sculptural way. But David has also appropriated Rembrandt's technique of skillfully juxtaposing light and shadow. While the neoclassicists sometimes paid homage to their distant past in subject matter, they also showed their reverence for the revolutionary ideals of their own time.

7. François Boucher. *The Toilet of Venus*, 1751. *(Metropolitan Museum of Art, NY.)*

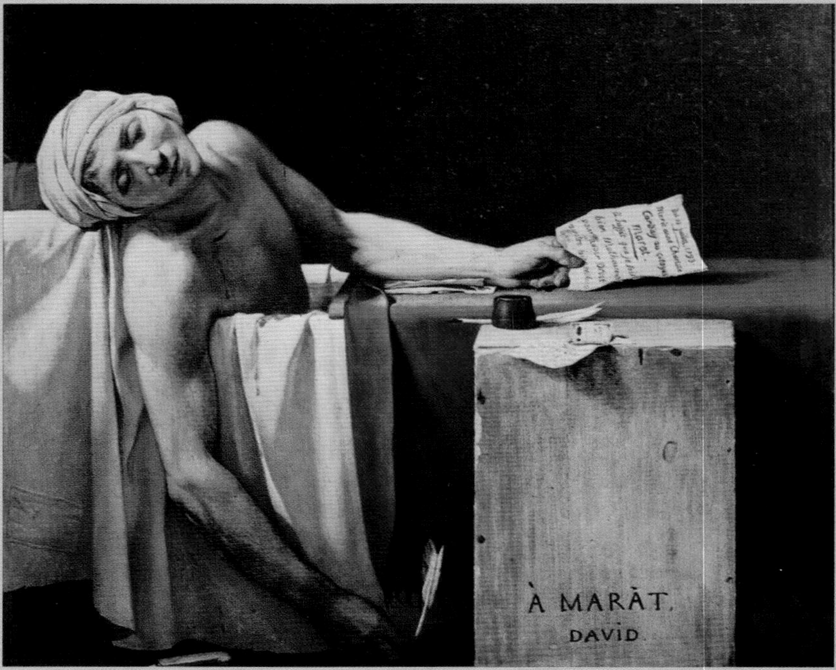

8. Jacques Louis David. *The Death of Marat,* 1793. *(Royal Museum of Fine Arts, Brussels/Giraudon/Art Resource, NY.)*

LA VÉRITÉ, BY BERNARD PICART. In the early eighteenth century, French critics of the existing order in church and state used Descartes as a symbol. Here he is pointing to the slaying of error and ignorance by truth. The engraver who created this picture was eventually forced to flee France and settle in the Dutch Republic. (*The Teylers Museum, Haarlem, The Netherlands.*)

God exists because Descartes had in his mind an idea of a supreme, perfect being, and, Descartes reasoned, this idea could have been put there only by such a being, not by any ordinary mortal. Therefore, God's existence means that the physical world must be real, for no Creator would play such a cruel trick and invent a vast hoax.

For Descartes, the new science meant confidence: in his own mind, in the knowability of the physical world, and in mathematics and reason. Scientific thought meant an alternative to everything he associated with the medieval: confusion, disorder, conflict between church and state, fear of the unknown, and magic. Turning his back on the centuries immediately preceding his own, Descartes, possibly as a result of knowing Bacon's ideas for practical science, proclaimed that "it is possible to attain knowledge which is very useful in life, and that, instead of that speculative philosophy which is taught in the schools [that is, scholasticism], we may find a practical philosophy by means of which . . . we can . . . render ourselves the masters and possessors of nature."[4] Descartes was the first person to dream about the capacity of science to control and dominate nature, though he could not imagine its potential to destroy nature.

Online Study Center

Improve Your Grade

Primary Source: Descartes' Discourse on Method Offers a New Method of Reasoning

In order to affirm the existence of anything other than the abstractions of mathematics, Descartes had to proclaim the existence of God and the Universe, largely because both were ideas in his mind. He radically separated matter from spirit, mind from nature, and in the process he widened a gap in Western thought that would haunt philosophers for centuries. What if a thinker who understood the implications of Descartes's separation of matter from spirit was to argue that only matter existed? The thinker who did so was Benedict de Spinoza (1632–1677). Born in Amsterdam of recently immigrated Jewish parents, he was trained in classical languages and Hebrew thought.

His genius drew him to the new science, and he became an early explicator of Descartes's philosophy, in which he spied a central weakness: its inability to explain the linkage between matter and spirit or to connect God to nature in any meaningful way. Spinoza's solution was radical, logical, and thoroughly heretical to Christian thinkers: he argued that God is Nature, that matter and spirit in effect are one.

To this day, philosophers dispute Spinoza's purpose. Was he an atheist who wanted to do away with the Judeo-Christian conception of God, or was he a mystic who wished to infuse God into Nature? His contemporaries of every religious persuasion (he was expelled from his Amsterdam synagogue) deemed him an atheist and thought that he had become one by reading too much science. Their condemnation made "spinozism" a byword for atheism and freethinking. In the Enlightenment, freethinkers and materialists would claim to have been inspired by Spinoza.

The thoughts and visions of Bacon and Descartes revealed the power and importance of scientific knowledge. Science could promote human well-being, as Bacon insisted; it could make human beings and nature the foundation of all meaningful knowledge, as Descartes assumed; it could express pantheism, as Spinoza showed; or it could justify a belief in Nature as God, as it did for Spinoza. Whichever position educated westerners embraced by the late 1600s, science would be used to challenge the traditional authority of the clergy, whether Catholic or fundamentalist Protestant. Why believe in dogmas and texts when nature offered another kind of truth—universal and, just as important, applicable to human problems? For good or ill, the Scientific Revolution gave its followers a sense of power and self-confidence unimagined even by Renaissance proponents of individualism or by the theorists of absolute state power.

Social Implications of the Scientific Revolution

Perhaps the critical factor in causing the historical phenomenon called the Scientific Revolution was the acceptance and use of the new science by educated elites. Without such acceptance, the science of Galileo, Kepler, Descartes, Boyle, and Newton would have remained the specialized knowledge of the few—or, worse still, a suspect, even heretical, approach to nature. Galileo could not have succeeded as much as he did in disseminating his theories (despite the hostility of the church) without his large European following and his many aristocratic patrons, particularly in Florence.

Access to the printing press in Europe was also critical to the acceptance of the new mechanical understanding of nature. Descartes understood that fact when he left France, after the condemnation of Galileo, and published and lived in the Netherlands. Persecution and censorship meant that the new science made far less of an impact in Catholic than in Protestant Europe.

Equally important, the new science offered the dream of power to both governments and early promoters of industry. In the seventeenth century, this dream enticed monarchs and statesmen to give their patronage to scientific academies and projects. The achievements of the new science were quickly institutionalized in academies dominated either by the state, as in France, or by the landed and commercial elite, as in England. Founded in the 1660s, scientific academies such as the Royal Society in England became centers for the dissemination of science at a time when many universities, still controlled by the clergy, were hostile to its attack on scholasticism.

The new mechanical learning—not widely communicated by Newton's *Principia,* which was far too technical for most people, but rather passed on as mechanical information in handbooks and lectures—began to be applied in Britain and Scotland during the second half of the eighteenth century. The applied mechanics that improved the steam engine and utilized it in coal mining and water engineering stemmed from Newtonian lectures and books, which proliferated in Britain during the 1700s. The road from the Scientific Revolution leads more directly to the Industrial Revolution than is often realized. James Watt, who perfected the steam engine, had been tutored in Newtonian mechanics. His engine revolutionized the manufacturing of cotton.

In the same period, the scientific gentleman and woman, like the French chemist Lavoisier and his wife, Marie Anne, became fashionable icons. Elite and mildly prosperous families brought microscopes and globes into their homes. Owning these objects caused the family's status to rise, even if no one in the family became an engineer or doctor. Science had captured the Western imagination.

The Meaning of the Scientific Revolution

The Scientific Revolution was decisive in shaping the modern mentality; it shattered the medieval view of the universe and replaced it with a wholly different world-view. Gone was the belief that a motionless earth lay at the center of a universe that was finite and enclosed by a ring of stars. Gone, too, was the belief that the universe was divided into higher and lower worlds and that different laws of motion operated in the heavens and on earth. Nature could be mastered conceptually and mathematically.

The methodology that produced this view of nature—the new science—played a crucial historical role in reorienting Western thought from medieval theology and metaphysics to the study of physical and human problems. In the Late Middle Ages, most men of learning were Aristotelians and theologians. By the mid-eighteenth century, knowledge of Newtonian science and the dissemination of useful learning had become the goal of the educated classes. All knowledge, it was believed, could emulate scientific knowledge: it could be based on observation, experimentation, or rational deduction; and it could be systematic, verifiable, progressive, and useful. This new approach to learning used the scientists of the sixteenth and seventeenth centuries as proof that no institution or dogma had a monopoly on truth; the scientific approach would yield knowledge that might, if properly applied for the good of all people, produce a new and better age. Such an outlook gave thinkers new confidence in the power of the human mind to master nature and led them to examine European institutions and traditions with an inquiring, critical, and skeptical spirit. Scientific societies and academies sprang up all over Europe. In the Dutch Republic in 1785, a society was also founded by women interested in receiving a scientific education. Most

James Watt (1736–1819). An engraved portrait of James Watt rendered in his successful years. His somewhat grim affect is consonant with the depression he often described in his letters. (*The Granger Collection.*)

scientific academies, however, excluded women into the twentieth century.

The Scientific Revolution ultimately weakened traditional Christianity. God's role in a mechanical universe was not clear. Newton had argued that God not only set the universe in motion but still intervened in its operations, thus leaving room for miracles. Others retained a place for God as Creator but regarded miracles as limitations on nature's mechanical perfection. Applied to religious doctrines, Descartes's reliance on methodical doubt and clarity of thought and Bacon's insistence on careful observation led thinkers to question the validity of Christian teachings. Theology became a separate and somewhat irrelevant area of intellectual inquiry, not fit for the interests of practical, well-informed people. Not only Christian doctrines but also various popular beliefs grew suspect. Magic, witchcraft, and astrol-

Profile

Sir Isaac Newton (1642–1727)

Today we know so much more about Sir Isaac Newton, about his beliefs and life, than did his contemporaries. Newton was very private, even secretive. He wanted to appear to the world solely as a natural philosopher interested in local motion and the motions of the heavenly bodies. He said sternly, "I do not frame hypotheses," when asked to explain what universal gravitation actually is. In his heart he believed it to be the will of God operating in the universe. This deeply religious man devoted as many hours of his workweek to theology and biblical prophecy as he did to experiments. Perhaps most surprising of all his labors are his alchemical pursuits. Like the magicians of old, he wanted to understand the secret workings of chemical action, and he believed that some day the truly pious natural philosopher would be able to transform ordinary metals into gold. Evidence of the private Newton sits amid his vast manuscript collections, which are now dispersed all over the world. At Imperial College, London, the Newton project has succeeded in putting many of these manuscripts online so that everyone can read them. Go to http://www.newtonproject.ic.ac.uk/.

(Art Resource, NY.)

ogy, still widespread among the European masses, were regarded with disdain by elite culture. The masses of people remained devoted to some form of traditional Christianity, and the uncertainty of a universe governed by devils, witches, or the stars continued to make sense to peasants and laborers.

In Catholic countries, where the Scientific Revolution began, hostility toward scientific ideas gathered strength in the early 1600s. The mentality of the Counter Reformation enabled lesser minds to exercise their fears and arrogance against any idea they regarded as suspicious. Galileo was caught in this hostile environment, and the Copernican system was condemned by the church in 1616. In Spain and Poland, it was not officially taught until the 1770s.

Gradually, the science of Newton became the science of western Europe: nature mechanized, analyzed, regulated, and mathematized. As a result of the Scientific Revolution, learned westerners came to believe more strongly than ever that nature could be mastered. Mechanical science—applied to canals, engines, pumps, and levers—became the science of industry. Thus, the Scientific Revolution, operating on both intellectual and commercial levels, laid the groundwork for two major developments of the modern West: the Age of Enlightenment and the Industrial Revolution.

❖ ❖ ❖

Online Study Center ACE the Test

Notes

1. Quoted in Jean D. Moss, *Novelties in the Heavens* (Chicago: University of Chicago Press, 1993), p. 33.
2. Excerpted in *Discoveries and Opinions of Galileo,* ed. Stillman Drake (Garden City, N.Y.: Doubleday, 1957), p. 28.
3. Excerpted in *Newton's Philosophy of Nature,* ed. H. S. Thayer (New York: Hafner, 1953), p. 177.
4. Excerpted in *Descartes' Philosophical Writings,* ed. Norman Kemp Smith (New York: Modern Library, 1958), pp. 130–131.

Suggested Reading

Appleby, J., L. Hunt, and M. Jacob, *Telling the Truth About History* (1994). Discusses the issues raised by the heroic model of science that came out of the Scientific Revolution and relates the issues to today's attitudes toward science.

Burns, Williams E., *Science in the Enlightenment: An Encyclopedia* (2003). An excellent source of information.

Gleick, James, *Isaac Newton* (2004). A great read.

Hellyer, Marcus, ed., *The Scientific Revolution: The Essential Readings* (2003).

Jacob, Margaret C., and Larry Stewart, *Practical Matter. Newton's Science in the Service of Industry and Empire* (2004).

Index

Glossary

Absolutism A form of government in which a single ruler and his court possess total and centralized power in the state.

Alliance system The complex web of alliances started in the late nineteenth century by Bismarck's Germany.

Anarchism The radical theory that all forms of government are oppressive and should be abolished. Anarchists denounced capitalist exploitation of workers and envisioned a new social order of individual freedom.

Anathema A person or thing loathed and detested; derived from the religious practice of damning, cursing or excommunicating.

Anomie Purposelessness and social instability as a result of lack of standards or values.

Anticlericalism Opposition to priestly influence in government, education, society, and ownership of land and property. It is most common in countries with a strong Catholic church and exercises an influence on politics in those countries.

Anti-Semitism Extreme fear and hatred of Jews and Judaism based essentially on irrational myths.

A priori A way of thinking that relies entirely on the mind's inherent capacities—as in mathematics—and not on sense experience.

Arêté The pursuit of arête, or excellence, was a crucial feature of the ancient Greek outlook.

Authoritarian A government in which authority is centered in a single person or a small group (elite) not constitutionally accountable to the people. Also the political attitude stemming from mistrust of the people or constitutions that favor such a government.

Autocracy The rule of a single head, usually king or emperor.

Bicameral legislature A law-making body that is divided into two parts or two "houses" with different responsibilities.

Blasphemy Scandalous words or actions that are demeaning and hostile to what is considered holy and sacrosanct.

Blitzkrieg Literally "lightning war"; the use of tanks and aircraft to strike swiftly and decisively.

Bolshevik A member of the Marxist revolutionary party that seized power in Russia in 1917.

Bourgeoisie Urban middle class citizens; in Marxist terms, those who own or control the instruments of production.

The Calculus A mathematical system of notation that allows us to depict bodies in motion.

Canon law The officially established rules governing the faith and practice of a Christian church; based on the Roman legal tradition.

Capitalism An economic system in which trade and industry are controlled by private owners or corporations.

Capitalist A person who invests in business enterprise; one who advocates an economy or political system in which investment in and ownership of production, distribution, and exchange of wealth is in the hands of private individuals or corporations.

Cereals production The growing of grain.

Chartist movement Political movement in the 1830s in England that culminated in 1848 with the presentation of a gigantic petition signed by hundreds of thousands of workers and middle class reformers to the Parliament asking for reforms including universal manhood suffrage, the secret ballot, and the abolition of property requirements for members of Parliament.

Chiliasm The religious doctrine that Jesus will reign on earth for 1000 years. Now used to describe a long-term vision of the future.

Citizenship A person, eligible by birth or nationality, for full rights, privileges, responsibilities in a country.

Civil disobedience The political tactic of a group or movement that refuses to obey or comply with laws that are thought to be discriminatory and immoral.

Civilization The intellectual, material, and cultural development of organized human society. The first civilizations are defined by cities, writing, monumental architecture, organized religion, and organized government.

Class The division of society into social strata according to economic or cultural characteristics.

Classical Referring to the culture of ancient Greece and Rome (500 B.C.– 500 A.D.)

Classicism The ancient Greco-Roman intellectual and cultural tradition that valued reason as the avenue to knowledge of nature, ethics, and the human community and aspired to the full development of human talent.

Colonialism The policy of a nation or state that tries to extend its power or authority over other peoples or territories.

Commercial monopoly A situation in which one trader or nation corners the market on a commodity.

Communism 1. An authoritarian system of government with state control of the economy. 2. A doctrine that advocates the overthrow of capitalism by revolution and the establishment of a communist government.

Conscription A general term for involuntary labor but generally in modern times means the requirement by the state that citizens serve in the armed forces.

Conservatism A political and social theory that values traditional institutions and standards.

Constitution The fundamental laws, either written or unwritten, of a political body or state.

Corpuscular The term used often in the seventeenth century to describe what we would call the atom.

Cosmopolitanism Open to influences and interests from all over the world.

Decolonization The process of moving to independence by a colony and the process of granting independence to a colony by the colonial state.

Deist Someone who believes in God but considers him irrelevant to the human situation.

Democracy Government by the population, either directly or through elected representatives.

Demonize The representation of a person, or group of people, as evil or as demons.

Despotism A government with the power to curtail individual liberty and to make and enforce the law without the approval of an elected legislature.

Dialectical conflict A means of arriving at the truth by stating a thesis (or argument), opposing it with a contradictory antithesis, and combining the two arguments into a coherent synthesis.

Dialectics A means of arriving at truth by the exchange of logical arguments.

Diaspora Jews who lived outside Palestine.

Diké Ancient Greek term for the principle of justice that underlies human society, formulated by Solon in 596 B.C.

Diplomatic crisis A conflict over foreign policy between governments.

Dollar Diplomacy The practice of using economic power to "buy" friends and allies in other states.

Dutch Republic What is today the Netherlands.

Dynastic state Traditional leadership of a state by a succession of rulers from the same family.

Ego In psychoanalysis, the conscious part of the psyche that controls thoughts and behavior and is most in touch with the outside world.

Ellipse The oval shape of a planet's orbit.

Empire A large area, usually encompassing different peoples, ruled by a single supreme authority, usually an emperor.

Empiricism The view that knowledge is derived from sense experience.

Ennobled Made noble or aristocratic.

Epic A long poem or other literary narrative celebrating heroic deeds and national glory.

Esprit de Corps Literally "spirit of the group." Comradeship and devotion to a cause that unites members of a group.

Estates The three orders into which French society was divided before the revolution. The First Estate consisted of the clergy, the Second Estate of the nobility, and the Third Estate of the rest of the population.

Ethics 1. Principles of human conduct governed by moral values. 2. Making intelligent moral decisions when confronted with problems.

Ethnic cleansing An attempt to make an area ethnically pure by killing or driving out people of a different nationality or religion.

Eucharist The doctrine essential to Catholicism that the bread and wine are miraculously transformed by the priest into the body and blood of Christ.

European Union (EU) The economic and political integration of 25 European countries for trade and mutual cooperation.

Evolution Darwin's theory, based on empirical evidence, which explained how a wide variety of species emerged over many millennia. The theory holds that human beings have emerged from earlier, lower, nonhuman forms of life. (See natural selection.)

Existentialism A philosophy popular after World War II that emphasized the importance of choosing one's way in a universe devoid of absolutes and indifferent to our existence.

Exodus To leave or immigrate.

Extraterritoriality The right of aliens to be tried according to the laws of their own nation or state rather than by the laws of the state or colony in which they reside or do business.

Fanaticism Extreme, unreasoning belief in something, usually a religion or ideology, that often incites violence against nonbelievers.

Fascism Term used to define antidemocratic, anticommunist, and highly nationalistic and militaristic movements that arose in European countries after World War I.

Feminism A movement against the subordination of women; it aims to achieve the same rights, opportunities, and treatment as men.

Fundamentalism A movement characterized by the strict maintenance of traditional orthodox religious beliefs and principles.

Genocide The planned and systematic extermination of an entire national, racial, or ethnic group.

Gentleman's agreement An informal agreement between individuals or states to do something or recognize something that might not be acceptable in law.

Globalization The spread of western ideals, free-market capitalism, trade, and technology throughout the world.

God-King A king who is believed to be an all-powerful, living god.

The Godly Those who are deemed to be true Christians and therefore destined, or at least the likeliest, to be saved.

Gothic The style of architecture, painting and sculpture in the twelfth through the fifteenth century. Gothic architecture is characterized by lofty vaulted ceilings, large windows and high pointed arches.

Grace The love and protection given to people by God.

Greco-Roman Age The period when the Roman Empire ruled the Mediterranean world and absorbed Greek civilization into its laws, institutions, thought, and art, 30 B.C. to ca. 500 A.D.

Guerrilla A member of a band of soldiers (not in a regular army of a state) who are fighting against a government or a colonial ruler.

Gunboat Diplomacy The name given to the practice of sending ships to intimidate another government.

Hellenic Age Ancient Greek civilization 800 B.C.–323 B.C.

Hellenistic Age The era succeeding Hellenic civilization 323 B.C.–30 B.C., when Greek culture spread through the Near East and was thereby changed.

Hellenization The spread and adoption of Greek language and civilization in the ancient world.

Heresy What is deemed by the authorities to be false religious belief, and therefore those who hold heretical views may be subject to punishment and persecution.

Heterodox Referring to beliefs that are not generally accepted and may be frowned upon or persecuted.

Hierarchy The order of elements (e.g. people) into higher or lower ranks or grades.

Holocaust The systematic extermination of European Jews by Nazi Germany during World War II.

Holy Roman Empire A collection of German speaking states, run by princes, and corresponding roughly with what is today Germany and Austria.

Hubris Excessive pride or arrogance, behavior that for the ancient Greeks produced ruin.

Humanism An approach to life that focuses on the value and worth of human beings and aspires to the maximum cultivation of human talents.

Id The subconscious part of the psyche that is impulsive, instinctual, irrational, and demands satisfaction of primitive needs. Denial of satisfaction results in frustration, anger and unhappiness.

Idealism A school of philosophy that holds that the outer world is not something objective that exists independently of individual consciousness. Rather, the human mind, the knowing subject, determines the form of the outer world.

Idol An image of a god used as an object of worship. A false god.

Incarnation Christian doctrine that Jesus was conceived and born as the Son or God, and is therefore both God and man.

Indigo The plant from which blue dye could be extracted. Indigo was a prized commodity inviting colonial domination in parts of Latin and Central America.

Indirect rule Imperial domination was often exerted indirectly, meaning the local elites and local armies controlled the people in ways that the imperial power wanted.

Individualism Self-reliance and independence in thought and action.

The Inquisition A church-controlled institution that sought to combat heresy and was particularly powerful in Spain and Italy.

Irrational A way of thinking and behaving not derived from reasoning but from impulses, feelings, instincts, and other forces below the level of consciousness.

Islamic radicalism Committed to a fundamentalist vision of Islam, some Muslims seek to create a theocratic state based on a strict interpretation of the Koran. Islamic radicals or jihadists see themselves engaged in a holy war against Western civilization in which terrorism is a legitimate weapon.

Isonomy Ancient Greek term meaning the equality of political rights for citizens of the polis.

Jesuits The "shock troops" of the Catholic Reformation who labored after 1534 to return Europe to the Catholic Church.

Jihad A Muslim holy war against nonbelievers

Judgment Day The day at the end of the world when, according to Christian belief, God will judge all mankind, sending the saved to heaven and the damned to hell.

Kulturkampf The struggle for culture in newly unified Germany (1871) was a campaign by Bismarck for the restriction of the power of the Catholic Church.

Laissez faire An economic theory held by nineteenth century liberals that economic competition should be free from government regulation and allowed to operate according to the laws of supply and demand.

Latifundia Large plantations in the Roman Empire.

Latin Christendom The Christian world in western and central Europe where western civilization developed after the fall of Rome, from 500 A.D. onwards

Lay Piety The religious beliefs and worship of ordinary believers as distinct from the clergy.

Lay preaching The giving of sermons by those who are lay people or laity rather than by ordained members of the clergy.

Lebensraum The German term for "living space." German nationalists deemed the acquisition of certain territories beyond its current borders necessary for the nation's well being.

Lent In the Christian religion, an annual season of fasting that lasts forty days to Easter.

Liberalism A political and social theory founded on individual freedom, equality under the law, and the safeguarding of basic rights from the power of government.

Logic A system of argument based on valid reason and consistent principles.

Logos For Greek philosophers, the fundamental order governing the universe; implanted in every human soul, it enables the individual to live in accordance with natural law. To Christians it means the creative word of God that became a human being in Jesus.

Manumission Granting freedom to a slave.

Maritime Referring to any ventures undertaken at sea; seafaring.

Martyrdom Accepting death or great suffering to demonstrate devotion to one's religion.

Marxism The political and economic theory of Karl Marx based on class conflict between the exploited working class and the capitalist ruling class that owned the means of production and wielded political power. Inevitable revolution would destroy capitalism, and a classless socialist society would emerge.

Mass production Large-scale manufacturing in which labor is specialized.

Mechanical conception of nature All motion occurs in the world because of contact action between bodies, their push and pull.

Mechanism The belief that the universe is analogous to a machine, all of whose parts operate with mathematical precision.

Mechanization Replacement of human labor with machine labor and power technology.

Messiah The anticipated savior and king of the Jewish people, whose coming was prophesied in the Old Testament. Christians believe Jesus Christ to have been the Messiah.

Messianic Age Hopes of ancient Hebrews for an era of peace and justice inaugurated by the Messiah.

Metaphysics The branch of philosophy that attempts to define ultimate reality, or Being.

Militarism The principle or policy of maintaining a strong armed force. Also the glorification of war as heroic and noble.

Millenarian thinking The widespread belief in early modern Europe that the world would end as foretold in the Bible, Christ would return, judge the saved and the wicked, and institute a 1000 year reign of peace.

Modern Referring to historical developments in the West since the fifteenth and sixteenth centuries, the time of the Renaissance.

Modern state The liberal, secular, democratic organization of a state in which citizens have liberty and equality under the law.

Modernism The movement starting in the late nineteenth century that departed from traditional artistic and literary in favor of innovative forms of expression.

Monasticism A secluded religious life of discipline and prayer practiced in a monastery.

Monotheism Belief that there is only one supreme god.

Monroe Doctrine A foreign policy of the United States since 1824 that declares that the United States will not tolerate the establishment or re-establishment of colonies by the European powers in the western hemisphere.

Mosaic law The ancient law of the Hebrews attributed to Moses.

Mystic A person who seeks transcendent union with God through spiritual discipline and surrender of self.

Myth A traditional story that seeks to explain the origins of the world and the actions of supernatural powers.

Mythopoeic thought The creation of imagery and stories that make sense of the world by endowing every object in nature with life or supernatural qualities.

Nationalism A conscious bond shared by a group of people who feel strongly attached to a particular land and who possess a common language, culture, and history, marked by shared glories and sufferings.

Natural law A law derived from nature and implanted in human beings so that they will do what is right and avoid what is wrong, especially in human relations.

Natural philosophy A more accurate term to describe investigation into nature during the Scientific Revolution, gradually replaced by what we call "science."

Natural rights Also called human rights. Basic rights and freedoms to which all people are entitled, including life, liberty, freedom of thought and speech, and legal equality.

Natural selection Darwin's theory which states that organisms more favored by nature than others of its species will have a better chance of survival and passing on their superior traits to their offspring. Over millennia, natural selection causes the death of old species that cannot adjust to the environment and the creation of new species, for genetic changes within a segment of a species can so differentiate its members from the rest of the species that interbreeding is no longer possible. (See evolution.)

Naturalism A literary movement that believed that human character is conditioned by the social environment.

Nazism Ideology of the German Nazi Party under Hitler. Its core principles were racial nationalism, glorification of war, German expansion, anti-Semitism, and idolization of the leader.

Neolithic Age The new Stone Age, beginning around 10,000 years ago with the development of agriculture.

Neo-Platonists The Renaissance followers of Plato who revived his philosophy and whose teachings influenced Kepler and Newton.

New science The term describes the understanding of nature put in place by Copernicus, Galileo, Descartes and Newton, among others.

Nihilism A form of extreme skepticism that rejects all traditional moral and social values and denies the validity of religious beliefs, and traditional truths.

Occupation Military control of territory, nation, or state.

Oikumene The inhabited world, united in a world community.

Old Christians Spaniards who claimed pure Christian ancestry without any intermarriage with Jews or Muslims.

Old Regime The structure of French society before the Revolution, based on clerical and aristocratic privileges under a despotic monarchy.

Oligarchy Rule by the few, a political elite.

Open Door policy The idea that anyone and any state or nation should be allowed to trade without restriction—specifically an American policy toward China at a time that China was being divided by imperialist powers.

Orthodox Referring to beliefs and practices, usually religious, which are generally accepted, taught, and even enforced.

Ostracism Banishment or exclusion from society of a person regarded as dangerous.

Overman For Nietzsche, the exceptional man who aspires to self-mastery; without fear or guilt, he creates his own values and defines his own self, his own life.

Paleolithic Age The Old Stone Age that began with the earliest chipped stone tools made by hunters and gatherers.

Pantheism The belief that nature is the same as God; that the creator and creation are essentially the same and most commonly associated with the seventeenth-century philosopher, Spinoza.

Papacy The office and authority of the pope; the system of church government headed by the pope.

Parlement of Paris Despite the similarity in name with "parliament," the French version was a court that helped to enforce the king's law and registered new ones.

Parochialism A narrow restricted outlook focused on a specific place or on a group of people who share a particular history or culture.

Patricians The noble families of ancient Rome.

Pax Romana The peace, stability and prosperity that characterized the Roman Empire in the first two centuries A.D.

Phenomenal world The physical world experienced by the senses, from which it constructs knowledge and reality.

Philosophy Literally "the love of wisdom." A system of enquiry based on logic and reason;

philosophers searched for basic truths and moral principles for the right conduct of life.

Plebeians The common people of ancient Rome.

Plebiscite A direct vote in which the entire voting public is asked to accept or reject a proposition or a candidate.

Pluralistic Referring to any group or society in which a variety of differing opinions are represented, expressed, tolerated, and perhaps even encouraged.

Polytheism Belief in and worship of more than one god.

Positivism The theory that the scientific method applied to the study of society is the only valid approach to knowledge and precise understanding.

Postmodernism A late twentieth century development that rejects universal principles and seeks the dismantling of all inherited systems and beliefs and that values cultural diversity in the arts and thought. A wide-ranging criticism of the Western tradition as a viable force in the contemporary world.

Productivity A term in economics that refers to how much it costs to produce goods. The less it costs to produce something, the higher the productivity.

Propaganda The deployment of lies, half truths, and myths in all forms of communication in order to win people over to a cause.

Protectorate The practice, common in the era of European imperialism, of a stronger state asserting power over a weaker state or territory. In effect, the protector warns all other powers that the weak state or territory is not available to any other power for colonization.

Providence The power of God acting in the world for, as is usually thought, the good of one and all; often referred to as Divine Providence.

Psyche The mind as the center of thought, emotion, and behavior.

Psychoanalysis The method originated by Freud for treating mental disorders by bringing to light unconscious impulses, desires and memories.

Racist A person who believes that race determines human ability and character, and that one particular race is superior to another.

Radicalism A doctrine advocating extreme change of existing conditions and standards.

Rationalism Reliance on reason as the avenue to knowledge.

Realism The representation in art and literature of social conditions, daily life, and ordinary people as they really are without idealism.

Realpolitik Political practice as a tough-minded, objective means of advancing national interest and power.

Redemption To be saved from the consequences of sin through the sacrifice of Jesus.

Relativism The belief that accepted truths and moral values are not universally valid, but are a matter of individual or group judgment.

Republic The political order in a country where the people or their elected representatives hold supreme power.

Respublica Christiana A universal Christian commonwealth envisioned by the Catholic Church, governed by an emperor under the pope's guidance.

Republicanism Belief in a republican system of government.

Revelation The making known of divine will or truth that was previously hidden.

Ritual A prescribed series of actions or rites used in a religious ceremony.

Romanesque The eleventh- to twelfth-century style of architecture that imitated ancient Roman buildings, with thick walls, rounded arches, and little ornamentation.

Romanticism A literary and artistic movement characterized by the liberation of human emotion with emphasis on the artist's imagination, intuition, and feelings.

Roosevelt Corollary A policy enunciated by Theodore Roosevelt in 1904 stating that European powers should not intervene in any government in the western hemisphere that appeared to be economically or politically unstable.

Royal hegemony The control exercised by a monarch over his or her subjects and territory.

Savior-God Christians view Jesus as both the Savior of mankind and God incarnate, leading humanity from sin to eternal life.

Scholasticism The attempt of medieval theologian-philosophers to explain and clarify Christian teachings by means of concepts and logic derived from Greek philosophy; to prove through reason what was held to be true by faith.

Scholastics Medieval philosopher-theologians who came to dominate the intellectual life of medieval universities.

Scientific Revolution The seventeenth-century movement that overthrew the medieval view of the universe and made physical nature a valid object for experimental inquiry and mathematical calculation.

Secession The act of withdrawing from a state, country, or polity.

Secular Referring to the world we live in as separate from any spiritual world; here and now; this life rather than the afterlife.

Secularization The process by which religious ideas, customs and traditions lose their political and social power in a society.

Self-determination The right of independence or self-government for a nation; also, an individual taking control over his or her life.

Sense perception Knowledge of the material world based on the observation and investigation of nature using the human senses (sight, touch, hearing, taste, and smell).

Skepticism An unwillingness or refusal to believe that something is true or certain unless adequate evidence or proof is provided. It is the opposite of dogmatism.

Social Darwinism The application of Darwin's theory to the study of human society. In the struggle for survival, some maintain, it is natural and beneficial to society for the fittest nations, races, and individuals to survive at the expense of the less fit.

Socialism A social and economic system based on cooperation not competition. The production and distribution of goods would be owned collectively, would benefit the community as a whole, and lift the laboring poor out of poverty and oppression.

Sophrosyne The ancient Greek idea of moderation and self-discipline.

Sovereignty The state's authority, which is absolute in matters of law within its borders.

Spheres of Influence A diplomatic term that describes the area or territory in which a foreign power or powers have great influence.

Stream of consciousness A literary technique that, through a punctuated and spontaneous flow of thought and feelings, attempts to reveal the mystery and complexity of the inner person.

Subsistence Having just enough food, clothing, and shelter to survive. A subsistence economy is one in which people live hand-to-mouth, everything produced is consumed, and there is no surplus.

Suffrage The right to vote.

Sui Generis The only example of its kind, without an equal.

Superman See Overman.

Syndicalism A political/economic philosophy and movement that advocates giving the control of government and industry to workers' federations.

Tabula Rasa A description of the mind as a blank slate before it organizes the impressions gained from experience.

Terror, Reign of The deliberate use of terror by the Jacobin regime to preserve the ideals of the French Revolution by execution of enemies of republican liberty.

Terrorism The use of force or violence against people or property in order to intimidate or coerce societies or governments for political or ideological reasons.

Teutonic cousins Germans and Englishmen (as well as Scandinavians) commonly referred to themselves as descendants of common ancestors—teutonic tribespeople.

Theocracy A country in which the government is dominated by clergy.

Tithe Tenth, referred to by Christians, as the portion of their income or revenues that ought to be given to the support of the Church.

Totalitarianism A form of government that exercises total control over all aspects of life, demanding submission of the individual to the state, and permitting no political opposition.

Tragedy A drama with an unhappy ending caused by human flaws or disastrous circumstances.

Trinity Christian belief in the union of three divinities, Father, Son, and Holy Ghost in one God.

Unconscious, The The inner life of the mind containing memories, repressed desires or passion, not consciously perceived, but affecting conscious thought and behavior.

Universalism 1. The unity and salvation of all people under God 2. Membership of all humanity in a worldwide community.

Utilitarian An ethical theory that all political, economic, and social actions should be directed toward achieving the greatest happiness for the greatest number of people.

Utopian Any visionary system of politics or society, named for Sir Thomas More's *Utopia* (1516).

Vernacular Referring to the language commonly spoken and written in a society.

Volkish thought A late nineteenth century movement glorifying the language, traditions, and history of the Germanic peoples.

World-view The perspective from which an individual or group sees and interprets the world and life. *Weltanschauung* in German.

Xenophobia An unreasoning fear and hatred of foreigners.

Zionism A movement to establish a Jewish state in Palestine, the Jews' ancient homeland.

SELECTED MATERIAL

China

A Cultural, Social, and Political History
by Patricia Buckley Ebrey

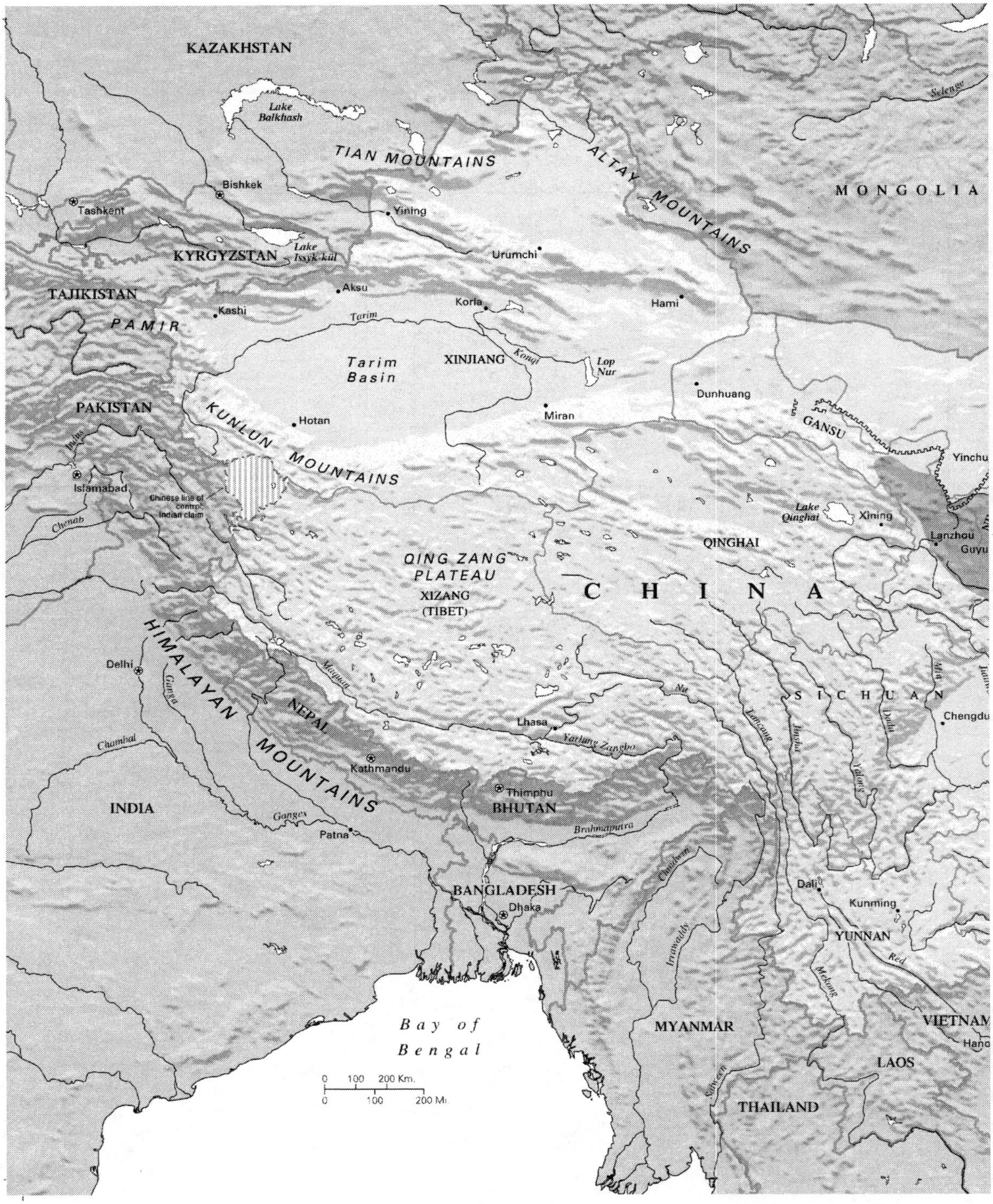
KAZAKHSTAN
Lake Balkhash
TIAN MOUNTAINS
ALTAY MOUNTAINS
MONGOLIA
Selenge
Bishkek
Tashkent
Yining
KYRGYZSTAN
Lake Issyk-kul
Urumchi
TAJIKISTAN
Aksu
Korla
Hami
Kashi
PAMIR
Tarim
Tarim Basin
XINJIANG
Konqi
Lop Nur
Dunhuang
PAKISTAN
KUNLUN MOUNTAINS
Hotan
Miran
GANSU
Yinchu
Indus
Islamabad
Chinese line of control, Indian claim
Chenab
Lake Qinghai
Xining
Lanzhou
Guyu
QINGHAI
QING ZANG PLATEAU
XIZANG (TIBET)
CHINA
HIMALAYAN MOUNTAINS
Delhi
Ganga
Miquan
NEPAL
Nu
Lhasa
Yarlung Zangbo
Lancang
Jinsha
SICHUAN
Chengdu
Yalong
Chambal
Kathmandu
Thimphu
BHUTAN
INDIA
Ganges
Patna
Brahmaputra
BANGLADESH
Dhaka
Chindwin
Dali
Kunming
YUNNAN
Irrawaddy
Red
Mekong
Bay of Bengal
MYANMAR
VIETNAM
Hano
LAOS
0 100 200 Km.
0 100 200 Mi.
Salween
THAILAND

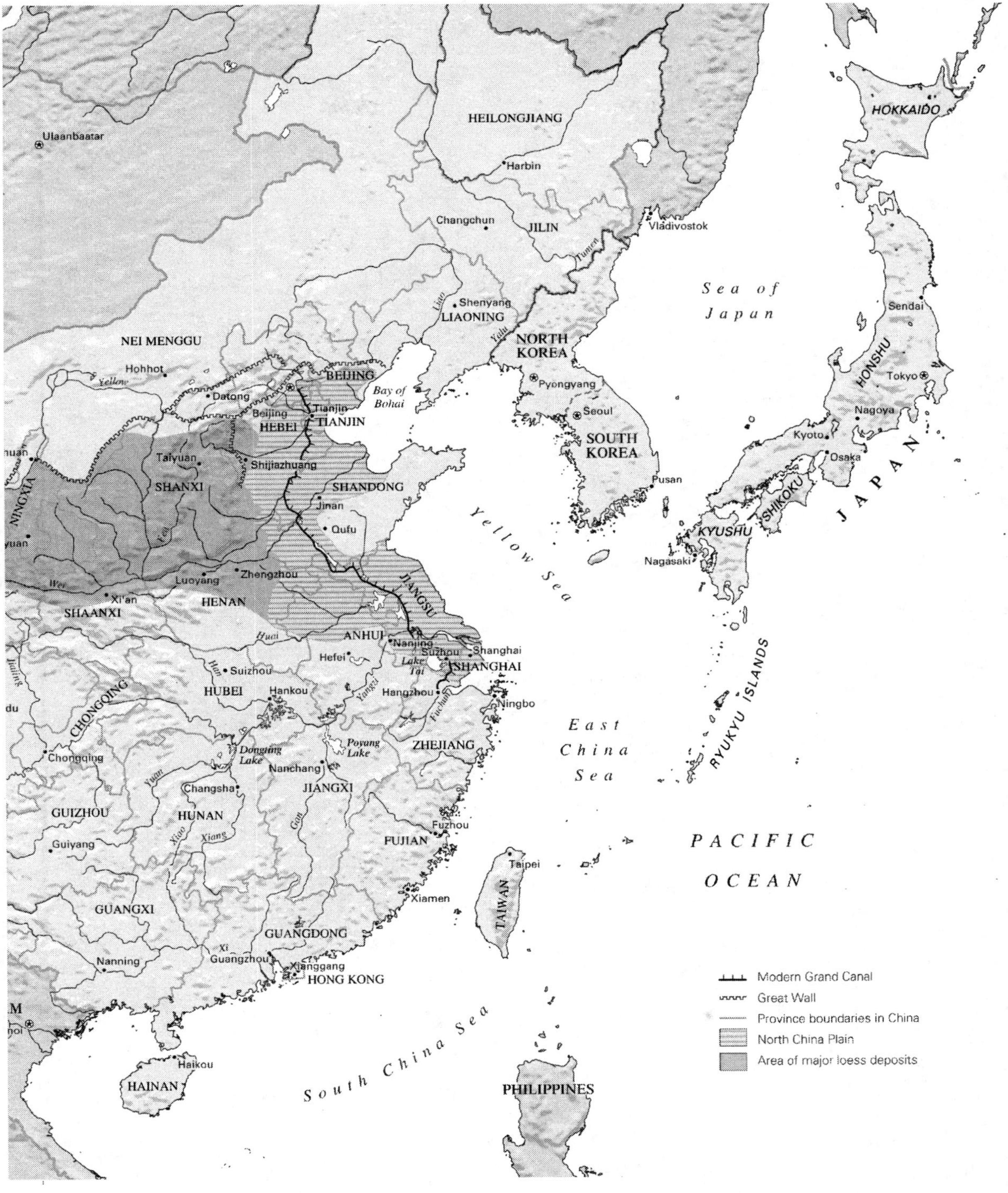

Ulaanbaatar
HEILONGJIANG
HOKKAIDO
Harbin
Changchun
JILIN
Vladivostok
Tumen
Sea of Japan
Shenyang
LIAONING
Liao
Yalu
NEI MENGGU
NORTH KOREA
Sendai
HONSHU
Tokyo
Hohhot
Yellow
BEIJING
Pyongyang
Datong
Bay of Bohai
Beijing
Tianjin
HEBEI
TIANJIN
Seoul
SOUTH KOREA
Nagoya
Kyoto
Osaka
Taiyuan
Shijiazhuang
SHANXI
SHANDONG
Pusan
NINGXIA
Jinan
Qufu
Yellow Sea
KYUSHU
SHIKOKU
JAPAN
Nagasaki
Luoyang
Zhengzhou
Wei
Xi'an
HENAN
JIANGSU
SHAANXI
Huai
ANHUI
Nanjing
Suzhou
Shanghai
Hefei
Lake Tai
SHANGHAI
Han
Suizhou
Jialing
CHONGQING
HUBEI
Hankou
Yangzi
Hangzhou
Fuchun
Ningbo
RYUKYU ISLANDS
East China Sea
Dongting Lake
Poyang Lake
ZHEJIANG
Chongqing
Nanchang
Yuan
Changsha
JIANGXI
GUIZHOU
HUNAN
Gan
Fuzhou
Xiao
Xiang
Guiyang
FUJIAN
PACIFIC OCEAN
Taipei
TAIWAN
Xiamen
GUANGXI
GUANGDONG
Xi
Nanning
Guangzhou
Xianggang
HONG KONG
South China Sea
Haikou
HAINAN
PHILIPPINES
Modern Grand Canal
Great Wall
Province boundaries in China
North China Plain
Area of major loess deposits

CREDITS

Chapter 1

p. 15: Copyright © 2005 The Metropolitan Museum of Art. Reprinted by permission of The Metropolitan Museum of Art. p. 19: Adapted from "The Announcement of Shao," translated by David S. Nivison in *Sources of Chinese Tradition*, 2nd Edition, compiled by Wm. Theodore de Bary and Irene Bloom (NY: Columbia University Press, 1999). Copyright © 1999 Columbia University Press. Reprinted with permission of the publisher. p. 21: Reprinted by permission of The Östasiatiska Museet (Stockholm Museum of Far East Antiquities). p. 21: Reprinted by permission of University of Hawai`i Press.

Chapter 2

p. 29: Reprinted by permission of Oxford University Press, UK. p. 39: The Yellow River's Earl by Ch'u Yuan, translated by Stephen Owen, from *An Anthology of Chinese Literature: Beginnings to 1911* by Stephen Owen, Editor & Translator. Copyright © 1996 by Stephen Owen and The Council for Cultural Planning and Development of the Executive Yuan of the Republic of China. Used by permission of W. W. Norton & Company, Inc.

Chapter 3

p. 43: Excerpted from the book *Journey into China's Antiquity*, vol. 2, Morning Glory Publishers, Beijing, China.

CONNECTIONS

Prehistory

THINKING ABOUT THE WHOLE OF EAST Asia before the invention of writing helps to remind us that East Asia has always been a part of Eurasia and did not develop in isolation. During the Pleistocene geological era (the last great Ice Age), plants and animals spread across Eurasia as far as Japan, then connected to the mainland. In later times, peoples, crops, and inventions traveled in many directions.

Early human beings *(Homo erectus)* appeared in East Asia over 1 million years ago, having gradually spread from Africa and West Asia during the Pleistocene. Peking Man, discovered in the 1920s, is one of the best-documented examples of *H. erectus,* with skeletal remains of some forty individuals found in a single cave complex. Peking Man could stand erect, hunt, make fire, and use chipped stones as tools. In recent decades, even earlier examples of *H. erectus* have been found in south China.

Modern human beings *(Homo sapiens)* appeared in East Asia around 100,000 years ago. The dominant theory in the West, supported by studies of the mitochondrial DNA of modern people, is that *H. sapiens* also spread out of Africa and displaced *H. erectus,* which became extinct. Chinese archaeologists have given more credence to the theory that *H. erectus* evolved into *H. sapiens* independently in many parts of the world, making Peking Man the ancestor of modern Chinese. They can point to similarities between Peking Man and modern Chinese, such as the shape of certain teeth.

During the period from 100,000 to 10,000 B.C.E., East Asia was home to numerous groups of Paleolithic hunters, gatherers, and fishermen. Many of these people were on the move, following the wild animals they hunted or searching for new environments to exploit. This was the period that saw the movement of people from northeast Asia to the Americas and also from south China and Southeast Asia to the Pacific and Australia.

During this long period, humans began to speak, and so the affinities of modern languages offer a rough clue to the spread of peoples in early times. In East Asia, three large language families can be identified. Korean and Japanese are related to each other and more distantly to other North Asian languages such as Turkic and Mongolian (the Ural-Altaic languages). Chinese has distant ties to Tibetan and Burman (the Sino-Tibetan-Burman languages). Many of the languages spoken by minorities in south China belong to a large group found widely in mainland and insular Southeast Asia (the Austro-Asiatic languages). Language affinities suggest at least three migratory routes through East Asia: from North Asia into Mongolia, Manchuria, Korea, and Japan; from China into Tibet and Southeast Asia; and from south China to both Southeast Asia and the islands of the Philippines and Indonesia. Other evidence suggests additional routes, for instance, from Southeast Asia and Micronesia to Japan.

All through Eurasia, much greater advance came after the end of the last Ice Age around 10,000 B.C.E. (see Map C1.1). Soon after this date, people in Japan began making pottery, some of the earliest in the world. Pottery is of great value for holding water and storing food. In China and Korea, the earliest pottery finds are somewhat later, but pottery was apparently in use by 6000 B.C.E. Throughout East Asia,

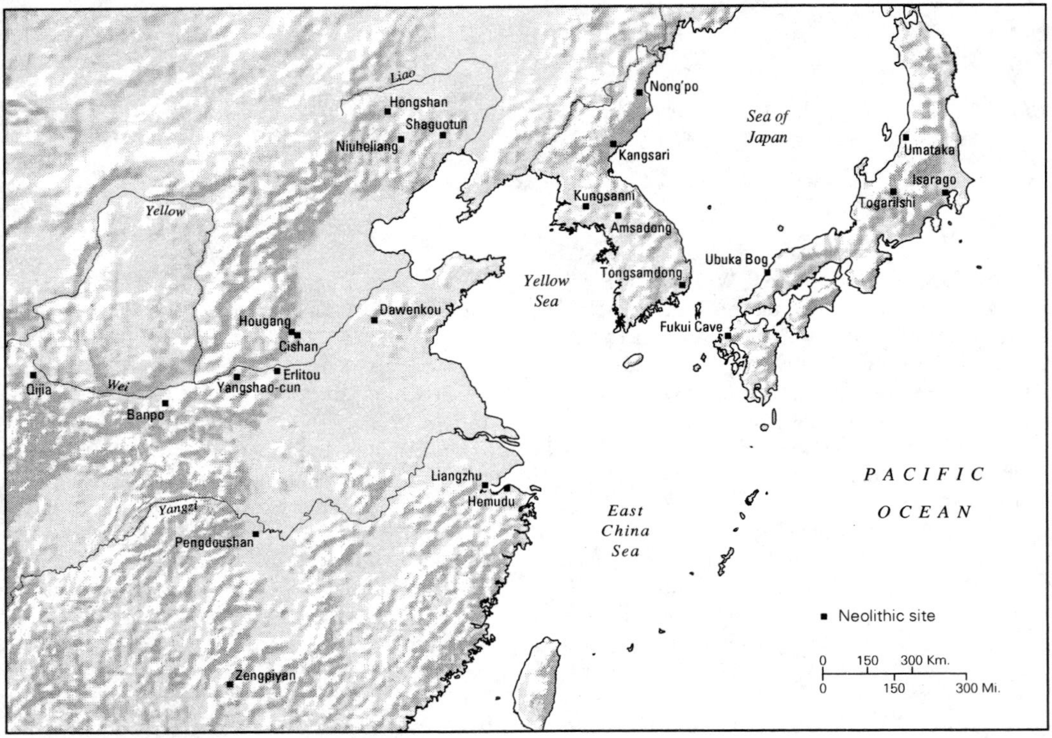

Map C1.1 Neolithic Sites in East Asia

early pottery was commonly imprinted on its surface to give it texture. In Japan this period is referred to as Jōmon and dated from about 10,000 to 300 B.C.E. The comparable period in Korea is called Chulmun and dated from about 8000 to 700 B.C.E. These cultures share many features. From shell mounds found in many places in both Korea and Japan, it is evident that sites were occupied for long periods, that shellfish were collected onshore, and that fish were caught from both rivers and the ocean. Other food sources were animals such as deer and wild boar, which were hunted. Dogs seem to have been domesticated, perhaps used as hunting animals.

China in the millennia after the last Ice Age followed more closely the pattern seen in western Eurasia involving crop agriculture, domestication of animals for food and work, pottery, textiles, and villages. Agriculture is a crucial change because cultivating crops allows denser and more permanent settlements. Because tending crops, weaving, and fashioning pots require different sorts of technical and social skills than hunting and gathering, it is likely that skilled elders began to vie with hunters and warriors for leadership.

The dozen or more distinct Neolithic cultures that have been identified in China can be roughly divided by latitude into the southern rice zone and the northern millet zone and by longitude into the eastern jade zone and the western painted pottery zone. Dogs and pigs were found in both areas as early as 5000 B.C.E. By 3000 B.C.E. sheep and cattle had become important in the north, water buffalo and cattle in the south.

Whether rice was independently domesticated in China or spread there from Southeast Asia is not yet certain. The earliest finds in China date to about 8000 B.C.E. At Hemudu, a site south of Shanghai and dating to about 5000 B.C.E., Neolithic villagers grew rice in wet fields and supplemented their diet with fish and water plants such as lotus and water chestnut. Hemudu villagers built wooden houses on piles, wove baskets, and made hoes, spears, mallets, paddles, and other tools of wood. They decorated their pottery and lacquered bowls with incised geometrical designs or pictures of birds, fish, or trees.

Millet, a crop domesticated in China, became the foundation of agriculture in north China. Nanzhuangtou, the earliest site found so far, is in southern Hebei and dates to about 8000 B.C.E. At Cishan, a site in Hebei dating to about 5500 B.C.E., millet was cut with stone sickles and stored in cord-marked pottery bowls, jars, and tripods (three-legged pots). Besides growing millet, the local people hunted deer and collected clams, snails, and turtles.

The east-west divide among Chinese Neolithic cultures in terms of expressive culture may well have had connections to less tangible elements of culture such as language and religion. In the west (Shaanxi and Gansu provinces especially), pottery decorated with painted geometrical designs was commonly produced from about 5000 to 3000 B.C.E. In the fully developed Yangshao style, grain jars were exuberantly painted in red and black with spirals, diamonds, and other geometrical patterns.

In the east, from Liaodong near Korea in the north to near Shanghai in the south, early pottery was rarely painted, but more elaborate forms appeared very early, with the finest wares formed on potters' wheels. Some had exceptionally thin walls polished to an almost metallic appearance. Many forms were constructed by adding parts, such as legs, spouts, handles, or lids. The many ewers and goblets found in eastern sites were probably used for rituals of feasting or sacrifice. Eastern cultures were also marked by progressively more elaborate burials.

Jade Plaque. This small plaque (6.2 by 8.3 cm, or 2.5 by 3.25 in) is incised to depict a human figure who merges into a monster mask. The lower part could be interpreted as his arms and legs, but at the same time resembles a monster mask with bulging eyes, prominent nostrils, and a large mouth. *(Zhejiang Provincial Institute of Archaeology/Cultural Relics Publishing House)*

At Dawenkou in Shandong (ca. 5000–2500 B.C.E.), not only were wooden coffins used, but even wooden burial chambers were occasionally constructed. The richest burials had over a hundred objects placed in them, including jade, stone, or pottery necklaces and bracelets. Some of those buried there had their upper lateral incisors extracted, a practice Chinese authors in much later times considered "barbarian," and which is also seen in some Japanese sites.

Even more distinctive of the eastern Neolithic cultures is the use of jade. Because jade does not crack, shaping it requires slow grinding with abrasive sand. The most spectacular discoveries of Neolithic jades have been made in Liaodong near Korea (Hongshan culture, ca. 3500 B.C.E.) and south of Shanghai (Liangzhu culture, ca. 2500 B.C.E.)—areas that literate Chinese in ca. 500 B.C.E. considered barbarian. In the Hongshan culture area, jade was made into small sculptures of turtles, birds, and strange coiled "pig dragons." In the Liangzhu area, jade was fashioned into objects with no obvious utilitarian purpose and which are therefore considered ritual objects. Most common are disks and notched columns.

In China, the late Neolithic period (ca. 3000–2000 B.C.E.) was a time of increased contact and cultural borrowing between these regional cultures. Cooking tripods, for instance, spread west, while painted pottery spread east. This period must also have been one of increased conflict between communities, since people began building defensive walls around settlements out of rammed earth, sometimes as large as 20 feet high and 30 feet thick. Enclosing a settlement with such a wall required chiefs able to command men and resources on a large scale. Another sign of the increasing power of religious or military elites is human sacrifice, probably of captives. The earliest examples, dating to about 2000 B.C.E., involved human remains placed under the foundations of buildings. At about the same time, metal began to be used on a small scale for weapons. These trends in Neolithic sites on the north China plain link it closely to the early stages of the Bronze Age civilization there, discussed in Chapter 1.

For China, prehistory conventionally stops soon after 2000 B.C.E. It is true that in the Chinese subcontinent outside the core of Shang territories, subsistence technology continued in the Neolithic pattern for many more centuries. In Korea and Japan, the period before writing lasted longer, but during the first millennium B.C.E., technologies from China began to have an impact.

To understand the links between early China and its East Asian neighbors, we must briefly consider the wider Eurasian context, especially the northern steppe region. In terms of contemporary countries, the steppe extends from southern Russia past the Caspian and Aral seas, through the Central Asian republics, into Mongolia and farther east. Horses were domesticated on the southern Russian steppe by about 4000 B.C.E. but spread only slowly to other regions. Chariots spread first, then riding on horseback. A fourteenth-century B.C.E. Hittite text on horsemanship discusses the training of chariot horses; within a century or so, chariots appeared in Shang China. The Scythians appeared as mounted archers in the tenth or ninth century B.C.E. East of them, the Karasuk, with a similar culture, dominated the region from western Mongolia into south Siberia. The Scythians and the Karasuk lived in felt tents, traveled in covered carts, and had bronze technology, including the bronze bit that made possible horseback riding. By the seventh century B.C.E. in the Altai region of Mongolia, there were two distinct groups of nomadic pastoralists: those who buried the dead under mounds and those who buried the dead in stone boxes. Their bronze implements, however, were much the same.

South of these groups on the steppe, but in contact with them, were pastoral-agricultural cultures in China's Northern Zone, stretching in terms of modern provinces from Gansu through northern Shaanxi, northern Shanxi, and northern Hebei, into Liaoning (southern Manchuria). During the late second millennium B.C.E., this zone was settled by a variety of cultures with distinct pottery and burial customs but bronze knives much like those of the steppe to the north. In the early first millennium B.C.E., warrior elites emerged in many of these cultures, and animal raising became more central to their economy, perhaps in response to a climate that was becoming colder and drier. From 600 to 300 B.C.E., evidence of horses becomes more and more common, as does riding astride. Some of these cultures adopted nomadic pastoralism, moving with their herds to new pastures. These cultures also adopted the art styles common on the steppe, such as bronze and gold animal plaques. They made increasing use of iron, which may have spread to them from the Central Asian steppe rather than from China, which was also beginning to use iron in this period. These Northern Zone cultures were in contact with the Chinese states, however, and early Chinese coins have been found at some sites.

The eastern end of this Northern Zone was directly north of Korea. Archaeologists have

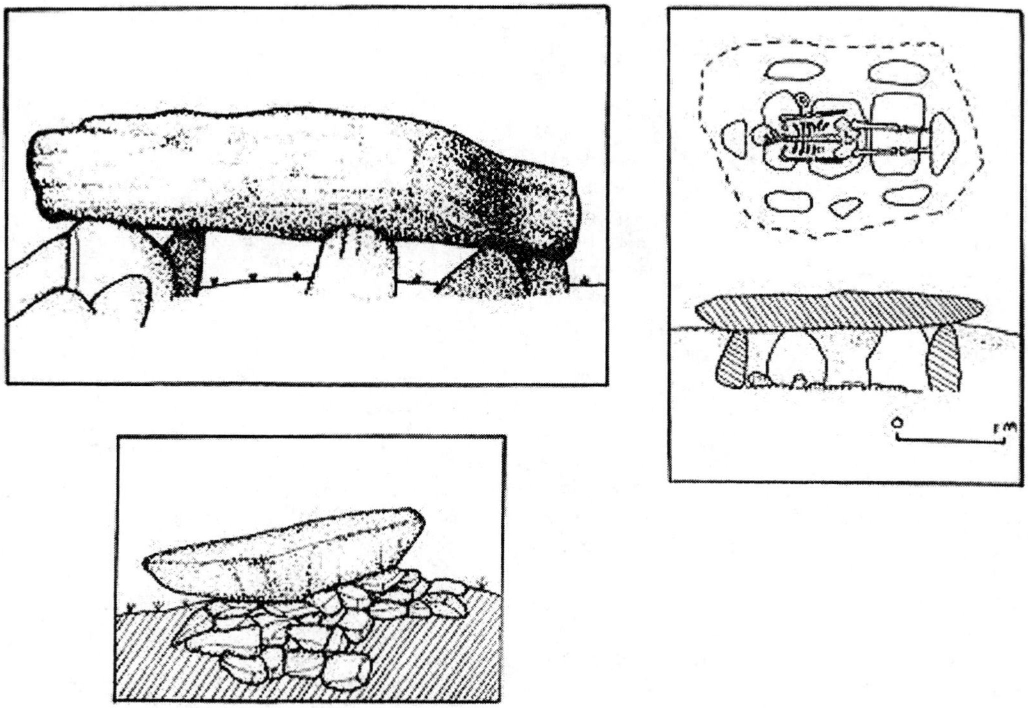

Figure C1.1 **Dolmens.** Burial structures capped with large stones, called dolmens, have been found in both the Korean peninsula and nearby parts of Japan. The two shown on the left were found in northern and southern Korea, respectively. The one on the right, which also shows the arrangement of the bones beneath the capstone, was found in Kyushu, across the Korean Strait.

identified a culture there that lasted eight centuries, from the eleventh to the fourth centuries B.C.E., called Upper Xiajiadian culture. Finds include an ancient mine, along with distinctive bronze knives, helmets, mirrors, and horse fittings. The faces of the dead were covered with a cloth decorated with bronze buttons. During the next phase there was such a radical change in burial practices that archaeologists suspect that a different, and militarily superior, horse-riding group entered the area. This new group used both wooden and stone-cist coffins. A cist burial is one with a burial chamber built of stones to form a box, with a flagstone or similar large, flat stone to cover it. By the third century B.C.E., the cultures of the Northern Zone became increasingly homogeneous in material culture and rituals, with similar warrior elites and ornamental art.

These societies came into contact with people settled farther south in the Korean peninsula. As mentioned previously, after the end of the last Ice Age, the Korean peninsula was home to the fishing and foraging Chulmun peoples. By the middle of the first millennium B.C.E., a new culture, called Mumun (from the name of its pottery), became established. Mumun sites, in contrast to the earlier Chulmun seaside ones, were on hillsides or hilltops. Grain production became more important, and metalworking was adopted. Bronze began to be used in Korea about 700 B.C.E. and iron by about 400 B.C.E. Mumun farmers grew barley, millet, sorghum, and short-grained rice, a similar mix of crops to north China. Another distinctive feature of this culture, the use of stone cist burials, links it to the Northern Zone. A fifth-century B.C.E. site in west-central Korea has a stone cist burial, twenty-one pit buildings, red burnished pottery, a pottery kiln, a stone mold for casting bronze implements, whetstones for sharpening blades, bronze daggers and swords, and a bronze dagger of the type found farther north in the Northern Zone. Soon, however, Korea was producing its own distinctive metalwork, such as finely decorated mirrors. A new burial form also emerged: large above-ground stone vaults called dolmens.

The shift from Chulmun to Mumun probably reflects the same movement of people seen in southern Manchuria. Without textual evidence, however, it is impossible to decide whether the local Chulmun quickly adopted the superior technology of the Mumun people or whether the Mumun moved into the area in large numbers, gradually pushing out those who were already there. Some scholars speculate that the newcomers were the speakers of languages that were the ancestors of the Korean and Japanese languages.

Another important technology that made its way to Korea and Japan before writing was rice cultivation. Studies based on stone reaping knives suggest that rice spread north along the China seaboard, reaching Korea and Japan by about 300 B.C.E. In the case of Japan, rice seems to have been grown by the end of the Jōmon period, but is more strongly associated with the next stage, called the Yayoi period. The Yayoi period is marked by distinctive pottery, found earliest in Kyushu, then spreading east through Honshu, though farther north more of the Jōmon style is retained in Yayoi pieces. Rice cultivation too was more thoroughly adopted in western Japan, with the marine-based way of life retaining more of its hold in northern Japan. Iron tools such as hoes and shovels also spread through Japan in this period, as did silk and associated spinning and weaving technology.

It is likely that the shift to Yayoi-style pottery and associated technologies was the result of an influx of people from Korea. Archaeologists have identified two distinct skeleton types in Yayoi period sites in western Japan, which they interpret as the indigenous Jōmon people and the new immigrants from Korea. The Jōmon type were shorter and more round-faced. The influx of the immigrants seems to have been greatest in Kyushu and western Honshu. Some scholars speculate that the Ainu, who survived into modern times only on the northern island of Hokkaido, are of relatively pure Jōmon stock.

Another sign that the influx of Yayoi people was not so great in eastern Japan is that bronze implements did not become important in the east, nor did easterners adopt the western Yayoi style of burying the whole body in a jar, a coffin, or a pit. Rather, in the east, reburial of the bones in a jar predominated. Because contact between southern Korea and western Japan continued through this period and because new technologies entered through this route, western Japan in this period was relatively more advanced than eastern Japan.

As we can see from this review of prehistory, contact among the societies of East Asia did not lead to identical developmental sequences. In China a millennium passed between the introduction of bronze technology and that of iron, in Korea only three centuries, and in Japan they were acquired together. Geography has much to do with the fact that Korea's direct neighbors frequently were not Chinese but nomadic pastoralists with distinctive cultures. Geography also dictates that passage from Korea to Japan was shorter and easier than crossing from China, giving Korea more direct influence on Japan than China had.

SUGGESTED READING

The best book for the archaeology of East Asia as a whole is G. Barnes, *China, Korea, and Japan: The Rise of Civilization in East Asia* (1993). For early China, see also K. C. Chang, *The Archaeology of Ancient China,* 4th ed. (1986), and D. Keightley, ed., *The Origins of Chinese Civilization* (1983). On the Northern Zone, see N. di Cosmo, *Ancient China and Its Enemies: The Rise of Nomadic Power in East Asian History* (2002), and V. Mair, ed., *The Bronze Age and Early Iron Age Peoples of Eastern Central Asia* (1998). On Korea, see S. Nelson, *The Archaeology of Korea* (1993), and for Japan, see R. Pearson, *Ancient Japan* (1992) and K. Imamura, *Prehistoric Japan: New Perspective on Insular East Asia* (1996).

CHAPTER ONE

The Bronze Age: Shang and Western Zhou (ca. 1500–771 B.C.E.)

China's Bronze Age began soon after 2000 B.C.E., and by 1200 B.C.E. there were bronze-based civilizations in several regions of China. The best known of these was centered on Anyang in north-central China, where the Shang Dynasty developed a complex state with writing and large settlements. The inscribed oracle bones found at Anyang confirm traditions about Shang rulers passed down in early texts.

In 1045 B.C.E. the Shang Dynasty was overthrown by an erstwhile ally-vassal, the state of Zhou. The early Zhou Dynasty is known not only from archaeological evidence, but also from transmitted texts, which provide the Zhou version of their righteous victory over the decadent Shang. The Zhou rulers sent out vassals to establish settlements in distant regions, creating a feudal-like system.

The issues that engage archaeologists, paleographers, and historians of China's bronze age remain the basic ones: Can we reconcile texts that talk of a sequence of dynasties with the archaeological evidence of distinct cultural centers? What were the consequences of the invention of writing? What can be inferred about Shang society and culture from surviving material artifacts such as bronze vessels? Is there any way to tell if cultures outside the core regions of the Shang and Zhou spoke the same language or considered themselves part of the same culture? How significant in political and cultural terms was the transition from Shang to Zhou? Was anything significant learned from other parts of Eurasia in this period, or were all advances locally generated?

Map 1.1 **Political Map of China Showing Modern Province Boundaries**

THE GEOGRAPHY OF THE CHINESE SUBCONTINENT

The term *China* as it is used in this book does not refer to the same geographical entity at all points in history. The historical China, also called China proper, was smaller than present-day China and changed in size over time. It can be thought of as the area settled by Chinese speakers or controlled by a Chinese state, or both. (To simplify complex issues of identity radically, references here to "the Chinese" can be taken to mean speakers of the Chinese language, a group that can also be referred to as the Han Chinese.) The contemporary People's Republic of China includes territories like Tibet, Inner Mongolia, Turkestan, and Manchuria that were the traditional homes of other peoples and not incorporated into Chinese states until relatively late in their histories. In this book, to indicate the location of historically significant places within China, modern province names are used for convenience (see Map 1.1).

The geographical context in which Chinese civilization developed changed slowly over time: rivers and coastlines have shifted, forests have been cleared, and climates have warmed and cooled. The human geography has undergone even more extensive changes as the area occupied by speakers of Chinese has expanded and they have faced different neighbors.

China proper, by the nineteenth century about a thousand miles north to south and east to west, occupies much of the temperate zone of East Asia. The northern part, drained by the Yellow River, is colder, flatter, and more arid than the south. Rainfall in many northern areas is less than 20 inches a year, making it best suited to crops like wheat and millet. The dominant soil is loess—fine wind-driven earth that is fertile and easy to work even with primitive tools. Much of the loess soil ends up as silt in the Yellow River, causing the river bed to rise over time. Once people began to dike the river, it became flood prone, since when the dikes break, huge floods result. Drought is another perennial problem for farmers in the north.

The Yangzi River is the dominant feature of the warmer, wetter, and more lush south, a region well suited to rice cultivation and to growing two crops a year. The Yangzi and many of its tributaries are navigable, so boats were traditionally the preferred means of transportation in the south.

Mountains, deserts, and grasslands separated China proper from the sites of other early civilizations. Between China and India lay Tibet, with its vast mountain ranges and high plateaus. North of Tibet are great expanses of desert where nothing grows except in rare oases, and north of them grasslands stretch from the Ukraine to eastern Siberia. Until modern times, Chinese civilization did not spread into these Inner Asian regions because they were not suited to crop agriculture. The northern grasslands, where raising animals is a more productive use of land than planting crops, was the heartland of China's traditional enemies, such as the Xiongnu and the Mongols.

THE SHANG DYNASTY (CA. 1500–1045 B.C.E.)

China's Neolithic Age has been discussed in **Connections: The Prehistory of East Asia.** China had agriculture from about 10,000 B.C.E.; by 4000 B.C.E. distinct regional cultures are evident; by 2500 B.C.E. settlements were sometimes walled and burials give evidence of increasing social differentiation. It was from these roots that China's first civilization emerged.

After 2000 B.C.E. a Bronze Age civilization appeared in north China. Early Chinese texts refer to the first dynasty as the Xia Dynasty and give the names of its kings. The earliest Bronze Age sites may have some connection to Xia, but they contain no texts to prove or disprove this supposition. The Shang dynasty, however, is documented in both excavated and transmitted texts, and no one today doubts that it existed. The key excavated texts are the oracle bone inscriptions found in and near the Shang settlement at Anyang, in modern Henan province. Although these inscribed cattle bones and turtle shells had been unearthed from time to time, it was only after 1898 that scholars connected them to Shang kings. Since then, rubbings of some 48,000 bone fragments have been published, giving paleographers much to study.

Pronouncing Chinese

Pinyin	English
c	ts in *tsar*
z	dz in *adze*
zh	j in *jack*
q	ch in *chin*
x	*sh*
ui	*way*

According to tradition, Shang kings ruled from five successive cities. The best known is the last, Anyang, first excavated between 1928 and 1937. The Shang kings ruled there from approximately 1200 B.C.E. to 1045 B.C.E. At the center of Anyang were large palaces, temples, and altars which were constructed on rammed earth foundations (see **Material Culture: Rammed Earth**).

The Shang kings were military chieftains who regularly sent out armies of three thousand to five thousand men on campaigns, and when they were not at war would go on hunts lasting months. Their armies fought rebellious vassals

MATERIAL CULTURE

Rammed Earth

From the late Neolithic period on, pounded or rammed earth was used in north China to build foundations and walls. In fact, in areas of loess soil, rammed earth is still used as a building material, primarily for the walls around houses or farmyards. The method used today begins with dumping loose soil into wooden frames, then pounding it into thin layers with wooden logs. At archaeological sites, the impressions of the pounders are often still visible on the top layer of the wall. Ancient rammed earth can be nearly as hard as concrete.

The most massive rammed earth structure of Shang date excavated so far is the wall surrounding the city of Zhengzhou (Henan province). It is about 1,800 meters on each side and about 9 meters tall. The base of the wall was as much as 20 meters thick. Chinese archaeologists have estimated that it contained 870,000 cubic meters of rammed earth, which would have required a labor force of 10,000 men working for eight years to dig the soil, transport it to the site, and pound it into a wall.

Earthen Walls. Walls are still constructed today of rammed earth. A frame of logs is constructed, the earth is pounded into place, and after it is dry, the frame is removed. *(Ronald G. Knapp)*

and foreign tribes, but the situation constantly changed as vassals became enemies and enemies accepted offers of alliance. War booty, especially the war captives who could be enslaved or sacrificed, was an important source of the king's revenue.

Bronze technology gave Shang warriors improved weapons: bronze-tipped spears and dagger-axes (blades mounted at right angles to the shaft), used for hacking and stabbing. Bronze was also used for the fittings of the spoke-wheeled chariots that came into use around 1200 B.C.E. There is no evidence of animal traction in China before the chariot or of the use of wheels, spoked or solid disk, leading to the conclusion that the chariot was introduced to China by diffusion across Asia. Shang chariots were pulled by two or four horses and provided commanders with a mobile station from which they could supervise their troops; chariots also gave archers and soldiers armed with battleaxes increased mobility.

Shang power did not rest solely on military supremacy. The oracle bone texts show that the Shang king also acted as the high priest, the one best qualified to offer sacrifices to the royal ancestors and the high god, Di, who could command rain, thunder, and wind. The king also made offerings to an array of nature gods, such as the spirits of the sun and moon, the Yellow River, the winds of the four directions, and specific mountains.

Royal ancestors were viewed as able to intervene with the remote Di. They also could send curses on their own, produce dreams, assist the king in battle, and so on. The king addressed his ancestors in prayers and made offerings to them of millet wine, cattle, sheep, grain, and human victims. He discerned his ancestors' wishes and responses by interpreting the cracks made on the oracle bones when they were heated. When King Wu Ding (ca. 1200 B.C.E.) had a toothache, he had his diviner ask whether it was his father who was causing it. Before building a new settlement, he asked if the high god Di would cause problems. Di or the ancestors were also asked about rain, the harvest, military expeditions, dreams, floods, tribute payments, sacrifices, and other matters of importance. It was common to verify the result of a divination by repeating the question in negative form, such as, "Di approves the king," followed by, "Di does not approve the king." Probably as a form of record keeping, these questions were often inscribed on the bones. Scholars of the oracle bone inscriptions have noticed that the style of the calligraphy decreased in size over time and the questions posed became more routinized and more focused on ritual matters.

Contents of Fu Hao's Tomb, ca. 1200 B.C.E.

468 bronze objects	including 195 ritual vessels 130 weapons 23 bells 27 knives 4 mirrors 4 tigers or tiger heads
755 jade objects	
63 stone objects	
5 ivory objects	
564 bone objects	including nearly 500 bone hairpins and over 20 bone arrowheads
11 pottery objects	
6,900 pieces of cowrie shell	
16 retainers	male and female, adults and children

Shang palaces were undoubtedly splendid, but they were constructed of perishable material like wood, and nothing remains of them today. What has survived are the lavish underground tombs built for Shang kings and their consorts. The one royal tomb not to have been robbed before it was excavated was for Lady Hao, one of the many wives of King Wu Ding. Although it was one of the smaller royal tombs (about 13 by 18 feet at the mouth and about 25 feet deep) and not in the main royal cemetery, it was nonetheless filled with an extraordinary array of valuable goods. The hundreds of bronze objects in the tomb weighed 1.6 metric tons (see the listing of its contents in the table). About sixty of the bronze vessels had Lady Hao's name inscribed on them. The weapons found in this tomb show that Lady Hao took an interest in military affairs. From inscribed bones found elsewhere at Anyang, we know that she led several military campaigns, once with thirteen thousand troops against the Qiang tribes to the west. Some of the objects in her tomb appear to be tribute sent to Anyang from distant places. These include both bronze vessels from the south and knives and mirrors from the Northern Zone (occupied by non-Han peoples, discussed below).

In addition to objects of symbolic value or practical use, the Shang interred human beings, sometimes dozens of them, in royal tombs. Why did they do this? From oracle bone texts, it seems that captives not needed as slaves often ended up as sacrificial victims. Other people buried with the king had chosen their fate; that is, his spouses, retainers, or servants could decide to accompany him in death. Those who voluntarily followed their king to the grave generally had their own ornaments and might also have coffins and grave goods such as weapons. Early Shang graves rarely had more than three victims or followers accompanying the main occupant, but the practice grew over time. A late Shang king's tomb contained the remains of ninety followers plus seventy-four human sacrifices, twelve horses, and eleven dogs. Archaelogists often can identify sacrificial victims because they were decapitated or cut in two at the waist.

Human sacrifice occurred not only at burials. Divination texts refer to ceremonies where from three to four hundred captives were sacrificed. In 1976, twelve hundred victims were found in 191 pits near the royal tombs, apparently representing successive sacrifices of a few dozen victims. Animals were also frequently offered in sacrifice. Thus, a central part of being a Shang king was taking the lives of others and offering the victims up on the altars.

What about those in Shang society who were not buried in well-furnished tombs? The Shang nobility lived in large houses built on platforms of rammed earth (see **Material Culture: Rammed Earth**). Those lower down on the social scale often lived in homes built partly below ground level, probably as a way to conserve heat. Animal husbandry was a major element in the Shang economy. The bone workshops at Anyang made use of the leg bones of cattle, sheep, pigs, deer, dogs, and horses. Divinations proposed the sacrifice of one hundred, two hundred, or three hundred cattle, sheep, pigs, or dogs.

In the urban centers, substantial numbers of craftsmen worked in stone, bone, bronze, and clay. Their workshops, concentrated in certain sections of the city, were often quite specialized. Some workshops specialized in hairpins, others arrowheads, others ritual vessels. Another important product was silk, made from the cocoons of the silkworm, which fed on the leaves of mulberry trees. Silk from Shang China has recently been discovered in an Egyptian tomb, evidence that its importance as an item of east-west trade began very early.

At the level of technology, the life of Shang farmers was not very different from that of their Neolithic ancestors. They lived in small, compact villages, surrounded by fields that they worked with stone tools. Millet continued to be the basic grain, but some new crops became common in Shang times, most notably wheat, which had spread from West Asia.

The primary difference between Shang farmers and their Neolithic predecessors is the huge gulf that separated them from the most powerful in their society. Shang rulers could command the labor of thousands of men for long periods of time. Huge work forces were mobilized to build the rammed earth city walls, dig the great tombs, open new lands, and fight in war. Some scholars assume that those laboring for the king were slaves, perhaps acquired through warfare. Others speculate that these laborers also included conscripts, called up as needed from among the serf-like farmers. Whatever the status of the workers, coercion, backed by violence, was an essential element of the Shang state.

Writing

The inscribed oracle bones demonstrate that writing was already a major element in Chinese culture by 1200 B.C.E. Writing must have been

Oracle Bone. The thousands of inscribed bones that survive from Shang sites are our best source for early Chinese writing. The questions they record were usually addressed to the king's ancestors. *(Institute of History and Philogy. Academia Sinica/Laurie Platt Winfrey, Inc.)*

invented earlier, but the early stages of its development cannot be traced, probably because writing was done on perishable materials like wood, bamboo, or silk. Late Neolithic pots sometimes have marks on them that some scholars speculate are early forms of writing. Not until the oracle bones from late Shang, however, is there evidence of full sentences.

What impact did writing have? Literacy is an ally of political control, facilitating communication across an expanding realm. From the oracle bones, we know that Shang kept records of enemy slain, booty taken, animals bagged in hunts, and other information, using lunar months and ten-day and sixty-day cycles to record dates.

Although only about 40 percent of the five thousand or so characters used on Shang divination texts have been deciphered, there is no longer any doubt that the language and the writing system of the Shang are directly ancestral to both the language and the writing systems of later Chinese. This script was logographic, like ancient Egyptian and Sumerian, meaning that each word was represented by a single graph (character). In the Chinese case, some of these graphs began as pictures, but for the names of abstract concepts, other methods were adopted to represent the word. Sometimes the graph for a different word was borrowed because the two words were pronounced alike. As in later times, sometimes two different graphs were combined; for instance, to represent different types of trees, the graph for tree could be combined with the graph for another word that sounded like the name of a kind of tree. More than half of the characters found on oracle bones combine components in these ways.

In western Eurasia, logographic scripts were eventually modified or replaced by phonetic scripts, but that never happened in China (though, because of changes in the spoken language, many words today are represented by two or three characters rather than a single one). Basic literacy requires knowing the characters for two or three thousand common words, and well-educated people learn a couple of thousand more. Because characters are composed of a couple of hundred components, this task is not as daunting as it may seem at first, but it still takes much longer than learning to read a phonetic script. Thus, because China retained its logographic writing system, it took many years of study for a person to master reading and writing.

Why did China retain a logographic writing system even after encounters with phonetic ones? Although phonetic systems make learning to read easier, there are costs to abandoning a logographic system. Those who learned to read Chinese could communicate with a wider range of people than those who read scripts based on speech. Since Chinese characters remained recognizable after the passage of many centuries, despite phonological change, educated Chinese could read texts written centuries earlier without the need for them to be translated. Moreover, as the Chinese language developed mutually unintelligible regional variants, readers of Chinese could read books and letters by contemporaries whose oral language they could not comprehend. Thus, the Chinese script played a large role in holding China together and fostering a sense of connection with the past.

For the history of East Asia, the Chinese script has a further significance. Korea, Japan, and Vietnam all began writing by adopting the Chinese script. For several centuries, reading and writing in these countries was done in a foreign language, Chinese. Since most available books had been written in Chinese, learning meant learning through a Chinese lens. In time, however, Chinese characters were used for their meaning or their sound to record the local languages. Those used for their meaning are much like Arabic numerals whose names are pronounced differently depending on the reader's language.

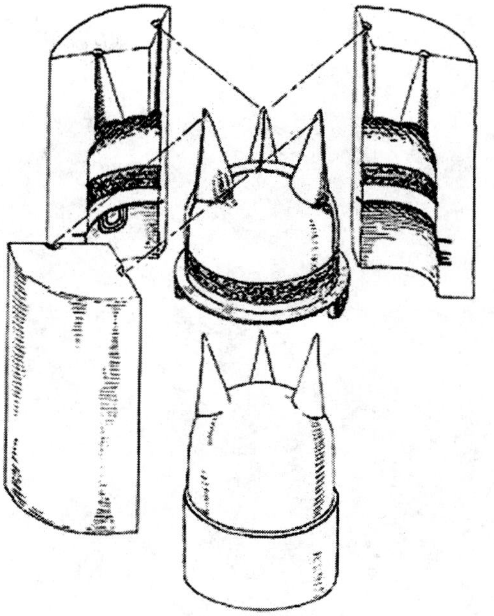

Figure 1.1 **Mold for Bronze Casting.** Shang bronze vessels were made with ceramic molds. After the molten bronze hardened, the pieces of the mold could be removed.

Metalworking

As in Egypt, Mesopotamia, and India, the development of more complex forms of social organization in Shang China coincided with the mastery of metalworking, specifically bronze. Beginning about 2000 B.C.E., people learned to prospect metals, remove them from their ores, and fashion them into tools or ornaments. The next stage, reached about 1500 B.C.E., involved large-scale production.

In Shang times, bronze was used more for ritual than for war. Most surviving Shang bronze objects are vessels such as cups, goblets, steamers, and cauldrons, which originally would have been used to hold food and wine offered to the ancestors or gods during sacrificial ceremonies. Both kings and nobles owned bronze vessels, but the kings had many more.

When compared to bronze objects made in other early societies, Chinese bronzes stand out for their quantity, their decoration, and the ways they were manufactured. Shang bronze making required a large labor force to mine, refine, and transport copper, tin, and lead ores and to produce and transport charcoal. To achieve the high degree of precision and standardization evident from surviving bronze vessels, there must have been considerable division of labor. Technically skilled artisans were needed to make clay models, construct ceramic piece molds, and assemble and finish each vessel. There also would have had to be managers overseeing the entire process. It has been estimated that two to three hundred craftsmen were needed to make the largest surviving Shang bronze vessel, which weighs 875 kilograms.

The technique used to make bronze vessels began with a clay model. After it hardened, soft clay was pressed against it, taking on the negative impression of its shape and decoration. These clay pieces were removed in sections to form the piece molds. The model was then shaved down to become the core (the walls of

Front View of a Shang Bronze Vessel. This rectangular covered vessel, about 10 inches (25 cm) tall, dates from the twelfth century B.C.E.. At the base and the top register are opposed dragons. Between them are stylized mask (*taotie*) designs, with eyes, eyebrows, ears, horns, mouth, and front paws all floating free. The designs on the sides are compressed versions of the designs on the front. *(The Metropolitan Museum of Art, Purchase, Arthur M. Sackler Gift, 1974 [1974.268.2ab])*

the bronze vessel would exactly equal the thickness of this shaved-off layer). After the piece molds were reassembled around the core, molten bronze would be poured into the space between the mold and the core. After cooling, the piece molds were removed.

Scholars have not reached a consensus on the meaning of the decoration on Shang bronzes. In the art of ancient Egypt, Assyria, and Babylonia, images of domesticated plants and animals match our understanding of the importance of agriculture in those societies, much as depictions of social hierarchy (kings, priests, scribes, and slaves) match our understandings of their social and political development. Why then did images of wild animals predominate in Shang China? The symbolic meaning of some animals is easy to guess. Cicadas, which spend years underground before emerging, probably evoked rebirth in the realm of ancestral spirits. Birds similarly suggest to many the idea of messengers who can reach realms in the sky. More problematic is the most common image, the stylized animal face called the *taotie*. To some it is a monster—a fearsome image that would scare away evil forces. Some hypothesize that it reflects masks used in rituals. Others associate it with animal sacrifices, totemism, or shamanism. Still others see these images as hardly more than designs. Scholars' inability to reach a consensus on something so basic as the meaning of the decoration on Shang bronzes reminds us of the huge gaps in our understanding of Shang culture.

DEVELOPMENTS OUTSIDE THE SHANG CORE

The Shang were constantly at war with other groups, tribes, or states, and the area in which the Shang king could safely travel was confined to northern Henan and western Shandong provinces. Key elements of their culture, however, such as their bronze technology, spread well beyond the area they controlled. In the middle Yangzi region, many bronzes have been found that share Shang technology but differ in design, some even using human faces in place of the *taotie*. Bells are particularly common in the Yangzi region, and at one site they were buried in groups in the side of a mountain. The profusion of objects in some tombs in Jiangxi province shows that the elites of this region were able to amass wealth on a scale similar to Shang elites. Their bronze vessels often have tigers on their handles, a style distinctive to the region. Whether this region should be considered a provincial version of Shang civilization or a different culture that borrowed extensively from Shang technology is still not certain. Without written documents like the divination texts of Anyang, there is no way to know if Chinese was the language used in this region.

As discussed in **Connections: The Prehistory of East Asia,** a more independent bronze culture existed north of the Shang core, where people grew millet and raised pigs, sheep, and cattle. Knives, axes, and mirrors are common finds there, but their bronze technology resembles that of Central Asia and Siberia more than the Shang core. Their practice of oracle bone divination, however, links them to Shang civilization. These finds could be evidence of the people who brought chariots to the Shang.

Another strong case for a distinct culture can be made for the civilization discovered at Sanxingdui in the western province of Sichuan. In 1986 two pits of Shang date were found packed with objects never found in Shang sites, including elephant tusks and huge masks, some covered in gold foil (see the table). Both pits were filled in layers, with small objects on the bottom, then the larger ones, then the elephant tusks, then rammed earth. (See Color Plate 1.)

Contents of the Pits at Sanxingdui, ca. 1200 B.C.E.

Pit 1	Pit 2
13 elephant tusks	67 elephant tusks
107 bronze rings	20 bronze masks
13 bronze heads	40 bronze heads
44 bronze dagger-axe blades	bronze statue
4 gold items	bronze trees
60 stone tools	4,600 cowrie shells
70 stone or jade blades	almost 500 small beads or tubes of jade, stone, or ivory
40 pottery vessels	burned animal bones
burned animal bones	

Why were these objects placed in the pits? Many of those in pit 1 had been burned before being deposited, and others had been purposely broken. Thus, one possibility is that these objects are the remnants of a huge sacrifice. Unlike major Shang sacrifices, however, there is no sign of human sacrifice. Some scholars speculate that the bronze figures of humans were being used to replace humans in a sacrificial ceremony. The heads most likely were originally attached to wood or clay statues and could have represented gods or ancestors. Thus, it is also possible that the statues with the bronze heads represented gods and the local people had for some reason decided that those gods or the representations of them had to be burned and buried.

Further archaeological exploration has revealed that the pits lay within a large walled city, nearly 2 kilometers square. Foundations of fifty or so buildings have been found, most rectangular but some round. Five other pits have been found, but they contained no bronze artifacts, only jade and stone ones. Perhaps because of flooding, the city was abandoned around 1000 B.C.E. No sites for later stages of this culture have been found, and there are no nearby sites from succeeding centuries that give evidence of comparable wealth. Perhaps whatever led to the abandonment of Sanxingdui also led to the collapse of the civilization.

The existence of sites like Sanxingdui has forced archaeologists to reconsider the political landscape during the centuries when the Shang ruled at Anyang. Shang rulers wished to see their own polity as the central one, but since we lack written records from sites of other cultures, there is no reason to assume that elites in other places had less self-centered notions of themselves.

THE WESTERN ZHOU DYNASTY (1045–771 B.C.E.)

Outside the Shang domains were the domains of allied and rival polities. To the west were the fierce Qiang, who probably spoke an early form of Tibetan. Between the Shang capital and the Qiang was a frontier state called Zhou, which shared most of the material culture of the Shang. In 1045 B.C.E., this state rose against the Shang and defeated it. The first part of the Zhou Dynasty is called the Western Zhou period (1045–771 B.C.E.) because its capital was in the west near modern Xi'an in Shaanxi province (to distinguish it from the Eastern Zhou, after the capital was moved to near modern Luoyang in Henan province).

In early written traditions, three Zhou rulers are given credit for the Zhou conquest of the Shang. They are King Wen (*wen* means "cultured" or "lettered"), who expanded the Zhou domain; his son King Wu (*wu* means "martial"), who conquered the Shang; and Wu's brother, the duke of Zhou, who consolidated the conquest and served as regent for Wu's heir.

These rulers and their age are portrayed in the earliest transmitted text, the *Book of Documents* (see **Documents: The Announcement of Shao**). The speeches, pronouncements, and reports in this book depict the Zhou conquest as the victory of just and noble warriors, supported by Heaven, over the decadent Shang court led by an evil king. Bronze inscriptions provide another important source for the early Zhou period. Court scribes would prepare written documents on bamboo or wooden strips to specify appointments to offices or fiefs. Later, during a court ceremony, an official would read the document on behalf of the king. A copy of the document would be handed over to the grantee, who then later had it reproduced in bronze so that it could be passed down in his family.

The early Zhou period did not mark an abrupt break with Shang culture, but some Shang practices declined. Divining by heating oracle bones became less common, as did sacrifices of human victims. Interring followers in tombs continued, though their numbers gradually declined.

The Mandate of Heaven

Like the Shang kings, the Zhou kings sacrificed to their ancestors, but they also sacrificed to the divine force called Sky or Heaven. The *Book of Documents* assumes a close relationship between Heaven and the king, who was called the "Son of Heaven." Heaven gives the king a mandate to rule only as long as he rules in the interests of the people. Because the theory of the Mandate of Heaven does not seem to have had any place in Shang cosmology, some scholars think it was elaborated by the early Zhou rulers as propaganda to win over the conquered subjects of the Shang. Whatever its origins, it remained a central feature of Chinese political ideology from the early Zhou period on.

The Zhou Political Structure

At the center of the Western Zhou political structure was the Zhou king, who was simultaneously ritual head of the royal lineage and supreme lord of the nobility. Rather than attempt to rule all of their territories directly, the early Zhou rulers sent out relatives and trusted subordinates to establish walled garrisons in the conquered territories, creating a decentralized, quasi-feudal system. The king's authority was maintained by rituals of ancestor worship and court visits. For instance, in 806 B.C.E., a younger son of King You was made a duke and sent east to establish the state of Zheng in a swampy area that needed to be drained. This duke and his successors nevertheless spent much of their time at the Zhou court, serving as high ministers.

Zhou vassals were generally able to pass their positions on to a son, so that in time the domains became hereditary fiefs. By 800 B.C.E., there were about two hundred lords with domains large and small, of which only about twenty-five were large enough to matter much in interstate politics. Each lord appointed officers to serve him in ritual, administrative, or military capacities. These posts and their associated titles tended to become hereditary as well. Each domain thus came to have noble families with patrimonies in offices and associated lands.

Some Zhou bronzes record benefactions from the king and mention the services that had earned the king's favor. One inscription, for instance, recorded the rewards given to Yu for obeying the king's command to repel attacks of the Southern Huai barbarians. After his successful return, the

DOCUMENTS

The Announcement of Shao

Several texts in the Book of Documents *record speeches and pronouncements of the early Zhou rulers. Scholars used to distrust the early attributions of these texts, but with the discovery and study of more and more inscriptions on early Zhou bronzes, scholars now believe that many of them were in fact written in the first century of Zhou rule. The "Announcement of Shao" records a speech by the duke of Zhou or his brother, the duke of Shao, in which the duke explains the Mandate of Heaven to the newly subjugated people of Shang.*

Ah! August Heaven, High God, has changed his principal son and has revoked the Mandate of this great state of Shang. When a king receives the Mandate, without limit is the grace thereof, but also without limit is the anxiety of it. Ah! How can he fail to be reverently careful!

Heaven has rejected and ended the Mandate of this great state of Shang. Thus, although Shang has many former wise kings in Heaven, when their successor kings and successor people undertook their Mandate, in the end wise and good men lived in misery. Knowing that they must care for and sustain their wives and children, they then called out in anguish to Heaven and fled to places where they could not be caught. Ah! Heaven too grieved for the people of all the lands, wanting, with affection, in giving its Mandate to employ those who are deeply committed. The king should have reverent care of his virtue.

Look at the former peoples of ancient times, the Xia. Heaven guided, indulged, and cherished them, so that they would strive to understand what Heaven favors, but by this time they have let their Mandate fall to the ground. Now look at the Shang; Heaven guided them, stayed near them, nourished them, so that they would strive to comprehend what Heaven favors; but now they have let their Mandate fall to the ground.

Now a young son succeeds to the throne; let him not, then, neglect the aged and experienced. Not only do they comprehend the virtue of our men of old—nay, more, they are sometimes able to comprehend counsels that come from Heaven.

Ah! Even though it be that the king is young, he is [Heaven's] principal son. Let him be grandly able to be in harmony with the little people. In the present time of grace, the king must not dare to be slow, but should be prudently apprehensive about what the people say. . . .

Those above and below being zealous and careful, let them say, "As we receive Heaven's Mandate, let it grandly be like the long years enjoyed by the Xia, and not fail of the years enjoyed by the Shang"—in order that [as one would wish] the king, through the little people, may receive Heaven's enduring Mandate.

Translated by David S. Nivison in *Sources of Chinese Tradition,* 2nd ed., comp. Wm. Theodore de Bary and Irene Bloom (New York: Columbia University Press, 1999), pp. 35–37, slightly modified.

king brought Yu into the ancestral temple, where he conferred on him two bronze ritual vessels, fifty strands of cowrie shells, and one hundred fields as reward for bringing back one hundred heads and forty manacled prisoners. The inscription concludes, "Yu dares in response to extol the

Chariot Burial. The type of chariot found in this Western Zhou burial pit, with large, many-spoked wheels, spread across Asia around 1200 B.C.E. *(Institute of Archaeology, Beijing)*

Son of Heaven's beneficence, herewith making this offertory tureen; may Yu for 10,000 years have sons' sons and grandsons' grandsons eternally treasure and use it."[1]

As in Shang times, there continued to be groups viewed as alien living in the same general region as the Zhou states as well as beyond its borders. Various groups of Yi ("eastern barbarians"), for instance, lived interspersed through the east, as did different groups of Rong ("northern barbarians") in the north and west. These groups spoke distinct languages, though they were not necessarily more primitive than the Zhou people in technology. Over the course of the nearly three centuries of Western Zhou rule, the Zhou kings drew many of these groups into the Zhou political order by recognizing their chiefs as the lords of their domains. To participate in this order, they had to use the Chinese writing system for matters of state.

Ties of loyalty and kinship linking the Zhou vassals to the king weakened over time, and in 771 B.C.E. the Zhou king was killed by an alliance of Rong tribesmen and Zhou vassals. Zhou nobles fleeing this attack buried their bronze vessels, expecting to unearth them after they returned. One such hoard discovered in 1976 contained 103 vessels belonging to Earl Xing of Wei cast by several generations of his family. Instead of returning, however, the Zhou royal house and nobles moved east to the area of modern Luoyang, just south of the Yellow River in the heart of the central plains. Eastern Zhou never fully regained control over its vassals, and China entered a prolonged period without a strong central authority, which will be discussed in Chapter 2.

Western Zhou Society and Culture

Western Zhou society was highly aristocratic. Inherited ranks placed people in a hierarchy ranging from the king, to the rulers of states with titles like duke and marquis, the hereditary great officials of these lords, and the lower ranks of the aristocracy called *shi,* men who could serve in either military or civil capacities. At the bottom were ordinary subjects. Patrilineal family ties were very important throughout this society, and at the upper reaches at least, sacrifices to ancestors were one of the key rituals used to forge social ties.

Land in this system was held on feudal tenures, and the economy was a manorial one. When the Zhou king bestowed land on a relative or subordinate, he generally also gave him people to work it. These farmers were treated as serfs, obliged to provide food and labor for the lord, who was expected in turn to look after their welfare.

Glimpses of what life was like at various social levels in the early Zhou period can be

1. Edward L. Shaughnessy, "Western Zhou History," in M. Loewe and E. Shaughnessy, eds., *The Cambridge History of Ancient China: From the Origins of Civilization to 221 B.C.* (New York: Cambridge University Press, 1999), p. 331.

found in the *Book of Poetry,* which contains the earliest Chinese songs and poems. Many of the folk songs are love songs. Others depict the farming life, which involved not merely the cultivation of crops like millet, hemp (for cloth), beans, and vegetables, but also hunting small animals and collecting grasses and rushes to make rope and baskets. The seasons set the pace for rural life, and poems contain many references to seasonal changes such as the appearance of grasshoppers and crickets.

The *Book of Poetry* also offers glimpses of court life and its ceremonies. Besides congratulatory court odes were ones with a critical edge. In the following stanza, the ancestors are rebuked for not providing aid to their descendants in distress:

> The drought has become so severe
> That it cannot be stopped.
> Glowing and burning,
> We have no place.
> The great mandate is about at an end,
> Nothing to look ahead to or back upon.
> The host of dukes and past rulers
> Does not help us.
> As for father and mother and the
> ancestors,
> How can they bear to treat us so?[2]

Men and women had very different roles at court, and one poem shows that these differences were marked from birth:

> A male child is born.
> He is made to sleep on a bed.
> He is made to wear a skirt.
> He is made to play with a scepter.
> His crying is loud.
> His red knee-covers are august.
> He is the hall and household's lord and
> king.
> A female child is born.
> She is made to sleep on the floor.
> She is made to wear a wrap-cloth.
> She is made to play with pottery.
> She has no wrong and right.
> Only wine and food are for her to talk
> about.
> May she not send her father and mother
> any troubles.[3]

SUMMARY

How different was China at the end of the Western Zhou period in 771 B.C.E. compared to China at the beginning of the Bronze Age in 2000 B.C.E.? Differences in technology were pervasive. At the beginning of this period, China was just beginning to fashion objects of metal; by the end, bronze workers had centuries of experience in casting all sorts of objects, and bronze was used not only for ritual vessels but also for helmets, swords, knives, axes, and other tools. Horses had been domesticated and trained to pull chariots. Writing had become a central feature in the life of the political elite, and a substantial body of literature was in circulation. Some elements of culture and organization had already undergone major transformations. Divination by oracle bones had largely disappeared, as had the practice of making offerings of human victims, except at the burial of rulers, where it continued somewhat sporadically. Previously alien groups were incorporated into the Zhou political order, and more and more of them participated in the culture associated with the Chinese written language. Thus, in all likelihood there were more people we can call Chinese by the end of this period.

2. Ode 258, in Shaughnessy, "Western Zhou History," p. 336.

3. Ode 189, in Paul Rakita Goldin, *The Culture of Sex in Ancient China* (Honolulu: University of Hawaii Press, 2002), p. 24.

SUGGESTED READING

For early China, the most authoritative volume is M. Loewe and E. Shaughnessy, *The Cambridge History of Ancient China: From the Origins of Civilization to 221 B.C.* (1999). The journal *Early China* often reports on important new archaeological finds. On the archaeology of early China, see K. C. Chang, *The Archeology of Ancient China,* 4th ed. (1986); *Shang Civilization* (1986); and *Art, Myth, and Ritual: The Path to Political Authority in Ancient China* (1983). For the development of the Chinese writing system, see W. Boltz, *The Origin and Early Development of the Chinese Writing System* (1994). S. Allan examines Shang cosmology and Zhou myths in *The Shape of the Turtle: Myth, Art, and Cosmology in Early China* (1991). For the Western Zhou period, see M. Lewis, *Sanctioned Violence in Early China* (1990), and C. Hsu and K. Linduff, *Western Chou Civilization* (1988). For a translation of the earliest Chinese history of the Shang and Western Zhou periods, dating to the first century B.C.E., see W. Nienhauser et al., *The Grand Scribes Records,* vol. 1 (1994).

Two attractive volumes on ancient art and technology are X. Yang, ed., *The Golden Age of Chinese Archaeology: Celebrated Discoveries from the People's Republic of China* (1999), and W. Fong, *Great Bronze Age of China* (1980). L. Ledderose, *Ten Thousand Things: Module and Mass Production in Chinese Art* (2000) offers fresh perspectives on both the Chinese script and the production of bronze vessels, among other subjects. Other good introductions to early Chinese art are J. Rawson, ed., *The British Museum Book of Chinese Art* (1992), and R. Thorp and R. Vinograd, *Chinese Art and Culture* (2001). On the discoveries in Sichuan, see R. Bagley, ed., *Ancient Sichuan: Treasures from a Lost Civilization* (2001).

CHAPTER TWO

2

Philosophers and Warring States During the Eastern Zhou (770–256 B.C.E.)

The foundations of Chinese thought were established in the five centuries that followed the transfer of the Zhou court to Luoyang in 770 B.C.E. In this period, the old Zhou fiefs came to function more and more like independent states, linked to each other in a multistate system. Gradually, warfare between the states intensified, and social, political, and cultural change also quickened. By the third century B.C.E., only seven important states remained. Over the course of these centuries, hereditary ranks meant less and less, and rulers made more use of the *shi,* the lower ranks of the old aristocratic order. As these *shi* competed to offer advice to rulers, they advanced the art of argument and set in motion a tremendous intellectual flowering. China entered one of its most creative periods, when the ideas underlying Confucian, Daoist, and Legalist traditions were developed.

Historians of ideas, warfare, and social and political change have all found the Eastern Zhou a fascinating period to study. Archaeological evidence remains fundamental to enlarging our understanding of this period and has been particularly valuable for showing the richness of the culture of the south, the region of the state of Chu. Few of the philosophical texts of this period were written by a single known author, so scholars have devoted much of their energy to distinguishing the earlier and later layers of texts. Knowing the importance of the strong, centralized state in later periods of Chinese history, historians have also drawn attention to the advances in statecraft of this period and the connections between the ideas articulated in this period and the social and political situation. Would comparable ideas have emerged if China had not been politically divided? How significant was the emergence of the *shi* to the intellectual history of this period? Is it more than coincidental that China's first intellectual flowering occurred in roughly the same centuries as that of ancient India, Greece, Persia, and Israel?

THE MULTISTATE SYSTEM OF THE EASTERN ZHOU

The Eastern Zhou Dynasty is conventionally divided into two periods named after books that recorded events of the time: the Spring and Autumn period, to 479 B.C.E., and the Warring States period after it. The history of the Eastern Zhou Dynasty is better documented than the history of the Western Zhou because of advances in the art of political narrative. For the Spring and Autumn period, the most important chronicle is the *Zuo zhuan,* a narrative covering the years 722 to 463 B.C.E., traditionally treated as a commentary to the much briefer *Spring and Autumn Annals.* For the Warring States period, *The Intrigues of the Warring States* presents lengthy narratives, arranged by state rather than chronologically. A third work, the *Discourses of the States,* also arranged by state, concentrates on speeches and covers both periods. The authorship and dating of all three of these works are uncertain, but at a minimum they contain Zhou material.

Although the Zhou kings were still considered the supreme monarchs, they no longer had the military might to force obedience. Sometimes supposed vassals would even attack the Zhou king. In this period, the ruler of one state would sometimes be recognized as the hegemon, the leader of the alliance of Zhou states (see **Biography: Guan Zhong**). These hegemons periodically called meetings of the allied states where rulers or leading ministers would swear to uphold the Zhou feudal structure. At a meeting in 657 B.C.E., the states

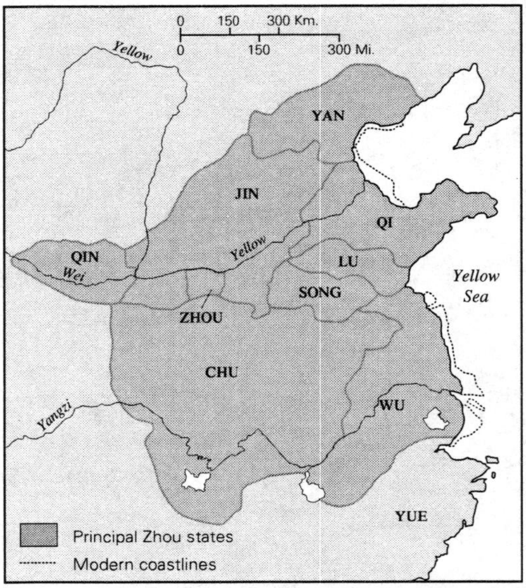

Map 2.1 **Zhou States in the Sixth Century B.C.E.**

swore not to dam irrigation waters, withhold sales of grain, replace heirs apparent, promote concubines to wives, or let women interfere in state affairs. The principal states of the early Warring States period are shown on Map 2.1.

Succession disputes were a common pretext for war between states. Rulers regularly had concubines in addition to a wife and thus would have children by several women. In theory, succession went to the eldest son of the wife, then younger sons by her, and only in their absence sons of concubines. In actual practice, however, the ruler of a state or head of a powerful ministerial family could select a son of a concubine to be his heir if he wished. During his lifetime, this led to much scheming for favor among the various sons and their mothers and the common perception that women were incapable of taking a disinterested view of the larger good. Sons who felt unfairly excluded often journeyed to other states in search of allies. Since rulers regularly took their wives from the ruling families of other states, a contender could try the state that his mother or grandmother had come from or the states his

BIOGRAPHY Guan Zhong

By the time of Confucius, the success of states was often credited more to the lord's astute advisers than to the lords themselves. To Confucius, the most praiseworthy political advisor was Guan Zhong (ca. 720–645 B.C.E.), the genius behind the rise of the state of Qi in eastern China.

The earliest historical sources that recount Guan Zhong's accomplishments are the commentaries compiled in the Warring States period to elaborate on the dry chronicle known as the *Spring and Autumn Annals.* The *Zuo zhuan,* for instance, tells us that in 660 B.C.E., Guan Zhong advised Duke Huan to aid the small state of Xing, then under attack by the non-Chinese Rong tribes: "The Rong and the Di are wolves who cannot be satiated. The Xia [Chinese] states are kin who should not be abandoned." In 652, it tells us, Guan Zhong urged the duke to maintain the respect of the other states by refusing the request for an alliance by a ruler's son who wished to depose his father. Because the duke regularly listened to Guan Zhong's sound advice, Qi brought the other states under its sway, and the duke came to be recognized as the first hegemon, or leader of the alliance of states.

Guan Zhong was also credited with strengthening the duke's internal administration. He encouraged the employment of officials on the basis of their moral character and ability rather than their birth. He introduced a system of drafting commoners for military service. In the history of China written by Sima Qian in about 100 B.C.E., Guan Zhong is also given credit for enriching Qi by promoting trade, issuing coins, and standardizing merchants' scales. He was credited with the statement that "when the granaries are full, the people will understand ritual and moderation. When they have enough food and clothing, they will understand honor and disgrace."

Sima Qian's biography of Guan Zhong emphasized his early poverty and the key role played by a friend, Bao Shuya, who recognized his worth. As young men, both Bao and Guan Zhong served brothers of the duke of Qi. When this duke was killed and a messy succession struggle followed, Bao's patron won out and became the next duke, while Guan Zhong's patron had to flee and in the end was killed. Bao, however, recommended Guan Zhong to the new duke, Duke Huan, and Guan Zhong took up a post under him.

In the *Analects,* one of Confucius's disciples thought this lack of loyalty to his first lord made Guan Zhong a man unworthy of respect: "When Duke Huan killed his brother Jiu, Guan Zhong was unable to die with Jiu but rather became chancellor to Duke Huan." Confucius disagreed: "Guan Zhong became chancellor to Duke Huan and made him hegemon among the lords, uniting and reforming all under heaven. The people, down to the present, continued to receive benefits from this. Were it not for Guan Zhong our hair would hang unbound and we would fold our robes on the left [that is, live as barbarians]" (*Analects* 14.18).

A book of the teachings associated with Guan Zhong, the *Guanzi,* was in circulation by the late Warring States period. Although today it is not thought to reflect the teachings of the historical Guan Zhong, the fact that later statecraft thinkers would borrow his name is an indication of his fame as a great statesman.

sisters or aunts had married into. The rulers of these states were often happy to see someone indebted to them on the throne of a neighboring state and would lend armies to help oust rivals.

There were, of course, other reasons for warfare. States tried to maintain a balance of power and prevent any one state from becoming too strong. States on the periphery had the advantage, as they could expand outward. Thus, the four states to gain the most over the course of the Spring and Autumn period were Qin in the west, Jin in the north, Qi in the east, and Chu in the south. As Chu expanded from its base in the south, Qi organized other states to resist it. Sometimes the states in the middle, weary of being caught in the fighting between the larger powers, organized peace conferences.

Another common reason for the hegemon to bring troops to the aid of a state was to help it fend off attack by various forces from beyond the Zhou world. But those labeled with the non-Chinese ethnic terms Di, Rong, or Yi were not always in a position of enmity to the Chinese states. For instance, Jin often enlisted Rong or Di polities to join it in fighting Qin. Moreover, some Rong and Di leaders were versed in Chinese literature. There was also intermarriage between the ruling class of Zhou states and the Rong and Di elites. Duke Wen of Jin's mother was a Rong, his wife a Di. The only written language in this world, however, was Chinese, which worked toward making Chinese the common language. In the south, the states of Wu and Yue emerged from outside the Zhou sphere but adopted Zhou cultural patterns; Yue, in fact, claimed to be descended from the Xia Dynasty, making it more ancient than the Zhou Dynasty.

Archaeological evidence confirms steady cultural exchange between Zhou and non-Zhou elements in this period. The rulers of the state of Zhongshan in the northeast were recognized as descended from White Di, who had been driven by other tribes from Shaanxi into Hebei in the sixth century. With help from the state of Wei, they established their own city there. Although Zhongshan was a very minor state, its rulers decided to call themselves kings when other states' rulers did. The tomb of King Cuo of Zhongshan, who died around 308 B.C.E., included inscribed bronzes that record historical events in typically Confucian language, full of stock phrases from the classics.

Rulers continued to be buried with followers in this period. Duke Mu of Qin had 177 people accompany him in death after he died in 621 B.C.E., and nearly a century later, in 537 B.C.E., Duke Jin was buried with 166. By this period, there were people who disapproved of the practice. In the state of Qin, the practice was outlawed in 383 B.C.E. Moreover, the sacrificing of war captives in ceremonies unrelated to burials no longer seems to have been practiced. Remnants of this practice could still be seen in the use of the blood of captives to consecrate newly cast war drums and the ritual of presenting captives at the ancestral temple or other altar.

WARFARE AND ITS CONSEQUENCES

The purpose and conduct of war changed dramatically in the Eastern Zhou period. In the Spring and Autumn period, a large army would have up to ten thousand soldiers, the chariot remained central to warfare, and states were ranked by how many hundreds of chariots they could deploy. A code of chivalrous conduct regulated warfare between the states. The two sides would agree on the time and place for a battle, and each would perform divination and sacrifices before initiating hostilities. One state would not attack another while it was in mourning for its ruler. Ruling houses were not wiped out so that a successor could continue to sacrifice to their ancestors. Battle narratives in the *Zuo zhuan* give the impression that commanders cared as much about proving their honor as about winning. In 638 B.C.E. the duke of the small state of Song felt compelled to fight a much stronger state. Because his forces were greatly outnumbered, his minister of war urged him to attack the enemy while they were fording a river, but the duke refused. The *Zuo zhuan* reports that he explained his behavior this way: "The gentleman does not inflict a second wound, nor does he capture those with gray hair. On campaigns the ancients did not obstruct those in a narrow pass. Even though I am but the remnant of a destroyed state, I will not drum an attack when the other side has not yet drawn up its ranks."[1] When combat was hedged with these ceremonial restrictions, war was less deadly—a wound ended the victim's combat status but not necessarily his life.

By the Warring States period, such niceties were being abandoned as advances in military technology changed the nature of warfare. Large, well-drilled infantry armies were becoming a potent military force, able to withstand and defeat chariot-led forces. By the late Warring States period military obligations were nearly universal for men. For Qin's campaign against Zhao in 260 B.C.E., it mobilized all men over age fifteen. By 300 B.C.E. states were sending out armies of a couple hundred thousand drafted foot soldiers, usually accompanied by horsemen. Conscripts with a year or two of training would not have the martial skills of aristocratic warriors who trained for years and tested their skills in hunts. But infantry armies won out through standardization, organization, discipline, and sheer size.

Adding to the effectiveness of armies of drafted foot soldiers was the crossbow, invented in the southern state of Chu. The trigger of a crossbow is an intricate bronze mechanism that allowed a foot soldier to shoot farther than a horseman carrying a light bow. One text of the period claimed that a skilled soldier with a powerful crossbow and a sharp sword was the match for a hundred ordinary men. To defend against crossbows, soldiers began wearing armor and helmets. Most of the armor was made of leather strips tied with cords. Helmets were sometimes made of iron.

Although most soldiers were drafted peasants, it became common to select and train elite corps of crack troops. The elite troops in the state of Wei had to wear heavy armor and helmets, shoulder a crossbow and fifty arrows, strap a spear to their backs and a sword by their waists, carry three days' supply of food, and march about fifty kilometers in a single day. Those meeting this standard earned their household exemption from all taxes and labor service obligations.

The development of infantry armies created the need for a new type of general, as rulers became less willing to let men lead troops merely because of aristocratic birth. Treatises on the art of war described the ideal general as a master of maneuver, illusion, and deception, ruthless in searching for the advantage that would lead to victory. He also had to be an organizer, able to integrate the efforts of the units under him.

Because cities were walled, attacks on them resulted in prolonged sieges, and generals were eager to try new ways to attack and defend walls. Portable ladders were brought to scale the walls. When attackers dug tunnels under the walls, defenders would use large bellows of the sort common in smelting iron to pump smoke into the tunnels and suffocate the attackers.

City walls were not the only defensive structure important to warfare of the period. States began building chains of watch stations and forts, often connecting them with long defensive walls. Permanent garrisons were left at strategic points to prevent the passage of armies. Barriers also allowed states to check those who entered or left their territories and to collect transit taxes from merchants.

The introduction of cavalry struck another blow at the chariot-riding aristocracy. Shooting bows and arrows from horseback was first perfected by non-Chinese peoples to the north of China proper, who at that time were making the transition to a nomadic pastoral economy. As the northern states expanded northward, absorbing non-Chinese communities of mixed shepherds and farmers, they came into direct contact with the horse riders of the steppe. In 307 B.C.E. the king of the northern state of Jin

1. Duke Xi, 22nd year. Translations cited by the traditional sections are by the author.

ordered his troops to adopt the nomads' trousers and practice mounted archery (see **Documents: The King of Zhao Persuades His Uncle to Wear Barbarian Dress**). Soon Zhao was using cavalry against other Chinese states, which then had to master the new technology to defend themselves. Larger infantry armies of 100,000 or 200,000 men would be supported by a few hundred mounted warriors. Cavalry were considered especially valuable for reconnaissance, pursuing fleeing soldiers, cutting supply lines, and pillaging the countryside. From this time on, acquiring and pasturing horses was a key component of Chinese military preparedness (see Color Plate 2).

As a result of all these developments in the art of war, conflicts came to be waged with greater intensity and on a much larger scale than ever before. Whereas Spring and Autumn period campaigns had lasted no longer than a season and battles no longer than a day or two, some campaigns in the Warring States period lasted for years, with separate armies operating independently on several fronts. Qin's defeat of Zhao in 260 B.C.E. came after a campaign that lasted three years and involved hundreds of thousands of soldiers on each side deadlocked across a front that stretched more than a hundred miles.

Because these developments in the art of war made commoners and craftsmen crucial, rulers of the warring states tried to find ways to increase their populations. To increase agricultural output, they brought new land into cultivation, drained marshes, and dug irrigation channels. By the sixth century B.C.E. some rulers were surveying their land and beginning to try to levy taxes on farmers. They wanted to undermine the power of lords over their subjects in order to get direct access to peasants' labor power. Serfdom thus gradually declined. Registering populations led to the extension of family names to commoners at an earlier date than anywhere else in the world.

The development of iron technology in the early Zhou period also promoted economic expansion. Iron was cast from the beginning, unlike in the west, where iron was wrought long before it was cast. By the fifth century B.C.E., iron was being widely used for both farm tools and weapons. By the third century B.C.E., the largest smelters employed two hundred or more workmen.

The economic growth of the late Zhou period is evident in the appearance of cities all over north China. In addition to the thick earthen walls built around the palaces and ancestral temples of the ruler and other aristocrats, outer walls were added to protect the artisans, merchants, and farmers living in the surrounding area. Another sign of economic growth is the emergence of a new powerful group in society: the rich, who had acquired their wealth through trade or industry rather than inheritance or political favor. Late Zhou texts frequently mention cross-regional trade in objects such as furs, copper, dyes, hemp, salt, and horses. To promote trade, rulers began casting coins, at first in the shape of miniature spades.

In the fourth century B.C.E., rulers of states started calling themselves kings, a step that amounted to announcing their intent to conquer all the other states. Rulers strengthened their control by dispatching their own officials rather than delegating authority to hereditary lesser lords. Rulers controlled these officials from a distance through the transmission of documents and could dismiss them if they proved unsatisfactory. For the *shi,* serving a ruler in this way offered new opportunities for advancement. There were plenty of *shi* eager for these opportunities because every time a state was destroyed, its old nobility sunk in status to *shi.* Although many *shi* did not have military skills by this period, they retained knightly values such as a sense of honor and an ideal of loyal service.

THE HUNDRED SCHOOLS OF THOUGHT

The late Zhou was a period when all sorts of ideas were proposed, debated, written down, and put to use, leading Chinese to refer to it as

DOCUMENTS

The King of Zhao Convinces His Uncle to Wear Barbarian Dress

The Intrigues of the Warring States *is a collection of late Zhou historical anecdotes and fables about the political ploys adopted by the various competing states. The book, full of speeches by kings and court advisers, has been appreciated as a work of literature, even by those who were dismayed by its morality. In this passage, the king of Zhao has decided to adopt the trousers of the northern nomads, the Hu (also called Xiongnu), but he worried that others would make fun of him. He sent a messenger to ask his uncle, Gongzi Cheng, to join him in changing his dress. We begin here with the uncle's response.*

[The uncle] Gongzi Cheng bowed twice: "I had, of course, heard of the king's Hu clothing but having been ill abed I had not yet gone to him to present my opinions. Since the king now sends me these orders, I must now make my clumsy gesture of loyalty.

"I have heard the Middle Kingdoms described as the home of all wisdom and learning, the place where all things needful of life are found, where saints and sages taught, where humanity and justice prevail, where the *Book of Poetry* and *Book of Documents* and *Canons of Ritual* and *Music* are used; a country where extraordinary skills and uncommon intelligence are given hearing, a land looked up to from afar, and a model of behavior for the barbarian. But now the king would discard all this and wear the habit of foreign regions. Let him think carefully, for he is changing the teachings of our ancients, turning from the ways of former times, going counter to the desires of his people, offending scholars, and ceasing to be part of the Middle Kingdoms."

When [the messenger] Wangsun Xie had reported, the king said merely, "I knew, of course, that he had been ill." Then, going in person to the home of Gongzi Cheng, the king urged his support: "Clothes exist to be useful and manners respond to conditions. Therefore the sage was guided by what was right and proper for each locality and encouraged behavior related to its conditions: always they sought to profit the people and strengthen their states," said the king. "To crop the hair, decorate the body, rub pigment into arms and fasten garments on the left side are the ways of the Ba and Yue [southern barbarians]. In the country of Daiwu the habit is to blacken teeth, scar cheeks, and wear caps of sheepskin stitched crudely with an awl. Their costumes and customs differ but each derives benefit from his own. . . .

"From Changshan to Dai and Shangdang, we border Yan and the Eastern Hu in the east, and Loufan, Qin, and Han in the west. Along this line we have not a single mounted archer. . . . I change our garments and mount archers to guard our borders with Yan, the Eastern Hu, Loufan, Qin, and Han. . . . With my men dressed as mounted archers I can today prepare for Shangdang nearby and exact vengeance upon Zhongshan at a distance. . . ."

Gongzi Cheng made deepest obeisance twice: "Such has been my stupidity that I had not even conceived of these arguments, your majesty. I had instead the temerity to mouth platitudes. But now that I too wish to carry out the hopes of Kings Jian and Xiang, the ambitions of our ancestral rulers, what choice have I but to make obeisance and obey your order?"

He was given the Hu garments.

Source: J. I. Crump, trans., *Chan-kuo Ts'e,* rev. ed. (Ann Arbor: University of Michigan Center for Chinese Studies, 1996), pp. 288–292, modified.

a period "when a hundred schools of thought bloomed." The political rivalry and constant warfare of the period helped rather than hindered intellectual creativity. Rulers turned to men of ideas for both solutions to the disorder around them and the prestige of attracting to their court wise and able men from across the country. Political strategists would travel from state to state urging rulers to form alliances. Lively debate often resulted as strategists proposed policies and challengers critiqued them. Successful men of ideas attracted followers, who took to recording their teacher's ideas on the rolls of silk and tied together strips of wood or bamboo that functioned as books.

Historians of later periods, beginning with Sima Qian in about 100 B.C.E., grouped these thinkers into schools, using labels that have survived until today, such as Confucianism, Daoism, and Legalism, which may give the mistaken impression that people of the time thought in those terms. Even the books we have today are not identical to the books that first circulated, as the works of an author were added to, subtracted from, and rearranged after his death, usually by his followers. Scholars today try to distinguish the different layers of texts to analyze the development of ideas and emphasize the extensive interchange of ideas among diverse teachers and thinkers.

Confucius and the *Analects*

Confucius (who early historians dated to 551–479 B.C.E.) was the first and most important of the men of ideas seeking to influence the rulers of the day. As a young man, Confucius served in the court of his home state of Lu without gaining much influence. After leaving Lu, he wandered through neighboring states with a small group of students, searching for a ruler who would follow his advice.

Confucius's ideas are known to us primarily through the sayings recorded by his disciples in the *Analects*. The thrust of his thought was ethical rather than theoretical or metaphysical. He talked repeatedly of an ideal age in the early Zhou, which he conceived of as a perfect society in which all people devoted themselves to fulfilling their roles: superiors looked after those dependent on them, inferiors devoted themselves to the service of their superiors, and parents and children, husbands and wives, all wholeheartedly did what was expected of them.

Confucius saw much of value in family ties. He extolled filial piety, which to him encompassed reverent obedience of children toward their parents and performance of the expected rituals, such as mourning them when they died and making sacrifices to them afterward. If one's parents were about to make a major mistake, the filial child should try to dissuade them as tactfully as possible but should try not to anger them. The relationship between father and son was one of the five cardinal relations stressed by Confucius. The others were between ruler and subject, husband and wife, elder and younger brother, and between friends. Mutual obligations of a hierarchal sort underlay the first four of these relationships: the senior leads and protects, the junior supports and obeys. The exception was the relationship between friends, which was conceived in terms of the mutual obligations between equals.

Confucian Virtues

ren	humanity, benevolence
xiao	filial piety
yi	integrity, righteousness
zhong	loyalty, constancy
xin	honesty
jing	reverence, respect
li	propriety, ritual decorum

Confucius urged his followers to aspire to become true gentlemen (*junzi*, literally "son of a lord"), a term that he redefined to mean men of moral cultivation rather than men of noble birth. He contrasted gentlemen of integrity to petty men seeking personal gain. The gentleman, he said, "feels bad when his capabilities fall short of the task. He does not feel bad when people fail to recognize him" (15.18).

The Confucian gentleman should advise his ruler on the best way to govern. Much of the *Analects* consequently concerns how to govern well:

> *The Master said, "Lead the people by means of government policies and regulate them through punishments, and they will be evasive and have no sense of shame. Lead them by means of virtue and regulate them through rituals and they will have a sense of shame and moreover have standards." (2.3)*

To Confucius, the ultimate virtue was *ren,* a term that has been translated as humanity, perfect goodness, benevolence, human-heartedness, and nobility. A person of humanity cares about others and acts accordingly:

> *Zhonggong asked about humanity. The Master said, "When you go out, treat everyone as if you were welcoming a great guest. Employ people as though you were conducting a great sacrifice. Do not do unto others what you would not have them do unto you. Then neither in your country nor in your family will there be complaints against you." (12.2)*

Treating people as though they were guests and employing them as though participating in a great sacrifice is another way of saying that they should be treated according to *li* (ritual, manners, propriety, good form). In other passages as well, Confucius stressed the importance of disciplining one's behavior through adherence to ritual: "Respect without ritual is tiresome; caution without ritual is timidity; boldness without ritual is insubordination; straightforwardness without ritual is rudeness" (8.2). But ritual must not be empty form: "Ritual performed without reverence and mourning performed without grief are things I cannot bear" (3.26).

In the Confucian tradition, studying texts came to be valued over speculation, meditation, and mystical identification with deities. Confucius encouraged the men who came to study with him to master the poetry, rituals, and historical traditions that we know today as the Confucian classics. Many passages in the *Analects* reveal Confucius's confidence in the power of study:

> *The Master said, "I am not someone who was born wise. I am someone who loves the ancients and tries to learn from them." (7.19)*
>
> *The Master said, "I once spent a whole day without eating and a whole night without sleeping in order to think. It was of no use. It is better to study." (15.30)*

Confucius talked mostly about the social and political realms rather than the world of gods, ghosts, or ancestral spirits. Moreover, although he is portrayed as deeply committed to ritual, he was said to have performed sacrifices as though the spirits were present, leaving open the possibility that he was not convinced that ancestors or other spirits were actually aided by the offerings people made to them.

Mozi

Not long after Confucius died, his ideas were challenged by Mozi (ca. 480–390 B.C.E.), a man who came not from the aristocracy but from among the master craftsmen. He was, however, well read and like Confucius quoted from the *Book of Documents* and *Book of Poetry.* Unlike Confucius, though, he did not talk of the distinction between gentlemen and vulgar "petty men," but rather of "concern for everyone," sometimes translated as "universal love." He put forward the idea that conflict could be eliminated if everyone gave other people's families and other people's states the same concern he gave his own. Mozi contended that all people recognize the validity of this idea because if they have to leave their family in someone else's care, they choose someone who accepts this ideal. To counter the argument that impartiality is not easy to achieve, Mozi said the sage kings of old had practiced it, proving its feasibility. Mozi also argued strongly for the merit principle, asserting that rulers should choose their advisers on the basis of their ability, not their birth.

The book ascribed to Mozi (called *Mozi*) proposes that every idea be evaluated on the basis of its utility: Does it benefit the people and the state? Using this standard, Mozi rejected many of the rituals emphasized by Confucius's followers, especially mourning parents for three years, which Mozi noted interrupts work, injures health, and thus impoverishes the people and weakens the state. Music, too, Mozi saw as a wasteful extravagance of no utility.

Mozi made a similar case against aggressive war, seeing no glory in expansion for its own sake. He pointed to the huge losses in weapons, horses, and human lives it causes. The capture of a city, he argued, is not worth the loss of thousands of men. But Mozi was for strong government and obedience toward superiors. He argued that disorder could be eliminated if everyone conformed his beliefs to those of his superior, the king conforming to Heaven.

Mozi had many followers over the next couple of centuries, and they organized themselves into tight groups. Because they saw offensive warfare as evil, these Mohists, as they are called, considered it their duty to come to the aid of cities under attack. They became experts in defending against sieges, teaching, for instance, that each soldier on the city walls should be held responsible for the two soldiers on his immediate left and right, a form of group responsibility later picked up by the Legalists.

After a few centuries, however, Mozi's school declined and eventually lost its distinct identity. Certain ideas, such as support for the merit principle and criticism of extravagance, were absorbed into Confucian thought in later centuries. Mencius, who lived a century after Mozi, borrowed his arguments against military aggression, and like him would often try to persuade rulers that they had not correctly identified where their advantage lay. Confucians, however, never accepted Mohist ideas about treating everyone equally, unnatural in their minds, or of applying rigidly utilitarian tests to ritual and music, whose value they saw in very different terms.

Mencius

Among the followers of Confucius eager to defend his teachings against Mozi's attacks, Mencius stands out. We know of Mencius (ca. 370–ca. 300 B.C.E.) largely from the book that bears his name, which Mencius may have written in large part himself. Mencius came from the small and unimportant state of Zou, next to Confucius's home state of Lu. He was born too late to have studied with Confucius himself, but he quotes Confucius approvingly and was said to have studied Confucian teachings with a student of Confucius's grandson.

The first two of the seven parts of the *Mencius* record conversations that took place from 320 to 314 B.C.E. between Mencius and a king of Qi and two successive kings of Wei. The opening passage in the *Mencius* records one such encounter:

> *Mencius had an audience with King Hui of Liang [Wei]. The king said, "Sir, you did not consider a thousand* li *too far to come. You must have some ideas about how to benefit my state."*
>
> *Mencius replied, "Why must Your Majesty use the word 'benefit'? All I am concerned with are the benevolent and the right. If Your Majesty says, 'How can I benefit my state?' your officials will say, 'How can I benefit my family,' and officers and common people will say, 'How can I benefit myself.' Once superiors and inferiors are competing for benefit, the state will be in danger." (1A.1)*

Like Confucius, Mencius traveled around offering advice to rulers of various states. He tried repeatedly to convert them to the view that the ruler able to win over the people through benevolent government would succeed in unifying "all under Heaven." Mencius proposed concrete political and financial measures for easing tax burdens and otherwise improving the people's lot. He also tried to get rulers to give up seeking military victories. To seek military domination will backfire, he argued, for it will turn the world against you, whereas those who are benevolent will have no enemies.

Men willing to serve an unworthy ruler earned Mencius's contempt, especially when they worked hard to fill his coffers or expand his territory. He pointed out that Confucius broke off his relationship with his disciple Ran Qiu when he doubled the tax collection but did not do anything to reform the ruler's character.

Although the bulk of the *Mencius* concerns issues of governing, Mencius also discussed issues in moral philosophy. He argued strongly, for instance, that human nature was fundamentally good, as everyone is born with the capacity to recognize what is right. He gave the example of the person who automatically grabs a baby about to fall into a well: "It would not be because he wanted to improve his relations with the child's parents, nor because he wanted a good reputation among his friends and neighbors, nor because he disliked hearing the child cry" (2A.6). Rather it was due to his inborn feelings of commiseration and sense of right and wrong.

Mencius quotes some conversations with a contemporary philosopher who disagreed with his interpretation of human nature:

> *Gaozi said, "Human nature is like whirling water. When an outlet is opened to the east, it flows east; when an outlet is opened to the west, it flows west. Human nature is no more inclined to good or bad than water is inclined to east or west."*
>
> *Mencius responded, "Water, it is true, is not inclined to either east or west, but does it have no preference for high or low? Goodness is to human nature like flowing downward is to water. There are no people who are not good and no water that does not flow down. Still, water, if splashed, can go higher than your head; if forced, it can be brought up a hill. This isn't the nature of water; it is the specific circumstances. Although people can be made to be bad, their natures are not changed." (6A.2)*

Sometimes Mencius related men's moral nature to Heaven. Heaven wants men to be moral and operates in history through men's choices. Heaven validates a ruler's authority through the people's acceptance of him. But Mencius did not think all rulers had been validated by Heaven; true kings tended to appear only about every five hundred years.

Xunzi

The *Xunzi* was written in large part by Xunzi (ca. 310–ca. 215 B.C.E.), who lived a half-century after Mencius and was Mencius's rival as an interpreter of Confucius's legacy. Xunzi explicitly opposed Mencius's view on human nature, arguing that people are born selfish and that it is only through education and ritual that they learn to put moral principle above their own interest. Much of what is desirable is not inborn, he said, but must be taught:

> *When a son yields to his father, or a younger brother yields to his elder brother, or when a son takes on the work for his father or a younger brother for his elder brother, their actions go against their natures and run counter to their feelings. And yet these are the way of the filial son and the principles of ritual and morality. (13)*

Neither Confucius nor Mencius had had much actual political or administrative experience. By contrast, Xunzi worked for many years in the governments of several of the states. Not surprisingly, he showed more consideration than either Confucius or Mencius for the difficulties a ruler might face in trying to rule through ritual and virtue. He strongly supported the view, earlier articulated by Mozi, that the worthy should be promoted even if they were descendants of commoners. In response to a question on how to govern, Xunzi said the ruler should promote the worthy and capable and dismiss the incompetent, and punish the evil without bothering to try to reform them. Xunzi, like Mencius, supported the basic message of the Mandate of Heaven: "The ruler is the boat, the common people are the water. It is the water that bears up the boat but also the water that capsizes it" (9).

Xunzi was a more rigorous thinker than his predecessors and developed the philosophical foundations of many ideas that Confucius or Mencius had merely outlined. Confucius, for instance, had declined to discuss gods, portents, and anomalies and had spoken of sacrificing as if the spirits were present. Xunzi went further and explicitly argued that Heaven does not intervene in human affairs. Praying to Heaven or to gods, he asserted, does not induce them to act. "Why does it rain after a prayer for rain? In my opinion, for no reason. It is the same as raining when you had not prayed" (17).

Although he did not think praying could bring rain or other benefits from Heaven, Xunzi did not propose abandoning traditional rituals. In contrast to Daoists and Mohists, who saw rituals as unnatural or extravagant, Xunzi saw in ritual an efficient way to attain order in society. Rulers and educated men should continue traditional ritual practices such as complex funeral protocols because the rites themselves have positive effects on performers and observers. Not only do they let people express feelings and satisfy desires in an orderly way, but by specifying graduated ways to perform the rites according to social rank, ritual traditions sustain the social hierarchy. Xunzi compared and contrasted ritual and music: music shapes people's emotions and creates feelings of solidarity, while ritual shapes people's sense of duty and creates social differentiation.

Daoism and the *Laozi* and *Zhuangzi*

Confucius and his followers believed in moral and political effort. They thought men of virtue should devote themselves to making the government work to the benefit of the people. Those who later came to be labeled Daoists disagreed. The authors of the *Laozi* and *Zhuangzi* thought striving to make things better generally makes them worse. They defended private life and wanted the rulers to leave the people alone. They sought to go beyond everyday concerns and let their minds wander freely. Rather than making human beings and human actions the center of concern, they focused on the larger scheme of things, the whole natural order identified as the Way or Dao.

Both the *Laozi* and the *Zhuangzi* date to the third century B.C.E. Master Lao, the putative author of the *Laozi,* may not be a historical figure, but the text ascribed to him has been of enduring importance. A recurrent theme in this brief, aphoristic text is the mystical superiority of yielding over assertion and silence over words. "The Way that can be discussed is not the constant Way" (1). The highest good is like water: "Water benefits all creatures but does not compete. It occupies the places people disdain and thus comes near to the Way" (8).

Because purposeful action is counterproductive, the ruler should let people return to a natural state of ignorance and contentment:

> Do not honor the worthy,
> And the people will not compete.
> Do not value rare treasures,
> And the people will not steal.
> Do not display what others want,
> And the people will not have their hearts confused.
> A sage governs this way:
> He empties people's minds and fills their bellies.
> He weakens their wills and strengthens their bones.
> Keep the people always without knowledge and without desires,
> For then the clever will not dare act.
> Engage in no action and order will prevail. (3)

In the philosophy of the *Laozi,* the people would be better off if they knew less, gave up tools, renounced writing, stopped envying their neighbors, and lost their desire to travel or wage war.

Zhuangzi (369–286 B.C.E.), the author of the book of the same name, was a historical figure who shared many of the central ideas of the

Laozi, such as the usefulness of the useless and the relativity of ordinary distinctions. He was proud of his disinterest in politics. In one of his many anecdotes, he reported that the King of Chu once sent an envoy to invite him to take over the government of his realm. In response, Zhuangzi asked the envoy whether a tortoise that had been held as sacred for three thousand years would prefer to be dead with its bones venerated or alive with its tail dragging in the mud. When the envoy agreed that life was preferable, Zhuangzi told the envoy to leave, as he would rather drag his tail in the mud.

The *Zhuangzi* is filled with parables, flights of fancy, and fictional encounters between historical figures, including Confucius and his disciples. Yet the book also deals with serious issues, including death. Zhuangzi questioned whether we can be sure life is better than death. People fear what they do not know, the same way a captive girl will be terrified when she learns she is to become the king's concubine. Perhaps people will discover that death has as many delights as life in the palace. When a friend expressed shock that Zhuangzi was not weeping at his wife's death, Zhuangzi explained that he had at first, but then began thinking back to before she had life or form or vital energy. "In this confused amorphous realm, something changed and vital energy appeared; when the vital energy was changed, form appeared; with changes in form, life began. Now there is another change bringing death. This is like the progression of the four seasons of spring and fall, winter and summer" (18). Once he had realized this, he stopped sobbing.

Zhuangzi was similarly iconoclastic in his political ideas. In one parable, a wheelwright insolently tells a duke that books are useless since all they contain are the dregs of men long dead. The duke, insulted, threatened to execute him if he could not give an adequate explanation of his remark. The wheelwright then explained that he could feel in his hand how to chisel but could not describe it in words. "I cannot teach it to my son, and my son cannot learn it from me. So I have gone on for seventy years, growing old chiseling wheels. The men of old died in possession of what they could not transmit. So it follows that what you are reading are their dregs" (13). Zhuangzi here questions the validity of verbal reasoning and the sorts of knowledge conveyed through words.

The ideas of the *Laozi* and *Zhuangzi* can be seen as a response to Confucianism, a rejection of many of its basic premises. Nevertheless, over the course of Chinese history, many people felt the pull of both Confucian and Daoist ideas and studied the writings of both schools. Even Confucian scholars who devoted much of their life to public service might find the teachings of Laozi or Zhuangzi helped them put their frustrations in perspective. Whereas Confucianism often seems sternly masculine, Daoism was more accepting of feminine principles (yin of the yin-yang pair) and even celebrated passivity and yielding. Those drawn to the arts were also often drawn to Daoism, with its validation of spontaneity and freedom. Rulers too saw merit in the Daoist notion of the ruler who can have great power simply by being himself without instituting anything.

Legalism

Over the course of the fourth and third centuries B.C.E., as one small state after another was conquered, rulers fearful that their state might be next were ready to listen to political theorists who claimed expertise in the accumulation of power. These theorists, labeled Legalists because of their emphasis on the need for rigorous laws, argued that strong government depended not on the moral qualities of the ruler and his officials, as Confucians claimed, but on establishing effective laws and procedures.

In the fourth century B.C.E., the state of Qin, under the leadership of its chancellor, Lord Shang (d. 338 B.C.E.), adopted many Legalist policies. Instead of an aristocracy with inherited titles, social distinctions were based on military ranks determined by the objective criterion of the number of enemy heads cut off in battle. In the place of the old fiefs, Qin divided the country into counties and appointed officials to administer them according to the laws decreed at court. To increase the population, migrants were recruited from other states with offers of land. To encourage farmers to work hard and improve their land, they were allowed to buy and sell it. Ordinary farmers were thus freed from serf-like obligations to the local nobility. Nevertheless, direct control by the state could be even more onerous, as taxes and labor service obligations were heavy.

In the third century B.C.E., Legalism found its greatest exponent in Han Feizi (d. 233 B.C.E.), who had studied with the Confucian master Xunzi but had little interest in Confucian virtues. Alarmed at the weakness of his own state of Han, Han Feizi wrote to warn rulers of the political pitfalls awaiting them. They had to be careful where they placed their trust, for "when the ruler trusts someone, he falls under that person's control" (17). This was true even of wives and concubines, who think of the interests of their sons. Given subordinates' propensities to pursue their own selfish interests, the ruler should keep them ignorant of his intentions and control them by manipulating competition among them. Warmth, affection, or candor should have no place in his relationships with others.

Han Feizi saw the Confucian notion that government could be based on virtue as naive. Even parents calculate their long-term advantage in favoring sons over daughters. One cannot expect rulers to be more selfless than parents. If rulers would make the laws and prohibitions clear and the rewards and punishments automatic, then the officials and common people would be easy to govern. Uniform laws get people to do things they would not otherwise be inclined to do, such as work hard and fight wars, essential to the goal of establishing hegemony over all the other states.

The laws of the Legalists were designed as much to constrain officials as to regulate the common people. The third century B.C.E. tomb of a Qin official has yielded statutes detailing the rules for keeping accounts, supervising subordinates, managing penal labor, conducting investigations, and many other responsibilities. Those who violated these statutes were fined.

Legalism saw no value in intellectual debate or private opinion. The ruler should not allow others to undermine his laws by questioning them. Rulers of several states adopted some Legalist ideas, but only the state of Qin systematically followed them. The extraordinary but brief success Qin had with these policies is discussed in Chapter 3.

Other Schools of Thought and Types of Learning

The thinkers and books discussed here had the greatest long-term impact on Chinese civilization, but the late Zhou "Hundred Schools of Thought" also included much else. There were logicians, hedonists, utopians, hermits, and agriculturalists who argued that no one should eat who does not farm. There were natural philosophers who drew lessons from their study of such fields as astronomy, medicine, music, and calendrical calculations. The concepts of yin and yang were particularly important to natural philosophy. Yin is the feminine, dark, receptive, yielding, negative, and weak; yang is the masculine, bright, assertive, creative, positive, and strong. Yin and yang are complementary poles rather than distinct entities or opposing forces. The movement of yin and yang accounts for the transition from day to night and from summer to winter. They are also involved in health and illness. The *Zuo zhuan* quotes Physician He on the six qi (vapors, forms of energy), which he defines as yin and yang, wind and rain, dark and bright. These six qi divide to make the four seasons, radiate to make the five colors and five sounds, and when they go to excess produce the six illnesses. Numerology of the sort apparent here is another feature of late Zhou natural philosophy.

Another important strand of thought of this period concerns military strategy. Sunzi's *Art of War,* dating probably to the third century B.C.E., warns against bravado. Since warfare causes loss of life and property, it is better to win without expending resources. "One hundred victories in one hundred battles is not skillful; what is skillful is subjugating the opponent's army without battle" (Chap. 3). Great generals are not those who charge up hills against overwhelming odds but those who advance when they know they can win. Heroism is a useless virtue that leads to needless deaths. Discipline, however, is essential, and Sunzi insisted that the entire army had to be trained to follow the orders of its commanders without questioning them. Spying on and manipulating the enemy are tactics worth learning, as is doing things the enemy will not anticipate. Often phrases in the *Art of War* echo ones from the *Laozi:* "The form of the military is like water. Water in its movements avoids the high and hastens to the low. The military in its victory avoids the solid and strikes the empty. Thus water determines its movement in accordance with the earth. The military determines victory in accordance with the enemy."[2]

The development of rationalistic and naturalistic ways of thinking does not mean that people no longer took an interest in the world of spirits. The records of divination found in the tomb of an official who died in 316 B.C.E. show that illness was seen as the result of unsatisfied spirits or malevolent demons, best dealt with through exorcisms or sacrifices to the astral deity Taiyi (Grand One). Some texts give incantations that could be used to exorcise offending demons. There were also ceremonies that could offer protection from evil spirits. To escape trouble on a trip, travelers were encouraged to perform a ceremony at the threshold of the gate to the city. They would call on the sage-king Yu to clear the road for them, draw five lines on the ground, then pick up some of the soil by the lines, and put it in the folds of their robe by their bosom. Texts on these occult and magico-religious subjects that have been found in excavation of late Warring States tombs have shown that traditions in these fields were transmitted in writing much as those of the philosophers were.

WARRING STATES LITERATURE AND ART: THE CASE OF CHU

Despite political division, all through the Eastern Zhou Dynasty, peoples on the periphery of the Zhou world were drawn into it. This does not mean, however, that all cultural differences were eliminated. As discussed in Chapter 1, the bronzes found south of the Yangzi River during the Shang Dynasty employed the same technology used at Anyang yet often featured highly distinctive decoration. For the Zhou period, because of the much greater survival of texts and an abundance of archaeological finds, it is possible to trace how the south steadily became a more integral part of the Zhou world and the ways it maintained a distinctive style.

The dominant state in the south was Chu. From Western Zhou times on, Chu gradually expanded, absorbing fifty or more small states as it pushed its borders northward and eastward. In the Eastern Zhou period, Chu became one of the strongest and most innovative states. In 548 B.C.E. it conducted a survey of its population to assess tax and military duties. Chu also was the first to form counties (*xian*) out of newly annexed land and to dispatch officials to administer them (instead of conferring the land on hereditary lords). In 334 B.C.E. Chu conquered the state of Yue, gaining control of the Lower Yangzi region. By the third century, Chu was a full participant in the alliances designed to maintain a balance of power. This does not mean those in the central regions no longer put it down as a primitive or barbarian region. Mencius chastised a man for following a teacher who came from Chu, saying, "I have heard of men using Chinese ways to transform the barbarians but not of being transformed by the barbarians" (*Mencius* 3A.4).

2. Translation by Kidder Smith in Wm. Theodore de Bary and Irene Bloom, eds., *Sources of Chinese Tradition,* rev. ed. (New York: Columbia University Press, 1999), p. 221.

MATERIAL CULTURE

Lacquer

Lacquer is made from the sap of a tree native to south and central China. When it is heated and purified, the sap makes a light, strong, smooth, and waterproof material highly resistant to decay. By Eastern Zhou times, craftsmen were using lacquer on furniture, coffins, bowls, cups, musical instruments, and sculpture. In most cases, many layers of lacquer were applied over a wooden core. Lacquer objects could be decorated with pictures or designs, using lacquer colored with pigments such as cinnabar for red and carbon for black.

Illustrated here is a small cup from Tomb 1 at Mashan, Jiangling, Hubei Province, decorated with images of two large birds. See also Color Plate 3, which shows the design painted in lacquer on a coffin from the late fourth century B.C.E. at Baoshan, Jingmen, Hubei province. It is covered with intertwining dragons and mythical birds.

Lacquer Cup. This 6 inch long lacquer cup is decorated in red, black, and yellow colors. It was one of many eating vessels found in a tomb in Hubei dating to the early third century B.C.E. *(Jingzhou Prefecture Museum, Hubei Province)*

It has been estimated that 70 percent of known Eastern Zhou tombs are in the Chu area. Much more in the way of lacquer and silk survives from tombs in this region than elsewhere in China for this period—a function of the high water tables in many places—giving us a remarkably full picture of the material life of the elite of Chu. Flowing, curvilinear lines, sometimes incorporating birds, dragons, snakes, and other creatures, are found on embroidered silks, inlaid bronzes, and painted lacquer (see **Material Culture: Lacquer**).

One of the most interesting of the Chu tombs, excavated in 1986–1987, was for an official who died in 316 B.C.E. The tomb had four chambers, filled with ritual vessels, furniture, and other objects of daily life such as fans, mirrors, boxes, weapons and chariot fittings, and books. The books include reports by the local government, texts on divination, and an inventory of the tomb's contents. Although the calligraphy of the books is elegant, many of the characters are in obsolete forms that have not yet been deciphered.

The distinctiveness of Chu culture can also be seen in the masterpiece of Chu literature, the *Songs of Chu* (Chu ci). The fantastic poems in this work are worlds apart from the poems in the *Book of Poetry.* The principal poem in this collection, titled *Encountering Sorrows,* is the lament of Qu Yuan (ca. 340–278 B.C.E.), an anti-Qin minister who lost the favor of the Chu kings and was sent into exile. Distraught that his loyalty to his ruler was not appreciated, he finally threw himself into a river. In the poem Qu Yuan describes his misfortunes, declares his virtue, maligns those who have defamed him, and goes on a cosmic quest for a lord worthy of his devotion. On that venture, he imagines him-

Bells of the Marquis of Yi. The tomb of a minor ruler who died in 433 B.C.E. contained 124 musical instruments, including drums, flutes, mouth organs, pan pipes, zithers, a set of 32 chime stones, and this 64-piece bell set. Five men, using poles and mallets, and standing on either side of the set of bells, would have played the bells by hitting them from outside. *(Henan Museum, Zhengzhou/Cultural Relics Publishing House)*

self wandering on the clouds and looking down on the earth. The structure of this lengthy poem (almost four hundred lines) corresponds to shamanic spirit quests in which the shaman declares his worth and goes to heaven to seek the god or goddess who had spurned him. Several of the shorter poems in the *Songs of Chu* fall into this tradition as well. The one that follows is titled the "Lord of the Yellow River":

> With you I will roam to the river's nine channels,
> when blasts of wind rise driving waves across stream,
> we will ride my coach of waters, its canopy, lotus,
> hitched to paired dragons, by basilisks flanked.
>
> I climbed Mount Kun-lun, I gazed all around,
> the heart flew aloft, it went sweeping off free.
> soon the sun was to set, I, transfixed, forgot going,
> and then to the far shore I looked back with care.
>
> My roofs are of fish scales, halls of the dragon,
> turrets of purple cowries, palaces of carmine—
> why is the holy one here, down in the water?
>
> We will ride on white turtles, goldfish attend us,
> with you I will roam by the river's isles,
> where the current is rushing, there we'll go down.
>
> You clasp your hands, journeying eastward;
> you go with the Fairest to the southern shores
> where the swell of the waves is coming to meet us,
> and the schools of fishes, will send off my bride.[3]

3. Stephen Owen, *An Anthology of Chinese Literature* (New York: Norton, 1996), p. 160.

SUMMARY

How did China change during the five centuries of the Eastern Zhou period? The Chinese world had grown by absorbing previously peripheral areas like Chu in the south and Zhongshan in the north. The economy had changed from one that was essentially manorial to one in which coinage was in use, trade was much more extensive, and iron was widely used for tools. The social structure had similarly been transformed from one in which membership in the elite depended almost entirely on birth to one in which there was considerable opportunity for advancement for talented *shi*. City-states had become territorial states, with rulers making use of officials to draw on the resources of their entire population. Conscription was nearly universal. Warfare was no longer hemmed in by notions of chivalry and as a consequence had become much more deadly. Intellectual discourse was much richer, with a great many texts in circulation that sought to persuade through argument and example. Distinct schools of thought had emerged. The writing of history had advanced, with much more in the way of extended narratives.

SUGGESTED READING

For both the history and the archaeology of Zhou China, the most authoritative volume is M. Loewe and E. Shaughnessey, *The Cambridge History of Ancient China: From the Origins of Civilization to 221 B.C.E.* (1999). On material history, see also X. Li, *Eastern Zhou and Qin Civilizations* (1985). On the texts surviving from this period, see M. Loewe, *Early Chinese Texts: A Bibliographical Guide* (1993). On the cultural and ethnic diversity of the Chinese subcontinent in this period, see W. Watson, *Cultural Frontiers in Ancient East Asia* (1971); C. Cook and J. Major, *Defining Chu* (1999); and N. de Cosmo, *Ancient China and Its Enemies* (2002).

Good overviews of the intellectual flowering of the Warring States period include A. C. Graham, *Disputers of the Tao: Philosophical Argument in Ancient China* (1989); Benjamin Schwartz, *The World of Thought in Ancient China* (1985); M. Lewis, *Writing and Authority in Early China* (1999); and, more briefly, F. W. Mote, *Intellectual Foundations of China* (1989).

J. Legge did a complete translation of *The Chinese Classics*, 5 vols. (1960) in the nineteenth century. More recent translators include A. Waley, D. C. Lau, and B. Watson. For Waley, see the *Analects of Confucius* (1938) and the *Book of Songs* (1937). Lao translated *Confucius: The Analects* (1979), the *Tao Te Ching: Chinese Classics* (1982), and *Mencius* (1970). Watson has published *The Tso Chuan: Selections from China's Oldest Narrative History* (1989); *The Complete Works of Chuang Tzu* (1968); and *Basic Writings of Mo Tzu, Hsun Tzu, and Han Fei Tzu* (1967). For military thinking, see *Sun-tzu: The Art of War,* translated by R. Ames (1993). For shorter selections of important Chinese texts, see W. de Bary and I. Bloom, eds., *Sources of Chinese Tradition* (1999), and P. Ebrey, ed., *Chinese Civilization: A Sourcebook* (1993).

CHAPTER THREE

3

The Founding of the Bureaucratic Empire: Qin and Han (256 B.C.E.–200 C.E.)

Qin's battle-hardened armies destroyed the Zhou royal domain in 256 B.C.E. and the last of the independent states in 221 B.C.E., thus unifying the Chinese realm. Although Qin rule did not last long, the succeeding Han Dynasty retained its centralized bureaucratic monarchy. Both Qin and Han mobilized huge armies to confront the emergence of a powerful enemy to the north, the Xiongnu tribal confederation. In part to deal with the Xiongnu threat, the Han government extended its territories to the east, west, and south.

In contrast to the Qin government, which favored Legalism, the Han government preferred that its officials be learned in the Confucian classics. With these officials, the Han government proved remarkably successful in coordinating administrative control of a population of about 59 million people. Still, the imperial institution proved vulnerable to manipulation by the families of empresses and by palace eunuchs.

The Han Dynasty is the first of the five major dynasties that lasted more than two and a half centuries (Han, Tang, Song, Ming, and Qing), and scholars often look at the Han with these later dynasties in mind. The structure and operation of the government have been major concerns: What enabled Han to succeed where Qin had failed? What was the impact of the centralized state on ordinary people's lives? What were the consequences of the support the government gave to Confucianism? What type of Confucianism did the government support? Later dynasties had difficulties on their northern borders reminiscent of the Han-Xiongnu confrontation, drawing

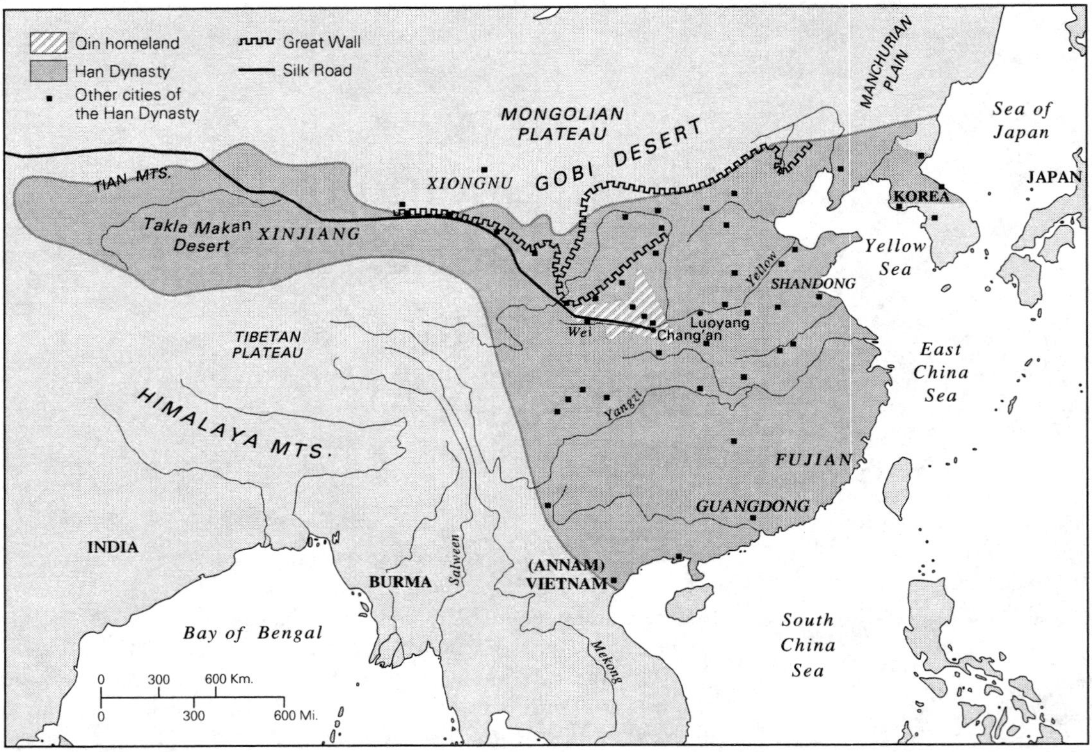

Map 3.1 The Han Empire at Its Maximum Extent, ca. 50 B.C.E.

scholars' attention to this initial stage. Was conflict between China and its northern neighbors inevitable, given the differences in the economies of the two regions, or could different policies have led to different outcomes? Did the Han Dynasty's great territorial expansion aid it in any way, or was it costly overextension?

THE QIN UNIFICATION (256–206 B.C.E.)

The year 221 B.C.E., one of the most important dates in Chinese history, marks the beginning of the Chinese empire. That year, the state of Qin, which had adopted Legalist policies, succeeded in defeating the last of its rivals, thus creating a unified China. (See Map 3.1.) As discussed in the last chapter, following the counsel of Legalist advisers, Qin had restructured itself in the fourth century B.C.E. The power of the old nobility and the patriarchal family were curtailed to create instead a direct relationship between the ruler and his subjects, based on uniformly enforced laws and punishments, administered by officials appointed by the king.

One of the most influential men in Qin in the decades before the conquest was a rich merchant, Lü Buwei. That a merchant could use his wealth to gain political favor is evidence of the high social mobility of the age. Lü was said to have decided that gaining control of a state offered more opportunities to grow rich than commerce did, and to have come up with a scheme to accomplish that by favoring a potential heir to the throne, then helping him succeed to it. Once Lü's protégé became king, Lü became chancellor. There followed a string of stunning victories over other states, allowing Qin to increase its territories steadily. This king died after only three years on the throne, and in 247 thirteen-year-old King Cheng came to the throne, with Lü as regent. One of the orders he issued was that common people who had amassed riches through their own enterprise be granted noble ranks. Those so honored included a man who traded silk for animals with the Rong barbarians and a widow who managed the family cinnabar mines.

Lü recruited scholars to come to Qin, where he put them to work on a book that would present a unified philosophy for the unified realm he envisioned. The resulting book, *The Annals of Mr. Lü,* combines cosmological correlative thinking using the five phases/agents and yin and yang with political philosophy from all the major schools. The ruler should be tranquil and unassertive, as *Laozi* had advised, but select wise ministers and trust their advice, an essentially Confucian attitude. The state should aid farmers, keep taxes low, and encourage merchants. Filial piety is extolled, as is learning.

After King Cheng began to rule on his own, he sent Lü Buwei away. Lü, seeing that he was losing favor, committed suicide. King Cheng's next chancellor was Li Si, a fully committed Legalist who, like Han Feizi, had studied under the Confucian scholar Xunzi. With Li Si's astute advice, Qin was able to reorganize each territory as it took it over. By 230 the tide of war had shifted in Qin's favor, and the final six states—Han, Zhao, Wei, Chu, Yan, and Qi—were defeated in rapid succession. All of a sudden Qin had to rule millions of people who had until then been desperately battling to avoid such a fate.

The First Emperor (r. 221–210 B.C.E.)

Once Qin ruled all of China, King Cheng decided that the title "king" was not grand enough and invented the title "emperor" (literarily, "august theocrat," *huangdi*), using words

Figure 3.1 Standardizing the Writing System

that linked him to the sage rulers of the mythical past. He called himself the First Emperor in anticipation of a long line of successors.

The First Emperor initiated a sweeping program of centralization that touched the lives of nearly everyone in China. To cripple the nobility of the defunct states, the First Emperor ordered nobles to leave their lands and move to the capital, Xianyang (near modern Xi'an). To administer the territory that had been seized, he dispatched officials whom he controlled through a mass of regulations, reporting requirements, and penalties for inadequate performance. These officials owed their power and positions entirely to the favor of the emperor and had no hereditary rights to their offices. To make it easier to administer all regions uniformly, writing systems were standardized, as were weights, measures, coinage, and even the axle lengths of carts. Private possession of arms was outlawed in order to make it more difficult for subjects to rebel. Thousands of miles of roads were built to enable Qin armies to move rapidly. Investment was also made in canals linking rivers, making it possible to travel long distances by boat. Most of the labor on these projects came from farmers performing required labor service or convicts working off their sentences.

The First Emperor shared the Legalist suspicion of intellectual diversity. In 213 B.C.E., after Li Si complained that scholars used records of the past to denigrate the emperor's achievements and undermine popular support, the emperor ordered the collection and burning of all useless writings. The only works excepted were manuals on topics such as agriculture, medicine, and divination. As a result of this massive book burning, many ancient texts were lost.

Some twentieth-century Chinese historians have glorified the First Emperor as a bold conqueror who let no obstacle impede him, but the traditional evaluation of him was almost entirely negative. For centuries, Chinese historians castigated him as a monster: cruel, arbitrary, impetuous, suspicious, and superstitious.

Qin Law

The Qin was always thought to have had a particularly harsh legal system, but little was known about its exact provisions until 1975 when 625 bamboo strips inscribed with Qin laws and legal texts were found in a tomb in Hubei province. The tomb was for a man who served the Qin government as a prefectural official. Some of the texts reconstructed from the strips contain statutes related to management of government granaries and labor service. One book explains legal terminology in question-and-answer format.

The penalties imposed by Qin law were hard labor, physical mutilation, banishment, slavery, or death. Labor could last from one to six years. Mutilation included shaving of the beard; shaving of the head; branding the forehead; cutting off the nose or left foot; or castration. Death also came in several forms, the most severe of which was being torn apart by horse-drawn chariots. To make sure that criminals were caught and offenses reported, Qin set up mutual responsibility units of five households, whose members were required to inform on each other or suffer the same penalty as the criminal. For particularly heinous crimes, even distant relatives could be enslaved.

Penal labor was a common punishment. Those guilty of theft or homicide were sentenced to long terms, but even those sentenced to pay fines often had to work the sentence off as labor, credited at the rate of eight coins a day (six if one received food rations). Those who owned slaves, oxen, or horses could receive credit for the work they did, or they could hire others to work in their place. Men and women were treated differently. Men had heavier work assignments but received larger rations. A man could volunteer for service on the frontier for five years to redeem his mother or sister but not his father or brother.

Government officials had to take similar responsibility for the performance of their department. Every year in the tenth month, officials had to send in detailed reports to be used for the evaluation of their performance. If they did more or less than expected, they were punished by fines calculated in sets of armor and shields.

The First Emperor's Tomb

The First Emperor started work on his tomb soon after he came to the throne. In 231 B.C.E. the area around the tomb was made a separate administrative district and the people of the district were made responsible for the construction and maintenance of the imperial tomb. Twenty years later, thirty thousand families were resettled to the district, and several hundred thousand forced laborers were sent there as temporary workers.

In 1974, about a kilometer from the tomb, a pit was discovered filled with life-sized terracotta figures of soldiers. Since then, as archaeologists have probed the region around the First Emperor's tomb, they have found more and more pits filled with burial goods of one sort or another. Sometimes actual objects were used, in other cases replicas. One pit had two finely made half-size bronze chariots, each drawn by four bronze horses. In another pit were thirty-

The First Emperor's Army. The thousands of life-sized terra-cotta soldiers placed in pits near the First Emperor's tomb were originally painted in bright colors and they held real bronze weapons. They testify both to the emperor's concern with the afterlife and the ability of his government to organize production on a large scale. *(Laurent Lecat/AKG-Images)*

one rare birds and animals that had been buried alive in clay coffins laid in rows. Although these were real birds and animals (probably from the huge imperial hunting park), they are guarded by a terra-cotta warden. Actual horses were buried in other pits. In many cases a small pit had a single horse and a terra-cotta groom. In one pit, however, were bones of three hundred horses. There is also a pit where more than a hundred human skeletons have been found; according to inscribed shards, these were conscript and penal laborers who died on the job.

By far the most spectacular of the pits discovered in the vicinity of the First Emperor's tomb are the three that contain the terra-cotta army. Historians had no knowledge of this army, so its discovery was a complete surprise. Pit 1 has more than six thousand figures of warriors arrayed in columns, most of them infantry, but with some chariots near the front. Pit 2 has cavalry plus more infantry and chariots and may represent a guard unit. Pit 3 seems to be the command post, with fewer soldiers. The floor of these pits had been made of rammed earth, covered by ceramic tiles (some 256,000 for pit 1). Wooden supports held up roof beams, strong enough to keep the roof from caving in from the weight of the earth above.

The soldiers were made of simple clay formed with molds. Although viewers often described the soldiers as individualized, in reality they were made of interchangeable parts. For instance, there were two basic forms for hands, with fingers straight or curved, but they could appear quite different depending on how they were attached to the sleeves and the angle at which the thumb was attached. Hand finishing, for instance of the hair, could make figures seem more distinct as well. After the soldiers were molded, they were painted with lacquer, which both preserved them and made them seem more lifelike. These figures carried real weapons, such as spears, halberds, swords, and bows and arrows. These weapons were of high quality (some of the blades are still razor sharp) and were mass-produced in state factories. To ensure quality control, each weapon was inscribed with the names of the worker who made it and the person who supervised him. Each also had a serial number.

Why did the First Emperor want so many replicas of soldiers buried near him? For several centuries, there had been a trend in Chinese burial practice to bury representations rather than real objects in graves. To some extent, this could have been a cost-saving measure: if replicas were just as good as the real thing in the afterlife, why take so much wealth out of circulation by placing it underground? But possibly replicas were considered in some way superior because they caught the unchanging universal aspect of the thing, not one particular manifestation. It is perhaps hard to believe that a ceramic representation of a bronze ritual vessel could be as useful in the afterlife as a real bronze one, but one can imagine that a ceramic guard, which will never decay, could be preferable to a mortal one.

The First Emperor's personal fears and beliefs undoubtedly also contributed to his decision to construct such an elaborate underground world. Three times assassins tried to kill him, and perhaps as a consequence he became obsessed with finding ways to avoid death. He sent a group of young men and women to search for Penglai, the famed isles of immortality in the Eastern Sea. He listened to seers and magicians who claimed to know other techniques for achieving immortality. Was his huge tomb a fallback plan—a way to reduce the sting of death if he couldn't escape it altogether?

Although the First Emperor filled the pits near his tomb with terra-cotta replicas of his minions, his successor saw to it that some human beings were buried there as well. According to Sima Qian, writing in about 100 B.C.E.:

> *The Second Emperor said, "Of the women in the harem of the former ruler, it would be unfitting to have those who bore no sons sent elsewhere." All were accordingly ordered to accompany the dead man, which resulted in the death of many women. After the interment had been completed, someone pointed out that the artisans and craftsmen who had built the tomb knew what was buried there, and if they should leak word of the treasures, it would be a serious affair. Therefore, after the articles had been placed in the tomb, the inner gate was closed off and the outer gate lowered, so that all the artisans and craftsmen were shut in the tomb and were unable to get out.*[1]

Presumably when the archaeologists excavate the tomb itself, they will find the bones not only of the First Emperor, but also those who accompanied him in death.

THE HAN DYNASTY (206 B.C.E.–220 C.E.)

The First Emperor died in 210 B.C.E. while traveling. He had trusted no one, and at this juncture no one proved trustworthy. The chief eunuch plotted with a younger son to send orders to the heir apparent and General Meng Tian to commit suicide. The younger son became the Second Emperor and had several of his brothers executed. The chief eunuch was elevated to chancellor after he got the Second

1. Burton Watson, trans., *Records of the Grand Historian: Qin Dynasty* (New York: Columbia University Press, 1993), p. 65.

Emperor to execute Li Si. By this time, the Qin state was unraveling. The Legalist institutions designed to concentrate power in the hands of the ruler made the stability of the government dependent on the strength and character of a single person.

In the ensuing uprisings, many of the rebels called for the restoration of the old states, but this was not what happened. The eventual victor was Liu Bang (known in history as Emperor Gao, r. 202–195 B.C.E.). The First Emperor of Qin was from the old Zhou aristocracy. Liu Bang, by contrast, was from a modest family of commoners, so his elevation to emperor is evidence of how thoroughly the Qin Dynasty had destroyed the old order.

Emperor Gao did not disband the centralized government created by Qin, but he did remove its most unpopular features. He set up his capital at Chang'an, not far from the old Qin capital. He eliminated some laws, cut taxes, and otherwise lessened the burdens on the people. After a century of almost constant war and huge labor mobilizations, China was given several decades to recover. Responding to the desire to restore the old order, Emperor Gao gave out large and nearly autonomous fiefs to his relatives and chief generals. Very soon he recognized that giving followers independent resources was a mistake, and he spent much of his reign eliminating the fief holders who were not relatives. After his death, the fiefs of imperial relatives were also gradually reduced in size.

The Han emperor in theory was all powerful but in actuality depended on his chancellor and other high officials for information and advice. Nine ministries were established to handle matters ranging from state ritual to public works. Officials, graded by rank and salary, were appointed by the central government for their merit, not their birth, and were subject to dismissal, demotion, or transfer, much in the way Qin officials had been. Local officials—magistrates and grand administrators—had broad responsibilities: they collected taxes, judged lawsuits, commanded troops to suppress uprisings, undertook public works such as flood control, chose their own subordinates, and recommended local men to the central government for appointments. The main tax was a poll tax of 120 cash (coins) on adults (less for children). Adults also owed a month of labor service each year. Land tax, largely retained by the county and commandery governments, was set at the low rate of one-thirtieth of the harvest.

When Emperor Gao died, his heir was a child, and the empress dowager (the widow of the former emperor) took control until her death, fifteen years later. This Empress Lü is described in the histories as a vicious, spiteful person, and after her fall her entire family was wiped out. For centuries to come, she would provide an example of the dangers of letting a woman take power, even if she was the mother of the emperor.

The Han emperor who had the greatest impact on Chinese culture and society was Emperor Wu, who came to the throne as a teenager in 141 B.C.E. and reigned for fifty-four years. Unafraid of innovation, Emperor Wu initiated many of the most significant developments in Han culture and government. He took an interest in the arts and patronized both music and poetry. Like many other men of his age, Emperor Wu was fascinated with omens, portents, spirits, immortals, and occult forces, yet he wanted his officials to study Confucian texts.

Emperor Wu expanded the empire through military means. To pay for his military campaigns, he took over the minting of coins, confiscated the land of nobles, sold offices and titles, and increased taxes on private businesses. A widespread suspicion of commerce—from both moral and political perspectives—made it easy to levy especially heavy assessments on merchants. Boats, carts, shops, and other facilities were made subject to property taxes. The worst blow to merchants, however, was the government's decision to enter into market competition with them by selling the commodities that had been collected as taxes. In 119 B.C.E. government monopolies were established on the production of iron, salt, and liquor, enterprises that previously had been sources of great profit for private entrepreneurs. Large-scale grain dealing also had been a profitable business, which the government now took over under the guise of stabilizing prices. Grain was to be bought where it was plentiful and its price low; it would either be stored in granaries until prices rose or transported to areas of scarcity. This policy was supposed to eliminate speculation in grain, provide more constant prices, and bring profit to the government.

The relative success of the Han form of government validated the imperial system, which drew from both Confucian rhetoric and Legalist bureaucratic methods. To put this another way, the Zhou notion of All-Under-Heaven ruled by the paramount Son of Heaven, an idea fully supported by Confucian thinkers, now had attached to it the structures of the centralized bureaucratic empire, indebted though these were to Legalist ideas.

Official Support for Confucianism

Emperor Wu was the first Han emperor to privilege Confucian scholars within the government. He listened to the Confucian scholar Dong Zhongshu, who gave him advice much like Li Si's to the First Emperor. "Because the various schools of thought differ," he said, "the people do not know what to honor," and he advised that "anything not encompassed by the Six Disciplines and the arts of Confucius be suppressed and not allowed to continue further, and evil and vain theories be stamped out."[2] Emperor Wu soon decreed that officials should be selected on the basis of Confucian virtues and established a national university to train officials in the Confucian classics.

The Han government's decision to recruit men trained in the Confucian classics marks the beginning of the Confucian scholar-official system, one of the most distinctive features of imperial China. Since one of the highest duties of the Confucian scholar was to admonish the ruler against misguided policies, officials whose educations imbued them with Confucian values did not comply automatically with the emperor's wishes. Still, emperors found employing Confucian scholars as officials efficient; because of their ingrained sense of duty, they did not have to be supervised as closely as the Legalist model required. That did not mean that emperors took all aspects of the Confucian model of governing to heart themselves or always treated their Confucian officials with respect. Emperor Wu was so averse to criticism that he once had an official executed on the charge that a wry twist of his lips showed that he disapproved in his heart, and his temper led him to put five of his last seven chancellors to death.

The Xiongnu and the Northern Frontier

As far back as written records allow us to see, the Chinese had shared the Chinese subcontinent with other ethnic groups. To the north were groups that the Shang and Zhou called Rong and Di. At that time, the economy of these northerners was similar to the Chinese settlements, with millet agriculture, animal husbandry, and hunting. Many of these groups were eventually incorporated into the northern Zhou states, which gradually expanded north. Over time, those not incorporated into China seem to have come to depend more and more on animal husbandry, perhaps because the climate grew colder or drier. They took to riding horses before the Chinese did, and by the seventh century B.C.E., many of these groups were making the move to nomadic pastoralism. Families lived in tents that could be taken down and moved north in summer and south in winter as they moved in search of fresh pasture. Herds were tended on horseback, and everyone learned to ride from a young age. Especially awesome from the Chinese perspective was the ability of nomad horsemen to shoot arrows while riding horseback. Their social organization was tribal,

2. William Theodore de Bary and Irene Bloom, eds., *Sources of Chinese Tradition*, rev. ed. (New York: Columbia University Press, 1999), p. 311.

with family and clan units held together through loyalty to chiefs selected for their military prowess. At the end of the Zhou period, there were three main groups of nomads in the Northern Zone: the Eastern Hu in the east (northern Hebei-Liaoning region), the Xiongnu in the Ordos (northern Shaanxi-Shanxi), and the Yuezhi to their west.

In 215 B.C.E. one of Qin's most successful generals, Meng Tian, led a huge army (said variously to be 100,000 or 300,000 strong) to attack the Xiongnu and drive them out of the Ordos region. Once he had succeeded, he built forty-four fortified towns along the river and moved people sentenced to guard the borders to settle them. He also built roads to the region and extended the defensive walls, projects that required tens of thousands of laborers. By connecting these walls, Meng Tian created the first version of the Great Wall.

At this time, the chief of the Xiongnu was Touman. The Xiongnu's failure to defend its territory against the Qin armies naturally weakened his authority, since Xiongnu chiefs were above all military leaders. Touman's own son Maodun soon challenged him. Maodun first trained his bodyguards to kill on command, executing anyone who failed instantly to obey his commands that they shoot his favorite horse and favorite concubine. When he was satisfied that they would do what he said, he ordered them to shoot his father and declared himself the Xiongnu chief.

During the next few years, Maodun led the Xiongnu to defeat both the Eastern Hu and the Yuezhi. Some of the Yuezhi simply moved west, but the Eastern Hu were incorporated into the Xiongnu tribal confederation. Maodun also campaigned north of the Gobi, uniting the tribes in modern Mongolia. His quick military victories made him a charismatic leader whom others wanted to follow. Some of the tribes he defeated were incorporated as tribute-paying vassals and other as slaves. By this time, the Qin Dynasty was falling apart, and Maodun was able to reclaim the Ordos region that Qin had taken from the Xiongnu only a few years earlier.

At the beginning of the Han, even before Emperor Gao had completed the consolidation of the empire, he came to realize the threat posed by the Xiongnu. In 200 B.C.E. the Xiongnu under Maodun attacked one of the recently appointed kings, who decided to go over to the Xiongnu. With his help, the Xiongnu then attacked the major city of Taiyuan. Emperor Gao personally led an army to retake the region, but his army suffered terribly from the cold. Maodun led a huge army of horsemen to surround the Han army. Given little choice, Emperor Gao agreed to make yearly gifts of silk, grain, and other foodstuffs to the Xiongnu. The Xiongnu considered this tribute, but the Han naturally preferred to consider it an expression of friendship.

After Emperor Gao's debacle, the early Han emperors had concentrated on pacifying the Xiongnu, supplying them not only with material goods but also with princesses as brides (which they hoped in time would lead to rulers with Chinese mothers). These policies were controversial, since critics thought they merely strengthened the enemy. Moreover, as they pointed out, no matter how much wealth the Han sent to the Xiongnu, they kept raiding the borders.

Emperor Wu decided to take a tougher stand. To push the Xiongnu back, he sent several armies of 100,000 to 300,000 troops deep into Xiongnu territory. These costly campaigns were of limited value since the Xiongnu were a moving target: fighting nomads was not like attacking walled cities. If the Xiongnu did not want to fight the Chinese troops, they simply decamped. Moreover, it was very difficult for Chinese troops to carry enough food to stay long in Xiongnu territory. What they could do was consolidate the land the Xiongnu had vacated by the same methods Qin had used: building forts, appointing officials, and dispatching settlers.

Wang Mang

The Han practice of hereditary succession to the throne from father to son meant that the heir might be a young child. During the last decades of the first century B.C.E., several children succeeded to the throne. Adult men of the imperial lineage did not serve as regents; they were regularly sent out of the capital to keep them from interfering in court politics. That left the mothers and grandmothers of the new rulers, along with the women's male relatives, as the main contenders for power during regencies. Wang Mang came to power as a relative of Empress Wang (d. 13 C.E.), who for forty years had been influential at court as the widow of one emperor, mother of a second, and grandmother of a third. After serving as regent for two infant emperors, Wang Mang deposed the second and declared himself emperor of the Xin (New) Dynasty (9 C.E.–23 C.E.).

Although he was condemned as a usurper, Wang Mang was a learned Confucian scholar who wished to implement policies described in the classics. He renamed offices, asserted state ownership of forests and swamps, built ritual halls, revived public granaries, outlawed slavery, limited private landholdings, and cut court expenses. Some of his policies, such as issuing new coins and nationalizing gold, led to economic turmoil. Matters were made worse when the Yellow River broke through its dikes and shifted course from north to south, driving millions of farmers from their homes as huge regions were flooded. Rebellion broke out, and in the ensuing warfare a Han imperial clansman succeeded in reestablishing the Han Dynasty. The capital was moved from Chang'an to Luoyang, leading to the references to the first half of the Han as the Western or Former Han and the second half as the Eastern or Later Han (reminiscent of the Western and Eastern Zhou).

Palace Eunuchs

During the second century C.E., Han court politics deteriorated as the eunuchs (castrated men) who served as palace servants vied with relatives of the empresses for control of the court. For centuries, eunuchs had been a part of palace life, charged with managing the women's quarters. Eunuchs were in essence slaves; a common source seems to have been boys captured from the "southern barbarians." Court officials looked on palace eunuchs with contempt. Emperors who had grown up with them, however, often saw them as more reliable than officials since they had no outside base of power.

During the Eastern Han period, eunuchs were able to build a base of power within the palace, with the result that weak emperors became the captives rather than the masters of the eunuchs. In 124 C.E., a group of eunuchs placed on the throne a child they could manipulate. They gained even more power after 159, when an emperor turned to them to help him oust a consort family faction. In 166 and 169, officials staged protests against eunuch power, but the eunuchs retaliated. In the purges that followed, the protestors were put in jail, banned from office, and even in a few cases killed.

INTELLECTUAL, LITERARY, AND RELIGIOUS CURRENTS

Perhaps stimulated by the Qin destruction of books, learning and literature of all sorts flourished in Han times. At the end of the Western Han period, the imperial library had some 596 titles, divided into six categories: classics, philosophy, poetry, military treatises, mathematics and natural science (including astronomy, the calendar, and divination), and medicine. Also important to the history of books in China is the development of paper. Over the course of the Han, a variety of plant fibers was tested, and by the end of the period, paper was produced that had a good, absorbent writing surface. Books were of course much less cumbersome when written on rolls of paper than on strips of wood or bamboo.

Early in the Han period, a form of Daoism called Huang-Lao Daoism became particularly influential; *Huang* (yellow) refers to the Yellow Emperor, *Lao* to Laozi, both of whom were treated as deities of vast powers. Emperor Wu was attracted to these teachings and tried to make contact with the world of gods and immortals through elaborate sacrifices. He marveled at stories of the paradise of the Queen Mother of the West and the exploits of the Yellow Emperor, who had taken his entire court with him when he ascended to the realm of the immortals. He inaugurated state cults to the Earth Queen in 114 B.C.E. and Grand Unity in 113. In 110 he traveled to Mount Tai to perform a sacrifice to heaven at the peak and a sacrifice to earth at the base. Although claims were made that these sacrifices were of ancient origin, in fact they were designed for him by court ritualists steeped in Huang-Lao ideas. Religious practices among ordinary people were influenced by Huang-Lao ideas, but also by a great variety of other ideas about spiritual beings and the forces of the cosmos (see **Documents: Lucky and Unlucky Days**).

Han Confucianism

The Five Classics

Book of Changes
Book of Documents
Book of Poetry
Spring and Autumn Annals
Book of Rites

Confucianism made a comeback during the Han Dynasty, but in a new form. Although Confucian texts had fed the First Emperor's bonfires, some dedicated scholars had hidden their books, and others could recite entire books from memory. The ancient books recovered in these ways came to be regarded as classics containing the wisdom of the past. Scholars studied them with piety and attempted to make them more useful as sources of moral guidance by writing commentaries to them that explained archaic words and obscure passages. Confucian scholars often specialized in a single classic, a teacher passing on to his disciples his understanding of each sentence in the work.

Perhaps inspired by the political unification of the realm, some Han Confucians attempted to develop comprehensive understandings of phenomena, drawing on ideas of diverse origins. Their cosmological theories explained all phenomena in terms of cyclical flows of yin and yang and the five phases (fire, water, earth, metal, and wood). This cosmos was a fundamentally moral one: natural disasters such as floods or earthquakes were viewed as portents indicating that the emperor had failed in his responsibility to maintain the proper balance in heaven and earth.

The emperor was of unique importance in this cosmology because he alone had the capacity to link the realms of heaven, earth, and man. The leading Han Confucian scholar Dong Zhongshu (195?–105 B.C.E.) wanted a ruler who would serve as high priest and fount of wisdom, who would be all-powerful but also deferential to learned scholars. Dong drew on ideas from earlier Confucian, Daoist, and Legalist texts to describe the ruler as the "pivot of all living

Correspondences of the Five Phases

	wood	fire	earth	metal	water
seasons	spring	summer		autumn	winter
directions	east	south	center	west	north
weather	wind	heat	thunder	cold	rain
colors	green	red	yellow	white	black
emotions	anger	joy	desire	sorrow	fear
organs	eyes	tongue	mouth	nose	ears

DOCUMENTS

Lucky and Unlucky Days

Some of our best evidence of common beliefs in Han China is found in the writings of critics, such as Wang Chong (27–ca. 100 C.E.). Wang's lengthy Balanced Discourses *includes refutations of a wide range of beliefs and practices, from the idea that people could become immortals and fly high above the earth, to the notion that ghosts could come back to harm people. In the passage here, he attempts to refute the idea that taking action on an unlucky day can cause people harm.*

People today commonly believe in evil influences. They think that when people fall ill or die, or there are repeated calamities, executions, or humiliations, some offense has been committed. If inauspicious days and months are not avoided when starting a project, moving, sacrificing, burying, taking up office, or marrying, then the demons and spirits that one encounters at these ill-fated times will work their harm. Thus illness, disaster, legal penalties, death, even the extermination of a family are all thought to be brought about by not taking care to avoid ill-fated times. In truth, however, this is wild talk. . . .

Rulers anxious about their office and commoners concerned about their bodies believe in this theory and do not raise doubts. Thus when a ruler is about to embark on an enterprise, diviners throng his halls, and when ordinary people have work to be done, they inquire into the best time. As a consequence deceptive books and false texts have appeared in large numbers. . . .

Rare are the diseases not caused by wind, moisture, or food and drink. After people have gone out in the wind or slept in a damp place, they spend money to find out which noxious influence [has attacked them]. When they overeat, they should practice abstinence, but if their illness does not improve, they say the noxious force has not been identified. If the person dies, they say the diviner was not careful. Among ordinary people, such talk is considered wisdom.

Among the 360 animals, man ranks first. Man is a living creature, but among the ten thousand creatures, man is the most intelligent. But he obtains his lifespan from Heaven and his *qi* from the origin in the same way as the other creatures. . . . It makes no sense that the misfortune caused by demons and spirits would fall on man alone, and not on other creatures. In man the minds of Heaven and Earth reach their highest development. Why do heavenly disasters strike the noblest creature and not the mean ones? . . .

If I commit a crime and am arrested by the magistrate and sentenced to punishment, no one says I did something wrong. Instead they say that someone in my family was negligent. If I have not been careful where I lodge or go overboard in food or drink, they do not say I have been immoderate, but that I have disregarded an unlucky time. When people die one after the other and dozens of coffins await burial, they do not say the air is contaminated but that the day of a burial was inauspicious. . . .

The city of Liyang one night was flooded and became a lake. Its residents cannot all have violated taboos on years and months. When Emperor Gao rose, Feng and Pei were recovered, but surely its residents had not all been careful in their choice of hours and days. When Xiang Yu attacked Xiangan, no one survived, but surely its residents had not all failed to pray. The army of Zhao was buried alive by Qin at Changping; 400,000 men died together at the same time. It is hardly likely that when they left home not one of them divined for a propitious time.

Source: Wang Chong, *Lunheng jiaoshi*, ed. Huang Hui (Taibei: Commercial Press, 1964), 24.1004–12. Translated by Patricia Ebrey.

things," who is "quiet and nonactive" yet "deliberates with his numerous worthies" and knows how to tell if they are loyal or treacherous.[3]

Sima Qian and the *Records of the Grand Historian*

History writing began early in China. In the early Zhou period, court chroniclers kept track of astronomical matters and advised rulers on the lessons of the past. Two of the Five Classics, the *Book of Documents* and the *Spring and Autumn Annals,* are historical works, the former a collection of documents and the latter a chronicle. By the Warring States period, not only did each of the states compile historical records, but citing examples from the past had become a common way to support an argument.

The art of history writing took a major step forward in the Han period. During Emperor Wu's reign, two historians, father and son, undertook to write a comprehensive history of the entire past. Sima Tan (d. 110 B.C.E.) served as the court astronomer under Emperor Wu and had access to the government archives. His son Sima Qian (145–ca. 85 B.C.E.) carried on his work and brought it to completion.

Before Sima Qian was able to complete his history, he angered Emperor Wu by defending a general who had surrendered to the Xiongnu. As a consequence, he was sentenced to castration and service as a palace eunuch. This punishment was so humiliating that it was expected that he would choose the honorable alternative of suicide. Sima Qian explained in a letter to a friend why he decided to accept his humiliating sentence: he could not bear the thought that the history would not be completed. "I have compiled neglected knowledge of former times from all over the world; I have examined these for veracity and have given an account of the principles behind success and defeat, rise and fall." His ambitions were large: "I also wanted to fully explore the interaction between Heaven and Man, and to show the continuity of transformations of past and present."[4] Only by finishing the work could he make up for the dishonor he had suffered.

Like the Greek historian Thucydides, Sima Qian believed fervently in examining artifacts and documents, visiting the sites where history was made, and questioning people about events. He was also interested in China's geographical variations, local customs, and local history. As an official of the emperor, he had access to important people and documents and to the imperial library. He quoted documents when they were available, and in their absence invented dialogues to bring events to life. The result of his efforts, ten years in the making, was a massive work of literary and historical genius, the 130-chapter *Records of the Grand Historian.*

The *Records* presents several perspectives on the past. A political narrative begins with the Yellow Emperor and continues through the Xia, Shang, and Zhou dynasties, down to Sima Qian's own day. It is supplemented by chronological charts with genealogical data and information on the organization of governments. Key institutions are given their own histories in topical chapters on state ritual, court music, the calendar, waterworks, finance, and other matters of concern to the government. Thirty chapters give the separate histories of each of the ruling houses of the states of the Zhou period. Biographies of individuals take up more than half the book. Although many of those portrayed played important political or military roles, Sima Qian also singled out other notable men, including philosophers, poets, merchants, magicians, rebels, assassins, and foreign groups like the Xiongnu. At the end of each chapter of biographies Sima Qian offered his own comments. Sima Qian's experiences with Emperor Wu did not incline him to flatter rulers. Not only did he give ample evidence of Emperor Wu's arbitrariness and policy errors, but he also found many ways to draw attention to those whose merit went unrecognized in their day.

3. Ibid., pp. 298–299.

4. Stephen Owen, *An Anthology of Chinese Literature: Beginnings to 1911* (New York: Norton, 1996), p. 141.

Reeling and Weaving. Many Han tombs had scenes of daily life depicted on their walls. In this example, seated below a finely-drawn tile roof are three women reeling, twisting, and weaving silk. The weaver is using a treadle-operated loom. *(National Museum of Chinese History, Beijing)*

By writing so well, Sima Qian had a profound impact on Chinese conceptions of history and personal achievement. In the centuries that followed, the *Records of the Grand Historian* was read as much for the pleasure of the narrative as for historical data. The composite style, with political narratives supplemented by treatises and biographies, became standard for government-sponsored histories. Subsequent histories, however, usually covered only a single dynasty. The first of these, *History of the Former Han Dynasty,* was the work of three members of the Ban family in the first century C.E. (see **Biography: The Ban Family**).

CHINESE SOCIETY IN HAN TIMES

During the Western Han, with the establishment of peace and the extension of the empire's frontiers, the Chinese population grew rapidly. The census of 2 C.E. recorded a population of 59 million, the earliest indication of the large size of China's population. These people shared status as subjects of the Han, but their daily lives varied enormously, depending on their social status and where they lived.

Common Farmers

The bulk of the population in Han times (and even into the twentieth century) were farmers living in villages of a few dozen or a few hundred households. At the technical level, agriculture continued to make advances. The new and more effective plow introduced during the Han period was fitted with two plowshares, guided by a pair of handles, and typically pulled by a pair of oxen. Farmers used fans to blow the chaff from kernels of grain, and they used either

BIOGRAPHY The Ban Family

Ban Biao (3–54 C.E.), a successful official from a family with an envied library, had three highly accomplished children: his twin sons, the general Ban Chao (32–102) and the historian Ban Gu (32–92); and his daughter, Ban Zhao (ca. 45–120).

After distinguishing himself as a junior officer in campaigns against the Xiongnu, Ban Chao was sent in 73 C.E. to the Western Regions to see about the possibility of restoring Chinese overlordship there, lost since Wang Mang's time. Ban Chao spent most of the next three decades in Central Asia. Through patient diplomacy and a show of force, he reestablished Chinese control over the oasis cities of Central Asia, and in 92 he was appointed protector general of the area.

Ban Gu was one of the most accomplished writers of his age, excelling in a distinctive literary form known as the rhapsody (*fu*). His "Rhapsody on the Two Capitals" is in the form of a dialogue between a guest from Chang'an and his host in Luoyang. It describes the palaces, spectacles, scenic spots, local products, and customs of the two great cities. Emperor Zhang (r. 76–88) was fond of literature and often had Ban Gu accompany him on hunts or travels. He also had him edit a record of the court debates he held on issues concerning the Confucian classics.

Ban Biao had been working on a history of the Western Han Dynasty when he died in 54. Ban Gu took over this project, modeling it on Sima Qian's *Records of the Grand Historian.* He added treatises on law, geography, and bibliography, the last a classified list of books in the imperial library.

Because of his connection to a general out of favor, Ban Gu was sent to prison in 92, where he soon died. At that time the *History of the Former Han Dynasty* was still incomplete. The emperor called on Ban Gu's widowed sister, Ban Zhao, to finish it. She came to the palace, where she not only worked on the history but also became a teacher of the women of the palace. According to the *History of the Later Han,* she taught them the classics, history, astronomy, and mathematics. In 106 an infant succeeded to the throne, and Empress Deng became regent. The empress frequently turned to Ban Zhao for advice on government policies.

Ban Zhao credited her own education to her learned father and cultured mother and became an advocate of the education of girls. In her *Admonitions for Women,* Ban Zhao objected that many families taught their sons to read but not their daughters. She did not claim they should have the same education; after all, "just as yin and yang differ, men and women have different characteristics." Women, she wrote, will do well if they cultivate the womanly virtues such as humility. "Humility means yielding and acting respectful, putting others first and oneself last, never mentioning one's own good deeds or denying one's own faults, enduring insults and bearing with mistreatment, all with due trepidation."[1] In subsequent centuries, Ban Zhao's *Admonitions* became one of the most commonly used texts for the education of girls.

[1]Patricia Buckley Ebrey, ed., *Chinese Civilization: A Sourcebook,* rev. ed. (New York: Free Press, 1993), p. 75.

mortars and pestles or hand mills to grind grain into flour. Irrigation of farmland was aided by brick-faced wells and pumping devices ranging from a simple pole with an attached bucket and counterweight to a sophisticated machine worked by foot pedals.

Because the Han Empire depended on free farmers to pay taxes and provide labor services, the government tried to keep farmers independent and productive. To fight peasant poverty, the government kept land taxes low, provided relief during famines, aided migration to areas where there was vacant land to be opened, and promoted agricultural advancements, such as planting two crops in alternate rows and planting a succession of carefully timed crops. Still, many farmers fell into debt and had to sell their land. Those who did not migrate in search of new opportunities usually became tenant farmers, often accepting quasi-servile status as the dependent of a magnate. Poverty also contributed to the supply of slaves, as men could sell their wives or children into slavery to pay debts.

Elite Groups

The old nobility of Zhou times did not survive Qin's destruction of the Zhou states and its determinedly anti-aristocratic policies. Still, Han historical sources are full of references to people who outranked ordinary farmers in wealth and power. Some of these gained power through proximity to the throne. Liang Ji, whose power derived from his position as father of the empress, was said to have had huge properties and mansions, forced commoners to become his slaves, used commoners doing labor service to work on his own properties, let his retainers extort property and favors, and so on. Members of the imperial clan and the adopted relatives of eunuchs could similarly take advantage of their position to accumulate wealth and power.

Other groups whose great wealth outraged observers were merchants and manufacturers. Zhao Cuo in 178 B.C.E. complained that merchants suffered none of the hardships of farmers and got the best food and clothing, associated with the nobility, and had more power than officials. Sima Qian spoke of how great merchants commanded the services of the poor. If a man's wealth was ten times their own, they would behave humbly toward him. If it was a hundred times their own, they would fear him. If it was a thousand times their own, they would work for him. And if it was ten thousand times their own, they would become his servants. Even those with noble titles, he added, depended on these rich merchants for loans.

Government officials had high standing in Han times, though rarely did they have the great wealth of the richest merchants or imperial relatives. In the Western Han, some men rose to high office from modest backgrounds. Kuang Heng, for instance, came from a farming family and hired himself out to get the money to study; he eventually became a respected classical scholar and high government official. Yet most of the time those who could afford to get the education needed to become officials came from families of means, most often landholders.

Access to office was largely through recommendations. At the local level, the county magistrate or commandery grand administrators appointed their own subordinates from among the local educated elite. The grand administrators also made recommendations to the central government of men who were "filial and incorrupt," who then became eligible for higher office. Another route to office was to study with a well-known teacher. Patron-client ties were very important in linking members of the elite, especially in the Eastern Han, when former subordinates and students could be counted on to come to one's assistance in political conflicts.

At the local level, better-off families were expected to act as the leaders of their communities and offer assistance to their neighbors and relatives in need. In the second century C.E., leading families in communities often erected stones inscribed with accounts of their good works, such as building or repairing bridges or shrines. Tombs and funerary monuments of the Eastern Han offer further evidence of the self-perception of such families. By decorating funerary architecture with pictures of famous filial sons, dutiful women, or loyal ministers, they were portraying their families as steeped in Confucian traditions. Not all those with power at the local level were Confucian scholars. Han sources are full of complaints of the "great families" or "powerful men" of local communities who intimidated their neighbors and built up their property by taking advantage of families in debt.

During the course of the Han, the educated elite (called the *shi,* the same term used in Zhou times for the lower level of the aristocracy) came to see themselves as participants, even if indirectly, in national literary, scholarly, and political affairs. The agitation against the eunuchs and consort families in the second century C.E. helped strengthen these feelings. The persecution of the leaders of the movement protesting eunuch power, which took place between 166 and 184, created a large group of articulate, energetic, concerned men excluded from office. Their prestige showed that social honor was something the elite conferred on itself rather than something the government controlled through its appointment of men to office.

The Family

During Han times, both the administrative structure of the centralized state and the success of Confucianism helped shape the Chinese family system. Since Shang times, at least at the highest social levels, patrilineal ancestors had been a central feature of the family. By the time of the registration of the population in Qin and Han times, everyone had patrilineal family names. Han laws supported the authority of family heads over the other members of their families. The state preferred to deal only with the family head and recognized this person's right to represent the family. The family head was generally the senior male, but if a man died before his sons were grown, his widow would serve as family head until they were of age. Family members were also held responsible for each other, and for serious crimes, relatives of a criminal were made slaves.

During the Zhou period, inheritance had favored the eldest son, who succeeded to both aristocratic titles and responsibility to maintain ancestral rites. By Han times primogeniture in ordinary families applied only to ancestral rites. Family property such as land was divided among all sons. Daughters did not get shares of the family property, though well-to-do families might provide a daughter with substantial goods as her dowry when she married. Because the family farm had to be divided every generation (at least when there was more than one son), a family with several sons risked rapid downward social mobility.

Marriages were arranged by family heads, generally with the bride joining the husband's family. Men could divorce their wives on any of seven grounds, which included barrenness, jealousy, and talkativeness, but could do so only if there was a family for her to return to. There were no grounds on which a woman could divorce her husband, but divorce by mutual agreement was possible.

The legal underpinnings of the family were closely connected to Confucian teachings. It was one of the Confucian ritual texts that first defined the seven grounds for divorce. Confucian ritual texts compiled in Han times also give elaborate descriptions of the proper deference that sons and daughters-in-law should show to parents. The *Book of Rites,* for instance, told daughters-in-law to rise at the cock's crow, wash and dress, and then call on their parents-in-law: "Getting to where they [the parents-in-law] are, with bated breath and gentle voice, they [the daughters-in-law] should ask if their clothes are too warm or too cold, whether they are ill or pained, or uncomfortable in any part; and if they be so, they should proceed reverently to stroke and scratch the place."[5] Male-female differentiation was much stressed in this book. For instance, in explaining why the man goes to fetch his bride in person, it says, "This is the same principle by which Heaven takes precedence over earth and rulers over their subjects."[6]

In Han times filial piety was extolled in both texts and art. Pictures of famous filial sons were used to decorate not only the walls of tombs but even everyday objects like boxes. The brief *Classic of Filial Piety* argued that at each level of society, sincere filial devotion leads people to perform their social duties conscientiously and prudently, creating peace and harmony.

Other Han texts addressed the virtues women should cultivate. The *Biographies of Exemplary Women,* compiled by Liu Xiang, told the stories of women from China's past who had given their husbands good advice, sacrificed themselves when forced to choose between their fathers and husbands, or performed other heroic

5. James Legge, trans., *Li Ki: Book of Rites* (Oxford: Oxford University Press, 1885), 1:450, modified.

6. Ibid., p. 440.

Painted Basket. Unearthed in the Han colony at Lolang, northern Korea, this basket provides excellent evidence of Han figure painting. The three-inch high figures that decorate the basket are all labeled and represent famous figures from history. Note that they are seated on the floor, not on chairs, not yet introduced. *(Central History Museum, Pyongyang, North Korea/Werner Forman/Art Resource, NY)*

deeds. It also contained cautionary tales about scheming, jealous, and manipulative women who brought destruction to all around them. Another notable text on women's education was written by the scholar Ban Zhao. Her *Admonitions for Women* urged girls to master the seven virtues appropriate to women: humility, resignation, subservience, self-abasement, obedience, cleanliness, and industry (see **Biography: The Ban Family**).

CENTRAL ASIA AND THE SILK ROAD

It was during the Han period that the Chinese first learned that theirs was not the only civilization with cities and writing, and also that these distant civilizations had been obtaining silk from China from merchants who crossed Eurasia.

This discovery was made when Emperor Wu decided to send Zhang Qian as an envoy to look for the Yuezhi, a group that had moved west after defeat by the Xiongnu several decades earlier and which Emperor Wu hoped would return to fight the Xiongnu for him. Despite being captured by the Xiongnu and delayed several years, Zhang eventually reached Bactria, Parthia, and Ferghana (in the region of modern Afghanistan). However, the Yuezhi, once found, had no interest in returning to help out the Han. In 115 B.C.E. Zhang was sent again, this time to look for another group, who proved just as unwilling to return. Zhang's travels, however, were not totally in vain. From the reports he made of these two trips, the Chinese learned firsthand of

MATERIAL CULTURE

Silk from the Silk Road

The Chinese product most in demand outside China was silk. The silkworm had been domesticated in China by the Shang period, and the excellence of Chinese silk technology in Zhou times is well documented through excavations of tombs. Silk is very strong and amazingly fine. A single silkworm can spin a filament 3,000 feet long but a minuscule .025 millimeters thick. Several of these filaments have to be twisted together to make the yarns used for weaving. Besides basic flat weaves and light gauzes, Chinese weavers also made patterned weaves, including multi-colored ones that required the use of a draw loom to separate the warp threads.

Many fragments of Han period textiles have survived in the arid climate of Chinese Central Asia, at sites along the Silk Road. The piece illustrated here was excavated from tomb 8 at Niya, along the southern arm of the Silk Road. The weave is exceptionally fine, with 220 warp threads per centimeter. The five-color woven design shows clouds, birds, a single-horned beast, and a tiger, along with Chinese characters. The inscription, which is the command of a Han emperor to a general leading troops to bring order to the north-west frontier, reads: "The Five Planets appear in the east. This is very auspicious for China. The barbarians will be defeated."

Silk Arm Cover. Excavated at Niya, along the Silk Road, this small piece (12.5 by 18.5 cm) is finely woven in five colors: blue, green, red, yellow, and white (the colors of the five planets). *(Xinjiang Institute of Archaeology)*

the countries of Central Asia and heard about the trade in silk with other ones farther out, such as Rome.

In 104 and 102 B.C.E. a Han general led Chinese armies across the Pamir Mountains to subdue Ferghana. Recognition of Chinese overlordship followed, giving China control over the trade routes across Central Asia, commonly called the Silk Road (see Map 3.1). The city-states along this route did not resist the Chinese presence, since they could carry out the trade on which they depended more conveniently with Chinese garrisons to protect them. (See **Material Culture: Silk from the Silk Road.**)

Much of the trade was in the hands of Sogdian, Parthian, and Indian merchants who carried silk and other goods by caravans all the way to Rome. There was a market for both skeins of silk thread and for silk cloth woven in Chinese or Syrian workshops. Caravans returning to China carried gold, horses, and occasionally handicrafts of West Asian origin, such as glass beads and cups (see Color Plate 4). Through the trade along the Silk Road, the Chinese learned of new foodstuffs, including walnuts, pomegranates, sesame, and coriander, all of which came to be grown in China. This trade was largely carried by the two-humped Bactrian camel, which had been bred in Central Asia since the first century B.C.E. With a heavy coat of hair to withstand the bitter cold of winter, each camel could carry about five hundred pounds of cargo.

BORDERLANDS

During the Qin and Han periods, the Chinese empire was extended by both armies and by migrants. Emperor Wu sent armies not only into Central Asia but also into northern Korea, where military districts were established to flank the Xiongnu on their eastern border. Armies were also sent south, extending the frontiers into what is now northern Vietnam.

In the south, migrants in search of land to till often were the first to penetrate an area. They moved south along the rivers, displacing the indigenous populations, who retreated farther south or up into marginal hillsides. A comparison of the censuses of 2 and 140 C.E. shows that between 5 and 10 million people left the north China plain for the Yangzi Valley or farther south between those dates.

The government fostered migration by building garrisons on the frontiers to protect settlers, merchants, and adventurers. Once enough settlers had arrived, the government created counties and sent officials to administer them and collect taxes. Often officials sent to the frontier counties tried to encourage the assimilation of the local population by setting up schools to train local young men in Chinese texts. The products of Chinese industry—iron tools, lacquerware, silks, and so on—were generally in demand and helped make Chinese merchants welcome.

Nevertheless, Chinese expansion often ran into active resistance. In the region of modern Yunnan, the Dian state was dominated by horse-riding aristocrats who made captured enemies into slaves. They drew wealth from trade conducted in both Chinese coins and in cowrie shells. Although the Dian did not have a written language, they were skilled metalworkers whose bronze drums often were decorated with images of people and animals. In 109 B.C.E. Emperor Wu sent an army that conquered Dian and made it a tributary state. Although the Dian repeatedly rebelled, the Han government was able each time to reestablish its overlordship.

The Case of Vietnam

To the north and west of China proper, there were natural boundaries to the Chinese way of life, as crop agriculture was not suited to the desserts, grasslands, and high mountains in those regions. The southern boundaries of China proper were not so clear and took centuries to become established. Crops that could be grown in modern Guangdong province could also be grown farther south, especially along the coast in what is today Vietnam. The rivers that are central to this region—both the Red River, which empties into the ocean near modern Hanoi, and the Mekong River, which empties near modern Saigon—start in the highlands of southwest China, and migrants following these rivers would end up in what is today Vietnam. Travel along the coast was also easy, even in early times.

Vietnam is today classed with the countries to its west as part of Southeast Asia, but its ties are at least as strong to China. The Vietnamese appear in Chinese sources as a people of south China called the Yue who gradually migrated farther south as the Chinese state expanded. In the Red River valley in northern Vietnam, they mixed with local people who had bronze technology, could kill elephants with poisoned bronze arrowheads, and knew how to irrigate their rice fields by using the tides that backed up the rivers.

The collapse of the Qin Dynasty in 206 B.C.E. had an impact on this area because a former Qin general, Zhao Tuo (Trieu Da in Vietnamese), finding himself in modern Guangdong province, set up his own kingdom of Nam Viet (Nan Yue in Chinese) that extended as far south as modern-day Da Nang. Trieu Da/Zhao Tuo called himself the Great Chief of the Southern Barbarians, incorporated local warriors into his army, encouraged the adoption of Chinese material culture, and supported intermarriage between Chinese settlers and the local population. Through these measures, he gained the support of the local population and was able to rule to the age of ninety-three, all the while resisting Han efforts to make him accept vassal status.

After almost a hundred years of diplomatic and military duels between the Han Dynasty and Nam Viet, Emperor Wu sent armies that conquered it in 111 B.C.E. As in Korea, Chinese political institutions were imposed, and Confucianism became the official ideology. The Chinese language was introduced as the medium of official and literary expression. The Chinese built roads, waterways, and harbors to facilitate communication within the region and to ensure that they maintained administrative and military control over it. Over time, Chinese art, architecture, and music had a powerful impact on their Vietnamese counterparts.

Chinese innovations that were beneficial to the Vietnamese were readily integrated into the indigenous culture, but the local elite were not reconciled to Chinese political domination. The most famous early revolt took place in 39 C.E., when two widows of local aristocrats, the Trung sisters, led an uprising against foreign rule. They gathered together the tribal chiefs and their armed followers, attacked and overwhelmed the Chinese strongholds, and had themselves proclaimed queens of an independent Vietnamese kingdom. Three years later, a powerful Chinese army reestablished Chinese rule.

China retained at least nominal control over northern Vietnam until the tenth century, and there were no real borders between China proper and Vietnam during this time. Many Chinese settled in the area, and the local elite became culturally dual, serving as brokers between the Chinese governors and the native people.

MAINTAINING THE EMPIRE

Maintaining the Han Empire's extended borders required a huge military investment. To man the northern defense stations along the Great Wall took about ten thousand men. Another fifty to sixty thousand soldier-farmers were moved to the frontiers to reduce the cost of transporting provisions to distant outposts. Drafted farmers from the interior did not make good cavalry troops, and as a consequence, a de facto professional army emerged on the frontiers, composed of Chinese from the northern reaches of the empire hired as mercenaries, reprieved convicts, and surrendered Xiongnu. In 31 C.E. the Han abolished universal military service, which it had inherited from the Warring States.

In the middle of the first century C.E., a succession struggle among the Xiongnu brought one of the rival claimants and his followers to the Chinese border seeking protection. These "Southern Xiongnu" were permitted to live in Chinese territory, primarily in the Ordos region in the great bend of the Yellow River. In 90 C.E. Chinese officials counted 237,300 Xiongnu living in China, of whom 50,170 were adult males able to serve in the army, and substantial numbers of other non-Han groups were also settled in Chinese territory. With the collapse of the Xiongnu confederation, a group from Manchuria, the Xianbei, rose to prominence and absorbed many Xiongnu into their tribal structure. The expeditionary armies of the Eastern Han included soldiers from all of these groups; in some campaigns, Han Chinese formed a tiny minority of the soldiers.

During the Han period, China developed a system of diplomacy to regulate contact with foreign powers. States and tribes beyond its borders sent envoys bearing gifts, which the Han emperor responded to with even more lavish gifts for them to bring back. Over the course of the dynasty, the Han government's outlay on these gifts was huge, perhaps as much as 10 percent of state revenue. In 25 B.C.E., for instance, the government gave tributary states twenty thousand rolls of silk cloth and about twenty thousand pounds of silk floss. But although the diplomacy system was a financial burden to the Chinese, it reduced the cost of defense and offered the Han imperial court confirmation that it was the center of the civilized world.

SUMMARY

What changed over the four centuries of the Han Dynasty? The area that could be called China was greatly expanded. Confucianism had become much more closely identified with the state and with the social elite. A canon of classics had been established, as well as a way of writing the history of a complex empire. The effects of the destruction of books by Qin had been largely overcome, and a great many books were in circulation. Paper was coming into common use. By 200 C.E. Chinese officials were much more knowledgeable about the military threats of China's northern neighbors and had much experience with all sorts of stratagems for dealing with them, such as setting up military colonies and recruiting auxiliary forces. China had knowledge of countries far to its west and knew that trade with them could be advantageous. Perhaps above all, by the end of the Han period, the centralized bureaucratic monarchy had proved that it could govern well; it could maintain peace and stability and allow the population to grow and thrive.

SUGGESTED READING

For solid scholarly studies of both the Qin and Han periods, see D. Twitchett and M. Loewe, eds., *Cambridge History of China,* vol. 1 (1986). On the political and military success of the Qin, see D. Bodde, *China's First Unifier: A Study of the Ch'in Dynasty as Seen in the Life of Li Ssu (280?–208 B.C.)* (1958). For Han material culture, see M. Perazzoli-t'Serstevens, *The Han Dynasty* (1982), and M. Loewe, *Everyday Life in Early Imperial China* (1968).

For China's relations with the Xiongnu, Xianbei, Turks, and other neighbors, see T. Barfield, *Perilous Frontier: Nomadic Empires and China, 221 B.C.–A.D. 1757* (1989); N. DiCosmo, *Ancient China and Its Enemies: The Rise of Nomadic Power in East Asia* (2002); Y. Yu, *Trade and Expansion in Han China: A Study in the Structure of Sino-Barbarian Economic Relations* (1967); and M. Elvin, *The Pattern of the Chinese Past* (1973).

Han view of their own history can be sampled in B. Watson's translations: *Records of the Grand Historian of China,* 2 vols. (1961), *Courtier and Commoner in Ancient China: Selections from the "History of the Former Han"* (1974), and *Records of the Grand Historian: Qin Dynasty* (1993). See also G. Hardy, *Worlds of Bronze and Bamboo: Sima Qian's Conquest of History* (1999). China's most important woman scholar is the subject of N. L. Swann, *Pan Chao: Foremost Woman Scholar of China* (1950).

For religion, see Mu-chou Poo, *In Search of Personal Welfare: A View of Ancient Chinese Religion* (1998); R. Yates, trans., *Five Lost Classics: Tao, Huang-Lao and Yin-Yang in Han China* (1997); and M. Loewe, *Chinese Ideas of Life and Death: Faith, Myth, and Reason in the Han Period (202 B.C.–A.D. 220)* (1982). Many of the works that deal with the intellectual history of the Warring States also cover the Qin and Han. On Qin thought, see in particular J. Knoblock and J. Riegel, trans., *The Annals of Lü Buwei* (2000). W. de Bary and I. Bloom, *Sources of Chinese Tradition,* rev. ed. (1999), has more than 150 pages on the Qin-Han period. Other aspects of social and cultural life can be found in T. Ch'ü, *Han Social Structure* (1972), and C. Hsu, *Han Agriculture: The Formation of the Early Chinese Agrarian Economy (206 B.C.–A.D. 220)* (1980). On Han funerary art, see H. Wu, *The Wu Liang Shrine: The Ideology of Early Chinese Pictorial Art* (1989), and M. Powers, *Art and Political Expression in Early China* (1991).

CONNECTIONS

Buddhism

EAST ASIAN CIVILIZATION WAS NEVER completely isolated from the rest of Eurasia. Wheat and the chariot arrived in China from west Asia in Shang times. Animal art spread across the steppe in late Zhou times. Nevertheless, ancient China had less contact with other early centers of civilization such as Mesopotamia, India, Egypt, and Greece than they had with each other. India was geographically the closest of those civilizations and therefore it is not surprising that it was the first to have a major impact on East Asia. The vehicle of its impact was one of its religions, Buddhism.

Early India differed from early China in a great many ways. Much farther south, most areas of the Indian subcontinent were warm all year. In the region of the Indus River there had been an ancient literate civilization that was already in decline by 1800 B.C.E. The Aryans, in India by 1000 B.C.E. if not earlier, were Indo-European speaking people who became the dominant group in north India. The culture of the early Aryans is known from the *Rigveda,* a collection of hymns, ritual texts, and philosophical texts composed between 1500 and 500 B.C.E., but transmitted orally for centuries. The *Rigveda* portrays the Aryans as warrior tribes who glorified military skill and heroism; loved to drink, hunt, race, and dance; and counted their wealth in cattle. It presents the struggle between the Aryans and indigenous peoples in religious terms: their chiefs were godlike heroes, their opponents irreligious savages.

Early Aryan society had distinguished between the warrior elite, the priests, ordinary tribesmen, and conquered subjects. These distinctions gradually evolved into the caste system. Society was conceived in terms of four hierarchical strata that did not eat with each other or marry each other: priests (Brahman), warriors or officials (Kshatriya), merchants and landowners (Vaishya), and workers (Shudra). The gods of the Aryans shared some features of the gods of other early Indo-European societies such as the Persians and the Greeks. The *Upanishads,* composed between 750 and 500 B.C.E., record speculations about the mystical meaning of sacrificial rites and about cosmological questions of man's relationship to the universe. They document a gradual shift from the mythical world-view of the early Vedic age to a deeply philosophical one. Associated with this shift was a movement toward asceticism. In search of a richer and more mystical faith, some men retreated to the forests.

Ancient Indian cosmology imagined endlessly repeating cycles. Central concepts were *samsara,* the transmigration of souls by a continual process of rebirth, and *karma,* the tally of good and bad deeds that determined the status of an individual's next life. Good deeds lead to better future lives, evil deeds to worse future lives—even to reincarnation as an animal. The wheel of life included human beings, animals, and even gods. Reward and punishment worked automatically; there was no all-knowing god who judged people and could be petitioned to forgive a sin, and each individual was responsible for his or her own destiny in a just and impartial world. The optimistic interpretation of samsara was that people could improve their lot in the next life by living righteously. The pessimistic view was that life is a treadmill, a relentless cycle of birth and death. Brahmanic mystics sought release from the wheel of life through realization that life in the world was actually an illusion.

The founder of Buddhism was Siddhartha Gautama (fl. ca. 500 B.C.E.), also called Shakyamuni ("sage of the Shakya tribe"), but best known as the Buddha ("enlightened one"). Our knowledge of his life is filtered through later Buddhist texts, which tell us that he was born the son of a ruler of one of the chiefdoms in the Himalayan foothills in what is now Nepal. Within the Indian caste system he was in the warrior, not the priest (Brahman) caste. At age twenty-nine, unsatisfied with his life of comfort and troubled by the suffering he saw around him, he left home to become a wandering ascetic. He traveled south to the kingdom of Magadha, where he studied with yoga masters. Later he took up extreme asceticism. According to tradition, he reached enlightenment while meditating under a bo tree at Bodh Gaya. After several weeks of meditation, he preached his first sermon, urging a "middle way" between asceticism and worldly life. For the next forty-five years, the Buddha traveled through the Ganges Valley, propounding his ideas, refuting his adversaries, making converts, and attracting followers.

In his first sermon, the Buddha outlined his main message, summed up in the Four Noble Truths and the Eightfold Path. The truths are as follows: (1) pain and suffering, frustration and anxiety, are ugly but inescapable parts of human life; (2) suffering and anxiety are caused by human desires and attachments; (3) people can understand these weaknesses and triumph over them; and (4) this triumph is made possible by following a simple code of conduct, the Eightfold Path. The basic insight of Buddhism is thus psychological. The deepest human longings can never be satisfied, and even those things that seem to give pleasure cause anxiety because we are afraid of losing them. Attachment to people and things leads to sorrow at their loss.

The Buddha offered an optimistic message, however, because people can all set out on the Eightfold Path toward liberation. All they have to do is take steps such as recognizing the universality of suffering, deciding to free themselves from it, and choosing "right conduct," "right speech," "right livelihood," and "right endeavor." For instance, they should abstain from taking life and thus follow a vegetarian diet. The seventh step is "right awareness," constant contemplation of one's deeds and words, giving full thought to their importance and whether they lead to enlightenment. "Right contemplation," the last step, entails meditation on the impermanence of everything in the world. Those who achieve liberation are freed from the cycle of birth and death and enter the blissful state called *nirvana*.

Although he accepted the Indian idea of reincarnation, the Buddha denied the integrity of the individual self or soul. He saw human beings as a collection of parts, physical and mental. As long as the parts remain combined, that combination can be called "I." When that combination changes, as at death, the various parts remain in existence, ready to become the building blocks of different combinations. According to Buddhist teaching, life is passed from person to person as a flame is passed from candle to candle.

The success of Buddhism was aided by the Buddha's teaching that everyone, noble and peasant, educated and ignorant, male and female, could follow the Eightfold Path. Within India this marked a challenge to the caste system, central to early Brahmanism and later Hinduism. Moreover, the Buddha was extraordinarily undogmatic. Convinced that each person must achieve enlightenment on his or her own, he emphasized that the path was important only because it led the traveler to enlightenment, not for its own sake. He compared religious practices to a raft, needed to get across a river but useless once on the far shore. Thus, there was no harm in honoring local gods or observing traditional ceremonies, as long as one kept in mind the ultimate goal of enlightenment.

In his lifetime the Buddha formed a circle of disciples, primarily men but including some women as well. The Buddha's followers transmitted his teachings orally for several centuries until they were written down in the second or first century B.C.E. The form of monasticism that developed among the Buddhists was less strict than that of some other contemporary groups in India, such as the Jains. Buddhist monks moved about for eight months of the year (staying inside only during the rainy season) and consumed only one meal a day obtained by begging. Within a few centuries, Buddhist monks began to overlook the rule that they should travel. They set up permanent monasteries, generally on land donated by kings or other patrons. Orders of nuns also appeared, giving women the opportunity to seek truth in ways men had traditionally done. The main ritual that monks and nuns performed in their monastic establishments was the communal recitation of the sutras. Lay Buddhists could aid the spread of the Buddhist teachings by providing food for monks and support for their monasteries, and could pursue their own spiritual progress by adopting practices such as abstaining from meat and alcohol.

Within India the spread of Buddhism was greatly aided in the third century B.C.E. by King Ashoka. As a young prince, Ashoka served as governor of two prosperous provinces where Buddhism flourished. At the death of his father about 274 B.C.E., Ashoka rebelled against his older brother, the rightful king, and after four years of fighting succeeded in his bloody bid for the throne. In 261 B.C.E., early in his reign, Ashoka conquered Kalinga, on the east coast of India. Instead of exulting like a conqueror, however, Ashoka was consumed with remorse for all the deaths inflicted. In this mood, he embraced Buddhism.

Ashoka used the machinery of his empire to spread Buddhist teachings throughout India. He banned animal sacrifices and in place of hunting expeditions, he took pilgrimages. Two years after his conversion, he undertook a 256-day pilgrimage to all the holy sites of Buddhism and on his return he began sending missionaries to all known countries. Buddhist tradition also credits him with erecting throughout India 84,000 stupas (Buddhist reliquary mounds), among which the ashes of the Buddha were distributed, beginning the association of Buddhism with monumental art and architecture. Also according to Buddhist tradition, Ashoka convened a great council of Buddhist monks at which the earliest canon of Buddhist texts was codified.

Gate at the Great Stupa at Sanchi. King Ashoka began the stupa at Sanchi in central India as a site for the preservation of the ashes of the Buddha. Each of its four gates, dating from the first century C.E., is decorated with Buddhist imagery. Note the depiction of a stupa on the horizontal support. *(Borromeo/Art Resource, NY)*

Under Ashoka, Buddhism began to spread to Central Asia. This continued under the Kushan empire (ca. 50–250 C.E.), especially under their greatest king, Kanishka I (ca. 100 C.E.). In this region, where the influence of Greek art was strong, artists began to depict the Buddha in human form. By this period Buddhist communities were developing divergent traditions and came to stress different sutras. One of the most important of these, associated with the monk-philosopher Nagarjuna (ca. 150–250), is called Mahayana, or "Great Vehicle," because it is a

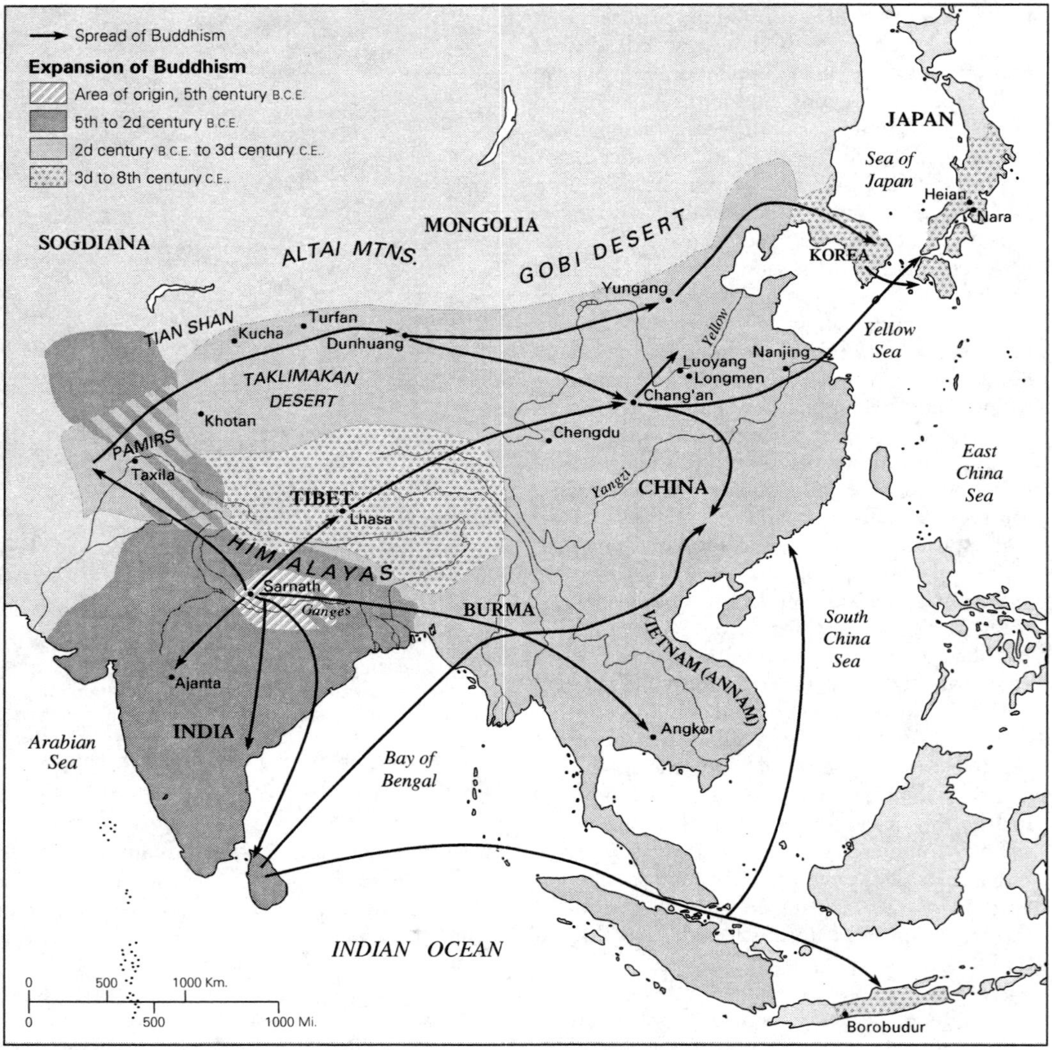

Map C2.1 Expansion of Buddhism from 500 B.C.E. to 800 C.E.

more inclusive form of the religion. It drew on a set of discourses allegedly preached by the Buddha and kept hidden by his followers for centuries. One branch of Mahayana taught that reality is "empty" (that is, nothing exists independently of itself). Emptiness was seen as an absolute, underlying all phenomena, which are themselves transient and illusory. Another branch held that ultimate reality is consciousness, that everything is produced by the mind.

Just as important as the metaphysical literature of Mahayana Buddhism was its devotional side, influenced by the Iranian religions then prevalent in Central Asia. The Buddha became deified and placed at the head of an expanding pantheon of other Buddhas and bodhisattvas (Buddhas-to-be who had stayed in the world to help others on the path to salvation). These Buddhas and bodhisattvas became objects of veneration, especially the Buddha Amitabha and the bodhisattva Avalokitesvara (Guanyin in Chinese, Kannon in Japanese, Kwanŭm in Korean). With the growth of Mahayana, Buddhism became as much a religion for laypeople as for monks and nuns.

Buddhism remained an important religion in India until about 1200 C.E., but thereafter it declined, and the number of Buddhists in India today is small. Long before it declined in India, however, it spread too much of the rest of Asia. One route was east to Sri Lanka and most of Southeast Asia, including Indonesia. Another was northeast to Nepal and Tibet. More important for the history of East Asia, however, was the route northwest through Central Asia. During the first few centuries C.E., most of the city-states of Central Asia became centers of Buddhism, from Bamiyan, northwest of Kabul, to Kucha, Khotan, Loulan, Turfan, and Dunhuang. The first translators of Buddhist texts into Chinese were not Indians but Parthians, Sogdians, and Kushans from Central Asia.

Central Asia in the centuries in which Buddhism was spreading east was ethnically diverse, though Indian and Persian languages were the most commonly used for administrative purposes. The economy of these city-states was dependent on the East-West trade. In Han times, the Chinese had become the overlords in the area, wanting both access to the fabled horses of Ferghana and to keep the area out of the hands of its foes, such as the Xiongnu. After the fall of the Han, most of these cities became independent and trade continued unabated. Buddhism thus reached China first as a religion of foreign merchants. Missionaries soon followed, however, and the hugely complex process of translating Buddhist sutras from Sanskrit or other Indian languages into classical Chinese was accomplished through the collaboration of Central Asian and Chinese monks.

Monk Contemplating a Skull. The painting is from the wall of a cave temple in Kizil, along the Silk Road in Central Asia, and dates from about 500 C.E. *(Museum of Indian Art, Berlin/Art Resource, NY)*

Kumarajiva (350–413 C.E.) was one of the most important of these translators. His father, from a high-ranking family in India, had moved to the Silk Road oasis city of Kucha, attracted by the quality of the Buddhist scholarship there, and he married the younger sister of the king of Kucha. At this time, Kucha reportedly had a population of 100,000, of whom 10,000 were monks. Already in this period spectacular cave temples were being constructed in the nearby small town of Kizil. At home Kumarajiva spoke Tokharian, an Indo-European language. He may also have learned some Chinese from merchants who came regularly to Kucha. From age seven he studied Buddhist texts in Sanskrit as part of his Buddhist training. By age twenty he had established himself as a brilliant Buddhist scholar, and the ruler of a small state in the modern Chinese province of Gansu sent a general to abduct him. He stayed in Gansu seventeen years, becoming fluent in Chinese. In 401 he was able to move to Chang'an where another ruler gave financial support to his plan to translate Buddhist sutras into Chinese. Kumarajiva recruited a large group of learned monks and set up a systematic procedure for checking draft translations. Rather than borrowing terms from Daoism, which often proved misleading, Sanskrit terms were retained, represented by Chinese words borrowed for their sound. About thirty-five sutras were translated, including some of the most famous and popular, such as the *Lotus Sutra* and the *Vimalakirti Sutra.* An exponent of Mahayana, Kumarajiva also translated treatises by Nagarjuna and lectured on their content.

Translating Buddhist texts into Chinese helped Buddhism spread throughout East Asia. Not only did these texts come to circulate throughout China (discussed in Chapters 4 and 5), but they also became the basis for Korean and Japanese schools of Buddhism. The Buddhism that reached Japan, for instance, was filtered through Central Asian, Chinese, and Korean lenses.

SUGGESTED READING

On early India, see L. Basham, *The Wonder that Was India* (1954) or R. Thapar, *History of India* (1966). A. Embree, ed., *Sources of Indian Tradition,* 2nd ed. (1988) has translations of central texts of all Indian religions. On Indian Buddhism, see A. Hirakawa, *A History of Indian Buddhism* (1990) and D. Lopez, *The Story of the Buddha* (2001).